EIM HABANIM
אם הבנים שמחה
SEMEICHAH

ON

ERETZ YISRAEL, REDEMPTION, AND UNITY

BY

HaRav **YISACHAR SHLOMO TEICHTAL** *zt"l*

Av Beit Din and *Rosh Yeshiva*

in Pishtian

Translated by

MOSHE LICHTMAN

KOL MEVASER

Jerusalem 5760

Published by
KOL MEVASER PUBLICATIONS
POB 85672
Mevaseret Tzion 90805, Israel
Tel. (02) 534-0502

ISBN 965-7108-17-9

First published 2000

Printed in Israel

Graphic design: Chayim Mushkin, Jerusalem

Distributed by:

Lambda Publishers, Inc.
3709 13th Avenue
Brooklyn, New York 11218 U.S.A
Tel: 718-972-5449 Fax: 718-972-6307
ejudaica@msn.com

Urim Publications
P.O.Box 52287, Jerusalem 91521
Tel: 051-671-553 Fax: 02-652-9895
UrimPub@netvision.net.il

Distributed in Australia by:
Gold's Books
36 Williams Street, Balaclava 3183
Victoria, Australia

And your eyes shall see your teacher (*Yeshayah* 30:20)

HaRav YISACHAR SHLOMO TEICHTAL *zt"l*

ובירושלים תנחמו

עזרי מעם ה׳ ספר עושה שמים וארץ

אם הבנים שמחה

מיוסד על גאולתינו ועל פדות נפשינו מגלות האחרון הזה אחר שנעשה כל מה שהבורא כל עולמים אלקינו ואלקי אבותינו מבקש מאתנו ומצוונו לעשות בענין קרבת הגאולה כמבואר בפנים כל דבר דבור על אופניו בשום שכל ודעת ממקורות נאמנים כולם נובעים ממעין הסהור של תורתינו הקדושה ומפי חכמינו ז״ל בש״ס בבלי וירושלמי במדרש וזהר ומשאר ספרותינו הקדושים ומבוקש מכל איש ישראל אשר כבוד ה׳ וכבוד אומה הקדושה וכבוד נפשו נוגע בלבו שיקח לו מועד לעבור במתינות ובדיוק על כל דברי הספר הזה אז אני ערב לו שבעזר הבורא יאירו עיניו ושכלו ולבבו יבין את אשר הוא חייב לעשות בעד נפשו בפרט ובעד כל אומתינו הקדושה בכלל ובעבור שמו הגדול יתברך ויתעלה בב״א.

מחובר ממני הצעיר באלפי ישראל

ישכר שלמה טייכטהאל

מלפנים אב״ד ותופס ישיבה נכבדה וכעת פה עיר הבירה בודאפעסט בעהמ״ס שו״ת משנה שכיר כמה חלקים עודם בכת״י ושני חלקים כבר יצאו לאור התחלתי בסידור הכת״י של ספר הנוכחי אור ליום ג׳ לסדר וארא בשנת תש״ג פה עיר הבירה הנ״ל בעמק עכור מצער חבלי משיח הנוראים אשר השתרגו על צווארנו במשך שנות המלחמה העולמית השנית הנוכחית וה׳ יזכני לגומרה בפתח תקוה לחזות במהרה בישועתן של ישראל ובהרמת קרנם ובשוב ה׳ את שיבת ציון בב״א.

כאיש אשר אמו תנחמנו, כן אנכי אנחמכם

וראיתם ושש לבכם ועצמותיכם כדשא תפרחנה

בודאפעסט תש״ג

בדפוס של משלם (זלמן) כ״ץ קאטצבורג

Druck von Salamon Katzburg Budapest, Kazincy-u. 34.

ונודעה יד ה׳ את עבדיו וזעם את אויביו (ישעי׳ ס״ו).

Title page of the original Hebrew edition

ישמח משה במתנת חלקו

THE TRANSLATION OF THIS BOOK IS DEDICATED
TO THE MEMORY OF MY GRANDFATHERS

MAX LAST

משה אהרן בן חיים זצ״ל

MOSHE HASS

משה נחום בן שמעון זצ״ל

ותפארת בנים אבותם

*

IN MEMORY OF THE LATE RABBI ISAAC BERNSTEIN

הרב יצחק יואל זצ״ל

THROUGH WHOSE INSPIRATIONAL *SHIURIM*
WE WERE FIRST DRAWN TO THE *SEFER*

אם הבנים שמחה

A TEACHER WHOSE MEMORY
WILL ALWAYS BE WITH US

מה אהבתי תורתך כל היום היא שיחתי

EDDIE LAST

LONDON, 1999

ספר זה מוקדש

לעילוי נשמת מורינו אבינו וסבינו

הר"ר שלמה בן הרב יהושע וויינבערגער זצ"ל

רב ומרא דאתרא של ק"ק תפארת ישראל

פאסיאק נו דגרסי

ניהל והדריך קהילתו יותר מארבעים שנה.

הקדיש חייו לתורה ועבודה ואהבת חסד

עשות משפט והצנע לכת עם אלקיו.

מסור היה לאשתו ולבניו, כלותיו, נכדיו ונינין

ולבני משפחתו

והניח אחריו בנים ובני בנים עוסקים בתורה ובמצוות.

יהי זכרו ברוך ותנצב"ה

משה וארין וויינבערגער ומשפחתם

DEDICATED BY THE SCHNIPPER FAMILY
IN EVERLASTING LOVING MEMORY OF THEIR

HUSBAND AND FATHER

ABE SCHNIPPER

אברהם חיים בן שמואל פנחס ז״ל

AND THEIR GRANDFATHER

MILTON COHEN

אלימלך בן רפאל מאיר הכהן ז״ל

DEDICATED BY

DAVID AND TAMAR ABELL

AND FAMILY

IN HONOR OF

DANIEL YEHUDAH'S BAR MITZVAH

May we merit to continue
to grow in our love for
HaShem, Torah, Am Yisrael, and Eretz Yisrael

זלמן נחמיה גולדברג
חבר בית הדין הרבני
ראש כולל "דעת משה" - סדיגורה

ב"ה, יום ב' ו' כסלו תש"ס

שמחתי לשמוע מידידי הרב חיים מנחם טייכטל שליט"א
שהספר המופלא שחיבר אביו הגאון הצדיק הקדוש
רבי יששכר שלמה טייכטל זכר צדיק וקדוש לברכה בעל המחבר שו"ת משנת שכיר
חיי העולם הבא שכולו קודש ומעורר את לבו
בני ישראל לאביהם שבשמים לחבב עליהם מצוה
הגדולה מצות ישוב ארץ ישראל
וכבר נתפרסם ספרו זה בשם אם הבנים שמחה
בכל תפוצות ישראל ועכשיו נתעורר הרב משה
ליכטמן שליט"א לתרגם הספר לשפה האנגלית
למען זכות את הרבים מבני ישראל אשר אינם
מבינים לשון הקודש והרב המתרגם מומחה לדבר
ואין ספק שיוציא מתחת ידו דבר מתוקן לתועלת
לכלל ישראל

הכותב לכבוד התורה והגאון הצדיק זצ"ל
זלמן נחמיה גולדברג

הרב זלמן נחמיה גולדברג
ירושלים

Monday, the 6th of Kislev, 5760

I was happy to hear from my dear friend, R. Chayim Menachem Teichtal *shlita*, that the wonderful book written by his brilliant, righteous, and saintly father, R. Yisachar Shlomo Teichtal *ztvk"l*..., author of Responsa *Mishneh Sachir*, [was being published in English]. This book, which is completely holy, arouses the hearts of Israel to their Father in Heaven and inspires them to cherish the great *mitzvah* of settling the Land of Israel.

For some time now, this book, entitled *Eim HaBanim Semeichah*, has been renowned throughout the Jewish world. Recently, R. Moshe Lichtman *shlita* took the initiative to translate this book into English, so that the Jewish masses who do not understand the Holy Tongue (Hebrew) can benefit [from it]. The translator has expertise in this field and, undoubtedly, will produce a proper work for the benefit of *Klal Yisrael*.

Written in honor of the Torah and in honor of the brilliant *tzaddik zt"l*,

Zalman Nechemyah Goldberg

Rabbi Hershel Schachter
24 Bennet Avenue
New York, New York 10033

הרב צבי שכטר
ראש ישיבה וראש כולל
ישיבת רבינו יצחק אלחנן

מכתב ברכה

לפני הרבה שנים קראתי כמה חלקים מהספר הנחמד "אם הבנים שמחה", ונהניתי מאוד. והמחבר הקדוש, הי"ד, בודאי אינו צריך — חלילה — להסכמתי. והנה היום, לדאבוננו, יש בלבול-המוחות גם אצל הרבה משומרי התורה בענייני ארץ ישראל, והוא מקצוע גדול בתורה. ואפריון נמטייה לכבוד ידידנו היקר והנחמד הר"ר משה ליכטמן, שיחיה, שתרגם את הספר החשוב הזה לשפה המדוברת. כי, בעוונותינו הרבים, הרבה בני תורה יש שאין ביכולתם לעבור על הספר במקור. ועברתי על כמה גליונות מתרגומו, ונהניתי אף מהם.

הכותב והחותם לכבוד התורה ולכבוד ארצנו הקדושה,

צבי שכטר

צבי שכטר,
יום ג' לס' ויצא, ז' כסלו תש"ס.

Many years ago, I read several sections of the beautiful work, *Eim HaBanim Semeichah*, and I enjoyed it tremendously. The saintly author, may HaShem avenge his blood, certainly does not need my approbation, God forbid.

Today, unfortunately, there is much confusion, even among Torah-Jews, on the issue of *Eretz Yisrael*, which is a vast discipline in the Torah. [Therefore], I commend our dear colleague, R. Moshe Lichtman (may he live), who translated this important book into the common vernacular. For, due to our numerous sins, many Torah-Jews cannot read this book in the original [Hebrew]. I reviewed several pages of his translation and enjoyed them, as well.

Written and signed in honor of the Torah and in honor of our Holy Land,

Tzvi (Hershel) Schachter
7 Kislev, 5760.

CONTENTS

FOREWORD

CHAPTER ONE

PERSECUTION AND THE PANGS OF *MASHIACH* – *THE SOUND OF MY BELOVED KNOCKING*

CHAPTER TWO

DELIVERANCE AND REDEMPTION

CHAPTER THREE
SETTLEMENT AND REBUILDING

TRANSLATOR'S PREFACE

The first time I read *Eim HaBanim Semeichah*, I was convinced that this *sefer* must be made available to the English-speaking public. Anyone with a discerning eye realizes immediately that its message is as crucial today as it was fifty-five years ago, when it was originally written. Therefore, when I was asked to translate it, I seized the opportunity, approaching the task with a deep sense of awe and trepidation.

I was awed by the saintly author, an exceptionally brilliant and holy man, a true *gadol beYisrael* who was murdered in sanctification of God's name; a man who felt Israel's pain and devoted himself to showing them the path to deliverance and salvation; a man whose words have often proven to be prophetic. Who was I to tread on the heels of this giant?

I was filled with trepidation because of the book's contents and the passion with which it was written. Who was I to render such lofty and powerful ideas into a foreign tongue?

But, *Chazal* instruct us, "In a place where there are no men, strive to be a man" (*Avot* 2:5). Thus, with a tremendous sense of purpose, I dedicated the past three years to translating this holy work. I can only hope that I lived up to the task and produced a work that will influence Jews the world over, as the author intended.

Because of the nature of this work, I was very apprehensive about adding to or subtracting from the author's holy words. At the same time, though, I wanted to make the book as readable as possible for an English-speaking audience. Fulfilling both of these objectives was not always easy, but I hope I have succeeded. When a choice had to be made, I preferred clarity and readability over strict literalness. But, I never (purposely) altered the author's intentions.

The reader must understand the conditions under which this book was written. Rav Teichtal wrote it during the unspeakable horrors of the Holocaust, often without books and always in hiding. He often writes very passionately, for he was desperately trying to awaken his fellow Jews to the truth that he had only recently recognized – that the return to Zion is the answer to our troubles. He also cites numerous proofs for the same point, which sometimes gives the (false) impression that he is repetitive or long-winded. I deliberately left such passages in, for they add to the flavor of the book; this is what makes it so unique and powerful. Occasionally, I omitted a few clearly repetitive words, but only after great deliberation.

Even though I did my utmost to make this book readable, one must realize that it is by no means light reading. It is not a storybook. It is a serious exposition on a serious topic, Israel's restoration and redemption. Rav Teichtal quotes from the entire gamut of Rabbinic literature – Talmudic, Midrashic, Halachic, Kabbalistic, and Chassidic. When I felt that important information was missing or not known to the general public, I added a bracketed statement or an explanatory footnote. I did not, however, spell out a conclusion which the text itself implies, even when considerable concentration and a second reading are required to understand it. I hope and trust that the reader will expend the efforts necessary to understand every part of this book; it is well worth it.

My publisher, R. Doni Cohen, put it best when he said that this book is like one long sermon. Rav Teichtal cites innumerable sources, original ideas, parables, stories, etc., all in an attempt to convince his fellow Jews of what he sees as the absolute truth. Like a rabbi delivering a sermon to his beloved flock, R. Teichtal exhorts and pleads that the Jewish people awaken from their slumber.

Throughout this "sermon," Rav Teichtal makes reference to previous sections of the work, advises us to see other sources, and inserts tangential (and even parenthetical) comments. These references and comments are acceptable and understandable in Rabbinic Hebrew. In English, however, they tend to break the flow of the text, making it hard to follow. Therefore, I moved them to the footnotes. Source references are placed in the footnotes and preceded by a "❖", indicating that they were originally in the body of the text. More substantive comments which, nonetheless, break the flow of the main idea are placed in notes immediately below the main text. Occasionally, the author himself separates tangential comments from the body of the text. I distinguish between these notes and the ones which I moved as follows: An asterisk (*) indicates the author's own note. A "❖" indicates a comment which I moved from the main text.

To summarize:

In the notes below the main text	**In the footnotes**
* – The author's own note	❖ – Author's reference notes
❖ – A comment originally in the main text which was moved for stylistic reasons	**No marking** – Sources or explanatory notes from the Pri HaAretz (now Kol Mevaser) Hebrew edition.
	[Brackets] – Translator's notes

Finally, I try to make it easier on the reader by dividing each chapter into major and minor sub-divisions. The major headings (preceded by Roman Numerals) appear in the main text. The minor headings appear in the margins so as not to hinder the flow of reading. All headings are mine except for chapter titles (and the one on p. 436). The table of contents provides a quick overview of these divisions.

I owe a great deal of gratitude to many people for helping me bring this project to completion. But, I must first thank the One without Whom I could not even have begun. There are simply no words with which to express my thanks to *HaKadosh Baruch Hu* for granting me the *zechut* and privilege to be involved in this lofty and sacred endeavor; for keeping me strong throughout; for providing my family and myself with all of our needs; and for enabling me to complete this work for the glorification of His name.

I am also greatly indebted to:

- HaRav Uri Cohen *shlita*, Rosh Kollel Meretz, for his help in clarifying some of the most difficult passages of this book.
- My publisher, R. Doni Cohen, for trusting me with this project, for his exceptional patience in answering all of my questions, and for his overall assistance.
- My friend and editor, Yoel Finkelman, whose insightful comments, corrections, and general advice greatly improved this work. I could not have done it without him.
- R. Micah D. Halpern, for his work on the historical introduction, and for his invaluable suggestions which enhanced many aspects of this book.
- My beloved parents, Rabbi Joseph and Elizabeth Lichtman, for their unending support and encouragement in all of my endeavors, including this one.
- My dear in-laws, Mr. Ralph and Sandra Rothschild, for their continuous generosity, kindness, and support.
- Sholom Menora, for his generous support, and for all of his efforts on behalf of this book.
- My team of proofreaders: Aaron Bayer, R. Yonah Fuld, Mordechai Gordon, Avi Lowell, Jeff Neiger, Yehoshua Paltiel, Shalom Sklar, and Roi Zadok.
- My close friends Alan and Stephanie Strauss, Alex and Dena Kaye, Jody and Michele Bardash, and David and Marcia Kreinberg for their generous help. A special thanks goes to Alan Strauss for his selfless efforts on behalf of this book. May the *zechut* of this *sefer* help all of them fulfill their dreams of *aliyah*.

- R. Yaakov I. Homnick, for his contribution to the early stages of this book.
- My many students who encouraged me throughout this project and gave up their time to allow me to pursue this lofty goal.
- אחרונה אחרונה חביבה: My *Eishet Chayil*, not only for the typing, and not only for her extraordinary patience in answering all of my questions, but also – and primarily – for her moral support, her dedication to me and my goals, and for selflessly enabling me to devote to this project all of my free time over the past three years. This entire book and all of my Torah is in her merit. רבות בנות עשו חיל ואת עלית על כולנה.

At the end of the second introduction Rav Teichtal prays, "May HaShem grant me the merit that my book will impact the restoration of the children to their borders and to their mother's bosom... And, may we go up to Zion joyously, speedily in our days. Amen."

Similarly, allow me to offer a closing prayer: May the English translation of this remarkable book help awaken the Diaspora Jews from their slumber and inspire them to leave the lands of exile and ascend to God's Land, in order to fulfill His will and expedite the coming of *Mashiach Tzidkeinu*, speedily in our days. Amen.

Moshe Lichtman
Mevaseret Tzion / Beit Shemesh
Tishrei, 5760

PUBLISHER'S ACKNOWLEDGMENT

I would like to take this opportunity to sincerely thank my dear friend, Mr. Eddie Last, for enabling me to turn this dream into reality. His support was the impetus for this entire project. His love for this *sefer*, and HaShem's Torah, knows no bounds. Surely, this is why God granted him the merit of helping make this sacred book available to the Jewish masses. May this merit stand by him and his family forever.

Doni Cohen
Kol Mevaser Publishing.

HISTORICAL INTRODUCTION*

Few theological works were written during the Holocaust. Fewer still address the status of the Jews during World War II and the reasons for the Holocaust. Rabbi Yisachar Shlomo Teichtal wrote one such work, *Eim HaBanim Semeichah* – "A Joyous Mother of Children." This seminal work was written and published in 1943, in Budapest, as millions of Jews were being murdered in the gas chambers of Poland.

It is truly impossible to understand the extent of the tragedy which befell the Jews of Europe between 1939 and 1945. The atrocities of the Holocaust are far beyond our comprehension. Yet, we continue to grapple with the pain as we try to find some lessons and some comfort from this horrific chapter of Jewish and world history.

Many questions arise concerning the Holocaust. Historical analysis can help us understand how it happened. By studying and probing, by piecing together the various parts of the puzzle, we can draw a clearer picture of the Holocaust. But even then, we are left asking, "Why?" *Eim HaBanim Semeichah* attempts to answer this question.

This work must be seen in the unique light in which it was written. While most responses to the Holocaust were written after the fact, with the advantage of hindsight, this book was composed in the middle of the *Churban*, during the destruction. Rabbi Teichtal grants us insight into what the rabbinic leaders, as well as the laymen, were thinking at the time. There is no better source through which to understand these issues than a work written inside the furnace, without the luxury and perspective of future knowledge.

Most importantly, R. Teichtal does not simply explain what happened, or even why it happened. He offers a concrete formula for the restoration of the Jewish people after the devastation and destruction. He proposes a practical plan for lifting the survivors out of despair and rebuilding the nation in its ancient Homeland, on the foundations of Torah. It is this that makes *Eim HaBanim Semeichah* truly unique.

I HISTORICAL CONTEXT

To truly appreciate this work it is essential to understand the historical events and developments that led to its writing.

Yearning for *Eretz Yisrael*

Ever since we, the Jewish people, were exiled from our Land, we

* Co-authored by R. Micah D. Halpern and the translator.

have continuously yearned to return to it. Three times a day we beseech God to end our bitter exile and bring us back to Zion. Some Jews even managed to brave the treacherous journey and make *Eretz Yisrael* their home, while the ones who remained in the Diaspora sent donations to help support them.

Particularly during troubled times, when pogroms and persecutions assailed them, the Jews turned their hearts eastward towards their sacred Homeland. The greater the persecutions, the greater the longing for the Holy Land. The greater the gap between the brutal reality of exile and the hoped-for redemption, the greater the anticipation of a miraculous salvation.

During the first few centuries of Jewish dispersion, this collective hope of recreating a national home in *Eretz Yisrael* was very real. As the years progressed, however, the distance between prayer and reality grew, and Jewry became further removed from the practical and viable realities of a potential state. The words, the prayers, the yearning to return all remained, but the reality of actually recreating a state was very distant. It began to seem as if the only possible way such an event could occur was through a divine miracle, through God's direct intervention into history.

False Messiahs

It is within this context that the false messiahs of the medieval period found fertile ground; and they devastated the Jewish world. These frauds took advantage of the traditional yearning for Zion and played upon the common belief that the Messiah would save the Jewish People from atrocity and persecution. Individuals like Shabbetai Tzvi, Jacob Frank, and David HaReuveni led untold numbers of Jews down paths of false hopes by offering their followers expectations of redemption and by revitalizing their dream to rebuild the Holy Land.

As a conscious response to these charlatans, rabbinic leaders downplayed the practical efforts needed to initiate the return to Zion and bring redemption. Instead, they fostered the simple belief that HaShem will redeem the Jewish people when He sees fit, without any human intervention. Thus, thoughts of reestablishing Jewish sovereignty in *Eretz Yisrael* were pushed aside. Jews still prayed for redemption, of course, and they continued to send donations to the few Jews who managed to settle in the Land. Nevertheless, those rabbis and men of deed – like R. Kalischer – who deviated from the accepted norms, attempting to initiate a practical, political movement to return to Zion, received little support. True, the great Torah authorities endorsed their plans, but little came of them.

The Enlightenment

At around the same time that the false messiahs were wreaking havoc on the Jewish world, the Enlightenment movement arose in Europe. This was yet another serious phenomenon which the Jewish people were forced to confront. Enlightenment philosophy can best be described as the belief that all people are equal. As such, great Enlightenment thinkers – Rousseau, Voltaire, Locke, Jefferson, and others – believed that even Jews should be granted rights as equal citizens in gentile societies.

Consequently, the Jews created their own type of enlightened thought to grapple with the problem of dual loyalty. They sought ways to preserve their Jewishness while becoming equal citizens of the host country. One of the earliest solutions was Moses Mendelsohn's: "Be a Jew at home and a man in the street." That is, Jews should continue their age-old traditions privately, but they should mimic gentile culture in public.

The upper class Jews of Germany and Austria had a different solution. Instead of trying to integrate their Jewish and universal commitments, they attempted to compromise between them. The result was the Reform movement, which tried to make Judaism resemble Christianity as much as possible. For example, they introduced musical instruments into the synagogue, removed the partition (*mechitzah*) between the sexes, and some even transferred the holy Sabbath to Sunday. In the home, as well, they eliminated most of the ritual *mitzvot*, making everything dependent on proper ethical intentions.

Most important for our discussion, Reform leaders renounced almost all ties to their ancient Homeland. They rejected the idea of reestablishing Jewish sovereignty in *Eretz Yisrael*, for they saw it as a major threat to their dreams of integrating into gentile society. Thus, they removed from the liturgy most references to Zion, Jerusalem, and *Eretz Yisrael*. Instead, they developed a new motto: "Berlin (or Paris or London or Vienna) is our Jerusalem."

When Reform began to influence great numbers of Jews in the middle of the 19th century, the religious leadership in Germany and Austro-Hungary reacted sharply. They decided to separate themselves completely from the reformers, establishing separate and autonomous religious communities. Not all religious leaders accepted this solution; some *gedolim* even opposed it strongly. For the most part, however, these rabbis lived in Eastern Europe, where the problem was less severe. In central Europe, though – in places like Galicia, Czechoslovakia, and Hungary – the rabbinic response tended to be one-dimensional: "Anything new is prohibited by the

Torah.ö They closed themselves in and zealously guarded every aspect of their age-old tradition. This extreme reaction caused further polarization. The two camps grew further apart, and mutual opposition, derision, and enmity prevailed. It came to the point (primarily in greater Hungary) that a Jew was either completely observant or completely irreligious.

The Rise of Zionism

Thus, the "enlightened," assimilated Jews reformed the Jewish religion and renounced all ties to *Eretz Yisrael* and Jewish nationalism. The Orthodox Jews, on the other hand, zealously guarded traditional Judaism and, of course, retained a holy reverence for their forefather's Land. Ironically, however, a significant shift took place on just this issue. These "enlightened" Jews, as far as they were from traditional Judaism, called for a renewal of Jewish nationalism, a rebirth of the Jewish nation in its ancient Homeland. They saw this as the only solution to the perpetual problem of anti-Semitism.

Initially, the Orthodox reaction to this unexpected development was mixed. Some (mainly in Czarist Russia) viewed Zionism as a return to authentic Judaism. Others (particularly in Austro-Hungary and Germany) remained silent, waiting to see how things would develop. It soon became clear, however, that the secular Zionists longed for a Jewish nationalism that mimicked European nationalism, with no ties to Torah and *mitzvot*. The Zionist Congress determined that "Zionism has nothing to do with religion." Many Orthodox groups saw this as a continuation of the Enlightenment movement, simply another attempt to strip the Jews of their sacred traditions.

Thus, the vast majority of Orthodox Jewry strongly opposed the Zionist movement. They still loved and longed for the Holy Land; they opposed only the call for a renewal of Jewish national independence. To underscore this difference, many religious leaders explained that it is inconceivable that God would fulfill our ancient hope of redemption through secular activism. Some even attributed the secular Zionists' success to the forces of evil, arguing that Satan wanted to confuse well-meaning Jews.

Orthodox Jews decided to continue their ways exactly as before. They would pray, study Torah, observe the *mitzvot*, accept the hardships of exile (or migrate to a different place in the Diaspora, if the suffering was too great to bear), and passively await *Mashiach*'s miraculous arrival. This alone, they felt, would expedite the true redemption, not political activism, mass *aliyah*, or land purchases in the Holy Land. In effect, then, the covert historical process which gradually distanced Jewry from a pragmatic outlook on the return to Zion, now became a determined ideology, which even found support in traditional Jewish sources.

At the same time, the secular, "enlightened" Jews began thinking and talking in concrete terms. Their entry into the "outside" world, with all of its modern disciplines and philosophies, enabled them to seek a real, practical solution to "the Jewish problem." Some, like the members of *Chovevei Tzion*, concentrated their efforts on the actual resettlement of the Land. Others, like Herzl, focused on the political arena, striving to gain international recognition for the future Jewish state.

There were, of course, religious Zionists, like the members of *Mizrachi*. However, they were not fully accepted by either group. The ultra-Orthodox condemned them for cooperating with sinners, and the secular Zionists accused them of not cooperating enough, of dual loyalties.

A Profile of the Author's Life

It is within this setting that R. Yisachar Shlomo Teichtal was born in 1885. Later on, we will present a somewhat detailed biography of this great man. For the time being, however, it is important to note that he was raised in a traditional religious environment and was naturally imbued with the prevalent, ultra-Orthodox world view, which included a strong opposition to Zionism. He invested all of his time and energy into Torah study, becoming a genuine Torah scholar at a young age. He frequented the courts of the era's most righteous and pious Torah leaders. To a large extent, these encounters molded his Torah personality. He never deviated from the accepted Orthodox framework; he was concerned only with serving God, improving his moral conduct, and studying Torah within the conventional areas of interest.

During the inter-war period, when R. Teichtal was reaching the height of his influence, the Jews of Europe enjoyed relative comfort. They were granted citizenship and equal rights in their respective countries, and Jewish political parties gained strength in Eastern European parliaments. The anti-Semitic parties tended to be in the opposition, and numerous governments promised freedom of religion to all of their citizens. These new circumstances helped strengthen the claims of the anti-Zionists. "All that fuss about the hopeless condition of European Jewry was a false alarm," they would claim. "The hard times were just a passing phase; we can easily study Torah and wait for *Mashiach* here in exile."

But then, World War II erupted; and the unthinkable became a dreadful reality, a reality far more savage than could have been described, far more terrifying than had been warned. While some people found it too difficult and terrifying to cope with this new reality, R. Teichtal began to reassess some of his fundamental positions. The Holocaust inspired him to reexamine the issue of Israel's redemption. It helped him better understand the sources which he already knew, for he now saw them in a different, more relevant, light. Previously, he viewed Zionism as "a desecration of holiness and a defilement of the supernal and earthly [Holy] Land" (Letter to the *Yiddishe Tzaytung* [the "Jewish Newspaper"] in Munkatch, 5696 [1936]). Now, however, he realized that the nationalistic movement and the rebuilding of the Land were revelations of Divine Providence and a clear sign of the imminent redemption. Despite his new outlook, R. Teichtal retained a profound respect for his righteous and holy mentors. After all, throughout the book he tries to reconcile their words with his findings.

R. Teichtal's new understanding drove him to awaken others, to show them the path of truth which he had found so recently. Thus, in the midst of the unspeakable Holocaust, with virtually no books, he wrote and published this sacred work. He hoped that it would help people understand the meaning of these horrifying events and help save them from the blindness and denial that once plagued him. Wherever he traveled, he spoke publicly about the importance of *aliyah* and building the Land, while exhorting his listeners to leave the Diaspora after the war. He was motivated by the profound hope that the survivors would live to see a brighter future, one in which the Jews would flourish in their ancient Homeland, in a Jewish state built upon the foundations of Torah and Tradition.

Apparently, however, God willed otherwise, and R. Teichtal shared the fate of so many other holy martyrs. May HaShem avenge their blood. We were not privileged to have him live among us, to teach us Torah and guide us in the pure service of God. The Talmud teaches that the death of the righteous atones for our sins; this is our only comfort.

This volume reveals R. Teichtal in his full stature: as a brilliant Torah scholar with a full command of classical Jewish sources; as a thinker whom few could equal; and above all, as a Jew who loved his fellow Jew with every fiber of his being. May the memory of the righteous be blessed.

II BIOGRAPHICAL SKETCH

Upbringing

Born in Hungary in 1885, Rabbi Teichtal grew up in a family with an illustrious lineage. Many of his ancestors were great rabbis and

Jewish leaders, and he perpetuated family tradition. His father, Yitzchak, was a noted scholar, teacher, and chassid. Yitzchak's father, Yisachar Shlomo (our author's namesake), served as a *Rosh Yeshiva* all his life and was one of the foremost chassidim of the Rebbe of Tzanz.

R. Teichtal's mother, Gittel, was known as a righteous and learned woman. R. Teichtal recounts in the introduction to his responsa: "She walked truthfully and perfectly before God. She despised worldly pleasures, caring only about Torah and fear of God. Her only goal was to instill in her children a burning love for these very ideals." He continues to describe how she used her great wisdom to draw her children to Torah.

His Mentors

At a very young age, Yisachar Shlomo showed signs of genius. Recognizing his special talents, his parents devoted extraordinary energies to his education. Until his Bar Mitzvah, Yisachar Shlomo was schooled by his father, as he writes: "[My father] ushered me into the inner chambers of the Torah. He provided me with a path through the sea of the Talmud, a course through the mighty waters of the Torah. He brought me through its width and breadth...from age three until thirteen" (ibid.).

Afterwards, he moved on to yeshiva study under the tutelage of Rabbi Shalom Weider – the *av beit din* of Nyrdhaza, Hungary, and one of the foremost students of the author of *Yitav Lev*. The following year he went to Tarnow, Galicia, to study at the famous *kloyz* (learning center) of the Tzanz Chassidim.

At age fifteen, he moved again, this time to the city of Gavne, Poland, where he was accepted as a student of one of the greatest minds in the Jewish world at the time, Rabbi Shalom Unger. The author of Responsa *Yad Shalom*, Rabbi Unger was the grandson and student of the Imrei Noam of Dzykov. He had a profound impact on the young Yisachar Shlomo. Not only did he teach him a great deal of Torah, but he also carefully fostered R. Teichtal's special talents. Rabbi Unger was very fond of his student, and he even asked him to tutor his own son. R. Unger also entrusted R. Teichtal with the task of editing his responsa, *Yad Shalom*. (At R. Unger's request, it was originally printed anonymously, only mentioning R. Teichtal's efforts.)

In 1905, after returning to Hungary, R. Teichtal studied under Rabbi Moshe Greenwald, the author of *Arugat HaBosem*. A year later, at age twenty-one, he received rabbinic ordination (*semichah*) from the great Rebbe of Talisheva, the author of *Yad Yitzchak*. In his letter of ordination, the Rebbe records R. Yisachar Shlomo's great skill and prowess in understanding Jewish law, as well as his sharp mind and keen insight.

A year later, Rabbi Teichtal received another ordination, this time from the great scholar of Unsdorf, Rabbi Shmuel Rosenberg, author of *Be'er Shmuel.* That same year he was ordained once again by the *av beit din* of Maad, Rabbi Mordechai Leib Winkler, author of *Levushei Mordechai.*

Marriage

At the age of nineteen, R. Teichtal married a woman with a pedigree as illustrious as his own. His wife, Freidel, was the daughter of R. Ya'akov Yosef Ginz, the rabbi of Hoida-Busermin, in Hungary, and author of *Harei Besamim.* Rabbi Ginz was a descendant of Rabbi Akiva Eiger and one of the foremost students of the Maharam Schick. Despite his young age, R. Teichtal was appointed judge and teacher in his father-in-law's community. His lectures and lessons were very popular and he quickly became renowned as a leader, scholar, and teacher. Unfortunately, however, Freidel passed away while still quite young.

R. Teichtal married again. His second wife, Nechamah, also came from a strong rabbinic family. Her father was Rabbi David Freidman, the *av beit din* of Tzahlim, who was a son-in-law of Rabbi Menachem Katz, one of the Chatam Sofer's prized students.

His Writings

In addition to his studies, lectures, and communal work, R. Teichtal was a prolific writer. He corresponded on matters of Jewish law and philosophy with his mentors and the other *gedolim* of Poland, Hungary, and Lithuania. As a result, many of his contemporaries mention him in their responsa. He also published numerous articles in Torah journals and periodicals.

R. Teichtal's masterpiece, and first major work, was *Mishneh Sachir.* It is a record of his responses to the numerous halachic questions he received from communities throughout Europe. He began working on this book at age twenty-four and published the first volume some fifteen years later, in 1924. The work received approbations from some of Europe's most illustrious rabbis, gaining him a reputation as an authority on Jewish law. The second volume appeared in 1926, while the third was printed in 1940, just after the beginning of the war. Unfortunately, the Nazis destroyed all the copies while they were still in the printing house. Only the author's personal copy was saved, together with the rest of his writings. The author's son, R. Chayim Menachem, recently published this volume, as well as a number of other manuscripts found after the Holocaust.

Fortunately, both of Rabbi Teichtal's major works – *Eim HaBanim Semeichah* and *Mishneh Sachir* – survived the Holocaust. Other manuscripts, including a personal journal, were also saved. R. Teichtal deposited these works with a Gentile and requested that any family member who survives the war return to retrieve them. After the war, his daughter, Hindel, fulfilled the request and retrieved the manuscripts from the Gentile, who miraculously managed to guard them. Most of these manuscripts have yet to be published. They include: novellae on the Talmud, homiletic discourses, ideas on the weekly *parashah*, and lessons from the lives of the great scholars.

In the Presence of the Generation's *Tzaddikim*

Rabbi Teichtal frequented the courts of the greatest chassidic masters, to bask in their glory and absorb some of their holiness. During his youth he would spend two months a year (Elul and Tishrei) in Belz to be with R. Yissachar Dov Rokeach, the Belzer Rebbe. He became even closer with the Rebbe during World War I, when the latter fled from his home town to a village near R. Teichtal's home.

R. Teichtal also used to visit the scions of the Tzanz Dynasty – the sons of the Divrei Chayim – i.e., the Rebbe of Shinev and the Rebbe of Rutzfort. He was especially close with the Rebbe of Munkatch, Rabbi Chayim Eliezer Shapira.

As the Rabbi of Pishtian

In 1921, R. Teichtal became the rabbi and *av beit din* of Pishtian, a mid-size city in Czechoslovakia. The local Jewish community lived quite comfortably at the time, so much so that people often referred to the area as ôLittle America.ö

The city of Pishtian was (and still is) famous for its mineral baths, which helped relieve the symptoms of rheumatism. Many people, including some of the era's greatest rabbis, flocked to these baths. While there, these *gedolim* would visit Rabbi Teichtal to discuss Torah and other pressing matters; and they quickly recognized his lofty stature. As a result of these meetings, R. Teichtal established close bonds with some of the greatest Torah scholars of the time, including R. Meir Shapira of Lublin, R. Meir Zamba of Warsaw, R. Shimon Greenfeld of Samihali, R. Eliezer Falkin of Pinsk, and Rabbi Eliezer Kahana Shapira of Kovno.

Yeshivat Moriah

R. Teichtal remained in Pishtian for twenty years. During that time, he achieved one of his life's greatest ambitions – he established a Yeshivah called Moriah. It was an elite institution for exceptional students; each year's class consisted of fifty of the best and brightest young minds in Europe. The yeshiva's goal was to train competent rabbis and equip them with the tools necessary to lead Jewish communities into a new era. Rabbi Teichtal wanted to ensure that no Jewish community would be left without a spiritual leader. He became a surrogate father to his students, taking a personal interest in each one, even providing financial assistance when necessary.

The Outbreak of World War II

Hitler invaded Czechoslovakia in 1938, while R. Teichtal was in Pishtian. Troubles mounted daily. In 1939, the Nazis began their campaign to degrade and demoralize the Jews. They deprived the Jews of their livelihood and severely restricted their movement. Despite this, the Jewish community tried its best to maintain normal religious life. During this period, R. Teichtal worked tirelessly for the members of his community, organizing relief efforts and encouraging them with words of hope.

The Great Vow

Deportations began in the spring of 1942 with the abduction of young women over the age of sixteen. To escape capture and deportation, R. Teichtal and his family hid in the attic of the local *beit midrash* along with ten other families. Through the cracks in the wall, he witnessed the massive deportation of his friends and neighbors right below. He heard their screams and watched helplessly as his fellow Jews were beaten ruthlessly and herded away.

In response, R. Teichtal took a vow, a *neder*. Should he survive this living hell and escape death, he would write a *sefer* in honor of the Land of Israel. The goal of this work would be to inspire every Jew to ascend to our forefathers' Land and help rebuild it. Rabbi Teichtal began fulfilling this promise immediately. There, in that attic, with virtually no books at his disposal, he began writing *Eim HaBanim Semeichah.*

Escape to Nitra

As the noose continued to tighten around the necks of Czechoslovakia's Jews, the *Tzaddik* of Nitra sent messengers to R. Teichtal, offering to provide refuge for him and his family. As the Chief Rabbi of Slovakia, the *Tzaddik* had been granted permission to remain where he was. He managed to save hundreds of Jews this way. Thus, in the month of Elul, 1942, R. Teichtal and his family escaped to Nitra. In early 1943, however, the Nazis decided to wipe out the population of Nitra as well. Thus, R. Teichtal and his family fled across the border into Hungary.

Refuge in Hungary

For a while, R. Teichtal wandered from place to place. Hungarian Jews were frightened and reluctant to harbor refugees, because of the potential dangers. Eventually, though, he found temporary refuge in different parts of Budapest – Hungary's capital – where he remained for almost two years. From time to time, he was forced to flee to the surrounding villages which were somewhat safer and where the Jews were more willing to harbor refugees. Despite the dangers, R. Teichtal taught Torah and delivered fiery sermons wherever he went. He urged his listeners not to lose faith, but to strengthen themselves in Torah and *mitzvot.* Most of all, he tried to impress upon his fellow Jews the dire need to return to *Eretz Yisrael* and build it upon the foundations of Torah and fear of God.

While still in Budapest, on Thursday night of *parashat VaYeira,* the 15th of Cheshvan, 5704 (1943), Rabbi Yisachar Shlomo Teichtal completed his seminal work, *Eim HaBanim Semeichah,* a little more than a year after beginning it.

The Nazis Invade Hungary

In 1944, the Nazis invaded Hungary and the local Jews were subjected to the same horrors that had befallen the rest of Europe's Jews. Thinking that the Nazis had already finished their evil work in Slovakia, the Teichtal family returned there and hid in a secluded house in Pressburg. They hoped to stay there until the imminent fall of the Nazis. Unfortunately, though, the Nazis stepped up their efforts to find the last remaining Jews, and Rabbi Teichtal and his family were captured and sent to Auschwitz.

A Martyr's Death

In January, 1945, as the Soviet army advanced through Poland, the Nazis began transferring the inmates of Auschwitz inland into Germany. R. Teichtal and his family were among them. Some inmates were made to walk the distance while others were sent by train. R. Teichtal perished on a train on his way to Mauthausen concentration camp, on the 10th of Shevat, 5705 (January 24, 1945). R. Chayim Menachem Teichtal recounts his father's death as follows:

> We know the details of the passing of this sacred soul from the testimony of one of his students, who was present at the time and now lives in *Eretz Yisrael.* During the month of Shevat, 5705 (1945), the allied forces advanced on all fronts, and the Russians reached the gates of Auschwitz. Still, even with the sword poised at their throats, the Nazis begrudged their tortured victims any chance of life. They used every means at their disposal to keep them from falling into the liberator's hands

> alive. The Nazis loaded the Jews onto locked freight cars together with Ukrainian prisoners – who harassed the Jews mercilessly – to transport them to an unknown destination, far from the front.
>
> After starving their victims for a number of days, the oppressors tossed each of them a meager crust of bread, with the evil intent of having them fight pathetically for their paltry allotment. Indeed, one of the Ukrainians grabbed the portion of a Jew – my father's neighbor – who was desperate for this crust of bread. This angered my father, who demanded the return of the theft. The other travelers begged my father not to get involved, since it might cost him his life. But he said, "How can I stand by when the wronged man's life depends on this food?" Indeed, he insisted on taking a stand, and the Ukrainians, with the cooperation of the Nazi soldiers, rose against him and killed him, after torturing him mercilessly.

Through the written word, the legacy and teachings of Rabbi Yisachar Shlomo Teichtal continue. This book is his legacy. It is his call for unity, his call for redemption, a call for the Jewish people to galvanize around the issue of *Eretz Yisrael* and, thus, set the stage for a new, Messianic era.

FOREWORD OF R. CHAYIM MENACHEM TEICHTAL

With the appearance of *Eim HaBanim Semeichah* in English, I find it my sacred obligation to clarify certain points about the author and about the purpose of the book.

This work is rooted in the pure wellsprings of our holy Torah and in the words of our great Sages throughout the generations. It was composed as an expression of absolute piety, at the very height of the unspeakable Holocaust, in the year 5703 [1943], in Budapest. It was written while the author was hiding from the rage of the oppressor, immersed in a sea of troubles. His saintly heart was fairly bursting with anguish over God's holy people bowed by the relentless pangs of exile beneath the boots of the ferocious Nazis, may their memory be eradicated!

Perhaps, for one who was not tried by the events of that period, in that hell-on-earth, for one who escaped the torment of the unbearable physical and emotional suffering of those days, some parts of this work may seem surprising, even "controversial." In fact, there have even been some who clothed themselves in zealousness and knew no peace until they distorted the pure and holy image of the author beyond recognition.

Even though some of them were motivated by sacred intentions, I, in turn, must lift up my voice with a passion every bit as holy and cry incessantly in the name of God: *Remove your shoes from your feet* (*Shemot* 3:5) when you come to speak of this wondrous man, exalted above the rest! Every aspect of his life was suffused with sanctity, piety, and supreme self-sacrifice for God and His Torah. Indeed, he selflessly gave up his pure soul in defense of another Jew (see above).

Our mental resources are insufficient to describe the greatness of my righteous father and teacher, whose entire life, within the narrow confines of *halachah*, was dedicated to guiding his precious flock – his congregation and the students of his yeshiva. But, as great as he was in Torah, he was greater still in fear of Heaven. He was a leader and guide of tremendous stature, always standing in the breach to defend pure Torah Judaism. He never yielded an inch on an issue of *halachah*, and he never deviated from the traditional path of Torah. Because of these qualities, he attracted many followers and admirers, who learned from his every word and exhibited absolute devotion to their master.

The greatest and most righteous scholars of the generation venerated my beloved father. They heaped titles of honor upon him while he was still a very young man, extolling his wisdom and extraordinary gift for discovering the truth of the Torah.

His whole life was centered around his precious congregation, his holy yeshiva, and the responsa he sent to the numerous questions he received from all over the world. During his lifetime, a portion of this great fountain of knowledge was indeed shared with the world when the first volume of *Mishneh Sachir* was published. (The remainder of my saintly father's responsa, saved miraculously in manuscript, are now, at last, appearing in print, with the help of the Almighty. They are being published by Machon Yerushalayim.)

This devout scholar worked day and night to serve the Almighty. The sounds of Torah and prayer constantly filled his home, and he never stopped writing, even in those darkest days. When unprecedented and unparalleled troubles befell the Jews, he poured out his pure heart to our Father in Heaven over every individual and collective misfortune.

During those stormy times, his yeshiva was banished from his *beit midrash*. Thus, his mind turned increasingly to the troubles of the generation. He began to scrutinize the history of our people, in an attempt to find an explanation for the terrible suffering we have endured ever since the destruction of the Temple, now reaching a peak before his eyes.

Observing the desperate circumstances of European Jewry, he arrived at his conclusion: The exile and our existence in foreign lands were the source of all the troubles of our people. And so, he embarked upon a campaign, from then until the end of his life, urging his brethren to flee these lands, to cease devoting their energies to the development of gentile countries, and to dedicate themselves, instead, to building our own Land in the spirit of the Torah.

When circumstances in his birthplace grew intolerable, he was forced to hide from the government forces. Along with some others – men, women, and children – he hid in the attic above his study hall. Through the slats of the attic, they were able to see their beloved neighbors and friends brutally forced onto transports for destinations which, at that time, were still unknown. My father's heart fairly burst within him at these terrible scenes, and his prayer was fervent: If only God's tortured people could escape from this nightmare and find themselves exclusively among Jews, on the sacred soil of *Eretz Yisrael*...

Such thoughts occupied his mind incessantly, giving him no peace. There, in that attic, he was able to raise himself out of his despair over the bitter fate of our people only through deep study. Now, exercising superhuman powers of concentration, he turned his attention and his writing to *Eretz Yisrael*.

The unendurable troubles and indescribable torture ignited the torch of love for the Land which had always been buried within him. This found its expression in *Eim HaBanim Semeichah*, a work encouraging the settlement and building of the Holy Land through the mass *aliyah* of Jews who "tremble at the word of God" (החרדים לדבר ה'). This masterful opus was invested with intense emotion; my father's very essence poured into every line. It was composed in 5703 (1943), in "a valley of troubles," Budapest, the capital of Hungary, to which he was forced to flee.

My revered father's love for the Land, his fervent desire to expand its settlement with Torah Jews, and his joy at its building were exhibited publicly at every possible opportunity. Alas, his fiery words in praise of our hallowed Land, were distorted more than once. Various groups misrepresented his views intentionally, for various reasons. Thus, concerned for the honor of this pure and righteous man, the family was hesitant to issue this work for some time.

Indeed, the author himself predicted this very eventuality. He expressed his fears in one of his last letters to me: "To my great dismay, there are some who did not understand my intent in writing *Eim HaBanim Semeichah*... God is my witness that when I write about our brethren resettling *Eretz Yisrael*, tears flow from my eyes uncontrollably because of God's people who suffer indescribable miseries. I see in the Land of Israel a ray of light, an anchor of salvation. I know that there will be those who will attribute to me words which I never said and never thought. Still, He Who Knows All Secrets can testify how fervently I prayed that my words not constitute a stumbling-block. And I am certain that the merit of our Holy Land will stand by all those who sincerely love her, so that ultimately no one will be turned away. I find support in the words of our sages, quoted often by the brilliant and holy author of *Minchat Elazar*, the righteous Rebbe of Munkatch: 'Israel will be redeemed only through repentance, and the Torah has already promised that Israel will repent at the end of their exile and immediately be redeemed.' On the basis of this guarantee I authored *Eim HaBanim Semeichah*."

And so, at this time, I find myself obligated to refute the views which were incorrectly attributed to the author by people who took his words out of context. It is my duty to reestablish the truth, that the goal of this work is to enhance the glory of Heaven and increase the settlement of *Eretz Yisrael* through the *aliyah* of masses of Torah-observant Jews.

The author quotes the words of the Rebbe of Gur *z"l*: "The more Orthodox Jews that ascend to *Eretz Yisrael*, the greater their influence will be in fashioning the image of the Land according to Torah tradition, and in preserving the holiness of the Land." Today we see concrete evidence of this in the increased numbers of Orthodox

Jews in the Land, bringing enhanced awareness of the Torah's demands. How much more so would this be true if they constituted a majority in the Land?! If a little bit of light can chase away much darkness, surely a great deal of light can eliminate the darkness entirely.

Indeed, we witness the proliferation of *yeshivot* in every part of the country, and the light of Torah is permeating even the thick darkness that precedes the advent of *Mashiach*. Increasingly, winds of purity are reaching our lost brethren. They are returning to their roots and casting away all of the false ideologies whose emptiness has become apparent. It is not hard to imagine how much better this situation would be if the Torah-true portion of the population were greater, and if centers of Torah learning filled every corner of the Holy Land. Clearly, the great light thus cast would bring all the people back, and "sins, not sinners, would cease to exist" (*Berachot* 10a).

The author speaks in praise of the builders of the Land. Although they may have left the Torah, it is undoubtedly to their credit that they are privileged to settle and build the Land. My saintly father even has answers for those who question why the Almighty saw fit to allow the initiative for the rebuilding to come specifically from such people. He explains that no human being can fathom the searchings of God, for the thoughts of He Who is Perfect in Knowledge are far beyond our thoughts. In his view, not only are the God-fearing Jews forbidden to refrain from building the Land based on such objections, but they have a sacred obligation to combine their strengths and contribute to this lofty endeavor. Then, when the wayward builders see that the religious Jews want to cooperate with them, they, in turn, will draw closer to them and improve their ways. After all, they, too, are descendants of Avraham, Yitzchak, and Ya'akov...

It should be clear to all that this author was not carrying the banner of a movement which announced "*Eretz Yisrael* without Torah!" Any organization whose goal was to establish Israel as a nation in its own Land, like all other nations, would have nothing in common with him. This was the very antithesis of my beloved father's goal.

There is a great danger in reading this work superficially, seeking a modern-day ideology with which to associate its message. To reduce the sacred, Torah principles laid forth on these pages to some "-ism" is a desecration, a blasphemy. The Torah precedes, transcends, and outlasts any man-made system of thought. In the Torah, and in all the holy books which explain it, love for the Land of Israel is a supreme value. Building and settling the Land are *mitzvot* of paramount importance. At this point in history, the author perceived a combination of factors making this *mitzvah* both more urgent and more available. He thus felt himself compelled to encourage the people of Israel to shoulder this precious obligation, to settle and build the Land on a firm Torah base.

Ideas fashioned by man are not addressed in this work at all. Indeed, there could be no greater distortion of its intent than to conclude that this book is a declaration of support for a man-made ideology. Beyond the straightforward restatement of Torah ideas, there is merely transcendent love: love for the Land of Israel, the people of Israel, the Torah, and the Almighty.

This love is displayed on all levels of my father's writing. At every opportunity, he addresses himself to the builders of the Land in an ardent plea to establish their efforts on a solid Torah base. He warns that without Torah, which is our only claim to the Land, the settlement of *Eretz Yisrael* can have no future. Whereas a Torah-true approach to building the Land is a guarantee for success, a nationalism stripped of Torah is a path to perdition, God forbid. Thus, while beseeching Torah Jews to join hands with the builders, he implores these very builders to subjugate themselves to Torah authority.

My father's love for the Jewish people expresses itself in almost every page of the work. He instructs us to invoke merit upon every Jew, encourage him to do what is right according to our holy Torah, and rebuke him lovingly where he falls short.

In his all-encompassing love for God and man, my saintly father served as a source of comfort and strength for all those around him. Even in the valley of tears and torment, his greatness of spirit never left him. When he understood that his own end was near, he spoke passionately to those around him: "Jews," he said, "soon this reign of evil will end, and you will merit a salvation so great that it will illuminate the entire world. In particular, those residing in our Holy Land will merit this. Let us all pray for the welfare of our brothers everywhere. I know that my time is limited, and I promise that I will pray on your behalf that you may speedily merit salvation and complete redemption."

With these words my father returned his pure soul to its Maker, on the 10th of Shevat, 5705 (1945). May God avenge his blood!

His very last request was: "Please, spread my wellsprings outward."

May his memory be blessed.

Chayim Menachem Teichtal,
son of my revered master and teacher,
the brilliant and saintly author,
Rabbi Yisachar Shlomo Teichtal *ztvk"l*

EIM HABANIM
אם הבנים שמחה
SEMEICHAH

A Cordial Letter from R. Shlomo Dov Heller

A cordial letter from my honorable friend, elder of the generation, unique in our time in brilliance, well-versed in the law as was Shmuel, the *halachah* always follows his opinion, the great and brilliant rabbi, paragon and glory of the generation, singular in this generation, the respected elder, *tzaddik*, foundation of the world, our holy master, R. Shlomo Dov Heller, rabbi and *av beit din* of Sighet, son-in-law of the mentor of the entire Diaspora, our master, the author of *Eirech Shai* and Responsa *Teshurat Shai*, from Sighet. May he still be fruitful and fresh in his good old age.[1] May his eyes behold Israel's salvation and the return of our captivity to Zion,[2] speedily in our days. Amen.

With God's help, Sunday of *parashat VaYishlach*, 5704 [1943], here in Sighet...

May HaShem grant abundant peace and blessing, a thousandfold, to my honorable friend, the brilliant rabbi, sharp and well-versed, the famed glory of Israel, the great author, the words of his palate are most sweet and he is altogether delightful,[3] our honorable and holy master, R. Yisachar Shlomo Teichtal *shlita*, who now lives in the capital, Budapest. May the pleasantness of HaShem hover over him forever.

After inquiring about his honor's well being, as is customary for those who love HaShem, I will begin with an apology so that his honor will not be distressed by my late reply to his pleasant letter. I actually received the letter on time, but due to my numerous sins I was sick in bed (may the Merciful One protect us). For six consecutive weeks, ever since the first day of *Rosh HaShanah*, I was bedridden because of the disease with which HaShem afflicted me. Doctors came and went, until HaShem had compassion on me, and my condition improved. I am still not totally cured, but I have left my bed. I hope and I am confident that by virtue of the prayers of the community and my friends, HaShem will help me return to my original strength and will complete my healing with His overflowing benevolence. Therefore, I publicly thank HaShem for the loving kindness He has shown me thus far, and I pray for the same in the future.

Therefore, his honor should not wonder why I have been silent until now. I hold his honor in great esteem, for I saw his great strength and wondrous expertise in every side and every corner of his booklet. I was astonished by the greatness of his pure and forthright intellect, by his charming rhetoric, and by his mastery of our holy language - to express every idea clearly. May there be many like him in Israel.

However, regarding the issue at hand: His honor asked me to express my humble opinion on the well-known idea. He has asked me a difficult thing, for I have always realized that I am too insignificant to become involved in issues which have been examined by the *gedolim* of the generation (such as this idea). What will come forth from someone as insignificant as me? I am afraid to stand in the place of *gedolim*. I have never overstepped my boundaries on any issue. Only when someone asked me to state my humble opinion on a halachic matter did I reveal whatever I knew, but not about communal issues. Therefore, his honor should not be distressed, for now too, I cannot overstep my boundary. I beg forgiveness.

I hereby remain his honor's friend and wholeheartedly wish him all the best. May he and all of Israel experience all types of salvation, consolation, and preeminence, speedily in our days, as his pure soul desires. I, too, await salvation, and honor and respect his exalted self.

Shlomo Dov Heller, Rabbi and *Av Beit Din* of Sighet

PS A certain scholar who came to my house saw his honor's booklet on the table and looked through it. He liked it very much and asked me to request of his honor to sell it to him. Therefore, please tell me how much money this man should send, and...I will give him this copy so that his honor should not have to print a new one. It goes without saying that if his honor wants me to return his booklet, I will do so immediately upon receiving his reply.

1 Based on *Tehillim* 92:15. 2 Based on *Tehillim* 126:1. 3 Based on *Shir HaShirim* 5:16.

APPROBATIONS [PREFACE][1]

In lieu of approbations, I hereby present at the beginning of this work the approbations of the holy and lofty *gedolim* to the volume, *Derishat Tzion*, by our brilliant and righteous master, R. Tzvi Kalischer *z"l*. He was the prime advocate of rebuilding our Land, and, in 5624 [1864], he wrote this work on the subject. I came across his book here in the capital after I had already completed mine, and I merited to concur with him on many points. Nevertheless, the *Mishnah* does not move from its place.[2] Thus, since I followed in his footsteps, I am certain that if these holy and brilliant scholars were still alive they would bestow their glory upon me and endorse my work as well. I am, therefore, using their approbations to *Derishat Tzion* for my work as well.

I Approbations

R. Yehoshua Kutner

The approbation of the renowned *gaon*, the honorable saint of HaShem, the mentor of the entire Diaspora, the prince of the Torah, the foremost teacher, our revered master and mentor, R. Yisrael Yehoshua *z"l, av beit din* of Kutno, known as R. Yusha'le Kutner, the author of many works including Responsa *Yeshu'ot Malko*.

Baruch HaShem, the 6th of Tevet, 5625 [1865].

A precious soul, a man of wisdom, from him comes forth the

1 [As the author presently explains, this is not a typical set of approbations. In addition, towards the end of the chapter, he adds some very significant points of his own which set the stage for the entire book. Therefore, we decided to add the title "Preface" to this chapter, to emphasize that it is an integral part of the *sefer* and cannot be overlooked (especially pp. 21ff.]

2 [Based on *Avodah Zarah* 35b. This expression indicates that even if a teaching is found to be repetitive, it is not discarded.]

peg, from him the cornerstone,[3] my honorable companion, the great rabbi renowned for pride and glory, our master, R. Tzvi Hirsch Kalischer, may his light shine brightly.

His honor's precious words have shed their light upon me, and I was glad to see that he has invested great efforts on behalf of the Organization for the Settlement of *Eretz Yisrael*.[4] Now, when one begins a *mitzvah*, we say to him, "finish it."[5] Continue and you will surely succeed. ***Do not become disheartened nor discouraged by the words of the antagonists, for they speak out of ignorance***. However, his exalted honor (may he live) has exaggerated a bit with regard to the renewal of the sacrificial service,[6] for this is a very difficult matter. Since the only permissible sacrifices are communal ones, we would need the approval of the majority of Israel. This is an almost impossible feat at this time, seeing that Israel is scattered to the four corners of the earth, both physically and ideologically (due to our numerous sins). With regard to the Organization for the Settlement of *Eretz Yisrael*, however, fortunate are those who work towards this.

I hereby say *shalom* to his honor and to the leaders of the organization, and although their beginning was insignificant, their end will be exceedingly great.[7] In accordance with their [elevated] souls, I seek their welfare with heart and soul.

Yisrael Yehoshua of Kutno

❋ ❋ ❋

R. Eliyahu of Greiditz

The approbation of the great *gaon*, the righteous and holy rabbi who is like an angel of the Lord of Hosts, our honorable master, R. Eliyahu, son of our master R. Shlomo *zt"l, av beit din* of Greiditz in Prussia.

I was asked by my beloved colleague, the renowned and righteous *gaon*, the glory of Israel, our master, R. Tzvi Kalischer

3 Based on *Zecharyah* 10:4.

4 See peface to *Derishat Tzion* (Mossad HaRav Kook, 5724 [1964]), pp. 23-33, concerning this organization.

5 *Yerushalmi*: *Pesachim* 10:5 (61a), *Rosh HaShanah* 1:8 (9a), *Megillah* 2:7 (21b); *Tanchuma, Eikev* 6.

6 R. Kalischer wanted to renew the sacrificial service. See *Derishat Tzion*, essays *HaAvodah* and *Kadishin*, pp. 122-72, and the preface.

7 Based on *Iyov* 8:7.

(may he live a long and productive life) to endorse this third volume,[8] which is called in Israel *Derishat Tzion* and *Chevrat Eretz Noshavet*. When I delved into his genuine and pleasant words, built upon the foundations of truth and justice, I said, perhaps HaShem will speedily have compassion and immediately fulfill through us the words of the prophet: *He confirms the words of His servant, and performs the counsel of His messengers; Who says to Jerusalem, "You shall be settled," and to the cities of Judah, "They shall be rebuilt, and I will raise up their ruins"* (*Yeshayah* 44:26). And, I felt dutibound not only to endorse its publication, but also to propose some ideas on this matter... Perhaps after we take some small initiatory step, HaShem will immediately think of us[9] and accept our actions, in order to fulfill: *Return to Me and I will return to you* (*Malachi* 3:7).* Therefore, we must also say, *I arose to open for*

---

* Behold, it appears that this holy *gaon* was unsure whether the Holy One Blessed be He would consider our return to *Eretz Yisrael* en masse a fulfillment of *Return to me and I will return to you*. Blessed is HaShem Who enlightened me to find this stated explicitly in *Midrash Tehillim*. Scripture states: *For the conductor, a psalm for the sons of Korach. O Lord You have favored Your Land, You have returned the captivity of Ya'akov... Return us O God of our salvation* (*Tehillim* 85:1-2,5). The *Midrash* comments:

> The sons of Korach said [to God], "Until when will You say, *Return O wayward sons* (*Yirmiyah* 3:14), and they [Israel] say to You, 'You return first,' as it says, *Return O Lord, until when? and relent...* (*Tehillim* 90:13). And You say, 'No, Israel must take the initiative.' You will not return by Yourself and we will not return by ourselves. Rather, both of us will return simultaneously, as it is written, *You have returned the captivity of Ya'akov... Return us*[10] *O God of our salvation*." (*Midrash Tehillim* 85:3)[11]

That is to say, Ya'akov will return and God will return, both together. Now, since the *Midrash* brings the claims of the Assembly of Israel (*Kenesset Yisrael*) and the Holy One Blessed be He, as well as the compromise of the sons of Korach, all upon the verse *O Lord You have*

8 This refers to *Derishat Tzion* which is the third section of a book entitled *Emunah Yesharah*.

9 Based on *Yonah* 1:6.

10 [The Hebrew word שובנו can also loosely be translated as "we will return."]

11 Buber edition. Hereafter, any reference to *Midrash Tehillim* will be from this edition.

my Beloved (*Shir HaShirim* 5:5). And when we take some small initiatory step, HaShem will completely and truthfully say, *My Beloved sent forth His hand through the hole and my innards stirred for Him* (ibid. 5:4). *Be strong and let us be strong for the sake of our people and for the sake of the cities of our God, and the Lord will do that which is good in His eyes* (I *Divrei HaYamim* 19:13). May we fulfill the verse, *You will arise and have mercy upon Zion, for it is time to favor her, for the appointed time has come* – When? – *For Your servants cherished her stones, and favored her dust* (*Tehillim* 102:14-15). The brilliant Sforno explains the reason for this (see there).[14]

Eliyahu, son of our master R. Shlomo *zt"l*, of ***Greiditz***

---

favored Your Land..., it seems clear that our return to *Eretz Yisrael* is unquestionably a fulfillment of God's plea, *Return to Me*.

Now, it is evident from the *Midrash* that the sons of Korach made a compromise between us and the Holy One Blessed be He that neither of us will take the first step. Rather, both of us will return simultaneously. Nonetheless, I discovered in the volume, *Tiferet HaGershuni*, by our mentor, R. Gershon of Metz *z"l* (a colleague of the Shach), that we still must take the initiative. If HaShem acts first, we cannot possibly reckon that exact moment and begin together with Him. On the other hand, if we act first, HaShem can certainly synchronize with us and begin at that very moment.[12]

Based on this, I explained the prophets declaration: "Your God will rejoice over you as a bridegroom rejoices over the bride."[13] Why does he compare our future joy specifically to that of a bride and groom? Based on the above, it is clear. It is well known that after the bride begins walking towards the *chuppah* [bridal canopy], the sexton proclaims, "Greet the bride," meaning that the groom should go forth to greet her. In fact, this custom is still practiced by pious and righteous men. The prophet says that the same will be true of us and our Father in Heaven. After we begin to return to *Eretz Yisrael*, Moshe Rabbeinu – who acts as the middleman between us and HaShem – will proclaim, "Greet the bride." HaShem will then come forth to greet us, and He will bring our efforts to a successful end. In any event, this *Midrash* explicitly concurs with our mentor *z"l*.

12 *Tiferet HaGershuni* (Munkatch, 5663 [1903]), *VeZot HaBerachah*, p. 98.

13 Based on *Yeshayah* 62:5.

14 Sforno, *Tehillim* 102:14-15. Also see *Kuzari* 5:27.

❋ ❋ ❋

R. Chayim David Chazan

The approbation of the great *gaon*, the holy Sefardic scholar, the *Rishon LeTzion*, R. Chayim David Chazan.

> He is strong and mighty in Torah. He uncovers the depths and the hidden, the renowned *gaon*, the righteous rabbi who cares for Zion, our revered master, R. Tzvi Hirsch Kalischer, may his light shine forth and illuminate like the light of the seven days of creation. So may it be God's will. Amen.
>
> Abundant greetings... His honor's words are pure utterances which enlighten the eyes. He has clearly proven to the wise that *Mashiach* will not come to Israel in the manner that people presume. The House of Israel says, "His time will come suddenly, a time for the beloved. HaShem will blow the *shofar* to illuminate the earth, to proclaim to the imprisoned, 'Go forth from darkness and the shadow of death to an intense light.'" This is not so. The truth is that the Children of Israel will indeed go forth from darkness to an intense light, but the great salvation will not shine and sprout all at once, to elevate us instantaneously from a pit of darkness to the loftiest level. Rather, the elevation will be gradual, from one level to the next. After becoming accustomed to a particular level they will lift up their heads to the next, closest level. An instantaneous elevation from the lowest extreme to the highest extreme is highly unrealistic. Also, the Children of Israel would not be able to cope with such abundant good. This is similar to a person who recently recovered from a difficult and dangerous illness. Due to his intense weakness, he cannot suddenly indulge in an excess of food and other physical pleasures. Experience also proves this, for if someone would suddenly shine a bright light on a person sleeping in a dark room, he would not be able to enjoy the luster of the light, as his honor cites in the name of the holy *Zohar* (*VaYishlach*).[15]
>
> These words are true, and befitting he who said them. The upright will follow them.[16] They teach the true belief that HaShem alone causes salvation and all of the awesome and wondrous miracles[17] which are beyond our comprehension. And, God will send the *Beit HaMikdash* from the heavens, already

15 See *Derishat Tzion*, p. 89.

16 Based on *Hoshea* 14:10.

17 Based on *Devarim* 34:11-12.

built and perfected by Him,[18] as well as wellsprings of wisdom. All of the complete blessings and prophetic promises [will be fulfilled]. We will receive the goodness from God at the end of days, [but only] after the proper preparation.* We must prepare our hearts to receive the good that HaShem will bestow upon us. We must do this through human acts: to fortify ourselves with strength and worthy deeds designed to arouse the love of the Beloved as in the days of our youth,[21] and to follow the ways of HaShem.

This does not violate the oath: *That you not wake or rouse*

---

* It seems to me that the words of the *gaon z"l* are stated explicitly in Yeshayahu's prophecy: *For the increase of dominion and for peace without end upon the throne of David and upon his kingdom, to establish it and support it with justice and righteousness from now to eternity. The zeal of the Lord of Hosts performs this* (*Yeshayah* 9:6). This verse seems to contradict itself. At first it says that we ourselves must establish and support it with justice and righteousness. But afterwards it says, *The zeal of the Lord of Hosts performs this*. We can understand this based on the *gaon*'s idea. In order to receive this great good from HaShem, we must first effect a great preparation through our deeds. Then, the zeal of the Lord of Hosts will bring our work to a successful end, for we cannot complete it with our strength alone. HaShem will only bring it to the utmost perfection after we perform some initial act which will serve as a preparation.

It seems to me that the prophet's statement, *To establish it and support it with justice* (במשפט) *and righteousness* (ובצדקה), hints to his statement elsewhere: *Zion will be redeemed with justice* (במשפט) *and those that return to her with righteousness* (בצדקה) (*Yeshayah* 1:27). That is to say, Zion takes us to task [lit., has a litigation (משפט) against us] because we are obligated to redeem her from the defiled ones (as the Rivash[19] and the Ramban[20] explain). *And those that return to her with righteousness* refers to the performance of highly righteous deeds, as *Chazal state*, "Charity (צדקה) is great for it brings the final redemption closer" (*Bava Batra* 10a). This is the preparation and the support that HaShem desires from us.

18 See below, pp. 217-20, and 436 -457.

19 *Teshuvot HaRivash* 101.

20 *VaYikra* 25:24.

21 Based on *Yirmiyah* 2:2.

the love until it pleases (*Shir HaShirim* 2:7).[22] For, although all prophecy about the final redemption has been concealed and we cannot assert decisively that the time of salvation has come, nevertheless, our eyes see HaShem's wondrous and lofty deeds and His Divine Providence over Israel. Behold, *The heart of a king is in the hands of the Lord* (*Mishley* 21:1), and HaShem has placed kindness and compassion in their hearts to free us from bondage. The kings wish to glorify and exalt the pride of Israel and elevate our name in the world, something which they have never done before. Furthermore, their hands are stretched out to make Jerusalem a source of pride.[23] Who can hear and see such things and not realize that *The Lord favors His people, He glorifies the humble with salvation* (*Tehillim* 149:4). HaShem desires us. Behold, *My Beloved sent forth His hand through the hole* (*Shir HaShirim* 5:4). He is awakening us to salvation and redemption, and HaShem will shine and illuminate our [path] like the morning light.[24] We will rise up in the name of HaShem, to aid HaShem against the mighty,[25] until *I arose to open for my Beloved* (ibid. 5:5). But if, God forbid, we act negligently in this matter and *my Beloved turned and left* (ibid. 5:6), and we search for Him but do not find Him, [at least] we will have the vision to know that through these things the Holy One Blessed be He awakens us and informs us that HaShem desires wholly burnt offerings (עולות).[26] [That is, He desires] to elevate (להעלות) Israel to the highest heights. This is the meaning of *until it pleases* (*Shir HaShirim* 2:7).

And since the King of Israel and its Redeemer[27] is drawing us[28] with wonders and signs, we, His nation and His servants, will run after Him.[29] Not with force nor with power[30] shall a man strengthen himself, God forbid. We must not rebel against the nations of the world and the benevolent kings, nor go up as a wall[31] to fight against the ruler. Rather, "to perform a

22 [The Talmud (*Ketuvot* 111a) derives from this verse that HaShem bound the Jewish people by three oaths, one of which is that they would not ascend to *Eretz Yisrael* en masse until the appropriate time.]

23 Based on *Yeshayah* 62:7.

24 Based on II *Shmuel* 23:4.

25 Based on *Shoftim* 5:23.

26 Based on I *Shmuel* 15:22.

27 *Yeshayah* 44:6.

28 Based on *Shir HaShirim* 1:4.

29 Ibid.

30 *Zecharyah* 4:6.

31 See *Ketuvot* 111a.

pronounced vow or a freewill offering,"[32] [meaning, we must] desire wholeheartedly to fulfill the will of the Creator by awakening from below. [We must] do whatever we can with God's help and with the support of the benevolent kings and their absolute good will. Then, God will grace us from the heavens and bring about good things through these worthy people, for our benefit as well as theirs. We will plow, harvest, and fulfill the commandments that are dependent on the Land in order to redeem the Holy Land.[33] Then, HaShem's salvation will sprout from the Land.[34] And it will be that when our eyes behold HaShem's assistance from above – as the words of the prophet indicate, *In a day of salvation* (the simple meaning being, at the time of the final redemption) *I have assisted you* (*Yeshayah* 49:8) – then, *I will make you a covenant of the people, to restore the Land* (Rashi explains, "To restore...*Eretz Yisrael* which I chose from all the other lands"), *and to bequeath you desolate inheritances..., they will not hunger and they will not thirst...* (ibid. 49:8-10). Afterwards, *The mountains will break forth in glad song for the Lord has comforted* (כי נחם) *His people and will have mercy on His humble ones* (ibid. 49:13). All of this is in the future tense. Even the words *for the Lord has comforted* (כי נחם) are in the future tense like the rest of the verse, as Yonatan ben Uziel interprets: "In the future, HaShem will comfort His people." Once we possess fields and vineyards from which the destitute of our people find sustenance, then *They will not hunger and they will not thirst*, and they will inherit an everlasting inheritance of fields, vineyards, and goodly houses.[35] HaShem's providence will watch over us in our homes and fields, and the nations of the land will see[36] the House of Israel dwelling on their own Land.[37] Nothing of the work of the field will be lacking. We will be like them [the nations], each man under his grapevine and under his fig tree.[38] None will envy the House of Israel. There will be no adversary nor evil affliction, because the kings of the earth and their glory will hover over us to bring us closer to the service of HaShem. This itself will be for us a sign and a great proof that this came from HaShem[39] and that He is the One Who grants strength

32 Based on *BeMidbar* 15:3.
33 Based on *VaYikra* 25:24.
34 Based on *Tehillim* 85:12-13.
35 Based on *BeMidbar* 16:14.
36 *Devarim* 28:10.
37 *Yechezkel* 36:17.
38 I *Melachim* 5:5; *Michah* 4:4.
39 *Tehillim* 118:23.

and courage. The Almighty will cause all of this as a sign, to teach, enlighten, and explain how to come even closer to HaShem – to stand before Him and serve Him through the sacred service. We will then establish a new altar in Zion,[40] as the *Yerushalmi*[41] (which his honor cited)[42] explains. I am reminded of *Chazal's* statement that this will take place forty years before the coming of *Mashiach*.[43] When we come near and prepare ourselves by the altar of HaShem and the people of Israel reside in their Land, we will dwell in peace, each man in his tent – i.e., the tents of learning. The more study, the more wisdom.[44] The Torah will go forth in her "bridal veil" to teach Israel the order of the sacrificial service, that which disqualifies it as well as its esoteric teachings. He who studies in order to practice[45] will find sufficient wisdom to understand all aspects of priesthood. There, chairs of learning will be set up[46] for the *kohanim* to know HaShem and the deeds that they should do.[47]

When HaShem is pleased with a man's actions,[48] the Holy One Blessed be He brings forth a light seven times as strong as the light of the sun.[49] This refers to the final redemption: the salvation of HaShem overlaid with sapphires,[50] with all of the promises that are unique to HaShem alone. And HaShem will be the King over all the land.[51]

I declare these words fearlessly, for this is the proper path. We must act in order to bring about the beginning of redemption. For every deed that we perform on our own at the beginning, HaShem Himself will show us the best path to the deed that follows after it. And when we see that we successfully carry out HaShem's will, we will pay attention and strengthen our hearts to draw as close to HaShem as possible.

Therefore, mighty one, be strong and of good courage.[52] And you, princes of Israel, be strong and let your hearts be

40 Based on *Musaf* for *Rosh Chodesh*.

41 *Berachot* 4:3 (30b); *Ma'aser Sheini* 5:2 (21b).

42 *Derishat Tzion*, pp. 159-62.

43 We were unable to locate a source for this. However, see *Zohar* 1:139a in *Midrash HaNe'elam*. Also see below, pp. 440-41.

44 *Avot* 2:8.

45 Based on *Avot* 4:5.

46 *Tehillim* 122:5.

47 Based on *Shemot* 18:20.

48 Based on *Mishley* 16:7.

49 Based on *Yeshayah* 30:26.

50 Based on *Shir HaShirim* 5:14.

51 *Zecharyah* 14:9.

52 Based on *Tehillim* 27:14.

courageous[53] and approach the task. Continue to buy houses, fields, and vineyards[54] to do righteousness in the Land,[55] as it says, [*So that your days may be multiplied and the days of your children*] *upon the Land* (*Devarim* 11:21).[56] May we merit that the Holy Land, the Land that HaShem your God cares for,[57] be the possession of Israel, and that the *mitzvot* which are dependent on the Land be fulfilled there. This is the charity (צדקה) that brings the redemption closer,[58] for these *mitzvot* are the source of life and sustenance for all that dwell there. From the heavens, HaShem will adjoin the final redemption to the redemption of the Land,[59] and the ultimate salvation and redemption of the people will arise speedily through our endeavors. And may HaShem establish for us the work of our hands.[60]

Hence, arise princes of the hosts of Israel. Be strong and let us make ourselves strong for the sake of the cities of our God.[61] Anoint the shield[62] for the rebuilding of Jerusalem. Grant a redemption for the Land.[63] Do not fear and do not be dismayed,[64] for HaShem is with us. The hearts of all the mortal kings are faithful to us and we to them, and they desire our welfare in order to fulfill the will of the Creator. HaShem will help us for the sake of His name, and a redeemer will come to Zion,[65] a savior [*Mashiach*] for Israel. So may it be His will. Amen.

I say: my desire, like that of the Almighty, is that the *Eretz Noshavet* (the Inhabited Land) Association be established. Please inform me of the manner and order of the rectifications (*tikkunim*) corresponding to the numerical value of *Shivtei Yisrael* (the tribes of Israel). HaShem is with us[66] and I longed for His word.[67] Let nothing but life and peace surround you and establish you. May you be successful and prosperous in all your endeavors,[68] and we will rejoice and be glad.[69] In accordance with his honor's elevated soul, I, the undersigned,

53 Based on *Tehillim* 31:25.
54 Based on *Yirmiyah* 32:15.
55 Based on *Yirmiyah* 23:5.
56 See *Berachot* 8a.
57 Based on *Devarim* 11:12.
58 *Bava Batra* 10a.
59 Based on *Berachot* 4b.
60 *Tehillim* 90:17.
61 II *Shmuel* 10:12.
62 Based on *Yeshayah* 21:5.
63 *VaYikra* 25:24.
64 *Yehoshua* 10:25.
65 *Yeshayah* 59:20.
66 Based on *Tehillim* 46:8.
67 *Tehillim* 130:5.
68 *Mishley* 17:8.
69 Based on *Yeshayah* 25:9.

seek his welfare and pray on his behalf for life and peace. This is the approval that the King sent to me.

The young ***Chayim David*** Chazan
Sefaradi Tahor

❋ ❋ ❋

Our author's comments

These are the approbations of three profound *gedolim*, the foremost *tzaddikim* of the past two generations, who fervently supported this lofty and sacred cause.

I have set for myself the words of R. Yusha'le Kutner *z"l* as an objective (he was unique in his generation in Torah and righteousness, and everyone testified that he was holy). He wrote, "***Do not become disheartened nor discouraged by the words of the antagonists, for they speak out of ignorance***."

When the kings allow us to build our Land it is considered a divine visitation

The brilliant and holy Kabbalist of Greiditz and the Sefardic scholar, the *Rishon LeTzion*, regard the fact that the gentile kings gave us permission to build *Eretz Yisrael* and Jerusalem as the fulfillment of the verse *My Beloved sent forth His hand through the hole* (*Shir HaShirim* 5:4). They concur with our Sages in the *Midrash* on this point:

> *My Beloved sent forth His hand through the hole.* (*Matnot Kehunah* explains: "He sent forth His hand through the hole to perform miracles through Cyrus.") R. Abba bar Kahana said: "The Assembly of Israel (*Kenesset Yisrael*) said to the Holy One Blessed be He, 'Master of the Universe, would it not have been better to perform all of these miracles through Daniel or another righteous individual, instead of Cyrus?' Nevertheless, *My innards stirred for Him* (ibid.)." R. Azaryah said: "The Holy One Blessed be He said, 'I enact good decrees. You have said, *My innards stirred for Him*, I have also said, *My innards My innards, I tremble* (*Yirmiyah* 4:19).' " (*Shir HaShirim Rabbah* 5:3)

(I will explain *Kenesset Yisrael*'s question and this entire *Midrash* later on.)[70] In any event, the *Midrash* states explicitly that the very fact that Cyrus gave us permission to build [the Temple] is a fulfillment of *My Beloved sent forth His hand through the hole* and is considered a miracle.

Similarly, these righteous and profound *gedolim* are correct that

70 Pp. 191-93.

today, as well, the fact that the kings of the nations permit us to come and build the Land is considered a miracle and a fulfillment of the verse *My Beloved sent forth His hand through the hole*. This is the handiwork of our God; the Holy One Blessed be He is performing miracles through them. Therefore, anyone who opposes this, opposes the will of the Almighty. We can say to him, as Moshe Rabbeinu said to Korach, *Your complaints are not against us, rather against the Lord*.[71]

It appears to me that this is why whenever the kings of the nations permitted us to ascend and build the Land and the *Beit HaMikdash*, Israel's leaders always accepted this permission lovingly. *Chazal* tell us that at the time of R. Yehoshua ben Chananyah, the kingdom gave the Jews permission to build the *Beit HaMikdash*. Papus and Lulinus set up tables from Akko to Antiochya, for they were the wealthiest men of the generation, and they cared for the finances. The Kutites interfered and convinced the kingdom to annul the decree (*BeReishit Rabbah* 64:10). In any event, R. Yehoshua ben Chananyah and the wise men of the generation accepted this permission with love. It must be because they saw this as the approval of *My Beloved sent forth His hand through the hole*.

The Chida, in *Sheim HaGedolim*, explains why *Mashiach* did not come in the period of the *Tana'im* and the *Amora'im* even though they were exceedingly holy and worthy of his coming: The decree had been, *He made me...mournful all the day* (*Eichah* 1:13). This means that the Jews would remain in exile one thousand years. Since the *Tana'im* and *Amora'im* lived during the first thousand years of exile, the time for redemption had not yet arrived.[72] Based on this, we can learn a *kal vachomer*: R. Yehoshua ben Chananyah lived only 250 years after the destruction. Nevertheless, when he received permission to go up to *Eretz Yisrael* he did not push it off, because he thought that the divine visitation might come before its time. *Chazal* also recount that 500 years after the destruction, the Jews thought that the visitation of redemption would take place, even though they were still in the middle of the first thousand years. They

71 The verse quoted here is *Shemot* 16:8 which refers to the episode of the quails. It, therefore, seems that the author's reference to Korach is a scribal error. [See, however, *BeMidbar* 16:11 where a similar verse can be found in reference to Korach.]

72 *Sheim HaGedolim, Ma'arechet Gedolim* 1:219, note s.v. *ve'od yesh lachkor madua*...

thought that perhaps it would be a time of special divine favor (see *Avodah Zarah* 9a). Now, if this was true in their days, then all the more so today, when we are standing at the eve of the sixth thousand (as I indicate below).[73] We should certainly not push off the visitation that HaShem sends us through mortal kings. Later on, in chapter three, I will elaborate on this (God willing). My intention here was only to demonstrate clearly that the words of these two "captains of the hosts" coincide with those of *Chazal* in the *Midrash*.

❋ ❋ ❋

R. Chayim Elazar Waks – Nefesh Chayah

I will now quote the beginning of Responsa *Nefesh Chayah*, written by the foremost *gaon* of the previous generation, the honorable holy man of HaShem, our master, R. Chayim Elazar Waks, *av beit din* of Kalisch in Russia. Through his first marriage he was the son-in-law of the brother of our mentor, the author of *Divrei Emet* from Tzanz. Through his second marriage he was the son-in-law of R. Yusha'le Kutner. He was remarkably brilliant and wondrously righteous. This will serve as another approbation to my work.

> I hereby quote a letter written to me by the brilliant, righteous, and holy rabbi who resembles an angel of the Lord of Hosts, our honorable and glorious master, R. Eliyahu, son of R. Shlomo *zt"l, av beit din* of Greiditz in Prussia.
>
> "*Baruch HaShem*. The 13th day of the *Omer*, 5634 [1874]. May HaShem grant a blessing to my beloved colleague..., our master, R. Chayim Elazar, *av beit din* of Kalisch, may his light shine forth.
>
> ôBehold, if I had the strength I would skip over mountains to travel and delight in the presence of his honor and the other great rabbis of Poland, in order to supervise the holy matter of the settlement of *Eretz Yisrael*. But, I have become weakened, may we hear good tidings. On the other hand, I do not have the audacity to request of his honor to find a way to come here. I, therefore, leave everything to the will of the Creator, may He be blessed.
>
> ôIt is already clear to me that if the people of Israel ensure that 130 families begin working the holy soil, the redemption will begin, even if Israel is unworthy. I can only explain briefly

73 Pp. 42-43, 155.

in a letter. It says in *Tehillim, It is time to favor Zion, for the appointed time has come, for Your servants cherished her stones...* (102:14-15). The Sforno explains that the Jews were exiled because they despised the Land, and the redemption will come with the rectification of this sin.[74]

ôIt says in *Tehillim, You have favored Your Land, You have returned the captivity of Ya'akov* (85:2). *Yalkut Shimoni* (2:833) states that when we reinstate the priestly gifts, then, *You have returned the captivity of Ya'akov*, even though the Jews do not possess much merit, as indicated a few verses later.

ô*And I will remember My covenant with Ya'akov, and also My covenant with Yitzchak, and also My covenant with Avraham I will remember, and I will remember the Land* (*VaYikra* 26:42). Seeing that the verse begins with the words *I will remember*, it is difficult to understand why it repeats them twice at the end. The Alshich[75] and the Akeidah[76] both explain that the Holy One Blessed be He was saying: '*And I will remember* – I would have remembered the merit of the Patriarchs and I would not have exiled [their descendants]. Instead, I would have punished them in their own Land. But, *I will remember the Land* – meaning, I will remember the wretched deeds that they committed in the Land, by violating the Sabbatical years and withholding the priestly gifts. For this, there is no forgiveness. Therefore, the Land needs to be appeased.'

ôFurthermore, human intellect dictates that we initiate the process of redeeming the Land, and then HaShem will complete it. One must understand the great importance of this matter, ***for the evil forces (kelipah) gain strength even among the most righteous individuals in order to nullify this good.*** This is so because the *kelipah*'s entire strength depends on exile; when the exile dissolves, so will the *kelipah*, as the Talmud states in *Sukkah* (52a).

Your beloved friend,

Eliyahu, son of our master R. Shlomo *zt"l*, of ***Greiditz***.

I have elaborated on this issue to our beloved comrade and master, R. Gershon, may his light shine forth."

74 ❖ It is surprising that our mentor did not remember that the Maharsha (*Ta'anit* 15a) also explains this verse in the same fashion. I will, God willing, cite his words in chapter 3 (pp. 277-78).

75 *VaYikra* 26:40 (end).

76 *Akeidat Yitzchak* 70, p. 153 (standard edition).

Says the author (of *Nefesh Chayah*): I desire to fulfill the wishes of this *tzaddik* (*ztvk"l*) with all my heart. I, therefore, found a *Midrash* on the verse *And when you shall come into the Land and you shall plant any food tree* (*VaYikra* 19:23):

ôR. Yehudah ben R. Simon began: *You shall follow the Lord your God* (*Devarim* 13:5). Is it possible for flesh and blood to follow the Holy One Blessed be He, about Whom it is written, *Your way was in the sea, and Your path was in the great waters* (*Tehillim* 77:20)?! And you say, *You shall follow the Lord*?! [Furthermore, it says], *And you shall cling to Him* (*Devarim* 13:5). Is it possible for flesh and blood to ascend to the heavens and cling to the *Shechinah*, about Whom it is written, *For the Lord your God is a consuming fire* (*Devarim* 4:24)?! It also states, *His throne was fiery flames, and A fiery stream issued and came forth from before Him* (*Daniel* 7:9-10), and you say, *You shall cling to Him*?! Rather, this means that at the beginning of creation the Holy One Blessed be He engaged in planting, as it is written, *The Lord God planted a garden in Eden* (*BeReishit* 2:8). Similarly, when you enter the Land, engage in planting first, as it is written, *When you shall come into the Land, and you shall plant* (*VaYikra* 19:23)." (*VaYikra Rabbah* 25:3)❖

Behold, last year, with the help of God, I purchased three gardens in K'far Chittin near Tiberias (there, one can find Yitro's grave). I planted 600 *etrog* trees there. This year, I hope, God willing, to plant several thousand *etrog* trees near the Chulah lake. This is the way we can hope to ascend onto

---

❖ I will enhance the words of the brilliant author of *Nefesh Chayah* with something I found in the holy work, *Tzror HaMor* (by the grandfather of the Beit Yosef's wife). He writes that Eretz Yisrael is so sanctified that it immediately follows the sanctity of the Holy One Blessed be He Himself. Thus, the verse states about Calev, *And he followed Me fully* (*BeMidbar* 14:24). That is to say, he literally followed Me by defending *Eretz Yisrael* which follows Me.[77] This explains how the *Midrash* derives the obligation to enter *Eretz Yisrael* and engage in planting from the verse *You shall follow the Lord your God*. That is to say, you shall follow the Lord by going to *Eretz Yisrael* which immediately follows HaShem, may He be blessed.

77 *Tzror HaMor, Matot*, s.v. *achar kach amar u'makneh*.

the path that leads to the House of God (בית ק"ל)[78] and settle families who will work the Land and guard it. In addition, the people of Israel will have unquestionably kosher *etrogim* for the *mitzvah*, as explained in the preceding responsa. With God's help, when our plan comes to fruition, we will send calendars from the Holy Land each year to fix the months and the years.✣ We will describe in these calendars every detail of what is happening in the Holy Land. This should quench the thirst of the faithful Jews who long for pure sanctity and who yearn to know the state of affairs in Jerusalem, as it is written, *Pray for the peace of Jerusalem, those who love you will be tranquil. May there be peace within your walls, tranquillity within your palaces* (*Tehillim* 122:6-7). May we merit to see the mountain of the Lord's Temple established as the highest of the mountains,[81] and the palace sitting in its proper place.[82] Amen, so may it be God's will.[83]

❋ ❋ ❋

R. Yehoshua Kutner

Now I will quote Responsa *Yeshu'ot Malko* by the brilliant teacher of Israel, the holy man of God, our master, R. Yusha'le Kutner. This is what he answered the Rebbe of Kotsk regarding this matter.

> *Baruch HaShem*. The eve of the holy Sabbath, *parashat Metzora*, 5651 [1891], here in Kutno. Near to the redemption, the honor of the great rabbi, the holy luminary, the progeny of nobility, our glorious master, R. Yisrael of Kotsk, will be raised up high.

✣ R. Waks determines that all calendars prepared outside of the Land are halachically invalid. One must only use calendars prepared in *Eretz Yisrael*.[79] I would add that the Chatam Sofer also writes that one must make the calculations based on the situation in *Eretz Yisrael*.[80] Thus, the author of *Nefesh Chayah* is correct.

78 [This alludes to the number 130 mentioned by R. Eliyahu of Greiditz. The numerical value of קל (which is the way God's name, א-ל, is written to avoid writing the ineffable name) is 130.]

79 *Teshuvot Nefesh Chayah* 1.

80 *Teshuvot Chatam Sofer* 6:35.

81 Based on *Yeshayah* 2:2.

82 Based on *Yirmiyah* 30:18.

83 *Teshuvot Nefesh Chayah*, immediately following sec. 1.

After inquiring about your well-being, I say: It is incomprehensible that his honor is concerned with the Rambam's opinion in *Hilchot Melachim*[84] (according to the *Kesef Mishnah*) that one who leaves Babylonia, even to go to *Eretz Yisrael*, transgresses a positive commandment. Behold, this only refers to Babylonia, not the rest of the Diaspora. This is so because the Jews of Babylonia were remiss and did not want to return with Ezra (for they did not deem this [redemption] a complete divine visitation). Therefore, they must stay there until the final visitation, as the prophet foretold. However, those who dwell in these countries, who were exiled from *Eretz Yisrael* by Titus, along with the people of all the other lands, are not included in this rule. On the contrary, it is a great *mitzvah*. Also, it seems to me that those Babylonian Jews who ascended to *Eretz Yisrael* while the Second Temple was still standing and were subsequently exiled from *Eretz Yisrael* to these lands, are also excluded from this rule.[85]

The Maharam of Rottenberg only hesitated [with regard to the *mitzvah* of *aliyah*][86] because of the dangerous journey and the lack of provisions, and because of the dispute that flared up at the time. It is well known that in the days of the Maharam of Rottenberg and R. Moshe Tiki there was a grievous dispute between the inhabitants of *Eretz Yisrael* and those of Germany and France over the *Moreh Nevuchim*. No one, however, concerns himself with the Talmudic statement: "He who ascends from Babylonia to *Eretz Yisrael* transgresses a positive commandment" (*Ketuvot* 110b). Therefore, now that there has been a change for the better (with God's help), both in terms of the dangers of the journey and in terms of sustenance, it is certainly a great *mitzvah*.

Even according to the Ramban who counts *Yishuv Eretz Yisrael* as a positive commandment,[87] the *mitzvah* is primarily fulfilled by taking possession of the Land and dwelling there like a person does in his own property. We are commanded to

84 5:12.

85 ❖ See *Siddur Ya'avetz, Sullam Beit El* (p. 13a); *Pe'at HaShulchan* (1:8); and *Derishat Tzion* (*Sha'ar Tzion*, p. 82) which determine that this statement of R. Yehudah [the Talmudic basis of the Rambam's ruling] is not difficult at all.

86 His opinion is cited in *Pe'at HaShulchan* 1:15.

87 Ramban's Addendum to *Sefer HaMitzvot,* Positive Commandments 4.

conquer *Eretz Yisrael* so that we control it,* not to come

---

* Our mentor writes that the main component of the *mitzvah* is to conquer the Land from the nations so that we control it, and that it is insufficient to come "empty-handed." This implies that even if an individual dwells there while keeping Torah and serving God, he does not fulfill the *mitzvah* properly. He further states that *aliyah* to *Eretz Yisrael* is also a *mitzvah*, albeit a preparatory *mitzvah* (הכשר מצוה). On all of these points, he concurs with the Rivash:

> There is no doubt that *aliyah* to *Eretz Yisrael* is a *mitzvah*.[88] Why, then, did the prophet tell the people in exile, *Build houses...* (*Yirmiyah* 29:5-7)? That was only because of the expulsion, for the One who exiled them forbade them to return until they received permission from Cyrus.[89] Today, as well, [the only reason we do not ascend to *Eretz Yisrael* is because] the Holy One Blessed be He adjured Israel not to "go up as a wall" (*Ketuvot* 111a).
>
> Furthermore, do not say that only dwelling in *Eretz Yisrael* is a *mitzvah*, while *aliyah* is not. After all, one who ascends with intention to dwell there is considered an "*oseik bemitzvah*" – one involved in a *mitzvah*...
>
> The respondent[90] derives a *kal vachomer* from the case of purchasing a field in *Eretz Yisrael*. The Talmud states that one is permitted to [tell a Gentile to] write the sales contract even on the Sabbath (*Bava Kama* 80b). For the sake of *Yishuv Eretz Yisrael*, our Sages waive the rabbinic prohibition of *amirah lenachri* (telling a Gentile to do work for you on the Sabbath), even in the case of a biblically forbidden work. The respondent considers buying land a lesser *mitzvah* than *aliyah*. I say that he is incorrect. On the contrary, buying land from a Gentile is a greater *mitzvah* than *aliyah*. *Aliyah* is a transitory *mitzvah* and affects only the one who performs it. *Yishuv Eretz Yisrael*, on the other hand, is not transient; it is a *mitzvah* that endures forever. It benefits the entire Jewish nation that the Holy Land not remain in the hands of the defiled ones. Therefore, one cannot infer other *mitzvot* from this one. The Ramban *z"l* already expressed these ideas.[91]

88 ❖ He cites proofs for this from *Chazal* (*Ketuvot* 110b).

89 ❖ The Rivash implies that if it is possible to return to *Eretz Yisrael*, it is forbidden to build houses outside of the Land. See the Shelah at the end of *Sukkah* (*Sh'nei Luchot HaBrit* 2:78b, s.v. *veho'il*); *Teshuvot Chatam Sofer* (*Yoreh De'ah* 138); and his novellae (*Sukkah* 36a, s.v. *domeh lekushi*).

90 [The Rivash is referring to *Teshuvot Tashbetz* 1:21.]

91 *Teshuvot Rivash* 101.

"empty-handed" like today. The *Acharonim* have compared this to the positive commandment of eating *matzah*. The essential component of the *mitzvah* is the eating. Taking the wheat for the sake of the *mitzvah*, kneading, and baking are not complete *mitzvot*. Nonetheless, they certainly are great *mitzvot*.[92] Concerning this it says, "He rewards man with kindness according to his actions,"[93] meaning, one receives reward even for the [preparatory] act of a *mitzvah*. It also says, *Fortunate are those whose way is perfect* (*Tehillim* 119:1); there is perfection even in the "way" of those who do *mitzvot*.

Furthermore, it is undoubtedly a great *mitzvah* because the ingathering is the beginning of redemption, and it says, *I will gather others to him, beside those already gathered to him* (*Yeshayah* 56:8). Also, the Talmud states that the *Shechinah* does not rest upon less than 20,000 Jews (*Yevamot* 64a). Especially now that we have seen the great desire [for *Eretz Yisrael* displayed by all types of Jews], including lowly, average, and upright people, it is almost certain that the spirit of redemption has sprouted. Fortunate is your portion, for you are among those who bring merit to the masses.

His honor writes in the name of the Maharit that the city of Gaza was not sanctified at the time of Ezra and is not included in this *mitzvah*, because it was not conquered by the Jews who ascended with him from Babylonia. I humbly disagree, and I have already discussed this at length in a treatise dealing with these issues.[94] When I have some free time, following the upcoming holiday, I will send you this treatise.

Your friend who constantly inquires about your well-being.

Wishing you holiday blessings.

Yisrael Yehoshua of ***Kutno***[95]

Behold, this agrees with R. Yehoshua Kutner. It is puzzling that the greatest of the *Acharonim* did not mention the Rivash's comments.

My beloved friend, the wondrously brilliant and knowledgeable R. Yisrael Veltz *shlita*, judge and mentor of the Orthodox community here in Budapest, showed me this Rivash.

92 [The same applies to *Yishuv Eretz Yisrael*. The essential component of the *mitzvah* is taking possession of the Land and dwelling there like a person does in his own property. The actual ascent (*aliyah*), however, is not a complete *mitzvah*. Nonetheless, it certainly is a great *mitzvah*.]

93 From the *Yigdal* prayer.

94 *Teshuvot Yeshu'ot Malko* 67.

95 *Teshuvot Yeshu'ot Malko* 66.

In the following section of *Yeshu'ot Malko*,[96] where the above-cited treatise is printed, R. Kutner determines that the *halachah* follows the Kaftor VaFerach,[97] who states that it is a *mitzvah* to reside both in the areas of *Eretz Yisrael* conquered by the Jews who ascended from Egypt, as well as in Transjordan. There is no reason to doubt his words. Therefore, even nowadays, if someone has the opportunity to buy land in *Eretz Yisrael*, it is a *mitzvah* to do so. The Kaftor VaFerach also writes that the rabbinic prohibition of *amirah lenachri* is waved even in the places conquered by the Jews who ascended from Egypt. This is derived by a *kal vachomer* from Syria [about which the Talmud explicitly states that this prohibition is waived]. In any event, do not deviate from the Kaftor VaFerach's conclusion that it is a *mitzvah*, even nowadays, to dwell in the areas conquered by the Jews who ascended from Egypt. Therefore, these areas do not cause ritual impurity, as do the lands of the nations.

II Author's Preface

The unanswered call of aliyah

My dear brothers, after presenting you the words of our brilliant and holy ancestors, you can clearly see that as early as eighty years ago a holy spirit arose within our exalted and glorious anointed ones, the leaders of the generation, to return to our mother's bosom and no longer embrace the bosom of the foreigner. They urged us to devote our strengths, our blood, and our money to the Holy Land, in order to raise it from the dust, establish it, perfect it, and elevate the dignity of our "king." It is well known from the Kabbalistic works[98] that *Eretz Yisrael* is in the *sefirah* of Kingship (*Malchut*), the highest *sefirah*, and Kingship is the mother of Israel. She awaits us and cries for us to return to her bosom.

In the same vein, in the year 5660 [1900], the holy *gaon*, our mentor, R. Hillel of Kalamoya, published a manifesto calling and urging our Jewish brethren to buy the Land of Israel from the Ishmaelites (Arabs). It was an opportune moment, for the sultan was at war and needed money. He was willing to sell *Eretz Yisrael*, Transjordan, and Syria for almost nothing. This holy man [R. Hillel] saw this as a divine visitation and called out vigorously in the streets to persuade the people of Israel to swiftly redeem our "king" from

96 Sec. 67.
97 Chapters 7 and 10.
98 ❖ Which I will cite below (p. 316).

foreign control and from the hands of the impure. He urged them to rebuild the ruins of *Eretz Yisrael*, to glorify the seat of our *Beit HaMikdash*, to restore the crown to its former glory, and to make *Eretz Yisrael* the most beautiful of sites, the joy of all the earth.[99] He was the original founder of the Petach Tikvah colony. All of this is recounted in the introduction to *Tosafot ben Yechiel* (a commentary on the holy work, *Tana DeVei Eliyahu*) by R. Hillel's son-in-law, the holy *gaon*, our master, R. Akiva Yosef, author of *Lev HaIvri*.

Due to our numerous sins, however, his words fell upon deaf ears. They hovered in the air, unable to find a place in the hearts of our Jewish brethren in which to rest. The Orthodox Jews[100] made silence their virtue and clung to the principle, "It is preferable to sit and do nothing,"[101] as has always been their policy. The irreligious extremists were swayed by the new era which ushered freedom into the world. They said, "Here, I will dwell, for I have desired it."[102] They expected to find tranquillity here in the lands of exile, seeing that they had received equal rights like all other citizens. In the meantime, they let our sacred mother [*Eretz Yisrael*] wallow in the dirt and remain in ruins. They let her eyes become a fountain of tears, to cry and lament over us because we remain in exile and do not contemplate longing to return to her bosom and to reestablish her home.

After some years passed in this new era of freedom, known as "The Golden Era," hatred sprang forth against the Jews in exile. Each time it occurred in a different location, until its flames spread so greatly that it endangered the entire community. We went from bad to worse until we reached the terribly dreadful state in which we find ourselves today.

The irreligious recognized their mistake

During the past few decades, the irreligious have opened their eyes and recognized their mistake in thinking that they will find their heart's desire here in exile. They have seen that hostility surrounds them from all sides. In response to their love, the Gentiles hate them and persecute them without reason. Hence, they opened their eyes

99 Based on *Tehillim* 48:3.

100 [The Hebrew word used here is חרדים (*chareidim*). Literally translated, it means ôthose who tremble.ö It is used as an appellation for Orthodox Jews based on verses which refer to such individuals as those who tremble at the word of God.]

101 Based on *Eiruvin* 100a.

102 Based on *Tehillim* 132:14.

and recognized that their hopes of finding peace and quiet here in exile are futile. The desire to return to the Land of our forefathers awoke within them, and they began working towards this goal.

The religious kept their distance

Those who tremble at the word of HaShem, however, stood on the side and refrained from sharing in the work. They stood by their age-old claim, "It is preferable to sit and do nothing." In the meantime, these "initiators" began rebuilding our Holy Land (so may it continue and prosper), while the Orthodox Jews and the *tzaddikim* stood aloof. It is clear that he who prepares prior to the Sabbath will eat on the Sabbath,[103] and since the Orthodox did not toil, they have absolutely no influence in the Land. Those who toil and build have the influence, and they are the masters of the Land. It is, therefore, no wonder that they are in control, for *He who guards the fig tree will eat its fruit* (*Mishley* 27:18).

Had we joined the builders, our Land would look very different today

Now, what will the Orthodox say? I do not know if they will ever be able to vindicate themselves before the heavenly court for not participating in the movement to rebuild the Land, and for not heeding the call of these *tzaddikim* of the generation. These *tzaddikim* were renowned as completely selfless, holy men of God, and all of their utterances were as complete and true as the Torah of Moshe from the Almighty. And since this awakening came from such holy mouths, they should have listened and joined in this sacred task. Had the God-fearing, religious Jews been involved in this undertaking, our Holy Land would have a completely different, more sanctified, appearance and form than it has now. In truth, though, our Father in Heaven desires and is pleased with the current appearance and form (as I will explain later on,[104] based on unequivocal proofs from *Chazal*). All agree, however, that if the Orthodox would have cooperated with and participated in the building effort, it would have been exceedingly lofty and holy. Now that they kept themselves at a distance, they should not wonder or question the situation, for they are at fault.

Who is responsible for the innocent blood spilled in our days?

Furthermore, if all of *Klal Yisrael* would have agreed to rebuild the Land it would have already been built-up and perfected enough to absorb a large portion of the Diaspora Jews. A great number of our fellow Jews who were recently killed (due to our numerous sins)

103 *Avodah Zarah* 3a.
104 Chap. 2, sec. י״ב-י״ג (pp. 183-94).

would have been saved, for they would have already been in *Eretz Yisrael*. Who will accept responsibility for the innocent blood that has been spilled in our days? It seems to me that all of the leaders who prevented the people of Israel from joining the builders cannot cleanse their hands and say, *Our hands did not spill this blood*![105]

Our Sages state in *Tana DeVei Eliyahu*:

> Not only Pinchas, but anyone who has the ability to protest or to bring Israel back to the proper path and does not do so, all of the Jewish blood that is spilled is on his hands. As it says, *So you, son of man, I have made you a watchman for the House of Israel...[when I say to a wicked person, "O wicked one, you shall surely die," and you do not speak to warn the wicked one concerning his way], that wicked one will die in his iniquity, but I will demand his blood from your hand* (*Yechezkel* 33:7-8). This is so because all Jews are responsible for one another... The great *Sanhedrin* that Moshe set up, which included Yehoshua and Pinchas, should have tied iron ropes around their loins, lifted their garments above their knees,[106] and gone around to all the cities of Israel; one day here and one day there... They should have taught Israel *derech eretz* in a year, or two, or three, until the people of Israel were settled in their Land, so that the Holy One's name be exalted and sanctified. They did not do so. Rather...each one entered his vineyard, his wine, and his field and said, "Peace be unto you my soul," so as not to overburden himself. (*Tana DeVei Eliyahu* 11:4-5)

The same is true today. The leaders should have become involved in this issue and taught the Children of Israel to go to the Holy Land in the spirit of the Torah. Where would we be now had this movement received the approval of all of the *tzaddikim* and God-fearing Jews of the previous generations, and of the present? How many thousands of Jewish souls would have been saved in this way?

Excessive caution is detrimental

Truthfully, one can judge these Orthodox Jews favorably by saying that they stood at a distance because of excessive caution. They were afraid that perhaps this movement would not be completely in the spirit of the Torah, as it should be. With all due respect, however, they overlooked the words of our pious mentor, the author of *Chovot*

105 *Devarim* 21:7. Also see *Or HaChayim HaKadosh* on *VaYikra* 25:25.

106 ❖ This is a metaphor showing how much they should have pained themselves.

HaLevavot. In his introduction he writes, "One of the components of caution is not to be overly cautious."[107] He further states that if every person who is involved in something positive would wait silently until all of his requirements are fulfilled, no one would accomplish anything. If every person who wishes to acquire all of the positive attributes would disregard a particular one because he cannot attain them all, then all of mankind would be void of goodness and lack pleasantness. The paths of goodness would be desolate, and the habitations of kindness would be abandoned.❖

These words were written with insight and wisdom and have indeed come to fruition regarding today's Orthodox Jews. Due to excessive caution they kept their distance from the builders, and now we are void of goodness. The paths of goodness are desolate, and the habitation of salvation has been abandoned. We could have saved thousands upon thousands of Jews who were killed or who died unusual deaths (may the Merciful One save us). Yirmiyahu's prophecy has indeed been fulfilled through us, *My tent has been plundered, and all my cords have been broken. My children have left me, and are no more* (*Yirmiyah* 10:20).

The extent of our afflictions

The holy *Zohar* explains the verse *The sun rose for him...and he was limping on his thigh* (*BeReishit* 32:32):

> While the Jews are still in exile they suffer pain, sorrow, and numerous afflictions. When the day grows brighter for them

---

❖ Our brilliant and holy mentor, the author of *B'nei Yissachar*, agrees:

> Behold, the *Yeitzer HaRa* lies in wait by all of man's paths and tries to entrap him in his net. He approaches him deceptively and makes him cautious in a way contrary to the Torah. In this way, he causes him to stray from the true path. Thus, the wise one [*Chovot HaLevavot*] warned, "One of the components of caution is not to be overly cautious."

The B'nei Yissachar elaborates on this and concludes:

> If a person is considering being cautious, he should analyze the Torah, for it will teach him wisdom, and he will find the path of understanding. Therefore, *Chazal* determine, "An unlearned man cannot be pious" (*Avot* 2:6), for he will not know how to measure his caution in matters of piety according to the ways of the Torah.[108]

107 *Chovot HaLevavot* (*Lev Tov* edition), vol. 1, p. 51.
108 *Tamchin DeOraita*, introduction.

and they enjoy peace and quiet, they will look back and feel sorrow over all of the afflictions and pains that they suffered, and they will wonder about them. Thus, the verse states, *The sun rose for him*, that is to say, the sun of the era of peace rose. *And he was limping on his thigh*, meaning, he felt the pain and suffering of his past troubles. (*Zohar* 1:170b)

The same is true of our present exile. We do not yet know what our enemies have done to us. But, when HaShem assists us in attaining peace and quiet from these great afflictions, we will know better what they did to us; and the breach that has befallen us will become well known to all. May HaShem bind up the breach of His nation and heal the wound of its blow,[109] speedily in our days.

Had the Orthodox Jews joined those who were engaged in this sacred endeavor sixty, fifty, or forty years ago, and had they inspired all of Israel to do the same, we would have found abundant relief in the Land. Thousands upon thousands of Jews would have settled there and would have been rescued from death. The Orthodox would have, thus, fulfilled the verse *To rescue those being taken out to be put to death* (*Mishley* 24:11).

The origins of hatred towards the Zionists

However, they opposed this undertaking. Not only did they oppose it, but they caused the simple, Orthodox Jews to despise the rebuilding of the Land so much that if one of them begins to speak or get enthused about it, they consider him repulsive and abominable. They all rebuke him, saying, "You are a Zionist, an abhorrence, and an abomination." Thus, they have truly caused the desirable Land to be despised and detested. The simple man who does not know enough Torah to decide whether this is true or not, chastises those who desire to rebuild the Land. He says, "You are a sinner and a Zionist," for he wants to be considered devout and pious. In this way, he defames both himself and our Holy Land. In reality, though, he is just a simpleton, someone who does not know how to ask. He cannot distinguish between his right and left.

Some of the true Torah scholars harbor a positive attitude towards this sacred endeavor. They admit to themselves the truth that our only objective must be to revive and establish the "House of Our Lives,"[110] to favor our Land, and to desire its stones and soil.

109 Based on *Yeshayah* 30:26.
110 From the second blessing recited after the *Haftarah*.

Nonetheless, these positive thoughts remain solely in the heart. They would not dare express their thoughts in words, for they fear that they will be rebuked and considered repulsive, abominable Zionists.

Modern-day "spies"

In this way, these zealots spread hatred and enmity throughout the Orthodox world against the group which devoted itself to building up our Land to its former glory. As a consequence of this, they also caused the desirable Land to be despised. They became entrapped in the sin of the spies, about whom it says, *They murmured in their tents... They despised the desirable Land* (*Tehillim* 106:25,24). What was the result of the spies? They caused everlasting sorrow.[111] Today's "spies," as well, have added sorrow onto sorrow, bringing us to our present situation in which we see horror after horror and weeping after weeping in the House of Israel. All of this has occurred because we despised the desirable Land, as I will prove later on[112] from the words of *Chazal*.

Our master, Maharam Chagiz, discusses the great punishment that awaits those who slander the inhabitants of *Eretz Yisrael*:

> HaShem decreed that just as *all the men who have seen My glory* (*BeMidbar* 14:22) – meaning, the generation of the spies – will not see the Land, the same is true of future generations. Anyone who spreads an evil report about the Land will be stricken and will receive the punishment of the spies. This is the meaning of [the next verse] *And all who provoke Me shall not see it* (ibid. 14:23), which refers to the future.[113]

Anyone who lives in Eretz Yisrael is considered a tzaddik

The divine Kabbalist, R. Avraham Azulai (the grandfather of our master, the Chida), writes in his holy work, *Chesed LeAvraham*:

> Anyone who lives in *Eretz Yisrael* is considered a *tzaddik* (righteous individual) even though it does not seem that way. For if he was not a *tzaddik*, the Land would vomit him out, as it says, *And the Land vomits out its inhabitants* (*VaYikra* 18:25). Since the Land does not vomit him out he must be considered a *tzaddik*, even though he is presumed to be wicked.[114]

111 See *Sotah* 35a, *Ta'anit* 29a.

112 Pp. 221-22, 330, 343, 399, 430.

113 *Sefat Emet* (Vilna, 5636 [1876]), p. 32b.

114 *Chesed LeAvraham, Ma'ayan* 3, *Nahar* 12.

❖ It seems to me that there is a Talmudic source for the words of this divine Kabbalist, whose every utterance was said with *Ruach HaKodesh*. It

Nachalah LeYisrael, written by a great Torah scholar from *Eretz Yisrael*,[115] cites this *Chesed LeAvraham* and adds the following:

> Thus, it is clear that we do not properly understand [the true nature of] the inhabitants of *Eretz Yisrael* with our physical eyesight. For man sees what his eyes behold, while HaShem sees into the heart.[116] Therefore, we cannot judge or degrade specific individuals, and certainly not the entire community, even those who do not find favor in our eyes or do not act in a manner befitting our nation.[117]

I would like to add to this. When we see from *Chazal* that the Omnipresent is pleased by the acts of today's builders (as I will demonstrate at length, God willing, in chapter three), then it is certainly forbidden to slander them. Hence, he who is not careful to guard his tongue about this, does not guard his soul from troubles.[118] He will be included in the decree *And all who provoke Me shall not see it* (*BeMidbar* 14:23), as explained by R. Moshe Chagiz (above). May HaShem protect us from them and their associates.

The author's confession

I must confess the truth and declare my sin. I, too, despised the rebuilding of the Land, because I heard unqualified statements made by many Orthodox Jews, which became firmly implanted in my heart. I did not concern myself with this matter at all, because I was preoccupied with learning, teaching, and writing volumes on the Talmud and its commentaries, as well as responses to questions regarding the word of HaShem. I only delved into this *halachah* after we suffered afflictions in this bitter exile. HaShem enlightened me, and I saw that I and all those who opposed this movement were mistaken. I admit and say, "That which I previously told you was

can be found in *Avodah Zarah* (26a) in the statement "Come and see the difference between the thieves of Babylonia and the highway robbers of *Eretz Yisrael*..." See Rashi's comments, as well as those of the brilliant Maharshak of Brod *zt"l* in *Avodat Avodah*.

115 This work speaks of the holiness and virtues of *Eretz Yisrael*, and prescribes worthy practices for those who dwell there. The author openly rebukes those who speak arrogantly against the Holy Land and its inhabitants. He served as rabbi in Ohel, Hungary for more than forty years and later moved to Tiberias. He wrote the book anonymously. It was printed in Jerusalem in 5642 [1882].

116 Based on I *Shmuel* 16:7.

117 *Nachalah LeYisrael*, chap. 12.

118 Based on *Mishley* 21:23.

mistaken," just like Rava and other great Talmudic Sages did.[119] When rabbis admit their mistakes, they are praiseworthy.

Thank God, I have no qualms about publicly expressing the truth that is in my heart. I am not afraid of any man, for I studied under great and righteous *gedolim* and was raised among the genuinely holy wise men of the generation. Thank God, I also studied Torah early on and was married young. At the age of nineteen I was united with the daughter of the foremost Torah scholar of the generation. Since then, Torah has never ceased from my table. I will not revoke my Torah opinion because of any *gadol* or *rebbe* of our generation, unless he debates the issues with me in the manner of Torah dialogue, using proofs from the words of *Chazal*. I will then concede to his words, if they are correct, but not if they are unfounded.

HaShem knows and can testify that I did not write this to be boastful or arrogant. I wrote it for the sake of truth and justice, for the sake of God's glorious name, for the sake of our nation's honor, and for the honor of our Holy Land. Furthermore, a person without ulterior motives will not be afraid nor hesitate to say the truth, as the brilliant R. Yosef Schwartz of Jerusalem writes in the introduction to his work, *Divrei Yosef*. The verse states, *Do not be afraid of any man, for the judgment is God's* (*Devarim* 1:17). He explains: "For truthful judgment is God's, and that is the determining factor. That is to say, if you are certain that your words are correct and true, do not be afraid to say them, for truth is the determinant."

Similarly, the *Yerushalmi* recounts that Reish Lakish stated [a *halachah*] which slightly disgraced R. Yehudah HaNasi. Reish Lakish said to him, "Do you think that I will refrain from relating the teachings of the Merciful One because I fear you?!" (*Sanhedrin* 2:1 [7b], *Horayot* 3:1 [9a]).

An exhortation to the Orthodox Jews

Let us return to the beginning. From the time that this movement began, until today, times have changed. Practically the entire order of nature has turned upside down. Events which previously took a thousand years to unfold, happen rapidly today. We are witnessing the constant and daily renewal of afflictions and misfortunes upon the people of Israel. They are cut off from all of life's vital necessities, and the very ground on which they stand has been stolen away. Furthermore, the younger generation has no future here, and they

119 See *Mesoret HaShas* on *Shabbat* 63b.

all long to emigrate to another land, if they only could. But to where? All the lands are closed to them. Hence, they aspire to ascend to *Eretz Yisrael*, for there is a new settlement there which needs all the manpower it can get.

Now, if the God-fearing, Orthodox Jews continue to refuse to participate in rebuilding the Land (in its totality and in its details), and if they do not keep a watchful eye over the state of affairs, refusing to dedicate their money, their minds, and their spirits to this cause, they will have no say whatsoever in the Land's management. They will be unable to assist the young immigrants with their physical needs, and they will lose their spiritual influence over them, as well. Thus, the entire young generation will fall into the hands of others. What will be the consequences of this?

Indeed, I heard from reliable, first-hand sources that our holy Rebbe from Unsdorf *ztvk"l* said in 1918 (according to their count): "Alas! I foresee that the Jews will be unable to remain here in these lands, God forbid. They will be forced to flee, but they will have nowhere to run, because they do not view the rebuilding of *Eretz Yisrael* favorably." He himself worked on this to some degree. Now, this was said twenty-five years ago, at a time when there was still peace and tranquillity here. It is clear that *Ruach HaKodesh* emanated from his holy mouth, for his words have been fulfilled (due to our numerous sins); there is no remnant of Israel left in these lands.

He intended to arouse the God-fearing Jews, to awaken them from their slumber, and to raise them up from their slothfulness on this issue. But, we cannot change the past. Now that our holy master's prophecy has been fulfilled, the God-fearing Jews – especially the leaders of the generation – have a sacred obligation to recognize the truth. They must internalize the words of our master, and the words of the other *gedolim* and *tzaddikim* which I cited above, and become involved in this matter with all of their strength. All the more so, since the masses and the young generation aspire to ascend to the Holy Land, the wise men of the generation must assist, encourage, and guide them. Then, they will be able to influence them spiritually as well.

Who is greater than our mentor the Chatam Sofer, who was renowned as an expert leader? He used to say, "Anything new is forbidden by the Torah," and he would not compromise at all on Torah and *mitzvot*. Nonetheless, we find in his novellae this interpretation to the verse *Your breasts* (שדים) *developed and your hair sprouted forth* (*Yechezkel* 16:7): *Your hair* refers to the masses. At a time when the masses "sprout forth" and aspire to something, and the wise men of the generation recognize that certain dangers exist, these wise men must not forcibly push the masses aside. If they do, they will lose their influence over them. Rather, they must deal patiently with the people of their generation and act in the capacity of "breasts" (שדים), for the word שדים is an abbreviation of "שמאל דוחה ימין מקרבת" – the left hand pushes aside and the right hand brings near.[120] This way, the connection between them will not be broken.[121]

Later on,[122] I will discuss this at length. I mention these things here only in order to adjoin my words to those of the *gedolim* of the previous generations who became greatly impassioned about our Holy Land. I have brought their words here in lieu of approbations to my work. With this I close.

Signed by he who is writing in the darkness of night, Monday evening, *parashat Tetzaveh*, in the year 5703 [1943], here in the capital, Budapest. And I am among the exile.[123] May HaShem put an end to our exile and speedily bring us to our Holy Mountain.

Yisachar Shlomo Teichtal

Note:

Our mentor, the Alshich, explains the verse *The Mighty One, God, the Lord, the Mighty One, God, the Lord, He knows and Israel shall know* (*Yehoshua* 22:22): When the Lord God knows that we are sincere and our intentions are for His sake, even if we are incapable of making this clear to all, we hope that HaShem will influence the people of Israel from the heavens so that they shall know. This means that our words will enter the hearts of Israel and they will trust them. This knowledge will root itself within the Jewish people and cause them to recognize the truth and not be skeptical.

It is revealed and known to HaShem (may He be blessed, and may His name be exalted through the exaltation of His sons – the people of Israel, His holy nation – speedily in our days) that I did not write this work for my honor, for my family's honor, or for any material

120 *Sotah* 47a.
121 *Chiddushei Chatam Sofer, Niddah* 48.
122 Pp. 104-6.
123 Based on *Yechezkel* 1:1.

benefit whatsoever. I wrote it only for HaShem's honor, for the honor of the Holy Nation which is now downtrodden, and for the honor of our Holy Land, the dwelling place of the House of our God. *Eretz Yisrael*, which is the mother of Israel,[124] cries, laments, and longs for us to return to her bosom. I wrote this in order to arouse the hearts of our holy people to desire and yearn to return to our mother and leave the stepmother, i.e., the lands of exile. For, this stepmother has thoroughly satiated us with bitterness for close to two thousand years. We are suffering all of these troubles now, at the end of days, because we have neglected the honor of our true mother, *Eretz Yisrael*. According to the secret of the *sefirot*, *Eretz Yisrael* is Kingship (*Malchut*), the lofty mother of Israel, as explained by the Kabbalists. When we covet our Land once again, then, and only then, we will deserve the redemption and the elevation of our glory and the glory of the Lord of Hosts,[125] even though we are unworthy. May we see this speedily in our days. Amen.

124 See *Yerushalmi: Berachot* 2:8 (18b); *Ketuvot* 13:11 (72).

125 ❖ See *Maggid Meisharim* (*Shelach*), and the sacred volume, *Divrei Emet*, by our holy mentor from Lublin (*BeHar*, s.v. *u'vechol*). I will elaborate on this below (pp. 258-59, 277-78, 282, 302, 314...).

FIRST INTRODUCTION

I discovered a letter written by the author of the *Tanya*[1] to the Rebbe of Berditchev, informing him of his release from prison in Petersburg.[2]

> I shall recount and declare that which is too great to tell. For HaShem has done wondrously in the land. Who am I, lowly of men, that HaShem has helped me glorify and sanctify His name... This was all HaShem's doing. He has arranged this by virtue of the merit of the Holy Land and its inhabitants. This is what stood by our side and will always assist in relieving us from the oppressor and delivering us from distress.[3]

I The Merit of Eretz Yisrael Protects Us

From his holy words I learned an entirely new concept, of which I was unaware until now and which I had not come across in any book. That is, when a Jew is in trouble, he can be saved through the merit of *Eretz Yisrael* and its inhabitants...

The mentor of the Ba'al HaTanya, our holy master, R. Baer of Mezhibuz,[4] testified in his will[5] that the Ba'al HaTanya's wisdom, intellect, and knowledge were limitless, and that his first thoughts on a matter were nearly prophetic. It is superfluous to express and describe the greatness of our master, the Ba'al HaTanya. After all,

1 Rabbi Shneur Zalman of Liadi *ztöl*, founder of Chabad *Chassidut*. [Hereafter, we will refer to him as the BaÆal HaTanya.]

2 The BaÆal HaTanya was imprisoned in Petersburg because informers accused him of treason. After a thorough investigation, he was set free. The date of his release, the 19th of Kislev, is celebrated by Chabad *Chassidim* until this very day.

3 The letter was written in 5559 [1799], and is printed in *Beit Rebbe*, chap. 18. Also see a similar letter in *Iggrot BaÆal HaTanya*, David Tzvi Hillman (Jerusalem, 5713 [1953]), no. 62.

4 Known as the Maggid of Mezeritch.

5 The will was written to his son, and dated the first day of *selichot* 5532 [1772]. See *HaToldot Rebbe Shneur Zalman MiLiadi,* R. Avraham Chanoch Glitzenstein, 3:13.

for some generations now, who does not know of his eminence? I only mention it in regard to the novel idea that I learned from his holy words – that the merit of *Eretz Yisrael* protects us and delivers us from distress. Even though I have not seen this concept in the teachings of *Chazal* or in our other holy writings, the words of our master are sufficiently trustworthy, for all his words were said with *Ruach HaKodesh*.

Torah sources which confirm this principle

After searching through many volumes, HaShem enlightened me and enabled me to find a genuine source for the Ba'al HaTanya's notion. I found it in the Torah itself! In *parashat BeChukotai* it is written, *And I will remember My covenant with Ya'akov, and also My covenant with Yitzchak, and also My covenant with Avraham I will remember, and I will remember the Land* (*VaYikra* 26:42). Our Sages discuss why the Land is mentioned in this verse (see their answer in *VaYikra Rabbah* 32:4). Based on the principle of the Ba'al HaTanya, the explanation is quite simple. Rashi, there, comments:

> Why were they [the Patriarchs] listed in reverse order? It is to tell us: Ya'akov, the youngest, is worthy of this [to bring about redemption]; and if he is not [sufficiently] worthy, behold, Yitzchak is with him; and if he is not [sufficiently] worthy, behold, Avraham is with him.

We can now take this one step further. Even if all of them are not worthy (in the eventuality that the merit of the Patriarchs has run out), still, *I will remember the Land*. That is, the merit of *Eretz Yisrael* will deliver us from distress. Thus, we have a ôpureö source from the holy Torah itself that the merit of *Eretz Yisrael* stands above all other merits. It is even greater than the merit of our forefathers. Therefore, even if they cannot come to our aid, the merit of *Eretz Yisrael* will protect and redeem us in our times of trouble.

Subsequently, I found another source for this. The *Mechilta* comments on the verse *Why are you crying out to me? Speak to the Children of Israel that they should travel* (*Shemot* 14:15): ôR. Yishmael says, æThrough the merit of Jerusalem I am splitting the sea' ö (*Mechilta, BeShalach* 3). This seems incomprehensible! What is the connection between Jerusalem and the splitting of the sea? According to the Ba'al HaTanya's principle, though, it is clear. The merit of *Eretz Yisrael* is always by our side in times of need to deliver us from distress. *Chazal* tell us that *Eretz Yisrael* is occasionally referred to as Jerusalem, since Jerusalem is its center (*Esther Rabbah* 1:9). The

Zohar similarly points out that all of *Eretz Yisrael* is included in Jerusalem (1:114a). Thus, the words of the Ba'al HaTanya are clearly derived from an explicit verse in the Torah and a *Midrash Chazal*, and they are as true as the words of Moshe from the mouth of the Almighty.

Since this is so, now that we, the Children of Israel, find ourselves in dire straits (may the Merciful One save us speedily), we certainly need the merit of our Holy Land to protect, guard, and rescue us from our persecutors. There is not a single day which is not more accursed than its precursor. Our hardships mount not only from day to day but from hour to hour. To recount them all would be impossible; I, therefore, leave that task to the historians. My purpose here was only to convey the severity of our situation.

II The Author's Vow

The Torah tells us that when Ya'akov Avinu was in distress he took a great vow to God, as it is written, *And Ya'akov took a vow saying: ôIf God will be with me, and guard me on this way that I am going, and will give me bread to eat and clothing to wear, and I will return in peace to my father's home...ö* (*BeReishit* 28:20-21). *Chazal* derive from here that one should take a vow in times of trouble (*BeReishit Rabbah* 70:1). Therefore, I, who was fortunate to see the Ba'al HaTanya's letter, would like to fulfill these words of *Chazal* and take a great oath to the God of Israel during these difficult times. I will pray, as our forefathers did, in the name of all of Israel. If God will be with me during these times of harsh decrees, and guard me from harm, and give me bread to eat and clothing to wear, and allow the merit of *Eretz Yisrael* to stand by me and my family, that no harm befalls us, and no disease or affliction comes upon us until the coming of salvation to the Jewish people as a whole and myself in particular... I plead in the name of all of Israel that the merit of *Eretz Yisrael* will arise on our behalf and save us from misfortune. Let it say to our troubles, ôEnough!ö May the following verse be fulfilled in our days, *The righteous one falls seven times, yet rises* (*Mishley* 24:15), while the wicked one falls but once.[6] May our Holy Land arouse mercy upon us so that we soon be redeemed, for we no longer have the strength to endure the pain. Let the persecutions of the last few years be considered the birthpangs of *Mashiach,* and may our

6 Based on *Mishley* 28:18.

righteous Savior come and redeem us from our enemies' clutches.❖

The purpose of this volume

In any event, if *Mashiach* still tarries even after the persecutions have ceased and HaShem has enhanced our status, then I accept upon myself a vow, like that of Ya'akov Avinu, to write a book dealing with the honor of *Eretz Yisrael*. Its aim will be to seek out the virtues of *Eretz Yisrael*, to raise its pride and honor, to demonstrate to everyone our great obligation to build it, perfect it, establish it on high, and raise it out of the dust. Through this work I will try to impress upon every Jew the importance of taking part in the rebuilding of our Holy Land, for our entire redemption depends on this. I intend to demonstrate that *Eretz Yisrael*, the ômotherö of the Jewish nation,[9] longs and awaits expectantly for all of us, young and old alike, to turn our attention towards her, to establish her, and to raise her walls in glory.

I will explain all of this (with God's help) in my book, in order to honor the Holy One Blessed be He and His *Shechinah*. In this merit, may HaShem protect us and all of Israel who are in dire straits, myself included. I hope that HaShem, the Guardian of Israel, will protect me from the oppressors, so that they will have no command over the Congregation of Israel, myself and my family in particular. May He keep me in good health and allow me to fulfill the vow that I have taken. May the merit of *Eretz Yisrael*, whose honor I will defend, stand by me and help free us from the oppressor and deliver us from distress, so that I may fulfill my vow with peace of mind and clarity of thought. May all of this come true speedily in our days. Amen. So may it be HaShem's will.

Ya'akov Avinu's vow

Now, it seems to me that this exactly was Ya'akov Avinu's vow during his time of trouble. He swore that he would return to *Eretz Yisrael*, enhance its glory, and put all of his efforts into improving

---

❖ But, one cannot know the CreatorÆs plan regarding *Mashiach*, for ôthe heart has not revealed [this matter] to the mouth.ö[7] The way in which he will come is hidden from all living beings. The Ran explains that just as the time of his coming is unknown, so too, the manner of his coming is also unknown, whether through manifest miracles or miracles hidden behind the guise of nature.[8]

7 *Midrash Tehillim* 9, *Kohelet Rabbah* 12:10.

8 *Derashot HaRan* 11 (end). ❖ See below (pp. 204-5).

9 ❖ As explained in the *Yerushalmi, Berachot* 2:8 (18b).

its settlement. By taking such a vow, he hoped to arouse the merit of *Eretz Yisrael* so that it would free him from distress. This is the meaning of the verse *And I will return in peace to my father's home and the Lord will be my God* (*BeReishit* 28:21), for this statement was itself the vow.

Based on this we can answer the question which troubled the commentators.[10] On the words, *And the Lord will be my God*, they ask, ôIs it possible that Ya'akov Avinu qualified his acceptance of God with a condition?ö Based on the above, though, it is quite clear. It is well known that *Chazal* say, ôHe who dwells in *Eretz Yisrael* is like one who has a God, and he who dwells outside the Land is like one who does not have a Godö (*Ketuvot* 110b). This, then, is the meaning of Ya'akov's statement *And I will return in peace to my father's home, and the Lord will be my God.* That is, he will return to *Eretz Yisrael* and then HaShem will be his God. Hence, this itself was the vow – that he would return to *Eretz Yisrael.*

I later found this interpretation stated explicitly in the *Midrash.* Our Sages write that Ya'akov Avinu longed for *Eretz Yisrael*, as it says, *And I will return in peace to my father's home* (*Tanchuma, Re'eh* 8).[11] I also found this in the *Zohar:* ô*And I will return in peace to my father's home,* for there lies the Holy Land, there I will be perfected, *and the Lord will be my God*ö (*Zohar* 1:150b). This is exactly how I explained Ya'akov Avinu's vow. Thus, I have merited to concur with the godly *Tana,* R. Shimon bar Yochai. Rejoice O innards that you have been so privileged.[12]

When I presented this idea to my beloved friend, the brilliant R. Yisrael Veltz *shlita*, judge and mentor of the Orthodox community here [in Budapest], he showed me a *Tosefta* which concurs with the *Zohar*:

> It says, *And I will return in peace to my father's home.* What is the meaning of [the continuation of the verse] *And the Lord will be my God*? [Similarly], it says, *To give you the Land of Cana'an to be for you a God* (*VaYikra* 25:38). [These verses

10 See Rashi, Ramban, Sforno, Or HaChayim HaKadosh, and others.

11 [The fact that they derive this lesson from YaÆEakov AvinuÆEs vow shows clearly that they, too, understand that the essence of his vow was to return to *Eretz Yisrael*.]

12 Based on *Bava Metzia* 83b.

> demonstrate that] as long as you are in the Land of Cana'an, I am your God. If you are not in the Land of Cana'an, I am not your God. (*Tosefta, Avodah Zarah* 5:2)

Thus, it is also clear from the *Tosefta* that Ya'akov's intention was to return to *Eretz Yisrael*. Blessed be HaShem; my words coincide with those of *Chazal*.

In any event, it is evident that Ya'akov, as well, vowed and prayed to the Holy One Blessed be He that the merit of *Eretz Yisrael* should stand by him and rescue him from distress.

Based on this, we can understand the *Midrash* on the verse *Ya'akov was very frightened* (*BeReishit* 32:8): ôYa'akov said, æAll of these years Eisav has dwelt in *Eretz Yisrael*, perhaps he is coming against me with the strength of living in *Eretz Yisrael*'" (*BeReishit Rabbah* 76:2). Although this appears difficult, it is quite comprehensible based on the above. Since the essence of Ya'akov Avinu's prayer was that the merit of *Eretz Yisrael* should protect him by virtue of his desire to return to it, he had good reason to be afraid. He was ôdwellingö there merely in thought, while the wicked Eisav was actually dwelling there. Therefore, Ya'akov was fearful that perhaps Eisav's merit would be greater than his own.

Our obligation during these difficult times

In any event, during his times of trouble, Ya'akov Avinu vowed to return to *Eretz Yisrael*, perfect it, and establish it, so that this merit would stand him in good stead. We, too, who find ourselves in times of difficulty, must learn from him and vow to return to our Holy Land and endeavor to raise its prestige. Then, the merit of *Eretz Yisrael* will arise to deliver us from distress, speedily in our days. Amen.

This is also the meaning of the following *Midrash*: ôThe Holy One Blessed be He turned the conversation of the Patriarchs into the key for the childrens' salvationö (*BeReishit Rabbah* 70:6, on the verse *And Ya'akov took a vow*). That is, just as Ya'akov Avinu vowed to return to our Holy Land, we, too, should take a similar vow, and then the merit of *Eretz Yisrael* will stand by our side.

Subsequently, I discovered that our godly mentor from Lublin explains, in his holy work *Divrei Emet*,[13] that Ya'akov Avinu's vow was entirely for us who are living in the era of ôthe footsteps of

13 (Germany, 5507 [1747]), p. 33.

*Mashiach.*ö Its purpose was to ensure that we return in peace to the Holy Land, our fathers' home. This is the meaning of the verse, *Ya'akov lifted up his feet* (*BeReishit* 29:1), [which immediately follows Ya'akov's vow]. It refers to ôthe footsteps of *Mashiach*ö which the *Zohar* calls ôfeet.ö[14] This idea is also found in *Beit Elokim*[15] by the brilliant and godly Mabit *zöl.*

Thus, according to our Sages *zöl*, the essence of Ya'akov's vow was intended to inform us what to do now, at the end of days, to bring the redemption closer. And, since I have already quoted the *Zohar* and the *Tosefta* as saying that Ya'akov vowed during troubled times to return to *Eretz Yisrael*, it follows that he was teaching us to do likewise in the era of ôthe footsteps of *Mashiach.*ö This alone will save us from the terrible hardships that we now face. This is a true Torah interpretation.

[In a similar vein], Rashi states that when a person is in distress and takes a vow to HaShem, he must mention Ya'akov Avinu, the one from whom we learn this tenet.[16] We also find this in the *Midrash*: ôBy our lives! We are doing this with Ya'akov Avinu's sanctionö (*see BeReishit Rabbah* 70:1).

I, too, have acted exactly as Ya'akov Avinu did, in order to arouse the merit of *Eretz Yisrael*. Therefore, its merit will surely protect us, as it did for Ya'akov Avinu. I will be able to fulfill my vow; and, God willing, my work will persuade the Jews of exile to abhor foreign lands and to once again desire the beloved Land that we inherited from our forefathers. With this merit, may we see the final redemption, speedily in our days. Amen.

The power of the merit of Eretz Yisrael

I wrote this introduction on the 7th day of Av, in the year, *Do not turn away* (תשב) *the face of Your anointed* (*Tehillim* 132:10),[17] at a time when my family and I escaped miraculously from great danger. There is no doubt in my mind that it was solely the merit of *Eretz Yisrael* that protected us, for its great merit always rescues us from oppression and delivers us from distress. We were only saved because I took a great vow to God to seek out the virtues of *Eretz Yisrael* as soon as HaShem would enable me to do so.

The Torah says, *Hear O Israel and be careful to fulfill..., as the*

14 See *Zohar* 1:72b.

15 *ShaÆar HaTefillah* 18, s.v. *tefillat YaÆakov.*

16 Rashi on I *Divrei HaYamim* 29:10.

17 [The numerical value of תשב is 702, corresponding to the year 5702 (1942).]

Lord, God of your forefathers, spoke concerning you – a land flowing with milk and honey (*Devarim* 6:3). The Chatam Sofer explains this enigmatic verse:

> In this entire section, the Torah repeatedly mentions *Eretz Yisrael* in its admonishment of the Jewish people. This is a wondrous property *(segulah)*, for the mention of the Holy Land generates holiness in the heart of the listener. With regard to impurity [the Torah states], *It shall not be heard from your mouth* (*Shemot* 23:13), and [the Talmud states], ôWhoever says æRachav Rachav' will immediately see a seminal emissionö (*Megillah* 15a). Similarly, the opposite is true concerning holiness, [for example], when mentioning the Holy Land or the Holy People. Thus, the Holy One Blessed be He is telling us that the people of Israel will become so sanctified that the mere mention of the name ôIsraelö will cause them to keep and fulfill HaShem's *mitzvot*. This is the meaning of *Hear O Israel*: When you hear the name ôIsrael,ö you will *be careful to fulfill*. Then, the verse concludes with an example of this concept, *As He spoke concerning you – a land flowing with milk and honey*. That is to say, [God mentioned *Eretz Yisrael*] at every point in order to enhance our holiness through its mention.[18]

Thus, the Torah deliberately mentions the Land countless times so that our holiness will be enhanced. This demonstrates its great strength. Therefore, it is no wonder that *Eretz Yisrael* has the power to deliver us from distress any time we mention its name. Let us yearn to return to *Eretz Yisrael* and dwell there, as in days of old. Amen. So may it be HaShem's will, speedily in our days. Amen.

18 *Derashot Chatam Sofer*, introduction.

SECOND INTRODUCTION

The destruction of European Jewry

With a broken spirit, I speak of the destruction of my people[1] which has befallen us in our days. The exile has overwhelmed us and become a virtual prison – the one misfortune which encompasses all others, as it is written, *Whoever is* [destined] *for death, to death; whoever for the sword, to the sword; whoever for famine, to famine; and whoever for captivity, to captivity* (*Yirmiyah* 15:2). The Talmud explains that each fate mentioned in this verse is worse than its precursor, for captivity includes all the previous fates (*Bava Batra* 8b, see Rashi). The pride of Israel has been cut down. In our entire history there has never been such calamity.

True, there have been difficult periods for Israel in the past, but only in distinct, isolated areas, and our ancestors were able to find refuge elsewhere. Misfortune on such an extensive and widespread scale, however, has never befallen us; except in the days of the wicked Haman, when a general decree was issued against the entire holy nation, and the gates of all countries were closed to them (see *Midrash Esther Rabbah* 7). Now too, Europe – which has always been the center for the Jews, and from which all of the *gedolim* and wise men of the last hundred years have emerged – has been utterly destroyed. *Raze it, raze it, to its very foundations* (*Tehillim* 137:7). There is nowhere to escape, for all of the nations have closed their gates to us. They are completely sealed; no one leaves and no one enters.[2]

I The Factors That Prompted the Writing of This Volume

1. Today's afflictions preclude ordinary Torah study

Now that we have encountered unwanted days,[3] my mind is preoccupied with the troubles of the generation. I am, therefore, unable to delve into ordinary halachic matters, as has been my practice since my youth, since such study requires clarity.[4] Moreover,

1 [Lit., *The breach of the daughter of my people*] from *Eichah* 2:11.

2 Based on *Yehoshua* 6:1.

3 Based on *Kohelet* 12:1.

4 See *Megillah* 28b.

the storms of exile which have assaulted us, have banished the yeshiva from my house of study. On the bitter day when the pogroms spread among the people and trampled all that was holy, yeshiva students were evicted from their study halls. I remained alone, isolated with my thoughts on the present-day destruction of the people and communities of Israel. Why has the Lord done this?[5] What is the meaning of this terrible anger?[6]

Thus, I decided to examine the history of our people during its 2,000 years in the tumultuous pit of destruction and exile in the lands of the nations. I have never dealt with these types of questions. Since my youth I have always been implanted in the house of God, hidden and concealed in the four cubits of *halachah*. HaShem (may He be blessed) has graciously allowed me to learn, teach, and author works which have been well received and praised by the great scholars of the generation.[7] I never took the time to concern myself with matters affecting the welfare of our holy nation, for this is a *mitzvah* that can be fulfilled by others. [I, therefore, felt] that one could apply the verse *All your desires cannot compare to it* [the Torah] (*Mishley* 3:15), and that one should not neglect Torah-study on its account.[8] Now, however, amidst this great upheaval, it is impossible to concentrate on the discussions of Abaye and Rava, and complicated *halachot*. My students have been driven away from me, and I have no one with whom to discuss halachic matters.

2. The time for redemption has come

Thus, I have been aroused to ask this question: It says in *Daniel* (12:6), *How long until the wondrous end?* Are we not yet close to the eve of the sixth day, about which is written, *It shall come to pass that at evening time, there will be light* (*Zecharyah* 14:7)? Rashi explains that prior to the end of the millennium there will be a glorious light. In addition, a hymn (*piyut*) which we recite on *Rosh HaShanah* alludes to the time when this will occur: "When the sun turns westward two parts, it is the time when the lights grow dim. So too, prior to the onset of evening, light will sprout forth for the upright,

5 Based on *Devarim* 29:23; I *Melachim* 9:8; *Yirmiyah* 22:8.

6 Based on *Devarim* 29:23.

7 ✣ See the approbations of the *gedolim* to my work, *Mishneh Sachir*, vol. 1 (5684 [1924]). Also see the letter of our godly mentor from Ostrovtza, published in my work, *Tov Yigal* (5686 [1926]).

8 ✣ As explained in *Mo'ed Kattan* 9b and as codified in *Yoreh De'ah* 246:18.

and it shall come to pass at evening time there will be light for the perfect."[9]

It appears to me that we have already reached this stage,✧ but *Mashiach* has not yet arrived. There certainly must be some obstacle preventing our redemption from this bitter exile. Therefore, we must ponder this matter and identify the obstacle so that we may remove it from our path. We will, thus, pave the way for our righteous Redeemer [*Mashiach*] who will arrive speedily in our days to deliver us from distress and raise the *Shechinah* from the dust. Thus, with the help of He Who Grants Knowledge, I have decided to investigate this matter to the best of my limited abilities.

3. One must care for the needs of Israel

Furthermore, I recalled the statement of *Chazal* cited in *Reishit Chochmah*:

> He who is proper and fears sin should involve himself in the needs of Israel... He should share their burden and suffer with them in times of trouble. He who acts in this manner sustains the world, as it is written, *Through justice the king establishes the land* (*Mishley* 29:4). On the other hand, he who refrains from sharing their burden and repairing their breaches, acting as if he was *terumah* separated from the dough, destroys the world, as it is written, *But a man set aside* (*ish terumot*) *destroys it* (ibid.).
>
> The story is told of Rabbi Abahu: When he was about to leave this world, the Sages of Israel entered and found him weeping. They said to him: "Why are you crying? All of your life you toiled in Torah. You taught so many disciples. Moreover, you even had a special quality: you did not engage in legal disputes." He replied: "That is exactly why I am crying, for I did not share the burden of Israel. Thus, I epitomized the verse: *But a man set aside destroys it.*"✧✧ (*Midrash Tanchuma, Mishpatim* 2)[11]

✧ I subsequently discovered in a commentary on *Tana DeVei Eliyahu,* called *Tosafot Ben Yechiel,* that we have actually reached this stage.[10]

✧✧ That is to say, he ôseparated himselfö from caring for the needs of Israel, like *terumah* which is separated from the rest of the wheat.

9 See *Machzor Rabbah (nusach sefard)*, p. 304, s.v. *"asher mi ya'aseh kema'asecha."*

10 *Tosafot Ben Yechiel* 2:1.

11 *Reishit Chochmah* (Jerusalem, 5732 [1972]), *Perek HaDinin*, p. 257a.

Thus, *Chazal* obligate us to be concerned with the plight of the Jewish people and care for their needs even during normal times – when everything proceeds naturally and peace and tranquillity reign in the world. How much more so must every Jew fulfill this obligation during times such as these, when the pride of Israel has been disgraced and cut down;[12] when Jews wallow in the dirt; when they have become scorned and degraded; and when they and their possessions have become abandoned like fish of the sea. Certainly, there is a manifold obligation upon every Jew to care for their needs, to be concerned with their condition, to help the Jewish people in any way possible, and to use his God-given wisdom to show them the way in which they can escape from distress.

Our mentor, R. Moshe Cordovero, writes in *Tomer Devorah* that one must think constructively on behalf of all of Israel, for their benefit.[13] The author of *Ya'arot Devash* also discusses this and writes that all the hardships that befall Israel are due to improper leaders.[14]

The purpose of this volume

This is what inspired me to examine the perseverance of this exile and, with God's help, to author this work. I intend to publicly express my opinion, to teach and advise our people, the Children of Israel, how to hasten the future redemption, speedily in our days. I have accepted this upon myself as a vow in times of trouble, as I explained above in the first introduction.[15]

Thus, since it is prohibited to delay fulfillment of a vow taken in times of distress,[16] and since I have enjoyed some respite ever since arriving in the capital,[17] I have begun to write a volume on the rebuilding of our Holy Land. The purpose of this work is to raise our Land from the dust and stimulate love and affection for it in the hearts of our Jewish brethren, young and old alike. Then they will yearn and strive to return to our Land, the Land of our forefathers, and leave the lands of exile. The *Midrash* states this explicitly, "It is preferable to dwell in the deserts of *Eretz Yisrael* than the palaces of *Chutz LaAretz*" (*BeReishit Rabbah* 39:8).

12 Based on *Eichah* 2:3.
13 *Tomer Devorah*, chap. 7.
14 *Ya'arot Devash*, vol. 1, on the blessing "Return Our Judges."
15 Pp. 35-39.
16 ❖ See *BeReishit Rabbah* 81:1-2, concerning Ya'akov Avinu.
17 Budapest. See the historical introduction for a description of our author's travels.

II The Purpose of Our Afflictions is to Arouse Us to Return to Eretz Yisrael

Furthermore, the sole purpose of all the afflictions that smite us in our exile is to arouse us to return to our Holy Land. This can be inferred from the story of King David and the plague. During the plague, God sent him Gad the prophet. *And Gad came to David...and said to him, "Go up and establish an altar to the Lord"* (II *Shmuel* 24:18). The *Midrash* explains:

> This can be likened to a father who beat his son, but the son did not know why he was being punished. After the beating, the father said, "For several days I have been commanding you to do something, and you have ignored me. Now go and do it!" So too, the thousands who fell at the time of David died only because they did not demand the building of the *Beit HaMikdash*. From this we can derive a *kal vachomer*. If they, in whose days the *Beit HaMikdash* was neither built nor destroyed, were punished for not having demanded its construction; then we, in whose days the *Beit HaMikdash* was destroyed..., certainly [deserve punishment], for we do not mourn nor supplicate. (*Midrash Tehillim* 17)

Rashi on *Hoshea* (3:5) cites the following:

> R. Shimon ben Menassiya said: "The Jewish people will not be shown a good sign until they once again request the kingdom of Heaven, the kingdom of the House of David, and the rebuilding of the *Beit HaMikdash*. It is thus written, *Afterwards, the Children of Israel will return and seek out the Lord their God and David their king...* (*Hoshea* 3:5)."

Behold, our desire to return to *Eretz Yisrael* encompasses these three elements. Firstly, "He who dwells in *Eretz Yisrael* is like one who has a God" (*Ketuvot* 110b). Also, the rebuilding of the *Beit HaMikdash* will occur (with God's help) when we assemble in *Eretz Yisrael*, as explained in *Megillah* (17b-18a). Afterwards, *Mashiach*, who represents the kingdom of the House of David, will arrive, as I will demonstrate in this volume.[18] First and foremost, though, we must strive to return to *Eretz Yisrael* and then, with God's help, we will attain these three objectives.

18 See pp. 140-41, 182, 199-201...

We only truly cling to God in Eretz Yisrael

The *Tosefta* comments on the verse *And I will truly implant them in this Land with all My heart and with all My soul* (*Yirmiyah* 32:41):

> If they are not upon the Land, they are not truly implanted before Me, neither with all My heart nor with all My soul. (*Tosefta, Avodah Zarah* 5:4)

It is striking that the Holy One Blessed be He says that when the people of Israel are not in *Eretz Yisrael* they do not cling to His heart and soul! Therefore, we should not be astonished by what has happened to us in our times, or by the lack of Divine Providence that we are experiencing, for we live in the lands of the nations and do not cling to God's entire heart and soul. However, when we strive to return to *Eretz Yisrael*, we will immediately cling to His entire heart and soul.

One who strives to reach Eretz Yisrael is considered already there

The Kuzari explains that even though *Chazal* say that the *Shechinah* does not reside outside the Land (*Mo'ed Kattan* 25a), it did rest upon Yechezkel, because he prophesied for the sake of *Eretz Yisrael*.[19] Rabbeinu Chayim, the brother of the Maharal of Prague, expresses a similar idea in his *Sefer HaChayim*. *Chazal* maintain that those who die outside the Land will be resurrected only after suffering the pain of rolling through underground tunnels. Nonetheless, explains R. Chayim, a person who strives to move to *Eretz Yisrael* but dies outside the Land, will be spared this pain. He is considered as one who resided in *Eretz Yisrael* and will, therefore, be resurrected in an upright position.[20] Our mentor, the Mabit, concurs with this view in his work, *Beit Elokim*.[21]

Thus, he who sets his eyes and heart upon moving to *Eretz Yisrael* is considered as if he is already there. It follows, then, that if we dedicate our thoughts to returning to our Holy Land we will immediately cling to God's entire heart and soul. His Divine Providence will keep a watchful eye over us to rescue us from our enemies and bring success to our endeavors. We will ascend to Zion joyously, and the Children of Israel will go forth with a high hand[22] from both physical and spiritual exile. HaShem will renew our spirit so that we will yearn to serve Him completely, by fulfilling the Torah and *mitzvot* as written in His holy Torah.

19 *Kuzari* 2:14, quoted in the gloss of *Maharatz Chayot, Mo'ed Kattan* 25a.

20 *Sefer HaChayim, Sefer Ge'ulah ViYeshuah*, chap. 1 (end).

21 See *Sha'ar HaYesodot*, chap. 55, quoted below, p. 392.

22 Based on *Shemot* 14:8.

We must take the first step and then God will assist us

The essential point is that HaShem is waiting for us to take the initiative, to desire and long for the return to *Eretz Yisrael*. He does not want us to wait for Him to bring us there. He, therefore, told us, *And I will truly implant them in this Land*. That is to say, when we, of our own volition, truly and with all our strength, desire and strive [to return to the Land], then God will bring our work to a successful end.

The Zohar writes in a similar vein. Although King Shlomo's Temple was erected miraculously, the Holy One Blessed be He waited for our initiative and only then completed the edifice (*Zohar* 1:74a). The same is true of settling *Eretz Yisrael*. We must strive with all our might, to the best of our abilities, and then HaShem will complete our handiwork. May the pleasantness of the Lord be upon us to establish and bring success to the work of our hands.[23]

When David consulted with the people of Israel it says, *And David said to the entire Congregation of Israel, "If it seems good to you and to the Lord our God, let us send abroad to our remaining brethren in all the lands of Israel"* (I *Divrei HaYamim* 13:2). One might ask, why did David mention the people of Israel before HaShem...when the [*Mishnah*] at the end of *Yadayim* (4:8) forbids this? It seems to me that the answer lies in Rashi's comment: "David said to them, 'You have already occupied yourselves with your own self-improvement, now occupy yourselves with God's honor.' " That is, the advice was to act for God's honor and restore the holy ark to Jerusalem. But, David wanted to begin with Israel, rather than God, in order to arouse them. Since God's honor was involved it was proper for the awakening to come from Israel first. Afterwards, assistance would come from above... This teaches that man must perform the initial act of any godly matter, and afterwards he will receive assistance from above.

The brilliant and holy rabbi who resembles an angel of the Lord of Hosts, our honorable R. Eliyahu, *av beit din* of Greiditz, concurs:

> Human intellect dictates that we initiate the process of redeeming the Land, and then HaShem will complete it. One must understand the great importance of this matter, for the evil forces (*kelipah*) gain strength even among the most

23 Based on *Tehillim* 90:17.

righteous individuals, in order to nullify this good. This is so because the *kelipah*'s entire strength depends on exile; when the exile dissolves, so will the *kelipah*, as the Talmud states in *Sukkah*.[24]

Thus, this holy Jew, whom the author of *Nefesh Chayah* calls, "the holy rabbi who resembles an angel of the Lord of Hosts," states explicitly that the reason there are *tzaddikim* who oppose this is because the *kelipah* has become strong within them. It entices them to nullify this great matter for which the Holy One Blessed be He constantly longs. He longs for us to yearn to return to our forefathers' inheritance, for every Jew has an obligation to strive to return to our Holy Land (as I will later prove, unequivocally, from the words of *Chazal*).[25] In this way, we can bring the final redemption closer, speedily in our days. Amen.

III This Work is Intended Only for Those Who Seek the Absolute Truth

I must, however, make it quite clear that my words are intended for those Jews who wish to arrive at the absolute truth by way of halachic debate and dialogue. For, the issue of the final redemption is also a matter of *halachah*, as *Chazal* demonstrate: "*The word of the Lord* (*Amos* 8:11) – this is *halachah. The word of the Lord* (ibid. 12) – this is the final redemption" (*Shabbat* 138b, *Tana DeVei Eliyahu* 16:11). Thus, anything which concerns the final redemption is akin to ordinary halachic matters and requires a dialogue of scholars.[26] This *halachah* should not differ from any other *halachah* in the Torah and must be discussed by scholars using proofs from our holy Torah to determine what course of action to take. Why should the *halachah* of rebuilding the Land – which concerns the honor of HaShem, the holy nation, and the Holy Land – be less important than any other *halachah* in the Torah? Therefore, one scholar builds [a proof] and the other refutes it until the matter becomes clear, as the Mabit explains in his responsa.[27]

24 ❖ This letter is printed in the beginning of *Nefesh Chayah*, by our brilliant master, R. Chayim Elazar Waks. I quoted it above [in its entirety] (pp. 14-15).

25 See pp. 156-62.

26 ❖ The righteous and brilliant R. Akiva Yosef of Jerusalem also says this in his wondrous commentary to *Tana DeVei Eliyahu*.

27 Sec. 116.

The Mabit, there, writes that the one who refutes must also bring proofs. He cannot simply argue without support, using mere chatter. The following are the words of our mentor, the Maharival, as cited by the Mabit:

> Any scholar who wishes to criticize a decision rendered by a colleague who elucidated the reasons for his ruling, may not do so unless he, too, clarifies his opinion with valid arguments. To merely chatter, however, and state that the law is not in accordance with the other's view is unacceptable.

Those who are biased or have ulterior motives will never concede to the truth

Therefore, those who have a predisposition on this matter will not see the truth and will not concede to our words. All the evidence in the world will not affect them, for they are smitten with blindness, and their inner biases cause them to deny even things which are as clear as day. Who amongst us is greater than the spies? The Torah testifies that they were proper individuals.[28] Nonetheless, since they were influenced by their desire for authority,❖ they rejected the desirable Land and led others astray, causing this bitter exile (as *Chazal* explain).[31] Yehoshua and Calev began to argue with them and attempted to prove the authenticity of Moshe and his Torah. They proclaimed, *Let us ascend at once* (*BeMidbar* 13:30). They even brought lengthy arguments and proofs to show that Israel would succeed [in entering the Land], as Rashi states. Nevertheless, they were unable to convince them [the spies], for the spies were prejudiced by hidden motives.

The same holds true in our times, even among rabbis, *rebbes*, and *chassidim*. This one has a good rabbinical position; this one is an established *Admor*;[32] and this one has a profitable business or factory, or a prestigious job which provides great satisfaction. They are afraid

---

❖ The *Zohar*[29] and the Shelah[30] explain that the spies were afraid that they would lose their positions of leadership upon entering *Eretz Yisrael*.

28 See Rashi, *BeMidbar* 13:3.

29 *Zohar* 3:158a, s.v. *vayishlach*.

30 *Sh'nei Luchot HaBrit, Torah SheBichtav – Shelach*, 2:68a, s.v. *be'inyan*.

31 See below, pp. 396-99.

32 [Hebrew acronym for אדוננו מורינו ורבנו – our master, our mentor, our rabbi – referring to a *chassidic rebbe*.]

that their status will decline if they go to *Eretz Yisrael*.[33] People of this sort are influenced by their deep-rooted, selfish motives to such an extent that they themselves do not realize that their prejudice speaks on their behalf.

In my responsa, *Mishneh Sachir*,[34] I cite our holy and godly mentor, R. Yeshayah Muskat of Praga, in a eulogy for the brilliant R. Meir Shapira, *av beit din* of Lublin. He says that most of the time a person fools himself and thinks that he acts for the sake of Heaven. In reality, though, he is controlled by his deep-rooted motives, and even he does not realize it... He proves this from the story of Avraham and Eliezer. *Divrei Chayim* (on Chanukah) states that a person sees only what he wants to see. Therefore, one who is prejudiced on a certain matter can no longer judge truthfully. This is why the Torah prohibits a judge from taking a bribe.❖

❖ The Divrei Chayim writes:

> Any kindness performed by the "mixed multitudeö (*eirev rav*) is done for their own benefit. We clearly see that the rabbis, *chassidim*, and laymen of this generation, for the most part, descend from the *eirev rav* (due to our many sins), and they want to rule over the masses. All of their deeds are done for their own benefit, to receive honor or monetary gain. Therefore, one should not associate with them, only with those who truly serve God and sacrifice themselves for His name, not for their own selfish gains.[35]

Frightening!

Our godly mentor, the Chatam Sofer, writes similarly:

> You should be aware of the expression of which I am fond: "There is no Ya'akov who is unharmed by Lavan, and there are few Lavans who are harmed by Ya'akov." Guard this principle for it is true; consider it and you will find it accurate. What I mean to say is, it is an established axiom that all Torah scholars and righteous individuals, referred to as "Ya'akov," have adversaries who are referred to as "Lavan." However, very few of these wicked people will find themselves opposed by someone who can equal their deception, as Ya'akov did against Lavan. You should know that many times I examined them [the "Lavans"] and concluded that one must guard himself from them and straighten out that which

33 ❖ The author of *Sefer HaBrit* (vol. 1, 9:16) writes in a similar vein as he bemoans the lengthiness of our exile.

34 Vol. 2. See author's footnote on p. 405, (n. 573) regarding this work.

35 *Divrei Chayim, VaYakhel* (addendum).

People of this sort will not be convinced to accept the truth, even if they are shown thousands of proofs from the Torah. This is what happened to Yehoshua and Calev with the spies. Therefore, this volume is intended only for those who wish to know the truth as it is; they will lend an attentive ear to my words. I do not allege that you must accept my view. I will simply provide halachic analysis, and whoever wishes to refute me, let him come and refute, but only with absolute proofs from the words of *Chazal*, as I have done. Then, I will debate him to the best of my God-given abilities. But, those who come with mere fabrications, without any substantiation from *Chazal*, will be disregarded (as the above-mentioned Mabit indicates).

IV The Call of Aliyah to Eretz Yisrael

Jews who live comfortably in exile tend to disregard this call

In reality, this movement of *aliyah* – the ascent and return to *Eretz Yisrael* – is not a new one. Since ancient times, great sages and *tzaddikim* have aroused themselves to this cause.[37] However, since

---

> is crooked. I also concluded that one must flee from the smallest of their deceptions, but I myself have stumbled at the greatest of them. Not only is this true of the simpletons and the masses, but even of Torah students and rabbis. Anyone who does not speak truth in his heart and who is not guided by integrity and righteousness, should be avoided. Remove your steps from his path.[36]

Now, if they wrote these things in their generation which, in truth, was still a knowledgeable generation, what are we to say in our generation? How are we to answer them?

The *Yerushalmi* comments:

> The same [distance] that exists between the Holy of Holies and the profane of profanes, exists between our generation and the generation of R. Yosi. R. Yishmael the son of R. Yosi said, "The same [distance] that exists between gold and dirt, exists between our generation and my father's generation." (*Gittin* 6:7)

This demonstrates the extent to which the son's generation dwindles and distances itself from that of the father. If so, how far have we fallen from the generation of those holy ones [the Divrei Chayim and the Chatam Sofer]? Yet, they wrote this about their generation. What, then, can be said about ours?

36 *Teshuvot Chatam Sofer* 6:59.

37 ❖ As I stated above (see approbations, pp. 2-23).

the Jews of those times enjoyed freedom and dwelt peacefully in exile, they did not listen to their divinely inspired words.

Rashi on *Kiddushin* (69b) states that the Jews who dwelt comfortably in exile did not go up with Ezra to *Eretz Yisrael*. Only the poor and dejected souls ascended with him. Furthermore, *Seder HaDorot* cites our mentor, the S'ma, who saw the following in *Ma'aseh Nissim* (by R. Eliezer of Worms, author of the *Roke'ach*): Ezra sent letters to all of the Diaspora communities urging them to ascend with him to *Eretz Yisrael*. One such letter arrived in the city of Worms, in Germany. The Jews residing there answered, "You may dwell in the great Jerusalem, we will dwell here in the small Jerusalem."[38] They said this because they were very important in the eyes of the ministers and the Gentiles. They were extremely wealthy, and they lived peacefully in exile.

Seder HaDorot further quotes the S'ma as saying that this is why such terrible decrees have befallen the Jews of Germany – Worms in particular – more than any other community. They settled there at the time of the destruction of the First Temple, but when Ezra asked them to return at the end of the seventy years, they refused. Indeed, we see from the history of our people that all of the troubles and evil decrees have emanated from Germany, just like today. It all stems from the sin of refusing to ascend with Ezra, which happened because they lived peacefully in exile. This has always been the case; when Jews live comfortably in exile, they do not want to hear about *aliyah* to *Eretz Yisrael*.

During times of adversity all should heed the call

Now, however, the Great Advisor and Mighty Doer,[39] Who is the Cause of All Causes, has, through His profound counsel,[40] caused all of our gentile neighbors to persecute us with harsh decrees. It is no longer possible to remain here amongst them. Every Jew would now be happy and fortunate if he were able to return to our Holy Land. With love and affection he would heed the call of *aliyah* and ascend to *Eretz Yisrael*.

Seemingly, this explains the *Midrash* on the verse *Draw me, we will run after You* (*Shir HaShirim* 1:4). *Chazal* comment, "Because You [God] incited my evil neighbors against me, we will run after You"

38 *Seder HaDorot* vol. 1, 5380.

39 Based on *Yirmiyah* 32:19.

40 Based on *BeReishit Rabbah* 84:13.

(*Shir HaShirim Rabbah* 1:4:4).[41] That is to say, for many years we lived in peace and harmony with our gentile neighbors. Then, suddenly, they turned into enemies and evil neighbors who persecute us. This can only be because some force incited them against us. HaShem, with His profound counsel, caused all of this to occur so that *we will run after You* to *Eretz Yisrael*, which immediately follows God.[42] This, then, is the meaning of the *Midrash*: From the fact that You incited my neighbors against me, I understand that we must run after You. That is, we must run to *Eretz Yisrael*, which is "after" You. Contemplate this for it is a true Torah interpretation.

In times like these, everyone will certainly heed our call to ascend to *Eretz Yisrael*, as our mentor, the Rosh, writes: "My heart tells me that now is the time to rectify that which I have wanted to rectify for some time, because people will surely listen to me during difficult times like these."[43]

All of our toil in foreign lands is in vain

The prophet Chaggai cries out: *And now, thus says the Lord of Hosts, "Consider your ways. You have sown much, but bring in little; you eat without being satiated...; you clothe yourselves, but no one is warm; and whoever earns wages earns for a bag with a hole." Thus says the Lord of Hosts, "Consider your ways"* (*Chaggai* 1:5-7). Rashi explains:

> *Consider your ways*, meaning, your business. You see that your labor achieves no blessing, as the verse says, *You have sown much, but bring in little..., and whoever earns wages earns for a bag with a hole.* Any profit you make perishes, just like one who places money in a pocket with a hole.

The prophet cautions us to pay attention to this matter, and he repeats his admonition – *Thus says the Lord of Hosts, ôConsider your waysö* – as a warning not to close our eyes to the fact that all of our toil is wasted in the hands of our enemies.

The *Midrash* indicates that this entire verse refers to those who refuse to ascend to *Eretz Yisrael*:

> You find that when the Children of Israel were exiled to

41 [Our Sages make a play on words between משכני (*Draw me*) and שכני (my neighbors).]

42 ❖ As I cited earlier (p. 16) from *Tzror HaMor*, by the grandfather of the Beit Yosef's wife.

43 ❖ *Teshuvot HaRosh* 4:10. See there that which pertains to our discussion.

Babylonia, Ezra said to them, "Ascend to *Eretz Yisrael.*" They, however, did not want to go. Ezra said to them, *You have sown much, but bring in little; you eat without being satiated...; you clothe yourselves, but no one is warm; and whoever earns wages, earns for a bag with a hole.* (*Midrash Tanchuma, Tetzaveh* 13)

Tzefanyah states, *And I will punish the men who sit complacently, who say in their hearts, "The Lord will not do good, nor evil." And their wealth will become a plunder, and their houses a desolation; they will build houses, but will not dwell in them; they will plant vineyards, but will not drink their wine* (*Tzefanyah* 1:12-13). Indeed all of this has occurred in our days in nearly all of the countries of Europe, because the Jews disregard *aliyah* to *Eretz Yisrael,* as the *Tanchuma* demonstrates.

The brilliant Ya'avetz also bemoans our lack of interest in returning to and dwelling in *Eretz Yisrael.* Since we subsist peacefully outside the Land, we imagine that we have already found a different *Eretz Yisrael* and Jerusalem. This caused great misfortune to the Jews who dwelt comfortably in Spain (and other lands), and they were expelled. There is no remnant of the Jewish people left in that land. HaShem is righteous, for they completely forgot that they were in exile, and they assimilated among the nations. All of this has happened because we neglected to return to our homeland, the Land of the Deer.[44]

Adversity awakens us to heed the call of aliyah

This is also the cause of the troubles that our nation is experiencing here today. My Beloved is knocking[45] to awaken our desire to return to our Land. After all that has happened to us during these difficult times, there is no doubt that my words will fall upon fertile ground and awaken the hearts of our Jewish brethren in exile to long and yearn to return to the desirable Land of our forefathers. They will realize that there is no blessing in all of their endeavors here in exile, for the fruits of their labor are snatched by Eisav. Not only does he steal their money and property, but also their bodies, their very lives (as is well known from current events throughout Europe). During such times, they will surely listen to me, as the words of the Rosh indicate (see above).

44 ❖ See the Ya'avetz's lengthy exhortation on this matter in his introduction to the *siddur* (*Sullam Beit El*, p. 13a).

45 Based on *Shir HaShirim* 5:2.

HaShem is delaying redemption until Eretz Yisrael is rebuilt

In the volume, *Hon Ashir*, by the author of *Mishnat Chassidim*, I found a comment on the *Mishnah* "The Galilee will be destroyed" (*Sotah* 9:15):

> It will become devoid of houses, as it says, *And your cities will be a ruin* (*VaYikra* 26:33). In the year 5478 [1718], when HaShem granted me the privilege to ascend to *Eretz Yisrael*, to Safed in the Galilee (may it be rebuilt and established speedily in our days), I saw with my own eyes how this curse has come true. Due to our many sins, it is completely filled with destroyed houses. In the two years that I remained there, however, I was happy to see that, day by day, it was being rebuilt, thank God. I claim that this is a sign of the imminent arrival of the Redeemer, for if he would come when *Eretz Yisrael* is in a state of ruin, there would be no place for the ingathered exiles to dwell.
>
> The same thing happened the first time we entered the Land. Our Rabbis state that the Holy One Blessed be He detained the people of Israel in the desert for forty years so that the Land could regain its original strength. When the Jews left Egypt, the Amorites destroyed and uprooted trees and buildings, thinking that Israel would enter the Land immediately and find it destroyed. God only brought them in when the Land was finally rejuvenated, (Shemot Rabbah 20:16). The same will happen (with HaShem's help) when *Mashiach* arrives, may he come speedily in our days, for he will reveal himself first in this Land, as the *Zohar* states.[46]

I was awestruck by this discovery, for I saw in it a Heavenly response to the question I posed earlier:[47] How much longer until the wondrous end? HaShem is detaining us in exile until *Eretz Yisrael* is rebuilt. I learned this from the holy words of the author of *Mishnat Chassidim* who possessed *Ruach HaKodesh* and achieved revelations from Eliyahu HaNavi, as is well known. Our master, the author of *Divrei Chayim,* writes about him: "It is fitting to rely upon the Mishnat Chassidim, particularly since it is well known that his words are clear and unerring teachings of the Ari *z"l* and his disciples, and the great early Kabbalists. Therefore, one should not deviate nor detract

46 *Hon Ashir*, end of *Sotah*.
47 P. 42.

from his words, for they are like fine flour."[48] This testimony of the holy Rebbe of Tzanz sufficiently demonstrates the greatness of the Mishnat Chassidim.

Thus, the author of *Mishnat Chassidim* writes explicitly, "The same will happen when *Mashiach* arrives, may he come speedily in our days." That is to say, the Holy One Blessed be He will delay the final redemption until our Land is built up with houses and trees. Hence, when we see that *Eretz Yisrael* is being rebuilt, we can perceive this as a harbinger of redemption. These are the words of the foremost Kabbalist of recent generations, whose every utterance was said with *Ruach HaKodesh*. Who, then, in our days is noble or arrogant enough to disagree with him?

According to the assertion of this holy Kabbalist, the fact that a large portion of the Land has recently been built up, and has actually become fertile, can be viewed as a sign of the redemption. It is therefore astonishing that some God-fearing Jews oppose this. It has practically become repulsive and loathsome in their eyes. This can only be explained according to the principle of the holy R. Eliyahu of Greiditz.[49] That is, the *kelipah* has overcome them and compels them to hinder the redemption process, for the *kelipah* knows that with the rebuilding of the Land comes its own downfall. Alternatively, they may have some selfish motive to remain here, as was the case with the spies.[50]

In any event, I have demonstrated to all of our fellow Jews in exile that now is the most opportune time to strive with all our might to leave the Diaspora, return to our Holy Land, and work to rebuild it. This way we will bring *Mashiach* closer, speedily in our days. Amen.

V *Eim HaBanim Semeichah – The Reason for This Title*

I have entitled this work ***Eim HaBanim Semeichah*** (A Joyous Mother of Children) based on the *Yerushalmi* which refers to *Eretz Yisrael* as the mother of Israel and the lands of exile as the stepmother (*Berachot* 2:8 [18b]). *Chazal* also state that our mother Zion cries and laments over us when we are in exile, and she waits for us to return to her bosom (see *Pesikta Rabbati* 27-32).

48 *Divrei Chayim, Even HaEzer* 101.

49 ❖ See above, p. 15.

50 ❖ See above, pp. 49-51.

From my flesh I see God![51] In the year 5702 [1942], before *Pesach* (Passover), the cursed oppressors issued the terrible decree to abduct young Jewish maidens in Slovakia, age sixteen and older, and deport them to an uninhabited, unknown land. To this day, the fate of thousands of pure Jewish souls who were transported there is unknown. May HaShem speedily take vengeance on our oppressors, on our behalf. The camp of Israel was in a great state of panic.

I know of an incident in which a certain individual attempted to smuggle his young daughters over the border, to save them from this horrible trap. It was the intermediary days of *Pesach*, and he promised his wife that he would send a telegraphed message from across the border informing her that he and his children had arrived safely. The mother sat at home anticipating and longing for the moment that she would receive the good news. It happened, however, that before they crossed the border, the father and his daughters were seized and transported to a nearby village, where they were placed in prison. There, they remained for the duration of *Pesach*. They were in great danger of being sent off immediately to an unknown place, for that was the punishment for someone who was caught attempting to escape; he would be deported to an unknown destination in a harsher manner than the other deportees.

In the meantime, his wife, the mother of the girls, was informed of the situation. We can imagine the bitter emotions which overcame her. Her joy at the prospect of deliverance was transformed into sorrow. Her holiday became a time of mourning for her husband and daughters. The entire holiday she cried endlessly. Her entire world became dark. It is impossible to describe the sorrowful state into which she fell from the time she became aware of her husband and daughters' fate, for she knew what awaited them.

However, the brilliant, righteous, and pious rabbi, a true self-sacrificing servant of HaShem, our master, R. Shmuel David Unger (*shlita*), the *av beit din* of Nitra, selflessly and vigilantly endangered his own life and labored until he redeemed these three captives with a large sum of money. May he be remembered for the good. On the last day of *Pesach* they were set free and permitted to return home, unharmed and in peace. The distraught woman was immediately informed, via telephone, that her husband and daughters were set free and that they would return home the next day, *isru chag*,

51 Based on *Iyov* 19:26.

unharmed and in peace. It is needless to describe what sort of an effect this good tiding had upon the soul of this unfortunate woman. From that moment on, she waited expectantly for the father and daughters to return home.

The following day, she was unable to restrain herself and wait for them inside the house. Instead, she sat by the entrance of the courtyard and, with great anticipation, awaited the moment of their return. When they arrived, she burst into tears and overwhelmingly poured out all the emotions of her heart. On account of the profuse outpouring of emotions, she was unable even to utter words of thanks to the Holy One Blessed be He for the great miracle He performed on their behalf. He who did not witness this reunion – the mother reunited with her daughters after such a dreadful captivity, the tears of the mother when she saw that her daughters had returned to their borders,[52] the joy of the joyous mother of children[53] – has never witnessed true feelings of joy. This is what I know about this incident which transpired in our days.[54]

I imagine that such will be the joy of our mother, *Eretz Yisrael*, when we all return to her bosom after the horrible captivity we now experience. This is how I picture the wondrous joy that the mother will share with her children, that is, *Eretz Yisrael* with us and we with her. Hence, I entitled this work ***Eim HaBanim Semeichah*** (A Joyous Mother of Children). May HaShem grant me the merit that my book will impact the restoration of the children to their borders and to their mother's bosom. May we see the fulfillment of *A joyous mother of children* (*Tehillim* 113:9), speedily in our days. Amen. And, may we go up to Zion joyously, speedily in our days. Amen. So may it be God's will.

I have concluded the second introduction on Thursday of the week in which we read, *And I have also heard the groaning of the Children of Israel* (*Shemot* 6:5), the first of the month of Shevat, the anniversary of the death of our mentor, Maharam Schick *z"l*, in the year 5703 [1943], here in the capital, Budapest.*

---

* Since it is the anniversary of the death of our mentor, the Maharam, I will mention an idea that I heard in his name from his foremost

52 Based on *Yirmiyah* 31:16.

53 Based on *Tehillim* 113:9.

54 See p. 525, where the author reveals that this incident actually happened to him and his family.

disciple, my father-in law, the *av beit din* of Busermin, our brilliant and righteous master, R. Ya'akov Yosef Ginz. The Maharam derives from the verse, *And I will betroth you to me in faithfulness, and you will know the Lord* (*Hoshea* 2:22), that our entire relationship with HaShem is based on faith, without logic or reason. Nonetheless, it says, *And you will know the Lord* (את ה'). This refers to the Torah scholar, who is derived from the words "את ה'".[55] If a scholar should say something contrary to the words of *Chazal*, we need not believe him unless we understand his logic and reasoning, and determine that his opinion is well founded. This concludes the Maharam's words. The same applies to our topic.

55 See *Pesachim* 22b [where the Talmud derives the obligation to revere Torah scholars from the word את in the verse *You shall fear the Lord your God* (את ה') (*Devarim* 10:20)].

FOREWORD

Torah and Eretz Yisrael were said in a single utterance.

They are two inseparable companions.

Concerning the Torah it says, Moshe commanded us the Torah, a heritage (morashah)[1] ***of the congregation of Ya'akov (**Devarim 33:4**).***

Concerning Eretz Yisrael it says, And I will give it to you as a heritage (morashah) (**Shemot 6:8**).

Thus, Torah and Eretz Yisrael were set apart and designated by the same expression, morashah, as a gezeirah shavah, demonstrating that, for us, they are equal and inseparable.

First, with God's help, I will explain the meaning of *morashah* when used with regard to the Torah. Then, I will explain its meaning in the context of *Eretz Yisrael*. We will clearly see that these two concepts are interconnected and inseparable.

I Torah as a Heritage

The prophet Yeshayahu says, *Any weapon that is formed against you will not prosper, and any tongue that will rise against you in judgment, you will condemn. This is the heritage of the servants of the Lord and the recompense of their righteousness appointed by Me, says the Lord* (*Yeshayah* 54:17). The Rambam (may his merit protect us), our divine teacher and great philosopher, discusses this verse at length in his famous epistle, *Iggeret Teiman*.❖ I will cite only the essential and relevant points.[2]

❖ *Iggeret Teiman* ("Epistle to Yemen") was written to our brethren living

1 [The Hebrew word *morashah* can be translated as heritage or inheritance. Throughout this foreword we will be using these two interchangeably.]

2 [In the following paragraphs the author intersperses both direct quotes and paraphrases of the Rambam's words in *Iggeret Teiman*. We have indicated direct quotes with quotation marks.] The sections cited here can be found in *Iggrot HaRambam* (Mossad HaRav Kook), pp. 114-17, 131-32.

The significance of the Sinai revelation

"Understand that the Torah we possess is HaShem's true Torah, given to us through the master of all prophets... By virtue of this Torah, the Creator distinguished us from all other peoples of the world." The truth of our Torah is not based on a miracle or sign, but on actual "seeing and hearing." With our own eyes we saw the revelation of our King, our Creator, on Mt. Sinai. With our own ears we heard Him as He spoke to Moshe and said, *I am the Lord your God* (*Shemot* 20:2), as well as the rest of the commandments. The Torah tells us clearly, *Behold, I come to you in a thick cloud, so that the people may hear when I speak with you, and believe in you forever* (*Shemot* 19:9).

We saw HaShem on Mt. Sinai with our own eyes, as Moshe did. We also heard the utterances of the Holy One Blessed be He, as Moshe did. We, thereby, developed a complete and everlasting faith in Moshe, as the verse says, *And believe in you forever*. We, the Jewish people, and Moshe Rabbeinu are, in this matter, like two witnesses who testify that they saw a certain event, each one knowing that the other's testimony is absolutely true. Similarly, we, the Congregation of Israel, know of Moshe Rabbeinu's authenticity not because of wonders or signs, but because we saw him on Mt. Sinai at the time of the revelation. (For, a sign's veracity can be doubted, but something one sees is unquestioned, as *Chazal* say, "Seeing is greater than hearing" [*Rosh HaShanah* 25b].) This is the greatness of the Sinai revelation.

"It is worthwhile for you, my brothers, to raise your children

---

in Yemen, at a time when they were in dire straits due to the overwhelmingly heavy hand of their oppressors. Numerous and dreadful misfortunes had befallen them, and it was decreed that they would have to abandon the Jewish faith, God forbid. Our teacher, "Moshe the man of God" [Rambam], wrote them fervent, divinely-inspired words to strengthen their faith and prevent them from slipping. [He tried to help them] endure their ever-increasing troubles and accept their suffering joyously; be it loss of money, exile, or general indignity. He explained that this brings us great honor and glory in the eyes of our Creator and that God considers all of our losses like a sacrifice completely consumed upon the altar. And He will say to us, *Consecrate yourselves today to the Lord...that He may bestow upon you a blessing this day* (*Shemot* 32:29). The Rambam continued with many wondrous words to strengthen the weak and encourage the downtrodden.

according to this great revelation. You should speak publicly about its greatness and glory, for it is the pillar upon which our faith rests and the claim which verifies the truth." Be assured, my brothers, that this great matter is as I have said, because "no other nation as a whole has ever heard the utterances of the Holy One Blessed be He or seen His glory so manifestly. This was done to strengthen our faithö in such a way that it would never falter, under any circumstances. God led us to the truth in order to prevent us from stumbling at a time when evil oppressors prosper and enact harsh decrees against us. If they should tempt us to abandon our holy religion, we reply to them, "Show us anything similar to the revelation at Sinai, when the camp of God stood opposite the camp of Israel, then we will accept your faith." Based on this, the Rambam explains the verse *For God has come to test you, and that His fear may be before your faces, so that you shall not sin* (*Shemot* 20:17). [He writes], "God revealed Himself in this manner, so that you will be able to stand up to any test that might confront you in the end of days, so that your hearts will not be turned astray, and so that you will not sin."❖

❖ In truth, our mentor, the S'mag, explains this grand revelation in the same way.[3] It is also cited by the Shelah[4] and *Sefer HaChinuch*.[5] The Chinuch expounds further upon the authenticity of our holy Torah. He notes that it seems to be universally accepted that if the testimonies of two witnesses match on a certain issue, their words are accepted as clear, undoubted truth. For example, if two witnesses say that so-and-so killed his fellow man, we put the convicted murderer to death. Now, if there was even the slightest doubt as to the accuracy of their testimonies, we would not spill blood based on their words. We, therefore, must conclude that this matter is considered true beyond a shadow of a doubt. The logic for this is as follows. No two people think alike; therefore, if they were not telling the truth their testimonies would not have matched so perfectly.[6] The fact that they agree proves that their declarations are true.

Now, if this is true of two individuals, how much more so if there are three, or four, or ten, or a hundred, or a thousand! Certainly if

3 *Sefer Mitzvot Gedolot*, Introduction to Positive Commandments.

4 *Sh'nei Luchot HaBrit, Sha'ar HaOtiot - Alef*, 1:43a.

5 Introduction.

6 ❖ See *Tosafot, Ketuvot* 19b, s.v. *ve'im*.

The two types of enemies of Israel

Ever since that momentous occasion, when HaShem brought us near to His service and unified us as His nation, thereby elevating us above the other nations of the world, the Gentiles have greatly envied us and our religion. *Chazal* thus state, "Why was it called Mt. Sinai? Because the hatred (*sinah*) of the nations of the world emanated from there" (*Shabbat* 89a). Their leaders and rulers girded their loins to arouse hatred and resentment against us because of Sinai. "From the moment the Torah was given until the present, there has never been a time that an oppressive gentile ruler or a powerful despot did not try, as his first objective, to destroy our Torah and forcibly abolish our religion by means of the sword. For example: Amalek, Sisera, Sancheriv, Nevuchadnetzar, Haman, Titus, Hadrian, and many others like them.

This is one of the two methods devised to foil the divine plan. However, the second method is used by the more clever rulers and wiser nations, such as the Edomites, the Persians, and the Greeks. They, too, set as their goal the destruction of our religion and the nullification of our Torah. [But, instead of accomplishing this by way of the sword, they attempt to do so] by means of arguments and questions aimed at refuting the Torah. Their purpose is to destroy the Torah and erase all traces of it through their writings, just as the tyrants intend to do through war."

Hence, we have two types of persecutors: those who use chariots, swords, and spears; and those who employ deceptive arguments and cunning speech. Neither of these shall succeed, for the Holy One Blessed be He has assured us, through Yeshayahu, that the weapons of any oppressor who attempts to physically destroy our Torah and

---

there are many thousands of people whose testimonies are identical, it is crystal clear, beyond the slightest shadow of a doubt, that their claim is true. For if it was a lie, and these people simply conspired to concur their claims, it would be impossible that not a single one of them deviated from the rest.

Now, [consider this]: The generation that stood at Mount Sinai consisted of 600,000 adult males, not to mention women and children. They passed on to the next generation an account of what they saw and heard directly from the Holy One Blessed be He. All of them reported clearly that they heard the Torah from the mouth of the Holy One Blessed be He. Not one of them distorted the truth. From here we have an unequivocal, crystal-clear proof of the authenticity of our Torah; and its existence in this world is evident to us.

abolish our religion will be broken and rendered ineffective. This metaphor means that his scheme will never succeed. The same holds true for anyone who tries to abrogate our heritage by means of arguments; he will be found "guilty," and his claims will be proven null and void.

This is the meaning of the verse *Any weapon that is formed against you will not prosper, and any tongue that will rise against you in judgment, you will condemn. This is the heritage of the servants of the Lord and the recompense of their righteousness appointed by Me, says the Lord* (*Yeshayah* 54:17). This means that neither of these two enemies will succeed "in destroying the foundations of our religion that are so deeply rooted... The edifice will stand firm. The truth will ridicule them and laugh. That is to say, the Holy One Blessed be He, Who is Truth, sits and scoffs at them. He laughs at the fact that they plot, with their limited intellect, a scheme that is doomed to failure. Similarly, King David said with his *Ruach HaKodesh, Let us cut their cords and cast away their ropes from us. He who sits in heaven will laugh, the Lord will mock them* (*Tehillim* 2:3-4). We have been continually tried and tested by these two groups, both in the days of our sovereignty and, in part, during the period of exile." This concludes the relevant passages from the Rambam.

The advantage of tradition over intellectual reasoning

In the edition of *Iggeret Teiman* published in Prague by R. Yisrael Landau, son of the Noda BeYehudah *z"l*, I found a note on these words of the Rambam which is more precious than pearls.

> I, Yisrael, son of our master, the famous *gaon*, R. Yechezkel Segal Landau, say: When I saw the words of "The Great Eagleö [the Rambam], I decided to bring my brilliant father's comments in *Doresh LeTzion*[7] as "golden apples in settings of silver."[8] He writes:
>
> "I am truly perplexed how the feeble, finite human intellect can comprehend such profound and infinite matters.❖ If

❖ I found that the Rambam writes something similar in a letter printed in *Iggrot HaRambam*:

I hold that man's intellect is limited. As long as the soul is in a

7 We were unable to locate this source. However, see *Ahavat Tzion, Derush* 12, which speaks of this topic.

8 Based on *Mishley* 25:11. [That is, to provide a commentary on the Rambam's words (cf. Introduction to *Moreh Nevuchim*).]

Avraham Avinu was capable of understanding such things on his own, it was only with divine assistance. He began to take notice, and the Holy One Blessed be He enlightened him beyond

---

body it cannot comprehend the metaphysical. Since it exists within nature, it cannot see that which is above. Therefore, when the intellect attempts to gaze at that which is higher, it is unable to do so, for this matter is too lofty for it. Anything in nature, on the other hand, can be perceived and seen [by the intellect].[9]

The *Mishnah* states, "He who does not have compassion on his Creator's honor should never have been born" (*Chagigah* 2:1). In his commentary to this *Mishnah*, the Rambam explains:

> The intellect is HaShem's honor. Therefore, he who does not have pity or compassion on his intellect – meaning, he who does not realize his limitations and seeks to comprehend matters which are outside his realm and beyond his natural capabilities – becomes carried away with his desires and is akin to the animals. Only someone who is a fool with regard to the form of created beings will imagine [that he can fathom] "that which is above and that which is below." When a person bereft of any wisdom thinks he can grasp that which is above the heavens and below the earth, comparing it (with his inferior imagination) to a house and an attic, his thoughts will drive him to madness and confusion.

Behold, the verse states, *It is hidden from the eyes of all the living and concealed from the birds of the heavens* (*Iyov* 28:21). *Chazal* tell us that this verse refers to the Torah (*Shavuot* 5a). That is to say, the Torah is concealed even from the angels who are *the birds of the heavens*, how much more so is it hidden from *the eyes of all the living*. Thus, may molten gold be poured into the mouths[10] of the Bible critics. The above-cited *Mishnah,* as explained by the Rambam, could be applied to them. For, they have the audacity to criticize our holy Torah. They have become carried away by their desire to go beyond the limitations of their feeble minds and to "climb" higher than their capabilities allow. [They presume] to judge our holy Torah which is not only above and beyond the human intellect, but is even beyond the separate intellects (השכלים הנבדלים), namely, the angels. Therefore, these critics are compared to the animals.

9 The letter was written to R. Chasdai HaLevi and can be found in *Iggrot U'Teshuvot L'HaRambam* (Jerusalem: Levin-Epstein, 5728 [1968]).

10 Based on *Sanhedrin* 92b. Rashi explains that this is a euphemistic curse.

natural human understanding. For us, it is sufficient that we have a tradition passed on from generation to generation, from 600,000 individuals who witnessed [the revelation] with their own eyes and received the Torah directly from God. They heard *I am the Lord* and *You shall have no other gods* (*Shemot* 20:2-3) from the Almighty Himself.

"King David *a"h* told Shlomo, *Know the God of your father* (I *Divrei HaYamim* 28:9). He was cautioning Shlomo to recognize that HaShem is the God of his father and, in turn, of all preceding generations. Furthermore, although a few individuals were privileged to comprehend the main principles of faith on their own, it all must start with faith. This is the crux of the matter, for [only] when they clung to the Creator did He, in His loving kindness, open within their intellects channels of influence, enabling them to comprehend matters beyond ordinary human comprehension. They were then able to see divine visions, some through prophecy, like the prophets; others through *Ruach HaKodesh*; and still others through the spirit of wisdom, like the holy and lofty *Tana'im* and *Amora'im*. Human intelligence itself, however, is too limited to comprehend such things. Tradition is paramount here.

"In this manner I explained the verse *Any weapon that is formed against you will not prosper, and any tongue that will rise against you in judgment, you will condemn. This is the heritage of the servants of the Lord and the recompense of their righteousness appointed by Me, says the Lord* (*Yeshayah* 54:17).

"The Rambam *z"l*, 'The Great Eagle,' explains the verse as follows. The first part refers to those who rise up to fight our religion. Some do so by way of the sword and spear, like Nevuchadnetzar (who erected an idol and forced the Jews to worship it), Haman, and many other oppressors throughout the generations. Others do so by way of disputation, like the philosophers and the Greeks. Indeed, all of them have vanished, while we who cling to HaShem, our God, and to His Torah and *mitzvot* have survived with our faith. The Rambam writes that this is the prophet's intention: *Any weapon that is formed* refers to those who oppose you with instruments of war to lead you away from the Torah. Nonetheless, *against you will not prosper*, because the Holy One Blessed be He rescues us for the sake of His glorious name, as He did for Chananyah, Misha'el, Azaryah, and their colleagues. *And any tongue that will rise against you in judgment*, by way of argument, *you will condemn*. This means that even the philosophers with their interrogations will be ineffective against our holy Torah. This concludes the Rambam's interpretation.

"I [the Noda BeYehudah] would like to add that the end of the verse comes to advise us how to ensure that their numerous, false arguments and inquiries will fail. *This is the heritage of the servants of the Lord*. We did not adopt our religion and our Torah based on intellectual reasoning, for if that were so someone might come and offer logical arguments proving the opposite. Rather, our faith is an inheritance from our forefathers, generation after generation, starting from the generation of the giving of the Torah who, as one entity, saw divine visions. The fact that certain famous individuals were able to grasp these things miraculously or intellectually, that was *the recompense of their righteousness* (צדקתם) *appointed by Me* – meaning, it was a gift (צדקה) from Me. God, in His great benevolence, helps those who wish to be purified,[11] granting His pious ones understanding beyond human capabilities."

The Torah is our inheritance

The Noda BeYehudah's comments teach us that had we acquired the Torah with our own faculties – that is, had we agreed to accept it based on our own intellectual inquiry – others could have brought counterarguments to convince us to abandon the Torah, God forbid. Now, however, since the Torah is not our own acquisition – rather, an inheritance from our forefathers, who actually saw the "Law-Giver" with their own eyes and heard the Holy One Blessed be He with their own ears, as one who speaks to a friend – no one has the power to dispute the Torah anymore.

I would like to explain this concept. The accepted practice is that if a person acquires a field, or the like, using one of the usual forms of acquisition, it is imperative that all the conditions of the acquisition be fulfilled in order for it to take effect. If someone protests, claiming that an essential factor was missing from the acquisition, and he brings proof or witnesses to affirm this, the acquisition will be deemed null and void, as if it had never taken place. This is only true of something that was obtained using one of the established forms of acquisition. If, however, it is well known that someone's property was an inheritance from his father, there is no longer any room for

11 Based on *Shabbat* 104a.

protest, because the ownership does not depend on any conditions. No one can claim that an element of the transaction was missing. Since it is well known that this is the son and that this property belonged to his father, what possible claim could be made against the inheritance?

This is just as true of our holy Torah as it is of worldly matters. We did not acquire the Torah intellectually, leaving room for protesters to arise and show us that we are mistaken. Rather, it is an inheritance from our forefathers who were convinced of its truth by way of a renowned revelation, when 600,000 men received it publicly from the Holy One Blessed be He Himself, in all His glory. They passed it down from generation to generation as an inheritance until this very day. We, in turn, will pass it down to our children, and they to theirs until the end of time, as it is written, *For us and our children forever, to do all the words of this Torah* (*Devarim* 29:28). Since it is all an inheritance, no one can lay claims against it. This is the implication of the Noda BeYehudah's interpretation of the verse *This is the heritage of the servants of the Lord* (*Yeshayah* 54:17).

Now, my brothers and friends, come and see how everything that our mentor *z"l* said is included in Rashi's comments on the verse *This is my God, and I will praise Him; my father's God, and I will exalt Him* (*Shemot* 15:2). Rashi comments, "I am not the beginning of the holiness; rather, it has been maintained and preserved for me from the days of my forefathers." That is to say, when I claim, *This is my God*, do not think that I attribute Him to me because of my own intellectual realization. Rather, He is *my fathers God,* a preserved inheritance from the days of my forefathers. This is exactly what the Noda BeYehudah said. I have thus proven that our entire claim to the Torah is based on the fact that it is an inheritance from our forefathers.

Torah and morashah

Now we can properly understand the word "inheritance" (*morashah*) mentioned in the verse *Moshe commanded us the Torah, an inheritance of the congregation of Ya'akov* (*Devarim* 33:4). This means that the congregation of Ya'akov did not acquire the Torah on their own, for this can be a risky acquisition. Instead, they acquired it as an inheritance. This is the strength of our claim to the Torah. Thus, the word "inheritance" used in reference to the Torah demonstrates the strength of its foundations, which are so deeply rooted, and our everlasting ownership over it, as indicated by the Rambam (quoted above).[12] This edifice cannot be undermined by any destructive force, and it will stand strong for all of eternity. Sooner or later, anyone who lifts a hand against it will be destroyed, as were all those who tried to do so in the past. We will not relinquish even the smallest detail of our Torah, and it shall never be annulled. This is what I wanted to explain about the word *morashah* used in reference to the Torah.

II Eretz Yisrael as a Heritage

The seventy nations and their lands are controlled by heavenly ministers

Now, with God's help, I will explain the word *morashah* used in regard to *Eretz Yisrael*. At the time of creation, HaShem decreed that the seventy nations (which proceeded from Adam) be placed in the charge of "heavenly ministers" (שרי מעלה), each nation being ruled and influenced by its own minister. The status of a particular nation below depends on the status of its minister above. When the latter prospers above, so does his nation below; when he falls, so does his nation. The verse thus says, *The Lord will punish the host of heaven in heaven, and the kings of the earth upon the earth* (*Yeshayah* 24:21). In the same fashion, He divided the world among these heavenly ministers, each one receiving a portion of land upon which his particular nation dwells. This was all revealed to us by our Sages *z"l*,[13] who were truly wise, and whose every word is sound and true. (The Rambam elucidates this so wonderfully in his introduction to the Mishnah. Whenever he refers to our Sages he calls them "our Rabbis, Sages of truth," for they were able to arrive at the clear truth with their *Ruach HaKodesh*).

Israel and its Land are under the direct providence of God

One land, however, was not entrusted to any minister. HaShem kept it for Himself, saying, I am keeping this Land...under My own dominion, and when I find a man upon the earth who will follow My heart and My desire, I will place him as a seal upon My heart and settle him in this Land. He will be guided directly by My providence and authority, without any intermediary among the heavenly ministers (unlike the other nations of the world who receive HaShem's influence through their heavenly ministers).

This individual was Avraham Avinu *a"h*. He acted completely in

12 P. 64.

13 See Zohar 1:69a, 2:6b, 2:18a, 2:46b, 2:54b, 2:175a, 2:232b. Also see *Sefer Chassidim* 1160, and R. Margolis' *Mekor Chesed* (ibid.).

accordance with the Creator's heart and desire, as the verse says, *You are the Lord, the God, who chose Avram and brought him out of Ur-Kasdim, and gave him the name Avraham; and You found his heart faithful before You* (*Nechemyah* 9:7-8). HaShem found him worthy to settle in the Land which He had chosen for Himself, as *Chazal* state:

> The Land of Israel is beloved since the Holy One Blessed be He chose it. You find that when God created the world He distributed the various lands to the heavenly ministers and chose the Land of Israel for Himself. How do we know this? Moshe said, *When the Supreme One apportioned to the nations their inheritance, when He separated the children of man, He set the boundaries of the people according to the number of the Children of Israel* (*Devarim* 32:8). He also chose the people of Israel as His portion, as it is written, *For the Lord's portion is His people; Ya'akov is the lot of His inheritance* (ibid. 32:9). Said the Holy One Blessed be He: "Let Israel, who became My portion, inherit the Land which became My portion." (*Midrash Tanchuma, Re'eh* 8)

Why did Avraham merit receiving Eretz Yisrael ?

We must realize, though, that Avraham Avinu *a"h* deserved to become God's portion because of his self-sacrifice for HaShem and the sanctification of His name. This eminence elevated him above all other people on the face of the earth and caused HaShem to choose him, as the verse proclaims, *You...chose Avram* (אברם), *and brought him out of Ur-Kasdim* (*Nechemyah* 9:7-8). That is to say, he deserved to be chosen because he sanctified Your name in public at Ur-Kasdim. This was the first of the ten tests which Avraham passed, as the Bartenura explains.[14] From then on, HaShem chose him and raised him above the rest of the nations. This is the meaning of the verse *And gave him the name Avraham* (אברהם) (ibid.). The addition of the letter *heyh* (ה) signifies that God designated him as the father of the host of nations, as *Chazal* tell us (*Berachot* 13a). Avraham deserved all this because God found his heart devoted to Him. This is also what enabled him to merit becoming HaShem's portion and to receive the Land which He had chosen as His portion.

I found this same idea in the holy work, *Beit Elokim*, by our master, the Mabit (a colleague of the Beit Yosef and co-member of his court). He explains that Avraham Avinu deserved *Eretz Yisrael* at the

14 *Avot* 5:3.

moment he sacrificed his life for the sanctification of God's name in Ur-Kasdim. At that time, HaShem vowed to give the Land to his descendants, as the verse says, *I am the Lord who brought you out of Ur-Kasdim to give you this Land to inherit it* (*BeReishit* 15:7). Now, [this is puzzling, for] Avraham was fifty-two years old at Ur-Kasdim, and this verse was said at the *Brit Bein HaBetarim,* when he was already seventy years old! [The explanation is]: God was telling him that from the time He took him out of Ur-Kasdim, He intended to give him the Land. It was as if HaShem had vowed to give him the Land at that moment because of his self sacrifice to sanctify HaShem's name.

Eretz Yisrael is our inheritance

Realize, my brothers, that when HaShem vowed to give Avraham the Land, He immediately revealed His intention to make it an inheritance. That is, Avraham would bequest it to his children, and they in turn would pass it on to future generations, as with every inheritance. Thus, we – the descendants of Avraham, Yitzchak, and Ya'akov – received *Eretz Yisrael,* which is the Holy One's portion, through Avraham Avinu, who is also the Holy One's portion. From the time God chose Avraham as His portion, we, too, became His, as it is written, *For the Lord's portion is His people; Ya'akov is the lot of His inheritance* (*Devarim* 32:9). *Chazal* express this beautifully:

> The Holy One Blessed be He said to Israel, "The Land of Israel is My portion, as it is written, *A Land which the Lord your God seeks out* (ibid. 11:12); and you are My portion, as it is written, *For the Lord's portion is His people*. It is befitting that My portion dwell in My portion." (*Midrash Tanchuma; Mas'ei* 6, Re'eh 8)

All this, however, came to us only as an inheritance from our forefathers, as *Chazal* say, "The Land of Israel is an inheritance from our forefathers" (*Avodah Zarah* 53b). This is the basis of our claim to *Eretz Yisrael*, for we are its rightful heirs, as the verse says, *To give you this Land to inherit it* (*BeReishit* 15:7). Our claim is not based on acquisition or military conquest, for a claim based on acquisition is weak and disputable, as stated above.[15] A claim based on military conquest is also imperfect, since another conquest can nullify the previous one.[16] Inheritance, however, has an advantage over all other

15 P. 67.

16 ❖ See Rambam, *Hilchot Beit HaBechirah* 6:16, with the *Kesef Mishnah*. The later commentators expound upon this (see *Teshuvot Devar Avraham* 1:10-11). This, however, is not the place to elaborate.

modes of acquisition, because it cannot be questioned, as explained above.[17] The holy Torah is our deed and our proof. It shows clearly that the Creator of the Universe presented the Land to Avraham Avinu, so that it be given over as an inheritance from generation to generation. This proof from the Torah is eternal and acknowledged by all the nations of the world.

Exile is unnatural

In the holy work, *Netzach Yisrael*, our divine and scholarly mentor, the Maharal of Prague, writes that nature is the most powerful of forces and triumphs over everything. It fulfills its duties, not allowing anything to deter it from its inherent task. No deterrent which stands in its way, preventing its normal functioning, will last forever. Eventually, nature will triumph over that deterrent, remove it from its path, and continue the natural process as originally set forth by the Holy One Blessed be He, Creator of the Universe. The same is true of our relationship with *Eretz Yisrael*. We can be certain that *Eretz Yisrael* will return to us (with God's help), because the Creator ordained, as a rule of nature, that each nation must have its own country in which to dwell. This country is where all of its people are to be concentrated so that they are not scattered throughout the world.

The same is true of us. HaShem chose *Eretz Yisrael* to be our dwelling place. Ever since we were exiled from our Land and scattered among the nations, we exist unnaturally. The existence of exile prevents nature from fulfilling its God-given task of implanting each nation in its homeland. Therefore, the Holy One Blessed be He, Who rules the world and gives nature the power to pursue its way without interference, will ensure (through various and diverse events) that our Holy Land will return to us and that we will return to it, as in days of old. Exile, the obstacle which prevents us from dwelling in our God-given Land, will be eliminated.

It is also natural for a son to inherit his father's possessions. Therefore, it is natural for us to inherit our Holy Land. Thus, our existence in exile and our inability to take hold of our inheritance is contrary to nature. This situation will not subsist forever, and HaShem will arrange events such that we will eventually return to our inheritance and to our Holy Land.[18]

17 P. 68.

18 *Netzach Yisrael* 1.

Eretz Yisrael is ours only if we emulate our forefathers

In any event, our entire claim to *Eretz Yisrael* is based on the fact that it is an uninterrupted inheritance from our first patriarch. However, it is important to point out that just as God promised Avraham the gift of *Eretz Yisrael* because he sacrificed himself for the sanctification of His name,[19] so too, this inheritance, which we desire to attain, is also bound by this condition. If we emulate the deeds of our forefathers and follow in their path, then we are considered their children and are worthy of their inheritance. If, however, we stray from their path (God forbid), we have no share in their inheritance.

Yishma'el was excluded from Avraham's inheritance

The Torah states this explicitly: *And Sarah saw the son of Hagar the Egyptian... mocking* (*BeReishit* 21:9). *Chazal*, followed by Rashi, comment that "he strayed onto a corrupt path" (*BeReishit Rabbah* 53:15). The Torah continues, *So she said to Avraham, cast out this maidservant and her son; for the son of this maidservant shall not inherit with my son, with Yitzchak* (*BeReishit* 21:10). It is clear that since Yishma'el went astray, he has no share in his father's inheritance. HaShem agreed with Sarah, as the verse testifies, *And the matter was very grievous in Avraham's eyes regarding his son. And God said to Avraham let it not be grievous in your eyes concerning the lad and your maidservant; all that Sarah tells you heed her voice; for through Yitzchak will your offspring be called* (ibid. 21:11-12). The *Midrash* comments on this:

> R. Yudan said, " 'Yitzchak' is not written here, rather, *through Yitzchak* (ביצחק). The letter *bet* (ב) [which numerically equals] two, [is added to teach] that he who believes in two worlds..., whoever affirms his faith in two worlds will be considered your descendant. But, whoever does not...will not be considered your seed." (*BeReishit Rabbah* 53:16)

Thus, whoever does not admit the existence of both worlds is not considered a descendant of Avraham and is not worthy of this inheritance.

In *Iggeret Teiman*, the Rambam explains this verse as follows:

> *For through Yitzchak will your offspring be called* (יקרא). The word יקרא is similar to what Ya'akov said, *And may my name be called* (ויקרא) *upon them, and the names of my fathers* (*BeReishit*

19 ∴ See above, pp. 70-71.

> 48:16). This means that only descendants who follow the ways of their forefathers, proclaiming and publicizing the latter's piety and righteousness, can be called "sons." HaShem said to Avraham, "Yishma'el will not be pious and will not reach sufficient human perfection in order for you to become recognized and renowned through him. Therefore, it is unfitting for your name to be associated with him. Your piety will only become recognized through your pious descendants, those emanating from Yitzchak."...[20]

Avraham Avinu followed HaShem's command, as the verse says, *And Avraham woke up early in the morning, took bread, and a bottle of water, and gave them to Hagar, putting them on her shoulder, along with the child, and sent her away* (*BeReishit* 21:14). The *Midrash* comments:

> Is it possible that Avraham – about whom it is written, *And Avram was very rich in cattle, in silver, and in gold* (*BeReishit* 13:2) – would send his wife and child away from his home empty handed, without clothing or support? This teaches that since Yishma'el became corrupt, Avraham no longer paid attention to him and ejected him from his house. (*Shemot Rabbah* 1:1)

This explains the juxtaposition in the Torah of *Akeidat Yitzchak* (The Binding of Yitzchak) and Sarah's statement *For the son of this maidservant shall not inherit with my son, with Yitzchak* (*BeReishit* 21:10). This proves that Yitzchak was worthy of inheritance because he sanctified God's name, as Avraham did. This is also the meaning of *After these things* (ibid. 22:1), which is the opening sentence of the *Akeidah* narrative. *These things* refers to the story of Sarah and Yishma'el (as just explained).

Thus, as soon as Yishma'el became corrupt, Avraham no longer considered him his son and excluded him from his inheritance. So too, we, who wish to enter our forefathers' portion and take possession of *Eretz Yisrael* by virtue of their inheritance, must hold fast to the deeds of our forefathers so that we can be worthy of bearing their names. Everyone must recognize that we are the descendants of Avraham, Yitzchak, and Ya'akov, and we must publicize their piety and righteousness, as the Rambam indicates. Then we will surely achieve our goal, for we will qualify as those descendants whom the Holy One Blessed be He promised would inherit the Land.

20 *Iggrot HaRambam*, 140-41.

God will then perform miracles and wondrous signs in order to bring us to our inheritance, and He will fulfill the verse *When the Lord your God will cut down the nations where you come..., and you drive them out and dwell in their Land* (*Devarim* 12:29). The *Midrash* comments on this verse: "Let Israel, who became My portion, inherit the Land which became My portion. Therefore it says, *When the Lord your God will cut down the nations*" (*Tanchuma, Re'eh* 8). This implies that we will receive our inheritance when we follow the ways of our forefathers and deserve to become the Holy One's portion. The nations who attempt to stop us, on the other hand, will be destroyed by HaShem and will be unable to prevent us from entering our inherited Land.

Yehoshua's conquest depended on Torah observance

We find that the Holy One Blessed be He made this condition with Yehoshua at the very beginning of his conquest of the Land, as it says:

> *Now, after the death of Moshe..., the Lord spoke to Yehoshua... "Now arise, cross over this Yarden, you, and this entire people, to the Land which I give to them, to the Children of Israel... Be strong and courageous, for you will cause this people to inherit the Land which I swore to their fathers to give them. Only be strong and very courageous to observe, to do, according to all the Torah, which Moshe My servant commanded you. Turn not from it to the right or to the left, that you may prosper wherever you go. This book of the Torah shall not depart from your mouth; rather, you shall meditate therein day and night..., for then you will make your way successful, and then you will act wisely. Have I not commanded you? Be strong and courageous; do not fear and do not be dismayed, for the Lord your God is with you wherever you go." Then Yehoshua commanded the officers of the people... "But you shall cross over armed before your brethren, all the mighty warriors."* (*Yehoshua* 1:1-15)

Thus, HaShem commanded two things to Yehoshua. First, to be strong and courageous in war; to encourage and rally the armed forces to fight against the indigenous nations and to seize the Land from them. God begins and ends with this first command... Second, in the middle, God introduces the concept of strength and courage in Torah; to keep and perform all that Moshe commanded in the holy Torah.

I discovered in the holy work, *Beit Elokim*, that the Mabit takes note of this point. He writes that in reality Yehoshua was supposed to conquer the Land through war, in the natural fashion.❖ Therefore, he attacked with troops and force. However, the Holy One Blessed be He explained to him that his success in conquering the Land was mainly dependent on maintaining Torah study and the performance of *mitzvot*, rather than mere military force. The verse thus says, *Be strong and courageous: for you will cause this people to inherit the Land.* This means that although it is necessary for you to be strong and courageous in battle, the main emphasis must be upon strengthening Torah observance. This is why the verse says about Torah, *Only* (רק) *be strong and very courageous to observe, to do, according to all the Torah*; while regarding military strength it does not use the word *only*. It merely says, *Be strong and courageous.* It is as if God was saying, "The strength and courage I spoke about previously is secondary to the strength and courage I am demanding of you concerning the Torah, which is primary." Therefore it adds the word *only*, which, as a rule, excludes something from the text.

Furthermore, the verse says about Torah observance, *Be strong*

❖ This idea, that we do not rely on miracles, is mentioned by the Ramban several times in his commentary to the Torah.[21] It is also cited by Rabbeinu Bachya,[22] Rashi,[23] and the *Yerushalmi*.[24] Also see *Zera Avraham* on *Midrash Rabbah*.[25]

The *Midrash* states: "*Yehoshua ben Nun sent two spies from Shittim* (*Yehoshua* 2:1)... There the Israelites sinned through lewdness" (see *BeMidbar Rabbah* 20:22). The author of *Zera Avraham* asks why the Torah hints to this here? He replies as follows: The Ramban explains that the reason for sending spies was in order to find a location from which *Eretz Yisrael* could easily be conquered. This is the practice of kings; when they wish to conquer a foreign country they send spies to find a vulnerable point of attack.[26] Therefore, explains the Zera Avraham, if the generation was worthy, there would have been no need for sending spies, because a miracle would have occurred. But now that they were unworthy, [for they sinned through lewdness], a "natural miracle" was necessary.

21 See *BeMidbar* 1:45 and 13:2.
22 Introduction to *Parashat Shelach*.
23 *Shabbat* 22b, s.v. *u'vah hayah mesayeim*.
24 *Yoma* 1:4 (6b). See *P'nei Moshe* (ibid.), s.v. *al shem lo tenasu*.
25 End of *Shir HaShirim*.
26 Ramban, *BeMidbar* 13:2.

and very (מאד) *courageous*, while it does not use the word *very* regarding physical and military strength. Thus, we find that as soon as the people of Israel were privileged to receive the entire Torah (which was on the day of Moshe's death, when the Torah was completed, as it is written, *Take this book of the Torah* [*Devarim* 31:26]) they were also privileged to enter the Land, led by Yehoshua (immediately following the completion of the days of mourning for Moshe). This is apparent in the verse *Now, after the death of Moshe...the Lord spoke to Yehoshua..., now arise, cross over*. That is to say, they shall inherit and take possession of *Eretz Yisrael* through the merit of the Torah, whose main fulfillment is in the Land. Therefore, it says, *For then you will make your way successful*. This refers to your efforts to capture the Land. *And then you will act wisely*, in terms of conquering it.[27]

It seems fitting to add another explanation of the word *only*, which is mentioned exclusively in relation to Torah observance, and not in relation to military matters. The Mabit's interpretation is certainly valid and true, but there is another meaning as well. I have already pointed out that in order for us to be worthy of inheriting *Eretz Yisrael* we must be proper children who follow the ways of our forefathers (as the story of Sarah and Yishma'el proves).[28] The same condition applies when we desire to conquer and take possession of the Land. If we follow the ways of the Torah, as our forefathers did, we will succeed. Yet, if we stray from their path and cease to keep the Torah and its *mitzvot*, God forbid, we have absolutely no portion in our forefathers' inheritance. We would be unsuccessful in conquering the Land, for it would not be rightfully ours. Therefore, immediately after God said, *Be strong and courageous* in battle, He said, *Only be strong and very courageous* in observing the Torah. It is as if He made a condition saying, "Be aware! Your strengthening in war will only help you if you also strengthen yourselves in Torah and *mitzvot*, because one without the other is insufficient." The word *only* is used here as a condition, as if to say, you will succeed in war *only* if you exert yourselves in Torah, to keep and guard all the words of this Torah. This is a true and proper explanation of these verses.

Our success depends on Torah observance (examples)

Similarly, we find that King David said to his son Shlomo, *Now, my son, may the Lord be with you; may you be successful..., only may*

27 *Beit Elokim, Sha'ar HaYesodot* 32, p. 96a.

28 See above, pp. 73-74.

the Lord give you wisdom and understanding, and give you charge over Israel, to keep the Torah of the Lord, your God. Then you will prosper, if you are careful to fulfill the statutes and judgments which the Lord commanded Moshe concerning Israel. Be strong and courageous! Do not fear and do not be dismayed (*I Divrei HaYamim* 22:11-13). Hence, King David also made the observance of Torah and *mitzvot* the principle condition for his son Shlomo's success.

This idea is also found in *Melachim* I (2:4). [King David says to his son Shlomo], *So that the Lord may uphold His word that He spoke concerning me, saying, "If your children will safeguard their way, to walk before Me in truth, with all their heart and with all their soul."* Our Sages comment on this, "Three things were given conditionally: *Eretz Yisrael*, the *Beit HaMikdash*, and the reign of the Davidic Dynasty" (*Yalkut Shimoni* 2:170).

We also find in *Divrei HaYamim* II (24:18,20): *And they forsook the House of the Lord, the God of their fathers..., and anger came upon Judah and Jerusalem for this transgression of theirs... And the spirit of God came upon Zecharyah ben Yehoyada the* kohen, *and he stood above the people and said to them, "Thus says God: 'Why are you transgressing the commandments of the Lord, though you will not succeed? You have forsaken the Lord, so He has forsaken you.'"* This is a clear proclamation that since the people abandoned HaShem, He abandoned them and gave them over to the enemy.

Likewise, Yoav, while battling Ammon and Aram, said, *Be strong and let us be strong, for the sake of our people and for the sake of the cities of our God; and let the Lord do that which is good in His eyes* (I *Divrei HaYamim* 19:13). He used the expression *the cities of our God*, implying that the cities should appear God-like through the observance of Torah and *mitzvot*, and then HaShem would bestow goodness upon them. This is the reason they won the war.

The following verse explicitly affirms this principle. *And David assembled all the leaders of Israel... Then King David stood up on his feet and said: "Hear me, my brothers and my people... And now, in the sight of all Israel, the congregation of the Lord, and in the hearing of our God, observe and seek out all the commandments of the Lord your God, so that you may possess the good Land and bequeath it to your children after you forever"* (I *Divrei HaYamim* 28:1-9). Thus, David, who was chosen to be our eternal king, proclaimed to the entire Congregation of Israel from the very outset that it is impossible to inherit the good Land without observing the *mitzvot* of our God. Furthermore, he clearly stipulated that this condition applies to all future generations, until the end of time.

Ezra acted similarly when he returned to *Eretz Yisrael* at the time of the Second Temple: *For Ezra prepared his heart to seek the Torah of the Lord, and to fulfill, and to teach in Israel statutes and judgments* (*Ezra* 7:10).

We have thus proven that adherence to Torah and *mitzvot* is a primary condition for Israel's success in conquering the Land and dwelling therein. Why? Because *Eretz Yisrael* originally became our inheritance only on condition that we remain proper children, worthy of bearing our forefather's names. This concurs with the Rambam's explanation of the verse *For through Yitzchak will your offspring be called* (*BeReishit* 21:12).[29]

Eretz Yisrael is our inheritance (summary)

After these introductory remarks, you will be able to understand the meaning of the word "inheritance" (*morashah*) in reference to *Eretz Yisrael*. It comes to teach us that our right to *Eretz Yisrael* is a matter of inheritance. If we are proper sons and worthy heirs – that is, if we strive to ensure that our deeds measure up to those of our forefathers – then, and only then, we will be privileged to receive our inheritance. As *Tana DeVei Eliyahu* says, "Every person is obligated to say, 'When will my deeds reach those of my forefathers?' " (*Eliyahu Rabbah* 22:2). If, however, we become negligent and divert our paths from those of our forefathers (God forbid), our efforts will all be in vain, and we will be unable to enter *Eretz Yisrael*'s borders. Accordingly, Zecharyah the *kohen* said, *You will not succeed, for you have forsaken the Lord, so He has forsaken you* (II *Divrei HaYamim* 24:20).

This idea clarifies a passage in the Yerushalmi:

> It is written, *I will bring you to the Land..., and I will give it to you as a heritage* (*Shemot* 6:8). R. Yochanan asked, "If it is a gift why is it a heritage? If it is a heritage why a gift?" We must conclude that after God gave it to them as a gift, He gave it to them again as a heritage. (*Bava Batra* 8:2 [18a])

This appears incomprehensible. What is the difference between a simple gift and a gift which is also a heritage? Based on the above, it is quite clear. One might have thought that *Eretz Yisrael* is an unconditional gift, to remain ours under all circumstances. The

29 See above, pp. 73-74.

Yerushalmi, therefore, says that after HaShem gave us the Land as a gift, He gave it again as an inheritance, to demonstrate that it is not an absolute, unqualified gift. Its bestowal is dependent on the conditions of the inheritance which were set down in the days of Avraham Avinu, as it says, *For he* [Yishma'el]...*shall not inherit with my son, with Yitzchak* (*BeReishit* 21:10). This implies that we shall receive the Land only if we are worthy of inheritance like Yitzchak was. Based on this explanation, the passage from the *Yerushalmi* illuminates like sapphires.

The relationship between Torah and Eretz Yisrael

Based on the above, we can understand the comparison between Torah and *Eretz Yisrael*, both of which are called *morashah*. That is, we enter both of these only by virtue of the fact that we inherited them from our forefathers, not by our own virtue (as I thoroughly explained above).[30] Accordingly, these two were set apart and identified by the same expression, because they are interconnected and inseparable.

The Mabit, in his holy work *Beit Elokim*, also equates Torah and *Eretz Yisrael*:

> You can perceive [the parallelism between these two] by the following. We find that...488 years passed from the time God promised to give us the Land until it was actually inherited. The same number of years elapsed from the beginning of the acceptance of the Torah until its completion. How so? Avraham's 52nd year, the 2,000th year from creation, is considered the beginning of the acceptance of the Torah. At that age Avraham completely recognized the Creator and fully appreciated all of the wondrous deeds that He had done for him. He saved him from Ur-Kasdim... Then, the Holy One Blessed be He vowed to give the Land to his descendants, as it says, *I am the Lord Who brought you out of Ur-Kasdim to give you this Land to inherit it* (*BeReishit* 15:7)...
>
> Since these two entities are equated, they were singled out and referred to by the same word. Regarding *Eretz Yisrael* it says, *And I will give it to you as a heritage* (*Shemot* 6:8), and regarding Torah it says, *Moshe commanded us the Torah, a heritage...* (*Devarim* 33:4). The Torah is hinting...that they are unique and similar in purpose... When Moshe's Torah is our

30 Pp. 67-69, 71-75, 79-80.

heritage, then *Eretz Yisrael* will also be our heritage. When, however, we stray from the Torah, to the right or to the left, disowning it as our heritage, *Eretz Yisrael* will also cease to be our heritage. This is precisely what happened to our forefathers and to us, due to our numerous sins.

Furthermore, we cannot fully grasp the Torah's true secrets anywhere outside of *Eretz Yisrael*, as our Sages say, "The air of *Eretz Yisrael* makes one wise" (*Bava Batra* 158b). They also extol the advantages of one who learns Torah in *Eretz Yisrael*.[31]

Now you can understand my previous statement: "Torah and *Eretz Yisrael* were said in a single utterance; they are two inseparable companions."[32]

"Moshe our teacher," the godly Maharam [R. Moshe] Cordovero, states in his work, *Or Ne'erav*:

> It is well known that the close relationship between Torah and *Eretz Yisrael* is parallel to the relationship between life and the heart. Torah is eternal life, as we say, "And eternal life He has planted in our midst."[33] The seat of life and of the soul is in the heart. The main instructions of life lie there, and life emanates to the rest of the body from it. The same is true of the Torah; it exists primarily in *Eretz Yisrael*.[34]

After writing these ideas, I found a passage in the *Yerushalmi* (*Bava Batra* 8:2) which also compares the inheritance of the Land to the inheritance of the Torah... When a person first studies Torah he encounters many doubts and difficulties. But, the more he learns, the more he succeeds, and the sweeter it becomes. The same is true of *Eretz Yisrael*. For, the word *morashah* also connotes "weak" or "doubtful." At the outset, we will encounter numerous doubts and deterrents, and the beginning will be very difficult. Nonetheless, if we exert ourselves to the greatest possible extent, it will eventually become pleasant for us, and we will find in *Eretz Yisrael* all that we had hoped for...

31 *Beit Elokim, Sha'ar HaYesodot* 32.

32 Beginning of this foreword, p. 60.

33 From the blessing recited after the Torah reading.

34 *Or Ne'erav* 5:4.

III Words of Encouragement and Reproof to the Pioneer Builders of Eretz Yisrael

After all I have said above, I will now address the builders of our Holy Land (may HaShem give them life, and may He help them succeed). It is as clear as day that the Holy One Blessed be He desires your deeds and your labor. You have built cities, and you have made flourishing gardens from fallow fields. This is the result of great toil and effort, and in many cases it involved genuine self-sacrifice. You have transformed swamps containing all sorts of disease into flourishing, prime soil. I have cited in this volume many sources which prove that the Holy One Blessed be He is pleased with your actions. I would like to cite here one additional proof which is impeccable and irrefutable.

The Talmud states, "R. Yochanan says, 'Why did Omri deserve kingship? Because he added on a city to the Land of Israel' " (*Sanhedrin* 102b). [The *Midrash* adds]:

> *Tana DeVei Eliyahu*: Once, I, [Eliyahu HaNavi], was sitting in a study hall. I asked, "My masters, why is it that all other kings were not succeeded by their sons, while Omri had three of his descendants inherit his throne?" They replied, "We do not know." I said to them, "My masters, it is because he added a great city to the Land of Israel. Omri thought, just as Jerusalem is [the capital] for the kings of Judah, so will Shomron be [the capital] for the kings of Israel." (*Yalkut Shimoni* 2:207)

In the Kabbalistic work, *Otzrot Yosef*, by the great R. Yosef Engel *z"l*, I discovered an insight to this *Midrash*. The Kabbalists ask, "It seems puzzling; why did the Holy One Blessed be He reward Omri with kingship for that particular deed? Why not a different reward?" They reply, "It is well known that *Eretz Yisrael* is in the supernal sphere of Kingship (*Malchut*). Thus, since Omri rectified an aspect of Kingship on earth by adding a city to *Eretz Yisrael*, he received the specific reward of kingship."[35]

Even sinners can effect spiritual rectifications by building the Land

Omri was considered one of the wicked kings, as the verse states, *Omri did evil in the eyes of the Lord, and did worse than all those who had preceded him. He went in the entire path of Yerovam ben*

35 *Otzrot Yosef, Ma'amar HaLevanah, Vav* (beginning).

Nevat and in his sins that he caused Israel to commit, to anger the Lord, God of Israel, with their vanities (I *Melachim* 16:25-26). The city he established was not built for the sake of glorifying God's name, but for Omri's own honor, as stated above: "Just as Jerusalem is [the capital] for the kings of Judah, so will Shomron be [the capital] for the kings of Israel." Nonetheless, even though it was built with great sins, it is clear that Omri fulfilled the positive commandment of settling *Eretz Yisrael*. After all, if he did not fulfill a *mitzvah* there would be no reward. Also, since he was rewarded specifically with kingship, we must conclude that he rectified the supernal sphere of Kingship. This is why he deserved such a great measure of kingship, that is, three generations of kings, as mentioned above.

Thus, Omri fulfilled the *mitzvah* of *Yishuv Eretz Yisrael* with all its rectifications, even those pertaining to the upper worlds. Through the physical act of building, he elevated and established the *mitzvah*, even though that was not his intention at all and even though he acted sinfully. The proof being the fact that he received his reward "a measure for a measure."

Hence, we have a clear, irrefutable proof that by building a city in *Eretz Yisrael*, even the greatest sinner – one who denies the entire Torah (heaven forbid), like Omri who worshipped idols, which is tantamount to denying the entire Torah – achieves all of the possible rectifications that this *mitzvah* can effect in the supernal worlds.

This principle can be applied to our times as well. Even though the men who currently build the Land have left the path of the Torah (due to our many sins), they are certainly no worse than Omri. The verse testifies that he was more wicked than all who proceeded him and that he followed the ways of Yerovam ben Nevat, who caused Israel to sin. Nonetheless, when Omri built *Eretz Yisrael*, he fulfilled the *mitzvah* properly and achieved unification in the upper spheres. In the same manner, it seems quite clear that the supernal sphere of Kingship has been rectified and glorified by the toil of today's builders, no matter who they are. Even if they are the greatest sinners, the Creator of the Universe desires their actions, and they achieve the appropriate rectifications and unifications. That is, by constructing buildings and transforming the Land into fertile soil, they have fulfilled the essential component of the *mitzvah* of *Yishuv Eretz Yisrael*.

Cultivation is the main fulfillment of Yishuv Eretz Yisrael

The Maharsha writes that the main element of the *mitzvah* of settling *Eretz Yisrael* is cultivating fields and vineyards.[36] The Chatam Sofer agrees. He explains that the land of Sichon and Og was not considered a settled land (even though it was inhabited), because it was not cultivated by Gentiles or Jews...[37] Hence, the essential component of *Yishuv Eretz Yisrael* is cultivation.

The following verse clearly proves this. *These are the sons of Se'ir the Chorite who settled the Land* (*BeReishit* 36:20). Rashi, quoting our Sages (*Shabbat* 85a), comments, "They were experts in settling the land. This plot is suitable for olive trees, this plot for vineyards. They would taste the soil and know for which plant it was best suited." Thus, planting is the main aspect of settling the Land. In addition, both the Rashbash[38] and the Chatam Sofer[39] compare cultivating the Land to the *mitzvah* of *tefillin, sukkah,* or *lulav* [i.e. it, too, is a *mitzvah*].

The actual fulfillment of a mitzvah is greater than lofty intentions

Moreover, it seems to me that the simple Jew who builds the Land without any spiritual intent (*kavanah*), merely for his own benefit, accomplishes a greater rectification (*tikkun*) in the supernal worlds than the greatest *tzaddik* with his tearful and lamenting midnight prayers (*tikkun chatzot*) recited for the sake of the *Shechinah* and the end of exile. The latter certainly accomplishes a great rectification, yet it cannot compare to the rectification caused by the simple Jew who physically builds the Land, even if he has no godly intent (as the above-mentioned passage from *Sanhedrin* indicates).

The introduction to *Reishit Chochmah* states that the essential rectification is achieved by one who actually performs a *mitzvah.* Similarly, the Yismach Moshe writes that the actual performance of a *mitzvah,* even without any intent, accomplishes more than a *mitzvah* which lacks an actual deed, even if it is accompanied by the loftiest intentions.[40] Thus, my thesis is clear and true and can only be contested by he who argues with the truth.

This is consistent with halachic principles as well. It is well known that the halachic authorities (*poskim*) maintain that a *mitzvah* which

36 The author cites as his source: Maharsha, *Berachot* 58a (s.v. *nitbarchu*). This reference, however, requires clarification, as the text implies the opposite.

37 *Derashot Chatam Sofer*, Sermon for *Shabbat HaGadol* 5558 [1798], s.v. *da.*

38 (❖ Written by the son of the Tashbetz). Responsa 1, 2, 3.

39 Novellae to *Sukkah* 36, s.v. *domeh lekushi.*

40 *Yismach Moshe* 2:33a.

involves an action does not require special intent; the *mitzvah* is fulfilled even without *kavanah*.[41] The Rashba writes that a *mitzvah* whose act is irrevocable is valid even if it is accompanied by a transgression (God forbid). The transgression does not harm the *mitzvah*.[42]

The same is true of our issue. Today's pioneers have caused the settlement to grow and expand, and it is impossible to retract or negate their actions, for we benefit from them. Therefore, even if transgressions were committed in the process (God forbid), the *mitzvah* was still fulfilled in all its strength and vigor, in both a revealed and esoteric sense. Thus, it is clear that the Omnipresent desires the work of today's builders and accepts their efforts before His glorious throne with love and abounding affection. This is true even if they act sinfully and even if they do not fulfill God's will when it comes to other *mitzvot* of the Torah (God forbid).

Later on I will cite many other proofs for this, but for now this one, conclusive proof should suffice. Therefore, any Jew whose heart is truly and completely loyal to HaShem, and to whom the love of God and His nation takes precedence over his own selfish interests, will respect and appreciate everything these pioneers have accomplished thus far in rebuilding our Holy Land.

The essence of our people is the Torah

My brothers and friends, nonetheless, you must remember that Moshe Rabbeinu entreated the Holy One Blessed be He, saying, *I and Your people will be differentiated from all of the people that are upon the face of the earth* (*Shemot* 33:16). The essence of our people is not nationalism alone, as is true with the other nations of the world. We are a holy nation, and this holiness is contingent upon the holy Torah commanded to us by HaShem. We are only a nation by virtue of the Torah, as it is written, *This day you have become a people* (*Devarim* 27:9).

The Arab sage [Muhammad] called us "The people of the book,"[43] and the sages of other nations call us "The people of the spirit." Therefore, those who believe that the concept of nationalism is all that we need (God forbid) are gravely mistaken, for this concept does

41 See *Tosafot Rabbeinu Yonah, Berachot* (Rif 6a); *Chochmat Shlomo* 60; *Aruch HaShulchan, Orach Chayim* 60:6, 589:13. Also see *S'dei Chemed, Mitzvot Tzrichot Kavanah*.

42 Rashba, *Yevamot* 103b, s.v. *echod*.

43 The *Even Shoshan* Dictionary (entry: *Am HaSefer*) cites the *Koran* as the source of this phrase.

not exist for us at all. Furthermore, this lowers us from the lofty level to which HaShem elevated us, above the other nations. They, too, have nationalism, but we have Torah, and that alone distinguishes us from them.

The *Midrash* states: "If someone should tell you that there is wisdom among the nations of the world, believe him. [If, however, he says that] there is Torah among the nations, do not believe him" (*Eichah Rab.* 2:13). In *Tiferet Yisrael*, our master, the Maharal, explains that the Torah removes us from the natural world and elevates us beyond the realm of nature. If we deem ourselves the Torah nation and regulate our actions in the spirit of the Torah, the Torah elevates us beyond the realm of nature. Then, that which is naturally unattainable can be attained through the merit of the Torah.[44]

Moreover, without Torah we are not a nation at all and we simply cannot exist (as demonstrated by R. Akiva in his parable comparing us to the fish of the sea [*Berachot* 61b]). Torah sets us apart from the other nations who have no connection to their religion. They can be a nation even without a religion; we cannot. This is the meaning of Moshe's request *I and Your people will be differentiated from all the people that are upon the face of the earth* (*Shemot* 33:16).

Our success in settling the Land depends on adherence to Torah and mitzvot

Know, that our claim to *Eretz Yisrael* is based entirely on the fact that it belongs to our forefathers who dwelt in it from time immemorial. As the saying goes, "We have but one historic claim to *Eretz Yisrael*; it is the Land of our forefathers."[45] The *Tanach* states this clearly. Furthermore, all the nations of the world acknowledge this fact, and with the strength of this claim we come to the powerful nations requesting that they restore the Land of our inheritance. Since our claim is based entirely on patriarchal inheritance, we must fulfill all the conditions of this inheritance. The condition was, *For* he [Yishma'el]...*shall not inherit with my son, with Yitzchak* (*BeReishit* 21:10). That is, he who does not follow the ways of our forefathers is not included in their inheritance. Rather, *through Yitzchak will your offspring be called* (ibid. 21:12), as explained above.[46]

[*Chazal* tell us that] before the days of Mordechai and Esther, the Torah was not legally binding, [because it was originally accepted through coercion] (Shabbat 88a). The Rashba and the Maharsha ask, if

44 *Tiferet Yisrael* 1.

45 [Originally in Yiddish.]

46 Pp. 73-74.

this is so, why were the Jews exiled and why was the First Temple destroyed before the days of Mordechai and Esther? They answer that God gave us *Eretz Yisrael* so that we can observe the Torah. *Eretz Yisrael* is an inheritance and God gave it to us on condition that we keep His Torah, as David said, *He gave them the lands of nations... that they might keep His statutes and observe His teachings* (*Tehillim* 105:44-45). Thus, since our forefathers did not fulfill this condition, the bequest was retracted.[47]

I would like to add the following. Yirmiyahu HaNavi said in his lamentation, *Her gates have sunk into the ground; He has destroyed and broken her bars; her king and her officers are among the nations; there is no Torah* (*Eichah* 2:9). One might ask, what connection is there between the prophet's outcry – *Her gates have sunk... He has destroyed and broken her bars* – and his statement that her king and officers have been exiled among the nations and there is no Torah in the Land? Clearly, the prophet is alluding to the fact that the Torah is the main protection (*bars*) of the Land. If there is Torah in *Eretz Yisrael*, the Land has *bars* which secure it from one end to the other, providing the utmost protection against enemies. If, however, there is no Torah, then the bars are broken, leaving the Land defenseless. Thus, the prophet laments, *He has destroyed and broken her bars*. Why? Because *her king and officers are among the nations, there is no Torah*. Her bars have been destroyed and broken because there is no Torah in the Land.

This also explains the *Midrash* on this verse: "If someone should tell you there is wisdom among the nations, believe him. [If, however, he tells you] there is Torah among the nations, do not believe him, as it is written, *Her king and her officers are among the nations; there is no Torah*" (*Eichah Rabbah* 2:13). That is to say, there is no Torah among the nations, only among the Jews. Hence, the prophet is referring to our Torah alone, the one that the Holy One Blessed be He gave us through Moshe Rabbeinu at Sinai. This Torah alone is the protective *bar* of *Eretz Yisrael*, not other doctrines espoused by the nations.

The *Midrash* comments on the verse *A prophet from your midst, from your brethren, like me* [Moshe], *shall He establish for you* (*Devarim* 18:15):

> *Like me shall He establish for you,* but not for the nations. How,

47 See *Ein Ya'akov, Shabbat* 88a. The Rashba is quoted in *Etz Yosef*.

> then, am I to understand the verse *I have made you a prophet to the nations* (*Yirmiyah* 1:5)? [This refers to a time] when the Jews follow the customs of the Gentiles. (*Yalkut Shimoni* 1:919)

Thus, when we behave like the Gentiles, our prophets are deemed prophets of the nations, not of the Jewish people. Yirmiyahu alluded to this when he said, *Her king and her officers are among the nations, there is no Torah* (*Eichah* 2:9). This implies that they abandoned the path of Torah and governed the Land in accordance with the spirit and ideologies of the nations. Thus it says, *Her king and her officers are among the nations*, meaning, in the ways of the nations. Therefore, *He has destroyed and broken her bars*. This is also the implication of the *Midrash* which declares that although wisdom can be found among the nations, Torah cannot, and that Torah is the primary and exclusive protection of *Eretz Yisrael*. These words are true and valid.

An impassioned plea to the chalutzim to return to the ways of the Torah

Therefore, you [the pioneers] and all of us must realize that the rebuilding, the governing, and all aspects of life must be founded on the spirit of our holy Torah. Only then, we will succeed;[48] only then, we will have a strong claim to our inheritance. If, however, we stray from the path of the Torah (God forbid), our entire claim to *Eretz Yisrael* dissipates, leaving us with no rights to it whatsoever. When the Supporter withdraws, he who is being supported stumbles. We have seen with our own eyes all of the difficulties and complications that you and all of Israel have encountered in recent years, ever since you began rebuilding the Land. How many innocent souls have perished in our Holy Land at the hands of Arab zealots? All this occurred because our claim to our inheritance is imperfect, for it is not completely in accordance with the spirit of our holy Torah.

I do not suspect that you act in this manner deliberately. The only reason you act this way is because you became imbued with the spirit of the nations while in exile, and you brought this spirit with you when you returned to the Land. The verse states, *They mingled with the nations and learned their deeds* (*Tehillim* 106:35). It is merely the spirit of foreign nations that swells up within you, yet it causes you to stumble and fall. Behold! The verse says, *If only My people would listen to Me...in an instant I would subdue their enemies* (ibid. 81:14-15). Discard the foreign ideas that you have brought with you, and act

48 ❖ As the verse in *Yehoshua* (1:7) indicates, as mentioned above (pp. 75-77).

only according to the council of the *gedolei Torah*. Everything must be done in the spirit of the Torah, for it is full of wisdom. Our holy Torah can solve, in the best possible manner, all of the problems that may arise concerning life as a sovereign nation. Then, the Land will flourish in every corner and in every way, assuring our continued political existence in the Land.

This is also found in the *Midrash*:

> *Daughters of Jerusalem* (*Shir HaShirim* 1:5): The Rabbis said, "Do not read it as, *daughters* (בנות), but 'builders' (בונות) of Jerusalem. This refers to the members of the great *Sanhedrin* who sit and enlighten[49] her concerning every question and judgment." (*Shir HaShirim Rabbah* 1:5:3)

That is to say, they determine how the edifice will stand, and they decide all questions concerning life and the state. Furthermore, our Sages in the *Yerushalmi* suggest that the verse, *For it is not an empty thing for you* (*Devarim* 32:47), implies that any Jewish court which exerts itself on a certain matter will succeed (*Pe'ah* 1:1 [3b]). We may conclude, then, that the *gedolei Torah* have the ability to solve everything in the spirit of the Torah.

My fellow Jews, all of us yearn to see the prosperity and preeminence of our Holy Land. Therefore, heed my words! If you wish to succeed, subjugate yourselves to the wise *gedolim* of our generation, those who bear the banner of Torah. Do not be stubborn and think that you can do without them. That would be unwise, for the Land cannot be built by might nor by power alone, only by My spirit, says the Lord of Hosts.[50]

We need you, for even Shlomo selected experts for each aspect of the work. The same is true today. Everyone will admit that without expert craftsmen we will be unable to rebuild the Land. Therefore, anyone who understands will acknowledge that we need you and your labor. You, however, must also understand that you need the *gedolei Torah*, so that everything will be done in the spirit of the Torah. Then, your labor will bear fruit. Similarly, *Chazal* state:

> Were it not for David who sat and occupied himself with Torah, Yoav ben Tzeruyah would not have been victorious in war. And, were it not for Yoav who fought the battles, David would not

49 [Literally: "impart wisdom," from the Hebrew root בינה.]
50 Based on *Zecharyah* 4:6.

> have been able to sit and occupy himself with Torah. (*Sanhedrin* 49a)

The merit of our holy forefathers will arouse divine desire to perfect your handiwork. There will be no obstacles nor misfortunes. No man will stand up against you.[51] All the workers of iniquity will be scattered.[52] Wherever we turn we will accomplish the will of HaShem. The Land will give its fruits abundantly, and divine blessing will descend upon us from the heavens, plentifully.

This coincides with Rashi's explanation of the verse *As your days so shall your strength* (דבאך) *be* (*Devarim* 33:25).

> As long as you do the will of the Omnipresent...all of the nations will make silver and gold flow (דובאות) into *Eretz Yisrael*. It will be blessed with produce, and all the nations will be sustained thereof. They will supply it with silver and gold, [until] their silver and gold run out, for they will constantly be sending it to your Land.

We will only deserve this blessing if the Land is built in the spirit of the Torah, according to the council of the *gedolei Torah*. So it was in the days of Ezra. They succeeded in building the Land because the masses subjugated themselves to those who bore the banner of Torah (see the Malbim). We must do the same. Then, all of the Land's original glory will be renewed. It will be the most beautiful of sites and the joy of all the earth.[53] God's name will be exalted and sanctified through our actions, and events will develop until the final redemption arrives, with our righteous Redeemer, the Son of David [*Mashiach*], may he come speedily in our days. Amen. So may it be the will of HaShem. Amen. Amen.

This completes the foreword to this work.
Praise God, Creator of the World.

51 Based on *Devarim* 11:25.
52 Based on *Tehillim* 92:10.
53 Based on *Tehillim* 48:3.

CHAPTER ONE

PERSECUTION AND THE PANGS OF MASHIACH – THE SOUND OF MY BELOVED KNOCKING

Belief in the coming of Mashiach

It is well known that faith in the coming of *Mashiach* is an assumed principle and an established dogma among our people, descendants of Avraham, Yitzchak, and Ya'akov, disciples of Moshe Rabbeinu, and subjects of King David. This belief is so deeply rooted in the hearts of our young and old that none of the upheavals or catastrophes that befall the world can uproot it. Even if *Mashiach* should tarry, we continuously await his arrival. May he come speedily in our days. Amen.

We do not determine the time of his arrival, nor do we attempt to derive indications of that time from Biblical sources, for it is hidden and unknown to any living being. R. Shimon bar Yochai states, "If anyone should tell you when the Son of David is to come, do not believe him, for the heart does not reveal this to the lips" (*Midrash Tehillim* 9:2). The Rambam, as well, discusses this at length in his commentary to the *Mishnah*[1] and in his prodigious and holy epistle, *Iggeret Teiman*.[2]

I Adversity is a Sign of the Advent of Mashiach

However, our prophets[3] and Sages (in the Talmud, *Midrashim*, and Kabbalistic works)[4] foresaw the horrible afflictions, massacres, and persecutions that would be inflicted upon the Jewish people in the end of days, before the advent of *Mashiach*. This alone demonstrates

1 *Sanhedrin* 11:1.
2 See *Iggrot HaRambam*, pp. 151ff.
3 See *Yechezkel*, chapters 38 – 39, *Zecharyah* 12 – 14.
4 See *Sanhedrin* 97a – 99a; *Eichah Rabbah*; *Zohar* 2:7b, 2:172b.

that the light of *Mashiach* has begun to shine. Our holy writings explain that the most difficult suffering of exile will begin only after the initial onset of redemption.[5]

Rashi concurs in his commentary on the verse *Like a pregnant woman close to giving birth, she is in pain, she cries out in her pangs. So were we before You, O Lord* (*Yeshayah* 26:17):

> We observe renewed afflictions and conclude that they are a sign of salvation and redemption, for we have been promised that we will be redeemed amidst trouble and hardship, like a woman in labor. *Before You* [means] because of Your decrees.

We must not lose faith during these troubled times

We must lovingly bear and courageously endure all of the hardships, evil decrees, and persecutions that have befallen us in these days, for they are considered wholly burnt offerings.[6] We must not become skeptical (God forbid), nor speak in the manner foretold by the last prophet. He prophesied about the era of "the birthpangs of *Mashiach*" when abundant and unusual afflictions will prevail:

> *You have said, it is useless to serve God, and what profit is there that we have kept His charge* (*Malachi* 3:14). *You have wearied the Lord with your words...when you say, everyone who does evil is good in the eyes of the Lord, and He favors them; or where is the God of justice?* (ibid. 2:17). *Then, those who fear the Lord spoke to one another, and the Lord listened and heard, and a book of remembrance was written before Him for those who fear the Lord and those who give thought to His name. And they will be Mine says the Lord of Hosts, on that day which I appoint as My particular day; and I will have mercy upon them as a man has mercy upon his son who serves him. Then you will return and see the difference between the righteous and the wicked, between one who serves God and one who does not serve Him* (ibid. 3:16-18).

Rashi explains:

> *Then...spoke to one another...* I [HaShem] am responding to your words: *Then*, when the wicked perpetrate evil and the righteous walk submissively before Me, *those who fear the Lord*

5 ❖ See *Avodat Avodah* (p. 9a) on Tractate *Avodah Zarah*, where the brilliant Maharshak explains *Chazal's* statement "Two thousand years are the days of *Mashiach*."

6 ❖ I cited this above (p. 61) from the Rambam's *Iggeret Teiman*.

> *spoke to one another*, [cautioning each other] not to cling to the evil ways of the wicked. And as for Me, I have not forgotten the conversation of those who fear the Lord. Even though I am not quick to reward, nonetheless, I *listened and heard*, and I commanded to write a *book of remembrance* for their sake. And their words will be preserved for *that day which I appoint as My particular day*, meaning, the day which I stored away and set aside to pay My reward. Then, I will show you the difference between the righteous and the wicked.

Thus, Malachi, the last prophet, foretold what would happen to us at the end of days, during the birthpangs of *Mashiach*. Troubles will besiege us to such a degree that some people will say, "It is useless to serve God, and what profit is there that we should keep His Torah; and everyone who does evil is good in the eyes of the Lord, and He favors them; and where is the God of justice?" This is exactly what we hear today, during these bitter times that have befallen us.

Those who cling to HaShem will be rewarded

However, those who fear and cling to HaShem spoke to one another [cautioning each other] not to cling to their evil ways. They strengthened and encouraged each other, as Yeshayahu said, *I will await the Lord who conceals His face from the House of Ya'akov, and I will hope for Him* (*Yeshayah* 8:17). That is to say, even though He conceals His face from the House of Ya'akov, I will await and hope for HaShem. The Holy One Blessed be He hears and pays attention to these words spoken during times of trouble by those who fear Him. He writes them down in a book of remembrance, and afterwards, on the day of recompense and salvation, the Holy One will show the difference between those who clung to Him and those who strayed from Him.

It seems to me that Daniel was referring to these righteous people who were written in a book of remembrance when he said, *And at that time...everyone who will be found written in the book will escape* (*Daniel* 12:1). That is to say, those who clung to the Holy One Blessed be He even during times of divine concealment, and were written in a book of remembrance, will escape the hardships of the birthpangs of *Mashiach*. I later discovered that one of the commentators of the *Tanach*[7] interprets this verse in the same manner. That is to say, Daniel was referring to the book about which Malachi had prophesied.

7 See Rav Sa'adya Gaon, Ibn Ezra, *Metzudat David*, and Malbim.

(Now, as I prepare the material for printing, I do not have any books; therefore, I am unable to cite the exact location).

Therefore, every Jew will certainly strengthen himself during these difficult times and guard himself from slipping, because the time will surely come when the prophecy will be fulfilled, and the difference between those who serve God and those who do not will become apparent. Each Jew will live up to the prayer "And despite all this we have not forgotten Your name."[8] It is worthwhile for us to bear the heavy burden of exile on account of the great reward that the Holy One Blessed be He will bestow upon us on the day that He will appoint as His particular day. For on that day, He will reward each individual based on the deeds he performed with God.[9]

II Why Must Mashiach Come by way of Afflictions?

It seems, however, quite incomprehensible why HaShem would do such a thing. Why would He bring us *Mashiach* by way of great afflictions? Is HaShem incapable (God forbid) of saving us without misfortunes? Could our righteous *Mashiach* not come with an overabundance of good?

1. We are unworthy of his coming amidst grandeur

The Or HaChayim HaKadosh reveals the answer with his *Ruach HaKodesh*. He explains that there are actually two aspects of the coming of *Mashiach*. The first is one of loftiness and grandeur, which is expressed by *Chazal* as, "If they are worthy" (*Sanhedrin* 98a). The second is one of poverty and distress. The prophet Zecharyah alludes to this, *Behold, your king will come to you...poor and riding upon a donkey* (9:9). This is the aspect of, "If they are not worthy" (*Sanhedrin* 98a). If we do the will of the Omnipresent and fulfill His commandments, redemption will arise amidst prosperity and grandeur. If, however, we do not fulfill His will, redemption will inevitably come amidst adversity, distress, and poverty. The hardships will serve as a substitute for the merit that we would have had by keeping the Torah and its *mitzvot*. (See the *Or HaChayim* inside.[10] I do not have it in front of me at this time).

8 From the *Tachanun* prayer.

9 Based on *VaYikra Rabbah* 27:2 and *Midrash Tanchuma, Emor* 7: "In the future, a Heavenly voice will thunder at the tops of the mountains and say, 'Whoever acted with God, let him come and receive his reward.' "

10 *VaYikra* 25:25-28.

Rashi also writes in this vein. The Talmud states: ôRav said, 'All of the predetermined times for redemption have passed, and this matter depends only on repentance and good deeds.' Shmuel said, 'It is sufficient for the mourner to remain in his state of mourning'" (*Sanhedrin* 97b). Rashi explains (as a second interpretation), "The pain of exile is sufficient for the Jews. They will be redeemed even without repentance."✧

2. The pangs of Mashiach serve as 'the absence' before 'the existence'

The Maharal of Prague explains the reason for our troubles. The pangs of *Mashiach* serve as "the absence before the existence" (ההעדר קודם ההויה). The extent of 'the absence' corresponds to the extent of 'the existence' that HaShem will bestow upon us at the time of redemption.[12] I also found this idea in the *siddur* of the brilliant Ya'avetz:

> Greatness and prosperity generally develop following the despair which is caused by enormous calamity. The same is true of 'existence', for one of its four causes is 'the absence' which precedes it. Accordingly, *Chazal* state, "[The chick] grows

✧ In my *Derashot*, I used this idea to explain the *Midrash* on the verse *Alas, who will survive when He does these things* (*BeMidbar* 24:23). The *Midrash* states: "*When He does these things* (מִשֻּׂמוֹ אֵל) [means] from Shmuel (משמואל), as it says, *Pardon my iniquity for it is great* (כי רב הוא) (*Tehillim* 25:11)."[11] This is truly perplexing. It seems to me that the explanation lies in the above-mentioned dispute between Rav and Shmuel... The *Midrash* maintains that there is really no dispute. In the absence of the pain of exile, even Shmuel admits that repentance is needed. When the exile is painful, even Rav admits that this suffering secures forgiveness for Israel's iniquities, and they will be redeemed without repentance.

This explains the *Midrash's* statement "מִשֻּׂמוֹ אֵל – משמואל." That is to say, *who will survive* if the redemption takes place as Shmuel stated, through the pain of exile, without repentance? The afflictions will be abundant and intense. Some of our greatest Talmudic Sages state, "Let *Mashiach* come, but let me not see him" (*Sanhedrin* 98b). The *Midrash* concludes, "As it says, *Pardon my iniquity for it is great* (כי רב הוא)." That is to say, in this scenario even Rav (רב) concedes, because Israel's iniquity is already pardoned.

11 We were unable to locate this *Midrash*.

12 *Netzach Yisrael* 26.

> when [the egg] decays" (*Temurah* 31a). This explains how we, the Chosen Nation, have declined so drastically in the exile before reaching a state of tranquillity and security. The last descent has been extremely difficult, proportionate to the absolute and everlasting good that will sprout after it. Hence, the Talmud states that when the Jews descend, they descend to the dust, but from there they ascend (*Megillah* 16a), as it says, *He lowers it...to the dust* (*Yeshayah* 26:5), and, *Our soul is bowed down to the dust... Arise, assist us* (*Tehillim* 44:26-27).[13]

According to this, it is natural that there be a great 'absence' before our great 'existence', as is the case with all existence, as *Chazal* state, "[The chick] grows when [the egg] decays."

3. The pangs of Mashiach generate within us a desire to return to Eretz Yisrael

There is another reason why the Holy One Blessed be He brings troubles and terrible persecutions before the coming of *Mashiach*. I found it in the words of the godly Kabbalist, the author of *Sha'arei Orah*, Rabbeinu Yosef Gikatilla. (He was one of the great Kabbalists of the past; even our mentor, the Beit Yosef, quotes him several times). In his commentary on the *Haggadah*, called *Tzofnat Pa'ane'ach*, he writes:

> Indeed, we must make a great and proper investigation into the reason for the Egyptian exile, for it contains a deep secret. HaShem (may He be blessed) chose the seed of Avraham, and He placed them in exile in order to enable them to receive the Torah. Had He increased them and made them prosperous without exile, and had they taken possession of the Land – and been successful upon it – without receiving any Torah from the Almighty, how could God have compelled them to go out to the desert? How could He have prohibited them from doing so many things to which they were accustomed, be it with regard to foods, marital relations, or anything else? If someone, today, is restricted from eating meat or drinking wine, he is greatly grieved, because he has become so accustomed to these things. This is certainly true of the 613 *mitzvot* that pertain to all future generations. Is there anything more difficult for a man's drives?
>
> Therefore, HaShem was compelled to exile the Jews to Egypt... They were not permitted to leave, for they were

13 *Siddur Ya'avetz, Ma'amadot LeYom Sheini*, p. 445a, s.v. *levarech*.

> subjected to the bondage of exile... And when the Holy One Blessed be He sent Moshe Rabbeinu *a"h*, He said to him, "Go forth and tell the Jewish people, 'You must accept 613 mitzvot; if you do so I will redeem you, but if not, you will stay where you are.'" This was the agreement in Egypt, as it says, *When you take the people out of Egypt, you will serve God on this mountain* (*Shemot* 3:12). This entire secret is hinted to in the verse *This is My name forever* (ibid. 3:15). Thus, the purpose of the Egyptian exile was to enable us to receive the Torah, and it is the cause for the great reward that HaShem bestows upon us.[14]

We learn from his holy words that the secret of the exile was to generate a desire to go out into the desert and receive the Torah. Had they been contented, they would have refused to go out into the wilderness, receive the Torah, and accept prohibitions against things to which they were accustomed.

Jews who live comfortably in exile generally have no desire to return to Eretz Yisrael

This also helps explain the afflictions that will befall us before *Mashiach* arrives. It is well known that this last redemption will be eternal; there will be no exile or subjugation following it. Furthermore, the Holy One Blessed be He does not want even a single Jewish soul to be lost among the nations, as it is written, *And you will be gathered up one by one* (*Yeshayah* 27:12), *So that none of us be banished* (II *Shmuel* 14:14). Now, if the redemption would occur while we live prosperously and tranquilly among the nations, there would be many, many of our Jewish brethren who would not want to leave. What are they lacking here in exile? They are wealthy and prominent officers among the nations, like the Rothschilds and the Jewish Barons, who attained distinction and honor, rising to positions of authority and prestige. Why should they care about *Mashiach* and *Eretz Yisrael*? They have a *mashiach* and a Jerusalem right here. They do not need a better *Mashiach* than the one they have.

This indeed is what the wealthy Jews of Ezra's time did when they dwelt peacefully in Babylonia. Rashi writes that the proper people who dwelt peacefully and comfortably in exile did not ascend to *Eretz Yisrael* with Ezra. Only the poor and downtrodden went with him.[15]

14 *Peirush HaHaggadah*, (Salonika), p. 3, s.v. *baruch shomer havtachato leYisrael*.

15 Rashi on *Kiddushin* 69b, s.v. *ve'avinah be'am*.

Why Germany has always been a source of trouble for Israel

This concept is cited in *Seder HaDorot*:

> In his youth, R. Yusfa Shamash studied in the yeshiva of our brilliant master, R. Pinchas Segal, who served as *av beit din* of Fulda. In the year 5380 [1620], he quoted his mentor, the brilliant R. Falk, author of the S'ma, explaining the reason why evil decrees are more prevalent in Worms than any other community or state. Jews settled in Worms at the time of the destruction of the First Temple. After the seventy years of Babylonian exile were completed, the exiles returned to Jerusalem and *Eretz Yisrael.* Those who settled in Worms, however, did not return. The people of Jerusalem wrote them, urging them to come and settle in *Eretz Yisrael*, so that they could ascend to Jerusalem on the three pilgrimage festivals. They paid no attention to this, replying, "You may dwell in the great Jerusalem; we will dwell here in the small Jerusalem." This occurred because they were extremely wealthy and very distinguished in the eyes of the ruler and the Gentiles. This is why evil decrees have been renewed upon them more than any other community or country.[16]

I would like to add that perhaps this is why Germany has always been a thorn in the side of Israel, from the Middle Ages until today.[17]

16 *Seder HaDorot*, 5380, in an addendum, citing *Ma'aseh Nissim* 9.

17 The following are just a few examples of anti-Jewish persecution in Germany in the Middle Ages. ***4856 [1096] – 4989 [1229]:*** The Crusades. ***4856 [1096]:*** First crusade; mass *Kiddush HaShem*. ***4941 [1181]:*** Pogroms against the Jews of Vienna. ***4955 [1195]:*** Pogroms against the Jews of Speyer. ***4981 [1221]:*** Pogroms against the Jews of Erfurt. ***4985 [1225]:*** Pogroms against the Jews of Mecklenburg. ***5001 [1241]:*** Pogroms against the Jews of Frankfurt on the Main. ***5058 [1298]:*** The Rindfleisch massacres against the communities of Franconia, Bavaria, and Austria. ***5081 [1321]:*** The Lepers Decree. ***5108 [1348] – 5109 [1349]:*** The Black Plague; pogroms against many communities. ***5141 [1381]:*** The expulsion of the Jews of Strasbourg. ***5149 [1389]:*** The Prague massacre. ***5159 [1399]:*** Blood libel in Poznan. ***5180 [1420]:*** The Vienna massacre. ***5186 [1426] – 5213 [1453]:*** Decrees of expulsion from Cologne, Augsburg, Bavaria, and Breslau.

There is simply not enough space to record all of the tragedies that have befallen the Jews from then until the Holocaust. Let us just point out that the modern anti-Semitic movement was conceived in the impurity of Germany, both in terms of the racist anti-Jewish ideology (for example – Friedrich Reiss, Karl Deering, Richard Wagner, Chamberlain, Rosenberg) and the consequent actions (for example – Adolf Steoker, Karl Lueger, Hitler and his evil associates – may their names be eradicated).

In any event, we see that they were afflicted with misfortune, evil decrees, and exile because they regarded themselves secure in their land. The same is true throughout the Diaspora. Since the Jews do not consider returning to and dwelling in *Eretz Yisrael*, the Great Advisor,[18] through His profound counsel, constantly afflicts them with exile and harsh bondage so that they will want to return to *Eretz Yisrael*. The Ya'avetz also agrees with this. He writes that harsh decrees swiftly come upon Israel when they disregard *Eretz Yisrael*.[19] This is true and clear, and it is the secret of the exile, as our Kabbalistic master explained.

We find no rest among the nations – a blessing in disguise

Now, come, O blessed of HaShem,[20] and see that this is stated explicitly in a *Midrash Chazal* on the verse *And he sent out the dove* (*BeReishit* 8:8):

> The dove represents the Jewish people. Just as the dove did not find rest for the sole of her foot, so too, Israel will find no rest in exile, as it says, *There will be no rest for the sole of your foot* (*Devarim* 28:65). And, just as the dove returned to the ark, so too, Israel will eventually return to its Land from exile because of the yoke of the nations who are likened to water, as it says, *Woe to the multitude of many nations who are as tumultuous as the tumult of the seas* (*Yeshayah* 17:12).[21]

Thus, it is clear from the *Midrash* that the pains of exile will push the Jews to their Land. This idea is repeated in *Midrash Eichah* (1:29) on the verse *She dwelled among the nations, but found no rest* (*Eichah* 1:3): "R. Shimon ben Lakish says, 'Had she found rest, she would not have returned.'" It is also found in *BeReishit Rabbah* (33:8):

> *And the dove did not find rest* (*BeReishit* 8:9): Yehudah bar Nachman said in the name of R. Shimon, "Had she found rest, she would not have returned." Similarly, *She* [Israel] *dwelled among the nations, but found no rest* (*Eichah* 1:3): Had she found rest, she would not have returned. Similarly, *And among those nations you will not be tranquil; there will be no rest for the sole of your foot* (*Devarim* 28:65): Had they found rest, they would not have returned.

18 Based on *Yirmiyah* 32:19.
19 *Siddur Ya'avetz, Sullam Beit El*, p. 13a.
20 Based on *BeReishit* 24:31.
21 *Midrash Aggadah* on the Pentateuch (Vienna: Buber, 5654 [1894]), *Noach* 8:11.

The Torah Temimah explains this:

> She dwelled complacently among the nations and did not contemplate returning to *Eretz Yisrael*. She failed, however, because she did not find rest. ***Behold, the clear outlook (hashkafah) of this dictum is very dear, and its echo resounds in every generation, to this very day.***[22]

The sound of my Beloved knocking

Thus, we understand from these words of *Chazal* that the purpose of the pains of exile and the harsh decrees that constantly befall us, from time immemorial, is to awaken us from the slumber of exile. It is the sound of our Beloved, the Holy One Blessed be He, knocking[23] on the doors of our hearts to arouse us with the desire and yearning to return to our Holy Land, which we have disregarded for almost 2,000 years. We have settled for a small measure of tranquillity dwelling among the nations, while denying the honor of HaShem, our nation, and our Holy Land. We have bartered Israel's birthright for a ôpottage of lentilsö[24] in the lands of the nations.

HaShem cries on account of this, on account of the pride of Israel which has been taken from us and given to the nations (see *Chagigah*). (At this time I do not have a Talmud in front of me to cite the page and the precise language, for I am writing without books.)[25] I discovered that one of the early *gedolim* explains this statement as follows. The Jewish people have lost the sense of national pride that each nation possesses. They feel no dignity or honor in being *Am Yisrael* (the Nation of Israel) and have lost all remnants of self-respect in being the holy nation. They have even sold all their pride and glory for a ôpottage of lentilsö extended to them in the lands of exile. Therefore, the Holy One Blessed be He is compelled to appear through *the sound of my Beloved knocking*. This refers to the harsh decrees that constantly befall us to awaken within us the desire to return to our Land and our glory.

Based on this we can explain the verse *When you come into the Land of Cana'an which I give you as a possession, and I will place a plague of* tzara'at *upon a house in the Land of your possession* (*VaYikra* 14:34). *Chazal* point out that the language, *and I will place*

22 *Torah Temimah, Eichah* 1:62.
23 Based on *Shir HaShirim* 5:2.
24 *BeReishit* 25:34.
25 The exact source is *Chagigah* 5b.

(ונתתי), implies good tidings.[26] [What good tiding is there in a plague of *tzara'at*]? Based on the above, however, it is clear. HaShem is telling us that at the moment the Jews assimilate to the extent that they consider their sojourn in the lands of exile as if they dwell in "the land of their possession," and they no longer contemplate returning to *Eretz Yisrael*, then HaShem will place a plague of *tzara'at* upon a house in "the land of their possession." That is to say, HaShem will place upon them numerous types of "*tzara'at* afflictions" in the lands of exile, which they consider the land of their possession. Then, they will open their eyes and realize, "Whom have you here and what have you here,"[27] and they will devote themselves to returning to their forefathers' possession, *Eretz Yisrael*.

This is exactly what we experience today. After all of the afflictions that have befallen us, each and every Jew longs and yearns for the Land of our forefathers. Every Jew would be happy and fortunate if he was permitted to return there. All of this is part of God's profound counsel, for our God, the God of our forefathers, thinks of good ways to ensure that we do not assimilate in exile. He wants us to return to the Land that He promised to give to our forefathers and their descendants after them.

Tana DeVei Eliyahu (18:49) states that landowners are uprooted from this world and sink to the ground (meaning, they lose their possessions and status) only because they eat, drink, and rebel despite all the good that they have. Also, they do not involve themselves with an occupation and Torah study (for "Torah study is good together with an occupation" [*Avot* 2:2]). About them the verse says, *Because of three things the earth is enraged, ...and a fool who is sated with bread* (*Mishley* 30:21-22). This prediction has come true for our Jewish brethren in Bohemia, Czechoslovakia, and Germany. They lived very affluent lives and rebelled to such an extent that they forgot that they are the seed of Israel. Therefore, God was compelled to send someone to remind them that they are the sons of Avraham, Yitzchak, and Ya'akov.

III Even the Wicked Will be Redeemed

Then, the Lord your God will return your captivity (*Devarim* 30:3). Rashi explains:

26 See *Horayot* 10a.
27 Based on *Yeshayah* 22:16.

> The day of the ingathering of the exiles is so awesome and difficult that God Himself (as it were), with His own hands, must actually seize each man from his place, as it says, *And you will be gathered up one by one, O Children of Israel* (*Yeshayah* 27:12).

An idea which I saw in the holy volume, *Ohev Yisrael*, by the Rebbe of Apt, will help explain this Rashi. The following *Midrash* expounds upon the verse *He has gathered them out of the lands* (*Tehillim* 107:3):

> Israel was immersed in Egypt like a bird in the hands of a hunter, as it says, *I will go down to rescue him* (*Shemot* 3:8). R. Abahu the son of R. Acha said in the name of Rabbeinu: "Israel was situated in Egypt like a fetus in the innards of an animal. Just as the shepherd places his hand inside and removes it, so did the Holy One Blessed be He [remove us from Egypt], as it says, *Or has any god ever ventured to come and take for himself a nation from amidst a nation...as...the Lord your God did for you in Egypt* (*Devarim* 4:34)." R. Eivo said in the name of R. Yochanan ben Zakkai: "Just as a goldsmith stretches out his hand and removes the gold from the furnace, so did the Holy One Blessed be He take Israel out of Egypt, as it says, *But the Lord has taken you...out of the iron furnace, out of Egypt* (ibid. 4:20)." (*Midrash Tehillim* 107:4)

[The Rebbe of Apt elaborates]:

> I would like to suggest an explanation of these three opinions, their reasoning, and the differences between them (seeing that each one uses a different parable). *Chazal* here allude to the three categories of Jews: the righteous, the ordinary, and the wicked. The one who compares Israel to a bird refers to the completely righteous Jews. A bird has absolutely no relationship with, or connection to, the hunter in whose hands it is imprisoned. It is an independent being and will escape the moment the hunter opens his hands, never to return again. So too, the righteous who were exiled in Egypt had absolutely no connection to the evil forces (*kelipot*); they were simply unable to escape. HaShem, in His loving kindness, came to rescue them and brought them out without any difficulty.
>
> The one who compares them to a fetus within an animal's innards refers to the ordinary Jew. A fetus has some connection to the animal [that carries it]; she is its mother and it follows her. Similarly, the ordinary Jews in Egypt were connected to

the *kelipot*, but not to a great extent (God forbid), just like the fetus which is clearly an independent being.

Finally, the one who compares them to gold in a furnace refers to the wicked Jews. Gold in a furnace is mixed with impurities. The gold and impurities are joined, neither being recognizable by itself. So too, the wicked in Egypt were thoroughly interconnected with the *kelipot*. But, the Holy One Blessed be He brought even them out of Egypt.[28]

HaShem will drag the wicked Jews out of exile

It appears to me that the verse mentioned above – *And you will be gathered up one by one, O Children of Israel* (*Yeshayah* 27:12) – which implies that God, with His own hands, must actually seize each person from his place, alludes to this third category. That is, the wicked will be so entangled and absorbed in the depth of the *kelipot* that the Holy One Blessed be He will have to grab them by the hand and deliver them from their utter immersion in the exile, a result of their adherence to the ways of the Gentiles. On the other hand, HaShem will have no difficulty with the ordinary Jews, and certainly not with the righteous ones. When the gates of exile open, they will immediately come running, of their own volition. There will be no need for HaShem to hold them by the hand and bring them out. This is true and clear.

Indeed, this has occurred in our own times. Many of our fellow Jews have become assimilated and entrenched among the nations. They no longer consider themselves members of our nation or sons of the living God. But, the wicked one [Hitler] came along and instituted the Racist Laws.[29] After a rigorous search into family origins, going back three generations,[30] he classified them as offspring of Avraham, Yitzchak, and Ya'akov. Thus, the prophecy was fulfilled – *And it will be that instead of that which was said to them, "You are not My people," it will be said to them,* "[You are] *the sons of the Living God"* (*Hoshea* 2:1). That is to say, when they reach the level where everyone considers them *not My people*, the Holy One Blessed be He will act for their sake and ensure that they are called *the sons of the Living God*. The prophet referred to these people when he said, *And you will be gathered up one by one*. Our master from Apt explained that even the completely wicked will be set apart, and the

28 *Ohev Yisrael, Likutim LePesach*, s.v. *bechol dor vedor chayav adam*.

29 [Probably a reference to the Nuremberg Laws of 1935.]

30 See *Hasho'ah BeTei'ud* (Yad VeShem, 5738 [1978]), p. 75.

Holy One Blessed be He will deliver them from the depths of the *kelipot*, as it says, *So that none of us be banished* (II *Shmuel* 14:14).

I also came across this idea in *Malbushei Yom Tov*,[31] by the holy one from Zhidachov *zt"l*. He cites R. Mendel of Rymanov (may his merit protect us) who says that even the second son mentioned in the *Haggadah* will have a *tikkun* (rectification) in the final redemption. Due to his abundant love for Israel, this holy man avoided using the name "wicked one" (*rasha*). Instead, he simply said, "the second son." This demonstrates the extent of *ahavat Yisrael* that one must have, for this holy Jew did not want to use the term *rasha* even for a completely wicked person like the second son of the *Haggadah*. (Let this be a lesson for all those who take a "measuring stick" in their hands to "measure" others and call them *resha'im*).

I also discovered this in *B'nei Yissachar*. He cites the Kabbalists who assert that even the completely wicked will achieve *tikkun* at the time of the final redemption, and all will be redeemed.[32] Subsequently, I found this stated explicitly in *Pesikta Rabbati* (*Piska Kumi Ori*): The Holy One Blessed be He says to *Mashiach*, "Due to the sins of these individuals, your tongue will be..."[33] He replied, "Master of the Universe, I accept this upon myself with a joyous soul and a glad heart, so that not a single Jew be lost." Further on (in *Piska Gili Me'od*), *Mashiach* states that he atones even for those who mocked him and did not believe that he would come, so that they should not be lost.

All of this demonstrates how precious even the lowliest soul of Israel is in the eyes of *Mashiach* and the Holy One Blessed be He. *Mashiach* agrees to suffer numerous afflictions just to prevent the loss of even the most corrupt Jewish soul, for all Jews are descendants of Avraham, Yitzchak, and Ya'akov.

We must love and befriend even the sinners of Israel

The holy *Zohar* states that even the sinners of Israel hold on to the right side[34] and are rooted in holiness. It is, therefore, forbidden to degrade or curse them. On the contrary, it is a *mitzvah* to love them and bring them near. (At this time I am unable to indicate the

31 R. Teichtal is referring to the work, *Malbush LeShabbat VeYom Tov* (Munkatch, 5687 [1927]), Commentary to the *Pesach Haggadah*, p. 51b, s.v. *be'arba'ah banim*.

32 See *B'nei Yissachar, Ma'amarei Sheva Nechemtot* 5:1:1.

33 The *Pesikta* goes on to describe various afflictions that *Mashiach* will suffer.

34 [In Kabbalah, the right side represents the forces of good and holiness.]

exact location of this source, for I am writing without books.)[35]

I saw a beautiful idea in *Likutei Beit Efrayim*, by the brilliant R. Naftali Sofer. Novellae of his mentor, the Chatam Sofer, are printed at the end of the volume. The following are the Chatam Sofer's words:

> The Talmud states that Beit Shammai was strict while Beit Hillel loved peace, pursued peace, and brought people closer to the Torah (*Shabbat* 31a). In my *Chiddushei Aggadot* I explained that this does not mean that Beit Shammai was unjustly strict (God forbid). Rather, Beit Shammai would distance those who legitimately deserved such treatment. Beit Hillel, on the other hand, was extraordinarily humble, and he brought people close even when the law did not call for it. That is to say, he befriended those who, by law, should have been distanced. And the *halachah* follows Beit Hillel.

Thus, our mentor, the Chatam Sofer, rules explicitly that the *halachah* follows Beit Hillel and that one must bring near even those who, according to the law, should be distanced, as Beit Hillel did.

R. Chayim Vital writes in *Sefer HaChezyonot* that he once asked his mentor, the Ari *z"l*, how he professed to have such a lofty soul when [in reality] even the most insignificant person of the earlier generations was incomparably more righteous and pious! The Ari *z"l* replied:

> Realize that greatness of the soul does not depend on man's perceivable deeds. Rather, HaShem probes the hearts and minds of men according to each time period and generation. A very small deed in this generation is equal to many *mitzvot* in the earlier generations. This is so because the *kelipah* and the evil forces have so vastly intensified in our generation that they are infinite and immeasurable. This was not the case in the earlier generations. Therefore, had I lived in those generations, my deeds and wisdom would have been wondrous, and they would have surpassed those of many of the earlier *tzaddikim – Tana'im and Amora'im.*

In his work, *Netiv Mitzvotecha*, the holy Kabbalist, R. Isaac'l of Komarno, comments on this:

> And now, my brother, take heed! If in the days of our master, the Ari, there was such an enormous intensification of the

35 See *Zohar* 3:36b-37a.

kelipot, what are we to say during these bitter times? Surely, we should embrace anyone who bears the name of Israel and invoke merit and love upon him. All of his sinful deeds are a result of the strengthening of the evil forces and are due to the hardships and suffering which have caused him to lose his understanding. I swear by the Eternal God that all of the wicked Jews in this country,[36] particularly those in Germany, are like infants who were kidnapped by Gentiles. They act under duress and speak out of ignorance. In an instant, they would all be willing to spill their blood like water – with love, happiness, and joyful dancing – for the sanctification of God's great name.[37]

This is true, for they are willing to sacrifice themselves for what they perceive as Judaism; and if they had a greater understanding, they would do more. In any event, observe, my brother, that this holy man of God states explicitly that we should embrace all those who bear the name of Israel. They suffer with the entire Jewish people, because they, too, are called Israel. He further states that it is a *mitzvah* to invoke merit upon them and accept them with abounding affection. He even swore by the Eternal God that all of today's sinners are like infants who were kidnapped by Gentiles, and that they act under duress. Pay close attention to and delve into his words, for he was renowned as a man who possessed *Ruach HaKodesh*.

All Jews will be accepted at the time of redemption

Nevertheless, it is clear that no Jew, not even the worst one, will be banished at the time of redemption. All Jews will return to their borders, and HaShem will accept them with love and affection. This already occurred in the days of Ezra, as it is written, *The people of exile who had come out of captivity offered burnt offerings to the God of Israel, twelve bulls...* (*Ezra* 8:35). R. Yehudah says that these sacrifices were brought to atone for the sin of idolatry that was committed in the days of Tzidkiyahu. (The Talmud explains that the idolaters of Tzidkiyahu's generation were still alive, and it was they who returned from the exile [see *Horayot* 6a and *Temurah* 15b].)

The Talmud queries, "Did they not act willfully?" Rashi explains, "The people of Tzidkiyahu's generation acted willfully and are deserving of death... How can they achieve atonement through these sacrifices?" The Talmud answers, "It was a temporary ruling."

36 Galicia.

37 *Netiv Mitzvotecha, Netiv Emunah* 6:10.

Rashi explains, "They were atoned even though they acted willfully." Rabbeinu Gershom Me'or HaGolah, commenting on the Talmud's answer, writes, "It was beyond the letter of the law."❖

Today's sinners are like infants kidnapped by Gentiles

Thus, the Holy One Blessed be He did not exclude even the absolute heretics (the ones who worshipped idols, which is the most grievous offense [see *Shavuot* 13a]) from the joy of redemption. Therefore, it is clear to me that now, too, when we merit redemption (speedily in our days) not a single Jewish soul will be cast aside, not even the greatest and most rebellious sinners. This is especially true in our days, because there is practically no one in the category of "one who knows his Master yet intentionally rebels against Him." Rather, they are like infants who were kidnapped by Gentiles. They do not know better, for they were not raised in the spirit of the Torah, and all of their sins are committed unwillingly (as the holy man of God from Komarno stated above).[38] Therefore, it is certainly a *mitzvah* to bring them near. This is similar to what the Rambam writes about the children of those who separated themselves from the congregation, like the Karaites. They should not be treated as outcasts. On the contrary, it is a *mitzvah* to bring them near, for they have been raised contrary to the spirit of the Torah.[39]

Therefore, the Holy One Blessed be He certainly loves the Jews of our generation, and they will be accepted at the time of redemption (speedily in our days). We are not permitted to distance them; on the contrary, we must bring them near. This is especially true now, after all of the misfortune that has befallen us in recent years. The sinners of Israel have not escaped the exile; they too have suffered because they bear the name of Israel. Their hearts have already

---

❖ It appears to me that this is similar to the custom of kings to grant amnesty to criminals on a day of royal celebration. The Shelah writes that all the practices common among mortal kings originated in sanctity. The trait of granting amnesty, as well, was stolen by the mortal kings from the Holy One Blessed be He. For, on the day of rejoicing over the redemption at the time of Ezra, God granted amnesty to those who willfully worshipped idols. He allowed them to achieve atonement through a sacrifice, as if they acted unintentionally, so as not to exclude them from the joy of redemption.

38 Pp. 105-6.

39 Rambam, *Hilchot Mamrim* 3:3.

softened. They surely realize that the reforms instituted by their fathers in recent generations are an inheritance of lies. They truly would return to us with all their hearts, but they have lost the way, and they have become estranged from us. We are certainly obligated to extend our hands to them and draw them near with affection and brotherly love. They indeed are included in the Rambam's description of...infants who were kidnapped by Gentiles, as mentioned above.

Yalkut Shimoni states: "*You have rebuked nations* (*Tehillim* 9:6), this refers to Amalek; *You have destroyed the wicked* (ibid.), this refers to Eisav. Could it be that even Ya'akov is included [among the wicked]? It does not say *resha'im* (wicked ones), rather *rasha* (wicked one)" (*Yalkut Shimoni* 2:643). The author of *Sheivet Mussar* comments on this in his holy work, *Azor Eliyahu*:

> This *Midrash* is quite puzzling when it asks, "Could it be that even Ya'akov is included?" It can be understood, though, if we read it carefully. It does not say, "even Yisrael is included," rather, "even Ya'akov is included." According to *Chazal*, the name Ya'akov refers to improper Jews.[40] Thus, the *Midrash* implies that perhaps the sinners of Israel, who are referred to as Ya'akov, will be destroyed because of their sins, just like Eisav is destroyed because of his wickedness... To this the *Midrash* replies, "It does not say *resha'im*, rather *rasha*." This alludes to the fact that only Eisav and his descendants will be destroyed. Indeed, had it said *resha'im*, all wicked ones would have been included, Jewish or not. *Rasha*, however, implies one specific type, that is, Eisav. Sinners of Israel, on the other hand, will not be destroyed. God forbid that even one "hoof" of Israel be lost, because the Jews can be rectified (*tikkun*) through afflictions and the like. Furthermore, there is not a single sinner among Israel who does not have thoughts of repentance.[41]

Will HaShem accept penitents during the days of Mashiach?

Tangentially, I would like to discuss a puzzling comment that I found in the Maharil:

> In the days of *Mashiach*, penitents will not be accepted. This is similar to *Chazal*'s assertion that we will not accept converts in those days, for he who converts then will not do so out of love for HaShem, but in order to share in Israel's joy. Thus,

40 See *BeMidbar Rabbah* 20:22. Also see *Sh'nei Luchot HaBrit* 1:14b.

41 *Azor Eliyahu*, chap. 140.

> since we anticipate salvation every day, he who does not repent before *Mashiach* comes will no longer be able to repent, and he will remain a sinner, God forbid.[42]

It is surprising that repentance will be ineffective in those times, for we find the opposite in a *Midrash* on the verse *The prophecy of the word of the Lord in the land of Chadrach* (חדרך) (*Zecharyah* 9:1): "*Chadrach* refers to the Messianic king, for he will ultimately guide (להדריך) the entire world in repentance before the Holy One Blessed be He" (*Shir HaShirim Rabbah* 7:5).[43]

The same principle is found in *Tana DeVei Eliyahu*:

> Father in Heaven, may Your name be blessed for all of eternity, and may You derive pleasure from Your servants Israel, wherever they may dwell. I bless You in this manner because You have said that You accept the repentance of the sinners of Israel. Even if a person commits many grave sins, when he repents You say, "I have compassion on him, and I will accept his repentance." Even if he arises and curses and blasphemes Your Exaltedness, when he returns and repents, You, O Holy One, forgive him for everything, as it says, *Then the eyes of the blind will be opened, and the ears of the deaf will be unstopped. Then the lame man will leap like a gazelle and the tongue of the mute will sing* (*Yeshayah* 35:5-6). The blind, deaf, and lame refer to those who lack Torah knowledge and good deeds, as it says, *For water will break out in the wilderness and streams in the desert* (ibid.). (*Eliyahu Rabbah* 22 [end])

A commentator explains:

> He means to say that if *the blind* and *the deaf* are to be taken literally, then how does the verse, *For water will break out...*, explain the healing of the blind and the deaf? If, however, we interpret these words referring to Torah, it makes sense. The eyes of the blind will be opened because water will break out in the wilderness, that is to say, because the earth will be filled with knowledge.[44]

42 Maharil, *Hilchot Aseret Yemei Teshuvah*, s.v. *haftarat*.

43 ❖ *Matnot Kehunah* explains that this inference is based on replacing the letter *chet* (ח) with a *heyh* (ה), following the principle that *alef, heyh, chet*, and *ayin* (א, ה, ח, ע) are interchangeable.

44 *Yeshu'ot Ya'akov* 16.

Thus, this verse refers to the days of *Mashiach*, for it is then that the earth will be filled with knowledge.[45] Nonetheless, repentance will avail those who curse and blaspheme God (Heaven forbid).

Rashi explains this verse, *Then the eyes of the blind will be opened...*, in a similar fashion:

> The eyes of those who have, thus far, been blind to the awe of God, and the ears of the deaf who did not, as of yet, hearken to the voice of the prophets, will be opened, for I will grant them a true spirit so that they will fear Me.[46]

The same thing occurred at the time of Ezra. The returnees were accepted with merely a sacrifice, as I mentioned above.[47] Therefore, the comments of the Maharil seem incomprehensible.

In order to explain his opinion, I would like to suggest that his sole intention was to frighten his readers into repenting immediately, before the coming of our righteous *Mashiach*. For, repentance of this sort is certainly on a higher level, as *Chazal* point out.[48] In reality, though, our mentor, the Maharil, would agree with our Rabbis of the above-cited *Midrashim* that *Mashiach* will accept the penitence of every single Jew.

Ahavat Yisrael – loving each and every Jew

For the Lord saw the affliction of Israel that it was very severe, and there was nothing left and nothing remaining, and there was no helper for Israel. But the Lord did not speak to erase the name of Israel from underneath the heavens, and He saved them through the hand of Yerovam ben Yoash (II *Melachim* 14:26-27). The *Midrash* comments on these verses:

> The Holy One Blessed be He does not want even one Jew to die, as it says, *Let not the foreigner say... ôThe Lord will surely separate meö* (*Yeshayah* 56:3). Now, if I [God] have said that I will not reject a foreigner, then obviously [I will not reject] My sons! (*Midrash Tanchuma, BeMidbar* 25)

Our master, the holy man of God, R. Yisachar Dov of Belz *ztvk"l* (may his merit protect us), expressed a similar idea. In the year 5674

45 Based on *Yeshayah* 11:9.

46 ❖ See the entire chapter there which speaks of the time of redemption.

47 P. 106.

48 See *Sanhedrin* 97b, *BeMidbar Rabbah* 7:10, *Tana DeVei Eliyahu Rabbah* 16:7.

[1914], at the outbreak of World War I, the Rebbe fled his glorious abode and escaped to the city of Rutzfort in Hungary. At that time I still lived in Busermin which is near Rutzfort, and for as long as our master resided there I took refuge under his wings.[49] I became close with him and his family and was a frequent guest in his home. (I found lodging in Busermin for some of his relatives, and many times I intervened with the authorities on their behalf.) People from all countries flocked to see his holy countenance.

Once, there was a great assembly of wise men at his home (for at that time Hungary was still a grand country filled with *gedolei Torah* and the most brilliant and sagacious men of the generation). The greatest men of the country, heavenly saints, were gathered before him. At their head was the holy elder, scion of illustrious lineage, our master, R. Moshe David Teitelbaum, *av beit din* of Madiar-Lapush in Zibanbergen,[50] grandson and foremost disciple of our master, the author of *Yitav Lev z"l.*[51] Being a prodigious orator and preacher, he petitioned the Rebbe of Belz as follows: "The people of Israel are in dire straits throughout almost the entire world, and their afflictions are extremely intense and frequent. There is no remedy for the wounds of Israel, save an awakening to repentance by all of Israel as one. It is befitting that his honor, who has been crowned the most righteous individual of our generation, initiate this movement of awakening to repentance. If he would do so, it would undoubtedly influence the entire generation to return their hearts to our Father in Heaven. This way, we would achieve the salvation that all of Israel so desperately awaits."

For almost an hour, R. Teitelbaum petitioned the Rebbe of Belz in this fashion. He embellished his pleas with beautiful and wondrous explanations illustrating that this obligation rests solely upon him. When he finished his plea, our master opened his holy mouth and answered him briefly and to the point: ***"O Rebbe of Lapush, have you concluded your petition? When Mashiach arrives, the Jews will repent. In the meantime, it is of utmost importance that the Jews love one another. One must love even the***

49 Based on *Tehillim* 91:4.

50 A city in Transylvania (Targul-Lapush in Romanian) situated on the Lapush river, near the city of Dash.

51 ❖ R. Teitelbaum published *Heishiv Moshe* – the responsa of his ancestor, teacher of Israel, the author of *Yismach Moshe* – in addition to all of the writings of his grandfather, the author of *Yitav Lev*.

lowliest Jew as himself. One must engender unity and keep far away from anything that causes disunity. The salvation of Israel during times of trouble rests on this." These holy words came from the depths of his heart with a sacred trembling.

Everything I cited from the *Midrash*, Talmud, *Tana DeVei Eliyahu, Netiv Mitzvotecha*, and the Chatam Sofer is included in the Rebbe of Belz's succinct statement. His words rend the heart of any Jew who feels the pain of the generation and who has a true feeling of love for Israel. Know and understand this, and do not be a pious fool who is quick to find fault with Israel. Do not cause disunity among those who are united, particularly at a time when the divine attribute of justice hovers over all of Israel. It is a time of trouble for Ya'akov, may the Merciful One protect us!

I subsequently discovered that our mentor, the man of God from Lublin, explicitly agrees with our holy Rebbe of Belz. In his holy work, *Divrei Emet*, he writes:

> Behold, there are those who pray solely for the generation to repent. This, however, is not proper, for it arouses divine justice, God forbid. The proper approach is to evoke wonders and miracles for the sake of Israel. Then, the Jews will repent out of love for the miracles. This is what happened at the time of Mordechai and Esther, as *Chazal* state, "They fulfilled that which they had already accepted" (*Shabbat* 88a). This is also the interpretation of the verse *As in the days of your leaving the land of Egypt, I will show him wonders* (*Michah* 7:15).[52]

Thus, he claims that if we pray for the generation to repent, we may actually arouse Divine Justice, God forbid. Rather, we must beg for miracles, and then all will return and serve Him. This is the truth, as a certain wealthy and distinguished woman from Trencin said regarding the difficult times that have befallen us, "If our Father in Heaven would perform but one miracle on our behalf we would all return to Him." Now, the religious level in the city of Trencin is well known, and she said this nonetheless. The words of our mentor from Lublin do not need strengthening, I simply wanted to bring an incident to illustrate this idea.

For He said, "Indeed they are My people, children who will not lie," and He became their Savior (*Yeshayah* 63:8). Rashi explains this

52 *Divrei Emet* (Warsaw, 5643 [1883]), p. 28b, s.v. *ve'od.*

verse as follows. "*Indeed they are My people*: Even though it is revealed to Me that they will betray Me, nonetheless, *they are My people*, and I consider them as *children who will not lie*." Also, on the verse, *And the people were as complainers* (*BeMidbar* 11:1), Rashi comments, "*The people* refers to the wicked..., and when they are fitting, they are called *My people*." Thus, it is clear that even though the sinners of Israel betray God, they do not cease being His children, for He called them *My people* (*Yeshayah* 63:8), as if they were fitting. It follows that it is a *mitzvah* to love them, bring them near, and treat them affectionately. In this way, we will achieve salvation, as the verse concludes, *And He became their Savior*. That is to say, then we will achieve the salvation that we await with great anticipation. This concurs with the words of the Rebbe of Belz *zt"l*.

Our obligation to invoke merit upon Israel

Yalkut Shimoni on *Hoshea* states:

> The Holy One Blessed be He said to Hoshea, "Israel has sinned..." He replied, "O Master of the Universe, the entire world is Yours; exchange them for a different nation." The Holy One Blessed be He said, "What am I to do with this elder [Hoshea]?... The people of Israel are My children, the sons of My tried ones – Avraham, Yitzchak, and Ya'akov. They are one of the three acquisitions that I have acquired in My world – Torah, *Eretz Yisrael*, and the people of Israel – and you tell Me to exchange them for a different nation?!" (*Yalkut Shimoni* 2:515)

Thus, the people of Israel are always HaShem's acquisition, even if they sin. How then is it permissible to degrade HaShem's acquisition? On the contrary, we are obligated to invoke merit upon Israel (ללמד זכות על ישראל), even at a time when they are improper.

Midrash Tanchuma on the verse, *And they shall judge the people with righteous judgment* (*Devarim* 16:18), expounds upon this:

> They shall incline the people towards the scale of righteousness. R. Yehudah ben Shalom said: "They shall...invoke merit upon them before the Holy One Blessed be He. From whom do we learn this? From Gideon ben Yoash. In his days, the people of Israel were in distress, and the Holy One Blessed be He was searching for a man who would invoke merit upon them. He could not, however, find one, for the generation was impoverished of *mitzvot* and good deeds. Once it was found that Gideon had this virtue, the angel immediately revealed

> himself to him, as it says, *And the angel of the Lord appeared to him... And the Lord turned to him and said, 'Go with this strength of yours'* (*Shoftim* 6:12,14). [That is to say, go] with the strength of the merit that you invoked upon My children." Thus, *And they shall judge the people with righteous judgment* means that they shall invoke merit upon the generation. (*Midrash Tanchuma, Shoftim* 4)

Let this be a lesson for those who scorn and slander the people of Israel. It is forbidden to invoke condemnation upon even the most corrupt Jews, for they are the seed of the tried ones, sons of Avraham, Yitzchak, and Ya'akov, and they are deeply rooted in holiness, as I cited above from the *Zohar*.[53] Remember and keep this principle; do not forget it, lest you fall into the trap of Satan, who incites you to denounce the people of Israel.

The importance of invoking merit upon Israel even when they are undeserving is also mentioned in *Midrash Shir HaShirim* (1:6:1), "R. Simon began"; *VaYikra Rabbah* (10), "We find by Gideon";[54] Rashi on *Shoftim* (6:14); *Pesachim* (87a-b); *Midrash HaNe'elam* (*Noach*);[55] *Or HaChayim HaKadosh* (*BeMidbar* 20:1); Rashi and Radak on I *Melachim* (19:16); *Shabbat* (117);[56] *Tana DeVei Eliyahu* (*Rabbah* 16:6-8); Rambam *Hilchot De'ot* (6:3-5); and *Devash LePhi* (*Chaf* 18, *Taf* 17). Examine all of these sources and you will realize how much one must invoke merit upon Israel in times of trouble and how much one must love even the most corrupt Jew with all one's heart and soul. This will surely cause HaShem to have mercy on the Jewish people and deliver them from distress. This was the Rebbe of Belz's intention when he said, "It is of utmost importance that Jews love one another, and the Holy One Blessed be He will assist us because of this merit."

Is Mashiach's arrival dependent on teshuvah or not?

However, it appears that the Rebbe of Belz's statement needs clarification. He claims simply, "When *Mashiach* arrives, the Jews will repent," which implies that *Mashiach* will arrive before Israel repents. From the Rambam, however, it seems that his arrival is dependent on Israel's prior repentance: "Israel will only be redeemed through repentance, and the Torah has already promised that Israel

53 See p. 104.

54 This needs clarification, for this source is not found there. See sec. 1-3.

55 *Zohar Chadash* (Mossad HaRav Kook), p. 23a, col. b.

56 This reference is unclear.

will repent at the end of their exile and immediately be redeemed."[57]

Apparently, though, this Rambam itself is problematic. In both the Talmud *Bavli* (*Sanhedrin* 97b) and *Yerushalmi* (*Ta'anit* 1:1 [2b]), R. Eliezer and R. Yehoshua dispute whether or not Israel needs to repent as a prerequisite for redemption. And it is clear that R. Eliezer eventually conceded to R. Yehoshua that Israel will be redeemed even without repentance.

The Rambam's intention is clarified with a true interpretation based on the *Yalkut Shimoni*:

> R. Yehudah said: "If the people of Israel do not repent they will not be redeemed. And, they will only repent amidst pain, wandering, and lack of sustenance. And, they will not repent until Eliyahu arrives, as it says, *Behold, I send you Eliyah the prophet*, which is immediately followed by, *And he will turn the hearts of the fathers with the sons* (*Malachi* 3:23-24)." (*Yalkut Shimoni* 2:595)

Thus, two conditions are necessary: first, the intense hardships, and afterwards, the coming of Eliyahu who will arouse their hearts to repent. Without the precursory hardships, however, even Eliyahu HaNavi would be unable to arouse them to repent, for these hardships will soften the hearts. R. Yehudah's statement in the *Yalkut* is the basis for the Rambam's position that Israel will not be redeemed without repentance. Afflictions and the coming of Eliyahu are the means by which redemption will arise. These two factors will cause Israel to repent and deserve immediate redemption... In any event, Eliyahu will come even before Israel repents, and he will bring us back to the proper path. This was also the Rebbe of Belz's intention. When he said, "When *Mashiach* arrives...," he was referring to *Mashiach* and the one who will accompany him, i.e., Eliyahu (as is well known).

Also, the Or HaChayim HaKadosh comments on the verse *When you are in distress and all these things have befallen you, at the end of days, you will return to the Lord your God and hearken to His voice, for the Lord your God is a merciful God* (*Devarim* 4:30):

> This verse speaks of the promise of redemption. For, when the Jewish people are in distress during the period of exile (this

57 Rambam, *Hilchot Teshuvah* 7:5.

> refers to the birthpangs of *Mashiach*; and *all* of the hardships will only come upon them at the end of days)... HaShem promises them that He will arouse their hearts to repent. This is the meaning of, *You will return to the Lord your God.* The verse provides a reason for this promise, *For the Lord your God is a merciful God, He will not forsake you.* Rather, He will strengthen your heart to repent. Perhaps this explains Micha'el's claim to HaShem, as cited in *Zohar Chadash* (*Noach* 23:4), for the end of days has arrived and all of these things have befallen us, so why does HaShem not arouse our hearts to repent? (I have explained this statement elsewhere.) Our eyes look expectantly towards HaShem, that He should open up a storehouse of purifying spirits, to open eyes that are blind, to incline hearts to HaShem, and to perceive the sweet pleasantness of His closeness.

Thus, the Torah promises that after all of the misfortunes befall the Jews, [HaShem] will awaken them to repent, and the redemption will subsequently ensue. It appears to me that this awakening will come through Eliyahu HaNavi, as the *Yalkut Shimoni* explains.

IV HaShem Will Arouse Us to Repent Only When We Return to Eretz Yisrael

The question still remains, have we not, in this generation, experienced all of these things in an overabundant measure? Also, are we not at the end of days, towards the end of the sixth millennium? Nevertheless, we have yet to witness any outpouring of a purifying spirit from above, or the coming of Eliyahu to arouse our hearts to repentance. We are ready for this because of the intense calamities that have befallen us in these days; the hearts of all of Israel have already been softened.

The answer to this is found in our holy Torah, in *parashat Nitzavim*:

> *And the Lord your God will bring you to the Land that your forefathers possessed and you shall possess it... And the Lord your God will circumcise your heart and the heart of your offspring, to love the Lord your God with all your heart and with all your soul that you may live.* (*Devarim* 30:5-6)

The Or HaChayim writes that there is no greater repentance than when HaShem will circumcise Israel's heart to love Him wholeheartedly. Thus, it is clear that the Torah made this matter contingent on our prior entry into the Land and our taking hold of our forefathers' inheritance. Then, HaShem will circumcise our hearts and bestow upon us a spirit of purity from above to incline our hearts towards Him.

Thus, as long as we are in a foreign land, this spirit of purity cannot come upon us. Therefore, it is befitting and a sacred obligation for all of us to strive to come to our Holy Land by way of the circumstances that the Prime Mover has generated (via His messengers) to bring us to the Land. This is the meaning of, *And He will bring you to the Land...*, that is, through His messengers and through the circumstances that He has generated for our sake. Then, the Holy One Blessed be He will fulfill His promise to send us a pure spirit from above, circumcise our hearts, and cause us to return to Him with all our hearts and all our souls. But, as long as we remain in the atmosphere of the lands of the nations there is no means by which to achieve this promise, for the impurity of these lands surrounds us. The Talmud determines that the *Shechinah* does not rest outside of the Land (*Mo'ed Kattan* 25a). Similarly, it is clear and true that the spirit of purity from above is unable to descend upon us in *Chutz LaAretz*.

It appears to me that this is also the meaning of the Rambam's statement "Israel will only be redeemed through repentance, and the Torah has already promised that Israel will repent at the end of their exile and immediately be redeemed."[58] The Rambam is consistent with his opinion stated elsewhere that before *Mashiach* comes, HaShem will direct the hearts of Israel and bestow upon them a spirit of purity, and they will ordain the elders (see there).[59] This is the aspect of "circumcision of the heart," which is the highest level of repentance, as the Or HaChayim HaKadosh explains.

According to the Chatam Sofer, this will occur in *Eretz Yisrael*. He explains that this Rambam implies that the people of Israel will gather together in *Eretz Yisrael* (without the *Beit HaMikdash*) even before *Mashiach* comes. *Mashiach* will then inevitably arrive, since the Jews will have already repented.[60] Israel will only deserve all of this, however, if they first assemble in *Eretz Yisrael*. Thus, the Rambam's opinion is clarified.

58 *Hilchot Teshuvah* 7:5.

59 Commentary to the *Mishnah, Sanhedrin* 1:3.

60 *Derashot Chatam Sofer*, Sermon of the 27th of Elul, 5580 [1820].

In any event, all of these sources imply that we have a sacred obligation to return to our Land, and then, with HaShem's help, we will attain all of the grand promises that our holy prophets have prophesied concerning us.

Now come, O blessed of HaShem,[61] and see that the prophet Yechezkel states this idea explicitly – namely, that HaShem will only bestow a spirit of purity upon us when we return to and live in *Eretz Yisrael*, not when we dwell in the lands of the nations.

> *I will take you from among the nations and gather you from all the lands, and I will bring you to your own Land. Then I will sprinkle pure waters upon you, and you will become cleansed from all your impurities... I will give you a new heart, and I will place a new spirit within you. I will remove the heart of stone from your flesh and give you a heart of flesh. I will place My spirit within you and I will cause you to follow My statutes, and you will guard My laws and fulfill them. You will dwell in the Land that I gave to your forefathers, and you will be for Me a nation, and I will be for you a God.* (*Yechezkel* 36:24-28)

Behold, the verse states explicitly that HaShem will circumcise our hearts to love and serve Him with all our hearts and all our souls, only after we enter our forefathers' Land.

Our mentor, the Chatam Sofer, explains that this entire section in *Yechezkel* refers to the time preceding the complete redemption, when we are still in exile. Nevertheless, after we experience intense afflictions, HaShem will have mercy on us and bring us to our Land. Then and there, HaShem will bestow upon us a pure spirit and give us a new heart to keep His statutes and laws.

Allow me to quote our mentor on another verse from the same prophecy in *Yechezkel: They will say, "This Land* [which was] *desolate has become like the Garden of Eden and the cities* [which were] *ruined, desolate, and destroyed have been fortified and inhabited." The nations...will know that I, the Lord, have rebuilt the ruins and I have replanted that which was desolate. I, the Lord, have spoken and I will do it* (ibid. 36:35-36). The Chatam Sofer explains:

> It has become like the Garden of Eden, which is the greatest delight. But, a person cannot merit this unless he first suffers afflictions (as *Chazal* say, *Eretz Yisrael* is acquired only through

61 Based on *BeReishit* 24:31.

> suffering [*Berachot* 5a]). Here too, after we suffer afflictions, HaShem will save us. Now, if this were to occur at the time of the final redemption it would not be considered novel. Rather, [it will happen] when "I am in the midst of the exile."[62] Nevertheless, HaShem will exalt the pride of His nation. This is wondrous and beneficial providence from HaShem.
>
> This also explains the verse *This Land* [which was] *desolate has become like the Garden of Eden*. That is, HaShem will save the Jews after they suffer afflictions. This will occur when *the cities are fortified* [i.e., during the time of exile]. After all, at the time of the final redemption, *Jerusalem will be inhabited without walls* (*Zecharyah* 2:8). Now, however, while the Jews are still exiled among the nations, the cities of *Eretz Yisrael* are considered fortified. Nonetheless, *This Land...has become like the Garden of Eden*. From this, everyone will understand and recognize that HaShem, may He be blessed, is the One Who delivers His nation from all their troubles. He is the One Who removes their sorrow and sighing, and may He bring great joy to dejected souls. Amen.[63]

Thus, "Moshe the great scribe (*sofer*)" affirms that this prophecy refers to the time preceding the redemption. After we suffer afflictions, the Holy One Blessed be He, with His wondrous providence, will bring us to *Eretz Yisrael* by way of His messengers and by way of the circumstances that He will cause to arise. *Eretz Yisrael* will then become the Garden of Eden; and while we are there, God will sprinkle upon us a pure spirit so that we may serve Him with a perfect heart. Hence, I was correct when I said that our existence in the atmosphere of the foreign lands prevents us from receiving a pure spirit from above.

I subsequently discovered that the Or HaChayim HaKadosh agrees with our mentor, the Chatam Sofer... He comments on the verse *He shall remove his garments and put on other garments, and he shall take the ashes outside the camp to a pure place* (*VaYikra* 6:4):

> The first garments are [designated for a time when God will] bring justice to our persecutors. Now, however, He comes to benefit us and take us out of exile. Therefore, He will wear

62 Based on *Yechezkel* 1:1.

63 *Derashot Chatam Sofer, Parashat Parah* 5568 [1808].

> "garments of benevolence." He will not delay the ingathering of the exiles (until after the evil-doers are destroyed). Rather, He will immediately gather the exiles, remove us (from the camp of the wicked), and bring us to a pure place. This place is *Eretz Yisrael*, for the lands of the nations are impure; they, their soil, and even their atmosphere. There is no place which can be called pure except the Holy Land.[64]

Now, since the Holy One Blessed be He will be compelled to remove us speedily from the hands of the wicked ones, even before He destroys them, it must be that the Or HaChayim is referring to a time before the final redemption. For after the Savior arrives, *They will not hurt nor destroy* (*Yeshayah* 11:9), as is well known.

In any event, two "prophets" – our mentors, the Or HaChayim and the Chatam Sofer – have "prophesied" in the same manner. After we suffer intense adversity, HaShem, with His wondrous providence, will bring us to *Eretz Yisrael*. Now, it is obvious and clear that this "prophecy" refers to our generation. This is true and evident.

The severity of our exile

Tangentially, I would like to quote the *Or HaChayim HaKadosh* on the afflictions that will befall us during this exile:

> When the Torah says, *He shall separate the ashes* (*VaYikra* 6:3), it refers to the evil that our enemies perpetrated by afflicting and torturing us. Now, if you look carefully [you will see that this exile] is more severe than the Egyptian exile. In the Egyptian exile, they enslaved the Jews, but also fed and clothed them, as *Chazal* explain, "*We remember the fish which we ate in Egypt for free* (*BeMidbar* 11:5): They ate everything for free" (*Sifrei*). In the Ishmaelite exile, however, (fortunate is he who has not seen it) they enslave and embitter the lives of the Jews. Not only do they withhold wages, but they levy heavy taxes upon them. Furthermore, they rob a man of what he has and demand from him what he does not have. They make him drink this "cup" until he dies.

All of this, and more, has indeed happened to us today. However, I am astonished by our mentor's statement, for it seems to imply that he only speculated that our present exile is more severe than the Egyptian exile. How did his holy lips fail to mention that the *Yerushalmi* states this explicitly?

64 [The parenthetical comments are R. Teichtal's.]

> The bondage of the other exiles is more severe than the Egyptian bondage. From the bondage of Egypt, Moshe saw the Heavenly Chariot (*Merkavah*) as a brick, as it is written, *And under His feet was the likeness of sapphire brickwork* (*Shemot* 24:10). Yechezkel, on the other hand, saw the *Merkavah* in the image of a sapphire stone;[65] and a stone is harder than a brick. (*Yerushalmi, Sukkah* 4:3 [17b])

Thus, our Rabbis in the Talmud already foresaw that the subsequent exiles would be more difficult than the Egyptian exile.

Further on, the *Yerushalmi* states that the Holy One Blessed be He records for Himself, in the *Merkavah*, all of the pain and suffering of the exile, no matter how insignificant. Every time the nations degrade us, He records it in full detail, and He will exact retribution from them for the affront to Israel's honor.[66] None of what they do to us is concealed from Him, may His name be blessed.

The sole purpose of our afflictions is to arouse us to return to the Holy Land

Let us now return to the beginning. I explained above that the sole purpose of all the blows that we have received is to arouse us to return to our Holy Land. I heard a beautiful idea on this concept in the name of the brilliant and holy man of God, our mentor, R. Bunim of Peshischa. He explains the verse *Draw me, we will run after You* (*Shir HaShirim* 1:4):

When acquiring an animal there are two types of *meshichah* [a means of acquisition by way of pulling].[67] The first is when the purchaser calls the animal and it follows him. The second is when he strikes it with a stick and it runs before him. Each of these methods is considered an acquisition by way of *meshichah*. The only difference is that in the first one, where the "pulling" is effected by way of calling, the owner walks in front and the animal follows; while in the second one, where the "pulling" is effected by way of striking, the animal walks in front and the owner follows. Which type of *meshichah* does the animal prefer? The *meshichah* by way of calling, of course, because the animal feels no pain. The *meshichah* by way of hitting, on the other hand, hurts, and the animal suffers the pains of the blow.

We are in the same position before the Holy One Blessed be He regarding the call to return to *Eretz Yisrael*. If we heed God's voice

65 See *Yechezkel* 1:26 and 10:1.

66 ❖ This is also stated in *VaYikra Rabbah* (23) on *parashat Acharei*.

67 See *Kiddushin* 22b.

that calls us to return to our Land, then we will personify the aspect of *meshichah* by way of calling. We will not suffer any pain or afflictions. Rather, we will go eagerly without any external coercion. HaShem will lead us and we will follow. If, however, we do not strive to return to our Land willingly, and we wait until the staff comes and strikes us, the *meshichah* will be in the form of hitting... We will suffer the agony and pain of the staff of our enemies until they force us to run before HaShem to *Eretz Yisrael.*

This is the meaning of our plea to HaShem: *Draw me* (משכני), *we will run after You.* That is to say, acquire us through the type of *meshichah* (משיכה) in which *we will run after You*, meaning, like one who calls and the animal follows. Place in our hearts the desire to follow You and return to our Holy Land by way of Your call alone. For You call us through the *tzaddikim* of the generation who appeal to us, in Your name, to return to our forefathers' possession. Do not acquire us through the *meshichah* of the staff, in which we are unwilling to return, and the staff alone will force us to do so. For then, we would have to run before You, and You would follow us.

I will support R. Bunim's interpretation with a *Midrash*. The *Midrash* states that all of the afflictions that come upon the people of Israel are because they do not crave *Eretz Yisrael.* After being afflicted, however, they immediately run to *Eretz Yisrael* (*Midrash Tehillim* 17:4). Current events prove this, for every Jew would run to *Eretz Yisrael* if he only could. Even those who incessantly opposed the *aliyah* movement would go, if they were given permission to do so. This type of going, however, is in the form of "He strikes it with a stick and it runs before him." If only they would have listened to the call of the *tzaddikim* who aroused themselves to this cause, they would have followed them in the manner of *Draw me, we will run after You.* Then, all of the afflictions that we recently encountered would have been unnecessary.

This explains the following *Midrash*:

> Had you [Israel] been worthy, you would have read in the Torah, *You will bring them and implant them on the mountain of Your inheritance* (*Shemot* 15:17). But now that you were unworthy, you read, *Let all their wickedness come before You* (*Eichah* 1:22). (*Petichta DeEichah* 11)

This means, had you been worthy, the ascent to *Eretz Yisrael* would have been in the form of "Draw us and we will run after You," that is, by way of "He calls it and it follows." This is expressed by the verse, *You will bring them*, for when a person leads or brings someone to a certain place he walks in front while the other follows behind. But now that you were unworthy, because you did not want to follow the call of the *tzaddikim*, the return to *Eretz Yisrael* must come the second way, "He strikes it with a stick and it runs before him." It must arise through numerous and dreadful afflictions and hardships. Thus, you will cry out, *Let all their wickedness* (רעתם) *come before You*. That is to say, because of the misfortunes (רעות) that have befallen you, you ran before HaShem. Hence, the verse, *Let all their wickedness* (רעתם) *come before You*, means that the misfortunes (רעות) caused you to be in the category of *before You*, like the animal that runs before its owner. Today, we see that everyone runs to *Eretz Yisrael* because of the afflictions that overtake them. This matter is extremely accurate and true.

The author of *Kapot Temarim* interprets the verse, *She is Zion, no one cares about her* (*Yirmiyah* 30:17), as follows:

> The people of Israel were complaining about their troubles. Therefore, HaShem said: "Why do you complain? I am not incapable of bringing salvation, but what am I to do? Your sins caused this. No one cares about Zion. She cries out to Me that you do not remember her. How, then, can I remember and redeem you?"[68]

Thus, if we remember Zion and seek out her well-being, our troubles will desist.

V *Redemption Will Come at a Time of Extreme Hardship and Poverty*

Tikkunei Zohar Chadash explains the verse *I am the Lord, in its time I will hasten it* (*Yeshayah* 60:22):

> Our Sages have determined: If they are worthy, *I will hasten it* [the redemption], and if they are not worthy, *in its time* – in HaShem's time. We must understand what HaShem's time is, for there is a time and there is a time, as Kohelet said, *A time to weep and a time to laugh* (*Kohelet* 3:4). The secret of this matter is, when the time of weeping arrives, a time of adversity for

68 *Yom Teruah* on *Rosh HaShanah* 30a, s.v. *gemara*.

Israel, we will immediately be redeemed. It is thus written, *It is a time of trouble for Ya'akov, but he will be saved from it* (*Yirmiyah* 30:7).

The *Zohar* asks, there have been many troublesome times; who can distinguish that time from all others? [The answer is], it is a time of weeping. The secret of this matter is, *They will come with weeping* (ibid. 31:8), with the weeping of extreme poverty. For the numerical value of *with weeping* (בבכי) is equal to that of ôextreme povertyö (דל). When Moshe foresaw Israel's oppressive poverty it was said about him, *And behold, a boy was crying* (*Shemot* 2:6). What is written immediately after the crying? *And she had compassion on him* (ibid.). This refers to redemption.[69]

Thus, the *Zohar* teaches us that the era of *in its time* will arrive at *a time to weep*, as Kohelet said. That is to say, when there is a time of weeping, it is the time of redemption. We have, therefore, undoubtedly reached this epoch, for today one can hear sounds of weeping in every corner of every Jewish home, and one can see that the House of Israel has been greatly confounded. May the Merciful One save us!

I need not recount what has befallen our Jewish brethren in Poland, Slovakia, and the other European countries. The destruction that has occurred there is well known to all: the murders, the massacres, and the numerous cruelties against young and old. Communities have been destroyed, great communities which were filled with Torah scholars, rabbis, and young children who were flourishing in Torah and fear of Heaven. They were utterly banished[70] to a barren land, stripped of all possessions. My heart, my heart grieves for their slain! My innards, my innards grieve for their slain![71] Do we need any greater time of weeping than this?

Furthermore, the *Zohar*'s assertion that the weeping refers to oppression and extreme poverty has also come true in our days. Israel's possessions have been devoured. Woe to the eyes that have seen how the plunderers stripped the Jews of their money in the streets of Slovakia. They took all that they owned: clothes, household

69 *Tikkunei Zohar Chadash* 80b. Also see *Zohar* 1:146b, 2:12b, 3:278b; and *Tikkunei Zohar, Tikkun* 11, p. 26b.

70 Based on *Shemot* 11:1.

71 From the *Nachem* prayer recited in the *Minchah* service of Tish'a B'Av.

utensils, and anything that could be moved. They decreed that any Gentile who sees an object belonging to a Jew may demand it, and the Jew is obligated to hand it over. Thus, the Jews remained stripped and indigent, in fulfillment of the verse *Because of the plundering of the poor, because of the sighing of the needy, "Now I will arise," says the Lord* (*Tehillim* 12:6). But, we have not yet been privileged to see [the fulfillment of the end of the verse].

Not only have these evil rodents done this to our movable property, but also to our immovable property, like our houses and fields. They seized everything from us while we were still in their midst, and then they stole away our very lives by sending us into exile. And they did not allow us to flee wherever we pleased. Rather, they sent us to an unknown land where the deportees are dying of starvation.

Everything that I have described here is merely a drop in the ocean compared to the cruelties that they have inflicted upon us for no reason. It is only because we are descendants of Avraham, Yitzchak, and Ya'akov. All of the Jews of Europe are defenseless. Is there any greater oppression and poverty than this? Indeed, we fulfill the words of the prophet Tzefanyah, *And I will leave in your midst a poor and destitute people, and they will take refuge in the name of the Lord* (3:12); and the verse *And you will save the afflicted people* (II *Shmuel* 22:28).

This coincides with the *Zohar* which states that poverty will abound during the final exile, as it is written, *And I will leave in your midst a poor and destitute people, and they will take refuge in the name of the Lord.* This will happen in order to fulfill the verse, *And You will save the afflicted people.* The wealthy individuals of the time will not want to assist, and they will say that they cannot help because of heavy taxes. This, however, is a lie, and they will hide their money and possessions in their homes (*Zohar* 3:153a). The *Zohar* continues: The merciful, gracious, and kind individuals will not require purification [even] in lukewarm water – like average people – to achieve the refinement of the pangs of *Mashiach.* They certainly will not require purification in boiling water like the absolutely wicked people, about whom it is written, *Everything that comes into the fire, you shall pass through the fire* (*BeMidbar* 31:23).

This has actually come true, for there are many wealthy people today who could have revitalized the souls of their unfortunate brethren, but they did nothing. In the end, they lost their wealth, for it went to waste in the hands of the wicked Eisav, as we have seen in Slovakia. Thus, the words of the *Zohar* have been fulfilled: *Everything that comes into the fire, you shall pass through the fire,* [meaning], they have come into the fire of exile.

VI An Expression of Gratitude to American Jews for Their Support

Let us be grateful, though, to our Jewish brethren in America. Without the support of their Joint [Distribution Committee], which sent aid for as long as it could before the outbreak of the war, we would have died of starvation. Indeed, ever since the war put an end to their support, many of our Jewish brethren have suffered the disgrace of starvation, and many have died of hunger in Poland. The American Jews, however, are not causing the stoppage, for they are willing to send their aid even now. May HaShem remember this on their behalf, and may they be spared all troubles and hardships in this merit. The prophet says about them, *Through charity you shall be established* (*Yeshayah* 54:14), and our Sages comment, "Great is charity for it brings the redemption closer" (*Bava Batra* 10a).

Our mentor, the author of *Heishiv Moshe*, cites the following *Midrash* in his work, *Tefillah LeMoshe*:[72]

> In the future, all of the heavenly ministers will come to God and say, "Do You show partiality? Both the Gentiles and the Jews commit adultery and murder... Why are these any different than those?"[73] The Holy One Blessed be He will say to Micha'el, "Give them an answer." Micha'el will become silent, as it says, *And at that time Micha'el will stand* (*Daniel* 12:1), and standing refers to silence... The Holy One Blessed be He will say to Micha'el, "[Since] you were silent, I will answer them. [I will save] the Jews because of the charitable deeds (צדקה) that they did for one another," as it says, *I speak in righteousness* (צדקה), *mighty to save* (*Yeshayah* 63:1). (*Yalkut Shimoni* 2:507; *Petichta DeRuth Rabbah* 1)

I am certain that HaShem refers to our Jewish brethren in America when He answers, *I speak in righteousness*. By this merit they will be saved and will deserve to see Israel's salvation. They will also be spared the severity of the pangs of *Mashiach*, as the above-mentioned *Zohar* states: Those who are gracious and kind and have compassion

72 On *Tehillim* 106.

73 [I.e., why do the Gentiles descend to purgatory while the Jews do not?]

on the poor and destitute will only require a mild purification. This can be likened to a utensil used for cold foods; it only needs to be rinsed in cold water [in order to become kosher]. Similarly, the Jews of America, who have been immeasurably kind, have escaped the refinement of the pangs of *Mashiach* with only a mild purification.

The refinement of the pangs of Mashiach

You might ask, is it not true that our Jewish brethren in the United States and England are living peacefully, tranquilly, and honorably, as in days of old? They have not experienced even the slightest refinement. Yet, the refinement of the pangs of *Mashiach* must affect the entire Jewish nation before the final redemption, as it is written, *Many will become purified, cleansed, and refined* (*Daniel* 12:10).[74] The troubles that have befallen us have not reached them at all. How, then, can they be part of the refinement if it has not affected them in the slightest?

In truth, the hardships that we now experience have affected them as well. They have not been affected to the same degree as us, but they have been affected in some way, as I will explain, with God's help. Let me preface with a comment of the Maharal of Prague in *Gevurot HaShem*. He cites a *Midrash* on the verse *The Lord saved Israel on that day* (*Shemot* 14:30): Uza, the ministering angel of Egypt, complained that Israel had not yet completed their exile, for it was decreed to last 400 years. HaShem responded that the angel Micha'el will answer this. Micha'el, however, did not know how to respond, so HaShem said, "I will answer. I never said that Israel will be in Egypt for 400 years, rather, *in a land not their own* (*BeReishit* 15:13); and we calculate this from the birth of Yitzchak" (*Yalkut Shimoni* 1:241).

This requires explanation. Why was Micha'el unable to give the answer to which the verse clearly alludes? The brilliant and godly Maharal explains that no angel could actually discern Avraham Avinu's status as an exile and a stranger. Avraham Avinu had great wealth, and everyone considered him honorable and great, as it says, *You are a prince of God in our midst* (*BeReishit* 23:6). Furthermore, the *Midrash* states that the masses wanted to accept him as their king and god, but he refused, saying that the world did not require his kingship or divinity (*BeReishit Rabbah* 58:7). If Avraham was exceedingly great and respected, how could he be called a stranger, and how is it possible to say that he was in exile? We must conclude that his

74 ❖ See the *Zohar* mentioned above (3:153a).

exile and stranger status was indiscernible to any man; and even the angels were unable to perceive it. Only HaShem Himself could detect the most minuscule trace of exile and stranger status. Therefore, the angel Micha'el was unable to respond. Only HaShem Himself, in His glory, was able to do so.[75]

Based on this, the brilliant Maharim Padua, *av beit din* of Brisk, explains the statement in the *Haggadah*, "Blessed is HaShem, for the Holy One Blessed be He calculated the end [of the bondage] in order to do." That is to say, He Himself was the only one who was able to make the calculation of the end, and no one else.[76]

Hence, we see that there are many aspects of exile. Similarly, I maintain that although our misfortunes have not directly affected our fellow Jews in the United States and other countries, still, in some manner and in some small measure, they too have been affected. They commiserate with us in our adversity, and they weep with us, for their respect is degraded along with ours. Just think of it: when their gentile neighbors read in the newspapers or hear on the radio descriptions of the degradations that we undergo here, isn't their own self-esteem lowered? The Gentiles say, "Look at what is being done to their brothers there;" and because of this, the Jews are disgraced and despised in their eyes, to some degree. In addition, the Jews of America actually join us with their monetary support. All of this is insignificant compared to our misfortunes. Nonetheless, it is considered a minor refinement and a small-scale exile on their behalf. Hence, they, too, are included in the refinement of the pangs of *Mashiach* and have fulfilled their "obligation." The Holy One Blessed be He knows how to calculate the end of the exile in order to act for their sake as well.

Conclusion: We must take the initiative and God will do the rest

In any event, we have undoubtedly reached the time of redemption according to the above-mentioned *Zohar*. Now all we have to do is generate the initial awakening, and HaShem will bring our efforts to a successful end.*

---

* The holy volume, *Zichron Zot*, by our mentor, the man of God from Lublin *z"l*, explains the Midrashic dialogue between the Assembly of Israel (*Kenesset Yisrael*) and the Holy One Blessed be He. The

75 *Gevurot HaShem* 47.

76 *Nachalei Mayim* (Warsaw, 5643 [1883]), *Derush* 9 for *Shabbat HaGadol*, p. 30b.

Assembly of Israel says, *Bring us back* (*Eichah* 5:21), and the Holy One Blessed be He says, *Return unto Me* (*Malachi* 3:7).[77] It is as if God stubbornly awaits our initiative. The holy man of Lublin explains that the Holy One Blessed be He intends this for our own benefit. It is well known that the first redemptions were likened to a woman. A woman who suffers the pains of labor is delivered from her distress when the child is born, but she eventually experiences this pain once again. The same is true of the first redemptions. Even though the people of Israel were redeemed, they were enslaved again. The future redemption, however, is likened to a male who never experiences the pains of labor. This is clear from the *Midrash*.[78]

Chazal comment on the verse *When a woman emits seed and gives birth to a male* (*VaYikra* 12:2): "If the man emits seed first, she will give birth to a female. If the woman emits seed first, she will give birth to a male" (*Berachot* 60b). It follows, then, that if we want the Holy One Blessed be He to bring us redemption in the "male" manner,[79] the initial step must come from us, so that we will be like the woman[80] who emits seed first and gives birth to a male. If, however, the Holy One Blessed be He takes the first step, it will be like the man emitting seed first, and the redemption will be in the "female" manner – it will not be everlasting. The reason why the first redemptions were temporary is because they came about without Israel's initial awakening. The Holy One Blessed be He awakened Himself.

Therefore, now that the Holy One Blessed be He seeks our welfare – that we should never be reenslaved and that the redemption should be everlasting – He awaits our initial awakening so that we will be like a woman who emits seed first and gives birth to a male. (This concludes his holy words, which he wrote several times in the above-mentioned volume.)[81] Since this has been revealed to us by the Rebbe of Lublin, who possessed *Ruach HaKodesh*, we must no longer tarry. We must take the initiative and return to our Holy Land. Then, HaShem will show us compassion and complete our redemption for the good. Amen. So may it be God's will.

77 See *Eichah Rabbah* 5:21.
78 See *Mechilta, BeShalach, Parashat HaShirah* 1.
79 [That is, if we want the redemption to be everlasting.]
80 [In Kabbalistic terms, the Assembly of Israel is considered the female, and God, the male.]
81 *Zichron Zot, Tetzaveh*, s.v. *midrash*. See also his novellae to *Berachot* (Germany, 5707 [1947]), p. 153.

Our main obligation is to awaken ourselves to return to our Holy Land, for that is the sole purpose of all of the hardships that we now experience, as I elaborated above. Then we will see the fulfillment of the verse *And the Children of Israel were going out with a high hand* (*Shemot* 14:8). Amen, so may HaShem say.

This concludes the first chapter (פרק ראשון). May HaShem protect us like the pupil of His eye (כאישון). And, may we merit to build Zion and Jerusalem which are called "the first" (ראשון).[82]

I have completed this on the Monday of the week in which we read, *And the Children of Israel were going out with a high hand,*[83] in the year 5703 [1943], here in the capital, Budapest.

82 See *Shemot Rabbah* 15:1. [I inserted the Hebrew words in parentheses to show that they rhyme.]

83 *Parashat BeShalach*.

CHAPTER TWO

DELIVERANCE AND REDEMPTION

I *The Ways of Redemption*

HaShem will redeem us even if we are unworthy

א * The book of *Melachim* (II 14:26-27) states: *For the Lord saw that Israel's affliction was very bitter. And there was none surviving and none remaining and there was no helper for Israel. But the Lord did not speak to erase the name of Israel from under the heavens, so He saved them by the hand of Yerovam ben Yoash.* The *Midrash Tanchuma*[1] comments:

> *But the Lord did not speak...* Why is Yerovam mentioned here? Was he not an idolater? The explanation is that [he deserved this] because he did not listen to gossip about Amos. At that time, the generation and its leader worshipped idols. Nevertheless, [God said], "The Land which I promised to give to the descendants of Avraham, Yitzchak, and Ya'akov,[2] give it over into the hands of he who did not listen to gossip." They say: that which was not given over into the hands of Yehoshua bin Nun and David, king of Israel, was given over into Yerovam's hands, as it says, *So He saved them by the hand of Yerovam ben Yoash.*[3]

Thus, when the Almighty wants to save Israel from exceedingly dire circumstances, He saves them even by way of the most wicked person, like an idolater. [However, this is] only when He finds in

* [Starting here, the author divides each chapter into sections. We left the Hebrew letters in, in order to facilitate comparison with the original.]

1 This Midrash does not appear in the *Tanchuma*, but in *Yalkut Shimoni* 2:232.

2 See *Shemot* 33:1, *Devarim* 34:4.

3 The *Yalkut* version reads, "As it says, *He restored the boundary of Israel* (II *Melachim* 14:25)."

him the virtuous, humanistic trait of love and unity, whose foundation is the rejection of gossip. Furthermore, that which was not given to the greatest *tzaddikim* like Yehoshua bin Nun and King David, was given to him, even though he and the entire generation were undeserving and unworthy (as stated in the *Midrash*).

It seems to me that the reason for this appears in the Sforno on the verse *I am God Almighty, be fruitful and multiply* (*BeReishit* 35:11):

> You need not worry that your offspring will perish (in the hands of the nations), even if they are unworthy. This is so because I do not need a suitable subject, for *I am God Almighty*. I will fulfill My word in any event, even without a suitable subject.

That is to say, He does not need any reason. Therefore, He will fulfill His word even if Israel is unworthy.

I discovered the following in the introduction to *Mishpetei Ya'akov*, a book on topics in the Talmud written by a brilliant scholar from Latvia.[4] He explains the prophecy *For the mountains will depart and the hills will be removed, but My kindness will not be removed from you* (*Yeshayah* 54:10). HaShem's kindness does not depend on any other cause, for if it did, the moment the cause would disappear the effect would also disappear. This can be compared to the mountains and the hills which hang upon the foundations of the earth. If the earth would move from its place, the mountains and hills would tumble down, as actual, natural phenomena demonstrate. Many mountains have sunk to the depths of the earth because of the shifting of the ground beneath them. This happens because the mountains and hills depend on an external cause, and when that cause dissolves, so do they. The kindness of HaShem, on the other hand, does not depend on any other cause. Therefore, it will never falter. This is the meaning of the verse *For the mountains will depart and the hills will be removed, but My kindness will not be removed from you*. This coincides with the Sforno's comments.

Our mentor, the Maharal, writes in *Netzach Yisrael* that none of God's prophetic promises to Israel are dependent on or bound by any

4 ❖ The owner of a flour business, [R. Ya'akov Aryeh Leib Kastin] is a disciple of our master, the brilliant R. Yitzchak Elchanan Spektor *z"l*. When I was in Kovno, in the summer of 5697 [1937], he honored me with this wondrous volume. An absolute genius, he sustains himself by the sweat of his brow, an attribute that is not found in these lands. May the merit of his Torah stand by him during these difficult times.

condition whatsoever. Even if we fail to do the will of HaShem (God forbid) He will fulfill His promises through us.[5]

Our mentor, the Rambam, writes in *Iggeret Teiman*:

> HaShem, may He be blessed, strengthened us with the good tiding that it is impossible for Him to reject us as a collective entity, even if we anger Him and transgress His *mitzvot*. For it is written, *Thus says the Lord: "If the heavens above could be measured and the foundations of the earth searched out beneath, then I too would reject the entire seed of Israel because of all that they have done," says the Lord, God* (*Yirmiyah* 31:36).[6]

The Noam Elimelech agrees:

> The entirety of Israel is righteous, as it says, *Your people are all righteous* (*Yeshayah* 60:21). Therefore, even though individuals occasionally sin, the whole [of Israel] always retains its sanctity, and there is no adversary nor evil affliction in them, God forbid. Their form is forever engraved [before God] above.[7]

It seems to me that the prophet's comparison of the entirety of Israel to the measurement of the heavens above hints to this comment of the Noam Elimelech. He states that the whole of Israel is perfect and flawless and their form is engraved [before God] above. Thus, the prophet declares that just as it is impossible to measure the heavens above, so too, it is impossible to measure the value of Israel, for they exist on the heavenly throne above. It is also impossible to search them out below, for they are the foundations of the earth, even at a time when they fail to do the will of the Omnipresent (God forbid).

Since this is so, we can be sure that HaShem will redeem us from this final, bitter exile, no matter what; as He promised in the Torah, the Prophets, and the Writings. We recite this in the *kiddush* and prayers of *Rosh Hashanah*: "Your words are true and enduring forever." The Beit Yosef writes (as one possible explanation) that this refers to the promise of redemption. That is to say, HaShem will fulfill His words and redeem us,[8] speedily in our days. Amen.

5 *Netzach Yisrael* 11.

6 *Iggrot HaRambam*, p. 129.

7 *Noam Elimelech, Devarim*, p. 88a. (In the Mossad HaRav Kook edition: vol. 2, p. 472.)

8 *Beit Yosef, Orach Chayim* 582 (end), s.v. *u'devarcha*.

The manner of redemption depends on our deeds

ב However, the manner of redemption – whether it occurs through outright, manifest miracles or miracles concealed in nature – depends on our deeds and our behavior. If we conduct ourselves according to the ways of the Torah, by fulfilling all the *mitzvot* that are written in the holy Torah, then we will deserve an unmitigated redemption with revealed and apparent miracles, above and beyond nature. However, if we fail to do the will of the Omnipresent (God forbid), then the redemption will occur through miracles hidden in nature, and it will develop naturally. The Talmud states this explicitly:

> R. Alexandri said: "R. Yehoshua ben Levi pointed out a contradiction. It says, *And behold, with the clouds of heaven, one like the son of man came* (*Daniel* 7:13). It also says, *Your king will come to you...poor and riding upon a donkey* (*Zecharyah* 9:9). [The resolution is]: If they are worthy – *with the clouds of heaven*. If they are unworthy – *poor and riding upon a donkey*." (*Sanhedrin* 98a)

That is to say, if we are worthy, the redemption will come in the form of *clouds of heaven*, which refers to manifest miracles. If we are unworthy, it will happen naturally. Thus, *poor and riding on a donkey* (חמור) refers to the materialism (חמריות) of nature, the element of poverty as opposed to grandeur, as the Or HaChayim HaKadosh writes.[9] He also explains that the *Zohar*'s assertion that the final redemption will occur miraculously[10] is only true if we are deserving. If we are undeserving, it will occur naturally (at this time I do not have the source in front of me to quote his holy words directly).[11]

In the *Mar'eh Yechezkel Haggadah*, I found a comment by the author's son, the brilliant author of Responsa *Sha'arei Tzedek*:

> The final redemption will essentially occur with manifest miracles, as it is written, *As in the days of your coming out of the land of Egypt, I will show it wonders* (*Michah* 7:15). But, some say that it will occur naturally (see inside where he cites this in the name of earlier authorities).[12] Let us suggest that it depends on whether or not the people of Israel are worthy. That

9 *VaYikra* 25:27. Also see *BeReishit* 49:11.

10 See *Sha'arei Zohar* by R. Reuven Margolis *zt"l, Sanhedrin* 98a, s.v. *zachu achishenah*.

11 *Or HaChayim HaKadosh, BeMidbar* 24:17.

12 Ya'avetz (beginning of *Or HaChayim*) and R. Sa'adya Gaon.

which comes in a natural manner does not come all at once. Rather, it evolves gradually, constantly changing forms. For example, when planting a tree, time and [many] transformations are required until it bears fruit. The staff of Aharon, however, blossomed instantaneously.[13] This is the aspect of, "If they are worthy – *I will hasten it*" (*Sanhedrin* 98a), by way of manifest miracles, which come swiftly. If they are unworthy, however, the redemption will still take place, but by natural means. And this requires time for development. This is the aspect of, "If they are unworthy – *in its time*" (ibid.). That is to say, time will be needed for the development of the natural process.[14]

This explains *Chazal*'s statement in the *Midrash*:

> One verse says, *A tower* (מגדול) *of salvation* (II *Shmuel* 22:51), while another verse says, *Great* (מגדיל) *salvation* (*Tehillim* 18:51). R. Yudan answers: "The redemption of this nation does not come all at once, but little by little. What does מגדיל mean? [Salvation] grows (מתגדלת) progressively for the people of Israel. If the redemption would come all at once, they would not be able to endure it because of the great hardships they now experience... Therefore, it comes little by little and grows progressively.
>
> The redemption is compared to the dawn, as it says, *Then your light will burst forth like the dawn* (*Yeshayah* 58:8). Why is it compared to the dawn? The hour closest to morning is the darkest one. If the entire sun would rise at that time, all of creation would be entrapped. Hence, the morning star rises first and illuminates the world. Afterwards, the sun rises and gives forth its light, and no creature becomes entrapped, as it is written, *And the path of the righteous is like the gleam of sunlight, growing brighter until the height of noon* (*Mishley* 4:18)." (*Midrash Tehillim* 18:36)

This *Midrash* speaks of a natural redemption. Therefore, it must come little by little – similar to the gradual rising of the sun – in order not to harm the people of Israel. If redemption occurs miraculously, however, it will come all at once, because when the Jews do the will of God, thus gaining the status of "worthy ones,"

13 [See *BeMidbar* 17:16-26.]

14 *Mar'eh Yechezkel* (Premyshl: 5654 [1894]), p. 25a.

they do not encounter great hardships. Therefore, they are able to tolerate the intense light of redemption, and it can come all at once. However, when they are sinful and gain the status of "unworthy ones," they are sure to encounter birthpangs of *Mashiach* and great suffering.[15] Therefore, they are unable to tolerate an instantaneous, intense light, and the salvation and redemption must come little by little, in the form of a natural process. This is true and clear.

Proofs that the redemption will occur naturally

The *Yerushalmi* concurs:

> R. Chiya the great and R. Shimon ben Chalafta were walking in the Arbel valley at dawn when they saw the glimmering of the morning star. R. Chiya the great said to R. Shimon ben Chalafta: "My master, so is the redemption of Israel – at first little by little, but as it progresses it grows greater and greater." Why so? *When I sit in darkness, the Lord is a light unto me* (*Michah* 7:8).
>
> Similarly: At first, *Mordechai was sitting in the king's gate* (*Esther* 2:21). Afterwards, *Haman took the garment* (ibid. 6:11). Then, *Mordechai returned to the king's gate* (ibid. 6:12). Afterwards, *Mordechai left the king's presence in royal apparel* (ibid. 8:15). And finally, *The Jews had light* (ibid. 8:16). (*Yoma* 3:2 [13a], *Berachot* 1:1 [4b])

The *Midrash* on the verse, *Who is this that gazes down like the dawn* (*Shir HaShirim* 6:10), agrees with this principle: "This is how the redemption of Israel sprouts forth; at first it comes little by little..." (*Shir HaShirim Rabbah* 6:10).

This idea is also found in the *Zohar* on the verse *Let me go, for dawn has broken* (*BeReishit* 32:26):

> R. Yehudah began: *Who is this that gazes down like the dawn, beautiful as the moon, clear as the sun, awesome as an army with banners* (*Shir HaShirim* 6:10). Our Sages explain this verse as follows: *Who is this that gazes down* refers to the people of Israel. When the Holy One Blessed be He elevates them and takes them out of exile, He will open for them a very minute orifice of light. Afterwards, He will open a slightly larger opening, until the Holy One Blessed be He will open for them the heavenly gates which are open to the four corners of the world... This can be compared to a man who...has always lived

15 ❖ As the Or HaChayim HaKadosh (*VaYikra* 25:27) and Rashi (*Sanhedrin* 97b, s.v. *dayo le'avel*) explain.

> in darkness. When people want to provide him light, they must first open an orifice like the eye of a needle, and afterwards, slightly larger...
>
> The same is true of Israel, as it is written, *Little by little, I will drive them away from you* (*Shemot* 23:30)... The light of Israel illuminates little by little, until they [Israel] gain strength, and the Holy One Blessed be He will shine [His] light upon them forever. Everyone will ask about them and say, *Who is this that gazes down like the dawn? The dawn* (שחר) refers to the darkness (שחרית) of the morning, which is the strong darkness that precedes the exceedingly faint, morning light. Afterwards, *beautiful as the moon*, for the moon's light is greater than that of dawn. And after that, *clear as the sun*, whose strong light illuminates more than the moon. And finally, *awesome as an army with banners*, which means, powerful, with an intense light.
>
> Come and see: When it is dark and the light is concealed, and the morning begins to glimmer, [the sky] first illuminates little by little until the light increases to its proper brightness. So too, when the Holy One Blessed be He will arouse Himself to enlighten the Congregation of Israel, He will first shine a light like that of dawn (שחר), which is black (שחור). Afterwards, *beautiful as the moon*; after that, *clear as the sun*; and finally, *awesome as an army with banners*. (*Zohar* 1:170a)

A hymn (*piyut*) which we recite on the second Sabbath after *Pesach* states, "The third *keitz*[16] of Daniel has been crowned, and the fourth *keitz* is concealed from all eyes."[17] Thus, there will be a third and a fourth *keitz*. The third *keitz* will occur in the manner stated above, with the permission of the rulers of the nations. This will serve as a preparation for the fourth *keitz* which is concealed from all eyes.

This also appears in the *Zohar* on *parashat Pinchas*: "There will eventually be four redemptions, corresponding to the four cups of *Pesach*" (3:252a). (Also see *Zohar, parashat VaYakhel* [2:216b].)

The *Midrash* states:

> When the Holy One Blessed be He reveals His *Shechinah* to Israel, He will not reveal it all at once. For if He would reveal

16 *Keitz* - a reckoned time for the coming of *Mashiach*.

17 *Siddur Otzar HaTefillot*, vol. 2, p. 130b, end of s.v. *shenoteinu*. ❖ This is also found in *Sifrei Zuta* (*BeMidbar*, 7:84) cited in *Yalkut Shimoni* (*Naso*, 717).

> all of His goodness at once, everyone would die, because they cannot tolerate [so much] good. Therefore, He reveals Himself little by little. (*Tanchuma, Devarim* 1)

The holy *Zohar* says, "When the Congregation of Israel returns to its place, the Holy King will return to His place, to Zion" (2:55b). Thus, first the Congregation of Israel must return to its place, and only then the Holy King will return to Zion.

Three Kabbalists – the K'li Paz,[18] Sh'tei Yadot,[19] and Rabbeinu Bachya[20] – explain that the verse, *He completes the counsel of His messengers* (*Yeshayah* 44:26), indicates that HaShem will not initiate [the redemption]. Rather, after Israel returns to the Land, HaShem will complete [the process]. *The counsel of His messengers* refers to natural processes, which are God's messengers.[21] [That is to say, when the Jews initiate these processes], HaShem will complete their work.

Hence, our veritable Sages explain that *Mashiach* will not come to the people of Israel suddenly like a flowing river [to redeem them] instantaneously from darkness to great light, as so many Jews imagine. Rather, they will ascend gradually, from one level to the next. Once they are accustomed to one level they will move on to the next, until they gradually reach the highest level on the ladder ascending to the House of God. An instantaneous elevation from the lowest extreme to the highest extreme is highly unrealistic. Also, the Children of Israel would not be able to cope with such abundant good. This is similar to a person who has recently recovered from a difficult and dangerous illness. Due to his intense weakness, he cannot suddenly indulge in an excess of food and other physical pleasures. This is also similar to a person who is sleeping in a dark room. If someone would suddenly shine a bright light upon him, he would not be able to enjoy the luster of light.[22] The *Yerushalmi* and *Zohar* (cited above) use the same parable. The same is true of Israel's redemption; it will come upon us gradually, not all at once.

18 We were unable to locate this source.

19 We were unable to locate this source.

20 See *Kad HaKemach* (*Nun* - נחמו) where Rabbeinu Bachya discusses this concept. He does not, however, mention this verse.

21 ❖ See *Menorat HaMe'or*, Sermon for *Shavuot* (Third *Ner*, 4:5:1). (Mossad HaRav Kook, p. 310.)

22 [This is an almost exact quote from a letter written by R. Chayim David Chazan, as cited in the approbations (p. 6).]

The reason why the redemption will occur naturally

It seems to me that the reason for this is based on the *Midrash*'s comment: "The Holy One Blessed be He said, 'If I look at Israel's deeds, they will never be redeemed. Upon whom, then, shall I look? Upon their holy forefathers' " (*Shemot Rabbah* 15:4). In *Even Sheleimah*, the Vilna Gaon also writes that the redemption will only occur by merit of our Patriarchs. We therefore say in *Shemoneh Esrei*, "He remembers the kindness of the Patriarchs and brings a redeemer to their children's children."[23] Thus, since we will not deserve redemption, it will not occur through manifest miracles, but miracles disguised in nature. Therefore, it will happen little by little, not all at once.

Apparently, this is the reason why the prophets called *Mashiach "Tzemach"* (the sprouting one), as it says, *For behold, I am bringing My servant, Tzemach* (*Zecharyah* 3:8); *Behold, there is a man whose name is Tzemach and he will sprout forth out of his place* (ibid. 6:12); *I will raise a righteous sprout from David* (*Yirmiyah* 23:5). We also recite this in our prayers: "May You speedily cause the sprout of Your servant David to sprout forth." The brilliant author of *Ezrat Kohanim*, quoting *Shiltei Giborim*, explains that Zerubavel was called *Tzemach*[24] "because just like a plant (*tzemach*) grows little by little, so too, his eminence will increase little by little until it is great."[25] This is also why *Mashiach* is called *Tzemach*, because his and Israel's eminence will ascend little by little until it is very great, just like a plant.

It is clear from all of this that our future salvation will sprout forth naturally, i.e., through miracles disguised in nature. Therefore, time will be needed for this natural process to develop.

This can also be proven from the words of our mentors, the Maharal and the Ya'avetz, cited in the first chapter.[26] They explain that the suffering of the pangs of *Mashiach* serve as 'the absence' before 'the existence'. The Ya'avetz supports this with the Talmudic statement that [the chick] hatches when the egg decays (*Temurah* 31a). Thus, they compare the development of the redemption to the development of an egg. Just as an egg develops naturally, so too, our redemption develops naturally.

Consider this matter closely, for all of the sources that I cited in these introductory remarks flow from the pure wellspring of our

23 *Even Sheleimah* 11:9.

24 *Zecharyah* 3:8 and 6:12.

25 *Ezrat Kohanim, Middot* 3:8, vol. 2, p. 80, s.v. *ha'atarot.*

26 Pp. 95-96.

Rabbis of the Talmud, *Zohar, Yerushalmi*, and *Midrash*, as well as great sages like the Maharal and the Ya'avetz who possessed *Ruach HaKodesh*.

Israel will return to Eretz Yisrael before Mashiach arives

ג After I have explained, with God's help, that the redemption, for which we so fervently yearn, will occur gradually, step by step, we can understand a comment found in the *Derashot* of the Chatam Sofer. He infers from the Rambam[27] that Israel will gather together in *Eretz Yisrael* before the advent of *Mashiach*, even though the *Beit HaMikdash* is not yet rebuilt.[28]

I discovered something similar in *Sh'vilei Emunah*, by the grandson of our mentor, the Rosh. He cites a *Midrash*[29] which says that many Jews from the four corners of the earth will volunteer to live and settle in *Eretz Yisrael* before the final redemption. When many people dwell there and pray frequently on the Holy Mountain, the Creator will listen [to their prayers] and hasten the final redemption.[30] The righteous *gaon*, R. Hillel of Kalamoya, cites this in his responsa, *Beit Hillel*.[31] Consequently, he wrote a very enthusiastic letter to the brilliant R. Zalman Spitzer of Vienna urging him to convince Baron Rothschild to become involved in this matter and finance it with his own capital. He reasoned that matters like this require the assistance of the wealthy Jews.❖ R. Hillel writes there, "Who among Israel, HaShem's nation, would not desire to take part in this *mitzvah*?"

A certain great rabbi enlightened me to Rashi's comments on the verses: *For God will save Zion and build the cities of Judah, and they will dwell there and possess it. And the offspring of His servants will inherit it, and those who love His name will dwell in it. For the conductor, by David, as a remembrance* (*Tehillim* 69:36 – 70:1). Rashi writes:

❖ The *Midrash* relates that in the days of R. Yehoshua ben Chananyah, the king gave the Jews permission to ascend to *Eretz Yisrael* and build the *Beit HaMikdash*. R. Yehoshua ben Chananyah delegated two extremely wealthy Jews to finance the endeavor (*BeReishit Rabbah* 64:10).

27 *Sanhedrin* 1:3.

28 *Derush* (sermon) delivered on 27 Elul, 5580 [1820].

29 Perhaps he is referring to the statement cited in *Yalkut Shimoni* (2:888) and *Midrash Tanchuma* (*Noach* 11): "There is an Aggadic tradition that Jerusalem will only be rebuilt after the exiles are gathered..."

30 *Sh'vilei Emunah*, Tenth *Netiv*, chap. 1.

31 Sec. 31.

> *By David, as a remembrance*: This is an expression of prayer... *Midrash Tehillim* (ibid.) compares this to a king who became angry with his flock. He, [therefore], destroyed its pen and banished the sheep and the shepherd. After a while, he retrieved the sheep and rebuilt the pen, but did not remember the shepherd. The shepherd said, "The sheep have returned; the pen is rebuilt; but I have been forgotten!" So too here. Above, it states, *For God will save Zion..., and those who love His name will dwell in it*. The pen is built, the sheep are gathered in, but the shepherd has been forgotten. Therefore, it says, *By David, as a remembrance*.

That is to say, David prayed that he, too, would return with Israel to his place. It is clear from this Rashi that Israel will return to *Eretz Yisrael* and build the Land before the Son of David arrives. Then, David will ask HaShem to allow him to return to the people of Israel, since they have already returned. This is a wondrous proof for the words of the Rambam cited above.

Eretz Yisrael will become a focal point for Jews throughout the world

It seems to me that the reason for this [order of events] is based on a comment of the Chatam Sofer himself.[32] He writes that

> the height of our evil lot is dispersion and exile. For even though the *Beit HaMikdash* was destroyed, had we remained in *Eretz Yisrael* matters would not have been so bad. Similarly, the Rambam writes, "The murder of Gedalyah ben Achikam caused the flame of Israel to be extinguished and the Jews to be dispersed among the exiles, due to our numerous sins."[33]

Now, I already mentioned that our Sages in the *Zohar, Midrash*, and *Yerushalmi* assert that the redemption will progress gradually, not all at once. Therefore, the ingathering of the Jews to *Eretz Yisrael* must precede the true redemption. First, they must leave the state of absolute evil, which is dispersion and exile, and proceed to the middle level of evil, which is when the people of Israel are in their Land but the Temple is in ruins. After this, peace will prevail among the Jews and there will be hope for the future, as the Chatam Sofer writes (ibid.). By virtue of this peace, the sons will return to their borders,[34] the *Beit HaMikdash* will be rebuilt, and there will be no

32 *Derashot Chatam Sofer*, vol. 3, p. 299, s.v. *vehineh bechol*.

33 *Hilchot Ta'anit* 5:2.

34 Based on *Yirmiyah* 31:16.

hatred among the Jews, like there was at the time of the destruction of the Second Temple.

I would like to add to the Chatam Sofer's holy words and explain how the ingathering to *Eretz Yisrael* will diminish the dispersion of the exiles even though it will occur before the rebuilding of the *Beit HaMikdash*. At the very beginning, it will be impossible for the entire nation to assemble in *Eretz Yisrael*, for the Land will have to first expand her "skin" to make room for all of her sons.[35] Therefore, some Jews will remain in the Diaspora until HaShem fulfills His promise to gather all of Israel into the Land. This coincides with the Ramban's comments on the verse *The Lord, God, Who gathers the dispersed of Israel says, "I will gather others to him, besides those already gathered to him"* (*Yeshayah* 56:8). He explains that God will gather many, but not all, of the dispersed Jews at the outset [of redemption]. Then, after the wars of Gog and Magog, there will be a second ingathering, as it says, *I will gather others to him, besides those already gathered to him.*[36]

Now, [even though all of Israel will not return right away], it seems to me that the Land will become a universal center for the entire Jewish nation, by the very fact that there will be an assembly of Jews in Jerusalem and *Eretz Yisrael*. Even those who remain in the Diaspora will keep their eyes and hearts on the Land. They will be bound and connected with all their souls to the universal center which will be established in *Eretz Yisrael*. It will unite them even in the Diaspora, and they will not be considered dispersed at all...

Today, on the other hand, the people of Israel are like lost and scattered sheep[37] among the nations. No Jew associates with his fellow Jew. Wherever they live, they are like dangling limbs without any connection to the individual, and certainly not to the community as a whole. This is true and utter dispersion (may the Merciful One save us). We have all been abandoned like fish of the sea. In these recent, difficult years, despots subjugate us and do with us as they please. They degrade and murder us without limit and without any liability for their actions. These scoundrels have no one to answer to for their deeds.

However, if we establish a universal center in *Eretz Yisrael* (with

35 ❖ It is well known that *Chazal* compare *Eretz Yisrael* to a deer, [whose skin expands to fit over its flesh] (*Gittin* 57a).

36 Commentary to *Shir HaShirim* attributed to the Ramban, 8:13.

37 Based on *Yirmiyah* 50:17.

God's help), our pride and glory will rise among the nations and we will be considered a dignified and important nation.❖ Then, even the individual who remains in exile will not be forsaken, because anyone who wants to cause him harm will know that there is someone who will demand a reckoning of his actions. He will know that he is liable for his deeds and will, therefore, refrain from doing anything improper.

Thus, the ingathering to the Land will free us from the state of absolute evil even in the Diaspora. It will also cause all of Israel, even the Diaspora Jews, to unite and live in peace. Then, we will reach the bright and hopeful future leading to the complete redemption, speedily in our days. Amen.

Eretz Yisrael expands for the Jewish people

ד Furthermore, it seems to me that if the Almighty agrees to gather the people of Israel into *Eretz Yisrael* by way of His earthly messengers,❖❖ the Land could receive all of her children even before the *Beit HaMikdash* is rebuilt. Not a single soul would be left in exile, if they wish to enter the Land.

Let me preface with the words of the Rama of Panow. He was asked to explain the Talmudic statement "The Sages spoke in exaggerated terms (הבאי)" (*Tamid* 29a). This is problematic, for the Talmud states elsewhere that even the casual conversations of our Sages require analysis (*Avodah Zarah* 19b). What can be learned from exaggerations? He answers as follows:

> Not only the Sages, but even the Torah spoke in exaggerated terms: *Cities great and fortified to the sky* (*Devarim* 1:28)! The prophets spoke in exaggerated terms: When Shlomo was anointed it says, *The earth split open from their noise* (I *Melachim* 1:40)!

❖ The *Midrash* comments on the verse *Ascribe to the Lord, O families of peoples, ascribe to the Lord honor and might* (*Tehillim* 96:7): "When you [Gentiles] bring them [the people of Israel], do not bring them in a disgraceful manner, but with honor and might" (*Yalkut Shimoni* 2:838).

❖❖ The Abarbanel writes in *Mashmia Yeshuah*, "This miracle will occur through the nations themselves."[38] The Maharivach concurs and writes that HaShem will cause the gentile kings to recognize the truth.[39]

38 *Mashmia Yeshuah*, p. 25.

39 Introduction to *Ein Ya'akov*.

> The masters of *Aggadah* explain that *Cities great and fortified to the sky* is meant literally. The cities of *Eretz Yisrael* are fortified up in heaven, because the ministering angels of the seventy nations do not enter the atmosphere of *Eretz Yisrael*.[40]
>
> We can explain the verse, *The earth split open from their noise*, in a similar fashion. *Eretz Yisrael* sometimes shrinks, as it says, *The Land upon which you lie* (*BeReishit* 28:13);[41] and sometimes it expands, as it says, *It became broader and turned upwards* (*Yechezkel* 41:7). This is why it is called "The Land of the Deer."[42] During Shlomo's reign, as well, the earth split open and expanded as much as existing conditions would allow, because he was destined to sit on the throne of the Lord.[43]

Further on, he cites every place where *Chazal* say, "The Sages spoke in exaggerated terms," and demonstrates how all of their words are significant and contain invaluable lessons. He writes:

> The letters of the word הבאי (exaggerations) represent **ה**נה **ב**רכו **א**ת **י**-ה-ו-ה – Behold, bless the Lord. For, there is not a word of nonsense in their statements. And certainly their casual conversations require analysis.

I would like to add to his holy words. During Shlomo's reign it was essential for *Eretz Yisrael* to expand and split open in all directions, for it says, *Israel was numerous like the sand of the sea* (I *Melachim* 4:20). Thus, since Israel assembled together in great numbers, the Land expanded and split open in all directions, even though the *Beit HaMikdash* was not yet built (for this occurred at Shlomo's inauguration which preceded the building of the *Beit HaMikdash*). This is *Eretz Yisrael*'s eternal nature; at times it contracts and at times it expands. It all depends on the needs of the Jews who dwell there.

In his annotations to *Mishnah Avot*, R. Yosef Sha'ul elucidates the following *Mishnah*: "Nor did any man say to his friend, 'There is not enough room for me to stay overnight in Jerusalem' " (*Avot* 5:5):

40 See Ramban, *VaYikra* 18:25; *Zohar*, 2:130a; and *Nitzotzei Zohar*, ibid. 6.

41 [Rashi explains that "The Holy One Blessed be He folded all of *Eretz Yisrael* underneath him (Ya'akov)..."]

42 *Daniel* 11:16, *Yechezkel* 20:6. [See *Gittin* 57a, which explains that just as the skin of a deer expands to fit its body, so too, *Eretz Yisrael* expands to accommodate the Jewish people.]

43 *Teshuvot Rama MiPanow*, sec. 73.

Our Rabbis state that *Eretz Yisrael* is called the Land of the Deer (*Gittin* 57a). This can be compared to a man who makes a garment for a young child. He folds it over and makes pleats so that when the child grows up the garment will grow with him. The same is true of *Eretz Yisrael*. If the Jews do not dwell there, it contracts. This is a sign that *Eretz Yisrael* belongs to the people of Israel. If they do settle there it expands in proportion to the amount of people dwelling there. And when they would come for the three festive holidays it would expand even more, and there was sufficient place for all to stay overnight. This was a great miracle.

In truth, the words of these *gaonim* are stated explicitly in the *Midrash* on the verse *When the Lord your God will enlarge your border* (*Devarim* 12:20):

> Is it possible that the Holy One Blessed be He will enlarge *Eretz Yisrael*? R. Yitzchak said: "A man does not know how wide or how long a scroll is until it is unrolled and revealed. The same is true of *Eretz Yisrael*. It consists mostly of mountains and valleys, as it says, *But the Land into which you cross over to possess it is a Land of mountains and valleys..., a Land that the Lord your God seeks out; the eyes of the Lord your God are always upon it...* (ibid. 11:11-12). When the Holy One Blessed be He straightens it out – as it is written, *Every valley will be raised, and every mountain and hill will be lowered, and the crooked will be made straight, and the rough places, a plain* (*Yeshayah* 40:4) – then its [true dimensions] will be known. (*Devarim Rabbah* 4:11)

Clearly, this *Midrash* encompasses all the words of our brilliant masters mentioned above. When the people of Israel dwell in the Land, they become aware of its limitless and immeasurable size. It always expands according to the size of its Jewish settlement. Therefore, the fact that *Eretz Yisrael* is presently undersized will not prevent HaShem from gathering us all into the Land, whenever He desires. For, the Land will open up like a scroll and expand in all directions according to our needs. There will be enough room for all those who ascend to her. The Tashbetz writes that this miracle occurred in his days as well.[44] When his community, along with all

44 *Teshuvot Tashbetz* 3:201 (end).

the surrounding communities, went to *Eretz Yisrael* for *Shavuot* there was enough space for all.[45]

Redemption will be a slow process

ח Let us return to the beginning. I proved that if we are unworthy, the redemption will occur naturally; and natural occurrences take time, periodically changing until they are completed. Accordingly, the brilliant R. Mende'le of Dash explains *Chazal*'s statement, "If they are unworthy – *in its time*" (*Sanhedrin* 98a), to mean, in the set time that every natural process takes to be completed.

Rashi's comments on the Talmudic discussion mentioned above[46] prove this point:

> R. Yehoshua ben Levi pointed out a contradiction. It says, *in its time* (*Yeshayah* 60:22), and it also says, *I will hasten it* (ibid.)? [The solution is]: If they are worthy – *I will hasten it*. If they are unworthy – *in its time*. R. Alexandri said: ôR. Yehoshua ben Levi pointed out a contradiction. It says, *And behold, with the clouds of heaven* (*Daniel* 7:13), and it also says, *poor and riding upon a donkey* (*Zecharyah* 9:9)? [The solution is]: If they are worthy – *with the clouds of heaven*. If they are unworthy – *poor and riding upon a donkey*.ö (Sanhedrin 98a)

Rashi explains, "*With the clouds of heaven* [means] quickly. *Riding on a donkey* [means] like a poor man who rides on his donkey sluggishly."

This is exactly as we stated above. If the Jews are worthy, the redemption will occur quickly, all at once, and with manifest miracles. This is the meaning of *with the clouds of heaven*, which symbolizes heavenly intervention. If they are unworthy, it will come through material (חמריות), natural means, as it says, *poor and riding upon a donkey* (חמור). Consequently, the redemption will come sluggishly, for it will evolve and change until it is completed.

Indeed, this is what happened at the time of Ezra. *Chazal* state that a miracle should have occurred, but sin prevented it (*Berachot* 4a). That is to say, their sin caused them to be unworthy, and the salvation had to come in the guise of nature, with the permission of the kingdom. Therefore, it did not occur all at once, but little by little. First, they ascended to *Eretz Yisrael*; Eighteen years later, they built the *Beit HaMikdash*; and afterwards, Nechemyah built the

45 ❖ Also see *Teshuvot Chatam Sofer, Yoreh De'ah* 234.

46 See p. 134.

city walls. Everything happened slowly, because they were unworthy of manifest miracles.

The same is true of the final redemption. Due to our numerous sins, we are unworthy (as I proved[47] from the Holy One's statement "If I look at Israel's deeds, they will never be redeemed" [*Shemot Rabbah* 15:4]). Therefore, it must proceed naturally and slowly.

This clearly refutes the outcry of our master and teacher, the holy *gaon* of Munkatch *z"l*, the author of *Minchat Elazar*, who opposed resettling and rebuilding the Land. I, too, was part of his entourage, and I know that he based his entire opposition on the idea that salvation must happen with miracles and wonders. In his opinion, anyone who tries to [bring salvation naturally] denies the redemption which will occur miraculously. His writings are filled with this,[48] and he cried aloud about it.

However, with all due respect, he, on his lofty level, assumed everyone to be in the category of "worthy ones," as he was. In reality, though, this generation is not worthy (due to our numerous sins). Therefore, the redemption must happen with miracles disguised in nature.[49] Everything that I have cited from the *Midrash, Zohar*, and *Yerushalmi* proves that it will come little by little, like all natural processes. Therefore, we have an absolute obligation to become involved in this undertaking with all of our strengths, as I will explain below. Then, HaShem will bring our efforts to a successful end, and we will see the final redemption speedily in our days, Amen.

Today, everyone would admit that we must return to Eretz Yisrael

I would like to add that if our mentor, the author of *Minchat Elazar*, was still alive today and saw all of the terrible decrees and massacres that have befallen us, he too would admit that we should leave the exile, go to *Eretz Yisrael* (which has been given to us by the kingdoms of the world), and no longer await the call of *Mashiach*.

R. Natan comments on the verse *To those who love Me and keep My commandments* (*Shemot* 20:6): "This refers to those who dwell in *Eretz Yisrael* and dedicate themselves to all of the *mitzvot*" (*Yalkut Shimoni, Yitro* 292). Our mentor, the Magen Avraham, explains in *Zayit Ra'anan*:

ôThis refers to those who dwell in *Eretz Yisrael*." For in *Eretz*

47 See p. 139.

48 See *Divrei HaIggeret* (Jerusalem, 5692 [1932]) and *Teshuvot Minchat Elazar* 5:12.

49 ❖ As I cited in the name of the Or HaChayim HaKadosh (see p. 134).

> *Yisrael* there were harsh decrees and the Jews could have fled to another land. Nonetheless, they sacrificed themselves to settle the Land. This is not true of those who dwell outside the Land. When there are harsh decrees, they are liable for their souls if they do not flee to another land.

Now, after all of the harsh decrees that have befallen us here in exile, and considering that we have a place of refuge in *Eretz Yisrael* (for the kings have permitted us to return), would anyone be so presumptuous to say that our mentor would deny that we should return?! He only cried aloud in his day when tranquillity prevailed here and the Jews were able to wait until the anointed (*Mashiach*) prophet of HaShem called upon them. This is clear and true.

The Ramban quotes the *Sifrei* on the verse *You shall seek out His dwelling place* (*Devarim* 12:5):

> You might think that you should wait until a prophet reveals it to you. Therefore, the verse says, *You shall seek out His dwelling place and come there.* Seek out and find it, and then a prophet will reveal it to you, just like we find by David.

This *Midrash* warns us not to wait until a prophet commands us to ascend [to HaShem's dwelling place]. Rather, we must go up and seek it out to the best of our abilities, and then HaShem will grace us with a prophet. Certainly now, during these troubled times, we are obligated to do our utmost and try with all our strength and courage [to return to our Land]. In addition, the Ahavat Yonatan states that harsh decrees will be enacted against the people of Israel in the end of days, and they will desire to go to *Eretz Yisrael*.[50]

Jerusalem will be rebuilt when the Jews long for it

The *Kuzari* states:

> Man is guilty if he does not bring his yearnings for the Holy Land to fruition. Mere intentions are insufficient. And when his deeds and intentions are perfected, then, there will be reward... When people awaken and arouse within themselves a love for the Holy Place, the long-awaited time will draw near with great reward and recompense. As it says, *You will arise and have mercy upon Zion, for it is time to favor her, for the appointed time has come. For Your servants cherished her stones and favored her dust* (*Tehillim* 102:14-15). That is to say,

50 *Ahavat Yonatan, Haftarat Eikev*, on *Yeshayah* 49:19.

> Jerusalem will only be rebuilt when the people of Israel long for it with a complete longing, until they favor her stones and dust.[51]

After citing numerous statements from *Chazal* which extol the inhabitants of *Eretz Yisrael*, this godly, ancient scholar continues:[52]

> If so, you are remiss in your obligation to your Creator, for you do not make this place the object of your ambitions. You say, "Have mercy on Zion for it is the house of our lives,"[53] and you believe that the *Shechinah* will return there...and that it is befitting for precious souls to yearn to return there... Also, your forefathers chose to dwell there rather than remain citizens in their birthplaces, even when the *Shechinah* was indiscernible in the Land. On the contrary, the Land was full of lewdness; and, nonetheless, they desired to stay only there.[54]

Hence, this godly man states explicitly that even if *Eretz Yisrael* is filled with lewdness (God forbid), it is preferable to dwell there than anywhere else. This should be an instructive lesson for today's "pious ones" who slander the resettlement of the Land on grounds that it is not kosher enough for them. A word to the wise is sufficient.

We must initiate the redemption

ו I discovered a very old commentary on *Seder Mo'ed*, based on *Pardes*,[55] which explains why our redemption will come about little by little, not all at once:❖

> The complete redemption will only occur when all of the worlds are completely rectified (*tikkun*); and we cannot do this now. All

❖ Since it is missing the first page I do not know to which sacred individual to attribute it, and I cannot call it by its name. However, it is clear from the work that he was a great man and a Kabbalist, one of our brilliant and sacred ancestors.

51 Conclusion of *Sefer HaKuzari*. [Our author's citation of this source is not exact and includes some of his own additions.]

52 [In this excerpt, the king of the Kuzar nation is speaking to the *Chaver* (Jewish scholar).]

53 From the second blessing recited after the *Haftarah*.

54 *Kuzari* 2:23.

55 [An abbreviation representing the four traditional ways of interpreting the Torah: פשט (the simple meaning), רמז (symbolism), דרש (homiletics), and סוד (the esoteric meanings).]

> we can do is draw a little closer to the beginning of the redemption, so that God will open the gates of prayer for us and eliminate the iron wall [separating us from Him].[56] The redemption will be small at first. Then, we will return in perfect repentance out of love [for HaShem]. Consequently, all of the prayers and repentance of previous years will accumulate to effect a great rectification, which will increase daily. Then the final redemption will come, and we will see the fulfillment of the verse *And I made you walk upright* (*VaYikra* 26:13)...

For all of this to occur, however, we need a small redemption first to eliminate the iron wall, so that it will no longer separate us from our Father in Heaven.

II Why Have Our Prayers for Redemption Not Been Answered?

Sefer HaBrit's answer: We do not pray or perform mitzvot with the proper intention

ז I saw that *Sefer HaBrit* greatly bemoans the fact that the exile has lasted so long and that there is still no sign of hope. He explains so wonderfully that our only transgression is that we do not pray with the proper intention (*kavanah*), to redeem the Holy One Blessed be He and His *Shechinah* from exile. We also do not act faithfully, with the intention of rectifying the *Shechinah*'s stature and hastening the end of days. He asserts that we should not pin our hopes on man, nor rely on the merits and prayers of great individuals to bring us the Redeemer. For He Who sees into the heart knows who is truly great, not one who merely sees with his eyes.[57]

He further states that although we constantly speak of the coming of *Mashiach*, it is insincere lip service. A person wants to finish the building that he is erecting, or wrap up the business deal that he has been developing with the authorities or the kingdom for four or five years, or any other profitable venture that he has here in the Diaspora. This is why the exile persists. The main thing is that every Jew, even one who does not know Torah, should perform the *mitzvot* with the sole intention of redeeming the Holy One Blessed be He and His *Shechinah* from exile. Then, and only then, we will be worthy of redemption.

With a passionate fear of Heaven and great fervor, he laments the

56 See *Berachot* 32b.

57 *Sefer HaBrit*, vol. 1, sec. 9, chap. 16.

perseverance of our exile. If only the Children of Israel would listen to him and perform the *mitzvot* with the intention of redeeming the Holy One Blessed be He and His *Shechinah* from exile. For the author of *Sefer HaBrit* determines that we should not rely on great and famous individuals, because we, who see only with our eyes, cannot know if they are truly great. Instead, each person should "fight" for the *Shechinah* by performing *mitzvot* and good deeds. Then *Mashiach* will come, but not otherwise. I wish that we would merit to see Israel act this way, for then we would all be worthy and reach the level of perfect penitents. If every individual Jew would fulfill the *mitzvot* and intend to redeem the *Shechinah* from exile, we would be in the category of "If they are worthy – *I will hasten it*," as *Chazal* state (*Sanhedrin* 98a). Could there possibly be a need for more merit than this? We would certainly reach the status of "completely worthy," mentioned by *Chazal* (ibid.), and the redemption would arrive speedily.

Regretfully, however, I must disagree with *Sefer HaBrit*'s determination that if we do not do this *Mashiach* will not come. God forbid to say such a thing! His Master is not pleased with such statements. Would you tarry for them and would you tie yourselves down for them[58] until this occurs, until all of Israel acts properly? If so, you would close the doors to those who await the coming of *Mashiach*. There would be no hope for our redemption, God forbid. All of the works of our *gedolim* are filled with the idea that even if the people of Israel fail to repent they will be redeemed. See Rabbeinu Bachya (*VaYikra* 25:47), *Yerushalmi* (*Ta'anit* 1:1), Rashi (*Sanhedrin* 97b),[59] the Gra (*Even Sheleimah* 11:9), and the rest of our great Sages whose words I cited at the beginning of this chapter.

The Mabit's answers

I discovered that the brilliant teacher of Israel, our master the Mabit, already pondered this issue of the perseverance of exile. He expresses great bewilderment in his work, *Beit Elokim*:

> Since communal prayers are always accepted, we must explain the prayer for the coming of our Savior. We have recited this prayer three times a day ever since the destruction of the *Beit HaMikdash*, but we have yet to be answered! And since this prayer is recited three times a day by all of Israel, wherever they live, it must have been said with proper *kavanah* by one

58 Based on *Ruth* 1:13.
59 S.v. *dayo* and lo *bekesef*.

of these communities and by righteous and upright individuals. Furthermore, our Sages declare, "He who mourns for Jerusalem will merit to see its rejoicing" (*Ta'anit* 30b). How many righteous and pious individuals have mourned, but have yet to merit seeing its consolation?[60]

To answer this query he writes:

1. The majority of Israel must repent

The acceptance of this prayer, which encompasses all of Israel, does not depend on a single community's devotion (*kavanah*) in prayer. Rather, it requires the devotion of the majority of Israel, since it encompasses them all. And even if they recite it with proper devotion, they must repent wholeheartedly in order to be answered, as it says, *Today, if you will only hearken to His voice* (*Tehillim* 95:7). Otherwise, their prayer will not be accepted, even if the majority of Israel recites it with devotion on a particular day. The reason for this is because exile is like a verdict accompanied by an oath; until its time is up, the verdict cannot be revoked, even for the sake of the community. Accordingly, it is written, *In its time I will hasten it* (*Yeshayah* 60:22): "If they are worthy – *I will hasten it*, if they are unworthy – *in its time*" (*Sanhedrin* 98a).

2. Numerous prayers from both past and present generations are needed

It seems to me that for such a wondrous event – Israel's everlasting redemption, after which there will be no exile – many prayers are needed from both earlier and later generations. The prayers of the ancestors assist those of their descendants. The prayers of the later generations, who are closer to the time of redemption, are more likely to be accepted than those of the earlier generations for two reasons. First, those who are five hundred years away from the time of redemption need to entreat and supplicate less than those who are a thousand years away, in order for their prayers to be accepted. And those who are only a hundred years away need even less effort, because their prayers are more applicable... This can be compared to one who is standing far from a city; he will not arrive as quickly as one who is standing close by.

Second, since the redemption is of such great importance, numerous prayers from many generations are needed. Once we reach the necessary amount of prayers, known only to God, the prayer of that particular generation will be accepted, even

60 *Beit Elokim, Sha'ar HaTefillah*, chap. 17.

> though it would not have been accepted in previous generations. That prayer will not be accepted on its own merit, but because it combines with all of the prayers that preceded it. Thus, all of the previous prayers contribute as well. And when this prayer is accepted in the last generation, it is as if the prayers of the earlier generations are being accepted, since they assist in having this prayer accepted.

The Mabit elaborates on this point and explains that the prophet Yeshayahu hints to these two reasons when he says, *Seek the Lord when He can be found, call upon Him when He is near* (55:6):

> This hints to the two reasons that I mentioned. *When He can be found* refers to the second reason, for all the prayers of years gone by will cause Him to *be found* to us. *Call upon Him when He is near* refers to the first reason, for the prayers of the later generations are more apt [lit., near] to be accepted than those of the earlier ones.

3. Our prayers have been answered to some degree in each generation

The Mabit gives an additional answer as to why our prayers for the redemption were not answered in previous generations:

> Besides all this, *Klal Yisrael*'s prayers for redemption are indeed heard in every generation. For HaShem redeems them and causes all of their captors to treat them kindly and honorably. Thus, some of the promises of the redemption are fulfilled through them. Accordingly, *Chazal* state that the verse, *Kings will be your foster–fathers* (*Yeshayah* 49:23), was fulfilled through Huna bar Natan (*Zevachim* 19a). There is not a single generation which does not experience some misfortune, but HaShem (may He be blessed) saves them and redeems them from the clutches of those mightier than them. Furthermore, even without misfortune, the very fact that the Jews exist and survive among the nations is on account of their prayers for redemption. HaShem oversees their affairs, and before they call out He answers them.[61] Before the blow, the flower of healing blossoms. If so, there is a quasi–redemption in every generation, as it says, *And despite all this, when they are in the lands of their enemies, I will not cast them away nor will I abhor them to obliterate them, to annul My covenant with them* (*VaYikra* 26:44).

61 Based on *Yeshayah* 65:24.

Our author disagrees

Thus, our mentor, the Mabit, was also hard–pressed to find an answer to *Sefer HaBrit*'s profound question concerning the continuance of our exile... However, based on Rashi's comments on *Megillah* (17b),[62] one could argue with his closing statement that although our prayers have not brought the complete redemption they have assisted somewhat in redeeming us from the troubles that befall us in each generation... Rashi explains that the blessing, "Redeemer of Israel" [in the *Shemoneh Esrei*], was specifically established for the redemption from the troubles of each generation. It is not a prayer for the redemption from exile. The blessings which concern exile are "And to Jerusalem Your city" and "The offspring of Your servant David." Therefore, according to Rashi, this latter answer is insufficient.

The S'mag, however, disagrees with Rashi and holds that the blessing, "Redeemer of Israel," was established for the redemption from exile.[63] According to him, there is a basis for our mentor's words.

Behold, the Mabit's primary answer is that for such a significant matter, which affects the entirety of Israel, the devotion of one community in prayer will not suffice. Rather, it requires the devotion of the majority of Israel, since it encompasses them all. And even this is not enough. In order to be answered, a perfect repentance is also needed. For exile is a verdict accompanied by an oath, and it cannot be annulled before its time, even by [the prayers of] the many, as *Chazal* state, "If they are unworthy – *in its time*" (*Sanhedrin* 98a). He also explains that numerous prayers from earlier and later generations are needed in order to bring the everlasting redemption, after which there will be no exile. We will achieve the complete redemption with the culmination of all the prayers from all the generations. And, based on the two reasons mentioned above, it is easier for the later generations than the earlier ones.

Allow me to take issue with a few of the Mabit's points. First of all, his assertion that the prayer and repentance of one community is insufficient...can be contested. *Zohar Chadash* states that even one group which prays with complete devotion and repentance can awaken the redemption.[64]

Moshe's prayers to enter the Land

In addition, I disagree with the Mabit's assertion that a specific number of prayers, known only to God, is required, and that when

62 S.v. *atchalta dege'ulah he*.

63 *Sefer Mitzvot Gedolot*, Introduction to Positive Commandments.

64 *Zohar Chadash, Noach*, p. 23b.

this amount is reached the redemption will occur. Behold, although we may not know the required amount of prayers (for this may be included in, "The heart has not revealed it to the mouth"),[65] perhaps we can derive it from Moshe Rabbeinu who was [equal to] the entirety of Israel.[66] He endeavored greatly to come to *Eretz Yisrael*; and had he succeeded, there would have been no exile, only a complete and everlasting rectification (*tikkun*), as is well known.[67] *Chazal* state that he wanted to recite 515 prayers, but when he reached the last one, HaShem said to him, *It is too much for you, do not speak to Me further about this matter* (*Devarim* 3:26) (*Yalkut Shimoni* 1:940). That is to say, HaShem prevented him from reciting this final prayer because had Moshe completed this sum, HaShem would have been forced, as it were, to answer him.

Clearly then, 515 prayers suffice to pursuade our Father in Heaven to allow us to enter our Holy Land and remain there forever. For, it is well known that had Moshe entered the Land, the Temple would never have been destroyed.[68] Therefore, perhaps this amount is sufficient for us as well. And if I am correct, the prayers of all of the generations have certainly surpassed 515.

The era of in its time has certainly arrived

Furthermore, I challenge the Mabit's assertion that since exile is a verdict accompanied by an oath, we must wait until *in its time*. Behold, we are now standing in the 703rd year of the sixth millennium (5703 [1943]), and we have certainly reached the stage of *in its time*. This is not only true according to our mentor, the Ari *z"l*, who holds that the period of *in its time* began in the year 5335 [1575],[69] and according to the Or HaChayim HaKadosh[70] and the Chatam Sofer[71] who maintain that the time of *Mashiach* began in the year 5500 [1740]. Rather, according to all opinions, now that two thirds of the sixth millennium have already passed, the stage of *in its time* has undoubtedly arrived.

The Maharsha explains David's statement *My days are like an evening shadow* (*Tehillim* 102:12):

65 *Kohelet Rabbah* 12:10.
66 *Zohar* 3:9a, in addition to other sources.
67 See *Or HaChayim HaKadosh* on *BeMidbar* 20:8 (end) and *Devarim* 3:25.
68 See ibid.
69 ❖ See *Zohar Chai*.
70 *VaYikra* 6:2, *BeMidbar* 26:19.
71 *Teshuvot Chatam Sofer* 6:61 (end); *Derashot, Pesach* 5560 [1800].

> This refers to the shadows of evening. David was intimating that the time of redemption had arrived, as it says, *And it shall come to pass that at evening time, there will be light* (*Zecharyah* 14:7). That is to say, [redemption will occur] when the Jews have reached the depths of degradation, as it says, *When He sees that their power is gone, and none is saved or assisted* (*Devarim* 32:36).[72]

Now, the Maharsha was forced to interpret *evening* as degradation because he lived in the first third of the sixth millennium. But we, who live at the end of the second third, can interpret *evening* according to its simple meaning, for it is already actually evening.

A hymn recited in the morning prayer of the second day of *Rosh HaShanah* states that after two thirds of the day there will be a fulfillment of the verse *And it shall come to pass that at evening time, there will be light* (*Zecharyah* 14:7).[73] This indeed corresponds to our times, for we have already reached two-thirds of the day. Furthermore, Tosafot and the Ritva explain[74] that *evening* implies the time prior to sunset, not nighttime.[75]

In addition, there is more than enough degradation in our times, as is well known to all. Thus, all of the reckonings of *in its time* have passed, and the Son of David has not yet arrived. There must be something hindering the redemption from coming, as *Sefer HaBrit* indicates.[76] We must search for and identify this hindrance.

Our author's answer: we must actually seek out Eretz Yisrael

After much toil, HaShem enlightened me to find the answer to the question: why does the exile endure despite the fact that the era of *in its time* has already arrived. Behold, the prophet Hoshea says, *Afterwards, the Children of Israel will return and seek out the Lord their God and David their king, and they will tremble for the Lord and for His goodness in the end of days* (*Hoshea* 3:5). *Chazal* comment:

> The Children of Israel were exiled because they despised three

72 Maharsha, *Ta'anit* 15a, s.v. *baruch atah HaShem merachem.*

73 See *Machzor Rabbah* (*nusach sefard*), p. 304, s.v. *asher mi ya'aseh kema'asecha.*

74 *Mo'ed Kattan* 19b, *Tosafot* s.v. *she'assur.*

75 ❖ See what I have written concerning the practical halachic ramifications of this concept in my work, *Mishneh Sachir* (2:10). It is still delayed at the printer in Tirna. May HaShem grant me the merit to see it published.

76 See above, p. 150.

> things: the kingdom of Heaven, the kingdom of David, and the *Beit HaMikdash*. R. Shimon ben Menassiya said: "The people of Israel will not be shown a good sign until they return and seek out these three things." Accordingly, it says, *Afterwards, the Children of Israel will return and seek out the Lord* – this refers to the kingdom of Heaven; *and David their king* – according to its simple meaning; *and they will tremble for the Lord and His goodness* – this refers to the *Beit HaMikdash*, as it says, *This good mountain* (*Devarim* 3:25). (*Yalkut Shimoni* 2:106)[77]

The *Yalkut* also states, "The people of Israel were exiled only because they despised *Eretz Yisrael*, as it is written, *And they despised the desirable Land* (*Tehillim* 106:24)."[78]

It seems to me that this *Yalkut* concurs with the first one, for all of these three things are included in *Eretz Yisrael*, because it is impossible to attain them anywhere else. [Concerning the kingdom of Heaven], it is well known that "He who dwells in *Eretz Yisrael* is like one who has a God" (*Ketuvot* 110b). The kingdom of the House of David is in *Eretz Yisrael*. And the *Beit HaMikdash*, of course, is only in *Eretz Yisrael*. According to this, the Jews will not deserve redemption until they seek out *Eretz Yisrael*, for then they will attain these three things.

I already cited[79] the *Midrash* which states that the plague of David's generation happened only because they did not ask for the *Beit HaMikdash* (*Midrash Tehillim* 17:4). The *Midrash* learns a *kal vachomer*: If the Jews at the time of David, who did not yet have a *Beit HaMikdash*, were punished for not requesting it, then we, who once had a *Beit HaMikdash* but it was destroyed, will certainly be punished for not requesting it. Therefore, our Sages instituted that we pray for the rebuilding of Jerusalem three times a day, everyday.

The question of the above-cited *gedolim* is now even stronger. Have we not prayed for this for many, many years since the destruction of the *Beit HaMikdash*? If so, we have already fulfilled the verse *And they will seek out the Lord their God and David their king* and the *Beit HaMikdash* (for our prayers include all three of these things). Why have we not yet been answered? Why have we not yet reached our inheritance and our resting place? Why have we not yet seen

77 ❖ This can also be found in *Midrash Shmuel* (13:4) and Rashi (*Hoshea* 3:5).

78 We were unable to locate this source.

79 P. 45.

any promising signs? R. Shimon ben Menassiya said, "The people of Israel will not be shown a good sign until they return and seek out these three things." Do we not do this three times every day? Yet, HaShem has still not shown us any promising sign of improvement. This is, seemingly, an incomprehensible wonder.

Prayer must be accompanied by action

With God's help, however, the answer is as follows. I will preface with a passage from the Talmud:

> What should a person do in order to become wise? He should intensify his studies... They said, "Many have done so but have not succeeded." Rather, he should beg for compassion from He Who possesses wisdom, as it says, *For the Lord grants wisdom; out of His mouth come wisdom and understanding* (*Mishley* 2:6)... What, [then], does this teach us?[80] One without the other is insufficient.
>
> What should a person do in order to become wealthy? He should increase his business dealings... They said, "Many have done so but have not succeeded." Rather, he should beg for compassion from He Who possesses wealth, as it says, *The silver is Mine, and the gold is Mine* (*Chaggai* 2:8). What, [then], does this teach us? One without the other is insufficient.
>
> What should a person do in order to have male children? He should marry a woman who is fitting for him... They said, "Many have done so but have not succeeded." Rather, he should beg for compassion from He Who possesses children, as it says, *Behold, children are the heritage of the Lord* (*Tehillim* 127:3). What, [then], does this teach us? One without the other is insufficient. (*Niddah* 70b)

Thus, concerning three distinct matters, upon which man's life depends, *Chazal* inform us that one without the other is ineffective. That is, prayer without action and action without prayer do not help. From these three examples we can infer all of man's affairs and all worldly matters, "One without the other is insufficient." That is to say, if a person prays to achieve something but makes no effort at all, he will never achieve it.❖

❖ I asserted that since *Chazal* taught us this rule with regard to three

80 [Rashi explains, "Why does the Talmud state that he should intensify his studies, seeing that this matter depends on prayer?"]

When I learned this Talmudic passage, that in order to have male children a man should marry a suitable woman, I was reminded of a story related to me by a certain elderly man who was a follower of Rebbe Eliezrel of Komarno *z"l*. This holy rebbe had an attendant called Peretz Gabbai. He was a feebleminded elderly bachelor who had never married, but he was a God-fearing man. They once asked him: "Peretz, why do you not marry?" He answered: "Why do I need a wife? What am I lacking by the rebbe?" They said to him: "Doesn't a man need children?" To which he replied: "Children?! I will write a *kvittle* (a note) to the rebbe and I will have children!" When they related Peretz's remarks to the rebbe, he laughed and said, "Someone who relies solely on the rebbe, looks like Peretz."

This is exactly the Talmud's lesson..., prayer without marriage will not suffice. One cannot rely on the rebbe's prayers alone and refrain from marrying a woman, as Peretz did. In any event, we learn from the Talmud that one who relies solely on prayer and does not take any action will look like a Peretz Gabbai.

The difference between asking (שאלה) and seeking (בקשה)

In a work by one of the great *gedolim*,✣ I discovered an explanation of the verse *One thing I asked* (שאלתי) *of the Lord, that thing I shall ask for* (אבקש): *that I may dwell in the House of the Lord all the days of my life* (*Tehillim* 27:4). All of the commentators[82] analyze the double language of שאלתי and אבקש. What does each one mean? Are they not identical? This *gadol* bases his answer on the passage from Tractate *Niddah*...which indicates that prayer alone is insufficient, even if it is recited with utmost concentration. Only if a person

---

matters that are essential to man, we can infer all other matters. I learned this from our master, the Beit Yosef, who quotes the Mizrachi as saying that since the Torah tells us concerning three prohibitions that one is forbidden to feed them to a minor, we can extend this law to all prohibitions in the Torah.[81] Hence, the same applies to the words of *Chazal*. Since they tell us that prayer without action and action without prayer is ineffective in three significant areas of life, it follows that the same is true of all of life's necessities.

✣ At this point I cannot indicate the title or reference, as I have fled from my birthplace because of the oppressors, and I am writing without books.

81 *Beit Yosef, Orach Chayim* 343, s.v. *vehavi*.

82 See Radak, Malbim, and others.

actually does his part will his prayers help him attain his desires. Let us take as an example a man who begs HaShem to make him into a Torah scholar. If he simply walks around the marketplace instead of sitting and learning in the *beit midrash*, he will never achieve his request, even if he prays tearfully all day long, because he does nothing on his part to promote it. If, however, he does his share by going to the *beit midrash* and learning with all his might; and, in addition, he prays to HaShem to open the gates of wisdom for him, then HaShem will surely fulfill his request.

Hence, the difference between שאלה and בקשה is as follows. שאלה means prayer. It is when a person asks of HaShem that which his heart desires. בקשה is concrete action. He seeks out and searches for what he desires to attain, as it says, *I will now arise and go about the city in the streets and in the broad ways. I will seek* (אבקשה) *him whom my soul loves* (*Shir HaShirim* 3:2). That is, she walks about in the broad places and actually searches for the one that she loves. This is similar to *Seek* (בקש) *peace and pursue it* (*Tehillim* 34:15), meaning, actually pursue peace. If, however, one does not search, he will not find.

Thus, when David says, *One thing I asked of the Lord...*, he implies: That which I ask (שואל) of HaShem – that I may dwell in His house all the days of my life – I also seek out (אבקש) with concrete actions. That is to say, I do all that is in my power to achieve my desire to sit in the House of HaShem. I go to the *beit midrash* to learn and engross myself in Torah study. But, I also ask HaShem to assist me...so that nothing should hinder me from sitting in His house all the days of my life. I perform concrete actions..., for if not, my request of HaShem is in vain. This explains the double language.

Based on this, we can understand the verse *Afterwards, the Children of Israel will return and seek out* (ובקשו) *the Lord their God and David their king* (*Hoshea* 3:5). That is to say, they will seek them out with actual deeds, not just prayer. They will actually search for ways to return to *Eretz Yisrael*. They will take action and not rely on prayer alone, because one without the other is useless... Then, they will be shown a good sign. Thus, R. Shimon ben Menassiya said, "The people of Israel will not be shown a good sign until they return and seek them out" (*Yalkut Shimoni* 2:106). Notice that it says "seek out," not "ask," for the word שאלה implies prayer, and prayer alone is insufficient. Instead, they will strive to return to our Land, to the kingdom of Heaven, and to the kingdom of the House of David.

They will take practical steps towards these three goals and do all that they are capable of doing. They will also pray for this. Then, the will of HaShem will succeed through them.[83] If, however, they rely on prayer alone, they will never achieve their goal.

This resolves the formidable question mentioned above.[84] Since we did not strive to return to our Holy Land, all of the prayers that we recited up until now were ineffective. This is why we have not yet seen any positive sign. If, however, we do our share, we will receive Heavenly assistance – by virtue of our prayers – to return to our Holy Land, and we will achieve our hearts' desire to enter our forefathers' inheritance, speedily in our days. Amen.

We must do our share and then HaShem will do His

Rashi comments on the counting of the *Levi'im*: "The Holy One Blessed be He said to Moshe, 'You do your part and I will do Mine.'"[85] This is a fundamental principle in all matters; we must first do our share and then the Holy One Blessed be He will do His.

The *Chaver* in *Sefer HaKuzari* states as follows:

> This sin (that is, the fact that few Jews long to actually return to *Eretz Yisrael*) prevented the fulfillment of that which was destined for the Second Temple. For Divine Providence was ready to reappear as at first❖ if all the Jews had willingly agreed to return. But, only a minority returned; the majority remained in Babylonia... Divine Providence only appears to a person in proportion to his preparedness for it. If he prepares a little, he will receive a little, if a lot, a lot. If we would be prepared to willingly and wholeheartedly draw near to the God of our forefathers, He would save us as He saved our ancestors from Egypt. [But since this is not the case], our utterances of "Who restores His presence to Zion"[87] and *Bow down at His*

❖ *Chazal* assert that the second redemption should have been everlasting but sin prevented it (*Sanhedrin* 98b). The Maharsha explains that the sin was that the Jews did not all return to *Eretz Yisrael*.[86] This corresponds fully with the words of the godly Kuzari.

83 Based on *Yeshayah* 53:10.
84 Pp. 151-52.
85 Rashi, *BeMidbar* 3:16.
86 Maharsha, *Yoma* 9b, s.v. *ke'chomah*.
87 From the seventeenth blessing of the *Shemoneh Esrei*.

holy mountain[88] are like the chirping of the birds, for we say these things without proper intent.[89]

The same is true to this very day. We say things with our mouths and tongues, but our hearts are indifferent. We do not arouse our souls to yearn and strive for the settlement of the Land – to encourage the Children of Israel to return to the Land and strengthen its settlement. This is the cause of all the troubles that have befallen us.

A proof for this from Ya'akov Avinu's prayer

ח Allow me to bring a proof for my thesis from the words of *Chazal*. The Holy One Blessed be He said about Ya'akov:

> ôThis righteous man came to My hostel and he should leave without lodging?!" Therefore, HaShem uprooted Mt. Moriah and brought it to Beit-El, as the verse states, *He* [Ya'akov] *encountered the place* (*BeReishit* 28:11). And if you should ask, when Ya'akov passed by the site of the *Beit HaMikdash* why did God not detain him there? [The answer is], if Ya'akov did not consider praying at the place where his forefathers prayed, should God detain him?! Ya'akov traveled until Charan, and when he arrived he said, "Is it possible that I passed by the place where my forefathers prayed and I did not pray there?!" He resolved to return and traveled until Beit El where the ground [of Mt. Moriah] leaped towards him. (See *Chullin* 91b; Rashi, *BeReishit* 28:17)

In his holy work, *Beit Elokim*, our master, the Mabit, lists and explains various biblical prayers which our righteous ancestors recited. With regard to Ya'akov's prayer he explains:

> The verse says, *He encountered* (ויפגע) *the place* (*BeReishit* 28:11). And, פגיעה (encounter) means prayer. From here *Chazal* derive that Ya'akov Avinu instituted the evening prayer (*Berachot* 26b). Now, the evening prayer is voluntary (ibid. 27b), because he did not originally intend to pray. Only in retrospect he thought about it and said, "Is it possible that I passed by the place where my forefathers prayed and I did not pray?!" Therefore, he went back and prayed. This is why our Sages determine that it is voluntary.
>
> Ya'akov Avinu prayed at this place for the redemption from our final exile. The Egyptian exile and the Jew's subsequent

88 *Tehillim* 99:9, recited at the beginning of *Pesukei DeZimrah*.

89 *Kuzari* 2:24. [The parenthetical comment is R. Teichtal's.]

> redemption hinged upon Avraham Avinu. The Babylonian exile and their subsequent redemption hinged upon Yitzchak. The present exile and our redemption hinge upon Ya'akov, as I mentioned in my epistle, *Ge'ulat Olam*, on the concealed end of days.[90] This explains Ya'akov's statement, "Is it possible that I passed by the place where my forefathers prayed and I did not pray?!" For this place is Beit El, which is Jerusalem. Just as they [his forefathers] prayed for the building of Jerusalem and the *Beit HaMikdash*, and their prayers were answered during the time of the first two Temples, so too, he wanted to pray for the future rebuilding of Jerusalem and the *Beit HaMikdash*. Hence, his prayer was close to sunset, which hints to our present, lengthy exile.[91]

Thus, everything Ya'akov did at this place alludes to the rebuilding of our Holy Land and the *Beit HaMikdash*. Now, Ya'akov Avinu prayed at the end of the day, which alludes to the end of this lengthy exile, when the stage of *in its time* has already arrived. Nonetheless, had he not contemplated returning, HaShem would not have inspired him to do so. God only helped him after he aroused himself to return and actually traveled from Charan back to Beit-El. That is to say, God awaited not only his desire to return but also concrete action. This is why our Sages specifically say, "and he traveled until Beit-El." Even though he had decided to return while still in Charan, he received Heavenly assistance only when he traveled from Charan back to Beit-El, not previously. Only then the ground leaped towards him. Hence, it is clear that good intentions are insufficient up in heaven. HaShem waits for concrete deeds to accompany our good intentions.

All of this alludes to our era, for we are living at the end of the exile. To simply desire to return to our forefathers' Land, while anticipating a divine awakening, is insufficient. We must resolve to return to our Land and actually begin to return, just like Ya'akov Avinu did. Then, we will receive divine assistance and the land will come forth to greet us. That is to say, the desire of HaShem will succeed through us.[92] If, however, we do not act on this matter, but await miracles and wonders, then our hopes are for naught. HaShem is waiting for us to initiate the process, as He waited for Ya'akov

90 ❖ I regret that I did not merit seeing this work.

91 *Beit Elokim, Sha'ar HaTefillah*, chap. 18.

92 Based on *Yeshayah* 53:10.

Avinu *a"h*. This is the lesson that Ya'akov Avinu taught us through his prayer and his return to the site of the *Beit HaMikdash*. We must learn from him and do the same, for this entire account alludes to our situation at the end of exile. This is true and clear.

Israel must act first

Chazal provide another reason why the land did not leap towards him at Charan, but only when he returned to Beit-El. The *Midrash* comments on the verse *For the conductor, a psalm for the sons of Korach. O Lord You have favored Your Land* (*Tehillim* 85:1-2):

> The sons of Korach said to the Holy One Blessed be He, "Until when will You say, *Return O wayward sons* (*Yirmiyah* 3:14), and they [Israel] say to You, 'You return first,' as it says, *Return O Lord, until when?* (*Tehillim* 90:13). And You say, 'No, Israel must take the initiative.' You will not return by Yourself and we will not return by ourselves, rather both of us will return simultaneously." (*Midrash Tehillim* 85:3)

Thus, the sons of Korach made a compromise between us and the Omnipresent, that each will return to one another simultaneously. Neither will begin. This way, the Land will be favored, as the verse begins, *O Lord You have favored Your Land.*

I discovered in the holy work, *Tiferet HaGershuni* (by a colleague of the Shach), that we must take the initiative nonetheless. For, if the Holy One Blessed be He acts first, we will be unable to determine the exact moment at which to begin, together with Him. On the other hand, if we act first, the Holy One Blessed be He will determine the exact moment and begin simultaneously with us.[93]

Now, Beit-El is situated exactly in between Charan and Mt. Moriah. The very moment that Ya'akov began to return from Charan, Mt. Moriah, which is the *Shechinah*, also began to move towards him. They proceeded at an equal pace, step by step, so that neither would precede the other, for the compromise of the sons of Korach indicated that they would both walk in unison. Ya'akov's actions on that occasion are a sign of what will happen to us now, at the end of days (as I cited in the name of our mentor, the Mabit). Therefore, the movement of Mt. Moriah could only occur in the fashion described above. When Ya'akov met up with the *Shechinah* at Mt. Moriah, it was in Beit-El, which is exactly in the middle. Thus, they returned to one another at the same instant. This seems to be the explanation

93 See above, pp. 4-5.

of this matter. It is exceedingly wondrous in my eyes. Blessed is HaShem Who enlightened me to this wondrous explanation.

In any event, this, too, is a proof that we must first strive to return to our Land, and then HaShem will come to greet us. We will return to one another in unison. However, if we do nothing (God forbid), simply waiting for a miracle from the heavens, it will be impossible to accomplish this, as the sons of Korach determined.

Our return to Eretz Yisrael is the essence of repentance

The Ahavat Yonatan writes that our very return to *Eretz Yisrael* is considered repentance, and it is, in fact, the essence of repentance:

> When numerous troubles will befall the Jews and, despite this, they will not forsake HaShem nor their inheritance – i.e., the Holy Land (may it speedily be rebuilt), their primary repentance will be achieved. For, repentance must be performed in the same place and concerning the same act.[94] Now, their main transgression at the time of the *Beit HaMikdash* was their descent to Egypt, as the verse says, *Woe to those who go down to Egypt* (*Yeshayah* 31:1). This gave rise to grave sins. Therefore, their future repentance will be that they will not forsake their inheritance.[95]

Now, today, when even the lowest Jews have decided to return to our inheritance, and they dedicate their lives to it, refusing to covet any other land, the Holy One Blessed be He certainly considers this repentance. The fact that they do not fulfill the commandments of the Torah is because they were not raised and educated in this spirit. They are like infants who were kidnapped by Gentiles, as the Rambam writes.[96] But, the act of *aliyah* is undoubtedly considered repentance, and through it they fulfill the positive commandment of *teshuvah* (repentance). This is the essence of repentance, as our mentor, R. Yonatan, explains.

Midrash Talpiot cites the *Zohar Chadash*:

> Micha'el, the great guardian angel of Israel, said: "Master of the Universe, when will Israel be delivered from the Edomite

94 [That is, in order to achieve complete repentance, a person must rectify the very sin he committed. Therefore, he must refrain from repeating the same sin when confronted with it under the same circumstances as before. (See Rambam, *Hilchot Teshuvah* 2:1.)]

95 *Ahavat Yonatan, Haftarat Balak*, s.v. *vehayah bayom hahu...*

96 *Hilchot Mamrim* 3:3.

exile? Did You not say that when they suffer myriad afflictions, they will be redeemed from exile?" The Holy One Blessed be He replied, "Let Sama'el, the guardian of Edom, come and debate you." Sama'el came and claimed, "You [God] said that the people of Israel will remain in exile until they repent, and now they are wicked"... The Holy One Blessed be He said to Micha'el, "You should have looked at the beginning of the verse – *You will return unto the Lord Your God*, and only afterwards, *For God is merciful* (*Devarim* 4:30-31)..." Micha'el retorted: "Master of the Universe, is it for naught that You are called a merciful God? You are merciful even if they are unworthy!" The Holy One Blessed be He said: "I have already sworn that I will not redeem them until they return to Me [to some small degree], even like the tip of a needle. Then, I will open for them a large opening."[97]

Thus, even the slightest repentance, like the tip of a needle, is enough for the Holy One Blessed be He to bring the redemption. Hence, according to R. Yonatan's assertion that returning to *Eretz Yisrael* is the essence of repentance, we may conclude that all those who have strayed from the path of Torah and *mitzvot* are repenting like HaShem desires by returning to the Land. Their return is considered at least a repentance like the tip of a needle. Afterwards, the principle of "One *mitzvah* leads to another" (*Avot* 4:2) will surely be realized, and the Holy One Blessed be He will open their hearts wide and sway them to love and worship Him wholeheartedly.[98]

In any event, since the pioneers perform a *mitzvah* by returning to the Land and since the Holy One Blessed be He is pleased with their actions,[99] every single Jew is undoubtedly obligated to assist, support, and join them in this endeavor. He who keeps a *mitzvah* will know no evil,[100] and nothing bad will come out of this, God forbid. On the contrary, HaShem's great name will be glorified and sanctified through it. This is true and clear.

Let us return to the beginning. I proved from Ya'akov Avinu, from the compromise of the sons of Korach, and from the Talmud (*Niddah*

97 *Midrash Talpiot, Erech Galut, Anaf Galut Mitzrayim*, p.128a, s.v. *inyan galut Edom*, citing *Zohar Chadash*, p. 23b.

98 ❖ I will demonstrate this below (sec. ט) from the Rambam, *Ahavat Yonatan*, and *Or HaChayim HaKadosh* (God willing).

99 ❖ As I proved in the foreword (pp. 82-83) and as I will further prove in the next chapter (pp. 291-98).

100 *Kohelet* 8:5.

70b) that everything depends on our initial, concrete actions. If we do our share, we can also expect heavenly assistance to come and complete the process for us. The *Zohar* states that the same thing happened with Shlomo's Temple. He began the work and then HaShem completed it miraculously. But, HaShem waited for him to take the initiative (*Zohar* 1:74a).[101]

This is also the reason why our future redemption is called *tzemach* (sprouting).[102] A person cannot expect his field to sprout grains before he works it. That is to say, if he does not plow, sow, and prepare the field, he will not achieve his goal. He will remain empty-handed, even if he prays all day and all night. Only after he does his part by plowing and sowing, can he pray to HaShem to bless his handiwork. The same is true of redemption. After we decide to return to our Land and after we actually begin the process, the Holy One Blessed be He will complete it for us. This is true and clear. Blessed is HaShem Who enlightened me to this principle.

III Redemption Through Sinners

Today's pioneers disregard the Torah only because of the influences of exile

ט In our days, there has been an awakening to return to our forefather's Land, and Jews have actually returned and begun rebuilding the Land. Surely, this is the realization of Hoshea's prophecy *Afterwards, the Children of Israel will return and seek out* (בקשו) *the Lord their God and David their king* (3:5). For, as I explained above,[103] the word בקשה implies actual, physical effort.

You may ask: Does the verse not state, *and seek out the Lord their God and David their king*? Today's builders have no inclination to seek out the Kingdom of Heaven or King David, and their conduct reflects this fact!

I will answer this question based on *Chazal*'s comment on the verse *Do not look upon me that I am black, the sun has tanned me* (*Shir HaShirim* 1:6): The Assembly of Israel said to the prophets, "Do not look upon me in my state of blackness,[104] and do not slander Israel, for the nations have tanned me." (*Shir HaShirim Rabbah* 1:6). That is to say, my blackness is not intrinsic. It is only because the sun – meaning, the nations – have tanned me. I was raised among the

101 ❖ I cited this in the second introduction (p. 47).
102 ❖ See above, p. 139.
103 Pp. 159-60.
104 Here ends the direct quote from the *Midrash*. The rest is a paraphrase.

nations, and my external appearance has absorbed their dross. My internal being, however, is clean and white. That is to say, it is not surprising that I have learned from the Gentiles' evil ways during the thousands of years that I was raised among them, as it says, *They mingled with the nations and learned their deeds* (*Tehillim* 106:35). But, the Jewish souls which descend from Avraham, Yitzchak, and Ya'akov are intrinsically pure and yearn to return to their roots. They simply do not know how to return to purity, for they have become accustomed to gentile upbringing.

Today's situation cannot be compared to that of the Temple era, when the Jews dwelt in their Land. At that time, the members of the *Sanhedrin* – who sat upon the thrones of judgment,[105] Torah, and piety – showed and taught them the ways of the Torah. Yet, the Jews rejected the *Sanhedrin* and HaShem's Torah. They did not listen to the voices of the prophets, therefore they were exiled. The people of our generation, however, were born in exile, and they assimilated with the Gentiles. They did not see or hear [the ways of the Torah], nor experience HaShem's honor. Therefore, the fact that they do not follow the ways of the Torah is no proof that they detest it. They have simply been blackened by the conduct of the Gentiles.

I already cited[106] our Kabbalistic master from Komarno who swore by the Eternal God that today's sinners are like infants who were kidnapped by Gentiles, for they act under duress and all of their sins are unintentional. The Rambam also writes that it is a *mitzvah* to bring those who were raised with foreign customs closer to the Torah, for they are like infants who were kidnapped by Gentiles.[107] It is a *mitzvah* to love them, for they are descendants of Avraham, Yitzchak, and Ya'akov. Hence, the Holy One Blessed be He certainly does not despise today's pioneers.

The *Midrash* comments on the verse *The House of Israel dwell on their Land, and they have defiled it* (*Yechezkel* 36:17): "The Holy One Blessed be He said, 'If only My children were with Me in *Eretz Yisrael*, even though they defile the Land' " (*Yalkut Shimoni* 2:1038). This *Midrash* expresses the same idea I just mentioned. Since they have spent so much time among the Gentiles, they are unaware of the severity of the prohibitions that they transgress, and all of their actions are

105 Based on *Tehillim* 122:5
106 Pp. 105-6.
107 *Hilchot Mamrim* 3:3.

under duress. Thus, they cannot be compared to the sinners of the Temple era.

Their love for the Land shows that they truly want to come close to God

Moreover, they cherish the Land and refuse to desire any other land besides that of their forefathers. They sacrifice their lives for it, as is well known. Many have even died for the sake of the Land. We heard that during the Arab uprisings, many Jews who were killed in battle said with their last breaths, "***There is nothing better than to die for the sake of our Land.***"[108]

The Chatam Sofer cites the Talmud in *Sanhedrin* (47a) which states that a Jew who is killed by Gentiles is called holy (*kadosh*) even if he was wicked.[109] This is certainly true of today's pioneers who risk their lives for the sake of our Land.❖ Is there any doubt that they are destined for the World to Come [*Olam HaBa*]?! Is this not a clear testimony that even though they do not "see," their inner Jewish souls "see" and yearn to return to their roots?!

Our Sages declare, "He who dwells in *Eretz Yisrael* is like one who has a God (*Ketuvot* 110b). That is to say, even if he does not know and understand how to seek God, his inner soul feels the need to do so. The words, "is like one," allude to this. That is, he has a God even if his conduct does not show it. Therefore, since today's pioneers seek out *Eretz Yisrael*, they are included in the verse *And they will seek out the Lord their God and David their king* (*Hoshea* 3:5). For, the return to *Eretz Yisrael* will lead to the establishment of the Davidic

---

❖ The *Sifrei Zuta* states:

> R. Shimon said: "Come and see how beloved is *Eretz Yisrael*. A person who goes off to war runs and runs, but when he reaches the battlefield, his legs buckle under. This did not happen to the Jewish people. When they approached *Eretz Yisrael* their legs lifted them up, and they said to one another, 'We are unworthy to enter *Eretz Yisrael* even if we die there immediately, for we are entering the place which HaShem promised our forefathers to give to us.'" (*Sifrei Zuta, BeHa'alotcha* 33, on *BeMidbar* 10:33)

The holy ones who died while fighting the Arabs did exactly the same thing.

108 This is a reference to Yosef Trumpeldor. See *Encyclopedia Ivrit*, vol. 18, p. 931.

109 *Teshuvot Chatam Sofer, Yoreh De'ah* 333.

Dynasty and the building of the *Beit HaMikdash* (when we eventually become purified). Then, we will see the fulfillment of the prophecy *And I will remove the iniquity of that Land in one day* (*Zecharyah* 3:9).

Furthermore, the Alshich and the Ran[110] explain that when one considers all of *Klal Yisrael* as a unit, each individual is included in all of the *mitzvot*, for different people perform different *mitzvot*. Indeed, there are astute individuals among *Klal Yisrael* who clearly know and understand how to seek out these three goals. Thus, if all the Jews unite, the prophecy of, *Afterwards, the Children of Israel will return and seek out the Lord their God...* (*Hoshea* 3:5), will be thoroughly fulfilled. If they also act on this matter,[111] HaShem will help them like He helped Ya'akov Avinu, and they will see a favorable sign and the final redemption, speedily in our days. Amen.

Most importantly, we all must long to return to our Land and do whatever we can to further this goal. Then, HaShem will complete the process and bring us to, and plant us upon, the mountain of our inheritance.[112]

HaShem will arouse us to repent after we return to Eretz Yisrael

The Rambam writes:

> The Holy One Blessed be He destined that our judges be restored as at first and our counselors as in the beginning.[113] Afterwards, "you will be called the city of righteousness."[114] This will undoubtedly occur when the Creator prepares the hearts of mankind, when their merits and their desire for HaShem and Torah increase, and when their perfection grows – [all] before the advent of *Mashiach*, as many verses in the Bible indicate.[115]

Thus, our mentor, the Rambam, writes that the Holy One Blessed be He will prepare the hearts of mankind before *Mashiach* arrives, so that they will long and desire to do God's will and fulfill His Torah. Now, this will take place after the Jews gather in His Land, as I cited above[116] in the name of the Chatam Sofer. He derives from the Rambam that Jews will gather in *Eretz Yisrael* before *Mashiach*

110 See *Derashot HaRan, Derush* 1. (We were unable to locate the Alshich.)
111 ❖ As I explained above (pp. 158-62).
112 Based on *Shemot* 15:17.
113 Based on *Yeshayah* 1:26 and the eleventh blessing of *Shemoneh Esrei*.
114 Based on *Yeshayah* 1:26.
115 Commentary to the *Mishnah, Sanhedrin* 1:3, s.v. *semichat zekeinim*.
116 Pp. 117, 140.

arrives. When they are in their Land, HaShem will bestow upon them a purifying spirit to cleanse their hearts of the impurities [they absorbed in] the atmosphere of the nations. Then, they will yearn and desire to cling to HaShem, do His will, and fulfill all that is written in the Torah.

This concurs with the *Or HaChayim HaKadosh* that I cited above,[117] which states that the Torah's promise of "circumcision of the heart" (see *Devarim* 30:6) will occur after we return to our Holy Land.

In light of all of the above, we must not be overly wise about this matter. Rather, we must do our share and return to our Land. We must also join all the Jews who are settling the Land of our possession, no matter who they are (just like the exiles did in the days of Ezra). Then, HaShem will do His share and prepare our hearts to love Him, serve Him, and fulfill His will wholeheartedly.

Israel can easily return to God

The Talmud asserts that if a person returns a stolen sheep to its flock he does not fulfill the positive commandment of returning a stolen object until he informs the owner. Even though the owner was unaware of the robbery, the replacement is invalid unless the thief informs the owner that he has returned the sheep. Rav Chisda explains the reason for this: "Since it has learned to go out" (*Bava Kama* 118 a-b). Rashi explains that since it has become accustomed to leaving the flock, and the owner is unaware of this, he will not guard it more carefully than the other sheep which have never left the flock. This is also the established *halachah* in the *Shulchan Aruch.*[118]

Based on this, our mentor, the Chatam Sofer, explains the verse *I have strayed like a lost sheep; seek out Your servant, for I have not forgotten Your commandments* (*Tehillim* 119:176). He writes that the *Yerushalmi* states explicitly

> that if the owner's flock has an old he-goat which walks in front of the sheep, or a *Pandora,*[119] or the like, by which the stolen sheep can recognize its flock, then any type of replacement is adequate. For even though it has learned to go out, these signs help it return easily to its former ways and become re-accustomed to its flock (*Yerushalmi, Bava Kama* 10:8 [33a]).

117 P. 120.

118 *Choshen Mishpat* 355:2.

119 *P'nei Moshe* explains that *Pandora* means ôdrumö in Greek... It is a bell which the shepherd rattles in front of the flock so that the sheep will follow him.

> Similarly, the *Yeitzer HaRa* and subjugation have caused the Jews to sin. They have learned to go out, away from the ways of the Torah. They *have strayed like a lost sheep*. Nonetheless, they can easily return (God forbid to say otherwise), for *I have not forgotten Your commandments*. When God gives us a small hint we will remember and return to the days of our youth when we leaned upon our Beloved,[120] may His name be blessed.[121]

These are the words of the living God, and they concur with my assertion that once the irreligious are inclined towards the good, they will easily return to God and His Torah. Amen. So may it be HaShem's will, after we all return to our Holy Land.

We must settle the Land without questioning God's hidden ways

Yeshayah HaNavi said to King Chizkiyah, *Command your household, for you shall die and not live* (II *Melachim* 20:1, *Yeshayah* 38:1). The Talmud comments:

> *For you shall die* in this world, *and not live* in the next world. Chizkiyah asked, "What is the meaning of all this?" Yeshayah answered, "It is because you did not procreate." He retorted, "I did this because I foresaw, through *Ruach HaKodesh*, that I would have unrighteous sons." Yeshayah responded, "Why do you involve yourself with the Merciful One's hidden matters? You must do as you are commanded, and the Holy One Blessed be He will do as He sees fit." (*Berachot* 10a)

The same applies to us. Since all Jews are commanded to perform this *mitzvah*, to ascend to *Eretz Yisrael* and rebuild our Holy Land, everyone must say to himself, "I will do as I am commanded, and the Holy One Blessed be He will do as He sees fit." Also, just as Chizkiyah was not exempted from the positive commandment of procreation because he foresaw that he would have unrighteous sons, so too, no Jew can exempt himself from the positive commandment of building the Land based on the claim that he is afraid of "unrighteous sons" (God forbid)... Indeed, "One *mitzvah* leads to another" (*Avot* 4:2), and the merit of settling the Land, which is greater than all *mitzvot* of the Torah,[122] will stand by him and help him have "righteous sons." That is, HaShem will incline the hearts of our Jewish brethren [to repent].

120 Based on *Shir HaShirim* 8:5.
121 *Derashot Chatam Sofer*, vol. 3, p. 560a.
122 *Sifrei, Re'eh* 28 (on *Devarim* 12:29).

Tana DeVei Eliyahu also cites this story of Yeshayah and Chizkiyah and concludes as follows:

> Therefore, a man should marry a woman so that he can have children; and he should learn from Chizkiyah. Chizkiyah knew, through *Ruach HaKodesh*, that he would not have righteous sons, and he, therefore, gave excuses to the Omnipresent. Nevertheless, he would have been punished in the next world had he not married a woman. (*Eliyahu Rabbah* 8:3-4)

The same is true of rebuilding the Land. A person must fulfill his obligation to God; and no excuse or rationale can exempt him from this. And if he neglects it, he will be subject to punishment, God forbid.

The great zealot, our brilliant and righteous master, R. Akiva Yosef *z"l*,[123] concurs with this in his wondrous work, *Tosafot Ben Yechiel*, a commentary on *Tana DeVei Eliyahu*. *Tana DeVei Eliyahu* states, "Blessed is the Omnipresent, blessed is He and blessed is His name, for He is entirely impartial. Since Israel wept without cause [in the episode of the spies], He decreed upon them eternal weeping" (*Eliyahu Rabbah* 8:3-4). R. Akiva Yosef comments:

> Indeed, there is no wisdom, counsel, or understanding against the Lord.[124] All of their wise and logical arguments against *Eretz Yisrael* are null and void, like the counsel of the spies. We must simply do the will of our Creator in accordance with His commandments. For the Lord has chosen Zion,[125] and the Land is exceedingly good,[126] both materially and spiritually. He who keeps the commandment will know no evil,[127] since he enters there [*Eretz Yisrael*] "like the Lord my God commanded me."[128] I will keep the word of the King of kings,[129] the Holy One Blessed be He.[130]

He has declared to His people the power of His deeds, that

123 ❖ R. Akiva Yosef Schlessinger, author of *Lev HaIvri*, and son-in-law of the brilliant and righteous R. Hillel of Kalamoya.

124 Based on *Mishley* 21:30.

125 *Tehillim* 132:13.

126 *BeMidbar* 14:7.

127 *Kohelet* 8:5.

128 Based on *Devarim* 4:5.

129 Based on *Kohelet* 8:2.

130 This ends the direct quote from *Tosafot Ben Yechiel*. The rest is a paraphrase.

He may give them the heritage of the nations (*Tehillim* 111:6). That is to say, God bestowed upon His people the power to obtain the heritage of the nations [i.e., *Eretz Yisrael*], but they have to strive to attain it. For, the deeds of the righteous are greater than the works of heaven and earth,[131] because when the Creator of the World brings redemption, it is not as glorious for us as when the work of our hands establishes it.[132] The entire order of redemption written in *Yechezkel* (34-36) proves this, to bless your handiwork.

HaShem will purify us during the final redemption

The Ahavat Yonatan explains the verse *The remnant of Ya'akov will be in the midst of many peoples like dew from the Lord* (*Michah* 5:6). The following is a synopsis of his words.

Yeshayah promises us that *They* [the Gentiles] *will bring all your brethren from all the nations as an offering to the Lord upon horses and in chariots and in wagons and upon mules and upon fleet camels, to My holy mountain, Jerusalem, says the Lord... And, from them, too, I will take* Kohanim *and* Levi'im, *says the Lord* (*Yeshayah* 66:20-21). [133]The Abarbanel explains that this refers to the Jews of Spain and Portugal who were forced to convert. Even though they assimilated with the Gentiles, the Holy One Blessed be He will eventually take them as *Kohanim* and *Levi'im* and bring them under the wings of the *Shechinah*. Even though these Jews have absolutely no awakening from below (for they have assimilated and intermingled with the Gentiles, and they have learned their ways), nevertheless, the Holy One Blessed be He will awaken them from above and place in their hearts the desire to love and fear Him.[134]

Now, [returning to our original verse], the difference between dew and rain is as follows. Not a drop of rain descends from above without some water ascending from below, as the verse states, *A mist ascended from the earth* (*BeReishit* 2:6).[135] Therefore, there must first be an awakening from the depths. Dew, on the other hand, comes from HaShem without any awakening from below. Hence, the future redemption will be similar to dew. HaShem will place a spirit of purity in the hearts of the Jews, without any prior awakening from below. This is the meaning of the prophet's statement *The remnant*

131 *Ketuvot* 5a.
132 Based on *Tehillim* 90:17.
133 This begins a direct quote from *Ahavat Yonatan*.
134 End of quote. The rest is a paraphrase.
135 [Also see *Ta'anit* 25b.]

of Ya'akov will be in the midst of many peoples. This refers to the Jews who assimilated in the midst of many peoples and who have no self–awakening to return to HaShem. They will be *like the dew from the Lord,* without any awakening from below.[136]

This concurs exactly with the above–cited Rambam which states that after the Jews gather in *Eretz Yisrael,* even before the advent of *Mashiach,* HaShem will prepare the hearts of man to yearn and desire to perform His will.

HaShem will gradually prepare the world for redemption

In *Gevurot HaShem*, the Maharal discusses the two remembrances (פקידות) of the redemption from Egypt:

> It says, *I have surely remembered* (פקד פקדתי) (*Shemot* 3:16). In the future, as well, the Jews will be redeemed with a double *tzadi* (צ), as it says, *Behold there is a man whose name is Tzemach* (צמח) *and he will sprout* (יצמח) *out of his place* (*Zecharyah* 6:12).❖ There are two "sproutings" here. This is necessary in order to bring about the redemption. It cannot come all at once, because it is on such a lofty level.[137]

Based on this, he explains the following *Midrash*: "*My beloved is like a gazelle* (*Shir HaShirim* 2:9): Just like a gazelle appears and disappears, so too, the first redeemer appears and disappears" (*Shir HaShirim Rabbah* 2:9). This corresponds to the two remembrances of, *I have surely remembered* (פקד פקדתי), which indicate that the exodus did not happen all at once. Similarly, the future redemption will not happen all at once, because great events cannot occur instantaneously. They must develop little by little.

With God's help, I came to this same conclusion independently. That is, HaShem must gradually prepare the world for grand events, [for] it is impossible to instantaneously bring the world to lofty heights without slowly preparing it beforehand. I derived this from a passage in *Iggeret Teiman*, where the Rambam explains the verse, *He appeared from Mount Paran* (*Devarim* 33:2), which refers to the giving of the Torah:

❖ *Pirkei DeRebbe Eliezer* explains that double letters represent the various redemptions. *Tzadi–tzadi* (צ״ץ) represents the final redemption, as derived from the verse *...whose name is Tzemach and he will sprout out of his place* (*Pirkei DeRebbe Eliezer* 48).

136 *Ahavat Yonatan*, beginning of *Haftarat Balak*.
137 *Gevurot HaShem* 30.

When Moshe Rabbeinu recounts the Sinai revelation, he explains that HaShem did not reveal Himself on Mt. Sinai like hailstones falling from the heavens. Instead, He appeared slowly and gradually, moving from one mountaintop to the next until He descended upon Mt. Sinai: *And he said, the Lord came from Sinai and shone forth to them from Se'ir; He appeared from Mount Paran, and He came from holy multitudes; from His right hand* [came] *a fiery law to them* (ibid.). It is clear that [the words *to them* refer to] the ones whom HaShem desires, the people of Israel.

Notice how precise the verse is. Regarding Paran, which is furthest, it says, *appeared.*❖ Regarding Se'ir, which is closer, it says, *shone forth*. And regarding Sinai, which was the destination and the mountain upon which God's Glory rested (as it says, *The glory of the Lord rested upon Mt. Sinai* [*Shemot* 24:16]), it says, *He came from Sinai*. In Devorah's account of the Sinai revelation, she also states that God's Glory appeared gradually from mountain to mountain, as it says, *Lord, when You left Se'ir, when You marched out of the field of Edom, the earth trembled, and even the heavens dropped...* (*Shoftim* 5:4).[138]

Subsequently, I discovered that Rashi concurs. He writes that HaShem did not appear on Mt. Sinai suddenly; rather, He revealed Himself little by little to prepare them in advance.[139]

We learn from here that momentous events cannot occur suddenly. The world must be prepared for them gradually. Therefore, an event as profound as our final redemption, upon which the entire creation depends,❖❖ will certainly not occur all at once. There must be a great and gradual preparation prior to its advent. I asserted this on my own, and when I discovered that I was privileged to concur

---

❖ On the Sabbath morning we say in *Kedushah*, "From Your place, our King, You will appear." Based on the Rambam's assertion that the word "appear" refers to a distant place, I explained this to mean, even though our deeds distance us from You, nonetheless, You will appear to us compassionately.

❖❖ As *Chazal* remark, "It does not say 'Israel rejoiced,' rather, *Israel will rejoice in its Maker* (*Tehillim* 149:2), meaning, in the future" (*VaYikra Rabbah* 20:2).

138 *Iggeret Teiman*, pp. 142-43.

139 Apparently, the reference is to Rashi on *Devarim* 32:11.

with this divine scholar [the Maharal], I was very pleased.

It seems to me that the prophet Malachi states this explicitly: *Behold, I send My messenger, and he will clear a path before Me, and the Lord Whom you seek will suddenly come to His sanctuary, and the messenger of the covenant whom you long for, behold he comes, says the Lord of Hosts* (*Malachi* 3:1). That is to say, after they [the messengers] have cleared the path before HaShem, through gradual preliminary steps that prepare the world for the ultimate redemption, the Lord will reveal *Mashiach*. By building and settling the Land; by gaining permission from the kingdoms to return to our Land, to perfect and exalt it; and by gaining autonomy in our Land, the Lord Whom we seek and the messenger of the covenant whom we long for will come.

Today's pioneers are God's messengers to prepare the Land for redemption

If you should ask, does it not say, *The Lord will suddenly come to His sanctuary*? How can it say *suddenly* if there was a preparation beforehand? The Rambam explains this in *Iggeret Teiman*:

> Understand that you will not recognize the rise of *Mashiach* before it happens. People will not say about him that he is so-and-so's son, or that he comes from a certain family. Rather, a previously unknown man will arise, and his signs and miracles will prove his authentic lineage. For, when the Holy One Blessed be He told us about this He said, *Behold there is a man whose name is Tzemach, and he will sprout out of his place* (*Zecharyah* 6:12). Yeshayah also said that he will appear without anyone knowing his father, mother, or family.[140]

Thus, the word *suddenly* refers to *Mashiach* himself. He will appear suddenly, without us knowing anything about him beforehand.[141] But, we will certainly prepare for his coming. In fact, the prophet says, *Behold, I send My messenger and he will clear a path before Me*, implying that he will clear a path before the anointed (*Mashiach*) of HaShem comes. This preparation is happening today, for we are preparing the Land to enable it to receive its children. This concurs with our holy mentor, the author of *Mishnat Chassidim* (whom I quoted in the second introduction).[142] He states that the rebuilding of the Land is a sign of the redemption, because it prepares

140 *Iggeret Teiman*, pp. 180-81.

141 ❖ The Chatam Sofer concurs (*Teshuvot* 6:98, s.v. *hareini nazir*), and it is surprising that he does not cite *Iggeret Teiman*.

142 See p. 55.

and enables the Land to receive the Jews who return from exile.

The builders of the Land and the kings who grant permission to build are the messengers referred to in this verse. The Menorat HaMe'or writes, "A person is considered a messenger of God even if he acts in accordance with his nature, as it says, *He makes the winds His messengers* (*Tehillim* 104:4)."[143] Therefore, the ones who currently prepare and build the Land are messengers of HaShem.

The Maharal writes in *Gevurot HaShem*:

> Nothing is coincidental. We have stated many times that one must not say that an aspect of the redemption is coincidental, and certainly not the order of its development. Rather, it is all by the word of HaShem.[144]

If so, all those who prepare for the redemption are messengers of HaShem and are included in the verse *Behold, I send My messenger, and he will clear a path before Me*. When there is a proper preparation and the majority of Israel gather in *Eretz Yisrael*,[145] our master, the *Mashiach*, whom we seek, will suddenly appear.

Why did the Jews only recently begin to resettle the Land?

יא Whenever our mentor, the Maharal, wants to emphasize a wonderful idea and inspire man to pay close attention to it, he writes, "There is no doubt that great phenomena do not happen coincidentally, but with the consent and providence of the Almighty, may He be blessed."[146] He repeats this often in his wondrous works, as experts in his holy writings know.

Therefore, I decided to examine a most wondrous phenomenon. One who surveys the history of our exile notices that we never found a place of rest. Even if we dwelt peacefully in a specific place, it did not last long. Our gentile neighbors promptly intensified their hatred and jealousy against us to such a degree that they stole all of our possessions and expelled us from their land, impoverished and destitute. Throughout our exile we wandered from nation to nation and from disaster to disaster, as is indeed happening today with intense cruelty in all of Europe. It is simply indescribable, as R.

143 *Menorat HaMe'or* 3:4:5:1 (Mossad HaRav Kook, p. 310).

144 See *Gevurot HaShem*, beginning of chap. 19 and 22.

145 ❖ As the Rambam and Rashi write - that the Jews will gather in *Eretz Yisrael* prior to the advent of *Mashiach ben David*. See above p. 140-41.

146 See *Gevurot HaShem*, beginning of chap. 19 and 22.

Shimon ben Gamliel said, "If we attempt to record all of the hardships, we will not succeed" (*Shabbat* 13b).

Our present situation is not new (as the saying goes, "History repeats itself").[147] Nonetheless, in days of old when we were forced to leave a particular place we never considered establishing a gathering place and a new settlement in our Holy Land. Only recently, in the past few decades, a movement arose to acquire fields and properties in *Eretz Yisrael*, to make them flourish, and to build houses and orchards. Portions of Land which for two thousand years were desolate, disease-filled swamps are now suitable for living. From the time this movement began, *Eretz Yisrael* has become a fruitful and marketable land, despite all of the obstacles that the pioneers encountered. It has become an ornate hill towards which thousands and tens of thousands of people face,[148] *the most beautiful of sites, the joy of all the earth* (*Tehillim* 48:3).

Why did the Jews never consider doing this in the past? Why did our ancestors, including many *gedolim* like the Abarbanel, never contemplate acquiring and settling *Eretz Yisrael* even during expulsions? The noble Don Yitzchak Abarbanel wrote a letter to the honorable president of Piza in which he complains about Israel's bitter lot:

> O great and noble one, open your eyes and see. From the day our city was destroyed, our Holy Temple laid waste, and the Jews were exiled from their Land, we have had no peace and quiet. Our enemies constantly provoke us, giving us no respite. They all follow the counsel of Edom, Yishma'el, Moav, and Hagrim.[149] And, if we enjoy tranquillity for a day or two, fearful reports from east, west, north, and south terrify us, for we hear that they have consumed the remnant of Israel and flayed their skin.[150]

At that time, the Abarbanel was still in a position of authority in the Portugal kingdom. Why did he not consult with this important minister and make an effort to acquire *Eretz Yisrael* and build it

147 [Originally in Yiddish.]

148 Based on *Berachot* 30a.

149 Based on *Tehillim* 83:7.

150 ❖ This letter was printed from a manuscript kept in the British Museum [end of author's note]. See *Sefer HaAtzamim*, edited by R. Menasheh Grossberg (London, 5661 [1901]).

anew, so that the dispersed and persecuted Jews of exile could gather there? [He and his fellow Jews] did nothing of the sort! Did they lack the financial means for this undertaking? Certainly not! They were highly prestigious and affluent. Also, from the Abarbanel's time until today, nobody conceived such a plan. This is truly striking and puzzling.

And now, after being in exile for so long, all of the Diaspora Jews are inspired by this idea. They are infused with a breath of life, a newfound aspiration to rebuild the Land by erecting houses, acquiring fields, working the Land, and planting gardens and trees. They want to make the Land livable, to prepare and enable it to receive its children. Is this mere coincidence, God forbid?

It is true that over 300 years ago[151] the noble Don Yosef HaNasi, a member of the sultan's court, made efforts to rebuild *Eretz Yisrael* and transform it into a gathering and dwelling place for the Jews. With the sultan's permission, he sent workers and artisans, and he even visited himself from time to time to supervise the workers. But, he was unsuccessful. The neighboring Arabs became extremely envious, interfered with the work, and abolished this endeavor.[152]

Today, on the other hand, efforts to rebuild the Land grow daily (may they increase and multiply),[153] despite the Arabs' envy. No obstacle or deterrent can stop the workers from doing their task. Day by day the Land expands and grows with new houses, trees, fields, vineyards, and orchards. This is certainly not a simple matter, and it is undoubtedly not a natural phenomenon.

HaShem is preparing the Land for redemption

HaShem enlightened me and I discovered [the answer] in *Hon Ashir*, by the brilliant Kabbalist, the author of *Mishnat Chassidim*. He comments on the *Mishnah* "The Galilee will be destroyed of houses" (*Sotah* 9:15):

> When HaShem granted me the privilege to ascend to *Eretz Yisrael*, to Safed (may it be rebuilt and established speedily in our days), I saw with my own eyes how this curse has come true. Due to our many sins, it is filled with destroyed houses.

151 In the year 5323 [1563].

152 ❖ See Eliyahu ibn Chayim's responsa [*Mayim Amukim*] (sec. 54), which speaks about the incident in which Don Yosef HaNasi elevated a confidant from a lowly state to the status of a great officer in his house. Eventually, this confidant falsely and libelously informed against him to the king, and all the wise men of the generation excommunicated him.

153 Based on *Shemot* 1:12.

In the two years that I remained there, however, I was happy to see that, day by day, it was being rebuilt, thank God. I claim that this is a sign of the imminent arrival of the Redeemer, for if he would come when *Eretz Yisrael* is in a state of ruin, there would be no place for the ingathered exiles to dwell.

The same thing happened the first time we entered the Land. Our Rabbis state that the Holy One Blessed be He detained the people of Israel in the desert for forty years so that the Land could regain its original strength. When the Jews left Egypt, the Amorites destroyed and uprooted trees and buildings, thinking that Israel would enter the Land immediately and find it destroyed. God only brought them in when the Land was finally rejuvenated.[154] The same will happen (with HaShem's help) when *Mashiach* arrives, may he come speedily in our days.[155]

This demonstrates that the Land must be built up with houses and trees before the advent of *Mashiach*. If not, Israel's entry into *Eretz Yisrael* and the final redemption will be delayed, God forbid. If the Land is built up, however, it is a promising sign of the imminent redemption. Realize that the author of these words was one of the greatest, holiest, and most formidable Kabbalists of the later generations. He experienced revelations of Eliyahu HaNavi, and all of his words were said with *Ruach HaKodesh*.[156] Who in our generation is noble enough to argue with him?

Thus, we have found the answer to our question. Since we are living at the end of the exile,[157] close to redemption, HaShem has inspired the Jewish people to dedicate themselves to rebuilding the Land and making it livable. He is preparing the Land so that the immigrants can gather there at the time of redemption. In any event, the rebuilding of the Land is a promising sign of redemption and is the beginning of redemption according to our mentor, the author of *Mishnat Chassidim*.

The flourishing of the Land is a sign of redemption

I just remembered a *Midrash* which clearly proves the Mishnat

154 *Shemot Rabbah* 20:16; *Mechilta*, beginning of *BeShalach*, s.v. *derech eretz Pelishtim*; Rashi on *Tehillim* 40:6.

155 *Hon Ashir*, end of *Sotah*.

156 ❖ See the second introduction (pp. 55-56) where I cited what the great and godly Rebbe of Tzanz testified about him.

157 ❖ As I explained above at length (pp. 155-56).

Chassidim's principle that the future redemption depends on the building of the Land. *Chazal* point out that in two places the open letter *mem* (מ) [used in the beginning or middle of a word] is interchanged with the closed *mem* (ם) [used at the end of a word]. The phrase, *for the increase of dominion* (לםרבה המשרה) (*Yeshayah* 9:6), is written with a closed *mem* in the middle of a word. And the verse, *the walls of Jerusalem which were breached* (המ פרוצים) (*Nechemyah* 2:13), is written with an open *mem* at the end of a word. The Maharalbach writes, "Our Sages explain[158] that this hints to the fact that as long as the walls of Jerusalem are breached like an open *mem*, the dominion is 'closed up' and removed from Israel, due to our numerous sins."[159] Thus, Israel's dominion depends on the building of our Holy Land.

I subsequently remembered that the Talmud states this explicitly:

> R. Abba said, "There is no clearer [sign of] the end of days than this verse: *But you, O mountains of Israel, will give forth your branches and yield your fruit to My people Israel, for they are soon to come* (*Yechezkel* 36:8)." (*Sanhedrin* 98a)

Rashi explains, "When *Eretz Yisrael* gives forth its fruit in abundance the end will be near, and there is no clearer [sign of] the end of days." This fully concurs with our holy master who asserts that the Land will be rebuilt and give forth its fruit abundantly before the end of days, and that this is a sign of the imminent redemption.

I also remembered that this is mentioned in Tractate *Megillah*:

> Why did the Men of the Great Assembly see fit to place the blessing for the ingathering of the exiles after the blessing of the years?[160] Because it is written, *But you, O mountains of Israel, will give forth your branches and yield your fruit to My people Israel, for they are soon to come*. (*Megillah* 17b)

Rashi explains, "This verse indicates that the ingathering of the exiles will occur when the years are blessed." That is to say, the Men of the Great Assembly established the blessing of "Sound the great *shofar* for our freedom and raise a banner to gather our exiles" after the blessing of the years which reads, "Bless for us...all the varieties of its crops, for goodness." They did so because this is how it is going

158 See Radak on *Yeshayah* 9:6.

159 *Teshuvot Maharalbach, Kuntras HaSemichah*, end of first *Kuntras*.

160 [In *Shemoneh Esrei* the blessing of "Sound the great *Shofar*" follows the blessing of "Bless for us...this year."]

to be in the future when the Redeemer arrives, speedily in our days. The mountains and hills, which were desolate during the entire exile, will yield their fruits when redemption draws near.

Hence, the authors of the *Shemoneh Esrei* – the Men of the Great Assembly, which consisted of 120 elders, including several prophets – agreed with this idea that the Land will become fertile and livable before the ingathering of the exiles. This fully concurs with the Mishnat Chassidim's assertion.

This is actually happening today! Many of our Jewish brethren came to the Land and built cities, villages, gardens, and orchards. They transformed great expanses of disease-infested swamps into dry land and fertile, prosperous fields. They sacrificed and endangered themselves to build the Land and make it fit for living. Is there even a shadow of a doubt that this is the wondrous work of HaShem,[161] and that it is a sign that our salvation is soon to come?! This is undoubtedly the beginning of redemption!

R. Shimon ben Menassiya's statement – that the people of Israel will only be shown a good sign when they return and seek out these three things...[162] – is being fulfilled through us. I explained his words to mean that Israel must actually strive to pursue these things and not rely on prayer alone. Thus, when a number of our fellow Jews overcame all of the obstacles that stood in their way and actually returned to our Land, HaShem granted them success and blessed their handiwork. They succeeded in rejuvenating the Land and making it fruitful, something that has not happened since the destruction of the *Beit HaMikdash*. This in itself is a sign that redemption is close at hand, as our godly mentor, the Mishnat Chassidim, declared. This is clearly true, and only a person smitten with blindness, who wishes to deliberately distort the truth, would deny it.

Why is God bringing redemption through sinners?

יב I know, my son, I know that you will challenge my position with a formidable refutation. If it is true that the rebuilding of our Holy Land is a sign of the imminent end of days and the beginning of the redemption, how could the majority of the builders, unfortunately, desecrate the Sabbath and commit other sins? They are practically like Gentiles, due to our numerous sins. How could the Creator of the Universe bring the beginning of redemption and

161 Based on *Shemot* 34:10.
162 See above, pp. 156-57.

a sign through them? Do we not maintain that good things are brought about by good people (*Shabbat* 32a)?

God's ways are unfathomable

My beloved son, although your refutation seems formidable, take heed and hear[163] my words. Know, my son, that no one can fathom the deeds of He Who is Perfect in Knowledge.[164] He is the God of the Universe, the Creator of All. Everything that happens in the world comes from Him. His thoughts are profound and He generates causes and effects, tying one strand to another until His decrees are fulfilled down on earth. He knows why He chose specifically these people to bring the beginning of redemption and a good sign.

An unclean bird will signal redemption

To understand this, take an example from a passage in the Talmud which discusses the unclean [i.e., unkosher] birds:

> *Racham* (*VaYikra* 11:18) is the sherakrak bird. R. Yochanan said, "Why is it called racham? Because when the racham comes, mercy (*rachamim*) comes into the world" (Rashi explains that mercy refers to rain). R. Bibi bar Abaye said, "This only occurs when it perches on something and makes a sherakrak sound" (Rashi explains, "When it chirps, it sounds as if it is saying, 'sherakrak'"). And, we have a tradition that if it sits on the ground and whistles, *Mashiach* will come, as it says, *I will whistle to them and gather them* (*Zecharyah* 10:8). (*Chullin* 63a)

Rashi, on this verse in *Zecharyah*, explains, "*I will whistle to them* like one who whistles to those who have lost their way as a signal for them to come towards him. *And I will gather them* at the time of the future redemption."

I was astonished when I read this statement. According to *Chazal*, the prophet promises us that an unclean bird will signal the final redemption. The Talmud states explicitly, "We have a tradition that if it sits on the ground...*Mashiach* will come." That is to say, they had a tradition that this bird will bring the good tidings of redemption...

What will you say about this, my son? You can now question God! Why would He do such a thing? Why would He bring the tidings of the most prodigious event, the one which we await with bated breath, specifically through unclean birds? Would it not have been more appropriate to do so through kosher birds and bring good tidings through meritorious and pure individuals?

163 Based on *Devarim* 27:9.
164 Based on *Iyov* 37:16.

However, the truth is as Iyov says, *Can you fathom the searchings of God?* (*Iyov* 11:7). Who can examine His deeds? Who can comprehend His ways? Only God understands His way,[165] why He specifically made this creature His messenger. Why do you involve yourself with the Merciful One's hidden matters?![166]

In any event, I have shown you, my son, an example which demonstrates that one cannot question God's deeds. His ways are above and beyond our ways, and our thoughts are not His thoughts.[167] Most importantly, it is self evident that these pioneers are God's messengers. Keep silent and do not ask questions against God. A word to the wise is sufficient.

If you wish, I will demonstrate more clearly that the builders of the Land, whom you consider sinners (God forbid), are in fact the harbingers of redemption. Our holy mentor, the Noam Elimelech, calls the sinners of Israel "unclean birds," and he explains, based on Kabbalah, that they are the unclean birds mentioned in the Torah.[168] ❖ Therefore, it is clear that the Sages of the Talmud revealed to us that unclean birds, meaning the sinners of Israel, will bring the sign of redemption. Thus, my son, I have proven that this concept was passed down to us as a tradition, and one cannot ask questions on accepted traditions, as the Talmud frequently states, "If this is *halachah*, we will accept it" (*Yevamot* 76b). Understand this, for it is clear! I hope you are satisfied with this, my son. ❖❖

❖ Also see *Bechor Shor* on *Bava Kama*[169] and *Torat Chayim on Perek Cheilek*[170] which concur with this. I am unable to cite the exact locations since I am now writing without books. I am in exile here in the capital, hidden in a secluded place in the cellar of a house.

❖❖ In passing, I will explain why the Talmud specifically says, "If it sits on the ground...*Mashiach* will come." This alludes to a *Midrash* on the verse *And the nation will go up from the land* (*Shemot* 1:10):

> Whenever the nation of Israel falls to the depths it rises, as it says, *And the nation will go up from the land.* David said, *For our soul*

165 Based on *Iyov* 28:23.

166 *Berachot* 10a.

167 Based on *Yeshayah* 55:8-9.

168 *Noam Elimelech*, *VaYikra*, p. 54, col. 4 (Mossad HaRav Kook, vol. 2, p. 291).

169 92b. It can be found at the end of *Tevu'ot Shor* (Jerusalem: Levin Epstein, 5726 [1966]).

170 We were unable to locate this source.

HaShem enwraps the redemption in "ugly wrappings" to deceive the accusers

יג My son, you asked how it is possible that the Holy One Blessed be He will initiate the redemption through transgressors and people with no recognizable vestige of Judaism, God forbid. Besides the answers I just gave to appease you, HaShem enlightened me to a fitting explanation which even our limited minds can comprehend. Let me preface with the Talmud's comments on the verse *Though it may tarry, await it* (*Chabakuk* 2:3):

> Perhaps you will say, "We are waiting, but God is not." Hence, the verse says, *And therefore, the Lord will wait, that He may be gracious to you, and therefore He will be exalted, that He may have mercy upon you* (*Yeshayah* 30:18). (Rashi explains, "HaShem Himself awaits and desires *Mashiach*'s arrival.") If we are waiting and He is waiting, then who detains [*Mashiach*]? The Attribute of Justice detains [him]. (*Sanhedrin* 97b)

Now, the Kabbalists explain that when HaShem wants to accomplish a great thing which affects both the celestial and earthly beings, He enwraps it in many types of coverings. He even uses unpleasant and ugly means so that the accusers will not take notice of it. For if it would be done openly, the accusers would immediately come to protest, and the Attribute of Justice would hinder the matter.

The Shach,[171] citing R. Ya'akov Ariz *z"l*, writes: "Why must Israel's lineage, dominion, and kingship appear in such a way that an onlooker will see in it an aspect of illegitimacy (God forbid)?" The Shach then describes how the entire development of *Mashiach* occurs in an ugly and licentious manner. He concludes:

> The Holy One Blessed be He does this in order to bring the Messianic King unexpectedly, so that the accuser will not protest... *Chazal* allude to this when they say that a snake,[172]

> *is prostrated to the dust, our belly cleaves to the earth* (*Tehillim* 44:26). [When we reach] that point, *Arise, help us, and redeem us for the sake of Your kindness* (ibid. 44:27). (*Shemot Rabbah* 1:10)

It seems to me that the Talmud's statement, "If it sits on the ground," means that when the pride of Israel is cut down and lowered to the ground, then *Mashiach* will come.

171 An acronym for *Siftei Kohen*, by R. Mordechai HaKohen. [Not to be confused with R. Shabbetai HaKohen, the commentator on the *Shulchan Aruch*.]

172 Our editions read, "a scorpion."

> a find, and *Mashiach* all come when the accuser is not expecting it (*Sanhedrin* 97a)... The Holy One Blessed be He does this so that Satan will pay no attention, saying that dominion and *Mashiach* will come only through nobility and holiness, not in this way.[173]

In the holy work, *Maggid Meisharim*, the angel reveals to our mentor, the Beit Yosef, the reason why David and the Messianic King were destined to come from Ruth the Moabite: This way, "there will be strength to overpower the evil forces."[174] The holy Noam Elimelech concurs: "If a man wants to break the strength of something, he must break it from within, using its own [tactics]."[175]

The *Midrash* states, "*I found David, My servant* (*Tehillim* 89:21): Where did He find him? In Sedom" (*BeReishit Rabbah* 50:10). The Noam Elimelech comments:

> Apparently, this parallels a Kabbalistic idea[176] which explains why Avraham descended from Terach and why many sacred *tzaddikim* descended from impure ancestry. When the evil accusers see an exalted and lofty soul, they employ every strategy to prevent it from coming into this world. What does the Holy One Blessed be He do? He places this soul in a defiled body, and the accusers leave it alone. Then, the soul is able to enter this world, for when the evil forces see it descend into an impure place they think that it will certainly not be able to ascend to the heights of sanctity.[177]

The Alshich[178] and the Iggeret Shmuel[179] also explain that a grand and sacred matter can only evolve through sin.❖

❖ *And Tamar, his* [Yehudah's] *daughter-in-law, bore him Peretz and Zerach* (I *Divrei HaYamim* 2:4). Rashi comments on this verse: "I am perplexed! How can the verse mention the disgrace of David's

173 *Siftei Kohen* on the Torah (Warsaw, 5643 [1883]), *VaYeishev*, p. 53a.
174 *Maggid Meisharim, VaYigash* (first edition).
175 *Noam Elimelech, VaYeishev*, p. 22, col. 3 (Mossad HaRav Kook, vol. 1, p. 117).
176 In the Mossad HaRav Kook edition, note 30, the following sources are cited: *Sha'ar HaGilgulim*, introductions 15, 27, and 38 (end); *Sha'ar HaPesukim, Iyov* 1; *Likutei Torah* of the Ari *z"l, Iyov* 1, s.v. *inyan Iyov*.
177 *Noam Elimelech, Korach*, p. 78, col. 3 (Mossad HaRav Kook, vol. 2, p. 420).
178 *Ruth*, chap. 3 and the end of the book.
179 *Ruth*, chap. 3 (Zolkiew edition), p. 43a, s.v. *lachain ani omer*.

ancestor?" We can answer this query based on these great Kabbalists who assert that the light of *Mashiach* is so lofty that it must come down to this world in unseemly wrappings, in order to sneak away from the accusers.

In the beginning of *Divrei HaYamim*, Rashi explains that Ezra (with the help of Chaggai, Zecharyah, and Malachi) wrote all of the genealogies of this book only in order to trace King David's lineage. Hence, he listed the lineage of Adam to Avraham and Avraham to David. And since it was all written for David's sake, scripture was very cautious of David's honor throughout the lineal order. Accordingly, Rashi comments on the verse, *The sons of Yitzchak – Eisav and Yisrael* (ibid. 1:34): "It says *Yisrael* and not Ya'akov for the sake of David's honor."

Rashi's question is now even more difficult. Certainly, his problem was that the verse should have omitted the word *daughter-in-law*. It simply should have written, "And Tamar bore him Peretz and Zerach." For, it is impossible to say that the verse should have completely omitted Peretz and Zerach's birth to Yehudah, because they are David's primary lineage. Rather, it is clear that Rashi was bothered by the fact that it mentions the word *daughter-in-law*, since that accentuates the disgrace of David's ancestor.

It seems to me that the answer lies in the Kabbalistic principle that God was compelled to enwrap *Mashiach*'s birth in ugly wrappings, like the incidents of Lot and Tamar. According to this, David's light shined in this world mainly because of the fact that Tamar was Yehudah's daughter-in-law. If not for that, she would not have been able to bear Peretz and Zerach, and David's arrival into this world would have been delayed. Thus, since the main objective of this genealogy is to tell us how David entered this world, and since the story of Yehudah's daughter-in-law is the essential element of David's entry into this world, the author [Ezra] was not apprehensive about the derogatory connotation of this word.

Moreover, it can be said that there is no disgrace at all, for his disgrace indicates his praise. David's light is so great and lofty that HaShem was compelled to obscure it with an unseemly covering. Hence, this is actually utter praise, and there is no disgrace whatsoever. Thus, Rashi's query is answered well, and this explanation is correct and true.

The sacred words of the Maharal of Prague, in *Gevurot HaShem*, shed light on current events in *Eretz Yisrael*:

> You must understand...that the holy kingdom of Israel, which has an inherent, divine status, sprouts from an unsanctified kingdom. For, this befits a kingdom which has a divine and inherent nature. The verse, *I brought forth fire from within you* (*Yechezkel* 28:18), alludes to this. Sanctity, which is compared to the fineness of fire, will arise from the profane and consume everything. Similarly, an unripe fruit stays in its peel, but when the fruit grows and ripens the peel decays. For, anything which has an inherent status sprouts from something external to it. This is why Moshe Rabbeinu *a"h* grew up in Pharaoh's house – so that his sacred and godly status could come from the mundane. Had this not occurred, he would not have been inherently 'separate' (*nivdal*). Understand this for it is very deep, and it is familiar to those who know about the development of spiritual [lit., 'separate'] things from material things. Similarly, *Mashiach* sits in Rome.[180]

Even though today's workers in *Eretz Yisrael* are extremely materialistic, their actions will lead to great spiritual heights. We must not alienate them nor hinder them from their work, God forbid. On the contrary, we must bring them near in any possible way and assist them. For it is God's will that events proceed specifically in this fashion. The essence and foundation of this process originate in the pinnacle of holiness. Its purpose is to produce from these laborers something awesome and lofty: the essence of our grand future and the elevation of our holy nation's pride, about which all of our holy prophets prophesied.

All of the great rabbis mentioned above agree that great things must come from the mundane, after which they ascend higher and higher. In this way, they enter the world unexpectedly and sneak away from the accusers.

Behold, I explained above[181] that our future redemption will develop gradually and that we will first gather in *Eretz Yisrael* and make it livable, with the permission of the kings.[182] I quoted the Talmud

180 *Gevurot HaShem* 18.

181 Pp. 175-78.

182 ❖ See Ramban (*Shir HaShirim* 8:13), Radak (*Tehillim* 146:3), *Yerushalmi* (*Ma'aser Sheini* 5:2) quoted in *Tosafot Yom Tov* (ibid. s.v. *u'tenai*) and *Sh'nei*

which states that the Holy One Blessed be He desires [*Mashiach*'s arrival] just like we do, but the Attribute of Justice detains it (*Sanhedrin* 97b). This shows that Satan continually "lies in wait" to delay the redemption. But, when we build the Land and lift the *Shechinah* out of the dust, we destroy and trample the evil forces (as is well known).

Now, had the Orthodox, God-fearing Jews initiated the movement to build and cultivate the Land, it would have been clear to all that a godly city was to be built. For example, if the initiators were the Rebbes of Belz, Shinev, Gur, Munkatch, or the other *tzaddikim* of the generation, would it have been possible to escape the Attribute of Justice and the evil forces, whom we have come to obliterate forevermore? The evil forces certainly would have realized what these *tzaddikim* wanted to accomplish by rebuilding the Land. The Attribute of Justice would have immediately ascended to prosecute the Jewish people, and he would have stopped them.

This actually occurred in the days of R. Yehoshua ben Chananyah. The *Midrash* explains that the king granted the Jews permission to ascend to *Eretz Yisrael* and build Jerusalem and the *Beit HaMikdash*. R. Yehoshua ben Chananyah chose two wealthy men to finance the undertaking, and they began working. Eventually, the Gentiles' envy brought an end to this effort (*BeReishit Rabbah* 64:10). Certainly, the evil forces opposed this matter because R. Yehoshua ben Chananyah was the leader. They recognized him as their chief rival and therefore prevented him from succeeding. Perhaps this was also the determining factor at the time of Don Yosef HaNasi.[183] He was a renowned *tzaddik*, the *gadol* of his generation in both Torah and righteousness. Therefore, the evil forces prosecuted him until they succeeded in nullifying his efforts.

The same is true today. Had the *tzaddikim* taken the initiative, the accuser would have certainly intervened and nullified the entire matter. The *tzaddikim* would not have been able to begin, or even talk about, a movement to rebuild the Land, for it would have immediately been aborted, never to see the light of day.

The Creator of the Universe, however, truly wanted the redemption to begin. And, the prerequisite for redemption is the building of the

Luchot HaBrit (vol. I, *Beit David*, p. 18a, col. b). God willing, I will elaborate on this in the next chapter [apparently, he means this chapter, pp. 199-201]. Also see *Tzror HaMor* (end of *VaYishlach*, s.v. *ve'lachain hitchilah*).

183 See above, p. 180.

Land,[184] or at least a beginning thereof. After the initial step is made, the redemption will grow brighter and brighter and the Attribute of Justice will no longer be able to hinder it. Similarly, the Akeidah writes that the beginning is the essence of any matter; once the initial step is made, nothing can stop it.[185]

Therefore, the Great Advisor,[186] through His profound counsel,[187] designated one man to propose this project of acquiring and building the Holy Land. This man did not know the difference between his right and his left[188] in terms of Judaism. All of his assistants were equally ignorant. When the Attribute of Justice and the evil forces saw this movement – those who initiated it, those who advocated it, and those who carried out the work – they were not afraid at all. They assumed that these builders were part of their camp. "What could they possibly do in the Land? They are on our side, not our enemies'." Therefore, they did not hinder this project.[189] Meanwhile, the process began and the evil forces can no longer nullify it, as the divine visitation will grow greater and greater.

[I already explained that] the original light of *Mashiach* developed in ugly wrappings and from the evil forces themselves. The same thing happened today during the era of the "footsteps of *Mashiach*." The time came for *Mashiach* to arrive, but the Land needed to be prepared and rebuilt.[190] Therefore, HaShem was compelled to steal away from the evil forces and destroy their strength using their own tactics, so He chose unworthy men. It was all part of the Omniscient's plan. This, too, is clear and true.❖

❖ Based on this we can answer the query raised by the Assembly of Israel (*Kenesset Yisrael*), as stated in the *Midrash*:

> *My Beloved sent forth His hand through the hole* (*Shir HaShirim* 5:4). (*Matnot Kehunah* explains: "He sent forth His hand through the hole to perform miracles through Cyrus.") R. Abba bar Kahana said, "What is the nature of a hole? Is it not a place where insects swarm?! [The explanation is as follows]. The Assembly of Israel

184 ❖ As I explained above (pp. 180-83).
185 *Akeidat Yitzchak, Devarim* 30:2.
186 *Yirmiyah* 32:19.
187 Based on *BeReishit Rabbah* 84:13.
188 Based on *Yonah* 4:11.
189 ❖ As our mentor, the Noam Elimelech, writes (see above, p. 187).
190 ❖ As I explained above (pp. 180-83).

> said to the Holy One Blessed be He, 'Master of the Universe, would it not have been better to perform all of these miracles through Daniel or another righteous individual, instead of Cyrus?' Nevertheless, *My innards stirred for Him* (ibid.)." R. Azaryah said, "The Holy One Blessed be He said, 'I enact good decrees. You have said, *My innards stirred for Him*, I have also said, *My innards, My innards, I tremble* (*Yirmiyah* 4:19).'" (*Shir HaShirim Rabbah* 5:3)

This is truly puzzling. Why did the Holy One Blessed be He build Jerusalem and the *Beit HaMikdash* through a Gentile and not through a righteous man? Based on the above, however, it is clear. When the Holy One Blessed be He wants to help His nation and bring them salvation, He is forced (so to speak) to bring it unexpectedly and hide the matter from the accusers, so that they will not oppose it. Therefore, HaShem was forced to hide the matter from the accusers, because Ezra's generation did not deserve a miracle. (The Talmud explains that a miracle should have occurred at the time of Ezra, but sin prevented it [*Berachot* 4a].) If the builders were *tzaddikim*, the accusers would have realized what they wanted to accomplish. Therefore, the Holy One Blessed be He caused a Gentile to initiate the building, and the accusers ignored it, for they said, "If Cyrus, who is one of us, is building it, it will certainly not be imbued with sanctity." Thus, they kept silent and did not protest nor interfere with the building. Once Jerusalem and the *Beit HaMikdash* were built, they were no longer able to interfere.

Moreover, this is apparently the reason why Ezra did not convince the *olim* to repent immediately when they arrived. Only twenty years later, when everything was already built and fixed in its place, he arose, purified them, and separated them from their gentile wives (see *Ezra* 9, *Nechemyah* 13). Why did he not do this immediately at the beginning of the return to *Eretz Yisrael*? The answer is as stated above. He wanted to deceive the accusers. Had he caused them to repent immediately, the accusers would have understood clearly that the Jews wanted to sanctify themselves in the Land. Therefore, they would have protested and put an end to the building. But, since the *olim* were sinners, who continued in their sinful ways, the evil forces were not afraid of them. They said, "These men are on our side," and they did not hinder the building. Then, after everything was already built, Ezra arose and separated the *olim* from their evil ways.

This is what the *Midrash* means, "The Holy One Blessed be He said, 'I enact good decrees.'" That is to say, My decree that the building should be carried out through Cyrus was a good decree. I

In reality, today's builders are not wicked

Know that I referred to the builders of the Land as wicked (God forbid) only because of the position of the zealots. They consider them wicked because they do not see them as God's messengers, with foundations in the apex of sanctity. But I, myself, disagree. In my opinion, these builders are not wicked. They are genuine descendants of Avraham, Yitzchak, and Ya'akov, seed of the tried ones.[191] They are simply like infants who were kidnapped by Gentiles, as I explained above.[192] It is a *mitzvah* to love them and bring them near, as the Rambam writes.[193] Our mentor, R. Mende'le of Rymanov, refrained from calling the second son of the *Haggadah* a *rasha* (wicked). Instead, he called him "the second son," as I cited above.[194]

Let this be a lesson for all those who are quick to call their fellow Jews "*rasha*." God forbid to do such a thing, for they are all descendants of HaShem's loved ones! HaShem will shower upon them a purifying spirit from above to purify their hearts, and He will draw them near to His service by virtue of the *mitzvah* of *Yishuv Eretz Yisrael*, for which they sacrifice themselves. Amen, so may it be God's will.

The *Midrash* comments on the verse *Therefore, I swore in My anger that they will not enter My* [Land of] rest (*Tehillim* 95:11): "When My anger subsides, they will enter My [Land of] rest" (*Torat Kohanim*).[195] The Magen Avraham, in his work *Zayit Ra'anan*, explains:

> The Talmud states that the Holy One Blessed be He regrets this oath (*Chagigah* 5b). He says, "As long as the anger – that is, the accuser – stands in My way, they cannot enter the [Land of] rest. When the anger subsides, however, they will enter the

---

enacted it in order to avoid opposition. "You have said, *My innards stirred for Him*, I have also said, *My innards My innards, I tremble*." That is to say, "It hurts Me, as well, to have a Gentile initiate the building. But, what can I do? I cannot do it through a *tzaddik* because of the accuser."

In any event, this *Midrash* is a clear proof for today's situation. The true God indeed knows how to arrange circumstances.

191 [That is, the Patriarchs. See *Avot* 5:4.]

192 Pp. 106-8, 165, 168.

193 *Hilchot Mamrim* 3:3.

194 P. 104.

195 R. A. Weiss edition, (Vienna, 5622 [1862]), p. 3a.

> [Land of] rest." From this we learn that HaShem gave the accuser permission [to interfere] until the nullifier [i.e., the accuser himself] is abolished.[196]

Thus, since the evil forces have permission to accuse, God must conceal this matter from them, as I have written.

A proof that HaShem tries to deceive the accusers

יד I explained above that the Holy One Blessed be He purposely refrained from initiating the building through *tzaddikim* in order to avoid protest. It seems to me that the following *Midrash* proves this. The [parenthetical] explanations are from *Matnot Kehunah*:

> Reish Lakish said: "The Temple was sanctified (that is to say, it was a fortunate, good, and sacred thing for the Temple) that Ezra did not ascend to *Eretz Yisrael* at that time. (At that time, Yehoshua ben Yehotzadak was not as worthy as Ezra to serve as High Priest.) Had Ezra ascended, Satan could have prosecuted and said, 'It is preferable that Ezra serve as High Priest, rather than Yehoshua ben Yehotzadak the High Priest.' Now, Yehoshua ben Yehotzadak was a High Priest the son of a High Priest, but since Ezra was a righteous man, [Yehoshua] was not as worthy as him to serve as High Priest." R. Simon said: "The Holy One Blessed be He does not like to uproot a lineal chain from its place." (For even though Ezra was more fitting to be the High Priest, HaShem arranged that Ezra would not ascend so as not to uproot Yehoshua the High Priest from his place). (*Shir HaShirim Rabbah* 5:5)

This seems incomprehensible... Why was this good and sacred for the Temple? On the contrary! There would have been more sanctity had the greater *tzaddik* served! Even more difficult is the *Midrash*'s assertion that had Ezra ascended, Satan would have demanded that the greater *tzaddik* be appointed to serve in the Temple. Does Satan usually search for the most perfect service of HaShem?! On the contrary! He tries to ruin and destroy such service.

It seems to me that the *Midrash* means as follows. Had Ezra ascended at that time, Satan could have brought destruction by arousing strife and disunity, which causes the *Shechinah* to abandon the Jewish people and the House of HaShem. He would have provoked people to say that Ezra deserves the High Priesthood, for he is a

196 *Zayit Ra'anan* on *Yalkut Shimoni, Naso* (end).

greater *tzaddik*. Others would have said that Yehoshua deserves it since he is a High Priest the son of a High Priest. This would have led to dispute and disunity, and in the meantime the *Shechinah* would have abandoned the Temple. Therefore, the Holy One Blessed be He delayed Ezra's ascent, so as not to give Satan a pretext to prosecute. Thus, the *Midrash* was correct that it was fortunate for the Temple that Ezra did not ascend at that time. Understand these words for they are true, in my humble opinion.

In any event, this indicates that the Holy One Blessed be He often prevents a *tzaddik* from ascending to *Eretz Yisrael* in order to avoid opposition. We can say the same about today's situation. The Holy One Blessed be He prevented the *tzaddikim* from ascending first, in order to keep the accusers away from us. May HaShem enlighten us to see the truth.

Redemption must come naturally so as not to arouse opposition

In this context I see fit to cite the comments of the brilliant and righteous Kabbalist, our master, R. Akiva Yosef Schlessinger *zt"l*, in his commentary on *Tana DeVei Eliyahu*. The *Midrash* states:

> The Holy One Blessed be He said... "I never performed miracles for Ya'akov, yet all his life he was righteous before Me, as it says, *And Ya'akov was an upright man* (*BeReishit* 25:27)"... And when the Holy One Blessed be He remembers him, He claps His two hands together,[197] as it says, *Thus, Israel shall dwell in safety, alone, in the likeness of Ya'akov* (*Devarim* 33:28).[198] (*Eliyahu Rabbah* 6:4)

R. Akiva Yosef explains:[199]

> ôI never performed miracles for Ya'akov": Rather, he was a shepherd [who lived by] the labor of his hands, and he was completely free of sin... Therefore, *Ya'akov arrived complete*[200]..., *and he bought the portion of land* (*BeReishit* 33:18-19). This is why the Holy One Blessed be He chose [Israel], as it is written, *For the Lord chose Ya'akov as His own, Israel as His treasure*

197 [To show His sorrow that there are none like Ya'akov anymore.]

198 [The next verse states, *Fortunate are you, O Israel. Who is like you?* We see that the Holy One Blessed be He praises upright and pious individuals (*Yeshu'ot Ya'akov* on *Tana DeVei Eliyahu*).]

199 [The comments in parenthesis are R. Akiva Yosef's. Those in brackets are either our author's or the translator's.]

200 [Unharmed by Lavan or Eisav (Rashi).]

(*Tehillim* 135:4). It also says, *Thus, Israel shall dwell in safety, alone, in the likeness of Ya'akov, in a Land...* (*Devarim* 33:28). Remember these things Ya'akov[201]...until *The Lord has redeemed Ya'akov* (*Yirmiyah* 31:10)...❖

For this reason, Ya'akov is called an *upright man* (*Zeir Anpin*). Miracles have the status of *Mochin DeGadlut* (*Chabad*).[203] Natural occurrences, on the other hand, are based on (*Zeir Anpin*) human intellect, which does not arouse much opposition. [If we act naturally], why should we be worse than any other nation?[204]

Therefore, the Ari HaKadosh is cited as saying, on the hymn (*DeVei Malka BeGilufin*),[205] that the word "nature" (הטבע) [in the phrase], "It is disguised in nature," has the same numerical value as "God" (אלהים). The hand of God is disguised in nature, and the one who experiences a miracle does not recognize his miracle. Therefore, "There are no strict judgments."[206] That is to say, the Attribute of Justice cannot prosecute like it did at the splitting of the sea, saying, "These and those are idolaters..."[207]

If we go up on the "king's highway," meaning, with the permission of the kings and through the toil of their hands, we will silence all of the accusers. For we will not [go forth] with great and wondrous [miracles] from HaShem. Rather, in the manner of, *We will go up on the highway..., I will pay their*

❖ That is to say, we should act in accordance with nature, as Ya'akov did, and not rely on miracles. The Ramban writes that Ya'akov acted only in accordance with nature and did not rely on miracles. And, it is well known that Ya'akov's deeds are a sign for his children at the time when Ya'akov will come to Se'ir [i.e., at the time of redemption].[202]

201 Based on *Yeshayah* 44:21.

202 Ramban, introduction to *VaYishlach*.

203 [*Zeir Anpin, Mochin DeGadlut* and *Chabad* represent deep Kabbalistic concepts. It is beyond the scope of this translation to define and explain them.]

204 [Meaning, the evil forces will not hinder us, just like they do not hinder the other nations who act only within nature.]

205 Part of the hymn, *Atkinu Se'udata*, recited at the third Sabbath meal.

206 [From the above-mentioned hymn.]

207 *Yalkut Reuveni, BeShalach*, on the verse, "*chail Paroh*." Also see *Midrash Tehillim* 15:5. [The *Midrash* explains that the Attribute of Justice tried to prevent HaShem from saving the Jews by saying that they worship idols just like the Egyptians do.]

> *cost, verily, nothing will happen. I will pass through on foot* (*BeMidbar* 20:19). If the [kings of the land] give permission, the accusers have no pretext to oppose this matter, not in the heavens above nor on the land below.
>
> In this way, *Israel shall dwell* – forever – *in safety, alone, in the likeness of Ya'akov,* as Eliyahu *z"l* explains.[208] All of the prophets prophesied that Eliyahu would show us the path in which to go before the coming of *Mashiach*, as it says, *Behold, I send you Eliyah the prophet before the coming of the great and awesome day of the Lord* (*Malachi* 3:23). He was chosen and destined to guide those who truly seek HaShem, through the paths of redemption.
>
> The third Sabbath meal corresponds to Ya'akov and saves us from the birthpangs of *Mashiach*.[209] Therefore, in keeping with Ya'akov's approach [of doing everything naturally and not relying on miracles], we say in the hymn, *Devei Malka BeGilufin*,[210] that the Holy One Blessed be He is hidden in nature: "Come near unto Me, see My strength, for there are no strict judgments."❖ When miracles occur, the accusers deduct from our merits. But, when matters proceed naturally, there is no room for opposition. Why should we be different than any other nation? Are they better than us? Therefore, "Those brazen dogs [the accusers] dwell outside and do not enter,"[211] [for their mouths will be shut].[212]

Thus, Ya'akov did not rely on miracles. He acted only in accordance with nature so as not to give the Attribute of Justice a pretext to prosecute. Ya'akov Avinu instructed us to act the same way when Israel will dwell in safety, alone, in the likeness of Ya'akov in a Land of grain and wine.[213] That is to say, we must first establish a settlement in the Land, and then the redemption will draw near. For the Attribute of Justice will be unable to prevent us and the Holy

---

❖ That is to say, "Come near unto Me" – O nation of Israel. "See My strength" – that I operate through natural means, which are not affected by judgments or the accusers.

208 [He is referring to the *Tana DeVei Eliyahu* cited above.]

209 See *Shabbat* 118a.

210 See note 205, above.

211 [From the above-mentioned hymn.]

212 *Tosafot Ben Yechiel* on *Eliyahu Rabbah* 6:4.

213 Based on *Devarim* 33:28.

One Blessed be He from doing as we please and achieving redemption. This is true and evident.

Eretz Yisrael precedes Torah

מו *Tana DeVei Eliyahu* comments on the verse *To guard the way to the tree of life* (*BeReishit* 3:24):

> *To guard the way* – this refers to the ôway of the landö (*derech eretz*); *to the tree of life*, for the ôway of the landö precedes the tree of life. *The tree of life* refers to Torah, as it says, *It is a tree of life for those who grasp it* (*Mishley* 3:18). (*Eliyahu Rabbah* 1:2)

The above-mentioned brilliant *tzaddik*, R. Akiva Yosef Schlessinger, explains:

> This requires clarification. Which "way of the land" is he referring to? The answer is based on the *Yalkut*'s statement: "'For they were banished from the Land' – this refers to *Eretz Yisrael*."[214] *Tana DeVei Eliyahu* is informing us not to...follow the ways of the spies who despised the Land. They said that Torah precedes *Eretz Yisrael*. Therefore, they did not want to enter the Land. They preferred to stay in the desert and learn Torah from Moshe Rabbeinu, for the Torah was only given to those who ate the Manna.[215] Thus, Eliyahu tells us that "the way of the Land" – that is, the way that leads to the Land of Israel – comes before Torah. Accordingly, the *Midrash* states, "Dwelling in *Eretz Yisrael* outweighs the entire Torah" (*Sifrei, Re'eh* 28, on *Devarim* 12:29).[216]

R. Schlessinger also writes that the reason the spies failed and were unwilling to enter *Eretz Yisrael* is

> because they were afraid of the transgressions committed there, which are more serious than those committed outside the Land. This was a sin on their part, for they were like the gentile nations who refused to accept the yoke of Torah for the same reason. Israel, on the other hand, said, *We will do and we will*

214 We were unable to locate this source. Perhaps it should read, *And I will banish them from the land* (*BeMidbar* 22:6). For, *Chazal* comment on that verse, "[Balak] wanted to drive them out only so that they would not enter the Land of Israel" (*BeMidbar Rabbah* 20:7, *Yalkut Shimoni* 1:765).

215 [Because they were able to study Torah without worrying about making a living.] *Mechilta, BeShalach, Parashat VaYasa* 2, s.v. *devar yom beyomo; Tanchuma, BeShalach* 20.

216 *Tosafot Ben Yechiel* on *Eliyahu Rabbah* 1:2, s.v. *lishmor*.

obey (*Shemot* 24:7), for they had great trust in God; and "HaShem assists those who come to be purified" (*Shabbat* 104a).[217]

Thus, we must not fear that perhaps we will sin while dwelling in *Eretz Yisrael* (God forbid), because HaShem assists those who come to be purified.

IV The Beginning of Redemption

Eretz Yisrael will be rebuilt with the permission of the kings

מז I have proven from many Rabbinic sources that our future redemption will develop gradually, with miracles disguised in nature, rather than all at once, with manifest miracles. This explains the *Yerushalmi* which quotes R. Acha as saying, "The *Beit HaMikdash* will be rebuilt before the reestablishment of the Davidic Dynasty" (*Ma'aser Sheini* 5:2 [21b]). The P'nei Moshe comments, "Good things come to Israel gradually... At first, the *Beit HaMikdash* will be rebuilt. Afterwards, the Davidic Dynasty will flourish and the complete salvation will occur, speedily in our days. Amen."

The Tosafot Yom Tov cites this *Yerushalmi* and comments:

> ...Our Sages decreed not to bring [the fruits of *kerem rivai* to Jerusalem] so as not to adorn the marketplace of Jerusalem, which is in the hands of our enemies. This is true even if...the *Beit HaMikdash* is rebuilt..., for the *Beit HaMikdash* will be rebuilt before the reestablishment of the Davidic Dynasty, as the *Yerushalmi* affirms... Thus, our enemies will have some control over us before the reestablishment of the Davidic Dynasty, just like at the beginning of the Second Temple...[218]

Thus, the *Beit HaMikdash* will be rebuilt with the permission of the kingdom.

Our mentor, the Shelah, also quotes this *Yerushalmi*,[219] as does the Ramban, who writes:

> The beginning of the future redemption will occur with the permission of the kings. Some of the exiles will gather in *Eretz Yisrael*, and afterwards, HaShem will extend His hand again [to gather the remaining exiles]. The verse, therefore, says, *Then the Lord your God will bring back your captivity* (*Devarim*

217 Ibid. 1:1, end of s.v. *vayegaresh*.
218 *Tosafot Yom Tov, Ma'aser Sheini* 5:2.
219 *Sh'nei Luchot HaBrit, Beit David*, vol. 1, p. 18a, col. 2.

> 30:3); and afterwards, *He will return and gather you from all the nations* (ibid.).[220]

The Radak writes:

> Salvation is solely in the hands of HaShem, and He brings it about through mortals, as He did with Cyrus during the Babylonian exile. In the future, as well, HaShem will bring Israel's redemption through gentile kings, by inspiring them to set the Jews free.[221]

Rabbeinu Bachya agrees:

> ôWhy is this nation [Edom] called a swine (חזיר)? For, it will eventually restore (להחזיר) the crown to its former glory" (*VaYikra Rabbah*, 13). This means as follows. The two Temples were built by Jews: the first one by Shlomo... and the second one by Zerubavel..., with Cyrus' permission. The third Temple, however, will be built by Edom..., since they destroyed it... In the future, they and all the other powers will come to assist and support Israel, for peace will abound.[222]

I also discovered in the *Pesikta*:

> Our Rabbis taught: When the Messianic King appears, he will stand upon the roof of the *Beit HaMikdash* and proclaim to Israel, "Humble ones, the time of redemption has arrived." (*Piska Kumi Ori*)

R. Zalman Margolis explains:

> ôStand upon the roof of the *Beit HaMikdash*" is meant literally. For the *Yerushalmi*, quoted by the Tosafot Yom Tov, affirms that the *Beit HaMikdash* will be built forty years before the coming of *Mashiach*.

This indicates that it will be built with the permission of the kings.

The brilliant Maharshak explains the prayer "Rebuild Your House as at first and establish Your Sanctuary on its prepared site. Let us see its rebuilding and gladden us in its rectification:"[223]

220 Ramban, *Shir HaShirim* 8:13.

221 Radak, *Tehillim* 146:3.

222 Rabbeinu Bachya, *VaYikra* 11:4-7.

223 *Musaf* prayer for *Pesach, Shavuot*, and *Sukkot*.

> This seems repetitive. Also, the phrase, "Rebuild Your House as at first," is particularly difficult, for it will not be as at first; rather, it will be made of fire... Apparently, however, this alludes to the Tosafot Yom Tov's statement. That is, at first the kings will build the *Beit HaMikdash*, and afterwards HaShem will build it with fire. This fits well with the wording of the prayer. At first we beseech, "Rebuild Your House as at first," i.e., through man. Afterwards, "Establish Your Sanctuary on its prepared site" – that is, the Holy One Blessed be He should establish it.[224]

Actually, the *Bavli* concurs. The Talmud comments on the order of the *Shemoneh Esrei* (which was authored by the Men of the Great Assembly): "Once Jerusalem is rebuilt, David will arrive, as it says, *Afterwards, the Children of Israel will return and seek out the Lord their God and David their king* (*Hoshea* 3:5)" (*Megillah* 17b-18a). Obviously, then, Jerusalem will be rebuilt with the permission and consent of the kingdoms, before *Mashiach* arrives.

In *Mashmia Yeshuah*, the Abarbanel explains that this miracle [of rebuilding the Land] will occur by way of the Gentiles themselves.[225] Maharivach, father of the Maharalbach, says that HaShem will inspire the kings to recognize the truth.[226]

Apparently, the prophet Yeshayahu supports all of these statements of *Chazal*:

> *I am the Lord...Who annuls the omens of the impostors and makes fools of the diviners; Who turns wise men backwards and makes their knowledge foolish; Who confirms the word of His servant and performs the counsel of His messengers; Who says of Jerusalem, "it shall be inhabited," and of the cities of Judah, "they shall be rebuilt, and I will raise up their ruins."... Who says of Cyrus, "He is My shepherd,*[227] *and he will perform all that I desire," to say of Jerusalem, "it shall be built," and of the Temple, "it shall be established." Thus says the Lord to His anointed one,*[228] *to Cyrus, whose right hand I have held...* (*Yeshayah* 44:24-45:1)

224 *Yeri'ot Shlomo*, commentary to the Ya'avetz's *Siddur Beit Ya'akov*, p. 256b.
225 *Mashmia Yeshuah*, p. 25.
226 Introduction to *Ein Ya'akov*.
227 ❖ Rashi explains this to mean, "My king."
228 ❖ Rashi explains, "Any title of distinction is referred to as anointing."

In *Iggeret Teiman*, the Rambam explains that this prophecy refers to the Messianic era, may it arrive speedily. The Gentiles thought:

> ôThis nation [Israel] will never gain autonomy and will never be redeemed from its subjugation.ö All of their wise men agreed with this... But, the Holy One Blessed be He will annul their schemes and deceiving logic, and then, *Mashiach* will appear. Accordingly, Yeshayah says, *Who annuls the omens of the impostors... Who turns wise men backwards... Who confirms the word of His servant... Who says of Jerusalem...*[229]

Thus, our mentor, the Rambam, states that this prophecy speaks of the future redemption. Now, since the prophet juxtaposed this prophecy to the one about Cyrus..., we can infer that our redemption will occur in the same fashion as the redemption at the time of Cyrus. At first, the kings will allow the Jews to return and rebuild *Eretz Yisrael*, Jerusalem, and the *Beit HaMikdash*. Then, the true redemption will ensue. In fact, *Chazal* say that Cyrus was destined to generate a true and complete redemption, but sin prevented it (*Berachot* 4a). Today's return to *Eretz Yisrael*, however, will certainly develop into the final redemption, but it will begin like Cyrus' redemption. This is why the prophet juxtaposed these two prophecies.

Thus said Cyrus king of Persia, ôThe Lord, God of Heaven, has given me all the kingdoms of the earth, and He has charged me to build Him a House in Jerusalemö (*Ezra* 1:2). Rashi comments:

> *He has charged me*, through the prophet Yeshayah, as it says, *Who says of Cyrus, "He is My shepherd"...to say of Jerusalem, "it shall be built"... Thus says the Lord to His anointed one, to Cyrus, whose right hand I have held.* And this prophecy was stated by Yeshayah (44:28-45:1).

Clearly, then, this prophecy refers to the Second Temple. If so, why was it necessary to juxtapose it to the prophecy about the rebuilding of Jerusalem in the future? We are forced to say that this teaches that the future restoration of Jerusalem and the *Beit HaMikdash* will begin the same way it did at the time of Cyrus, with the permission and consent of the kingdom. Based on this, *He performs the counsel of His messengers* refers to the kings who consent to this, for they are God's messengers, as I explained above.

229 *Iggeret Teiman*, pp. 159-60.

I also discovered this idea in R. Sa'adya Gaon's work, *Emunot VeDe'ot*. He writes that the *Beit HaMikdash* will first be built with the permission of the kings of Edom. This will serve as a preparation for the heavenly *Beit HaMikdash*.[230]

The Abarbanel concurs:

> It is possible that the redemption will occur when the kings decide that the Holy Land should return to the people of Israel. He who desires to go up to *Eretz Yisrael* will do so, like the Jews did after the Babylonian exile. Afterwards, when the Holy City of Jerusalem is rebuilt, all the Jews will ascend together.[231]

Similarly, the Malbim writes that the exiles will begin to gather in *Eretz Yisrael*, where they will enjoy some autonomy and sovereignty. Afterwards, they will have a permanent kingdom, namely, the Davidic Kingdom, for the Messianic King will reign permanently. The Davidic Kingdom will develop gradually, however. At first, it will only [have the status of] a judge, and it will develop little by little until HaShem reigns sovereign.[232]

The *Pesikta* states, "When the Assembly of Israel ascended from Babylonia to *Eretz Yisrael* after the seventy years of exile, they were loaded with kindness before the kingdoms" (*Pesikta Sos Asis*).[233] R. Efrayim Zalman Margolis explains: "When the Jews were to be redeemed from Babylonia, they were scattered around the world, and they were subordinate to the kings of the nations. But, they found favor [lit., kindness] in their eyes."

Apparently, the *Pesikta* learns this from the end of the verse,[234] *For as the earth brings forth its growth...so will the Lord God cause righteousness and praise to sprout forth before all the nations* (*Yeshayah* 61:11). That is to say, Israel will find favor in their eyes. Tzefanyah also says, *For I will make you a name and a praise among all the peoples of the earth, when I return your captives* (*Tzefanyah* 13:20). Thus, the future redemption will depend on the favor and kindness of the nations, and it will begin like it did with Cyrus. It is surprising that none of these *gedolim* realized that Yeshayahu's prophecy

230 *Emunot VeDe'ot* 8:5.
231 Abarbanel, *Tehillim* 147:2.
232 Malbim, *Michah* 4:8.
233 On *Yeshayah* 61:10.
234 See previous note.

alludes to this, as I mentioned above. Perhaps, HaShem set this aside for me to discover.

The time and manner of redemption are hidden

יז[235] The Rambam writes in *Iggeret Teiman*:

> Regarding your mention of the end of days... First of all, you must realize that no man can ever possibly know the true end of days, as Daniel said, *For these matters are hidden and sealed until the time of the end* (*Daniel* 12:9)...
>
> We can infer a *kal vachomer*: Although the Torah revealed that the Egyptian exile would last 400 years,[236] Israel did not know [the precise moment] of the end until it actually occurred. (For, when they left Egypt they realized that the calculation started from Yitzchak's birth)... All the more so, we cannot know the end of this exile, the length of which caused the prophets to fear and tremble. David wondered, *Will You be angry with us forever? Will You draw out Your anger for generation to generation?* (*Tehillim* 85:6). Yeshayah said about this lengthy exile, *They will be gathered together as captives are gathered in a pit, and they will be imprisoned in a prison, and after many days they will be remembered* (*Yeshayah* 24:22). Daniel explained to us how deep and hidden is the knowledge of the end of days.[237]
>
> Therefore, our Sages discouraged us from reckoning the appointed times of the coming of *Mashiach*. They feared that this would cause the masses to stumble, for perhaps people would go astray upon seeing that the reckoned days have passed and *Mashiach* did not come. Thus, *Chazal* said, "May those who reckon the end of days perish" (*Sanhedrin* 97b). They are an obstacle to the nation. Therefore, our Sages prayed that their knowledge should perish and their calculations should be destroyed.[238]

It seems to me that the manner in which the redemption will occur – how it will begin and how it will develop – is just as obscured and hidden as the time of the end of days. The Ran writes:

> Behold, we notice that at the very time the redemption from

235 [In the original Hebrew edition, the next five sections are numbered incorrectly. יז is missing, and כא appears twice. We have corrected this.]

236 See *BeReishit* 15:13.

237 *Daniel* 12:9.

238 *Iggeret Teiman*, pp. 151, 153-55.

> Egypt was nearing, the Jews perceived that they were being redeemed. In addition, they saw the circumstances and deeds which were the cause of their redemption. Nevertheless, they were unable to comprehend the reason for these things until HaShem revealed it to them. If so, we certainly are even more ignorant about the future redemption. Therefore, the Rambam *z"l* writes that no one will know how these things will occur until they occur.[239]

Thus, we do not clearly understand how the redemption will unfold until it actually unfolds. The Rambam himself also writes, "But, you will not know how *Mashiach* will arise until he arises."[240]

We must not disregard anything that might be the beginning of redemption

Therefore, we must not disregard anything that might be the beginning of redemption. For perhaps God wants it to happen specifically in this manner, especially since *Chazal*, our true Sages, predict that the beginning of redemption will occur with the permission of the kings. It is even possible that the prophet Yeshayahu states this explicitly (as I explained above).

The verse states, *When I return your captives before your eyes, says the Lord* (*Tzefanyah* 3:20). Our mentor, the author of *Yismach Moshe*, explains that in reality the manner and time of the redemption are written explicitly in the Torah, but our eyes are closed, and we do not know how to interpret the words. However, after HaShem returns our captives we will understand the words, and our eyes will recognize that HaShem foretold the time and manner of the redemption.[241] At that time, perhaps we will realize that Yeshayahu's prophecy (mentioned above) indeed compares the future redemption to the story of Cyrus.

In any event, just as we cannot say for sure that the redemption will occur in a particular way, so too, we cannot reject it and say that it will not. We must accept all of the circumstances, means, and opportunities that come to us, for perhaps the Creator wants it to happen specifically this way. Anyone who desires the truth will acknowledge this point.

Today's pioneers are God's messengers

יח In the beginning of the winter of 5703 [1942], on Wednesday of *parashat VaYeishev*, during my exile, circumstances brought

239 *Derashot HaRan*, end of *Derush* 11; quoting Rambam, *Hilchot Melachim* 12:2.
240 *Iggeret Teiman*, p. 105.
241 See *Yismach Moshe*, vol. 1, p. 129b, s.v. *u'bazeh*.

me to Busermin, my former residence. While there, I visited my honorable and beloved student, an eminent Torah scholar, a famous magnate, our distinguished and pious master, R. Avish Ruttman.[242] He was a prominent member of his community and one of the most extraordinary and devout followers of the great and brilliant rabbi, the prince of the Torah, the holy luminary, the light of the world, the prince of the house of the *Zohar*,[243] expert in both the revealed and esoteric aspects of the Torah, our honorable and holy master, R. Aharon Yeshayah Fisch *ztvk"l*, *av beit din* of Yudess. (R. Aharon was one of the foremost disciples of the Rebbe of Komarno *z"l* who ordained him as rabbi.) When I was young and lived in Busermin, I was privileged to know him and bask in the light of his Torah. Once a year he would visit Busermin to spend a Sabbath with his followers and admirers. I simply cannot describe his righteousness and piety, which surpassed even his greatness in Torah. A man's wisdom illuminates his face.[244] He was a distinguished sage who understood and knew how to differentiate between truth and falsehood. He was truly a giant among giants.[245]

This R. Avish related to me a speech about the Zionist movement that he heard from R. Aharon Fisch's holy mouth. Although many of the generation's Torah leaders strongly opposed [lit., "stoned"] this movement, R. Fisch said as follows:

> Leave them alone! We do not truly know how the redemption will unfold. In one place the *Zohar* states that Jerusalem will be rebuilt and the exiles will be gathered before the redemption.[246] Elsewhere the *Zohar* states that redemption will occur without our intervention.[247] Thus, it is unclear what the Creator of the Universe wants. Therefore, if we see that

242 ❖ When I was young and sharp, I resided with my brilliant and righteous father-in-law, our master and teacher, R. Ya'akov Yosef Ginz *z"l, av beit din* of Busermin. During those years, R. Avish used to come to me every day to learn a set lesson in Talmud and *Tosafot*.

243 [I.e., a great Kabbalist.]

244 Based on *Kohelet* 8:1.

245 ❖ In my responsa, *Mishneh Sachir* (1:86), I printed an answer he gave me concerning whether or not it is permissible to remove the last from a sandal on the Sabbath.

246 See *Zohar* 1:139a, *Midrash HaNe'elam*. Also see *Sha'arei Zohar* on *Berachot* 49a, and *Tanchuma, Noach* 11.

247 See *Zohar* 3:221a.

> many Jews desire to rebuild the Land, even if they are the greatest sinners, who could be so brazen and arrogant to interfere with their work?! Perhaps HaShem wants the rebuilding to be done specifically by people like these. Why must you involve yourself with God's hidden matters?![248] God, the Cause of All Causes, knows how to cause things to happen. Leave them alone!

Keep in mind that these words come from a man who was truly unique in his generation, in this country. The revealed and the hidden, as well as supreme wisdom, were all unified in him. His statement coincides exactly with what I wrote in the previous section.

I subsequently heard this same idea in the name of the *Admor* of Vizhnitz, a man of God, brilliant in both the revealed and hidden, our master and teacher, the honorable and holy R. Yisrael *ztvk"l*, who lived in Grossvardine. Reliable sources told me that they heard directly from his holy mouth that he did not want to join in the ostracism of the Zionists. He felt that God purposely wanted them to rebuild the Land, because the ruffians (*biryonim*) destroyed our Land and the Second Temple.[249] Therefore, they must rectify their wrongdoing and rebuild our Land now. Rabbeinu Bachya (whom I quoted above)[250] agrees.

Now, notice and consider how these two great men looked into the handiwork of today's builders with a discerning eye and saw the will of the Almighty.

At the end of days, the time and manner of redemption will become less obscure

יט *As for you, O Daniel, hide the matter and seal the book until the time of the end; many will wander and knowledge will increase* (*Daniel* 12:4). The Malbim explains that things will be hidden only until the time of the end.

> But at the time of the end, doubt will disappear. The closer the time, the smaller the doubt. We know that the redemption must come before the seventh millennium.[251] Therefore, in the past, there was little certainty and much doubt. (That is to say, little time had passed without the redemption coming, which we knew for certain was not the destined time; and much

248 *Berachot* 10a.
249 See *Gittin* 56a.
250 P. 200.
251 See *Avodah Zarah* 9a; *Zohar* 1:116b; 117a; 119a. Also see *Sha'arei Zohar* on *Sanhedrin* 97a.

> time was left in the future until the seventh millennium.) However, as we approach the seventh millennium, there is more certainty and less doubt. In this way, *Knowledge will increase.*

Thus, at the time of the end, doubt will disappear, knowledge will increase, and we will know that the time of redemption is approaching.

Now, although the Malbim wrote this as if it was his own idea, I found the exact same idea in *Kisei HaMelech*:[252]

> Even though the heart does not reveal this matter to the mouth, when the time of redemption approaches, it will be revealed to the upper and lower worlds. Most of the world will know the end, as the *Zohar* states, "At that time it will be revealed..."[253]

Thus, the Malbim's explanation is true.

A wonderful story

כ Allow me to relate a wonderful story that I heard from my friend, the brilliant teacher, our honorable and holy master, R. ***Yisrael Veltz*** *shlita*, judge and mentor of the Orthodox community here in the capital city. When the Malbim published and distributed his commentary on the book of *Daniel*, the *gedolim* of the generation criticized him for calculating the end of days (see the end of his commentary). They wrote him a letter of rebuke asking how he dared publicize this in disregard to *Chazal*'s statement "May those who reckon the end of days perish" (*Sanhedrin* 97b). Many such letters came in and he was unable to answer each one individually, so he published a manifesto explaining his position. (This manifesto is kept in the museum of the holy community of Prague.):

> My venerable masters, I will tell you of an incident which took place in the Bucharest province, which is subsumed under my rabbinic authority. A certain wealthy man, the head of a large leather trading business, had an only son who became Bar Mitzvah. At his Bar Mitzvah, the boy delivered a good and intricate discourse, which pleased his father greatly. In order to reward his beloved son for learning so well and for delivering such a wonderful discourse in public, the father said, "My son, I am about to take a long and difficult business trip to the

252 *Kisei HaMelech* on *Tikkunei Zohar* 21:4 (see p. 50b).

253 *Zohar* 1:118a. Also see there *Nitzotzei Zohar* 1.

Leipzig market. I would like to take you along in order to please you, just like you pleased me with your discourse." The son was overjoyed when he heard this.

His mother and the servants prepared for this great trip, which, at that time, was very arduous and would last three to four weeks. The journey, of course, was dangerous for it passed over mountainous terrain.

When the time came to leave, the father and son bid a tearful farewell to their wife and mother. They assured her that nothing bad would happen to them on the way, and that HaShem would help them return safe and sound. The father and son sat in the wagon and began their long journey. After two hours, the son asked his father, "Father, how many more hours until we arrive in Leipzig?" When the father heard this question he became enraged. He stared at his son with an extremely embittered look, but remained silent, not answering his question. The son, too, remained silent and never asked that question again.

After three or four weeks of the journey, the father asked the wagon driver, "Moshe, how much longer until Leipzig?" The driver answered, "In another hour and a half we will reach the city, God willing." When the son heard this question he was astonished. He said to his father: "I do not understand. When I asked this very question – how much longer until Leipzig – you became enraged and looked at me indignantly. But now, I hear that you asked the same question yourself!" The father replied jovially, "My son, both now and then you asked foolishly. Then, we had just begun the journey and had traveled only a few hours. You should have realized from the preparations and from the tears that flowed when we left your mother that this would not be a two-hour trip, but a long and arduous one. Why, then, would you ask, after two hours, 'How much longer to Leipzig?' Therefore, I rightfully got angry at your question. But, now that we are already very near to Leipzig, the time has come to ask and inquire how much longer until we reach Leipzig."

My masters, this is exactly what has happened to us during this long and bitter 2,000-year journey through exile. Of course, at the beginning of the exile *Chazal* forbade us to calculate the end of days, because the great weeping and the great preparations indicated that the exile was not going to last a day or two. When Ya'akov Avinu foresaw the destruction and

> the exile he trembled and became frightened.[254] Therefore, there was no reason to calculate the end. On the contrary, by doing so, people would see that the exile would last an exceedingly long time, and who would have the strength to endure? R. Shimon bar Yochai cried when he saw how long it would last, and he said, "Woe that the exile will last so long; who can bear this?"[255] But now that we are so near to Leipzig, it is permissible and proper to ask such questions, "How much longer until Leipzig?"

It seems to me that this is why the *Zohar* (mentioned above)[256] states that when the time of redemption approaches most of the world will know. We will already be so close to Leipzig that it will be permissible to know how much longer the journey will last. A word to the wise is sufficient.

The return of Jews to Eretz Yisrael is a sign of redemption

כא The *Midrash* states: "R. Abba bar Kahana said, 'If you see benches filled with Babylonians in *Eretz Yisrael*, anticipate the footsteps of *Mashiach*. Why? For, it says, *He spread* (פרש) *a net for my feet* (*Eichah* 1:13)' " (*Eichah Rabbah* 1:41). The Torah Temimah explains:

> The *Midrash* interprets the word פרש (*He spread*) as פרס (Persia).[257] The Babylonians are the same as the Persians.[258] *For my feet* alludes to *Mashiach*, as it is written, *How beautiful upon the mountains are the feet of the harbinger of good tidings* (*Yeshayah* 52:7). "If you see benches filled with Babylonians in *Eretz Yisrael*" means, if you see many Diaspora Jews ascending from Babylonia to *Eretz Yisrael*, it is a sign that the Holy One Blessed be He calculated the end of days. The verse hints to this: "Persia (פרש) is *a net* [– a sign] *for my feet* [– *Mashiach*]."
>
> Furthermore, it is possible that the *Midrash* alludes to *Chazal*'s statement: "He who ascends from Babylonia to *Eretz Yisrael* transgresses a positive commandment, as it says, *I have adjured you, O daughters of Jerusalem, by the gazelles and by the hinds of the field, if you should stir or arouse the love* (to

254 See *Zohar* 1:23b.
255 *Zohar Chadash*, p. 55a.
256 P. 208.
257 Using the rule that "ש" and "ס" are interchangeable. (Torah Temimah's note)
258 The *Midrash* mentions these two because Persia and Babylonia are known as places of our exile. They are not meant exclusively. (Torah Temimah's note)

ascend to *Eretz Yisrael) until it pleases* (*Shir HaShirim* 2:7)" (*Ketuvot* 111b). That is to say, do not arouse the love until the Holy One Blessed be He desires it. Thus, when there is a universal awakening to ascend to *Eretz Yisrael*, it is a sign that the time of divine desire has arrived. This is the meaning of, "If you see benches..." That is, if you see many people return, "anticipate the footsteps of *Mashiach*," for it is a sign that *the feet of the harbinger of good tidings* are already standing in the gates of Jerusalem.

In addition, it is possible to say that the *Midrash* interprets the word *net* (רשת) as inheritance (ירושה). That is to say, the inheritance [*Eretz Yisrael*] will come to the feet of *Mashiach*.[259]

Now, in recent years thousands and tens of thousands of our Jewish brethren have flowed into *Eretz Yisrael* from all corners of the Diaspora. This is certainly a sign of the beginning of redemption.

War is a sign of redemption

The wars of recent times are also a sign of redemption. There have been constant conflagrations ever since the outbreak of world-war in 5674 [1914], sometimes here and sometimes there. And now, war has once again returned and flared up in the world, even worse than before.

Our Sages say, "War is the beginning of redemption" (*Megillah* 17b). *Midrash Rabbah* (*parashat Lech Lecha*) states, "If you see kingdoms provoking one another, expect the footsteps of *Mashiach*. From whom do we derive this? From Avraham, for there was a war between the kings, and Avraham was redeemed." (See the *Midrash* inside;[260] at this point I do not have it in front of me.)

The author of *Brit Menuchah*, a great and prodigious Kabbalist,[261] writes:

> It says about the time of redemption, *I will cause Egypt to fight against Egypt..., city against city, kingdom against kingdom* (*Yeshayah* 19:2). Afterwards, there will be peace and tranquillity, rest and calm. The peace of earlier generations, like the generation of the desert and that of King Shlomo *a"h*, will not compare to the peace of *Mashiach*'s generation...

259 *Torah Temimah, Eichah* 1:141.

260 *BeReishit Rabbah* 42:4.

261 R. Avraham Merimon HaSefaradi. ❖ He lived a hundred years before the Ari *z"l*, who testified that all of his Kabbalah was divinely inspired.

A great and boundless war will break out in heaven; and there will be a corresponding war down on earth. Spiritual and mortal beings will battle one another...[262] [The earthly war will take place] in order to inform the Jews of the establishment of the three luminaries[263] that are destined to gather them from the lands of their enemies. Destructive angels will run towards them [the Jews] with destructive forces in hand. Evil will expand its dominion and strive to intensify the exile. There will be great confusion, and many Jews will contemplate saving themselves by forsaking our religion (may the Merciful One protect us). But, each Jew must remain perfect in faith.

This is what happened in Egypt. The Jews were in grave danger because of the destructive forces that descended to destroy and eradicate them. But, the people of Israel persevered and held fast to the perfect faith of their forefathers.

This is why the place [where the Jews first encamped after leaving Egypt] is called *Eitam* (*Shemot* 13:20), [which means strength]. It also says, *Between Migdol and the sea* (ibid. 14:2). The place is called *Migdol* because that is where the people of Israel strengthened themselves and saw all of the greatness (*gedulah*)[264] that was going to come to them. They also saw that their greatness was going to reach a place called "The Sea of Wisdom" (ים החכמה), as it says, *Between Migdol and the sea*.

It seems to me that Chaggai's prophecy alludes to this and to current events: *For thus says the Lord of Hosts, "Yet again, in just a little while, I will shake the heavens and the earth and the sea and the dry land. I will shake all the nations, and the precious things of all the nations will come, and I will fill this House with glory," says the Lord of Hosts* (2:6-7). This coincides with the Kabbalist's description of the time of redemption and is exactly what has happened today. Therefore, this is a great sign that we are close to redemption. The current war, the great confusion that has arisen in the world, and the fact that so many Jews are flowing into *Eretz Yisrael* all demonstrate that we are close to Leipzig.[265] May HaShem

262 This ends the direct quote from *Brit Menuchah*, p. 21b, col. a. What follows is a paraphrase from p. 21a, col. b.

263 [A reference to some deep Kabbalistic concept.]

264 [From the same root as *Migdol*.]

265 See above, pp. 208-10.

save us and deliver our souls, speedily in our days. Amen.

I concluded this chapter with 21 (כא) sections. May this be a good sign that Israel will only (אך) have goodness, speedily in our days. Amen. Today is Wednesday of *parashat Mishpatim*, 5703 [1943], here in the capital, Budapest.

CHAPTER THREE

SETTLEMENT AND REBUILDING

Before I discuss the *mitzvah* of settling and building the Land, I will begin this chapter with an introduction.

I Introduction

God sends afflictions to awaken us from our indolence

א The following is a quote from the introduction to *Ezrat Kohanim* on Tractate *Middot*.

> Let us contemplate, deliberate, and investigate: Perhaps all of the hardships, evil afflictions, and misfortunes that befall us bang like a hammer on the doors of our hearts to arouse and awaken us from our indolent sleep. They replace the prophets' utterances in days of old, as *Chazal* state in the holy books: Today, afflictions and evil diseases fulfill the mission of rebuke that the prophets used to fulfill (when prophecy was prevalent in Israel). I think this is stated in the *Zohar*.❖

❖ I found this stated explicitly in the *Midrash*:

> The Holy One Blessed be He said to the prophets: "If you do not fulfill My mission, do you think that I have no [other] messengers?! *Land has the advantage over everything* (Kohelet 5:8). I will achieve My mission even through a snake, a scorpion, or a frog." This can be proven, because were it not for the hornet, how would the Holy One Blessed be He have punished the Amorites? Were it not for the frog, how would He have punished the Egyptians? Therefore, it says, *Behold I will strike* (נוגף) *all your borders with frogs* (Shemot 7:27). What does this mean? The Holy One Blessed be He said, "Behold, I will push the plagues upon you." [For, נוגף can also mean "push"] as in the verse *If a man's ox pushes* (יגוף) *another's* (ibid. 21:35). (*Shemot Rabbah* 10:1-2)

Thus, the *Midrash* states explicitly that evil afflictions and misfortunes replace the prophets' utterances.

I will prove the absolute clarity and truth of this concept from the words of our sacred seers. Notice how our holy prophets aroused the hearts of our ancestors in a similar fashion at the beginning of the Second Temple era. Our ancestors stopped building the Temple because the enemies of Judah and Jerusalem halted them by force and power.[1] So the prophets aroused them in the name of HaShem, saying, *Is this a time for you, yourselves, to dwell in your roofed houses while this House lies in ruins?... Consider your ways... You have sown much, but bring in little;* [you] *eat without being satiated... Why is this? says the Lord of Hosts. Because of My House which lies in ruins, and you run, each man to his own house. Therefore, because of you, the heavens withheld their dew, and the Land withheld its produce. I called for a drought upon the Land* (*Chaggai* 1:4-11, see Rashi).

Once they became inspired to build the Temple, the prophet said, *Now, consider* [what happened] *from this day and beforehand, before a stone was laid upon a stone in the Lord's sanctuary. When they would come to a* [grain] *heap of twenty* [measures], *there were only ten... From this day on, I* [God] *will bless* [you] (ibid. 2:15-19). That is to say, notice the difference between the past and the present, and realize that your pain and suffering will turn into blessings because you now build the Temple. In reality, they were not only blessed physically, but also spiritually. They advanced to great heights and transformed everything from bad to good, as is well known. When they first came to *Eretz Yisrael* they were on a lower level, for the "craftsmen and smiths"[2] remained in Babylonia. ❖ After a few years, however, this changed, and people sought

---

❖ I will add to the words of the brilliant author of *Ezrat Kohanim*. The immigrants were not simply on a lower level, as he put it, but they were extremely low and wicked. The Radak writes:[3]

> Most of the people who ascended from Babylonia performed improper deeds. They married gentile women, as [is evident] from Ezra[4] and Malachi's admonition – *He has married the daughter*

1 Based on *Ezra* 4:23.

2 Based on II *Melachim* 24:16. *Chazal* explain that this refers to Torah scholars (*Gittin* 88a).

3 *Malachi* 1:1.

4 See *Ezra* 9.

Torah only from Zion. All this occurred because of the sanctity of the *Mikdash* (Temple). See *Pirkei Heichalot*[9] which describes their lofty status.

We also find that the inhabitants of Beit Shemesh were severely punished because they did not search for the Holy Ark when it was in the hands of the Philistines (*Sotah* 35a-b; *BeMidbar Rabbah* 5:9). *Yefeh To'ar HaKatzar* explains that they were

---

of a foreign god (*Malachi* 2:11); they desecrated the Sabbath; and [sinned] in other areas, as is written in the book of *Ezra*.[5]

Ezra states this explicitly: *The officers approached me saying, "The people of Israel, the* Kohanim, *and the* Levi'im *have not separated themselves from the peoples of the lands, like their abominations to the Canaanites..."* (*Ezra* 9:1). *Metzudat David* explains, "They were still performing the abominations of the Canaanites."

These are the ones who went up from Tel-Melach (Pillar of salt)... *They could not tell their father's house and their seed, whether they were from Israel* (*Ezra* 2:59). The Talmud comments, "*Tel Melach* refers to people who acted like [the people of] Sedom, which turned into a pillar of salt" (*Kiddushin* 70a). Rashi explains, "[The people of] Sedom were adulterous, as it says, *wicked and sinful* (*BeReishit* 13:13) - wicked with their bodies and sinful with their money." This demonstrates how wicked the *olim* really were.

The Sforno writes that the Holy One Blessed be He complained to Chaggai, Zecharyah, and Malachi about the Jews who remained in Babylonia and failed to ascend to *Eretz Yisrael*. He explained to them that since the righteous men stayed in Babylonia and only the wicked ones came, He was unable to let His *Shechinah* rest among them. Therefore, He requested that they try to convince the righteous men to ascend to *Eretz Yisrael* so that He can let His *Shechinah* rest there.[6]

R. Yosef Albo writes in *Sefer HaIkarim*, "Only a small number ascended with Ezra. The great ones (*gedolim*), the wise men, and the nobility of Israel remained in Babylonia."[7] Rashi writes, "The majority remained in Babylonia."[8] That is to say, the majority both quantitatively and qualitatively.

5 See *Ezra* 9-10, *Nechemyah* 13:14-31.
6 Sforno, *Shir HaShirim* 6:11.
7 *Sefer HaIkarim* 22:3.
8 *Ketuvot* 25b (top).
9 By the *Tana'im*, R. Yishmael Kohen Gadol and R. Akiva (Jerusalem, 5641 [1881]), chap. 29-31.

punished, [and no one else], because their city was the closest to the Philistines.[10] The *Midrash* states, "The Holy One Blessed be He said, 'If one of them lost a chicken, he would search for it extensively. But, My Ark is in the fields of the Philistines for seven months and they pay no attention... I will attend to it'" (*BeReishit Rabbah* 54:4). Now, all of this was said of the Ark itself, without the Tablets (as will be explained below). Certainly, then, we must search for the entire *Beit HaMikdash*, with the Tablets and all of its holy vessels.

Our obligation to build the Beit HaMikdash

The author wondrously explains that every Jew must strive to come to *Eretz Yisrael*, so that he can merit to build the *Beit HaMikdash*. He writes that the [story of] creation alludes to the fact that this is Israel's main prayer and hope. *Chazal* comment on the verse *No plant of the field was yet on the earth* (*BeReishit* 2:5): "All of Israel's prayers are for the *Beit HaMikdash*. O Master, when will the *Beit HaMikdash* be built" (*BeReishit Rabbah* 13:2).[11] *Chazal* further state that the Holy One Himself has prayed for the building of the *Beit HaMikdash* since the days of Avraham, and even before (*BeReishit Rabbah* 56:10). [*Ezrat Kohanim* continues]:

> Undoubtedly, all of Israel, together as one, is responsible to build the *Beit HaMikdash*. Everyone has an equal share, and it is invalid if an individual does it. It is the community's task, and everyone is obligated [to participate]. The Rambam states, "Everyone, both men and women, are obligated to build and support it with their very selves and their money."[12] We also find that King David collected money from all the tribes of Israel to buy the site of the *Beit HaMikdash*. He specifically wanted the foundations of the building to come from all of Israel, together. The essential component is the land; once the land belongs to everyone, so does the entire edifice.

The author discusses this at length and proves from the *Midrash* that we will build the future *Beit HaMikdash* by ourselves. He also writes that he discussed this with the honorable and saintly *gaon*, the holy luminary, the pious and sacred *Admor*, our master, R. Ya'akov of Radzin (*shlita*) *ztvk"l*. This rabbi stated clearly that we will build

10 *Yefeh To'ar* on *BeMidbar Rabbah* 5.

11 [See *Etz Yosef* as to how the *Midrash* derives this from the verse.]

12 *Hilchot Beit HaBechirah* 1:12.

the *Beit HaMikdash* by ourselves. Afterwards, during the time of the ultimate *tikkun* (rectification), when *Mashiach* arrives, Yechezkel's edifice will descend from the heavens. This concludes the words of the brilliant author of *Ezrat Kohanim*, who published his work in 5632 [1872].

We must build the earthly Temple before HaShem can send us the supernal one

ב Behold, later on[13] I will discuss at length the *Admor* of Radzin's statement that we will build the *Beit HaMikdash* before the advent of *Mashiach*. I will show that *Aspaklariya HaMe'irah* on the *Zohar* concurs.

However, it is puzzling that none of these *gedolim* mention that *Tikkunei Zohar* states explicitly that man will build the *Beit HaMikdash* first, and afterwards, when the *tikkun* is completed, a heavenly edifice will rest upon it.[14] Similarly, R. Sa'adya Gaon[15] writes that we will build the *Beit HaMikdash* first, with the permission of the kings, and this edifice will serve as the foundation for the one that will come from the heavens.[16]

Using my limited intellect, I will explain why we must build the earthly *Beit HaMikdash* before the supernal *Beit HaMikdash* descends from above. The Shelah states:

> ...It is known that the Holy One Blessed be He clings to us and we to Him. We cause this great ôclingingö (*d'veikut*), for when we effect an awakening from below, a great emanation awakens from above. This explains Rashi's comments on the verse *To bring you to the place which I have prepared* (*Shemot* 23:20). Rashi writes: "His [God's] place is already perceivable opposite it [the *Beit HaMikdash*]. This is one of the sources which indicate that the upper *Beit HaMikdash* is situated directly opposite the lower *Beit HaMikdash*." This is difficult! Who compares himself to whom? Surely, the smaller one compares himself to the greater one. Rashi should have said that the lower *Beit HaMikdash* is situated directly opposite the upper one. Furthermore, he contradicts himself. At first he says, "His place is already perceivable," implying that the upper *Beit*

13 Essay: The Sanctuary of HaShem, pp. 436-57.

14 *Tikkunei Zohar* 21, p. 60b.

15 *Emunot VeDe'ot* 8, chap. 5-6.

16 ❖ This is also found in the *Pesikta* (*Piska Kumi Ori*). See the commentary of the brilliant R. Zalman Margolis (ibid.). It is also found in the *Yerushalmi*, as I already mentioned in chapter two (p. 199).

> *HaMikdash* came first. But afterwards he says, "is situated directly opposite the lower one," implying that the lower one came first, God forbid!
>
> The explanation is as follows. The upper *Mikdash* existed first. HaShem commanded that the lower *Mikdash* be made according to the secrets of the upper one, for the divine service causes the lower *Mikdash* to be prepared to receive the influence from the upper *Mikdash*. But, this influence does not descend from above until a preparatory awakening ascends from below. Thus, in terms of this influence, the upper *Mikdash* is situated directly opposite the lower one. For, there must first be an awakening from below, that is, a seat and a foundation upon which the influence from the upper *Mikdash* can rest. *Chazal* allude to this: "Even though the fire [on the altar] descends from the heavens, we must bring [fire] from mortals" (*Yoma* 21b). The fire that we bring from below awakens the spiritual fire from above.[17]

Thus, if we want to receive influence from above we must first cause an awakening from below. This is why HaShem commands us to build a *Beit HaMikdash* on earth.

Based on this we can answer our original question. Prior to the complete *tikkun* of the Messianic era, we have only the ***influence*** of the upper *Beit HaMikdash*. That is, when we awaken and build the earthly *Beit HaMikdash*, we receive spiritual influence from the upper *Beit HaMikdash*. However, when we achieve the complete *tikkun*, the supernal *Beit HaMikdash* will actually descend and rest upon the lower *Beit HaMikdash*. We will not simply receive its influence, like the first two Temples did; rather, the building itself will descend. The Creator of the World will leave the supernal worlds and establish His abode in the lower worlds, for this is the purpose of all of creation. But, in order to be worthy of this, we must first effect an awakening from below, as the Shelah writes. Therefore, we must first build the *Beit HaMikdash*, and afterwards the Holy One Blessed be He will place the upper *Beit HaMikdash* upon the lower one. In my humble opinion, this explains the matter, and based on the Shelah's interpretation it is evident and true.

ג This also explains the *Midrash* I cited above,[18] that the Holy One Blessed be He prays for the building of the *Beit HaMikdash*. This

17 *Sh'nei Luchot HaBrit* 2:48b, col. a.
18 P. 217.

seems difficult. Why should He pray for this? It all depends on Him! Whenever He desires to send it down, He can do so! However, based on what we just said, that it all depends on an awakening from below, we can easily understand HaShem's prayer. He prays for our awakening – for the building of the earthly *Beit HaMikdash* – so that He can lower the supernal *Beit HaMikdash* upon it.

Returning to Eretz Yisrael is a pre-requisite for building the Beit HaMikdash

Now, it is well known that Israel must assemble in *Eretz Yisrael* before the *Beit HaMikdash* can be rebuilt, as the Talmud and the Rambam posit.[19] Therefore, when the author of *Ezrat Kohanim* says that the Holy One Blessed be He gets angry and punishes us because of our indolence, he certainly refers to our indolence in returning to *Eretz Yisrael*. Even the smallest assembly of Jews in *Eretz Yisrael* is extremely important to HaShem, and no one is allowed to belittle it. The prophet thus says, *Who scorns the day of small things?* (*Zecharyah* 4:10). The Ibn Ezra explains that this refers to someone who scorns small salvations, considering them insignificant... *And it will come to pass that just as you, O House of Judah and House of Israel, were a curse among the nations, so will I save you, and you will be a blessing. Do not fear. Let your hands be strong* (ibid. 8:13). *Metzudat David* explains, "Do not fear the words of those who belittle the honor of the Temple and the divine visitation. Let your hands be strong to take hold of the building and to complete it."...

When we return to the Land HaShem will cause us to repent

After Jews gather there and build up the Land, the [completion of the] building will be done by those who were blessed both physically and spiritually, as *Ezrat Kohanim* stated above. For, the Holy One Blessed be He will oversee the project vigilantly. The prophet states this explicitly:[20] *Upon one stone are seven eyes* (ibid. 3:9). "That is to say, the Omnipresent will guard this building." *Behold I engrave its inscription, says the Lord of Hosts.* "God Himself will carve designs on the stones in order to beautify them. Meaning, HaShem will give strength and assistance for the work." *And I will remove the iniquity of that Land in one day.* "That is to say, I will remove the iniquity of the Land all at once, for I will renew a proper spirit within the Jews. They will refrain from sin, and iniquity will no longer be found."

The prophet's intention is quite clear. He is saying that we must not prevent people from joining the builders by denouncing them as

19 ❖ See above, pp. 117, 140.

20 The comments after each verse are from *Metzudat David*.

sinners, because HaShem promised that He will remove the iniquity of the Land in one day. In other words, suddenly, one day, they will find that their hearts have been turned to the good (as the saying goes, "One morning they will wake up from their slumber").[21] Iniquity will no longer be found and there will be a new spirit in their hearts to fulfill the will of God.

Do not wonder how a generation as sinful as ours could possibly mend its ways, for the Holy One Blessed be He has the power to renew everyone's spirit to do His will. This is the meaning of the above-mentioned promise, *And I will remove the iniquity of that Land in one day*. Moreover, the Rashbam writes that it is possible that [more than] 900 generations will anger God, and the thousandth generation will be upright.[22]

Thus, since the prophet promised this in the name of HaShem, we must not be overly wise and say, "The builders of the Land are improper; we do not want to join them because they transgress God's will." Realize that Satan blinds us in order to keep us from accomplishing the rebuilding with a general consensus. Alternatively, he tries to prevent large numbers of people from doing this *mitzvah*, for one cannot compare a small group which fulfills a *mitzvah* to a large group which fulfills one (*Torat Kohanim, VaYikra* 26:8). We must join the builders and not be lax. We must do our share, then HaShem will do His and fulfill the verse *And I will remove the iniquity of that Land in one day*. This is genuine and clear in accordance with the truth of the Torah.

If we fail to return to the Land, our troubles will increase

Anyone who neglects this will be punished severely, as *Ezrat Kohanim* asserts.[23] This is why we have suffered so many hardships of late. We have disregarded *Eretz Yisrael*, over which the Lord our God constantly watches,[24] forever and ever. We have also disgraced and scorned its builders. If we do not change our way of thinking (God forbid), our troubles will increase. All of the troubles and evil afflictions that have befallen us are in place of the prophets' utterances. They speak to us, rebuke us, awaken us from our idle

21 [Originally in Yiddish.]

22 Rashbam, *Devarim* 7:10.

23 See above, pp. 214-17.

24 Based on *Devarim* 11:12.

sleep, and cause us to aspire to return to our Holy Land.[25]

We also find this in *Midrash Tanchuma* regarding Elimelech and his sons:

> *They dwelt there* [Moav] *about ten years* (*Ruth* 1:4). All of these years, the Holy One Blessed be He gave them warnings, perhaps they will repent and return to *Eretz Yisrael*. When they did not repent, He began to smite their cattle and camels. When they [still] did not realize that they must repent, they died immediately. (*Tanchuma, BeHar* 3)

Behold, God's warnings were not delivered by prophets (for we do not find that prophets went to them in Moav). Rather, the afflictions and mishaps that befell them took the place of the prophets to arouse them to repent. Now, in what way were they to repent? Only by returning to *Eretz Yisrael*. But, since they did not repent, and they did not even realize that they needed to repent, they were punished with loss of property and, eventually, death (may the Merciful One protect us). The *Midrash* also says that a number of times Ya'akov Avinu did not understand why he was being punished, and it was because he did not hurry to return to the Land of his forefathers.[26] Now, it is well known that all of Ya'akov Avinu's experiences reflect what will happen to his descendants at the end of days.[27] Therefore, *Chazal* were referring to us when they said these things, for we too do not understand why we are being punished so frequently. It is because we do not hurry to return to the Land of our forefathers.

The "promise of exile"

ד The Ramban comments on the verse from the Admonitions (*Tochachah*), *You will bring abundant seed out to the field, but you will gather in a little...* (*Devarim* 28:38):

> All of these admonitions apply only when the people of Israel are in the Land, for it says [later on], *You will be plucked from off the Land* (ibid. 28:63), which refers to exile... But, when we are in exile in the lands of our enemies, our handiwork, our cattle, our flocks of sheep, our vineyards, our olive trees, and our fields will not be cursed. Rather, we will dwell in these lands like, or even better than, the rest of the nations, for

25 ❖ I mentioned this concept above (pp. 214-15) in the name of the *Midrash*, and in the name of *Ezrat Kohanim* citing the holy *Zohar*.

26 We were unable to locate this source.

27 See *BeReishit Rabbah* 70:6; Ramban, Introduction to *Parashat VaYishlach*.

> HaShem has mercy on us. Our sojourn in exile fulfills His promise: *And yet despite this, when they are in the land of their enemies, I will not despise them nor will I reject them to destroy them, to annul My covenant with them, for I am the Lord their God* (*VaYikra* 26:44). In *BeChukotai*,[28] I explained the secret of this covenant, that it refers to our present exile in the hands of the fourth beast.[29] Afterwards, HaShem promises to redeem us from this exile.[30]

Today's hardships are God's way of telling us to return to our Land

Thus, the Holy One Blessed be He made a special covenant with us and promised that we would live peacefully and comfortably during our exile in the lands of the nations, just like the inhabitants of the land and perhaps even better than them. Now, however, the Gentiles have taken away our very right to live; they have deprived us of all means of sustenance; they have broken our staff of bread.[31] Therefore, it is clear that the Holy One Blessed be He has removed this "promise of exile." It is as if He is telling us explicitly, "My children, I do not want you to remain in the lands of exile anymore. Therefore, I will no longer protect your stay in the Diaspora. Rise up, go to your mother's bosom, and return to the Land of your forefathers."

To'aliyot HaRalbag (by the Ramban's grandson)[32] discusses the verse in *parashat Lech Lecha*, *There was a famine in the Land, and Avram went down to Egypt to sojourn there, for the famine was severe in the Land* (*BeReishit* 12:10):

> Man should diligently pursue what is needed to sustain his body, like food. Notice that after Avraham had already been promised monetary success, he went to Egypt because of the famine in the Land of Cana'an. The fact that HaShem commanded him to dwell in Cana'an did not prevent him from leaving. HaShem's commandments are meant to be beneficial to man, not painful. Therefore, Avraham knew that HaShem wanted him to go there to look for food. Furthermore, the [whole] reason God sent Avraham to the Land of Cana'an was to prepare him to receive His abundance. This would be impossible during a famine, without any food. Thus, it was

28 *VaYikra* 26:16.

29 [See *Daniel* 7:1-8. The ôfourth beastö refers to Rome.]

30 Ramban, *Devarim* 28:42.

31 Based on *VaYikra* 26:26.

32 ❖ The Shelah HaKadosh often quotes him and praises him greatly.

> better for him to leave and go to a place where he could find food until the famine ended.

Thus, even though HaShem commanded Avraham to go to the Land of Cana'an, the harsh conditions there and the relief that was in Egypt caused him to infer that HaShem wanted him to leave Cana'an and go to Egypt. This was truly the Creator's will, as the *Midrash* states (regarding the commandment of *lech lecha* – Go forth): "The Holy One Blessed be He said to Avraham, 'Go out and pave the way for your descendants' " (*BeReishit Rabbah* 40:6). That is, this will be a sign for them for the future. In any event, the Holy One Blessed be He did not tell Avraham explicitly to go down to Egypt. Instead, Avraham assessed the Creator's will based on the circumstances that he encountered.

The same is true today. It is no longer possible to remain here in the Diaspora, due to the hardships and expulsions. On the other hand, the gates are open for us to return to the Land of our heritage. Let us take a lesson from our elder, Avraham. When living conditions became difficult in the Land, he deduced that the Creator wanted him to leave the Land and go to Egypt, where he could find sustenance. And so he did; he left *Eretz Yisrael* and went to *Chutz LaAretz*. We can derive a *kal vachomer* from this. If he did this even though he received an explicit command from HaShem to go to *Eretz Yisrael*, and he was already there, all the more so in our situation. We are in *Chutz LaAretz*; living conditions are unbearably harsh; and the gates of *Eretz Yisrael* have opened up before us. Certainly this is an adequate hint to make us realize that the Creator wants us to leave the Diaspora and return to *Eretz Yisrael*. We must do as our venerable forefather did, with one amendment. He went from *Eretz Yisrael* to *Chutz LaAretz*, while we will go from *Chutz LaAretz* to *Eretz Yisrael*, an act which our Father in Heaven will certainly cherish. This is genuine and clear in accordance with the truth of the Torah, beyond a shadow of a doubt.

One can recognize God's will through the type of suffering He sends

ח *Chazal* state that three precious gifts are acquired through suffering: Torah, *Eretz Yisrael*, and the World to Come (*Berachot* 5a; *Shemot Rabbah* 1:1). The Talmud and *Midrash* cite a separate biblical source for each gift. The Rif (on *Ein Ya'akov*) asks, why is this necessary? They all could have been derived from one verse! I found an answer in the introduction to *Eirech Dal* (on Tractate *Arachin*), by our brilliant and pious master, R. Mordechai Eliezer Waber *zt"l*:[33]

> It seems to me that each of these three types of suffering has [unique] signs which show a person the direction in which the finger of God is leading him, and the specific area in which God wants him to awaken. If God wants him to awaken [to go] to the Holy Land, (then) the afflictions will pertain to his place of dwelling. He will feel that he can no longer exist in this country.
>
> The Ramban's comments on the verse that the Talmud cites (to demonstrate that *Eretz Yisrael* comes through suffering) prove this: "*Just as a man chastises his son, so the Lord your God chastises you* (*Devarim* 8:5): At first He tormented you in the desert and tested you with the Manna, so that your soul would delight in the goodness of the Land and its fruits. Therefore, it says afterwards, *For the Lord your God brings you into a good Land* (ibid. 8:7)."[34] This teaches that the nature and make-up of the afflictions can show a person that God is pointing him towards the Holy Land. The same is true of the other [two examples, Torah and the World to Come]. This is why the Talmud cites three (separate) verses: to make us aware of the signs of the afflictions, so that we can recognize through them (the will of the Creator).
>
> This explains *Chazal*'s statement "The walls (קורות) of a person's house testify about him" (*Ta'anit* 11a). That is to say, occurrences (קורות) and afflictions testify to him, warn him, and show him the path he should take. HaShem will steer him in the direction He wants him to go.[35]

Now, after these pleasant and godly words, and after all that has befallen us in our times, do we need any further confirmation from the heavens that the King of All Kings, the Holy One Blessed be He, wants us to return to the Holy Land?! He caused all of this to happen so that we will no longer be able to exist among the nations. He removed the "promise of exile,"[36] because He wants us to leave the

33 ❖ He was the *av beit din* of Ada and one of the greatest of the Tzanz Chassidim. Our mentor, [the Rebbe of Tzanz], endearingly called him "Rav Ada bar Ahavah" [the name of one of the Talmudic Sages]. He immigrated to *Eretz Yisrael* in 5634 [1874].

34 Ramban, *Devarim* 8:5.

35 *Eirech Dal*, beginning of the introduction called *Midbar Kedumot*, s.v. *amar*. [The parenthetical comments are R. Teichtal's.]

36 See above, p. 222.

Diaspora and arise and strengthen ourselves[37] to once again dwell honorably in our Land.

Three statements used by the antagonists to oppose aliyah

ו This explains a comment found in *Ahavat Yonatan* on the verse *I have adjured you* (*Shir HaShirim* 2:7). Our mentor explains that the Assembly of Israel (*Kenesset Yisrael*) declared under oath that they would not go to *Eretz Yisrael* even if the nations consent, for the end is concealed.[38] All of the antagonists base their opposition to the lofty and sacred idea of rebuilding the Land upon this statement. However, based on what I presented above, it is clear that the Ahavat Yonatan is correct [only] as long as there is no heavenly sign indicating that HaShem wants us to leave the lands of exile. That is to say, he is indeed correct that we should not return to *Eretz Yisrael*, even with the consent of the nations, when the Jewish world enjoys peace and tranquillity, the Ramban's "promise of exile"[39] is still in effect, and Jews are able to live here comfortably (like in the Ahavat Yonatan's lifetime).

Today, however, the words of the prophet have come true: *And the remnant of Ya'akov will be among the nations...like a lion among the animals of the forest, like a young lion among flocks of sheep, who, if he passes by, tramples and tears in pieces, and there is no savior* (*Michah* 5:7). On the other hand, the kingdoms have given us permission to return to our Holy Land! Is there any doubt that HaShem wants us to return to *Eretz Yisrael*?! I am certain that if our mentor, the author of *Ahavat Yonatan*, were alive today and saw our condition in this bitter exile, he too would say, "My Jewish brethren, the time has come to go up to Zion and the Land of our forefathers, for this is God's will. What is happening to us here in exile is not by chance. The finger of God is instructing us to leave the Diaspora and ascend to our forefathers' inheritance."

Our mentor, the Chatam Sofer, writes that at times it is possible for an incomplete redemption to occur, like the redemption of the Second Temple, but this is undesirable. It is preferable for Israel to suffer through the lengthy exile in order to eventually enjoy the complete redemption.[40] This statement, as well, refers to a time when

37 Based on *Tehillim* 20:9.

38 *Ahavat Yonatan, Haftarat VaEtchanan.*

39 Above, pp. 222-23.

40 *Torat Moshe* (5666 [1906]), vol. 2, p. 161a, s.v. *behaftarah* (on *Haftarat Shoftim*).

there is no heavenly sign and we are able to dwell in exile and engage in Torah and *mitzvot* with prosperity and tranquillity. This is evident from another statement of the Chatam Sofer. He writes that the great Torah scholars did not ascend to *Eretz Yisrael* because the entire world is fitting for them. That is to say, the peace and quiet that exist in exile allow them to devote themselves to Torah and divine worship. "In every place, offerings are dedicated to My name."[41] The Torah scholars enjoy the sanctity of *Eretz Yisrael* here [in the Diaspora].[42]

Similarly, the statement of the holy Rebbe of Shinev at the end of *Divrei Yechezkel* (at this time, I do not have the book in order to cite his words)[43] refers to his era when Israel enjoyed tranquillity in exile. Today, however, when our very lives have been taken from us, even the Chatam Sofer, the Ahavat Yonatan, and the Rebbe of Shinev would admit that HaShem is ordering us to leave the lands of exile and go to the Land that the Lord our God seeks out.[44]

In the *Yerushalmi*, R. Kahana asks R. Yochanan, "He whose mother degrades him but his father's wife [i.e., his stepmother] honors him, where should he go?" R. Yochanan responds, "He should go to the one who honors him" (*Berachot* 2:8 [18b]).[45] The *Yerushalmi* there explains that R. Kahana was more comfortable in *Chutz LaAretz* than in *Eretz Yisrael*. Therefore, R. Yochanan agreed that he should go to *Chutz LaAretz*. This also explains the statements of the Ahavat Yonatan, the Chatam Sofer, and the Rebbe of Shinev. Today, however, when the stepmother (*Chutz LaAretz*) gives us no honor – on the contrary, she degrades us, she gives Ya'akov over to plunder,[46] and she places an iron yoke upon our necks – everyone would agree that we should go to our mother, *Eretz Yisrael*.

I made this distinction between the different times and situations... independently. But now I discovered that the Ahavat Yonatan himself states this:

> ...In the future, when the "time of love"[47] arrives, the kingdom

41 Based on *Malachi* 1:11.

42 Novellae of the Chatam Sofer, *Gittin* 44a, s.v. *chutz mimelachto*; *Likutei Chaver Ben Chayim*, vol. 4, p. 27.

43 See below, pp. 463-68.

44 Based on *Devarim* 11:12.

45 ❖ This is cited by Rashi (*Bava Kama* 117b, s.v. *ve'iy lo ho'il vechalif sha'ata*) and the Ya'avetz (*Siddur Beit Ya'akov, Sullam Beit El*, p. 13b, col. a.).

46 Based on *Yeshayah* 42:24.

47 Based on *Yechezkel* 16:8.

> will enact harsh decrees against Israel. Then, the Jews will devote themselves to going to and living in *Eretz Yisrael*. It will be a difficult time for Ya'akov, and HaShem will hear their prayers and have pity on them. He will send them His anointed one (*Mashiach*) who walks upright,[48] and return the captivity of Zion as at first.[49]

This seems to clearly contradict his commentary on *Haftarat VaEtchanan* which states that even if the nations give us permission to go to *Eretz Yisrael* we are not to go... We must answer that troublesome times are different.

Now, his statement that HaShem will have pity on them and send *Mashiach* does not necessarily mean that He will send *Mashiach* immediately, and that they will not go unless He does. Rather, they will devote themselves to going to *Eretz Yisrael* because the decrees will make it impossible to stay in exile. If they are worthy, our righteous *Mashiach* will certainly arrive immediately. However, if they do not deserve this right away (God forbid), they will still devote themselves to going to *Eretz Yisrael*, until our righteous Savior comes. Their ascent to *Eretz Yisrael* will prepare the way for the coming of the Son of David, speedily in our days.[50] Amen.

In any event, our mentor states explicitly that when the "time of love" arrives, the kingdom will enact harsh decrees against Israel, and the Jews will devote themselves to going to and living in *Eretz Yisrael*. Therefore, now that we have encountered all of these evil decrees, we must realize that the "time of love" has arrived. Every Jew must devote himself to going to and living in *Eretz Yisrael*. We must no longer remain in exile, even if the nations reconcile with us. In this merit, HaShem will have compassion on us, immediately send us His anointed one who walks upright, and return our captivity as at first. Amen, so may it be God's will.

Thus, today, every single Jew is obligated to devote himself to leaving the lands of the nations and living in *Eretz Yisrael*. The Chatam Sofer himself concurs, as I will cite below.[51]

This concludes the introduction.

48 From the fifth *HaRachaman* recited at a circumcision feast.

49 *Ahavat Yonatan, Haftarat Eikev* (on *Yeshayah* 49:19).

50 ∴ See above (pp. 160-65...).

51 Sec. ט, p. 237.

II The Mitzvah of Yishuv Eretz Yisrael

ז Now, with God's help, I will begin to discuss whether or not there is an obligation and a *mitzvah* to build and settle the Land during the period of exile.

The Ramban's opinion

It is well known that according to the Ramban there is a positive, biblical commandment to take possession of the Land, even today. "We must not leave it in the hands of any other nation."[52] He derives this from the verse *You shall dispossess* [the inhabitants of] *the Land and dwell in it, for I have given you the Land to possess it. You shall divide the Land as an inheritance...* (*BeMidbar* 33:53-54). The Ramban discusses this at length and proves that it is a positive commandment for all generations. Thus, according to the Ramban it is one of the 613 *mitzvot*.

The Megillat Esther's opinion

The Megillat Esther[53] claims that the Rambam did not count this *mitzvah* among the 613 because he holds that it is not a perpetual *mitzvah*. Rather, it applies only when the *Beit HaMikdash* stands and the Jews dwell in their Land. Once they are exiled, however, the *mitzvah* no longer applies, until *Mashiach* comes.[54] The Megillat Esther supports this with Rabbeinu Chayim's opinion, cited in *Tosafot*, that nowadays there is no *mitzvah* to dwell in *Eretz Yisrael*.[55]

However, all of the later authorities dismissed Rabbeinu Chayim's opinion. The Shelah writes that we may ignore his opinion because it is an isolated one, and his reasoning is unsound.[56] The Maharit discusses this at length and proves that the *halachah* follows the Ramban.[57] Also, all of the great *poskim* who came after the Megillat Esther rejected his opinion, because it has no basis or substance.[58] There is no need for me to elaborate on this for it is well known.

52 Ramban's Addendum to *Sefer HaMitzvot* of the Rambam, Positive Commandments 4.

53 [*Megillat Esther*, written by R. Yitzchak de Leon, is a commentary on the Rambam's *Sefer HaMitzvot*. He named it thus in memory of his mother whose name was Esther. It is not to be confused with the book in the Bible with the same name.]

54 *Megillat Esther*, ibid.

55 *Tosafot, Ketuvot* 110b, s.v. *hu*.

56 *Sh'nei Luchot HaBrit* 1:75b.

57 *Teshuvot Maharit* 2:28.

58 See *Pitchei Teshuvah, Even HaEzer* 75:6.

Why did the Rambam fail to count this as a mitzvah?

In 5658 [1898], a certain *gadol*[59] from Dvinsk (Dynaburg) published, in Vilna, a most wonderful booklet called *Mitzvat Yeshivat Eretz Yisrael*. The entire purpose of the work is to examine and analyze the Megillat Esther's opinion, to determine whether or not it is a valid explanation of the Rambam's position... This *gadol* refutes all of the Megillat Esther's words, from beginning to end, using accurate and genuine proofs from the Talmud and the Rambam himself. The author posits that the Rambam holds this to be a biblical commandment in effect at all times. However, he does not count it as one of the 613, because it does not fit into the fourteen rules which the Rambam set down to determine which *mitzvot* are included in this number. There are several biblically ordained *mitzvot* which are not included in this number because they do not fulfill the conditions of the Rambam's fourteen rules. The *mitzvah* of *Yishuv Eretz Yisrael* is in the same category.

Study this booklet, for the author discusses this *halachah* thoroughly. It was printed with the approval of the *gedolim* of his generation. They all praised his words, saying that they "hit the target of truth." I need not elaborate on this because many great scholars before me did so, and they all rejected the Megillat Esther's opinion.

I would like to add just two comments. One comment I later found in *Yeshivat Eretz Yisrael*. The other one is original; even the author of that booklet did not mention it (even though he delved deeply into this issue). [The novel idea is as follows.]

An original proof against the Megillat Esther

The Torah commands, *Do not harass* Moav and Ammon (*Devarim* 2:9,19). It also says, *Do not provoke* Se'ir [Eisav] (ibid. 2:5). The Rambam writes that these *mitzvot* are temporary and do not apply to all generations.[60] The Ramban challenges this:

> Behold, it says, *Do not harass Moav...for I will not give you an inheritance from their land, for I have given Ar to the children of Lot as an inheritance* (ibid. 2:9). It also says, *For I have given Mt. Se'ir to Eisav as an inheritance* (ibid. 2:5). Now, it is well known that the word "inheritance" applies only to things which are given for all generations, as it says about our Land, *As Israel did to the Land of its inheritance* (ibid. 2:12). The Rambam himself learns from the expression, *An inheritance of the*

59 Rabbi Yonah Dov Blumberg *zt"l*.

60 *Sefer HaMitzvot, Shoresh* 3.

> *congregation of Ya'akov* (ibid. 33:4), that the Torah is for all generations.[61] Our Sages state, "An inheritance is everlasting" (*Bava Batra* 129b). [They also say]: "*Resting place* (*Devarim* 12:9) refers to Shiloh; *Inheritance* (ibid.) refers to Jerusalem" (*Megillah* 10a), for it is the eternal House [of God]. They also explain, "The Torah juxtaposes *ma'aser* (tithes) to inheritance to teach that just as an inheritance is everlasting, so too, *ma'aser* is everlasting" (*Rosh HaShanah* 12b).
>
> Now, since HaShem explained that the reason for the prohibition against going to war with these nations is because He gave them their lands as an inheritance, it follows that this prohibition applies to all generations. We must not steal their inheritance, and they will forever possess what HaShem bequeathed them.[62]

The Megillat Esther defends the Rambam as follows:

> The Rambam is correct that they are temporary *mitzvot*. And in terms of the Ramban's assertion that the word "inheritance" indicates that they are everlasting: It seems to me that the Holy One Blessed be He originally gave them the lands for all generations. However, after they treated Israel cruelly, He permitted [us to take] their lands and their bodies. At that time He wrote about them, *Do not seek their peace* (*Devarim* 23:7). By saying this He permitted what He had originally prohibited.[63]

In any event, the Megillat Esther also agrees with the Ramban that the word "inheritance" implies forever and uninterrupted. However, these nations are an exception, because the Torah eventually permitted what it originally prohibited.

Since this is so, I am astonished at this brilliant author. How can he say that the *mitzvah* of inheriting the Land...only applied in the days of Moshe, Yehoshua, and David; and that ever since the Jews were exiled from their Land it is not in effect, until *Mashiach* comes? If so, the *mitzvah* is suspended. But, the word "inheritance" implies permanence! And we do not find anywhere in the Torah even the slightest hint that HaShem retracted the original obligation of, *You shall dispossess...and dwell in it* (*BeMidbar* 33:53), making it into a

61 Ibid.
62 Ramban's Addendum to *Sefer HaMitzvot*, Negative Commandments (end).
63 *Megillat Esther*, ibid.

temporary *mitzvah* (as we find by the *mitzvot* of *Do not harass* and *Do not provoke*).

Furthermore, the Rambam himself writes that the verse, *Moshe commanded us the Torah, an inheritance* (morashah) *of the congregation of Ya'akov* (*Devarim* 33:4), applies to all generations, because it uses the term *morashah*. Surely, the same is true of the Land, for the Torah says, *And I will give it* [the Land] *to you as an inheritance* (morashah) (*Shemot* 6:8)! Therefore, it is clear that the Rambam, who holds that the word *morashah* implies perpetuity, agrees that [the *mitzvah* of dwelling in] the Land is forever, for *Eretz Yisrael* is also referred to as *morashah*.

This explains a passage in the *Yerushalmi*, commenting on the verse just cited:

> If it is a gift why is it an inheritance? If it is an inheritance why a gift? We must conclude that after God gave it to them as a gift, He gave it to them again as an inheritance. (*Bava Batra* 8:2 [18a])

Based on the above, *Chazal*'s intention is quite clear. If *Eretz Yisrael* had remained simply a gift, this would have implied that it is not continuously ours for all generations. It might have been ours only temporarily, just like "And after you, so-and-so [will inherit it]" (*Bava Batra* 129b). But, when God gave it again as an inheritance, He implied that it is ours forever.

In any event, based on the above, the Megillat Esther's opinion is very difficult, for he contradicts himself. Serious investigation is needed to reconcile his words.

This concludes the novel comment that none of the earlier *gedolim* mentioned.

Our existence as a nation depends on Eretz Yisrael

ח Secondly, I am astonished that the brilliant author of *Megillat Esther* thinks that our mentor, the Rambam, holds that there is no *mitzvah* nowadays to settle the Land. He even states that it is forbidden to do so. He and his words are completely perplexing. How can the Rambam's opinion be explained in this way? Notice what the Rambam writes (in *Sefer HaMitzvot*) about the positive commandment of *Kiddush HaChodesh* [establishing a Jewish calendar]. He explains that the calculations we make in the Diaspora [to determine when the new month begins] are meaningless. We rely solely on the calculations made in *Eretz Yisrael*. Our calculations merely reveal [what was determined in *Eretz Yisrael*, for we use the same system as they do]. [The Rambam elaborates]:

> I will explain further. Let us suppose, for example, that there would be no Jews living in *Eretz Yisrael* – God forbid that He should do such a thing, for He has promised not to destroy the remnants of the nation completely. [Let us suppose] also that there would be no Jewish court (*beit din*) there, and that there would be no *beit din* in the Diaspora which was ordained in *Eretz Yisrael*. [Under these circumstances], our calculations would not help us at all. For we may not calculate the months or establish leap years in the Diaspora, unless we fulfill the conditions mentioned above. *For, out of Zion the Torah will go forth* (*Yeshayah* 2:3).[64]

I quoted this in its entirety because it helps us fully comprehend the Rambam's opinion. He considers the settlement of our Holy Land an essential foundation [of our faith]. His statement teaches that the existence of the entire holy nation is bound to the settlement of the Land to such a degree that the entire nation would dissolve if the Jewish people would cease to exist in *Eretz Yisrael*, God forbid. The commentator on the Rambam's *Hilchot Kiddush HaChodesh*[65] quotes him as follows: "If, God forbid, the Jews would perish from *Eretz Yisrael* – may HaShem be blessed because He has promised us in the Torah not to destroy this nation completely." Thus, he, too, understands the Rambam to mean that the Jewish people would be destroyed, God forbid, if they would not dwell in *Eretz Yisrael*. This concept is utterly astounding!

Eretz Yisrael is the heart of the nation

In my opinion, this is so because *Eretz Yisrael* is the heart of the nation, as our mentor, the godly man from Cordovero, writes in his holy work, *Or Ne'erav*.[66] The Chacham Tzvi writes that no creature can live without a heart.[67] Therefore, when the Jewish nation is not in *Eretz Yisrael*, it is as if its heart is removed and its entire life force is abolished.

We can further explain this matter based on *Chazal*'s statement in the *Midrash*:

> The Holy One Blessed be He said, "Israel is My portion, as it

64 *Sefer HaMitzvot*, Positive Commandments 153.

65 5:13.

66 5:4. ❖ See above, p. 81.

67 *Teshuvot Chacham Tzvi* 74.

> says, *For the Lord's portion is His people* (*Devarim* 32:9). *Eretz Yisrael* is also My portion, as it says, *A Land which the Lord your God always seeks out* (ibid. 11:12). Let My portion dwell in My portion." (*Tanchuma, Re'eh* 8)

That is to say, Israel's connection to the Holy One Blessed be He comes specifically through *Eretz Yisrael*, which is God's portion. This is especially true according to the author of *Tzror HaMor*, who writes that *Eretz Yisrael* immediately follows HaShem Himself. The Torah, therefore, says about Calev, *And he followed Me fully* (*BeMidbar* 14:24), [meaning, he] literally followed Me [by defending *Eretz Yisrael* which follows Me].[68] This also explains *Chazal*'s statement "He who dwells outside the Land is like one who has no God" (*Ketuvot* 110b). Understand these words, for they are based on the foundations of truth.

Thus, it is clear why *Eretz Yisrael* is the heart of the Jewish nation and its life-giving force. Now we can understand the words of our luminary, the Rambam, who writes that every fiber of life of the Jewish nation is bound to *Eretz Yisrael*. So much so, that if no Jews would live in *Eretz Yisrael*, God forbid, it would be equivalent to the destruction of the entire nation. We would be like a person without a heart, whose entire life force is gone. We can infer from all of this that strengthening the settlement in *Eretz Yisrael* strengthens the heart of Israel, and helps the Jewish people grow higher and higher.

Now, given that the Rambam values settling the Land so much that he considers it the soul of the Jewish nation..., how can any intelligent person entertain the thought that according to him there is no *mitzvah* nowadays to settle the Land and that it is even forbidden to do so?

By my life! I realized this on my own when I began delving into this matter. And now, after I arrived here in the capital, HaShem brought to my attention this most wonderful booklet [*Yeshivat Eretz Yisrael*] by a *gadol* from Dvinsk, our master, R. Yonah Dov Blumberg. (He wrote the work in 5650 [1890].)... I discovered there that he stated this idea before I did:

> Every fiber of life of the Jewish nation is connected and linked specifically to this Land, as our mentor, the Rambam, writes regarding the *mitzvah* of *Kiddush HaChodesh*: "I will explain further. Let us suppose, for example, that there would be no Jews living in *Eretz Yisrael* – God forbid that He should do

68 *Tzror HaMor, Matot,* s.v. *achar kach amar u'makneh.*

> such a thing, for He has promised not to destroy the remnants of the nation completely... Then, our calculations would not help us at all." One who studies his words carefully will see that the words, "God forbid...completely," are totally unconnected to the subject of the passage... These words are parenthetical. When his holy pen recorded the words, "there would be no Jews living in *Eretz Yisrael*," this profound *tzaddik* withdrew for a moment because of the fear of HaShem that hovered over him. He shuddered out of awe and fear of HaShem, like someone who mentions some dreadful concept or word (for a specific purpose) and, within the same breath, withdraws and says, "God forbid that this should be." This is exactly what happened here, as is clear to anyone who studies his words carefully.
>
> Any forthright thinker will shudder [at the thought] that the Rambam trembled and shook [when he wrote] the dreadful words, "there would be no Jews living in *Eretz Yisrael*." He even went back and wrote a special parenthetical statement, "God forbid...for He has promised not to destroy the remnants of the nation completely." Let us reflect on the fact that the Rambam shuddered, while we do not tremble nor care at all whether the Jews will be in *Eretz Yisrael* or not, God forbid. A word to the wise is sufficient.[69]

Thus, the Rambam's sacred mind viewed the absence of the people of Israel from *Eretz Yisrael* as the total destruction of the Jewish nation, God forbid. If so, our existence depends solely on settling the Land, and we cannot imagine any revival of the Jewish nation at any time without it.

This *gaon* [R. Blumberg] explains the following *Midrash* based on this idea:

> One verse says, *For the Lord will not abandon His people, for the sake of His great name* (I *Shmuel* 12:22). Another verse says, *For the Lord will not abandon His people, nor will He forsake His inheritance* (*Tehillim* 94:14)... One refers to *Chutz LaAretz* and the other refers to *Eretz Yisrael*. In *Chutz LaAretz* He acts for the sake of His name. In *Eretz Yisrael* He acts for the sake of His people and His inheritance. (*Ruth Rabbah* 2:11)

This can be explained according to the Rambam. In *Eretz Yisrael* HaShem acts for the sake of His people and His inheritance, for if

69 *Yeshivat Eretz Yisrael*, pp. 112, 138.

He would abandon the Jews of *Eretz Yisrael* [it would mean] the destruction of the nation, God forbid. Since the primary status of the Jewish nation is attained when they dwell in *Eretz Yisrael*, it is sufficient for the Holy One Blessed be He to act for the sake of His nation alone. In *Chutz LaAretz*, however, since the existence of the nation does not depend on [the Jews living there], He acts only for the sake of His great name.

Yishuv Eretz Yisrael encompasses the entire Torah

Based on this principle, [R. Blumberg] also explains why the Rambam fails to count the positive commandment of *Yishuv Eretz Yisrael* as one of the 613 *mitzvot*, even though he holds it to be of biblical origin. The fourth rule that the Rambam sets down in *Sefer HaMitzvot* is: Commandments which encompass the entire Torah are not to be counted. Now, settling *Eretz Yisrael* is an extremely precious *mitzvah*. It is the sum-total of all other *mitzvot*, and it encompasses the entire Torah. The fixing of the holidays and the months, and all related *mitzvot*, depend on it, as the Rambam writes, *For out of Zion the Torah will go forth.* ❖ Our nation's entire existence depends on it. Therefore, it is not included in the enumeration of the *mitzvot*, for only particular *mitzvot* are counted, and this *mitzvah* is a general one.

This is similar to what the Ramban writes on the *mitzvah* of, *You shall be perfect with the Lord your God* (*Devarim* 18:13). He explains that the Rambam does not count it as a *mitzvah* because it is a general, rather than a particular, *mitzvah*.[71] The same is true of *Yishuv Eretz Yisrael*. Since the Rambam raised it so high, making it an inclusive *mitzvah*, it is not counted.

R. Blumberg's work is filled with wondrous and true words, and it is a *mitzvah* for every Jew to read it carefully. It will enlighten the reader about the great *mitzvah* of *Yishuv Eretz Yisrael* and make him understand that he must no longer degrade it. Then, the merit of *Eretz Yisrael* will stand by us to deliver us from distress.[72]

In any event, I was privileged to concur with this *gadol* on the

---

❖ The *Or HaChayim HaKadosh*, on *parashat Nitzavim*, agrees that settling the Land is a *mitzvah* which encompasses the entire Torah.[70]

70 *Devarim* 30:20.

71 Ramban's Addendum to *Sefer HaMitzvot*, Positive Commandments 8.

72 ❖ As I mentioned in the first introduction (p. 33) quoting our mentor, the Ba'al HaTanya.

proof from the Rambam in *Hilchot Kiddush HaChodesh*. I will repeat myself: How can we possibly agree with the Megillat Esther that according to the Rambam one should not engage in settling and building the Land. Our nation's entire existence depends on this! I am bewildered!

The entire Torah depends on Jewish settlement in Eretz Yisrael

מ I will now strengthen this position with the words of our mentor, the Chatam Sofer. He also cites the Rambam's comments in *Hilchot Kiddush HaChodesh* and explains:

> Even though Hillel and his colleagues sanctified all of the months and years until the coming of *Mashiach*, this will not help unless one Jew lives in *Eretz Yisrael*. Hillel and his colleagues – the last men to receive traditional ordination – calculated and sanctified [the months and years] for this one Jew, and the sanctity emanates from there [*Eretz Yisrael*] to all of Israel. However, if the settlement in *Eretz Yisrael* would cease to exist in our days (God forbid), this sanctification (*kiddush*) would become null and void, and most of the *mitzvot* would dissolve, God forbid. Therefore, we must support [Jewish] settlement [in the Land] with all of our strength.[73]

The brilliant author of *S'dei Chemed* comments on this:

> The Chatam Sofer does not assert that we must strengthen the settlement of *Eretz Yisrael* in order to help the inhabitants of the Land [fulfill] the *mitzvah* of *Yishuv Eretz Yisrael*. Rather, we must do so for ourselves, so that we can fulfill the words of the Torah. For if Jews would not live there, the Torah would vanish, God forbid, as the Rambam writes in *Hilchot Kiddush HaChodesh*...
>
> Our master, the Chida, concurs in *Yosef Ometz*:[74] "I will further reveal that the Rambam writes in *Hilchot Kiddush HaChodesh* that...we rely on the calculations and fixings of the inhabitants of *Eretz Yisrael*... He also states in *Sefer HaMitzvot* that if, God forbid, there would be no Jews [in *Eretz Yisrael*] our calculations would be meaningless... Therefore, all Diaspora Jews are obligated to ensure that there are Jews in *Eretz Yisrael*, for if not, [the Diaspora Jews] would forget about the new months and holidays."[75]

73 *Teshuvot Chatam Sofer, Orach Chayim* 203.
74 Sec. 19.
75 *S'dei Chemed, Ma'arechet Eretz Yisrael*, Collection of Laws, p. 680, sec. 4.

Behold, all of these *gedolim* state that the Torah would have been abrogated, God forbid, if not for the continuous Jewish presence in *Eretz Yisrael*. Therefore, the *gaon* from Latvia, [R. Blumberg], was correct when he said that the *mitzvah* of *Yishuv Eretz Yisrael* is an inclusive, rather than a particular, *mitzvah*.❖ And, according to the fourth of the fourteen rules set down by the Rambam, an inclusive *mitzvah* is not counted, even if it is biblical. This is also logical, because the Rambam holds that most of the Torah's *mitzvot* depend on this one. Hence, there is certainly a biblical obligation to strengthen the settlement of the Land in order to enable us to keep the rest of the *mitzvot* of the Torah. This is the clear and true explanation of the Rambam's opinion, without any shadow of a doubt.

The Rambam's three reasons for this mitzvah

Thus, according to the Rambam we are obligated to strengthen the settlement in *Eretz Yisrael* for three reasons:

1. For the survival of the Jewish nation: We cannot imagine our nation's revival without it, as the Rambam writes in *Sefer HaMitzvot*... Undoubtedly, the Rambam's intellect soared higher than ours to find a source for this concept – that the existence of the Jewish nation depends specifically on Jewish settlement in *Eretz Yisrael*. Therefore, it follows that the stronger the settlement, the stronger the nation as a whole, wherever they may live. Human logic, as well, dictates this, as I explained at length in the previous chapters.

2. [To enable us] to fulfill the Torah: As our illustrious rabbis – the Chatam Sofer, the S'dei Chemed, and the Chida – write. The Chatam Sofer also cites these words of the Rambam elsewhere and explains fervently that [if no Jews would live in *Eretz Yisrael*] the entire Torah would be abrogated, God forbid, and there would be no Jewish nation.[76]

3. Because of the positive commandment of *Yishuv* [*Eretz Yisrael*], which is of biblical origin even according to the Rambam. He does not include it in his count of the *mitzvot* only because it is an inclusive *mitzvah* (as stated above). I studied the *Chatam Sofer* again and

---

❖ I already cited above that our mentor, the Or HaChayim, also considers *Yishuv Eretz Yisrael* a *mitzvah* which encompasses the entire Torah. If this *gaon*, [R. Blumberg], would have seen this he would have been overjoyed to find a "*Tana*" who supports him.

76 *Teshuvot Chatam Sofer, Yoreh De'ah* 234.

discovered that he agrees with the Latvian *gaon*, [R. Blumberg]:

> Even though the Rambam does not count the positive commandment of *Yishuv Eretz Yisrael* as the Ramban does, he emphatically acknowledges *Eretz Yisrael*'s sanctity [even] nowadays. Thus, he writes with regard to *Kiddush HaChodesh* that if there would be no Jews in *Eretz Yisrael* our calculations would not help us at all.[77]

He explains that this is why the inhabitants of *Eretz Yisrael* take precedence [over Diaspora Jews in terms of charity].[78] Since the Land is sanctified, it is a *mitzvah* to dwell there; and it is proper to give precedence to people who do *mitzvot*.

Thus, the Chatam Sofer agrees that according to the Rambam there is a *mitzvah* to settle *Eretz Yisrael* at all times, because the sanctity of *Eretz Yisrael* is eternal; it has never changed and never will change. "It is not at all dependent on the fulfillment of the *mitzvot*; the Land itself is holy."[79]

From this we may conclude that, on the contrary, the obligation of *Yishuv Eretz Yisrael* is many times greater according to the Rambam than it is according to the Ramban. In the latter's opinion, the obligation has only one facet – it is one of the *mitzvot* of the Torah. According to the Rambam it has three.

The Minchat Elazar's opinion

I came across a copy of Responsa *Minchat Elazar*, [by the Rebbe of Munkatch], and I saw that he refutes the Avnei Neizer, who advocates the positive commandment of *Yishuv Eretz Yisrael*.[80] (I do not have a copy [of *Avnei Neizer*] at this time. I searched for one here in the capital, but did not find it.) The holy *gaon* of Munkatch *zt"l* explains the Rambam's omission of this *mitzvah* the same way the Megillat Esther does, i.e., because it does not apply to all generations. He refutes the Avnei Neizer, who refutes the Megillat Esther, and concludes that according to the Rambam there is no *mitzvah* nowadays to promote settlement of the Land.

How puzzling are his words! With all due respect, they have no basis. I proved above from our rabbis – the Chatam Sofer, the S'dei

77 Ibid., s.v. *hayotzei mi'devareinu*.

78 See *Sifrei, Re'eh* 63 (on *Devarim* 15:7); *Shulchan Aruch, Yoreh De'ah* 251:3; *Derishat Tzion*, pp. 76-77.

79 *Teshuvot Chatam Sofer*, ibid.

80 *Teshuvot Avnei Neizer, Yoreh De'ah* 454.

Chemed, and the Chida – that according to the Rambam we have a great obligation to strive for and support the settlement of the Land, because the existence of the Torah and our nation rests on it. Furthermore, everyone rejects the Megillat Esther's opinion. The Sefardic sage, R. Yehudah Ayash,[81] disproves his words and decides the *halachah* in accordance with the Ramban.[82] The brilliant R. Yosef Sha'ul also challenges the Megillat Esther's words and cites several proofs for the Ramban's opinion. He concludes, "Therefore, [the *halachah*] clearly follows the Ramban; and may HaShem grant us the merit to fulfill this *mitzvah*."[83] The brilliant author of *Pe'at HaShulchan*, a disciple of the Gra,[84] also concludes that the *halachah* follows the Ramban.[85] Earlier *gaonim* as well, like the Maharit[86] and Mabit,[87] follow this course and reject Tosafot's opinion in *Ketuvot*,[88] [one of the Megillat Esther's proofs]. There is no need to cite their words for they are quoted in *Pe'at HaShulchan*.

The Megillat Esther brings a proof from Rav Yehudah's statement: "He who ascends from Babylonia to *Eretz Yisrael* transgresses a positive commandment, as it says, *They will be brought to Babylonia, and there they will be* (*Yirmiyah* 27:22)" (*Ketuvot* 110b). Profound *gedolim*, like the Ya'avetz,[89] disprove this as well. He points out that this was merely the Talmud's postulation. The Talmud concludes, however, that this verse refers to the vessels of the Temple. The *gaon* of Dvinsk concurs in his booklet, *Yeshivat Eretz Yisrael*.[90]

Thus, there is no basis whatsoever for the brilliant and holy Minchat Elazar's refutation of the Avnei Neizer. He adhered to an isolated opinion which was rejected by practically all of the *gaonim* of the generations following the Megillat Esther. The Latvian *gaon*, as well, disproved all of his arguments with good reasoning and

81 ❖ He lived at the same time as the Yad Malachi and the Or HaChayim HaKadosh, and he printed in his work many responsas which he exchanged with them.

82 *Teshuvot Beit Yehudah* 2:124.

83 *Yosef Da'at* 372.

84 R. Yisrael of Shklov zt"l.

85 *Pe'at HaShulchan, Hilchot Eretz Yisrael* 1:3.

86 *Teshuvot Maharit* 2:28.

87 *Teshuvot Mabit* 1:139.

88 110b, s.v. *hu*.

89 *Siddur Beit Ya'akov*, p. 13a.

90 *Ma'aneh* 13, sec. 4-5 and n. 7.

knowledge. This is not the place to engage in lengthy dialectics, for that is not my purpose here.

Keeping the mitzvot in the Land

The Tashbetz writes about the *mitzvah* of immigrating to *Eretz Yisrael*:

> [One is permitted to go] as long as, from now on, he will be ascetic, careful of all sin, and will fulfill all the *mitzvot* that apply there. For if he sins, he will be punished more severely... One cannot compare someone who rebels against the king in the palace to someone who rebels outside the palace. This is the meaning of the verse *It is a Land which devours its inhabitants* (*BeMidbar* 13:32)... Those who act frivolously and quarrel recklessly in the Land are included in the verses: *You came and defiled My Land* (*Yirmiyah* 2:7) and *Who asked this of you, to trample My courtyards* (*Yeshayah* 1:12).[91]

Based on this, the Minchat Elazar exhorts [his readers] not to collaborate with today's builders in any way whatsoever, for they do not have the life-giving spirit of our holy Torah, nor the sacred belief in the imminent arrival of our righteous Redeemer. He also quotes the well-known statement of the Ahavat Yonatan[92] and concludes that we should not join them in any aspect of the building.

I am astounded by this! Behold, Tosafot cite Rabbeinu Chayim's opinion that there is no *mitzvah* to live in *Eretz Yisrael* nowadays because there are several *mitzvot* dependent on the Land which entail several punishments, and we are unable to keep them properly.[93] Our mentor, the Shelah, comments on this:

> Rabbeinu Chayim's opinion is an isolated one,❖ and his reasoning is unsound. For it says about such matters, [*The ways of the Lord are straight*]; *the righteous will walk in them and the sinners will stumble in them* (*Hoshea* 14:10). Of course,

❖ The Maharit writes that this statement in *Tosafot* was not authored by the Tosafists. Rather, some erring student wrote it.[94] Therefore, the Maharit and everyone after him reject this opinion.

91 *Tashbetz Kattan* 559.

92 See above, p. 226.

93 *Tosafot, Ketuvot* 110b, s.v. *hu*.

94 *Teshuvot Maharit* 2:28.

> he who dwells in *Eretz Yisrael* and does not fulfill his obligations is a sinner. However, he who sanctifies himself and fulfills...his obligations is fortunate. Also, I do not understand his assertion that we are unable to keep the *mitzvot* properly. Why is this so? Who prevents us? Therefore, one may ignore his words.[95]

These words of our mentor, the Shelah, also apply to the Tashbetz's statement.

In addition, the brilliant and holy R. Yusha'le Kutner comments on this statement of the Tashbetz, [which was said] in the name of the Maharam of Rottenberg:[96]

> The Maharam of Rottenberg only hesitated because of the [dangerous] journey and the lack of provisions, and because of the dispute that flared up at the time. It is well known that the debate over the *Moreh Nevuchim* flared up again in the days of the Maharam of Rottenberg and R. Moshe Tiki... Therefore, now that there has been a change for the better (with God's help), both in terms of the dangers of the journey and in terms of sustenance, it is certainly a great *mitzvah*.[97]

Coope-rating with the irreligious pioneers

יא I am also astounded that the brilliant and holy Minchat Elazar considers it obvious that we must not join today's builders in any way since they do not follow the ways of the Torah. That is to say, he holds that it is preferable to leave the Land in their hands and let them do with it as they please, according to their spirit, than to join them with our labor and spirit.

I cannot understand this. Why should we not join them? Granted, if there was a chance that our refusal to build would cause them to do the same, then there would be room to agree that it is better to sit back and do nothing than to build in a sinful manner. ❖ However,

---

❖ Although, in my humble opinion, this is not so clear. In the foreword,[98] I cited a Talmudic statement which proves that the Holy One Blessed be He is pleased by the building of the Holy Land, even if it is done sinfully, God forbid. Therefore, if we were faced with a situation in which we were only able to fulfill the positive commandment of *Yishuv*

95 *Sh'nei Luchot HaBrit, Sha'ar HaOtiot* 1:72b.

96 ❖ I already cited this in the preface (p. 18).

97 *Teshuvot Yeshu'ot Malko, Yoreh De'ah* 66.

98 Pp. 82-83.

they will not stop building even if we do. (This has actually happened; they have been building for years, even without the cooperation of the God-fearing Jews.) If so, why should we completely divorce ourselves from them? Why should we not combine our strengths and spirit with their work, so that at least some spirit of Torah and sanctity will be present in the building effort (to whatever degree we can influence them)? Perhaps if the God-fearing Jews cooperate, they will be able to cause this undertaking to be completely in accordance with the spirit of the Torah (with God's help). However, if they stand aloof and leave everything in the hands of the irreligious, it will certainly be contrary to the spirit of the Torah.

Current events prove this. Ever since the Zionist movement began, the Orthodox Jews refrained from building the Land, and the irreligious did their work without us. Consequently, and mournfully, a non-Torah spirit pervades there. What did the Orthodox

---

Eretz Yisrael through sin, and without the sin the Land could not be built, perhaps we would conclude that it is preferable to build it and let the positive commandment of building, which is equal to the entire Torah,[99] push aside the sin (especially since the entire existence of our holy nation depends on the settlement of the Land, as I proved above[100] from many sources). For there is a well-known rule of the Talmud that a great and important positive commandment (*asei*) overrides a positive (*asei*) and negative (*lo ta'asei*) commandment, even if they do not coincide.[101]

99 *Sifrei, Re'eh* 28 (on *Devarim* 12:29).

100 Pp. 232-36.

101 See *Tosafot, Pesachim* 59a, s.v. *ati*; *S'dei Chemed*, vol. 7, *Ma'arechet Ayin, Klal* 35, and *Klal* 42, s.v. *vekatav beYishrei Lev*.
[In general we maintain that an *asei* overrides a *lo ta'asei*, but not an *asei* and a *lo ta'asei*. And, an *asei* can only override a *lo ta'asei* if it is fulfilled at the same time that the *lo ta'asei* is transgressed. For example, a *kohen* is permitted to wear his special belt (*avneit*) even though it contains *sha'atnez* (wool and linen together - *kil'ayim*), because the *asei* of wearing the priestly garments overrides the *lo ta'asei* of *kil'ayim*. But, he may only wear it while performing the Temple service, for then the *asei* is fulfilled at the same time the *lo ta'asei* is transgressed. If he wears it at some other time, however, he transgresses the *lo ta'asei* without immediately fulfilling the *asei* (see *Menachot* 43a). A great and important *asei*, however, (like *Yishuv Eretz Yisrael*) overrides even an *asei* and a *lo ta'asei*, even if the *asei* is not fulfilled exactly when the *lo ta'asei* is transgressed.]

accomplish by detaching themselves from this sacred endeavor? Would it not have been better for them to join the builders, whoever they may be, in order to contribute their strengths and sacred spirit to this endeavor? Had they done this, the Land would now have a completely different appearance, one of sanctity and purity. For it is well known that a little light repels the darkness of a large room. Therefore, I do not understand this holy *gaon*'s reasoning at all.

Matters will be worse if we leave everything in the hands of the irreligious

יב My brother, do not think that I invented all of these refutations of the Minchat Elazar's opinion. That is not so, my son. Actually, this is the opinion of our mentors, the Chatam Sofer and his disciple, the Maharam Schick. *Chazal* state:

> From the day the *Beit HaMikdash* was destroyed..., and from the day the kingdom which enacts harsh decrees against us arose..., we rightfully should decree that no one marry a woman or beget children. This way, the seed of Avraham Avinu would perish on its own. But, leave Israel alone; [it is better for them to act unintentionally than intentionally]. (*Bava Batra* 60b)

The statement, "This way, the seed of Avraham Avinu would perish on its own," is quite puzzling. It seems to imply that *Chazal* wanted Avraham Avinu's seed to perish, God forbid.

The Chatam Sofer explains this based on the following *Midrash*:

> When Pharaoh decreed, *Every son that is born, you shall cast him into the river* (*Shemot* 1:22), Amram arose and divorced his wife. All the righteous men arose and divorced their wives. Miriam said to him [Amram], "Your decree is harsher than Pharaoh's." (*Shemot Rabbah* 1:17)

Our master explains:

> The Holy One Blessed be He made a covenant with our forefathers to preserve their seed after them and give them *Eretz Yisrael* as an inheritance. Now, if the Jews would decree upon themselves not to beget children, a generation would end but a new one would not begin. There would then be concern that the seed of Avraham Avinu would perish. Thus, HaShem would be forced to save Israel immediately and return the children to their borders.[102] (Since there would be no future generations

102 Based on *Yirmiyah* 31:16.

> and the seed of Avraham Avinu would perish, HaShem would have no one through whom to fulfill the covenant. Therefore, salvation would come immediately.) However, this is [only] true if the entire congregation follows the decree. But, if only the righteous and proper Jews do so, while the wicked ones marry women, the Holy One Blessed be He would no longer be forced to bring salvation immediately, for the wicked ones are also the seed of Avraham. The result would be that only the righteous would perish, while the seed of the wicked would endure. Then, the evil would be twofold (the salvation would not come and the righteous would perish, leaving only the wicked).
>
> When the Talmud states, "We rightfully should decree that no one marry a woman; this way the seed of Avraham Avinu would perish on its own," it means that the Holy One Blessed be He would be compelled to save us immediately. "But, leave Israel alone...," because the wicked ones and the simpletons will not listen to us, and the seed of Israel will be preserved through them, while the righteous will vanish from the world.
>
> This was also Amram's intention. He divorced his wife so that everyone would divorce their wives. (Thus, the seed of Avraham Avinu would perish) and the redemption would ensue immediately. However, only the righteous ones divorced their wives, while the masses kept theirs. Therefore, Miriam cried, "Your decree is harsher than Pharaoh's." Since only the righteous cooperated, their seed will perish, God forbid, while the wicked will multiply. Thus, the evil is twofold...[103]

His disciple, the Maharam Schick, applies this to all areas of Jewish life. If the *tzaddikim* detach themselves from something which is necessary for the community, and the simpletons stay with it, the evil is twofold. This matter will turn out to be exclusively in accordance with the spirit of the simpletons, God forbid. Therefore, it is better for the proper Jews not to detach themselves.[104]

The same is true of building our Holy Land. Ever since the beginning of this movement, the God-fearing, Orthodox Jews separated themselves from it and opposed it. The simpletons, on the

103 *Teshuvot Maharam Schick, Orach Chayim* 70. [The parenthetical comments are R. Teichtal's.]

104 ❖ See this inside the text. Also, see the end of the approbations (pp. 30-31), where I cited a similar idea from the Chatam Sofer's novellae on *Niddah*.

other hand, took the matter into their own hands and exerted themselves greatly to achieve their goals. They toiled and labored until HaShem's desire succeeded through them.[105] Now, since the God-fearing Jews kept their distance from this entire undertaking, is it surprising that the building was accomplished with a free [non-religious] spirit? Had we all cooperated from the very beginning, an abounding spirit of Torah and devotion would undoubtedly have pervaded the Land. Now that the simpletons have already established a fine settlement, it is obvious that they are the lords of the Land, for it is the fruit of their labor. Thus, the words of our mentor, the Chatam Sofer, have been proven true.

In any event, we see that our mentors, the Chatam Sofer and his disciple, the Maharam Schick, disagree with the brilliant and holy author of *Minchat Elazar*; and the *halachah* always follows the Chatam Sofer and Maharam Schick. Therefore, the God-fearing, Orthodox Jews must not withdraw from the building effort. On the contrary, they have a sacred obligation to contribute, from now on, to this holy endeavor and unite all of the forces. They must accompany the initial builders in this lofty endeavor, in order to elevate it higher and higher. The *Midrash* thus states: "One verse says, *Great* (מגדיל) *salvation* (*Tehillim* 18:51), while another verse says, *A tower* (מגדול) *of salvation* (II *Shmuel* 22:51). R. Yudan answers, 'The redemption of this nation does not come all at once, but little by little. What does מגדיל mean? [Salvation] grows (מתגדלת) progressively for Israel' " (*Midrash Tehillim* 18:36).

We must bring the irreligious back to God

When these simpletons see that we, the Orthodox Jews, do not reject them and that we want to work together with them, they will come closer to us and improve their ways. After all, they are also descendants of Avraham, Yitzchak, and Ya'akov, and are rooted in holiness. Our mentor, the author of *Shulchan Aruch HaRav*, writes in his introduction to *Sefer HaTanya* that even the lowest Jews are connected to and rooted in the letters of the Torah; and the Torah binds them to HaShem. Their souls yearn to return to their source, as I explained above.[106] If we choose this path, we will proceed without fail towards the completion of the building, and HaShem's name will be sanctified through us.

105 Based on *Yeshayah* 53:10.
106 P. 168.

Our mentor, the man of God from Komarno, explains the saying "Distance yourself from a bad neighbor, and do not associate with a wicked person" (*Avot* 1:7):

> The *Tana* does not say "Distance yourself from a wicked person" as it says of a bad neighbor. Rather, "Do not associate." That is, do not distance yourself from a wicked person, God forbid. On the contrary, it is a *mitzvah* to come close to him, because in this way you will influence him to become good. Just, "Do not associate" with him in the confines of your heart. But you must certainly not distance him from you or yourself from him.[107]

The same applies to our discussion.

We erred

Tangentially, I will mention what I heard yesterday, Monday of *parashat Emor*, 5703 [1943], when I visited the great *gaon*, the holy luminary, our honorable master, R. David Meisels, *av beit din* of Ohel, author of Responsa *Binyan David*, who is in the Varush Meyer hospital here in the capital. May HaShem cure him and grant him a speedy recovery, so that he will be healthy and strong for his sacred work, until the coming of *Mashiach*, speedily in our days. Amen.

Last *Pesach*, on the Sabbath of the intermediary days, I was honored to speak in front of a large audience in the Orthodox synagogue of the Talmud society here. In the middle of my sermon, I introduced the issue of building our Land. I enthusiastically explained that we must all work for this cause after all that we have been through, and that our only option is to rebuild the Land together. Many people complained about me, and the brilliant R. Meisels heard the complaints. He said, "In truth, it turns out that we were wrong for ignoring the movement to build the Land." These are the words of the brilliant *gadol ha'dor*. He also said that many of our Jewish brethren would have been saved had we all engaged in building the Land from the outset, instead of arguing about this. He then sighed and said that his sons were also caught in the enemies ensnaring trap in Slovakia.

Today, the halachah follows those who advocate settling the Land

יג Furthermore, after the utter chaos that our Jewish brethren have experienced, it is obvious that the *halachah* does not follow those lofty saints who opposed the settlement. The earth has crumbled beneath the feet of millions of Jews here in Europe. Some of them

107 *Notzer Chesed*, Commentary to *Avot* (1:7).

had their blood spilled like water; others remained like a mast at the head of a ship, with no shelter or shade above their heads and no ground beneath their feet. They are like a lone ship in the waves of a sea of troubles; they do not know where to turn and what direction they are facing. In this situation, the *halachah* follows those *gedolim* who advocated settling and rebuilding the Land, as I will explain.

Eliyahu HaNavi's advantage over Moshe Rabbeinu

I will preface with the wondrous words of our mentor, the Kedushat Levi. Often, when there is an unresolved question in the Talmud, *Chazal* say "תיקו"[108] which stands for "תשבי יתרץ קושיות ובעיות – [Eliyahu] the Tishbi will solve difficulties and questions:"[109]

At first glance, one might ask: Behold, this will occur after the Redeemer comes (speedily in our days. Amen). Why, then, must Eliyahu solve the difficulties and questions? Moshe Rabbeinu *a"h*, who gave us the Torah and *mitzvot*, will be alive; why won't he solve all the difficulties that we have with our holy Torah?

The answer is as follows: *Seder HaDorot*, commenting on the dispute between Rashi and Rabbeinu Tam concerning *tefillin*, says that Rashi *z"l* was the "Moshe Rabbeinu" of his group. Rabbeinu Tam ignored this, saying that Moshe already gave us the Torah. Now it is up to us to teach according to our intellect's understanding of the holy Torah.[110]

We will explain this briefly. *Chazal* say about the disputes between Beit Shammai and Beit Hillel, "These and those are the words of the living God" (*Eiruvin* 13b). For there is a level at which a man's essence determines the way he understands our holy Torah. If he comes from the world of loving-kindness (*chesed*), then, according to his understanding of our holy Torah, everything is pure, permitted, and kosher. If he has the attribute of strength (*gevurah*), the opposite is true. Now, Beit Hillel had the attribute of *chesed*; therefore, they were [more] lenient. Beit Shammai had the attribute of *gevurah*; therefore, they were strict. This is the meaning of "These and those are the words of the living God": In truth, each one [expressed] the words of the living God, according to their level.[111]

Behold, our Sages *z"l* who lived after the generation of Beit

108 *Berachot* 8a, 25b; *Shabbat* 5a...
109 See *Tosafot Yom Tov, Eidi'ot* 8:7.
110 *Seder HaDorot* 1:104b.
111 ❖ See Rashi, *Ketuvot* 57a, s.v. *ha kamashma lan*.

> Shammai and Beit Hillel saw that the world needs to operate through *chesed*. Therefore, they determined that the *halachah* always follows Beit Hillel's leniencies. Now, who is capable of discerning the attribute through which the world needs to function, so that the *halachah* can be decided accordingly? Only someone who is alive and exists in this world knows which attribute the world needs. Someone who is not alive, however, does not know this at all. Eliyahu is still alive and always exists in this world, for he never tasted the taste of death.[112] Therefore, he will resolve all the difficulties and questions, for he knows the attribute through which the world needs to function. This also explains Rabbeinu Tam's statement that once Moshe Rabbeinu *a"h* gave us the Torah, it is up to us to teach it.[113]

The Kedushat Levi means that since Moshe Rabbeinu does not exist in this world, he cannot determine the *halachah* now, [at the time of redemption], based on the world's needs at the time [of the giving of the Torah]. These words are befitting a godly man such as himself.

HaShem enlightened me, and I found that one of the great *poskim*, whose teachings radiate every day in every house of study, our great mentor, R. Moshe Mabit,[114] agrees with our master, the Kedushat Levi, on this point. In his work, *Beit Elokim*, he provides the same explanation as the Kedushat Levi as to why Tishbi will resolve our difficulties and not Moshe Rabbeinu. Thus, two "prophets" prophesied in the same manner.[115] I will quote his words, for they are the words of the living God:

> Eliyahu *z"l* will be renowned in those days (that is, at the time of the resurrection). Tishbi will resolve our difficulties and questions, and he will turn back the hearts of the fathers through the sons and the hearts of the sons through their fathers.[116] [This is true] of all things, especially acceptance of the Torah.
>
> Eliyahu HaNavi will reveal all matters which were hidden

112 Based on the song, *Eliyahu HaNavi*, recited after the Sabbath.

113 *Kedushat Levi* (Jerusalem: HaMosad LeHotza'at Sifrei Mussar VeChassidut, 5718 [1958]), *Likutim*, vol. 1, p. 316.

114 ∴ A colleague of the Beit Yosef and a member of his court.

115 Based on *Sanhedrin* 89a.

116 Based on *Malachi* 3:24.

in this world. When the other prophets, judges, and wise men, who lived in previous generations, come back to life, they will not know what happened in this world since their deaths. This is true even of the Patriarchs, the Tribes, and all those who lived from the time of Moshe Rabbeinu until the resurrection. For they were in the upper and lower Garden of Eden, detached from the concerns of this physical world. Eliyahu, on the other hand, who lived from the time of Moshe Rabbeinu until the time of Yehoram, knew everything that occurred in his days. Also, after he departed [this world] with body and soul, his body became purified like one of the celestial bodies, if not greater. God prepared him to be available in Israel's time of need, so that He [God] could save them through him and in his merit. Eliyahu also appears to the wise men of Israel in order to reveal the secrets of the Torah to them, according to each generation's preparedness. Not to mention our tradition that he is present at [every] circumcision, for he was zealous about this *mitzvah*. We even prepare a chair in his honor.

He is also involved in areas that are hidden and concealed from man in this world. Accordingly, *Chazal* say, "Let it be put aside until Eliyahu comes" (*Bava Metzia* 3a). He comprehends every aspect of this world; there is nothing hidden from his wisdom. This is because of his longevity as a prophet. Several things that *Chazal* say about Moshe Rabbeinu apply to him, as well.[117] But, these levels of perception are not given even to Moshe Rabbeinu *a"h*, because his soul is separated from his body and he cannot grasp this-worldly matters. Even the angels are unable to grasp these matters, except regarding the mission on which HaShem sends them to this world; and an angel cannot accomplish two missions [simultaneously].[118] On the other hand, God sustained Eliyahu *z"l* in a pure body and a delicate soul and chose him from among all the other prophets, because He recognized in him (more than in others) a certain readiness for these levels of perception... Thus, because of his delicate soul, he knows all of the lofty matters that occur in the supernal worlds; and because of his pure body, he knows everything that occurs in this world. For even though he is delicate and pure, he retains a small amount – in quantity and quality – of corporeality, which is undetectable in [physical]

117 [See Rambam, *Hilchot Yesodei HaTorah*, chap. 7.]
118 See *BeReishit Rabbah* 50:2.

> circumstances and movements. He hovers around the world...
>
> Even though he exists in the manner that we described, he will undergo a quasi-resurrection at the time of the resurrection. His pure body will thicken a bit and become more physical, in order to make him visible to all of the redeemed and resurrected people, and to enable him to dwell permanently among them and act as they do. This is also what the Patriarchs, the prophets, and their leader, Moshe Rabbeinu *a"h*, will do at that time. Eliyahu will achieve more than anyone else because of his knowledge of all of the secrets of this world. He lived a very long life in this world before ascending to the heavens in a whirlwind. From that moment until the redemption and resurrection, he roams the world [and reveals himself to] the righteous and pious ones, and he saves Israel from their troubles (as mentioned above). Therefore, in every generation he achieves the knowledge of every aspect of this lowly world, and he is able to clarify all of the doubts that the Sages have and anything that is hidden from us. In this way, he will cause Torah study to be complete, clear, and doubtless.
>
> Even Moshe Rabbeinu, through whom the Torah was given, will not be able to clarify the uncertainties of the Torah, even though they are clear to him. This is so because when God brings him back to life, he will speak as if from the heavens, since his soul was separated from his body. But, the verse says, *It is not in the heavens* (*Devarim* 30:12), and [*Chazal* state] "We pay no attention to a heavenly voice" (*Bava Metzia* 59b)... Whatever we receive from Eliyahu, however, will be as if [it was handed down from generation to generation], for he has existed forever with both body and soul and can clarify the uncertainties and secrets of the Torah.[119]

Behold, this is the same thing that our mentor, the Kedushat Levi, says. That is, since Eliyahu never left this world, and he knows the situation of every generation, he can decide the *halachah* whenever necessary. On the other hand, a *tzaddik* who already departed this world and does not know the circumstances of a [later] generation, cannot decide the *halachah* for that generation. All of this demonstrates the greatness of the Kedushat Levi's intellect, for he was worthy enough to concur with our master, the Mabit, who lived at the time of the Beit Yosef. Had he seen this work, he would

119 *Beit Elokim, Sha'ar HaYesodot* 60 (end).

have been overjoyed to find a "companion" like himself.

We may conclude from the words of these two profound *gedolim* that when a *tzaddik* renders a *halachic* decision on a particular issue and then ascends to the heavens, the *halachah* does not necessarily follow his opinion. If circumstances change, making it very difficult for the generation to follow this *tzaddik*'s stringent opinion, and some good will result from following the opinion of the other *tzaddikim*, then we do not follow his opinion. This is so because he is no longer in this world and he does not know what the world needs. Therefore, today, when it is impossible to remain in the Diaspora because of the great calamity that has befallen Israel, it is obvious that we need not be concerned with the opinion of those *gedolim* who opposed the settlement. Rather, the *halachah* follows those who advocated it, because the times require it. Moreover, perhaps if the former *gedolim* were alive today and saw our predicament, they too would agree.

III Redemption and Yishuv Eretz Yisrael

The redemption may occur naturally

יד I already mentioned in the previous chapter[120] that our master, the brilliant and holy author of *Minchat Elazar*, opposed the building movement only because, in his opinion, the third redemption will occur miraculously, not naturally. Anyone who anticipates a natural process denies the coming of *Mashiach*, God forbid. His works are filled with this idea. I explained there[121] (citing the Sages of the Talmud and *Midrash*, the Or HaChayim HaKadosh, and other holy men) that it all depends on the two aspects of redemption – whether we are worthy or, God forbid, not. If we are unworthy, it will have to come through miracles disguised in nature.

The hatred against Babylonian Jews for not ascending with Ezra

I will now add [another refutation] to this. Many sources indicate that the inhabitants of *Eretz Yisrael* harbored a hatred against the Babylonian Jews for not ascending to *Eretz Yisrael* with Ezra. For had they all ascended, the redemption would have been everlasting. This hatred lasted from the time of the rebuilding of the Temple until after its destruction. *Tosafot* and *Tosafot Yom Tov* state that since the Torah scholars of *Eretz Yisrael* hated the people of Babylonia, they referred to them derogatorily as "Babylonians" and said about them, "The Babylonians eat [the *Yom Kippur* he-goat]

120 P. 147.
121 Pp. 134-40.

raw."[122] This occurred while the *Beit HaMikdash* was standing. After it was destroyed we find:

> Reish Lakish said to Rabbah bar bar Chanah, ôBy God, I hate you. (Rashi explains: 'I hate...all Babylonians, because they did not ascend to *Eretz Yisrael* at the time of Ezra. They prevented the *Shechinah* from returning to rest upon the Second Temple.') It is thus written, *If she be a wall, we will build upon her a battlement of silver; and if she be a door, we will enclose her with a cedar board* (*Shir HaShirim* 8:9): Had you made yourselves like a wall and ascended all together to *Eretz Yisrael* at the time of Ezra, you would have been compared to silver which does not decay (and the redemption would have been complete). Now that you went up like doors,[123] you were compared to cedar which decays (meaning, the edifice was destroyed).ö (*Yoma* 9b)[124]

The Ya'avetz explains [the homiletic passage in which Eliyahu] appears to R. Chiya as a fiery bear (*Bava Metzia* 85b):

> For he [the angelic minister of Persia, who appears as a bear] prosecutes against the Babylonian Jews who did not ascend when Cyrus, king of Persia, gave them permission to do so. Had they ascended during that divine visitation, [their efforts] would not have decayed and the redemption would have been complete... Therefore, there is room to prosecute, because the Babylonians caused the exile to be lengthened.[125]

Thus, even at the time of R. Chiya (who lived after the destruction), the prosecutor prosecuted because many Jews did not ascend when Cyrus granted permission.

The *Midrash* comments on the verse *If she be a wall* (*Shir HaShirim* 8:9):

> Had Israel ascended from Babylonia as a wall, the Second Temple would not have been destroyed. R. Ze'ira went to the marketplace to buy some goods. The seller said to him, "You are not leaving here, you Babylonian whose ancestors destroyed

122 [This is considered gluttonous behavior.] See *Tosafot, Menachot* 100a, s.v. *she'son'im*; *Tosafot Yom Tov, Menachot* 11:7, s.v. *haBavli'im*.

123 [Rashi: "A gate which has two doors is opened one door at a time. Similarly, you ascended by halves," meaning, in insufficient numbers.]

124 [The parenthetical comments are R. Teichtal's.]

125 *Siddur Beit Ya'akov, Sullam Beit El*, p. 14b.

> the *Beit HaMikdash*!" R. Ze'ira wondered, "Are my ancestors any different than his?" He entered the study hall and heard the voice of R. Shilah, who was sitting and expounding, "*If she be a wall*: Had Israel ascended from the Diaspora as a wall, the Second Temple would not have been destroyed." [Upon hearing this], R. Ze'ira said to himself, "That ignorant Jew taught me well." (*Shir HaShirim Rabbah* 8:9:3)[126]

Responsa *Chavot Ya'ir* explains that when R. Zeira called someone a "stupid Babylonian" because of his love for *Eretz Yisrael*, he had this very idea in mind.[127]

Thus, it is clear that this hatred [against Babylonian Jews] for not returning to *Eretz Yisrael* with Ezra, continued from generation to generation. The other Jews could not forgive them for this, so much so that even a simple, ignorant Jew did not want to sell his goods to a Babylonian Jew, saying that his ancestors destroyed our city and desolated our *Beit HaMikdash*.

Now, according to the brilliant and holy Minchat Elazar, who holds that the future redemption will come only through manifest miracles and not with the permission of the kings, what was the sin of Ezra's generation? Why should there be such a long-lasting, pent-up hatred for them? Surely, the Jews of Babylonia did not want to be redeemed by Cyrus. They wanted to be redeemed by the Holy One Blessed be He Himself, with manifest and glorious miracles. [So, what was their sin?] We are forced to say, "Why do you involve yourself with the Merciful One's hidden matters?!" (*Berachot* 10a). Perhaps, the Holy One Blessed be He wanted it to unfold specifically in that manner.

The same applies to our situation. If the kings grant us permission to return to our Land, this is the Creator's will. It will develop into what should have developed at the time of Cyrus, had all the Jews returned. All we have to do is see to it that everyone returns. Then, we will attain our heart's desire, the final redemption, with God's help. This is an irrefutable proof!

This was also R. Yehoshua ben Chananyah's reasoning, as the above-cited *Midrash* states.[128] In his days, the king granted the Jews permission to go to *Eretz Yisrael* and build the *Beit HaMikdash*. R.

126 [The translation incorporates the comments of *Matnot Kehunah* as quoted by our author.]

127 *Teshuvot Chavot Ya'ir* 152.

128 *BeReishit Rabbah* 64:10. See above, p. 190.

Yehoshua accepted this permission, even though he knew that there would be no more redemptions after the third one and that the final redemption would undoubtedly develop from this.

We must not delay redemption through our sins

The Talmud states that the Holy One Blessed be He made the Assembly of Israel swear that they will not delay (ירחקו) the end of days (*Ketuvot* 111a). Rashi explains:

> They will not delay the end of days through their sins. Another version reads, "They will not precipitate (ידחקו) [the end of days]," from the word דוחק (to press). [That is to say], they will not pray for this excessively. ❖

A hymn (*piyut*) from the morning prayers of the first day of *Pesach* states, "I made you swear רחוק דחוק"[132] It seems that the author of this hymn holds that both versions are true. That is, the Jews took an oath on both of these matters. The poet (*paytan*) himself writes explicitly[133] that we must not precipitate the end of days; i.e., we must not leave the exile before its time, like the tribe of Efrayim did.[134] (This is unlike Rashi's explanation above.) In any event, it is clear from this hymn that the version which reads, "They will not delay (ירחקו) the end of days" is also valid.

Now, Rashi's explanation - "They will not delay it through their sins" - seems difficult. If he refers to sins in general, why is a new oath necessary? Were they not already adjured at Mount Sinai not to sin?[135] Furthermore, we already swore not to delay the end of days through our sins by virtue of the verse *Do not do this to the Lord your God* (*Devarim* 12:4).[136] Rashi comments: "R. Yishmael said, 'Do you

---

❖ The Chatam Sofer explains what Rashi means when he says, "excessively": "That is to say, like Yosef Della Reina[129] and the like. However, we are obligated to pray every day."[130] I found this same interpretation in the new *Yismach Moshe* on *Shir HaShirim*.[131]

129 He lived at the time of the expulsion from Spain and attempted to bring the redemption closer using practical Kabbalah, but failed.

130 *Teshuvot Chatam Sofer* 6:86.

131 *Yismach Moshe*, *Nevi'im* and *Megillot*, p. 81a (on *Shir HaShirim* 2:7).

132 S.v. *or yesha*.

133 Letter *Lamed*.

134 See *Sanhedrin* 92b, *Shemot Rabbah* 20:10.

135 Based on *Nedarim* 8a.

136 [The preceding verses read, *You shall utterly destroy all of the places in which*

really think that Israel would smash the altars [of HaShem]? Rather, do not act as the Gentiles do, lest your sins cause your forefathers' Sanctuary to be destroyed.'" The *Yerushalmi* also states, "Any generation which does not witness the rebuilding of the *Beit HaMikdash*, is considered as if it destroyed it" (*Yoma* 1:1 [4b]). Therefore, Rashi's comments above require explanation.

It seems to me that Rashi is not referring to a general sin, but to a sin that relates to the end of days itself. *Chazal* state, "A miracle should have occurred at the time of Ezra, but sin prevented it" (*Berachot* 4a). The Maharsha[137] explains that Ezra's redemption was supposed to last forever, but the sin of not returning to *Eretz Yisrael* en masse prevented this from happening.[138] The true end of days was delayed (נתרחק) because of this.

This is the sin referred to in the oath "They will not delay (ירחקו) the end of days through their sins." They swore that if the kings permit them to ascend to *Eretz Yisrael*, they will take this opportunity and ascend en masse, in order to generate an everlasting redemption. They will not do like the Jews did at Ezra's time and delay the end of days... And if they completely refuse to accept the divine visitation, they will certainly delay the end of days. This is the true interpretation of Rashi's words.

The wealthy Jews who do not donate to this cause

מט This explains King David's statement to HaShem (when he was collecting donations for the building of the *Beit HaMikdash*), *And now, I have seen Your people, who are present here, offering donations to You with joy* (I *Divrei HaYamim* 29:17). Rashi comments:

> *Who are present here*: This refers to those who are mentioned above, *David assembled all the princes of Israel...* (ibid. 28:1). But, the wealthy Jews of each city are not present here. Therefore, O Master of the Universe, the donation is humble. For, if the rest of Israel were here, the donation would be greater.

This is a disgrace to our nation's wealthy individuals. They continually refrain from donating even to the loftiest causes, like building the *Beit HaMikdash*. This is true until this very day.

Thus, David criticized the wealthy Jews for staying at home and

the nations served...their gods... You shall smash their altars... (*Devarim* 12:2-3).]

137 *Yoma* 9b, s.v. *kechomah*.

138 ❖ I also cited this above (p. 161) in the name of the *Kuzari*.

failing to donate. As a result of this, not every Jew had a share in the *Beit HaMikdash* and it did not endure; it was not "like silver which does not decay" (*Yoma* 9b).

The *Tosefta* also describes how great *aliyah* is when all of *Klal Yisrael* participate in it:

> [The verse says, *About forty thousand soldiers* (of Reuven and Gad) *passed before the Lord for the battle* (*Yehoshua* 4:13).] It also says, *The Lord has delivered the entire Land into our hands* (ibid. 2:24). Do you really think that Israel conquers the Land before the Omnipresent?[139] Rather, when all the Jews live in the Land, it is conquered; when they do not all live in the Land, it is not conquered.[140] (*Tosefta, Avodah Zarah* 5:2)

Why do today's builders desire God's Land when they reject His Torah?

מז The founders of the movement to return to and settle in our Holy Land, along with their comrades, are very weak in our holy religion (due to our numerous sins). They have broken virtually all ties with it. Nevertheless, we notice that they refuse to choose any plot of land, other than our forefathers' Land, to turn into a settlement. They sacrifice themselves for the Holy Land, as numerous incidents demonstrate. Many of these simpletons endangered their lives for it, and countless sacrifices have been offered on the altar of this sacred soil. May God remember this for their benefit.

This seems puzzling. Since they do not adhere to God's Torah, what have they to do with *Eretz Yisrael*, which is only sanctified through the sanctity of the Torah? The Torah is fulfilled mainly in *Eretz Yisrael*, as I explained above[141] citing the godly Maharam Cordovero. Moshe Rabbeinu desired to enter the Land only because of the sanctity of the Torah, as *Chazal* state (*Sotah* 14a). Avraham Avinu, as well, desired it[142] only in order to gain the wisdom of Torah, for "There is no Torah like the Torah of *Eretz Yisrael*" (*BeReishit Rabbah* 16:4). If so, since the members of this movement do not adhere to HaShem's Torah (due to our numerous sins), what have they to do with *Eretz Yisrael*?

139 [The second verse implies that God conquers the Land for us. The first verse, however, implies that numerous soldiers are necessary!]

140 [I.e., conquering the Land depends on *Klal Yisrael*. Thus, all the tribes – including Reuven and Gad, who lived across the Jordan river – needed to help conquer the Land. (See *Chasdei David* on the *Tosefta*.)]

141 P. 81.

142 See *Midrash Tehillim* 1:13.

Merely desiring the Land makes Israel worthy of inheriting it

I found the solution to this problem in the divine words of *Maggid Meisharim*. There, the angel explains the entire episode of the spies to our mentor, the Beit Yosef:

> The eve of the Sabbath, 23rd of Sivan. The Lord is with you, O mighty man of valor[143]... Behold, we can ask [several questions] on this *parashah* (*Shelach*): Why does it say, *Send forth men, for yourself* (*BeMidbar* 13:2)? This implies that it was a commandment from the Holy One Blessed be He and not Israel's initiative. In *Devarim*, however, it says, *All of you approached me...* (1:22)? Furthermore, why was it necessary for Moshe Rabbeinu *a"h* to degrade the Land and arrange for the spies [to find out], *Is it fat or lean...* (*BeMidbar* 13:20)? This implies that if the Land is not fat and good they would not go! Furthermore, it seems that Moshe Rabbeinu *a"h* caused them to err and not believe the Holy One Blessed be He. God promised, "I will bring you up from the affliction of Egypt to a good Land" (see *Shemot* 3:17), and Moshe said, *Is it fat or lean*!
>
> The explanation of this matter is as follows, and it will answer many of the commentator's questions. You must understand that the people of Israel did not deserve to enter the Land, because they tested the Holy One Blessed be He many times. However, through His abundant mercy and kindness, God placed in their hearts the desire to send men to spy out the Land. Had they performed this mission properly, HaShem would have brought them into the Land (because of this merit), and afterwards, slowly but surely, He would have taken retribution for their previous sins. The Torah does not mention here that they approached God, as it does in *Devarim*, to hint to the fact that the Holy One Blessed be He placed this request in their hearts.
>
> HaShem commanded them to send their princes, meaning, their greatest sages. [The sending of] Yehoshua proves this, for he was great in Torah, and all of them were like him. Moshe told them to see if *it is fat...*, because it is well known that the Land is certainly fat, good, and [full of] trees.[144] Moshe was hinting that they should praise *Eretz Yisrael* so that the Jews would yearn to enter the Land. Then, they would merit to enter therein.[145]

143 Based on *Shoftim* 6:12.

144 Based on *BeMidbar* 13:20.

145 *Maggid Meisharim, Shelach* (beginning).

Every utterance of this holy angel is the word of the living God... This teaches that simply yearning for and desiring the Land makes Israel worthy of inheriting it.

Maggid Meisharim continues to explain that Moshe specifically chose *gedolei Torah*, and not the princes from the inauguration of the altar, because he was worried that they would deviate from their mission. Nonetheless, his efforts were to no avail. Even though they were the greatest Torah scholars, they deviated from their mission.

The holy *Zohar*[146] and the Shelah[147] explain that selfish motives caused the spies to do this. They feared that they were fit to be princes [only] in the desert, but once they enter the Land new princes would be appointed. Let this be an instructive lesson. Even the greatest *gadol* in Torah and righteousness should not trust himself when he opposes the movement to build the Land. He should not think that his intentions are fully for the sake of Heaven, for he is certainly no greater in Torah and righteousness than the princes whom Moshe sent. Consider and study this well and you will see that it is the truth.

In any event, we see that HaShem motivated the Jews to send men to *Eretz Yisrael* for Israel's benefit. He wanted to awaken within them a yearning and desire for the good Land, so that they would be worthy to enter and inherit the Land.

This also explains our issue. There is no doubt that the Holy One Blessed be He, Who always has our best interest in mind, placed this desire for the Land of our forefathers into the hearts of our Jewish brethren (who have learned the ways of the nations during this long and bitter exile), so that none of us will be banished.[148] He inspired them to yearn and sacrifice themselves for the Land, and this makes them worthy to inherit and dwell in it. Undoubtedly, one *mitzvah* leads to another,[149] and eventually, after many Jews dwell there, the Holy One Blessed be He will purify their hearts and they will return to His service.[150]

146 3:158a, s.v. *vayishlach*.

147 *Sh'nei Luchot HaBrit, Torah SheBichtav - Shelach*, 2:68a, s.v. *be'inyan shilu'ach*.

148 Based on II *Shmuel* 14:14.

149 *Avot* 4:2.

150 ❖ I cited this above (pp. 118-20) in the name of our mentors, the Or HaChayim HaKadosh and the Chatam Sofer. May their merits protect us and all of Israel.

Israel's return to Eretz Yisrael is considered repentance and makes them worthy of redemption

יז The Rambam writes in *Hilchot Teshuvah*, "Israel will only be redeemed through repentance, and the Torah has already promised that Israel will repent at the end of their exile and immediately be redeemed."[151] I believe that this statement can be explained based on something I saw in *Minchat Yehudah*,[152] by the Sefardic scholar, R. Yehudah Alcalay, a disciple of the holy author of *Pele Yo'etz z"l.*[153] He cites the Rambam's statement that a person who performs one *mitzvah* properly deserves a portion in the World to Come.[154] The Rosh agrees. The Ran also quotes this Rambam and adds that this *mitzvah* must be one of great value, a *mitzvah* that is equal to many other *mitzvot.*[155] R. Alcalay adds that the same applies to repentance. A person who performs one *mitzvah* perfectly is considered a complete penitent.[156]

Now, if this is true of individual repentance, it is certainly true of communal repentance. Accordingly, R. Alcalay writes that if the masses perform one *mitzvah* perfectly they are considered complete penitents and will merit redemption through it. *Chazal* state this [clearly]: "Anyone who performs one *mitzvah* will receive goodness and long life and will inherit the Land" (*Kiddushin* 39b). If this is true of an individual, then it is certainly true of many people who do a *mitzvah*. For it is well known that one cannot compare a few people who do a *mitzvah* to many people who do it.[157]

R. Alcalay then quotes Rashi on the verse *Afterwards, the Children of Israel will return and seek out the Lord their God and David their king, and they will tremble for the Lord and for His goodness in the end of days* (*Hoshea* 3:5). Rashi writes:

> After the days of exile, Israel will return. It was taught in the name of R. Shimon bar Yochai: The Children of Israel despised three things: the kingdom of Heaven, the kingdom of the House

151 *Hilchot Teshuvah* 7:5.

152 *Kitvei Rebbe Yehudah Alcalay* (Mossad HaRav Kook), vol. 1, p. 213ff.

153 ❖ This precious work [*Minchat Yehudah*] was printed a hundred years ago, in 5603 [1843]. I obtained it through Divine Providence, for it is very hard to find. The entire book speaks about Israel's redemption.

154 Commentary to the *Mishnah, Makkot* 3:16.

155 *Derashot HaRan, Derush* 6 (beginning).

156 ❖ He also cites this in the name of his mentor, the Pele Yo'etz (in his work *Elef HaMagen, Ki Tavo*), quoting the godly Kabbalist, our master, R. Shalom Sharrabi.

157 ❖ See Rashi on *VaYikra* 26:8.

> of David, and the *Beit HaMikdash*. R. Shimon ben Menassiya said, "Israel will not be shown a good sign until they return and seek out these three things. Accordingly, it says, *Afterwards, the Children of Israel will return and seek out the Lord their God* – this refers to the kingdom of Heaven; *and David their king* – according to its simple meaning; *and they will tremble for the Lord and His goodness* – this refers to the *Beit HaMikdash*, as it says, *This good mountain and the Lebanon* (*Devarim* 3:25)" (*Yalkut Shimoni* 2:106).

R. Alcalay comments on this: [158]

> Since he said that Israel will not see a good sign until they seek out those three things, we certainly have a great obligation to devote ourselves to them.
>
> "*Afterwards, the Children of Israel will return and seek out the Lord* – this refers to the kingdom of Heaven": The holy *Zohar* states, "The Holy One Blessed be He is called 'King' only in *Eretz Yisrael*" (*Zohar* 3:276a). Thus, the first act of repentance that Israel will do in the end of days will be to seek out the kingdom of Heaven. That is, they will return to *Eretz Yisrael* so that the Holy One Blessed be He can be called 'King.' This is the meaning of *And seek out the Lord their God*, for "He who dwells outside of the Land is like one who has no God" (*Ketuvot* 110b).
>
> I heard from the holy lips of the great rabbi, the ôfortress and tower,ö R. Yehudah Bibas, that this explains the verse *Return to Me and I will return to you* (*Malachi* 3:7). That is to say, Israel will return and find shelter with God in *Eretz Yisrael*, and then He will cause His *Shechinah* to rest among us...
>
> The *Zohar* similarly states: "R. Chiya said, 'The nations will rule over Israel for only one day, a day of the Holy One Blessed be He, which is a thousand years. It is thus written, *He has made me desolate, faint throughout the day* (*Eichah* 1:13), one day and no longer.' R. Yosi said, 'If [the Jews] are subjugated longer than this, it is not because of the King's decree, but because they refuse to return towards Him (לקבליה)' " (*Zohar* 2:17a).
>
> It seems to me that the words, "towards Him (לקבליה)," hint to the fact that the Jews will return to *Eretz Yisrael*, as R.

158 *Minchat Yehudah*, sec. 18, p. 237.

Yehudah Bibas states. For, it does not say, "to return in repentance" as *Chazal* usually say. ❖

Now, it is well known that the *mitzvah* of *Yishuv Eretz Yisrael* is equal to the entire Torah (*Sifrei, Re'eh* 28). It is also well known that many Jews presently ascend to *Eretz Yisrael* with genuine effort and self-sacrifice. Furthermore, [we already explained that] by performing one of the preeminent *mitzvot*, the Jews are considered penitents and deserve redemption. Therefore, the Rambam's statement – "Israel will only be redeemed through repentance, and the Torah has already promised that Israel will repent...and immediately be redeemed" – has come to fruition. That is to say, the very fact that the Jews yearn to return to *Eretz Yisrael*, which is a preeminent *mitzvah*, is their repentance,[160] and it makes them worthy of seeing the final redemption (with God's help). Their yearning stems from HaShem's promise to stir their hearts to repentance at the end of their exile. For, I stated above that the Holy One Blessed be He will place in their hearts the desire and yearning to return to *Eretz Yisrael*. This itself will be their repentance, as Hoshea the prophet says, *Afterwards, the Children of Israel will seek out the Lord their God*. "This refers to the kingdom of Heaven," [meaning, they will strive] to return to *Eretz Yisrael* so that the Holy One Blessed be He can be called "King."

By fulfilling even one mitzvah we are free from Eisav's dominion

יח Based on the principle that fulfilling one *mitzvah* makes us worthy of redemption, I would like to explain a puzzling *Midrash* on the verse *It is a gift sent to my lord to Eisav* (*BeReishit* 32:19). The *Midrash* states, "He [Ya'akov] sent him an eagle" (*Yalkut HaReuveni*, ibid.).

HaShem told Rivkah, *And the elder shall serve the younger* (*BeReishit* 25:23). Thus, at the very beginning of their creation, it was determined that Eisav would serve Ya'akov. However, Yitzchak said in his

---

❖ [I.e., as *Chazal* usually say] in the *Zohar*.[159] Rather, it says "towards Him (לקבליה)," meaning, to return to *Eretz Yisrael* and approach the Holy One Blessed be He. For God can always be found in *Eretz Yisrael*, even when it is destroyed.

159 See *Sha'arei Zohar* by R. Reuven Margolis *zt"l*, *Sanhedrin* 97b, s.v. *kalu kol ha'kitzin*.

160 ❖ As *Minchat Yehudah* and the holy R. Yehudah Bibas state, that this fulfills the verse, *Return to Me*.

blessing to Eisav, *It shall be that when you are distressed,*[161] *you will remove his yoke from upon your neck* (ibid. 27:40). But, we do not know the parameters of "*when you are distressed,*" for we have 613 *mitzvot* to keep![162] There are two possible explanations:

1. Ya'akov avoids "*when you* [Eisav] *are distressed*" only if he keeps all 613 mitzvot, not neglecting even one of them. However, if even one *mitzvah* is lacking, the situation is one of "*when you are distressed,*" and Eisav is free from Ya'akov's yoke. In fact, Ya'akov will serve Eisav.

2. Ya'akov avoids "*when you are distressed*" as long as he keeps just one of the 613 *mitzvot*, even though he neglects all of the rest.

Apparently, the first explanation is correct, because Ya'akov informed Eisav, *I have sojourned* (גרתי) *with Lavan* (ibid. 32:5), which *Chazal* interpret to mean, "I have kept the 613 (תרי"ג) *mitzvot.*"[163] However, Ya'akov took precautions for the sake of his descendants and sent Eisav an eagle. By doing so, Ya'akov was telling Eisav that he should not conclude, based on Ya'akov's actions, that the Jews must keep all 613 *mitzvot* in order to avoid "*when you are distressed.*"

[How does an eagle show this]? The Talmud asserts that if a bird has only one sign [of *kashrut*] it is kosher. From where do we learn this? From the eagle. Why did the Torah include the eagle [in its list of unkosher birds]?[164] It must be to teach that only a bird like the eagle, which has no signs of *kashrut*, is unkosher. But, if a bird has one sign of *kashrut*, it is kosher (*Chullin* 61a-b).

Thus, the eagle proves that one sign is sufficient. Therefore, for us as well, it is sufficient to keep only one *mitzvah* in order to avoid "*when you are distressed.*" [You may ask]: Why, then, was Ya'akov careful to keep all 613 *mitzvot*? He wanred to act in the best possible way. But, one *mitzvah* is sufficient to prevent Eisav from subjugating us.

We will return to our Land with the permission of the kings

יט *Minchat Yehudah* also explains that the verse, *And they will seek out* (ובקשו) *the Lord their God* (*Hoshea* 3:5), does not merely imply entreaty (בקשה) through prayer, rather:

161 [Rashi explains: "When Israel will transgress the Torah and you (Eisav) will have reason to be distressed over the blessings that he took..."]

162 [In other words, since there are so many *mitzvot*, it is unclear what is the definition of "When Israel will transgress the Torah and Eisav will have reason to be distressed."]

163 Rashi, ibid.

164 [Since it does not have even one sign of *kashrut* it is obviously prohibited.]

This great matter requires us to entreat the kings of the earth... The Holy One Blessed be He will motivate them to set us free and allow us to return to our possession and our forefathers' inheritance... Israel will not be shown a good sign until they entreat and create an opening like the tip of a needle, and then the Holy One Blessed be He will create an opening like the entrance to a hall.[165] The Torah also promises, *From there* [exile] *you will seek* (ובקשתם) *the Lord, your God, and you will find Him* (*Devarim* 4:29).

The author of *Yefeh To'ar* concurs: "*Mashiach* is not going to come to gather the exiles; he is not needed for that. HaShem Who scattered Israel will gather them,[166] as it says, *He will raise a banner for the nations and assemble the outcasts of Israel* (*Yeshayah* 11:12), and *They will bring all your brethren from all the nations as an offering to the Lord* (ibid. 66:20). HaShem will do these things in the way of the world."[167]

Today, the "way of the world" is to ask for mercy (חנינה) from the kings of the earth... Ya'akov Avinu hinted to this when he returned from exile, *And he encamped* (ויחן) *before* (את פני) *the city* (*BeReishit* 33:18). *Chazal* learn, "He asked for mercy (חנן) from the important people (הפנים – lit., 'the faces') of the city. He began to send them gifts" (*BeReishit Rabbah* 79:6).

The Radak comments on the verse "*Do not put your trust... in a son of man who holds no salvation* (*Tehillim* 146:3): Salvation is solely in the hands of HaShem, and He brings it about through mortals, just as he brought salvation from the Babylonian exile through Cyrus. In the future, as well, HaShem will bring Israel's redemption through gentile kings, by inspiring them to set the Jews free..." The same can be found in *Shir HaShirim Rabbah* on the verse *Come with me from Lebanon, O bride* (*Shir HaShirim* 4:8).

Ascribe to the Lord, O families of the peoples, ascribe to the Lord honor and strength (*Tehillim* 96:7). The *Midrash* comments, "When you [nations] bring them [the Jews], do not degrade them. Rather, bring them with honor and strength" (*Midrash Tehillim* 87:6). The Abarbanel concurs: "Zion will be astounded by the return of her children. Therefore, the prophet states that

165 Based on *Shir HaShirim Rabbah* 5:2.

166 Based on *Yirmiyah* 31:9.

167 *Yefeh To'ar, BeReishit Rabbah* 98:14:9, s.v. *im kein lamah...*

this event will take place with great strength, and this miracle (נס) will occur through the Gentiles themselves, as it says, *Behold, I will lift up My hand to nations and raise My banner* (נסי) *to peoples* (*Yeshayah* 49:22)."[168]

This also explains the verse *Kings will be your nurturers and their queens, your wet nurses* (ibid. 49:23). That is to say: During the redemption from Egypt, HaShem commanded Moshe, *Carry them in your bosom as a nurse carries the suckling child* (*BeMidbar* 11:12). Similarly, during the final redemption, kings will be your nurturers. During the redemption from Egypt, Israel encamped and traveled according to the commandment of HaShem through Moshe. Similarly, during the final redemption, they will travel according to the commandment of HaShem through the kings of the earth. Thus, the statement, *Kings will be your nurturers and their queens, your wet nurses...*, means that all of the rulers will agree that it is proper to return the crown to its rightful owners, as stated in *VaYikra Rabbah* (13:5).

This is the meaning of the verse *And I will bring you to the wilderness* (מדבר) *of the nations* (*Yechezkel* 20:35). The *Midrash* states: "מדבר (wilderness) connotes speech (דיבור), as it says, *And your speech* (ומדברך) *is comely* (*Shir HaShirim* 4:3)" (*Shemot Rabbah* 2:4). Thus, our verse means, I will bring you to the "speech" of the nations, for they will consider and discuss the lengthiness of our exile. For instance, I have heard that the High Priest of Hungary (called, His Majesty ôPrimas" in their language) pronounced sagaciously before the king and his officers, "We have never heard of or seen a people imprisoned for 1,800 years like these unfortunate Jews. They are mournful and oppressed by kings and officers, but they still act properly." ✣ ...

✣ Nowadays, we see how accurate are the words of this Sefardic scholar... Today, the question of how to end Jewish subjugation, return the crown to its former glory, and restore our Holy Land to us is discussed in every parliament, and the nations struggle to solve it. One hundred years ago, however, when this scholar lived, it was not a pressing issue in their parliaments. Only one, kind priest praised the nation of Israel... Today, on the other hand, it is an open question, like all of their other ordinary questions, and they are attempting to solve

168 *Mashmia Yeshuah*, p. 21b.

Thus, the verse, *And their queens will be your wet nurses*, means that all of the rulers will agree, and they will nourish us with honey and milk under our tongues.[170] Accordingly, it says, *You will nurse from the milk of the nations and you will nurse from the breast of kings* (*Yeshayah* 60:16). *They will bow down to you with their faces towards the earth* (ibid. 49:23). That is to say, the Holy One Blessed be He will perform these things respectfully, honorably, and through political means. *And they will lick up the dust of your feet* (ibid.). Even some of the Gentiles will accompany HaShem on that day. They will come to *Eretz Yisrael* to dwell and trade amidst love, brotherhood, and companionship. *And you will know that I am the Lord, and those who wait for Me will not be ashamed* (ibid.).[171]

My beloved reader, examine and contemplate these words of the Sefardic scholar, for he was a great and righteous man. He was also the disciple of a great and righteous man, our master, the Pele Yo'etz, whose work has been accepted throughout the world. He cites the Yefeh To'ar (who was one of the great, earlier scholars) and other profound gedolim who state that the restitution of our Land will become an international issue and will happen respectfully, naturally, and through political means. Now, he wrote this before there was even a hint of this in the world, before the parliaments of the nations ever discussed how to solve the Jewish problem, because there was no such problem in his days. And now that we have reached the era in which the Jewish question actually permeates all of their parliaments, can you possibly ignore this? Whoever has a brain in his head must admit that we are living through the era about which all of our prophets prophesied. Our time of remembrance has arrived by way of the circumstances that the Cause of All Causes has arranged.

---

it in a way that will benefit us forever. This is all part of the profound counsel[169] of the Creator of the World.

In any event, this shows that the words of this Sefardic scholar are true. He was practically granted prophecy! From here we can infer that all of his utterances are true words of the living God.

169 Based on *BeReishit Rabbah* 84:10.
170 Based on *Shir HaShirim* 4:11.
171 *Minchat Yehudah*, sec 19, p. 238.

The gedolim must accept any chance of redemption

כ In the introduction to *Minchat Yehudah*, this wise author writes very accurately that we must not disregard or ignore any redemptive event, for the issue of redemption is very obscure. The Holy One Blessed be He says, "The heart has not revealed this to the mouth" (*Kohelet Rabbah* 12:10, *Midrash Tehillim* 9:2). Our Sages who were endowed with godly perception also did not explain these matters clearly, only with hints and parables, as the Rambam writes.[172]

Therefore, the *gedolim* and "shepherds" of Israel must lovingly accept any opportunity for redemption and strive to bring it to completion. They are responsible for this *mitzvah*. They must have compassion on the remnants of our people and use their wisdom to gather our scattered ones from the four corners of the earth, to be united as one. Then, [the ingathered Jews] will return and seek out the Lord their God and David their king. HaShem will bless all of their handiwork with success,[173] and all of their accomplishments will endure. This is why "the heart has not revealed it to the mouth," because this matter is entrusted to the mighty ones of Israel and its leaders, to do as they see fit.[174]

R. Alcalay compares this to *Chazal*'s exposition on the fixing of the festivals: "*These are the festivals...which you shall proclaim them* (אֹתָם) *in their appointed times* (*VaYikra* 23:4). You (אַתֶּם), even if you are mistaken and even if you [err] deliberately" (*Rosh HaShanah* 25a). The Ibn Ezra explains this as follows. The Torah does not describe the fixing of the months [in detail], even though a mistaken calculation can lead to a prohibition which carries the penalty of excision (כרת), like eating leavened bread on *Pesach* or eating on *Yom Kippur*. On the other hand, there are many *mitzvot* which the Torah describes in great detail, even though they only apply to specific people, in specific places, and at specific times. The true and clear explanation is that the Torah conceals this matter because it is entrusted to *Beit Din* (the courts), even if they are mistaken and even if they [err] deliberately.[175]

Similarly, the Torah does not specify how the redemption will evolve, because this great matter is entrusted to Israel's *gedolim*. It is up to them to do as they see fit, according to the place and the

172 *Hilchot Melachim* 12:1.
173 Based on *BeReishit* 39:3.
174 *Minchat Yehudah*, introduction entitled *Mizmor LeTodah*, p. 204.
175 Ibn Ezra, Introduction to the Torah, and *Shemot* 12:2.

time. Therefore, it says about the redemption, *The fasts...will become for the House of Yehudah...cheerful festivals* (*Zecharyah* 8:19). This teaches that the redemption is entrusted to *Beit Din* just like the fixing of the festivals.[176]

This explains events that you witness today. Do not be so quick to conclude that we should sit back and do nothing about redemption, and that we should wait for *Mashiach* to come and carry us off on the wings of eagles to our Land and our inheritance. Many of our fellow Jews, even rabbis and *gedolei Torah*, imagine that the redemption will occur in this way. One great rabbi [even] preached in public that we must not act at all, not even to build and settle the Land. Rather, we must wait for *Mashiach* to swoop down and carry us to *Eretz Yisrael* on clouds. He came to this conclusion because he did not delve deeply into this *halachah*, which is one of the deepest and most obscure *halachot*.[177] He who does not delve deeply into it has no grasp on it whatsoever.

Redemption is a gradual process

I will now cite a proof for this from a "*Tana*," the righteous Kabbalist, the Sefardic scholar mentioned above:

> Do not entertain the thought that the end (קץ) and the redemption... and the coming of *Mashiach* are the same thing, and that they will all occur simultaneously, in one day. Actually, they are separate things.[178] Each one has its own time and boundary, a time for every purpose.[179] We thus say in *selichot*, "Bring the appointed time (קץ) of redemption near." Its beginning is minute and undetectable, as the *Yerushalmi* states: "R. Chiya and R. Shimon, the son of Rebbe, were walking in Karitzta (name of a place). They saw the glimmering of the morning star. R. Chiya said to R. Shimon: 'So is the redemption of Israel – at first little by little, [but] as it progresses, it grows greater and greater.' Why so? *When I sit in darkness, the Lord is a light unto me* (*Michah* 7:8)" (*Berachot* 1:1 [4b]).
>
> *Chazal* also state: "Once the exiles are gathered, the wicked

176 ❖ This concludes the citation from the introduction to *Minchat Yehudah*.

177 ❖ As I cited in the second introduction (p. 48), from the Talmud and *Tana DeVei Eliyahu*.

178 ❖ See the beginning of this book (Approbations, p. 6) where the brilliant and holy Sefardic scholar, the Kabbalist and *Rishon LeTzion*, R. Chayim David Chazan, concurs with this.

179 Based on *Kohelet* 3:1.

will receive justice.❖ And once the wicked receive justice, the heretics will be destroyed.❖❖ And once the heretics are destroyed, the pride of the righteous will be exalted. And where will their pride be exalted? In Jerusalem, as it says, *Pray for the peace of Jerusalem* (*Tehillim* 122:6). And once Jerusalem is rebuilt, [the Son of] David will arrive. And once [the Son of] David arrives, prayer arrives. And once prayer arrives, [Temple] service arrives" (*Megillah* 17b).

The author of this statement repeats the words, "And once...," at each interval, to teach that each stage has its own defined time. The coming of *Mashiach* is the final and most wondrous event before the resurrection of the dead. Accordingly, I mentioned above that the *Beit HaMikdash* is destined to be built before [the establishment of] the Davidic Dynasty.[182] This is why the Davidic Dynasty is called "sun" (*shemesh*), as it says, *And his throne shall be like the sun before Me* (*Tehillim* 89:37). For, the redemption is like the rising of dawn,[183] the more it progresses the greater it becomes; and the Davidic Dynasty will follow it like the sun coming out in all its might.[184]

He who says that Mashiach ben David will initiate the redemption, as the lowly masses anticipate, is like someone who says that the sun will rise before dawn. Nonsense! The great evil that arises from this harmful outlook is tangible, as experience proves. It is a mitzvah

❖ This refers to the wicked Gentiles who oppress the Jews. This proves the Or HaChayim's claim[180] that the Holy One Blessed be He will not delay the ingathering of the Jews until He punishes their wicked oppressors. Rather, He will take the Jews from their midst and bring them to *Eretz Yisrael* even before He punishes their oppressors. This is what the Talmud says here explicitly.

❖❖ That is to say, everyone will see HaShem's providence, incline their hearts to Him, and believe in Him. Thus, all of the heretics among Israel will be rectified. Above,[181] I discussed this at length and cited our great Rabbis *z"l* who say that even the heretics will achieve *tikkun* at the time of the future redemption.

180 ❖ Which I cited above, p. 120.
181 Pp. 101-8.
182 ❖ As the *Yerushalmi* explains (*Ma'aser Sheini* 5:2 [21b]). [See above, p. 199.]
183 Based on *BeReishit* 19:15.
184 Based on *Shoftim* 5:31.

to publicize this matter to the ignorant, and blessed is he who sanctifies God's name among the multitudes.[185] ***In my opinion, he who hides this matter, desecrates God's name in private***. For due to our numerous sins, several simpletons who pinned their hopes on the year 5600 [1840] have opened their mouths without measure[186] and fabricated things that are not so[187] about HaShem and His anointed one.[188] Thus, this wondrous destiny, for which our sacred ancestors yearned and about which all of the prophets promised, has become a laughing matter (in the eyes of the masses). Woe to the ears that have heard this.

The eyes [i.e., the leaders] of the congregation did this evil thing unintentionally[189] (God forbid [to say otherwise]). Even if the Almighty commands us directly not to speak about the promise of redemption for better or for worse, (nonetheless), it says, *It is a time to act for the Lord; they have nullified Your Torah* (*Tehillim* 119:126). If the Holy One Blessed be He has compassion on the honor of the *tzaddikim* more than His own honor,[190] certainly the *tzaddikim* must have compassion on their Master's honor more than their own. They must, therefore, pay no attention to the vain and impetuous ones who put their mouths before their ears. Compassion and forgiveness belong to the Lord our God,[191] for I have spoken until now out of the greatness of my grievance and anger.[192] God will bless the man who is zealous for His name and who stops up the mouths of the liars[193] when they speak nonsense. All of Israel is commanded to sanctify God's name.[194]

We have a tradition, which is familiar to all of Israel, that *Mashiach ben Yosef* will precede *Mashiach ben David*; and the redemption – meaning, the deliverance from the decrees and afflictions that storm upon (Israel) – will precede even him...

185 From the morning blessings.
186 Based on *Yeshayah* 5:14.
187 Based on II *Melachim* 17:9.
188 Based on *Tehillim* 2:2.
189 Based on *BeMidbar* 15:24.
190 *Tanchuma, Toledot* 12.
191 *Daniel* 9:9.
192 Based on I *Shmuel* 1:16.
193 *Tehillim* 63:12.
194 Rambam, *Hilchot Yesodei HaTorah* 5:1.

> However, the heart has not revealed to the mouth[195] the way in which this redemption will occur, nor its essence, for the Omnipresent has many channels. Nothing prevents HaShem from saving,[196] and He does not save with the sword and spear.[197] (Rather, He saves with His faithful messengers. I explained this above[198] when I quoted *Minchat Yehudah* as saying that we must ask for kindness and mercy from the kings of the earth.)
>
> These words will make you wise..., for gold and glass cannot equal them,[199] and anything that may be desired cannot compare to them.[200] This is certainly true when we take into account the testimonies of the mighty ones mentioned above: the Radak, the Abarbanel, and the Yefeh To'ar. These three reliable witnesses establish this matter.[201] We are aware of the statements of *Chazal* [which imply that the redemption will occur miraculously], but they [these three "witnesses"] knew that these statements do not refer to the beginning of redemption. For, the beginning is a small thing, like the breaking of dawn (and it is up to us to achieve this through HaShem's messengers).[202]

He further elaborates on this issue wondrously. However, I cannot transcribe it all, for that would require a book in itself.

Thus, a "Tana" supports everything I said above and contradicts the rabbi who preached that we should do nothing but wait for Mashiach to come flying through the air on a chariot of fire to carry us to Eretz Yisrael. Behold, my brother! This wise Kabbalist considers such a position to be harmful and a desecration of God's name. He writes that anyone who keeps silent and fails to inform the masses that such an opinion is untrue desecrates God's name in private. It is a mitzvah to publicize to the masses that we must do our share, to the best of our abilities, and beseech the kind kings to

195 Based on *Kohelet Rabbah* 12:10.
196 Based on I *Shmuel* 14:6.
197 I *Shmuel* 17:47.
198 See above, sec. ט' (pp. 263-66).
199 Based on *Iyov* 28:17.
200 Based on *Mishley* 8:11.
201 Based on *Devarim* 19:15.
202 *Minchat Yehudah*, sec. 34, p. 254. [The parenthetical comments are R. Teichtal's.]

have mercy on us. Then, HaShem will perfect our efforts and fulfill His will through us. Examine these words, for they are accurate and true, with HaShem's help.

We must not rely on miracles

כא Thus, we must not rely on miracles alone. Instead, we must do what we can, naturally, and then HaShem will send us assistance from the heavens. I will prove this from a letter that our mentor, the Rambam, wrote to the scholars of Marseilles regarding astrology.[203] First, he tells them that astrology books have no content, are absolutely foolish, and that he who studies them simply wastes his time and gains nothing. Afterwards, he writes:

> This is what abolished our kingdom, destroyed our *Beit HaMikdash*, prolonged our exile, and brought us to our present predicament. Our fathers sinned and are no more.[204] For they found many astrology books, followed them, and went astray. They imagined that these wisdoms were glorious and greatly beneficial, ***and they did not study warfare and land conquest***. Instead, they imagined that these wisdoms would help them. Therefore, the prophets called them fools; and they certainly were fools, for they followed vanities which cannot avail nor rescue, for they are vain.[205]

Thus, our master, the Rambam, blames our ancestors for the destruction of our Land and our Temple because they did not study warfare and land conquest. Instead, they wasted their time and relied on vanities and nothingness. Now, why did he not blame them for their failure to study Torah and serve God properly? The answer must be, because that alone is insufficient. The Ramban writes in many places that we must not rely on miracles. Rather, we must do whatever is humanly possible, and then God will send us heavenly assistance.[206] The Rashba concurs,[207] as does the *Midrash* on the verse *If the Lord will not build the house, its builders labor on it in vain* (*Tehillim* 127:1). The *Midrash* explains that this does not mean that a person should do nothing and rely solely on HaShem to build his house. It means that when a person works and toils, he should not

203 *Iggrot U'Teshuvot LeRambam, Iggrot Shonot*, p. 21.
204 Based on *Eichah* 5:7.
205 Based on I *Shmuel* 12:21.
206 Ramban: *VaYikra* 21:17; *BeMidbar* 1:45, 13:2.
207 *Teshuvot HaRashba* 419.

rely on his work alone, for then *its builders labor on it in vain.* Instead, he should rely on God's heavenly assistance. This can be inferred directly from the verse: *It's builders labor on it in vain* implies that there is someone toiling and building. The only qualification is that one should not rely on his toil alone, but put his trust in HaShem (*Midrash Tanchuma* [Buber], *Pekudei* 8).

The *Yerushalmi* states that the Jews studied Torah and kept *mitzvot* at the time of the Second Temple (*Yoma* 1:1 [4b]). Thus, the reason the Land and the Temple were destroyed was not because they lacked the merit of Torah and *mitzvot.* It must be, as the Rambam states, that they relied on vanities and did not engage in the natural activities that were needed for the Land to subsist, like the study of warfare and land conquest. This caused the destruction of the Land and the *Beit HaMikdash.*

The Rambam (above) also states that this is the reason for our lengthy exile and our present predicament. Clearly, he does not mean that we should learn how to wage war and conquer lands while in exile. That would be impossible, for our dispersion among the nations has made us weak. That obligation only applied when we were together in our Land. Besides which, we are bound by oath not to go up to *Eretz Yisrael* "as a wall" (*Ketuvot* 111a).

Undoubtedly, the Rambam means that we should use the natural means that become available to us and not rely on miracles alone. For example, we should ask the kings to show us kindness and end our exile; we should "conquer" the Land by acquiring it;* and we should engage in other natural endeavors. Then, HaShem will send us heavenly assistance, bring us to our Land, and put an end to our

---

* Our brilliant and righteous master, R. Tzvi Kalischer *z"l*, discusses this at length in *Derishat Tzion.*[208] Other *gaonim* discuss it as well and cite the *Yerushalmi* (*Mo'ed Kattan* 2:4 [7b]) to prove that buying land from the Gentiles is like conquering the Land, and that it is a *mitzvah* to redeem the Land from their hands. See the Rivash which I cited above in the approbations.[209] Also see *Yeshivat Eretz Yisrael*, by the great *gaon*, our master, R. Yonah Dov Blumberg of Dvinsk (printed in Vilna, 5658 [1898]).[210]

208 We were unable to locate this source.
209 P. 19.
210 *Ma'aneh* 9.

exile. However, if we do nothing, the Rambam's words – "This is what prolonged our exile and brought us to our present predicament" – will pertain to us. That is to say, we will have only ourselves to blame for the lengthy exile and our present predicament. We are abandoned like the fish of the sea, anyone can do to us as he pleases, and our blood is spilled like water (due to our numerous sins). May HaShem help us recognize the truth, and may He arouse the people of Israel to once again long for their "mother's" bosom and work towards this goal. May He open the eyes of those who have been blinded by Satan's false and unfounded claims which clearly contradict *Chazal*'s words.

Our redemption depends on the redemption of the Land

כב Commenting on the verse, *The Land shall not be sold permanently* (*VaYikra* 25:23), the brilliant and godly Kabbalist, R. David Lyda, writes that "Our redemption depends on the redemption of the Land, and our subjugation depends on its subjugation."[211] Similarly, the Ramban cites a *Yerushalmi* which indicates that we must not let our Land remain in gentile hands forever (*Demai* 5:9 [19b]). He concludes:[212]

> This implies a prohibition, that we may not leave the Land permanently in the hands of the Gentiles. The reason for this is as follows. If we sell our bodies to the Gentiles, we are commanded to regain them from their possession, and the Torah explains why: *For the Children of Israel are servants to Me* (*VaYikra* 25:55). Similarly, we are commanded to take possession of the Land and not leave it in their hands. The Torah gives the same reason here as it does in reference to our bodies. That is, because the Land belongs to Him (may He be exalted)... He does not want to settle anyone there but us... Therefore, it will return to us. ❖

❖ In *Derishat Tzion*, R. Kalischer explains that, nowadays, [the *mitzvah* of] conquering the Land is primarily accomplished through acquisition.[213] This concurs with *Tosafot*.[214]

211 *Ir Miklat, Mitzvah* 335, p. 38a, citing מוהרמ"ש. [It is unclear to whom he is referring.]

212 Ramban's commentary to *Sefer HaMitzvot*, Negative Commandment 227.

213 We were unable to locate this source.

214 *Kiddushin* 26a, s.v. *amar*.

This Ramban sheds light on R. David Lyda's statement that our redemption depends on the redemption of the Land, and our subjugation depends on its subjugation. This seems difficult! Why should they depend on one another? Now, however, it is clear. The Ramban writes that HaShem insists that we regain the Land from the hands of the Gentiles, just like we are commanded to regain Jewish bodies from their possession. Therefore, when we do not care to regain the Land from their possession, we are punished measure for measure, and our bodies, as well, are subjugated to them. However, if we strive to regain the Land from their possession, our bodies will also deserve to go free. This is true and clear, with HaShem's help.

A proof that our redemption depends on the settlement of Eretz Yisrael

כג Subsequently, I found another proof that our future redemption depends on *Yishuv Eretz Yisrael*, that is, redeeming the Land from the Gentiles and engaging in its construction and settlement. The *Mishnah* states:

> What is the order of the [prayers on the] fast days?... They stand in prayer... He [the leader] says twenty four blessings – the eighteen daily blessings plus another six. And these are [the additional ones]... Then he says their endings. For the first blessing he says, "He Who answered Avraham Avinu on Mt. Moriah, may He answer you... Blessed are You HaShem Redeemer of Israel." For the second one he says, "He Who answered our forefathers at the Red Sea, may He answer you... Blessed are You HaShem Who remembers all forgotten things." For the third he says, "He Who answered Yehoshua in Gilgal, may He answer you... Blessed are You HaShem Who hears the *teruah*." For the fourth he says, "He Who answered Shmuel in Mitzpah, may He answer you... Blessed are You HaShem Who hears crying." For the fifth he says, "He Who answered Eliyahu on Mt. Carmel, may He answer you... Blessed are You HaShem Who hears prayer." For the sixth he says, "He Who answered Yonah from the innards of the fish, may He answer you... Blessed are You HaShem Who answers in time of trouble." For the seventh he says,[215] "He Who answered David and Shlomo, his son, in Jerusalem, may He answer you...

215 [The Talmud reconciles the obvious contradiction between the beginning of the *Mishnah* - "Plus another ***six***" - and this statement.]

> Blessed are You HaShem Who has mercy on the Land." ❖ (*Ta'anit* 15a)

The Talmud comments on the last blessing:

> Seeing that Yonah lived after David and Shlomo, why is he mentioned first? Because they [*Chazal*] wanted to conclude with "Who has mercy on the Land." It was taught in the name of Sumchus, "Blessed [are You] Who humbles the arrogant." (Rashi explains that according to Sumchus, this blessing takes the place of "Who has mercy on the Land.") (ibid. 17a)

The Maharsha discusses the Talmud's question...[and is bothered by the fact that] the Talmud does not ask the same thing about Eliyahu, who also lived after David and Shlomo. Granted, according to the opinion that Eliyahu is really Pinchas there is no difficulty.[219] However, several *Midrashim*[220] indicate that Eliyahu was not a *kohen*[221] [like Pinchas was]. Therefore, why did the Talmud fail to ask about Eliyahu? He answers that the Talmud was not bothered by [the fact that Eliyahu was mentioned before David, because it understood that] this was a hint that Eliyahu would come before *Mashiach ben David*.[222]

Thus, all of the prayers of these fast days were instituted and arranged according to the order of the coming of our righteous *Mashiach*. This explains the Talmud's answer... – "Because they wanted to conclude with 'Who has mercy on the Land.'" This answer seems difficult. Why did the author of the *Mishnah* place so much importance on concluding with this blessing, to the point that he

---

❖ Rashi,[216] Tosafot,[217] and the Maharsha[218] explain that David and Shlomo prayed for *Yishuv Eretz Yisrael*. This is evident from the psalm, *A prayer of the afflicted* (*Tehillim* 102), which was founded on the prayers of the exiled Jews. It is recited to bring the redemption closer. The Maharsha demonstrates at length how the entire chapter speaks of the troubles of exile and the redemption.

216 *Ta'anit* 15a, s.v. *uShlomo*.
217 Ibid. 16b, s.v. *baruch*.
218 Ibid. 15a, s.v. *baruch ata HaShem merachem*.
219 See *Bava Metzia* 114b; *Sha'arei Zohar*, ibid.; *Yalkut Shimoni*, beginning of *Pinchas*.
220 *BeReishit Rabbah* 71:12, 99:12; *Shemot Rabbah* 40:4.
221 ❖ As *Tosafot* explain (*Bava Metzia* 114b, s.v. *amar*).
222 Maharsha, *Ta'anit* 17a, s.v. *michdi*.

changed the chronological order, mentioning Yonah before David and Shlomo?

Based on the Maharsha's suggestion that these prayers hint to the coming of *Mashiach*, it is clear. This blessing – "Who has mercy on the Land" – deals with *Yishuv Eretz Yisrael*, for that is what David and Shlomo prayed for (as I cited above from Rashi, Tosafot, and the Maharsha). But not only did they pray for it, they also built and settled the Land. (The only reason the Talmud mentions their prayers [and not their actions] is to teach that one without the other – actions without prayer – is insufficient.)[223] Therefore, *Chazal* specifically conclude with this blessing, because the conclusion denotes the essence of a thing.

Thus, the most important thing to do to bring *Mashiach* closer is to engage in *Yishuv Eretz Yisrael*, as David and Shlomo did. This concurs with the godly Kabbalist, the author of *Mishnat Chassidim*, who states that HaShem delays *Mashiach*'s arrival until the Land is built up.[224] Therefore, the Sages of the Talmud insisted on concluding with "Who has mercy on the Land," to teach that if we have mercy on the Land by rebuilding it, if we put all of our strength into settling it, and if we also pray for this, then we will bring *Mashiach* closer. For, these things show HaShem that we hope, desire, and yearn for our Holy Land.

By doing this, we will hasten the appointed time of our redemption from this bitter exile, as the verses state: *You will arise and have mercy upon Zion, for it is time to favor her, for the appointed time has come. For Your servants cherished her stones, and favored her dust* (*Tehillim* 102:14-15). The Maharsha explains:

> *For the appointed time has come*, meaning, the appointed time of which Daniel spoke[225]... *For Your servants* in the bitter exile already *cherished her stones*, and they *favored her dust* even more. They did not act like the generation of the desert who despised the Land and were, therefore, condemned to be exiled from it.[226]

(Now, however, the Jews have been afflicted in exile, and they desire

223 ❖ See above (p. 158) where I proved this from *Niddah* 70b.
224 ❖ I cited his words above, pp. 180-81.
225 See *Daniel* 8:19, 12:7.
226 Maharsha, *Ta'anit* 15a, s.v. *baruch ata HaShem merachem*.

the Land once again. Therefore, they deserve Your mercy.)

Allow me to explain these words of our mentor, the Maharsha, further. Why does the verse specifically mention, *her stones* and *her dust*? It should have said "For Your servants cherished the Land." Clearly it comes to teach that the exiles desire to build the Land, for stones and dust are the materials used to build houses and walls. Because of this, HaShem (may He be blessed and exalted for all of eternity) is pleased with them, and they will hasten the appointed time mentioned by Daniel, speedily in our days. Amen. This is as clear and luminous as the sun.

Now we can explain Sumchus' opinion that the blessing ends, "Blessed are You Who humbles the arrogant." Rashi explains that Sumchus argues with the first *Tana* who holds that the blessing ends, "Blessed are You Who has mercy on the Land." If not for Rashi's interpretation, I would have said that Sumchus does not argue with the first *Tana*, but comes to add to the *Mishnah*. According to him the blessing ends with both – "Blessed are You Who has mercy on the Land and Who humbles the arrogant."[227]

This addition also alludes to our redemption. If we have mercy on the Land by perfecting and building it, the merit of *Yishuv Eretz Yisrael* will assist us in humbling the arrogant. Anyone who stands in our way, even if he is as high as the cedars and as strong as the oaks, will be humbled and cut down before us, for HaShem is with us. This concurs with the Ya'avetz's dictum: "All heavenly matters succeed if they are done wholeheartedly, as the verse says about Chizkiyah, *With every deed that he began in the service of the House of God...he acted with all his heart, and he succeeded* (II *Divrei HaYamim* 31:21)."[228] The same will happen to us. This is what Sumchus meant by his addition. HaShem will humble the arrogant people who try to hinder us, and our handiwork will be established.[229] Amen, so may HaShem proclaim, speedily in our days. Amen.

Thus, it is clear that the merit of *Yishuv Eretz Yisrael* brings the redemption closer.

227 ❖ We find this many times in the Talmud - "Therefore, we say them both." See *Megillah* (21b) and *Berachot* (11b). (Also see *Sotah* 40a with *Gilyon HaShas*.)

228 *Siddur Beit Ya'akov, Sullam Beit El*, p. 6b (top).

229 Based on *Tehillim* 90:17.

Another proof

כד The Talmudic Sage, R. Nachman bar Yitzchak, says that one who brings joy to a bride and groom is considered "as if he has built one of the ruins of Jerusalem, as it says, *For I will return the captivity of the Land as at first, says the Lord* (*Yirmiyah* 33:11)" (*Berachot* 6b). The Maharsha comments, "For this, [marriage and procreation], is the preservation and settlement of *Eretz Yisrael*."[230] That is to say, if we preserve and settle *Eretz Yisrael*, HaShem promises that He will return the captivity of the Land, as at first.

The merit of the Patriarchs protects us only if we cherish the Land

כה With God's help, I will prove that even the merit of the Patriarchs does not protect us unless we cherish the Land. The *Midrash* states:

> Why does the Torah mention the merit of the Land alongside the merit of the Patriarchs?[231] Reish Lakish says, "This can be compared to a king who has three sons, and a maidservant who raises them. Whenever the king inquires about his sons he [also] inquires about the woman who raises them. Similarly, whenever the Holy One Blessed be He mentions the Patriarchs, He mentions the Land with them, as it says, *And I will remember My covenant with Ya'akov,* [*and also My covenant with Yitzchak, and also My covenant with Avraham I will remember*] *and I will remember the Land* (*VaYikra* 26:42)." (*VaYikra Rabbah* 36:5)

I believe that the Ramban's comments in *parashat Shelach* help explain this *Midrash*. After the sin of the spies, Moshe prays for Israel, *And now, may the strength of my Lord increase... Please pardon the iniquity of this people according to the greatness of Your kindness... And the Lord said, "I have pardoned according to your word"* (*BeMidbar* 14:17-20). The Ramban writes:

> Moshe did not mention *Keeper of kindness for thousands of generations* [as he did after the sin of the calf], because in this instance Moshe did not use the merit of the Patriarchs in his prayer. He did not mention Avraham, Yitzchak, and Ya'akov at all. The reason for this is [as follows]. The Land was given to the Patriarchs, and their descendants were to inherit it from them. [But now], the descendants rebelled against their forefathers and rejected the gift which the Patriarchs greatly

230 Maharsha, *Berachot* 6b, s.v. *over be'chamishah kolot.*
231 [In *VaYikra* 26:42, as quoted at the end of the *Midrash*.]

desired. Therefore, how could Moshe say, *Remember Avraham, Yitzchak, and Ya'akov Your servants to whom You swore by Your Own Self and said to them, "...This entire Land...I will give to your seed"* (*Shemot* 32:13), when the people were saying, "We do not want this gift"?[232]

Furthermore, I already cited the *Midrash* on the verse *I gave you a desirable Land* (*Yirmiyah* 3:19): "A Land which the fathers of the world desired. Avraham craved it; Yitzchak craved it; and Ya'akov craved it" (*Tanchuma, Re'eh* 8). (The *Midrash* cites verses to prove this.)

We can now explain the meaning of our [original] verse and *Midrash*. The Torah reveals to us that HaShem will remember the merit of the Patriarchs only if we emulate them by desiring and cherishing the Land. If we cherish, desire, and crave the Land as they did, HaShem will remember their merit for our sake. Thus, the verse says, *And I will remember My covenant with Ya'akov...*, but only on condition that *I will remember the Land*, [meaning, only if I see] that you cherish the Land. This also explains the *Midrash*'s statement: "Whenever the Holy One Blessed be He mentions the Patriarchs, He mentions the Land with them." Examine this closely, for it is clear and true. The more we cherish our Holy Land, the more we will receive the merit of the Patriarchs.

The bond between the Patriarchs and the Land

כו The brilliant mentor of all of Israel, our master, R. Yosef Engel *zt"l*, cites this *Midrash* in his work, *Otzrot Yosef*.[233] He explains that according to the wisdom [of Kabbalah] the unification of Kingship (*Malchut*) with Beauty (*Tiferet*) is tantamount to the unification of Kingship (*Malchut*) with the three attributes of: Love (*Chesed*), Strength (*Gevurah*), and Beauty (*Tiferet*). For *Tiferet* encompasses these three, as is well known. This is evident from the *Midrash* which states that whenever the Holy One Blessed be He mentions the three Patriarchs, He mentions the Land with them. For, it is well known that Land (*Eretz*) is considered *Malchut*. Thus, the mention of *Eretz Yisrael* with the Patriarchs is the secret of the unification of *Malchut* with *Chesed*, *Gevurah*, and *Tiferet*, which represent the three Patriarchs: Avraham, Yitzchak, and Ya'akov.

232 Ramban, *BeMidbar* 14:17.

233 ❖ This is the only one of his Kabbalistic works that has been published so far. The others remain in manuscript. The greatness of his wisdom in the "wisdom of truth" is unfathomable. He was as profound a genius in the esoteric wisdom as he was in the revealed.

This is also the meaning of the verse *The Almighty, God, Lord, spoke and called the land* (*Tehillim* 50:1). The names Almighty (קל), God (אלקים), and Lord (ה') represent respectively *Chesed*, *Gevurah*, and *Tiferet*, and these three unify with the Land, as explained.

[R. Yosef Engel continues]: Now, behold something astounding. The *Midrash* is not the only source which states that the Holy One Blessed be He always mentions the Land with the Patriarchs. R. Eliezer HaGadol says the same thing in his testament:

> Make the evening prayer first and foremost of all the prayers, for Ya'akov Avinu instituted it,[234] and the Torah made him the "first" of all the Patriarchs, as it says, *And behold, the Lord was standing over him* [Ya'akov] *and He said, "I am the Lord, God of Avraham your father, and God of Yitzchak, the Land"* (*BeReishit* 28:13).[235]

That R. Eliezer HaGadol would include the words, *The Land*, is incomprehensible. In the verse, these words come after the Patriarchs because of the context: *I am the Lord, God of Avraham..., and God of Yitzchak. The Land on which you are lying, to you I will give it and to your descendants*. For R. Eliezer's purposes, however, they are not needed at all. Why did he bring them here?

You must know and understand that this coincides with *Chazal*'s statement that the Land is always mentioned with the Patriarchs, alluding to the unification of *Malchut* with the three Patriarchs. The Torah mentions *The Land* immediately after the Patriarchs... in order to juxtapose the two. The *Tana*, R. Eliezer HaGadol, intended the same thing. He did not want to divide this unification even with words. Therefore, once he cited the first part of the verse, he also mentioned the words, *The Land*, in order not to divide the holy unification alluded to in the verse. The enlightened will understand. (This concludes the words of the profoundly brilliant R. Yosef Engel.)[236]

This shows you the magnitude of the bond between the Patriarchs and the Land. It is so great that one must avoid disuniting them even verbally, as the Torah and the great *Tana*, R. Eliezer, were cautious to do. Therefore, realize that my interpretation of the *Midrash* is true according to the hidden wisdom as well. I explained,

234 *Berachot* 26b.
235 *Tzava'at R. Eliezer HaGadol*, also known as *Orchot Chayim*, sec. 4.
236 *Otzrot Yosef, Ma'amar David*, sec. 4.

based on the Ramban, that we cannot mention the merit of the Patriarchs unless we cherish the Land as they did. Now, since the Land and the Patriarchs are interconnected like two inseparable companions, and the complete unification is achieved [only] through both of them, how can we possibly arouse the merit of the Patriarchs when we do not fully cherish the Land? Therefore, we must cherish our Land with all our might, in thought, speech, and action. Then, the merit of the Patriarchs will automatically arise on our behalf.

Redemption depends on our love for the Land

Based on this, you will also realize that the redemption depends solely on our love for the Holy Land. The more we cherish it, the closer the redemption comes. In *Even Sheleimah*, our mentor, the Gaon of Vilna *z"l*, writes that the future redemption depends on the merit of the Patriarchs, not repentance.[237] Accordingly, we say three times a day, "Who remembers the kindnesses of the Patriarchs and Who brings a redeemer to their children's children."[238] Thus, redemption depends on the merit of the Patriarchs, which depends on how much we cherish the Land. Therefore, I am correct that everything depends on the love of the Land. May HaShem place in our hearts the desire to sacrifice ourselves for the sanctity of our Land and build it on its original site, for the honor of His blessed and exalted name. And, may we be worthy of the final redemption speedily in our days. Amen.

IV Sinners and Yishuv Eretz Yisrael

HaShem wants His beloved nation in His beloved Land

כז The *Midrash* states:

> The Holy One Blessed be He said: "*Eretz Yisrael* is more beloved to Me than anything. Why? Because I spied it out..." This teaches that there is no love like the love for *Eretz Yisrael*. The Holy One Blessed be He said to Moshe: "The Land is beloved to Me, as it says, *A Land that the Lord your God constantly seeks out* (*Devarim* 11:12); and the people of Israel are beloved to Me, as it says, *Rather, because of the Lord's love for you* (ibid. 7:8). I will bring the people of Israel, who are beloved to Me, into *Eretz Yisrael*, which is beloved to Me, as it says, *When you come into the Land of Cana'an* (*BeMidbar* 34:2)." (*BeMidbar Rabbah* 23:7)

237 *Even Sheleimah* 11:9.

238 First blessing of *Shemoneh Esrei* (The Eighteen Blessings).

The Maharal explains at length that HaShem's love for the people of Israel is unconditional. His love never leaves them, whether they do His will or not (God forbid).[239] Our mentor, the Rambam, writes this explicitly (in *Iggeret Teiman*),[240] as does our mentor, the Noam Elimelech.[241] If so, HaShem always wants His beloved children to enter the Land, for they are always beloved to Him. The only difference is: if they are worthy He will bring them in with manifest miracles, and if they are unworthy (God forbid), He will do so naturally, as I explained above at length.[242] This is clear.

HaShem wants us in the Land even if we transgress His will

כח The *Midrash* further comments on the verse *This is the Land that shall fall to you as an inheritance* (*BeMidbar* 34:2):

> What does *to you* mean? The Land befits you. This can be compared to a king who had servants and maidservants. He used to marry off his servants to maidservants of a different family, and his maidservants to servants of a different family. The king stopped and thought, "The servants are mine and the maidservants are mine. It is preferable for me to marry my servants to my maidservants; my own to my own." So too, the Holy One Blessed be He said (as it were): "The Land is Mine, as it says, *The Land is the Lord's* (*Tehillim* 24:1) and, *For the Land is Mine* (*VaYikra* 25:23); and the people of Israel are Mine, as it says, *For the Children of Israel are servants to Me* (ibid. 25:55). It is preferable for Me to give My Land as an inheritance to My servants; My own to My own." Therefore it says, *This is the Land that shall fall to you as an inheritance.* (*BeMidbar Rabbah* 23:11)

Why did *Chazal* need this parable? They simply should have said, "The word 'Mine' is written about both *Eretz Yisrael* and the people of Israel etc." Furthermore, why did the *Midrash* cite the verse, *For the Children of Israel are servants to Me*? They should have cited the verse from the giving of the Torah, *And you shall be to Me...* (*Shemot* 19:6). Why did they mention the verse which refers to Israel as servants?

It seems that the *Midrash* was bothered by a question. Why does the verse ascribe the act of inheriting to the Land, as it says, *This*

239 *Netzach Yisrael* 11.
240 P. 129.
241 *Parashat Devarim*, p. 88a.
242 Pp. 134-40.

is the Land that shall fall to you as an inheritance? This implies that the Land itself will "fall to you"! It should have said, "This is the Land that you shall inherit," for the act of inheriting comes from Israel, not the Land.

The *Midrash* brings its parable to answer this. For let us consider this matter. A king will certainly not entertain the thought of marrying off his children to servants or maidservants from the outside. Rather, he will marry them to people similar to them. However, he will not hesitate to marry off his servants and maidservants to servants and maidservants from the outside. Eventually, though, he realizes that it is preferable to marry even his servants and maidservants to his own. This is the meaning of the word "preferable." That is, even though this way is good, the other way is slightly better.

Now, we are familiar with *Chazal*'s statement that when we do the will of the Omnipresent we are considered His children, and when we fail to do His will (God forbid) we are considered servants (*Bava Batra* 10a). This explains everything. When the people of Israel do the will of the Omnipresent and act properly, thereby becoming God's children, there is no doubt that they will receive the Land. For then, the match (*shidduch*) is like "grapes of the vine with grapes of the vine" (*Pesachim* 49a). But when they fail to do His will, and are considered merely servants, one might think that perhaps the Holy One Blessed be He will "marry off" the Land to servants from the outside, meaning, the nations of the world. Therefore, the *Midrash* brings its parable to teach that even when the people of Israel are considered servants, HaShem says, "It is preferable to 'marry off' My Land to My servants."

Thus, the need for the parable is clear, for it alludes to the fact that even when the people of Israel fail to do the will of HaShem, He still wants the *shidduch* between them and *Eretz Yisrael*. This also explains why the *Midrash* specifically cites the verse *For the Children of Israel are servants to Me*. It hints to a time when the Jews are considered servants. The *Midrash* does not cite the verse from the giving of the Torah because that refers to a time when they listened to God, as it says, *Now, therefore, if you will hearken to My voice* (*Shemot* 19:5).

This also explains why the verse says, *This is the Land that shall fall to you as an inheritance*, and not, "that you shall inherit." "That you shall inherit" would have implied that you, by your own virtues, deserve this. Then it makes sense to ascribe the act of inheriting to Israel. It would have referred specifically to a time when the people of Israel do the will of HaShem. Therefore, the Torah says, *that shall fall to you.* This implies that you will not receive the Land because you acted properly, but because the Land desires it. The Land says, "It is preferable for me to fall to you than to other servants." With HaShem's help, this *Midrash* is now clear, and this explanation is very sweet.

In any event, it is clear from *Chazal* and the Torah that the Creator always wants the Jews to dwell in the Holy Land, even when they do not fulfill His will, and even when they do not deserve the Land on their own merits, God forbid.

Subsequently, I found this stated explicitly in *Midrash Eichah.* The Holy One Blessed be He said:

> "If only My children were with Me, even though they anger Me." This is the meaning of the verse, *Oh, that I were in the desert in a lodging place* (מלון) *of wayfarers* (*Yirmiyah* 9:1). The Holy One Blessed be He said, "If only My children were with Me as they were in the desert when they complained (מלינין) against Me." (*Eichah Rabbah* 3:7)

כט The *Midrash* continues:

Why doesn't the Land vomit out the sinners?

> *The House of Israel dwell on their Land and they have defiled it* (*Yechezkel* 36:17): The Holy One Blessed be He said, "If only My children were with Me in *Eretz Yisrael*, even though they defile it." (*Eichah Rabbah* 3:7)

This *Midrash* is extremely puzzling. How could the Holy One Blessed be He look forward to this...? Surely, the Land does not tolerate the Jews when they defile it, as the verse says, *So that the Land will not vomit you out when you defile it* (*VaYikra* 18:28)? At first, I thought that perhaps the *halachah* does not follow this *Midrash*, because it is so perplexing. Afterwards, however, I discovered that the ancient volume, *Kaftor VaFerach,* cites it. Thus, one of the Tosafists cites and agrees with this *Midrash.*[243]

HaShem enlightened me to explain this perplexity and understand

243 ❖ It is well known that the Kaftor VaFerach was one of the Tosafists. Also see *Teshuvot R. Betzalel Ashkenazi* (p. 49), by the author of *Shittah Mekubetzet*, who refers to the Kaftor VaFerach as wise and pious.

the intention of the Sages of truth, our Rabbis of the *Midrash*.❖ I will preface with a most wonderful idea suggested by our mentor, the Or HaChayim HaKadosh. In his commentary to the Torah, he writes that not every sin causes the Land to vomit out the people of Israel. Only one sin does. However, the holy Torah did not reveal which sin it is. Therefore, we are forbidden to violate any of them. ❖❖

[The Or HaChayim elaborates]:[247] Do not say that this one sin

---

❖ When our mentor, the Rambam, quotes *Chazal* in his letters[244] he refers to them as "Sages of truth, our Rabbis *z"l*." He means that they alone are the true Sages, and that all of their words are one hundred percent true. (See his lengthy discussion in the introduction to *Zera'im*.)[245] Everything they say comes from a divine source which is totally infallible, not from a fallible, human source. This is why our Sages *z"l* are greater than the other sages of the world. See the Rambam's words inside for they will inspire you to believe the words of *Chazal*.

Realize that it is our master, the Rambam, whose praise fills the entire world, who bears witness to the truth of *Chazal*'s words. A few years ago all the sages of the world celebrated his 800th birthday[246] in recognition of his great wisdom. This remarkable man speaks so reverently about the words of *Chazal* and testifies that they are absolutely true, beyond a shadow of a doubt. Remember this and do not let it out of your sight.

❖❖ Truthfully, only a holy man like the Or HaChayim HaKadosh could say such a thing. In the introduction to his work, *Pri To'ar*, he testifies that he did not formulate any novel Torah insight until he first bound his soul to the Torah-Giver, the Holy One Blessed be He. See the text inside and you will be awe-stricken by the intensity of his holiness.

244 See *Iggrot U'Teshuvot LeRambam, Iggrot LeChachmei Marseilles*, p. 27.

245 I.e., the introduction to his commentary on the *Mishnah*.

246 In the year 5695 [1935].

247 [An example will help clarify the following paragraphs. Normally, the *halachah* follows the principle of *batel be'rov*. This means, "[the minority is] annulled by the majority," or, the majority prevails. Thus, if nine out of ten stores in a row sell kosher meat, and only one sells non-kosher meat, we assume that a piece of meat found in front of the stores came from one of the kosher stores and is kosher. But, this is only true in the case mentioned (where the meat was found outside the stores), because then we apply the rule "Anything that departs (*pa'rish*), departs from the majority." However,

should be annulled (*batel*) by the majority [of sins which do not cause Israel to be vomited from the Land]. This is not so, because since this one sin exists alongside all the others, our case is considered "stationary" (*kavua*), and [the rule is], "Anything which is stationary is considered like [a case of] fifty-fifty" and is biblically prohibited (*Ketuvot* 15a).[248] Also, do not say [that all sins should be permitted because] whenever something departs (*pa'rish*) from a stationary medium it is permitted on account of [the rule] "Anything that departs (*pa'rish*), departs from the majority."[249] This is not so, because in our situation there are 613 *mitzvot* in front of us [which are considered *kavua*] and someone "takes" one of them and transgresses it. This is considered taking away from the *kavua* [as opposed to something which departs on its own], and it retains the law of *kavua* [and is prohibited]. Therefore, we are forbidden to perform any of the practices of the Gentiles, and [that one sin] can cause us to be vomited from the Land, because "anything which is stationary (*kavua*) is considered like [a case of] fifty-fifty." This concludes the godly words of the Or HaChayim HaKadosh.[250]

Now, with regard to the rule that if someone takes something away from the *kavua* it retains the law of *kavua*, the halachic authorities maintain that this is only true if the one who takes it is an intelligent person who understands the circumstances and recognizes that there is a doubt in this *kavua* situation. Then, the stationary (*kavua*) status continues even though the object departs (*pa'rish*) from its original place. However, if a mentally incompetent,

if a person buys a piece of meat but does not remember from which store, we apply the rule "Anything which is stationary (*kavua*) is considered like [a case of] fifty-fifty." That is to say, since the stores are stationary we consider it as if there are five kosher stores and five non-kosher stores. Therefore, *batel be'rov* does not apply and the meat is forbidden. (Some opinions indicate that this is a biblical decree with no logical reason. See *Sanhedrin* 79a.) See *Shulchan Aruch, Yoreh De'ah* 110:3.]

248 ❖ This is a proof for the Bach's opinion (*Yoreh De'ah* 110) that a case of *kavua* which is not recognizable is [still prohibited] by the Torah.

249 See *Ketuvot* 15a; *Shulchan Aruch, Yoreh De'ah* 110:3. [That is, we should be permitted to do any sin without worrying that perhaps we are transgressing the one which causes us to be vomited from the Land. How so? When a person commits a sin, that sin has, in effect, departed (*pa'rish*) from the other transgressions written in the Torah. Thus, we can assume that any particular sin is not the one which causes us to be vomited out, because "Anything that departs (*pa'rish*), departs from the majority."]

250 *VaYikra* 18:24.

unintelligent person takes it away, all the *poskim* agree that it assumes the law of *pa'rish*, is annulled (*batel*) by the majority, and is permitted.[251]

Today's sinners act unintentionally

Based on this introduction, the words of *Chazal* in the above-cited *Midrash* illuminate like a brilliant light, without any questions or perplexities. When Israel dwelt in its Land and had the Great and minor *Sanhedrins*, each city had courts (*beit din*) which would instruct and teach Israel.[252] All of the Children of Israel were raised in the spirit of the Torah and knew its laws and statutes. Therefore, if a Jew transgressed a *mitzvah* of HaShem, he certainly knew and recognized which transgression he violated, and he took on the law of "someone who takes away from the *kavua*."

But, ever since the Jews were exiled and dispersed among the nations, there is no teacher nor prophet, and *They mingled with the nations and learned their deeds* (*Tehillim* 106:35). The majority of our Jewish brethren in exile do not truly recognize the value of the *mitzvot*. Those who were raised and educated under the influence of the wise men of the nations have certainly lost every spark of the Torah. There are countries and districts in which the Jews have completely forgotten all of the Torah's ways (due to our numerous sins). Undoubtedly, people like this fall in the category of infants who were kidnapped by Gentiles, as the Rambam writes.[253] The godly Kabbalist, our master, R. Isaac'l of Komarno, also invoked merit upon them, as I cited above in chapter one.[254] Thus, in terms of the law of "someone who takes away from the *kavua*," these people are considered mentally incompetent, unintelligent people, and they assume the law of *pa'rish*: "Anything that departs (*pa'rish*), departs from the majority." Therefore, that specific sin which causes its transgressor to be vomited from the Land is indeed annulled (*batel*) by the other 613 *mitzvot* of the Torah, and the Land will not vomit them out...

Thus, *Chazal* were correct when they said that the Holy One Blessed be He yearns for His children to be in *Eretz Yisrael*, even though they defile it, God forbid. The *Midrash* refers to the period of exile, when HaShem's children are scattered among the nations

251 See *Shulchan Aruch*, ibid., and *Darkei Teshuvah* 55.
252 See *Sanhedrin* 16b.
253 *Hilchot Mamrim* 3:3.
254 Pp. 105-6.

and have lost their recognition of Torah and *mitzvot*. The Talmud states, "There was no greater abrogation of the Torah than when the Jews were exiled from their place" (*Chagigah* 5b). Under these circumstances, they will not be vomited out of *Eretz Yisrael* even if they act like the Gentiles, because they "take" the sins unintentionally and assume the law of *pa'rish*, in which [the minority] is annulled by the majority. Even though they defile the Land, the Land loves them, because they sin unwittingly. The Land is waiting until they become more knowledgeable and recognize the value of our holy Torah. This will occur when HaShem bestows upon them a purifying spirit from above and removes their heart of stone.[255]

I discussed this at length in chapter one[256] and explained that after the people of Israel assemble in *Eretz Yisrael*, HaShem will arouse them to serve Him wholeheartedly. He will bestow upon them a pure spirit from above and circumcise their hearts, as He promised in the Torah, *And the Lord your God will circumcise your heart...* (*Devarim* 30:6). Then, the earth will be filled with even their knowledge,[257] and they will keep the Torah and its *mitzvot*. Thus, this *Midrash* is clear and simple. Consider this explanation, for, in my opinion, it is true. Blessed is HaShem Who enlightened me to this.

Do not retort by asking: If so, why did the Land vomit out the Gentiles? They, too, have no knowledge or recognition! We should apply the law of *pa'rish* to them as well, and say [that this one specific sin] is annulled by the majority! I will give several answers.

1. The later *poskim* determine that the law of annulment by the majority (*bitul be'rov*) does not apply to Gentiles.[258] Therefore, the rule of "Anything that departs, departs from the majority" does not apply to them either.

2. When it comes to Gentiles we say, "Their warning is their death" (*Sanhedrin* 58b).[259] Therefore, here too, the Torah was strict with them.

3. The *Yalkut* comments on the verse *The Land into which I bring you to dwell* (*VaYikra* 20:22):

> I bring you into the Land only so that you will take possession

255 Based on *Yechezkel* 36:26.
256 Pp. 116-20.
257 Based on *Yeshayah* 11:9.
258 See *S'dei Chemed*, vol. 2, p. 11, letter *Chaf*.
259 [That is to say, if they transgress any of the seven Noachide Laws they are put to death, even if they were not warned beforehand.]

> of it and dwell in it, unlike the Canaanites who were watchmen over the place... Similarly, it says, *And I will give it to you to inherit it* (ibid. 20:24). In the future, I [God] will give it to you [Israel] as an everlasting inheritance. Perhaps you will say, "It is not Yours to give to us, for it belongs to others." [I will answer]: "Surely, it is yours [Israel], for it is Shem's portion and you are Shem's descendants. They [the Canaanites] are Cham's descendants. What, then, are they doing in the Land? They are guarding it until you come." (*Yalkut Shimoni* 1:626)

Thus, since the Land is not theirs, it vomits them out even for a minor infraction.

My beloved friend, our brilliant master, R. Yisrael Veltz, judge of the Orthodox community here [in Budapest], pointed out that there is a proof for this *Midrash*[260] in the verse *And so shall he do for the Tent of Meeting that dwells with them amidst their defilement* (*VaYikra* 16:16). The Torah states explicitly that HaShem wants to dwell with the people of Israel even when they defile the Land, God forbid. However, we still need the distinction that I made between intentional and unintentional defilement. For without it, the verse itself is difficult: How could God dwell with them amidst their defilement if the Land vomits them out?

It is possible that the Chesed LeAvraham (whom I quoted above)[261] had this distinction in mind when he said that it is forbidden to degrade the inhabitants of *Eretz Yisrael* even if we see them acting improperly. Since the Land does not vomit them out they must be *tzaddikim*. That is to say, since they act unintentionally they are, in effect, not considered sinners. All of their sins are committed under duress, for they were not raised in the spirit of the Torah, as the holy man of Komarno writes.

The merit of building the Land outweighs many sins

Furthermore, the Rambam writes that the Holy One Blessed be He does not weigh our merits according to our way of thinking, but according to His. He knows how to weigh one merit such that it will outweigh many evil deeds.[262] Therefore, it is possible that the merit of settling our Holy Land, which is equal to the entire Torah,[263]

260 [The one quoted at the beginning of this section.]

261 P. 27.

262 *Hilchot Teshuvah* 3:2.

263 *Sifrei, Re'eh* 28 (on *Devarim* 12:29).

outweighs many sins, especially since the pioneers often act with true self-sacrifice.

Today's situation is incomparable to the time when the Jews dwelt in their Land and followed the evil ways of the Gentiles. For then, this one sin [mentioned above] "prosecuted" against them, and the Land vomited them out. Nowadays, however, the Land is in the hands of the defiled ones [the Gentiles], and the pioneers sacrifice themselves to redeem it and build it up. This earns them great merit and outweighs the sins that they perform in the Land, especially since they act unintentionally. The Land loves and awaits them. She says, "It is preferable for me to marry them than to marry servants and maidservants from the outside," as I cited above from the *Midrash*.[264] This is true, in my opinion.

It goes without saying that I wrote all of this only to arouse merit on their behalf, not to approve of their actions, God forbid. I merely expressed my opinion that we should not alienate them, for the reason stated above. However, I look forward to the time when a spirit of purity will enter their hearts, and they will love HaShem with all their hearts and all their souls. Amen, so may it be God's will.

A proof that God is pleased with the deeds of today's pioneers

ל I already demonstrated in the foreword to this work[265] that building the Land is very desirable and proper in God's eyes, no matter who does it. The most important thing is that the Land should be built up so that people can settle there. At this point, I would like to add another proof from the *Midrash*:

> R. Yosi bar Chanina said: "There are four categories with respect to names: There are those whose names are becoming and whose deeds are becoming. There are those whose names are ugly and whose deeds are ugly. There are those whose names are ugly and whose deeds are becoming. And, there are those whose names are becoming and whose deeds are ugly... 'Those whose names are ugly and whose deeds are becoming' refers to the people [who returned from the Babylonian] exile: *The children of Bakbuk, the children of Chakufa, the children of Charchur* (*Ezra* 2:51, *Nechemyah* 7:53). They were worthy to ascend and build the *Beit HaMikdash*." (*BeReishit Rabbah* 71:3)

264 P. 283.
265 Pp. 82-83.

This *Midrash* is repeated elsewhere: " 'Those whose names are ugly and whose deeds are becoming' refers to those who ascended [to *Eretz Yisrael*] from the exile: *The children of Barkos, the children of Sisera, the children of Temach* (*Ezra* 2:53, *Nechemyah* 7:55)" (*BeMidbar Rabbah* 16:10).[266] It also says in *Ezra*, *And these are the ones who went up from Tel Melach, Tel Charsha, Keruv, Addan, and Immer; they could not tell their father's house and their seed, whether they were from Israel* (*Ezra* 2:59, *Nechemyah* 7:61). Rashi explains, "Because they lost their lineage, and they did not know whether they were from Israel." Thus, our Rabbis of the *Midrash* state that the names of the people who ascended at the time of Ezra were ugly because they were gentile names. We can infer this from *Sisera* which is known to be a gentile name. In addition, some of the returnees were on such a low level that they could not tell whether or not they were from Israel.

We can also recognize their low spiritual level from the gentile names mentioned in the verse. I will explain based on our own experiences living in exile. The Rosh writes that the common practice in the Diaspora is for a Jew to have a gentile name besides the holy name he receives in the "Jewish camp." He uses the gentile name in his dealings with Gentiles, like in business, etc.[267] However, when he is among Jews, he uses only his holy name, especially for holy purposes like being called up to the Torah in Synagogue, dancing with the Torah on *Simchat Torah*, or at a ritual feast. His gentile name will not be mentioned or remembered there. On the contrary, he would be utterly disgraced and humiliated if he was called by that name in the presence of other Jews, and certainly in the presence of a *tzaddik*, especially the greatest *tzaddik* of the generation.

Let us imagine [the following scenario]. A righteous rabbi of Israel, like the *tzaddik* of Belz or any other prominent *tzaddik* of the generation, calls and presides over a meeting to discuss an issue which affects all of Israel. All of the assembled must approach the *tzaddik* and tell him their names so that he can know who is joining him. When they approach and are asked to say their names, each one says, "I am Shimon ben Moshe," "I am Ya'akov ben Levi," etc. Now, if someone would answer, "My master and rebbe, I am Franz, Heinrich, Adolf," etc., he would be the laughingstock of the assembly,

266 ❖ [Our version of] the *Midrash* reads, "The children of Brak" (*b'nei Brak*). However, this is a printers error, as the verse itself reads, *The children of Barkos*.

267 Rosh, *Gittin* 1:10 (on page 11b of the Talmud).

because one does not use these names in front of the greatest *tzaddik* of the generation... Jews who were raised among God-fearing people know that in the presence of other Jews, and certainly in the presence of a renowned *tzaddik*, one uses only his holy name, and that it would be a disgrace to call himself by a gentile name.

However, there are places, like Bohemia, Moravia, etc., where the Jews have forgotten about Judaism and have been raised completely in the spirit of the nations. They do not even know their holy names, for they use their gentile names in all of their affairs. If a Jew like this would come before the greatest *tzaddik* of the generation...and say innocently, "Rebbe, my name is Franz, or Adolf," the assembled would laugh at him and the rebbe himself would smirk a bit. But, this man would not understand why everyone is laughing. "All I did was tell the rebbe my name. What is all this laughter about? What sin did I do?"

In any event, we see that presenting a gentile name before the *tzaddikim* of the generation (even if done innocently) indicates a low spiritual level and is extremely bad. This is exactly what happened with the people who returned from exile at the time of the Second Temple. The verse says, *These are the people of the country who went up out of the captivity of the exile...who came with Zerubavel, Yeshua, Nechemyah, Serayah, Re'elayah, Mordechai, Bilshan...* (Ezra 2:1-2). These were the generation's *tzaddikim* under whose banner everyone gathered to ascend to *Eretz Yisrael*. They asked for and recorded the names of everyone who ascended with them. Surely, everyone gave his holy name, for it would be disgraceful to use a gentile name in front of such *tzaddikim*. However, there were some who were on such a low spiritual level that they did not realize the disgrace of using a gentile name in front of a *tzaddik*. Therefore, when asked to give their names, they answered unabashedly, "Barkos, Sisera, Temach" etc. They had become so assimilated with the Gentiles that they had absolutely no knowledge or conception of Jewish life. Thus, the verse concludes, *They could not tell their father's house and their seed, whether they were from Israel*, as Rashi writes, "They lost their lineage...ö Apparently, this verse alludes to what I just mentioned and explains why they were not ashamed to use gentile names in front of these *tzaddikim*. That is, they were so assimilated that they did not know whether or not they were from Israel, and they did not realize that this was disgraceful. With God's help, this is a true and clear explanation of the verses.

In any event, ...this demonstrates that the people who returned at the time of the Second Temple were on a low level. Nevertheless, our Sages in the *Midrash* (above) testify that even though their names were ugly, their deeds were becoming to the Creator of the Universe.

Now, anyone who sees these words of *Chazal* will be astounded. How can the deeds of such people be considered becoming? It is well known that those who returned with Ezra were extremely evil and sinful. The Radak writes:[268]

> Most of the people who ascended from Babylonia performed improper deeds. They married gentile women, as [is evident] from Ezra[269] and Malachi's admonition, *He has married the daughter of a foreign god* (*Malachi* 2:11); they desecrated the Sabbath; and [sinned] in other areas, as is written in the book of *Ezra*.[270]

Scripture states this explicitly: *The officers approached me saying, "The people of Israel, the* Kohanim, *and the* Levi'im *have not separated themselves from the peoples of the lands, like their abominations to the Canaanites* (Metzudat David explains, "That is to say, they were still doing the abominations of the Canaanites.")... *And the hand of the officers and the deputies has been primary in this offense"* (Metzudot explains, "The rest of the nation learned from them.") (*Ezra* 9:1-2). *And they did not repent from their evil deeds* (*Nechemyah* 9:35). *The Land that you are coming to inherit is an impure land, because of the impurities of the peoples of the lands, with their abominations, for they have filled it from one end to the other with their defilement* (*Ezra* 9:11). *I contended with the nobles of Judah, and I said to them, "What is this evil thing that you are doing that you desecrate the Sabbath day? Did not your forefathers do this, and our God brought all this evil upon us and upon this city? And yet you bring more wrath upon Israel by desecrating the Sabbath!"* (*Nechemyah* 13:17-18).

On the verse cited above – *And these are the ones who went up from Tel Melach* – *Chazal* explain that they acted like [the people of] Sedom, which turned into a pillar of salt (*tel melach*) (*Kiddushin* 70a). Rashi explains that the people of Sedom were wicked and sinful to HaShem,[271] because they stole and committed adultery.

268 *Malachi* 1:1.
269 See *Ezra* 9.
270 See *Ezra* 9-10, *Nechemyah* 13:14-31.
271 Based on *BeReishit* 13:13.

Furthermore, the Sforno writes that the Holy One Blessed be He complained that He had no one upon whom to let His *Shechinah* rest, for the *tzaddikim* and men of deed remained in Babylonia and did not ascend to *Eretz Yisrael.*[272]

After seeing all of these sources, how is it possible to say that the deeds of those who ascended with Ezra were becoming, and only their names were ugly? *Chazal* even use them as the example of "Those whose names are ugly and whose deeds are becoming"! How can it be said about such an evil and deceitful generation that their deeds were becoming? In what way were their deeds comely?! This is utterly perplexing and most astonishing!

Aliyah and working the Land make a Jew worthy in the eyes of HaShem

We are forced to say that their comeliness and beauty was the act of *aliyah* itself and the fact that they built the Land and the *Beit HaMikdash*. HaShem was very pleased by this, even though they transgressed practically the entire Torah. Nonetheless, in this one area their deeds were desirable and becoming to God. For this reason alone they were worthy to be called "becoming" and to serve as the example of "Those whose names are ugly and whose deeds are becoming." Perhaps this is because the *mitzvah* of settling *Eretz Yisrael* is equal to the entire Torah.[273] Their involvement in this *mitzvah* tipped the scales so greatly that it could be said of them that their deeds were becoming. In any event, this shows how much the Holy One Blessed be He loves when the Holy Land is built, no matter who does it, even the lowliest Jew... This is an irrefutable proof.

You are beautiful, my love, as Tirtzah, comely as Jerusalem (*Shir HaShirim* 6:4). Rashi explains that this refers to the builders of Jerusalem and the Temple at the time of Ezra. Behold, the Holy One Blessed be He Himself called these *olim* beautiful and comely! Thus, *Chazal* were correct that the deeds of those who returned from exile were becoming. The act of *aliyah* and building made them fitting to be called *comely*.

The book of *Ezra* states that Ezra devoted himself to separating the Jews from their foreign wives [only] twenty years after the building.[274] He cried out, plucked his hair, cursed, and did whatever he did until he succeeded in purifying and cleansing them from their

272 Sforno, *Shir HaShirim* 6:11.
273 *Sifrei, Re'eh* 28 (on *Devarim* 12:29).
274 *Ezra*, chap. 9.

terrible sins. At first, however, at the time of the *aliyah*, he did nothing about this. He simply gathered and assembled whoever came, no matter who they were, and did not ask about their deeds. He did not distance them, even though he knew quite well of their evil deeds. Instead, he received them with open arms. He knew that the building and settlement effort required plenty of manpower and that the more people that would join, the more complete it would be. And perhaps he knew, through *Ruach HaKodesh*, that their deeds were becoming and pleasing to HaShem; therefore, he did not inquire about them.*

---

* The Talmud states, "Come and see the difference between the thieves of Babylonia and the highway robbers of *Eretz Yisrael*..." (*Avodah Zarah* 26a, see Rashi's explanation). In his work, *Avodat Avodah*, the brilliant R. Shlomo Kluger *z"l* explains this as follows. The difference between *Chutz LaAretz* and *Eretz Yisrael* is that in *Eretz Yisrael* HaShem derives benefit and pleasure even from wicked people. The Psalmist underscores this difference and says, *Glorious things are spoken of you, O city of God, Selah* (*Tehillim* 87:3). That is, in *Chutz LaAretz* HaShem only regards those who recognize Him, and He derives no honor or pleasure from the wicked ones who do not recognize Him. Thus, the Psalmist says, come and see the difference between *Eretz Yisrael* and *Chutz LaAretz*: Behold, *I mention Rahav and Babylonia* (only) *to those who know Me* (ibid. 87:4), i.e., I will only mention the places of those who recognize and know Me. *Behold Peleshet and Tzor with Kush* (ibid.). They are only important to Me because *this one was born there* (ibid.), meaning, a person who knows Me was born there. In terms of those who do not know Me, however, these places are absolutely unimportant to Me. On the other hand, *But of Zion it will be said, "This and that man was born in her," and He, the Most High, will establish her* (ibid. 87:5). This place is important to Me on account of both the righteous and the wicked (*this and that man*), for all of them were born in her.

[R. Kluger continues]: This is a sign that the Holy One Blessed be He will eventually renew Zion as at first. For, if the difference between the wicked people of *Eretz Yisrael* and those of *Chutz LaAretz* is apparent even today, when we are exiled and the Land is in ruins, then it must be that the Land is still holy and will eventually be renewed as at first. This is the meaning of the verse *But of Zion it will be said, "This and that man was born in her"*: HaShem's honor is recognized through both the *tzaddik* and the *rasha*, because they

Behold, who in our days is noble or arrogant enough to call today's *olim* "ugly" or "wicked" (God forbid)? Who can condemn their actions or denigrate and slander them?[275] With true self-sacrifice they have succeeded in building a flourishing Land. Unwittingly, they have fulfilled the great, positive commandment of *You shall possess it and dwell in it* (*Devarim* 17:14, 26:1), with all of its revealed and hidden rectifications, as I proved in the foreword.[276] I say unhesitatingly that their deeds are becoming to the Holy One Blessed be He and their reward is exceedingly great. I only wish that my lot could be with theirs in this matter. We only have to ask them to follow the ways of HaShem from now on, and do everything in the spirit of the Torah, according to the instructions of the *gedolim* of the generation. We will achieve this, with God's help, if we bring them close to us, lovingly and respectfully. The gentle words of the wise will be heard,[277] but not loud noise and yelling. Then, they will subject themselves to the spirit of Torah and fear of God, and we will succeed in purifying them, just like Ezra did. He was able to bring the sinners closer to Torah and sanctity because they saw that he befriended them and did not alienate them. This is true and clear to anyone who wants to see the truth.

Rashi writes on *Shir HaShirim* (7:14):

> *The baskets give a fragrance*: [This refers to] baskets of good and bad figs, as it says, *The Lord showed me, and behold two baskets of figs..., one basket had very good figs...and one basket had very bad figs* (*Yirmiyah* 24:1-2). This refers to the sinners of Israel. Now, both of them give a fragrance, [meaning], they all seek Your countenance.

---

were born in *Eretz Yisrael*. This is not true of the wicked ones of *Chutz LaAretz*. This is a sign that *He, the Most high, will establish her* once again, and that her holiness has not expired completely.

This proves my assertion that one must not degrade [the secular pioneers], God forbid. HaShem's honor will be glorified through them, their deeds are desirable to Him, and they will rise to the heights of perfection. Amen, so may it be God's will.

275 ❖ See what I cited above (p. 27) from Maharam Chagiz and *Chesed LeAvraham* on the punishment of those who slander the residents of *Eretz Yisrael*.

276 Pp. 82-85.

277 Based on *Kohelet* 9:17.

This alludes to the *aliyah* and building that occurred at the time of the Second Temple, and it can also apply to today's situation.

Above,[278] I stated that the people of *Eretz Yisrael* harbored a hatred for the Diaspora Jews because they did not ascend to *Eretz Yisrael* with Ezra. This, too, proves my assertion. After all, why should they hate them? Maybe the Diaspora Jews did not want to join the *olim* because they were, for the most part, lowly and extremely sinful men, as the Talmud states in *Kiddushin* (70a).[279] We must conclude that the Diaspora Jews were wrong for not returning, because they caused the redemption to be imperfect. Had they ascended, holiness and purity would have pervaded the entire nation of Israel, the sinners would have improved their ways, and everything would have been perfect. The same applies today. If everyone joins in, the holiness of the Land will be complete, as I cited above[280] in the name of the Chatam Sofer and Maharam Schick. Our holy Rebbe of Gur *shlita* also agrees, as I will demonstrate below, God willing.[281]

V The Importance of Settling the Land

The cities of Judah have the sanctity of HaShem's name

לא The prophet says, *Lift up your voice with strength, O you who brings good tidings to Jerusalem..., say to the cities of Judah, "Behold, your God"* (*Yeshayah* 40:9). The end of this verse is incomprehensible. It seems as if the prophet wants to say that God will do something to the cities of Judah, but then the verse ends abruptly. Also, the word *behold* [usually] introduces something new (as is known from the rules of etymology). But here, the verse ends without saying anything new.

With HaShem's help, I would like to suggest a proper and true explanation of this verse. I will preface with the well-known comments of the Or HaChayim on the verse *But you who cling to the Lord your God* (בה' אלקיכם) *are alive, every one of you, today* (*Devarim* 4:4). There are seven names of God which may not be erased. The Rambam rules that it is permissible to erase a prefix but not a suffix, like the "ך" of אלקיך (your God) or "כם" of אלקיכם. The suffixes

278 This chapter, sec. י"ד (pp. 252-54).

279 ❖ See above, p. 294.

280 Pp. 244-46.

281 P. 312.

are like the letters of the name, for the name sanctifies them.[282] Based on this, the Or HaChayim explains:

> This is the meaning of the phrase *who cling to the Lord* (בה'): This unique name, the Tetragrammaton (י־ה־ו־ה),[283] has no suffixes, only prefixes, like לה' or בה'. These prefixes have no sanctity and may be erased. If so, [the verse seems to imply that] Israel will cling to HaShem in a way that "The Name" (*HaShem*) does not sanctify them [Israel]. Therefore, the verse continues and says, *your God* (אלקיכם). This indicates that Israel's clinging to HaShem is not like the "clinging" of the prefixes, rather, like the suffixes ("כם" of אלקיכם), which are as holy as the rest of the letters of the name.

He also explains that the verse uses the word בה' (*to the Lord*), and not only אלקיכם (your God), to teach that Israel clings to the unique Name [the Tetragrammaton] itself. See the text inside, for his words are wondrous, true, and the words of the living God.

We may conclude from these comments of the Or HaChayim HaKadosh that the name אלקיכם signifies Israel's clinging to the holy name in a way that the people of Israel become affixed to this holiness and sanctified like the name itself.

Behold, I saw a beautiful idea in the holy work, *Tzror HaMor*, by the grandfather of the Beit Yosef's wife, our master, R. Avraham Sabba, who was among those expelled from Spain. He writes that the sanctity of *Eretz Yisrael* is second only to that of the Holy One Blessed be He Himself. That is, first comes the Holy One Blessed be He, and immediately after Him comes *Eretz Yisrael*. This is why the verse says that Calev ben Yefuneh *followed the Lord fully* (*Devarim* 1:36).[284] That is to say, he literally followed the Lord, because *Eretz Yisrael* comes after HaShem.[285] This demonstrates that *Eretz Yisrael* is affixed to the end of ôThe Nameö (*HaShem*). Therefore, it is sanctified like the letters of The Name itself, just like the "כם" of אלקיכם.

This clarifies the prophet's intention in saying, *Say to the cities of Judah, "Behold, your God"* (אלקיכם). The one who brings good tidings to Jerusalem will proclaim to the cities of Judah that they are exactly

282 *Hilchot Yesodei HaTorah* 6:3.
283 [Abbreviated as ה' (HaShem).]
284 [By defending *Eretz Yisrael*.]
285 *Tzror HaMor, Matot*, s.v. *achar kach amar u'makneh*.

like the name אלקיכם. In this name, the letters of the suffix are sanctified like the letters of the name itself. Similarly, the cities of Judah are affixed to the end of ôThe Nameö (*HaShem*) and are actually אלקיכם. This is the novel idea that the prophet teaches us, and he, therefore, uses the word *Behold*, [which usually introduces a new idea]. The verse is not abridged at all, it informs us that the cities of Judah are אלקיכם. This explanation is wonderful and true. Blessed is HaShem Who enlightened me to it.

HaShem loves Eretz Yisrael primarily when it is inhabitable

It seems clear to me that the reason the prophet says, *cities of Judah*, and not *Eretz Yisrael*, is because the Land of Israel is most beloved when it is inhabitable, as the *Midrash* states:

> The Land of Israel is beloved since the Holy One Blessed be He chose it. You find that when God created the world He distributed the various lands to the [heavenly] ministers of the nations and chose the Land of Israel for Himself... He also chose the people of Israel as His portion, as it is written, *For the Lord's portion is His people; Ya'akov is the lot of His inheritance* (*Devarim* 32:9). Said the Holy One Blessed be He: "Let Israel, who became My portion, inherit the Land which became My portion." (*Midrash Tanchuma, Re'eh* 8)

The *Midrash* also explains that this is why the Holy One Blessed be He detained the people of Israel in the desert for forty years. When the [Canaanite] nations heard that Israel was about to enter *Eretz Yisrael*, they destroyed and desolated everything. But, the Holy One Blessed be He wanted Israel to enter a built-up Land, full of houses, fields, trees, and gardens. Therefore, He told Moshe to bring them in only after the nations restored everything (ibid., *Re'eh* 7).

Thus, the Holy One Blessed be He loves *Eretz Yisrael* primarily when the people of Israel can live there, not when it is desolate and unlivable. We may conclude from this that when *Eretz Yisrael* is desolate, it is not fitting to be affixed to the Holy One Blessed be He, and ôThe Nameö (*HaShem*) does not sanctify it. Accordingly, the Taz rules that if someone affixes letters [to God's name] which have no meaning in connection with the name, they do not become sanctified.[286] The same is true of *Eretz Yisrael*. When it is desolate and uninhabited it is not fitting to be affixed to the Holy One Blessed be He, and it does not become sanctified with the holiness of אלקיכם

286 Taz, *Yoreh De'ah* 276:5, s.v. *ha'derech ha'sheini* (end).

(your God). Therefore, the prophet specifically uses the word *cities* (*Say to the cities of Judah*), because it implies built-up and inhabitable places, as the children of Gad and Reuven said, *We will build...cities for our young children* (*BeMidbar* 32:16). Thus, the prophet says, *Say to the cities of Judah, "Behold, your God"* (אלקיכם), meaning, when the cities are built up and inhabitable, they have the sanctity of אלקיכם.

This also explains the following *Midrash*:

> R. Yehudah ben R. Simon began: *You shall follow the Lord your God* (*Devarim* 13:5). Is it possible for flesh and blood to follow the Holy One Blessed be He...? Rather, at the beginning of creation the Holy One Blessed be He engaged in planting, as it is written, *The Lord God planted a garden in Eden* (*BeReishit* 2:8). Similarly, when you enter the Land engage in planting first, as it is written, *When you shall come into the Land, and you shall plant* (*VaYikra* 19:23). (*VaYikra Rabbah* 25:3)

On a simple level, this *Midrash* teaches that the verse, *You shall follow the Lord*, means that we should imitate God's ways...and cultivate the Land first. However, we can add another fitting interpretation based on the above. I already cited from the Kabbalistic work, *Tzror HaMor*, that *Eretz Yisrael* is second only to HaShem Himself. Therefore, we can say that *Chazal* derive this lesson – that we should plant upon entering the Land – from the very words of the verse *You shall follow the Lord your God* (אלקיכם). That is, you shall go to *Eretz Yisrael*, which follows HaShem, and build it up so that it can be sanctified with the holiness of אלקיכם. This will happen if you make the Land inhabitable for the Children of Israel by planting, building, and perfecting it immediately when you arrive there... With God's help, this explanation is as sweet as honey and illuminates like a radiant light.

We derive from all of this that when a Jew comes to the Holy Land and works the sacred soil, by planting trees, building houses, or doing anything that is vital for its settlement, he causes the Land to become sanctified with the holiness of God's sacred name. This is true even if he has no intention whatsoever to do this. We can support this with the Shach's ruling that it is forbidden to erase any name of God, even if it was written unintentionally.[287] All the later

287 Shach, *Yoreh De'ah* 276:12.

authorities establish this as *halachah*.[288] Similarly, the sanctity of *Eretz Yisrael*, which follows HaShem and is sanctified with the holiness of His name, comes about by itself, even without any special intention. Anyone who builds the Land fulfills the verse, *You shall follow the Lord your God...and cling to Him* (*Devarim* 13:5), according to both its plain and homiletic meanings. With God's help, all of the above is clear and true, in accordance with the truth of the Torah.

It seems to me that all of this is alluded to in the verse *You will arise and have mercy upon Zion, for it is time to favor her, for the appointed time has come. For Your servants cherished her stones and favored her dust. And, the nations will fear the name of the Lord, and all the kings of the earth* [will fear] *Your glory* (*Tehillim* 102:14-16). The Maharsha explains that by cherishing and desiring her stones and dust (i.e., by building and settling the Land), the Jews bring the appointed time of redemption closer.[289] In light of this, the verse concludes, *And the nations will fear the name of the Lord...* That is to say, the act of building sanctifies the Land with the holiness of HaShem's name and causes all the kings of the earth to fear the glory of the Lord that is in the Land... Amen, so may it be God's will.

The pre-eminence of the mitzvah of Yishuv Eretz Yisrael

לב The words of our godly mentor and master, the Chatam Sofer, whose teachings and halachic decisions radiate daily in study halls throughout the world, demonstrate the magnitude of our obligation to work the soil of our Holy Land, a *mitzvah* which surpasses almost all others. The Talmud states:

> The master [in the *Mishnah*] said, "A *Kushite* (black) *etrog* is unfit for use (*pasul*)." But, did we not learn in a *Beraita*, "A *Kushite* one is fit for use (kosher), while one that is similar to a *Kushite* is *pasul*"? Abaye answers: "Our *Mishnah* also refers to one that is similar to a *Kushite*." Rava answers: "There is no contradiction, one [the *Beraita*] refers to us [in Babylonia], and one [the *Mishnah*] refers to them [in *Eretz Yisrael*]." (*Sukkah* 36a, see Rashi)

The Chatam Sofer comments:

> "Our *Mishnah* refers to one that is similar to a *Kushite*": The Talmud concludes the dispute between R. Shimon bar Yochai

288 See the commentaries to *Shulchan Aruch, Yoreh De'ah* 276:9.

289 Maharsha, *Ta'anit* 15a, s.v. *baruch ata HaShem merachem*.

and R. Yishma'el (*Berachot* 35b)✣ with the following statement, "Many acted like R. Shimon bar Yochai but were unsuccessful." I heard from my master and teacher, the Hafla'ah *zt"l*, that this means that they acted ***like*** R. Shimon but were not truly R. Shimon.✣✣ For, someone who acts for the sake of HaShem (the One Who examines his thoughts and knows his plans) will certainly succeed. However, they acted ***like*** R. Shimon. They were similar to him but did not possess his true qualities. Therefore, they were unsuccessful. The Hafla'ah explains that this is the meaning of "A *Kushite etrog*." It represents a *tzaddik* whose ways are different, just like the skin of a black man (*Kushite*) is different. Such a *tzaddik* is kosher. However, "one that is similar to a *Kushite*" – someone who wants to compare himself to R. Shimon bar Yochai – is *pasul* (unfit), for he will not succeed.

This concludes the words of the teacher; what follows is an addition of his insignificant disciple. In my humble opinion, R. Yishma'el only applies the verse, *You shall gather your grain*, in *Eretz Yisrael* when the majority of Israel dwells there. For then, the very act of tilling the land fulfills the *mitzvah* of *Yishuv Eretz Yisrael* and brings forth her sacred fruits. Thus, the Torah commands, *You shall gather your grain*. Also, *Boaz winnows barley tonight on the threshing floor* (*Ruth* 3:2), because of the *mitzvah*. ***It is like saying, "I will not don tefillin, because I am studying Torah." So too, one must not say, "I will not gather my grain, because I am studying Torah." Furthermore, it is possible that other trades which involve social welfare are also included in the mitzvah.***

However, when we are scattered among the nations of the world (due to our numerous sins), the more the world develops

---

✣ R. Shimon bar Yochai asks, ôIf a person plows during the plowing season and sows during the sowing season, what will become of the Torah?ö Therefore, he holds that a person should learn Torah, and others will do his work. R. Yishma'el holds that a person should act in the way of the world, as it is written, *You shall gather your grain* (*Devarim* 11:14). He should plow during the plowing season etc., and when he is free from work he should study Torah. The Talmud concludes that many acted like R. Shimon bar Yochai but were unsuccessful, while those who acted like R. Yishma'el succeeded.

✣✣ That is to say, they made themselves out to be R. Shimon bar Yochai, but were not really in his category.

> the more divine service deteriorates.[290] Then, R. Yishma'el agrees with R. Shimon bar Yochai (that one should only study Torah and not engage in social welfare). We [in exile] rely on R. Nehurai [who says], "I leave aside all the trades in the world and teach my son only Torah" (*Kiddushin* 82a). This is true outside the Land, as explained above.
>
> This is what Rava teaches regarding a *Kushite etrog*. Even if it is not [merely] similar, but a real *Kushite* – meaning, R. Shimon bar Yochai and his true adherents – nonetheless, "One [the *Beraita*] refers to us [in Babylonia], and one [the *Mishnah*] refers to them [in *Eretz Yisrael*]." That is to say, for the inhabitants of Babylonia (*Chutz LaAretz*) it is fitting (to act like R. Shimon bar Yochai and only study Torah...). But, for the inhabitants of *Eretz Yisrael* it is *pasul*, because the people of Israel need to settle *Eretz Yisrael*.[291]

These words are utterly astounding. Our mentor, the Chatam Sofer, values the work of settling the Land so much that he forbids the inhabitants of *Eretz Yisrael* to act like R. Nehurai and R. Shimon bar Yochai, [who advocate] studying Torah exclusively while neglecting the Land. Instead, we must act like R. Yishma'el and engage in *Yishuv Eretz Yisrael*, because it is a *mitzvah*. He even compares someone who neglects this *mitzvah* to someone who says "I will not don *tefillin...*"

This is the ruling of one of the greatest *poskim* of the later generations, our mentor, the Chatam Sofer, whose decisions have been accepted like the Torah of Moshe from the Almighty. Who, then, is so noble or arrogant to degrade what our mentor, the Chatam Sofer, values so highly? He even compares working the Land to the daily, positive commandment of donning *tefillin*. Without the *mitzvah* of *tefillin* a Jew is simply not a Jew, and he descends [to purgatory] and does not rise.[292] Therefore, those who degrade the positive commandment of *Yishuv Eretz Yisrael*, using fabricated and shaky proofs, should be utterly ashamed. Their words are null and void in comparison to those of our mentor, the Chatam Sofer *z"l*, and we may disregard them completely.

290 ❖ See *Teshuvot Chatam Sofer, Yoreh De'ah* 138; *Sh'nei Luchot HaBrit, Hilchot Sukkah* (end) 2:78b.

291 *Chiddushei Chatam Sofer, Sukkah* 36a, s.v. *domeh le'kushi*. [The parenthetical comments are R. Teichtal's.]

292 ❖ See *Rosh HaShanah* (17a).

The importance of working the Land

לג The *Midrash* states:

> R. Yehudah ben R. Simon began: *You shall follow the Lord your God...and cling to Him* (*Devarim* 13:5). Is it possible for flesh and blood to follow the Holy One Blessed be He...? Rather, at the beginning of creation the Holy One Blessed be He engaged in planting, as it is written, *The Lord God planted a garden in Eden* (*BeReishit* 2:8). Similarly, when you enter the Land engage in planting first, as it is written, *When you shall come into the Land, and you shall plant* (*VaYikra* 19:23). (*VaYikra Rabbah* 25:3)
>
> *Who placed wisdom* ba'tuchot [בטוחות – lit., *in the innards*] (*Iyov* 38:36)? What is *ba'tuchot*? *Ba'tavya* (בטויא – in the *tavya*. *Matnot Kehunah* explains that this is a type of bird). *Or who gave the sechvi* (שכבי) *understanding* (ibid.)? This is the hen. R. Levi said, "In Arabic the hen is called *sechvi*." When the hen's chicks are small, she gathers them under her wings and keeps them warm. She digs and pecks in the refuse [to find food] for them. But when they are big, if one of them wants to get close to her, she pecks at its head with her beak and says, "Go and dig in the refuse." So too, when the people of Israel were in the desert for forty years, the Manna came down from heaven, the well came up for them, quails were available to them, the clouds of glory surrounded them, and the pillar of cloud traveled before them. But, when they entered the Land, Moshe said to them, "Everyone of you shall take up his spade and plant trees." This is the meaning of the verse *When you shall come into the Land, and you shall plant*. (*VaYikra Rabbah* 25:5)[293]

Thus, Moshe Rabbeinu commanded Israel to plant immediately upon entering the Land...

Therefore, Levi had no portion nor inheritance with his brethren; the Lord is his inheritance (*Devarim* 10:9). Rashi explains, "They were set aside for the service of the altar and were [therefore] not free to plow and sow." *Siftei Chachamim* comments that Rashi does not mean to say that tilling the soil is degrading for the servants of the Most High. Rather, he means that they have no time to do so.

Midrash Tanchuma states:

> *When you shall come into the Land, and you shall plant* (*VaYikra*

293 [The translation incorporates the comments of *Matnot Kehunah*, as cited by our author.]

> 19:23): The Holy One Blessed be He said to Israel, "Even though you find the Land filled with everything good, do not say, 'We will refrain from planting.' Rather, be sure to plant, as it says, *And you shall plant all types of food trees* (ibid.). Just as you entered and found trees that other people planted, so too, you should plant for your children." A person should not say, "I am old. How many years am I going to live? Why should I toil for others?"... Therefore, even if a person is old, he should add plants to those that he found. The Holy One Blessed be He said to Israel, "Learn from Me. Do I need plants?!" [Nevertheless] it says, *The Lord God planted a garden in Eden* (*BeReishit* 2:8)."[294] (*Tanchuma, Kedoshim* 8)

The *Midrash* comments on the verse *Do not go down to Egypt; dwell* (שכון) *in the Land* (*BeReishit* 26:2): "Make a settlement (שכונה) in *Eretz Yisrael*; plant, sow, and graft trees" (*BeReishit Rabbah* 64:3). The *Midrash Tanchuma* cites this same idea on David's statement *Trust in the Lord and do good; dwell in the Land, and find sustenance faithfully* (*Tehillim* 37:3): "*Dwell* (שכן) *in the Land* – Make a settlement (שכונה) of Land; sow, plant... *And find sustenance* (ורעה) *faithfully* – See (ראה) the faithfulness of the Patriarchs" (*Tanchuma, Re'eh* 11). Both of these *Midrashim* also interpret *Dwell* (שכן) *in the Land* to mean, "Cause the *Shechinah* to dwell (שכון השכינה) in the Land." The commentators explain that if the sowing and planting are done faithfully and in the spirit of the Torah, the *Shechinah* will dwell in the Land.[295]

The importance of studying and supporting Torah

This is also the meaning of another *Midrash* on the verse *When you shall come into the Land, and you shall plant all types of food trees* (*VaYikra* 19:23):

> *It* [the Torah] *is a tree of life to those who uphold it* (*Mishley* 3:18)... R. Huna said in the name of R. Binyamin ben Levi: "This is analogous to a king who told his son to travel for business. The son responded, 'Father, I am afraid of robbers on the highway and pirates at sea.' What did the father do? He took a staff, carved it, placed an amulet on it, and said to his son, 'Keep this stick in your hand and you will not fear any other

294 [I.e., God certainly does not need plants. So why does the Torah say that He planted? To teach us that we should imitate Him and plant in *Eretz Yisrael*.]

295 See *Etz Yosef* on the *Midrash Tanchuma*.

being.' So too, the Holy One Blessed be He said to Moshe, 'Say to Israel: "My sons, engage in Torah and you will not fear any other nation."'"

Had the verse said, "It is a tree of life to those who toil in it," Israel would not have been able to endure. Instead, it says, *to those who uphold it*. [Similarly], had the verse said, "Cursed is he who does not learn," Israel would not have been able to endure. Instead, it says, *Cursed is he who does not maintain the words of this Torah* (*Devarim* 27:26)...

For, [to be] *in the shelter of wisdom* [is to be] *in the shelter of money* (*Kohelet* 7:12)... R. Huna and R. Yirmiyah said in the name of R. Chiya bar Abba: "In the future, the Holy One Blessed be He will make shelters and canopies in the Garden of Eden for people who do *mitzvot* (meaning, for wealthy individuals who sustain the Torah with their money), [and He will place them] alongside the people who study Torah. There are three verses [which indicate this]: 1. *For,* [to be] *in the shelter of wisdom* [is to be] *in the shelter of money*. 2. *Fortunate is the man who does this* (*Yeshayah* 56:2). 3. *It is a tree of life to those who uphold it*.

Shimon said [a *halachah*] in the name of his brother, Azaryah. [The *Midrash* asks]: But, was Shimon not greater than Azaryah? (So why did he quote Azaryah?) [The answer is], since Azaryah engaged in business and provided Shimon with food, the *halachah* was attributed to him. Similarly, *And of Zevulun he said: "Rejoice, Zevulun in your journeys, and Yissachar in your tents"* (*Devarim* 33:18). Was Yissachar not greater than Zevulun? [The answer is], Yissachar gave Zevulun part of his reward for toiling [in Torah], because Zevulun went off on business, far from civilization, and provided Yissachar with food. Therefore, the verse begins with his name, as it says, *Rejoice Zevulun in your journeys, and Yissachar in your tents*.

R. Tanchum said, "Anyone who goes off on a journey without preparing himself for war will eventually fall in war, except for the tribe of Zevulun. Whether they prepare or not, they go out to war and win, as it is written, *Of Zevulun, those who go out to the army, experts in war...fifty thousand, and who set themselves in array without a heart and a heart* (I *Divrei HaYamim* 12:34). What is the meaning of *without a heart and a heart*? Whether they prepare or not they go out and win." (*VaYikra Rabbah* 25:1-2)

We need both Torah scholars and workers

Apparently, these different expositions of the verse, *When you shall come into the Land*, contradict each other. At first *Chazal* explain that Moshe told Israel to plant, hoe, and grow trees when they enter *Eretz Yisrael*. Afterwards, they explain that Israel should engage in Torah! It must be that *Chazal* want to teach us that both are necessary. The Land needs yeshiva students who study Torah, as well as people who work the ground. And, they must strengthen each other. Thus, *Chazal* explain that had the verse said, "It is a tree of life to those who toil in it" or "Cursed is he who does not learn," Israel would not have been able to endure. Instead, it says, *to those who uphold it* and *who does not maintain*, to teach that some people will learn and some will till the ground. But, everything must be done in the spirit of the Torah. Then, the workers will succeed and win their wars, like Zevulun and Yissachar.

Similarly, the Talmud states that had David not sat in yeshiva and learned Torah, Yoav ben Tzeruyah would not have been victorious in war. And had Yoav not gone out to war, David would not have been able to sit in yeshiva (*Sanhedrin* 49a). The same is true today. If there are no yeshiva students, the pioneers will not succeed in tilling the Land; and if there are no laborers, the yeshiva students will not be able to sit and learn. Each group must complement the other, and then everyone will succeed. Accordingly, David said, "Half of them will go off to war, and half will remain with the supplies."[296] The *Midrash*[297] states explicitly that David informed Israel that not everyone will be Torah scholars. Rather, half will engage in Torah and divine service and half will be ordinary people.[298]

The Rambam writes in his introduction to *Zera'im*:

> The second reason for the existence of unintelligent people is because Divine Wisdom determined that there must be very few wise men. One should not ask why this is so, just like one should not ask why there are nine heavenly spheres, seven planets, and four basic elements...
>
> The masses were created in order to form a society for the wise men, so that they will not be alone. Perhaps you think that this benefit is insignificant, but it is more necessary and befitting than the first reason. For, the Holy One Blessed be He placed the wicked ones [the seven gentile nations] in *Eretz*

296 An apparent reference to I *Shmuel* 30:24.

297 We were unable to locate this source.

298 ❖ See *Ahavat Yonatan, Haftarat Terumah*, s.v. *vaya'al ha'melech*.

> *Yisrael* to form a society for [Israel], so that the pious ones will not feel lonely... Our Sages explained this and said, "What is the meaning of, *For this is man's entire duty* (*Kohelet* 12:13)? The entire world was created to accompany the [righteous one]" (*Berachot* 6b), meaning, to eliminate his sadness and loneliness.[299]

Thus, our master, the Rambam, asserts that the few wise men need the society of the masses who engage in settling the Land. It is impossible for one to exist without the other.

Therefore, from the very outset we must arrange the settlement of the Land in a way that the people who can succeed in Torah-study should be allowed to sit in the tents of Torah and grow to be Torah scholars, while the masses engage in settling the Land. But this, too, must be done in the spirit of the Torah, so that their efforts will succeed and flourish.

This is actually what happened in the days of Ezra. The verse says, *This Ezra ascended from Babylonia; and he was a brilliant scribe of the Torah of Moshe, given by the Lord, God of Israel. The king granted him his every request, according to the hand of the Lord his God upon him* [Ezra] (*Ezra* 7:6). The Malbim comments:

> Shimon HaTzaddik, one of the remaining members of the Great Assembly, said, "The world is sustained by three things: Torah, [divine] service, and deeds of kindness" (*Avot* 1:2). During the time of the Great Assembly, three specific individuals fortified these three pillars. Zerubavel and Yehoshua the High Priest built the *Beit HaMikdash* and fortified the pillar of [divine] service. Afterwards, Ezra came to establish the pillar of Torah. And then, Nechemyah built the walls of the city and engaged in politics, in order to fortify the pillar of kindness. Thus, the verse says that Ezra ascended to *Eretz Yisrael* because he was a brilliant scribe of HaShem's Torah and he came to establish the pillar of Torah. He requested this of the king, and the king acquiesced. In this way, God's providential hand helped him ensure that Israel would not forget the Torah.

We, too, must appoint specific individuals to establish the pillars of Torah and [divine] service,[300] as well as people to settle the Land.

299 Rambam's Introduction to the *Mishnah* (Mossad HaRav Kook), pp. 82-83.

300 ❖ For, we have not yet been worthy to see the building of the *Beit HaMikdash* (due to our numerous sins). May it be God's will that we see it speedily in our days. Amen.

Then, our Land will be a Land of delight,[301] HaShem's desire will succeed through us,[302] the edifice will last forever, and the complete redemption will ensue, with the coming of *Mashiach ben David*, speedily in our days. Amen.

The *Mishnah* states:

> When they [the ones who participated in the *Simchat Beit HaSho'eivah*] arrived at the gate that exits from the east, they turned their faces from east to west and said, "Our fathers who were in this place [stood] with their backs to the Temple of the Lord... and bowed eastward towards the sun.[303] But as for us, our eyes are towards God." R. Yehudah said that they would repeat this: "We are to God and our eyes are towards God." (*Sukkah* 51b)

This is astonishing! Why would they disgrace their fathers? The author of *Hon Ashir* explains that they did this in order to prevent the onlookers from saying, "The end of joy is sorrow,[304] the proof being that the First Temple was destroyed." Therefore, the participants said, "Our fathers...bowed eastward," [as if to say], this is why it was destroyed. But as for us, our eyes are towards God, and therefore, our handiwork will last.[305]

The same applies to us. If we act in the manner stated above, there will be no need to fear that the end of joy will be sorrow (God forbid), because our eyes will be to God and we will do everything in the spirit of the Torah. Then, as a matter of course, *The pleasantness of the Lord our God will be upon us and establish our handiwork for us, and establish our handiwork* (*Tehillim* 90:17). The godly Kabbalist, Maharam Gabbai, explains this verse at the end of his work, *Avodat HaKodesh*. If we initiate [a process] with our own efforts, but are unable to complete it, the pleasantness of God will descend upon it and complete it with absolute perfection. Then, our handiwork will endure forever.[306]

I explained above[307] that the two contradictory *Midrashic* interpretations of the verse, *When you shall come into the Land* (*VaYikra*

301 Based on *Malachi* 3:12.
302 Based on *Yeshayah* 53:10.
303 Based on *Yechezkel* 8:16.
304 Based on *Mishley* 14:13.
305 *Hon Ashir* on this *Mishnah*.
306 *Avodat HaKodesh* (Warsaw, 5662 [1902]), vol. 4, chap. 36, p. 100b.
307 P. 308.

19:23), are true. Israel must plant and work the Land, and also study Torah... I just discovered that our mentor, the Or HaChayim HaKadosh, agrees:

> *When you shall come into the Land, and you shall plant all types of food trees*: Three *mitzvot* are enumerated here: 1. To come into the Land, as *Chazal* say, "Anyone can force [others] to ascend to *Eretz Yisrael*" (*Ketuvot* 110b).[308] 2. To plant all types of food trees, in order to enhance the Land. 3. To keep the [laws] of *Orlah*.
>
> Furthermore, the phrase, *When you shall come into **the** Land* (הארץ, with the definite article), alludes to the fact that one should not enter the Land in order to [fulfill his] physical desires. Rather, one should come for the love and desire of HaShem's chosen Land, which contains the Mountain of the Lord. This does not mean that one should refrain from trying to settle the Land, for the verse says, *You shall plant*. This teaches that the Torah's condition, [implicit in] the words *into **the** Land*, refers to ideal intentions. That is to say, ideally one should be motivated by the spiritual virtues of the Land and not by physical pleasures. ❖
>
> In addition, perhaps the term *food trees* alludes to those who study Torah, for they are called "plants," and "trees." [How so]? R. Yosi says, "I had marital relations five times and I planted five plants" (*Shabbat* 118b);[309] and it is written, *The days*

❖ The Or HaChayim's intention is clear. The *mitzvah* is primarily to settle the Land by planting and building. That is why the verse states definitively, *You shall plant*, implying that this is the main part of the *mitzvah*. However, one must make sure not to think about physical pleasures alone, but [also] about the spiritual virtues of the Holy Land. It is clear that if a person is not on this level, he should certainly not refrain from performing the simple aspect of this *mitzvah*. This is true of all *mitzvot* of the Torah. The simple man fulfills them on a simple level, and the rectifications (*tikkunim*) are effected by themselves.

308 [The Talmud explains this to mean that both men and women can force their spouses to move to *Eretz Yisrael*; and if they refuse, they forfeit their rights to the *Ketuvah* (marriage contract).]

309 [Printed editions of the Talmud read, "I planted five cedars." That is to say, he fathered five great Torah scholars.]

of My people will be like the days of a tree (*Yeshayah* 65:22). Also, the *Zohar* explains that *Do not destroy its trees* (*Devarim* 20:19) refers to people who study Torah (*Zohar* 3:202a). Thus, HaShem tells us that our main purpose in entering the Land must be to plant food trees, meaning, people who study Torah. For, the air of *Eretz Yisrael* makes one wise (*Bava Batra* 158b) and purifies the soul.[310]

Thus, according to the Or HaChayim HaKadosh, this verse refers to the two themes mentioned above, planting and studying Torah. It is a bit surprising that he did not bring a proof from our Rabbis of the *Midrash* who also interpret the verse in reference to these two themes... Our mentor, the Chatam Sofer, also aroused the people of Israel to support the settlement in *Eretz Yisrael*.[311]

Orthodox Judaism's influence will grow with numbers

לד I found the following in *Osef Michtavim*,[312] a collection of letters from the Rebbe of Gur *shlita*:

This indeed is my opinion. The *mitzvah* of *Yishuv Eretz Yisrael*, which our holy Torah commands us, does not depend on a specific time, only on capabilities and opportunities.✣ Therefore, we must take advantage of today's opportunities and exert all of our strengths [for this *mitzvah*]. ***The more Orthodox Jews that ascend to Eretz Yisrael, the greater their influence will be, and this will help preserve the holiness of the Land... In this way, Orthodox Judaism's influence will grow, and the settlement of the Holy Land will be founded on the spirit of our holy, written and oral Torah.***

✣ Undoubtedly, he wrote this in order to reject the Megillat Esther's opinion (cited above)[313] that this *mitzvah* is only in effect during the Messianic era, not during the period of exile. Our brilliant mentor, R. Yosef Sha'ul, also challenges the Megillat Esther's words and cites several proofs for the Ramban's opinion. He concludes, "Therefore, [the *halachah*] clearly follows the Ramban; and may HaShem grant us the merit to fulfill this *mitzvah*."[314] *Sefer Chareidim* states, ôThere

310 *Or HaChayim, VaYikra* 19:23.

311 Our author cites *Teshuvot Chatam Sofer, Orach Chayim* 205 as the source. Apparently, he means responsa 203.

312 *Osef Michtavim* (Jerusalem, 5727 [1967]), pp. 75, 77.

313 P. 229.

314 *Yosef Da'at* 372.

...The Rebbe of Gur, *shlita*, intimates that when there are many God-fearing people in a particular place, they influence their surroundings even if they do nothing. Their influence comes automatically. I believe that the words of the Ramban clearly prove this. He asks: Why is it that wherever Avraham and Yitzchak went they called aloud in the name of HaShem (as it is written, *And he called in the name of HaShem* [*BeReishit* 12:8]), but Ya'akov did not? He answers that Avraham and Yitzchak were [leaders of] a small group, and those who surrounded them did not recognize the work they did for HaShem. Therefore, it was essential for them to call aloud. Ya'akov, on the other hand, had twelve married sons who each had children. His family was already a large group, a multitude of people.

---

is a positive, biblical commandment to dwell in *Eretz Yisrael*, as it says, *You shall possess it and dwell in it* (*Devarim* 17:14, 26:1). *Chazal* say that this *mitzvah* is equal to all the *mitzvot* of the Torah (*Sifrei, Re'eh* 28), and it is one of the 613 *mitzvot* according to the Ramban and the Rashbetz."[315] The Maharam Schick agrees,[316] as does the Maharsham.[317] The latter cites the Maharam[318] who asserts that there is no difference between today and the Temple era; it is always a *mitzvah*. In his holy work, *Azor Eliyahu*, the author of *Sheivet Mussar* writes that the *mitzvah* of dwelling in *Eretz Yisrael* is in effect even when the Land is in ruins.[319] The holy volume, *Aspaklariya HaMe'irah*, also states, "This implies that it is forbidden to leave *Eretz Yisrael* even when it is in ruins. After all, there was no Temple at the time of Ya'akov."[320] Furthermore, I already stated above[321] that even the Rambam holds that dwelling in the Land is biblically ordained. The reason he does not count it as one of the 613 *mitzvot* is because it encompasses the entire Torah. I just discovered that our mentor, the Or HaChayim HaKadosh, writes, "Settling the Land is a *mitzvah* which encompasses the entire Torah."[322]

315 *Sefer Chareidim* (Jerusalem, 5718 [1958]), *Mitzvot Asei HaTeluyot B'Eretz Yisrael*, chap. 1, sec. 15.
316 *Yoreh De'ah* 225.
317 Vol. 1, sec. 18.
318 *Teshuvot Maharam* (Krimona, 5317 [1557]), sec. 199.
319 *Azor Eliyahu* 194.
320 *Aspaklariya HaMe'irah, VaYeitzei*, p. 21b, s.v. עמ' שנ"ה. ❖ It is cited in *Nitzotzei Orot* on *Zohar, Parashat VaYeitzei* (1:153a).
321 Pp. 232-39.
322 *Or HaChayim, Devarim* 30:20.

They did not need to call aloud, because the people of the generation recognized them through their deeds, which drew the hearts of the masses closer to their Father in Heaven.[323] This clearly concurs with the Rebbe of Gur's statement that the influence of many God-fearing people comes by itself. It is a bit surprising that he failed to bring this Ramban as a proof. In any event, the Rebbe of Gur was absolutely correct that the most important thing is to ensure that many Orthodox Jews ascend to *Eretz Yisrael*. Then, with God's help, the sanctity of the Land will increase.

Mashiach will come when we devote ourselves to Eretz Yisrael

לה During the summer of 5703 [1943], I spent a few weeks in Bekescsaba with my family. I found a close friend from youth there, our brilliant master, R. Natan Tzvi Brisk *shlita*, *av beit din* of Nadislanta.[324] He showed me the holy volume, *Ach Pri Tevuah*, by the holy Rabbi of Liska *zt"l*, which cites the following from *Nachal Kedumim*: ארץ ישראל (*Eretz Yisrael*) has the same numerical value as תת לב ("put one's heart," or dedicate). That is to say, if all the Jews dedicate themselves to dwelling in *Eretz Yisrael*, our righteous Savior (*Mashiach*) will arrive.[325]

I will prove this... from something I cited above.[326] *Chazal*, followed by Rashi, state: "If Ya'akov did not consider praying at the place where his forefathers prayed, should God detain him?! Ya'akov traveled until Charan, and when he arrived he said, 'Is it possible that I passed by the place where my forefathers prayed and I did not pray there?!' He resolved to return and traveled until Beit El where the ground [of Mt. Moriah] leaped towards him."[327] Thus, from the moment he considered returning, and actually returned, a miracle occurred. Now, *Chazal* assert that this incident is a sign for the final redemption, which we anticipate every day.[328] Therefore, we will only be redeemed if we consider returning to *Eretz Yisrael* and actually return there. Then, miracles will happen to us as they did to Ya'akov Avinu *a"h*.

323 Ramban, *BeReishit* 12:8.

324 ❖ He is the son-in-law of the brilliant author of *Beit Naftali*, who was the son of the brilliant author of *Kol Aryeh, z"l*.

325 *Ach Pri Tevuah* (Bronx, 5721 [1961]), *VaYechi*, p. 52a, s.v. *od katav*.

326 P. 162.

327 See *Chullin* 91b; Rashi, *BeReishit* 28:17. [I quoted this passage as it appears in chapter two, because our author quotes only fragments of it here, making it difficult to understand.]

328 See *BeReishit Rabbah* 68:18, 70:1.

You, son of man, thus says the Lord...to the soil of Israel, "An end! The end has come upon the four corners of the earth. Now, the end is upon you" (*Yechezkel* 7:2). This verse is self-explanatory based on the above. When the people of Israel strive to make *an end for the soil of Israel* – meaning, when they strive to redeem it from the defiled ones[329] by dedicating themselves to returning there – then, *the end will come* for the Jews [who are scattered] *upon the four corners of the earth*. According to this, it is obvious that the phrase, *The end is upon you*, means that it is all in your hands. Whenever you put your hearts into this, you will achieve it. God will assist you, but it mainly depends on your "putting of the heart."

My close friend, R. Natan Tzvi Brisk, also told me that his father, our brilliant and righteous master, R. Yehoshua *zt"l*,[330] heard directly from the holy mouth of his teacher, our master from Liska, that he sent money to *Eretz Yisrael* to buy a portion of land. He said that every Jew is obligated to ensure that our Holy Land is settled by the people of Israel and filled with houses, fields, and vineyards.

I, the insignificant one, will enhance his words with Rashi's comments on the verse *A redeemer will come to Zion* (*Yeshayah* 54:20). He writes, "As long as Zion is in ruins, the Redeemer has not yet come." Therefore, we must build our Land to bring the redemption closer. The holy Kabbalist, the author of *Hon Ashir*, also says that our redemption depends on the rebuilding of the Land, as I cited above.[331] Now we see that Rashi also states this explicitly.

VI A Plea to the Survivors: Return to Your Motherland!

Eretz Yisrael is the mother of Israel

לו In Tractate *Berachot*, the *Yerushalmi* calls *Eretz Yisrael* "the mother of Israel" (2:8 [18b]). Elsewhere it says, "He left his mother's bosom (*Eretz Yisrael*) and embraced the foreigner's bosom (*Chutz LaAretz*)" (*Mo'ed Kattan* 3:1 [8b], *Ketuvot* [end]). On the other hand, the *Yerushalmi* calls the Diaspora "the father's wife," i.e., the stepmother.

The reason for this, in my opinion, is based on an idea I saw in

329 ❖ As I cited above (p. 7) from *Teshuvot HaRivash* (101) and the Ramban (*VaYikra* 25:24).

330 ❖ He was the *av beit din* of Tesadada. I knew him when I was a young child, and he was renowned as a wondrous *tzaddik*. Many people came to him to have him request things of God.

331 Pp. 55, 180-81.

Otzrot Yosef, by the brilliant mentor of the entire Diaspora, our master, R. Yosef Engel *z"l*. He explains, in the name of the Kabbalists, that *Eretz Yisrael* is an aspect of Kingship (*Malchut*).[332] Now, Kingship is an aspect of the mother of Israel, as implied in the verse *Your mother has been sent away because of your transgressions* (*Yeshayah* 50:1). The Kabbalists explain that this verse refers to the *Shechinah*, as *Chazal* state, "Come and see how beloved the people of Israel are to the Holy One Blessed be He: Wherever they are exiled, the *Shechinah* is exiled with them" (*Megillah* 29a). And, it is well known that *Shechinah* represents Kingship, and Kingship is the mother of Israel. Therefore, the verse says, *Your mother* [i.e., the *Shechinah*] *has been sent away because of your transgressions*. This concludes the words of the Kabbalists.[333] Now we understand why the *Yerushalmi* calls *Eretz Yisrael* the mother of Israel, [because it is an aspect of Kingship and Kingship is the mother of Israel]. This is a true explanation of the *Yerushalmi*.

Based on this *Yerushalmi*, I explained a *Midrash* on the verse *Your sons and daughters will be given to another nation* (*Devarim* 28:32): "Do not read it as, *to another nation* (לְעַם אַחֵר), rather, 'to another mother' (לְאֵם אַחֵר)."[334] That is to say, your sons and daughters will be sent into the Diaspora, which is the stepmother. They will devote their hearts and souls to this stepmother and her foreign ideologies until she becomes like another mother. And they will completely disregard the Land which is their true mother. [The verse continues], *And your eyes will see and languish for them all day long* (ibid.). [This means that you will long] to see their greatness, because the whole reason you handed them over to the stepmother was for them to become great. You educated and raised them in the spirit of the foreign mother, and your entire goal was for them to live in and toil for the lands of exile.

The *Midrash* thus says: "*They made me the keeper of the vineyards* (*Shir HaShirim* 1:6), for the honor of the nations. *But my own vineyard*, meaning, the Holy One Blessed be He, *I did not guard* (ibid.)" (*Yalkut Shimoni* 2:982). What will happen because of all this? *Your hand will have no might* (*Devarim* 28:32). All the effort that you expended for the stepmother (the lands of exile) will be wasted, because the Gentiles

332 *Otzrot Yosef, Ma'amar HaLevanah* 6, 12.

333 See *Zohar* 1:27b; 3:253b in *Ra'aya Mehemna*.

334 See *Yevamot* 63b where the Talmud uses a different expression: "This refers to the stepmother."

will take it away from you, and you will remain naked and indigent. Due to our many sins, we have seen all of this with our own eyes, throughout the lands of Europe.

We must no longer give our strengths to the lands of exile

Realize this, O fellow Jew! From now on do not seek rest anywhere except by your true mother, *Eretz Yisrael*. Only our true mother will console us after all of the severe hardships that have befallen us, and after all of the pain that the stepmother has inflicted upon us. The prophet says, *Like a man whose mother consoles him, so will I console you, and in Jerusalem you will be consoled* (*Yeshayah* 66:13). That is, we will only find safety and consolation by our true mother, *Eretz Yisrael*. Thus, the prophet says, *And in Jerusalem*, which represents all of *Eretz Yisrael*,[335] *you will be consoled*. Let us no longer put our faith in our stepmother and, thereby, remain in the lands of exile.

How much money did our ancestors invest in these lands? They built palaces, castles, and great halls, because each one of them thought, *This is my resting place forever; here I will dwell, for I have desired it* (*Tehillim* 132:14). They completely disregarded their true mother, *Eretz Yisrael*. The Shelah[336] and the Chatam Sofer[337] bemoan the fact that some Jews become completely absorbed in *Chutz LaAretz*. They build themselves houses and palaces and invest all of their silver and gold in "*Chutz LaAretz*" property, in order to enhance and expand the stepmother's boundaries. But, they neglect to establish the boundaries of the widow, our righteous mother who cries and laments over us. They do not even consider doing anything for her benefit. They only care and desire to make an honorable living and build a big house with a courtyard made of hewn stones. [They build it] to last for many years, so that they can bequeath it to their children and grandchildren who will be born on foreign soil, [for] they hope to see many offspring and live long lives in exile.

In this way, we lost hundreds and thousands of years in exile and gave all of our strength and wealth to our stepmother. And now, we "merited" to receive her expression of gratitude for all of the effort that we expended on her behalf. She took a staff and hit us cruelly and mercilessly. She wounded our entire body; from the sole of the foot to the head, there is nothing whole.[338] She also banished

335 ❖ As I mentioned in the first introduction (pp. 34-35), quoting the *Zohar*.
336 *Sh'nei Luchot HaBrit* 2:78b (the end of Tractate *Sukkah*).
337 *Yoreh De'ah* 138.
338 Based on *Yeshayah* 1:6.

us completely[339] and took our money from us. We were forced to leave her house naked and indigent. Thousands and tens of thousands of our Jewish brethren died unnatural deaths at her hands.

These are the deeds of our stepmother. Now, should we put our faith in her for the future and return to her once again? How can we be so sure that after a few decades she will not do this to us again? Indeed, we see that the Gentiles have treated us this way during every period of our history. But, we have yet to learn that we must no longer put our trust in the lands of exile. Therefore, my brothers and sisters, No! No! We will no longer return to our stepmother. Instead, we will arise and go up to our true mother and devote all of our strengths to her, from now and forever, to build up her walls and repair her ruins. Be strong and let us be strong for the sake of our people and for the sake of the cities of our God, and the good Lord will make a good sign for us,[340] and our enemies will see and be ashamed.

After all of our suffering, everyone must advocate aliyah

לז The *Midrash* states:

> The day the *Beit HaMikdash* was destroyed it was decreed that the Torah scholars will learn amidst pain, poverty, and confusion, so that they will pray for the coming of *Mashiach*.[341]

It seems to me that the explanation of this *Midrash* is based on something I heard from my brother-in-law, the brilliant rabbi, son of saints, our master, R. Moshe Klein *shlita*, the spiritual leader of Grossvardine. The brilliant R. Meir Shapira *z"l*, *av beit din* of Lublin, traveled around Hungary to speak to the *gedolim* and leaders of the generation about settling and building the Land (for it is well known that they opposed this matter). Despite all of his arguments and proofs, he was unable to convince them to give their approval. [At the end of his trip] he spent a Sabbath with a certain rebbe, one of the leaders of the generation in this country. He noticed that this rebbe had a custom of eating two portions of fish during *Se'udah Shlishit* (the third festive Sabbath meal), one before lighting the [*Havdalah*] candles and one afterwards. The one before the lighting

339 Based on *Shemot* 11:1.

340 Based on II *Shmuel* 10:12.

341 See *Tana DeVei Eliyahu Zuta* 4:4, *Yalkut Shimoni* 1:391. ❖ This *Midrash* is cited in *Kol Ya'akov*.

was called "fish of darkness" and the one after was called "fish of light." "Now I understand why you oppose *aliyah* and the building of the Land," said the Rabbi of Lublin to his host. "As long as you eat 'fish of light' you do not need *Eretz Yisrael*. But, due to our numerous sins, the majority of *Klal Yisrael* eat only 'fish of darkness,' and you are unaware of Israel's pain."

Therefore, after all that we have been through here in Europe, where we have all eaten "fish of darkness," everyone must certainly approve of *aliyah* and building the Land. The fact that there are still individuals, and especially rebbes, here in Hungary who oppose this, is only because they have not yet "tasted" what most of *Klal Yisrael* has "tasted." May HaShem protect them from this. This explains the *Midrash* cited above, "It was decreed that the Torah scholars will learn amidst pain, poverty, and confusion, so that they will pray for the coming of *Mashiach*."

After experiencing our step-mother's wrath we can better appreciate our mother

לח Our brilliant and holy master, R. Tzvi Elimelech *zt"l*,[342] writes in *Iggra DeParka*:

> I heard in the name of a certain *tzaddik* that one attains a greater level of "dwelling in *Eretz Yisrael*" when he leaves the Land for a period of time and then returns. He "tastes" the sanctity more the second time. In my opinion, we learn this from Avraham Avinu, because his main stature and eminence came the second time, [as it says], *And Avraham ascended from Egypt* (*BeReishit* 13:1).[343]

I will add to the words of our mentor. *Sefer Chareidim* cites a *Midrash* which states that the Holy One Blessed be He originally told Avraham to go to *Eretz Yisrael*, see it, and return [to his birthplace]. After he returned, HaShem did not allow him to go back to *Eretz Yisrael* for five years. During this time, he longed to return to the Land, and he said: *O that I had wings like a dove! I would fly away and be at rest. Behold, I would wander far off; I would dwell in the desert* (*Tehillim* 55:7-8). [*Chazal* comment on this], "It is preferable to dwell in the deserts of *Eretz Yisrael* than the palaces of *Chutz LaAretz*" (*BeReishit Rabbah* 39:8). Before he entered the Land, however, he did not long for it. He only truly did so after he was

342 The author of *B'nei Yissachar*.

343 *Iggra DeParka*, sec. 108. [Apparently, the author understands the word *ascended* also in a spiritual sense.]

there once and saw, with prophetic vision, the splendid glory of the sanctity of the Land. We, his descendants, must learn from him and yearn for the Land as he did.[344] This is an explicit proof that one feels more sanctity the second time he enters the Land, as the above-mentioned *tzaddik* asserts.

According to this, we can explain the Rambam's ruling about the sanctity of *Eretz Yisrael* in relation to *shevi'it* (the laws of the sabbatical year) and *ma'asrot* (tithes). He states that the destruction of the First Temple dissolved the sanctity [of the Land] and exempted us, biblically, from [keeping the laws of] *ma'asrot* and *shevi'it*. On the other hand, the sanctity generated by Ezra never dissolved, and the Land is still holy today, even though it is not in our possession. Therefore, we are biblically obligated [to keep the laws of] *shevi'it* and *ma'asrot*.[345] Based on the preceding idea, this Rambam is clear. At the time of the second *aliyah* the sanctity of the Land became more deeply rooted than it did at first, and it never dissolved. Even though the sanctity was less complete than it was during the First Temple era (it is well known that five things were missing from the Second Temple),[346] that was only because all of the Jews did not return, as is well known.[347] However, the sanctity that existed became more deeply rooted than it did at first.

I would like to give a simple explanation as to why *Eretz Yisrael* "tastes better" the second time around. Let us imagine a child who is always by his mother's side. She raises him and takes care of him, and he never leaves her, even for a moment. This child cannot appreciate all that his mother has done for him. However, if he is taken away from her (for some reason) and given over to a stepmother for a period of time, then, when he returns to his mother's bosom, he understands and appreciates what it means to be by his mother's side. While he stays with the stepmother, he gets a taste of what a stepmother is. He sees and feels how she acts towards him, how she supports him half-heartedly, and how everything she does is forced, unwilling, and insincere. Especially if she beats him with abounding hatred, then, when he returns to his true mother, he will say wholeheartedly what King David said, *Surely I have stilled and quieted my soul, like a just weaned child by his mother's side, like a just*

344 *Sefer Chareidim* (Jerusalem, 5718 [1958]), p. 196.

345 *Hilchot Beit HaBechirah* 6:16.

346 See *Yoma* 21b.

347 See *Yoma* 9a with the Maharsha.

weaned child is my soul (*Tehillim* 131:2).❖ He will feel that his soul is bound up with his mother's soul, and he will enjoy his mother's meager portions of bread more than his stepmother's quarrelsome feasts.[348] Therefore, since I explained above that *Chutz LaAretz* is considered the stepmother and *Eretz Yisrael* the true mother, we can easily understand why a person who returns to *Eretz Yisrael* a second time has a "better taste" for the Land than someone who never left it.

The same is true today. We have experienced the true nature of our stepmother, the lands of exile, in the fullest measure. She has placed her cup of poison before us in all the countries of Europe, and we have drunk and drained its sediments.[349] Therefore, every Jew will undoubtedly wake up from his slumber and intensify his aspiration and yearning for his true and proper mother, our Holy Land. He will refuse to stay in the Diaspora any longer, even in exchange for all of the treasures in the world. He will strive with all his might, with all his heart and soul, and with all his wealth to return to his mother's bosom as soon as possible. He will say what Avraham Avinu said when he longed to return to *Eretz Yisrael*, "It is preferable to dwell in the deserts of *Eretz Yisrael* than the palaces of *Chutz LaAretz*" (*BeReishit Rabbah* 39:8). The *Midrash* states [the same idea] on the verse *Better is a dry piece of bread with tranquillity in it than a house full of quarrelsome feasts* (*Mishley* 17:1):

> *Better is a dry piece of bread with tranquillity in it*: R. Yochanan said, "This refers to *Eretz Yisrael*, for even if a person eats (dry) bread and salt every day while dwelling in *Eretz Yisrael*, he is assured a portion in the World to Come. *Than a house full of quarrelsome feasts*: This refers to *Chutz LaAretz*, which is full of violence and robbery." (*Yalkut Shimoni* 2:956)

Even if conditions improve we must leave the Diaspora at once

לט Behold, I write these words at a time when we still suffer the hardships of exile, surrounded on all sides by fear and dismay. In every corner and on every side of the camp of Israel one can hear

❖ The *Yerushalmi* comments on this verse, "Like a baby which has left its mother's womb, so has my soul been to me" (*Sanhedrin* 2:4 [9a]). That is to say, in *Eretz Yisrael* one feels like a baby which has left its mother's womb, because *Eretz Yisrael* is his mother.

348 Based on *Yalkut Shimoni* 2:956 [cited at the end of this section].

349 Based on *Yeshayah* 51:17, *Yechezkel* 23:34, *Tehillim* 75:9.

sounds and yearnings to return to the Land of our inheritance, to rebuild the city's walls, and to raise our Holy Land from the heaps of dust. However, there is reason to fear that after the harsh decrees subside, with HaShem's help, and the lands of exile return to their original strengths ❖ – thereby ushering in a time of rest and tranquillity for Israel – the Jews will once again content themselves with their original situation and remain in the Diaspora. All the more so, if they find a good business or a good means of support here, they will reconsider [returning to *Eretz Yisrael*] and use various excuses to once again cling to their stepmother and betray their true mother. They will fool themselves into thinking that their stepmother will be better to them this time, and they will relapse into their old flaw of neglecting *Eretz Yisrael*.

This concurs with something I heard from my beloved friend, the brilliant and righteous rabbi, our master, R. Yisrael David Margolis Schlessinger *shlita*.[350] The Ba'al HaTurim cites a *Mesorah*: *The thunder ceased* (ויחדלו) (*Shemot* 9:33), and *They ceased* (ויחדלו) *to build the city* (*BeReishit* 11:8).[351] R. Schlessinger explained that as long as the *thunder* and cries of the harsh decrees can still be heard (may the Merciful One protect us), the Jews awaken themselves to build the Holy City. But, when the thunder ceases and the decrees subside, the Jews cease to build the City. They return to their original places and become enamored with their situation in the Diaspora, as in the past.

It is forbidden to derive benefit from these lands anymore

Therefore, I say that we must caution our fellow Jews who have gone through this calamitous period, and we must remind them of the following *Mishnah*:

❖ As *Chazal* explain: "Decrees against the Jewish people come and go, but Israel will always survive. They were never abandoned and never will be abandoned. They were never destroyed and never will be destroyed, as it says, *For I am the Lord, I have not changed, and you, the sons of Ya'akov, have not been destroyed* (*Malachi* 3:6)" (*Derech Eretz Zuta, Perek HaShalom*). Furthermore, "A decree is liable to be annulled" (*Ketuvot* 3b).

350 ❖ He was the *av beit din* of Solanak and is now the rabbi of Linat HaTzedek, a chassidic *beit midrash* in the capital, Budapest.

351 *Ba'al HaTurim, Shemot* 9:33.

> If a man copulates with an animal, or a woman brings an animal upon herself, both [the human and the animal are executed] by stoning. Granted, the man sinned, but what sin did the animal commit? Since it caused a man to stumble [i.e., sin], the Torah said that it should be stoned. Another explanation: [We stone it] so that the animal should not walk around the marketplace where people will say, "This is the animal that caused so-and-so to be stoned." (*Sanhedrin* 54b)

In addition, the Talmud (ibid. 45b) and the Rambam[352] determine that one is forbidden to derive benefit from a sword with which a person was executed, even though it helped fulfill the *mitzvah* of *You shall destroy the evil from your midst* (*Devarim* 13:6). It is completely forbidden since a man was killed with it. All the more so, one is forbidden to derive any benefit from a sword that was used in a murder.

Thus, the Torah says that something which causes a man to stumble or which might cause people to say, "This is what caused so-and-so to be stoned," is completely forbidden. Therefore, it is forbidden for us to derive benefit from these countries anymore, because they have caused *Klal Yisrael* tremendous misfortune, especially in our times. Moreover, how can we continue to walk around these countries and say, "Here and there so-and-so and so-and-so were killed, burned, stoned, plundered, and abducted." There is not a single Jewish family in which one of its members was not ensnared in their trap: a father, brother, son, or daughter. Hundreds, thousands, tens of thousands [have perished], as is well known throughout the world. How is it possible to look at these places anymore? How can anyone with any pure emotions associate with such places after they poured contempt and disgrace upon us? They afflicted us so intensely that nothing in our entire history can compare to it. We must mention this and similar ideas to the survivors of this exile, in order to awaken them.

Furthermore, it is well known that a mark remains on a place where a person was killed or injured. An evil spirit rests there and lies in wait for other human souls. The *Yalkut* comments on the verse *For the blood pollutes* (יחניף) *the Land* (*BeMidbar* 35:33): "R. Yoshiyah says, '[The word יחניף] is an acrostic for יחון אף, anger will dwell on the Land'" (*Yalkut Shimoni* 1:788). This *Midrash* states explicitly

352 *Hilchot Sanhedrin* 15:9.

that anger dwells on the land where there is bloodshed. This is also why the above-cited *Mishnah* forbids us to derive benefit from anything that causes man to stumble. How many thousands, tens of thousands, and hundreds of thousands of evil spirits remain in these lands upon which our fellow Jews have "stumbled" in recent times? According to this *Yalkut*, all of these lands are filled with anger because of all the blood that was spilled in them. How can we remain here any longer? For this same reason, our forefathers who were expelled from Spain did not want to return, even after the decrees ended.[353]

Therefore, one should not become blinded or enticed by a good business opportunity that he might find here, for he will not see any blessing from it. An evil spirit rests on it, and in the end it will be to his detriment, God forbid. I said this long ago about individuals who use bribes and "protectionism" to remain in places from which practically all of the Jews were expelled. They use the prevailing market conditions to amass huge sums of money. Others take advantage of war-time market conditions to become wealthy. However, they forget that the Creator of the Universe sent these afflictions to awaken us, His children, to leave the lands of exile and yearn to return to our forefathers' inheritance.[354] They do not understand this. They have fattened their hearts[355] and become engrossed in accumulating wealth through the great business opportunities that have developed during these turbulent times. Nothing will come out of this but disappointment. I cited a *Midrash* about the plague of locusts [to prove this]:

> What is the meaning of the verse *Not a single locust remained* (*Shemot* 10:19)? R. Yochanan said, "When the locusts came, the Egyptians rejoiced, saying, 'We will gather them and fill barrels with them.' The Holy One Blessed be He retorted, 'You wicked ones, you are happy with the plague that I have brought upon you?!' Immediately, *The Lord turned a very strong west wind, and it carried the locusts* (ibid.). What does it mean *Not a single locust remained*? Even the ones that were salted in their pots and barrels flew away." (*Shemot Rabbah* 13:7)

353 See *Teshuvot Mabit* 1:307, *Teshuvot Kol Mevaser* 1:13 (end).

354 ❖ I already proved from *Chazal* that this is the purpose of all the troubles that have befallen us. (See pp. 45, 54, 96-101, 121-23, 223-26.)

355 Based on *Yeshayah* 6:10.

The same is true of those who rejoice over the market conditions that have resulted from today's misfortunes. The Holy One Blessed be He says to them, "You are happy with the plague that I have brought upon you?! I swear by your lives that you will remain empty-handed, because the wind will carry everything away!" Similarly, we must not expect anything from the market conditions that will arise after the war. The only outcome of these misfortunes should be that we leave the Diaspora, go up to the cities of Zion, and dwell therein. Then, we will succeed and attain everlasting peace and tranquillity. This is HaShem's will, as I proved above at length.[356]

HaShem afflicts us so that we will return to our Land

Let no one imagine that after the war ends and the countries of Europe return to their normal routine, the Jews will be able to do good business with the Gentiles. [For one could argue], only a few Jews will remain, because the vast majority has been annihilated during the horrors of the war (due to our numerous sins). Therefore, the Gentiles will not be jealous, for jealousy is only caused by many Jews, not a few scattered ones. I do not suspect that any Jew would say or think such a thing. First of all, who gave him the right to inherit the multitude of Jews who were killed in sanctification of God's name (*Al Kiddush HaShem*)? Also, which pure-hearted man[357] would want to build himself up and derive some selfish benefit from spilt Jewish blood? Furthermore, what does he think? – that all of this blood was spilled just so that he can build his house and elevate his pride?! No! No! All of this Jewish blood was spilled to make Israel want to go to *Eretz Yisrael*. I already proved this several times from the *Midrash* which states that HaShem brought a plague on the people of David's generation so that they would request the building of the *Beit HaMikdash* (*Midrash Tehillim* 17:4). In fact, immediately after the plague stopped, David went to Aravnah and purchased the site where the *Beit HaMikdash* would be built.[358] In this way, he rectified the souls of the fallen Jews, because they caused the site of the Temple to be purchased sooner.

The same is true today. If we arise and go up to Zion, we will rectify the souls of the Children of Israel who died in sanctification of God's name, because they caused us to return to our forefathers'

356 See note 354.
357 Based on *Tehillim* 24:4.
358 See II *Shmuel* 24:18ff.; I *Divrei HaYamim* 21:18ff.

inheritance. And if we are worthy to see the ingathering of many Jews to *Eretz Yisrael* – at which time HaShem will direct our hearts to love and serve Him sincerely – ❖ then we will merit to see the resurrection of all those who perished in exile. They will arise first, as the Ritva[360] and *Ikkarei HaDat*, citing the Radvaz, explain.[361] Thus, if we leave the Diaspora and return to *Eretz Yisrael*, not only will we rectify the souls of our fellow Jews who were killed in exile, but we will even hasten their resurrection. Then, their deaths and the *Kiddush HaShem* that they caused will not have been in vain.

The Ari HaKadosh explains that the Ten Martyrs were killed in order to weaken the evil forces (*kelipot*) with the *Kiddush HaShem* that their deaths caused. The same is true today. It is well known that when the *kelipot* intensify they prevent us from returning to our Holy Land. Thus, the *Kiddush HaShem* generated by the deaths of thousands and tens of thousands of Jewish martyrs has weakened the *kelipot* and allowed the gates of our Holy Land to be opened, as the prophet prophesied, *The gates of your Land have been opened wide* (*Nachum* 3:13).

However, this will only happen if we understand the purpose of our afflictions. I explained above,[362] citing the brilliant author of *Eirech Dal*, that one can understand the Creator's will from the afflictions He sends. If the situation in *Chutz LaAretz* makes it difficult to live there, then we know that the Creator wants us to leave the Diaspora and return to our forefathers' Land. If we do this, we will achieve the Creator's desired goal and rectify our souls and the souls of our fellow Jews who perished in the horrors of exile. However, if we do not do this (God forbid), but let the *Yeitzer HaRa* entice us to remain here in the Diaspora, not only do we transgress the Creator's will, but we are also guilty for the Jewish blood that

---

❖ I already[359] quoted the Rambam as saying that many Jews will gather in *Eretz Yisrael* before *Mashiach* comes, and HaShem will send a purifying spirit to direct their hearts to return to Him sincerely and wholeheartedly.

359 P. 117.

360 *Ta'anit* 30b, s.v. *kol ha'ochel basar*. It is also cited in *Teshuvot HaRadvaz* 3:1069.

361 R. Daniel Tyrani, *Ikkarei HaDat* (Amsterdam), p. 121b, sec. 66; quoting *Teshuvot HaRadvaz* (Venice), vol. 2, sec. 639. ❖ It is surprising that he did not realize that the Ritva concurs.

362 Pp. 224-25.

was spilled in vain. Therefore, my brothers and friends, let us take these words to heart, and then the Almighty will be exalted through us in the heavens above and on the earth below. Amen, so may it be His will.

Subsequently, I saw that the daily newspapers quoted the wise, great, and pious Mr. Roosevelt, the president of the United States of America, as saying that we cannot simply return to the good days before the war. Rather, people anticipate that the future, after this horrific war, will bring something of immense value. Now, what should we, the Children of Israel, say after all of the sacrifices that we offered? Should we be satisfied with the days gone by? A word to the wise is sufficient.

My anger will burn against them [the Jewish people] *on that day, and I will forsake them, and I will hide My face from them, and they will be as prey, and many evils and troubles will befall them. They will say on that day, "Have not these evils come upon us because our God is not in our midst?" And I will surely hide My face* (הסתר אסתיר פני) *on that day, because of all the evil that they have done* (*Devarim* 31:17-18). All of the commentators ask:[363] Since the Jews confessed their sin, admitting that all this happened because God was not in their midst, why should God's anger burn (and He even doubled the hiding of His face – הסתר אסתיר)?

I saw a beautiful answer to this in *Yad Yosef* by the *Chacham*, R. Yosef Tzarfati *z"l*, who lived in 5377 [1617]. We find that Pharaoh also repented, saying, *The Lord is the Righteous One, and I and my people are the wicked ones* (*Shemot* 9:27). However, his repentance lasted only as long as the plague afflicted him. As soon as there was relief he became the old Pharaoh again, and God was forced to smite him again and again. The same applies here. If we repent only *on that day* – i.e., as long as the troubles affect us, but when they pass we return to our old ways – then our repentance is not really repentance. On the contrary, HaShem's anger will burn even more, God forbid. Thus, the verse says, *They will say* ***on that day***. As long as they are in distress they will confess and say, *These evils have come upon us because our God is not in our midst*. When the troubles pass, however, they will not recognize this, and they will return to their abominations. Therefore, *I will surely hide* (הסתר אסתיר) *My face...*[364]

363 See Ramban, Sforno, *Or HaChayim*, etc.

364 *Yad Yosef* (Amsterdam, 5466 [1706]), p. 278a (end).

The same is true today. If we forget all that we went through and our vows to return to our Homeland when the troubles pass, acquiescing once again to remain in exile, then HaShem's anger will burn with a double hiding of His face.[365] May HaShem place in our hearts the desire to return to Him sincerely and with a pure heart, and may He [grant us the privilege] to serve Him wholeheartedly in *Eretz Yisrael*, speedily in our days. Amen.

We must loath our sojourn in exile

מ The *Midrash* states:

> R. Simlai says: "What is the meaning of the verse *Until when, O fools, will you love folly?* (*Mishley* 1:22)? The Holy One Blessed be He says [to Israel]: 'Usually, a man who eats *tzachnah* (an offensive food) for two or three days will loath it. But, you have been serving false gods for many years and you do not loath it, [even though] it says, *You will say to it* [your false god], *"Go away"* (צא) (*Yeshayah* 30:22). [This means], you will say to it, "You are excrement" (צואה)!' " (*Yalkut Shimoni* 2:998)

It seems clear that God's statement, "You have been serving false gods for many years and you do not loath it," does not refer to actual gods, but to the nations who serve false gods. The Torah says, *The Lord will scatter you among the nations..., and there you will serve gods, the handiwork of men* (*Devarim* 4:27-28). Rashi explains the words, *And there you will serve gods*, to mean, "And there you will serve the nations who serve false gods," as the Targum translates it.❖

It is clear that the *Midrash* refers to the same thing. The Holy One Blessed be He reproves and castigates Israel: "For many years you have lived among the nations and become their servants, but this does not disgust you. Surely, such a situation...should be to you as repulsive as excrement, and you should say to it 'Go away!' You should desire once again to go to your forefathers' Land, to live a 'family life' with your own nation and your own brothers, in your mother's bosom." This is what the Holy One Blessed be He expects from us, and He complains that the Jewish people are on such a low spiritual level that they do not loath living in exile among the nations.

❖ *Siftei Chachamim* explains that Rashi was bothered [by the Torah's implication] that when HaShem scatters the Jews among the nations they will inevitably serve false gods (God forbid). Therefore, he accepts the Targum's explanation.

365 ❖ See what I wrote on this issue in the addendum to this chapter (pp. 463-69).

Instead of it being to them as repulsive as excrement, it is as pleasant as wafers made with honey.[366]

I am reminded of a story I once heard. A village dweller came to one of the *tzaddikim* of the generation to ask him to pray that he make a decent living. The villager gave a note to the rebbe, and the rebbe blessed him that he should have blessings (*berachah*) and success. The villager answered, "No rebbe! I do not need blessings, only success." The rebbe, not understanding his words, asked, "Why do you not want a blessing?" The villager explained, "Rebbe, I own an inn. I do not make a living from people who make blessings (*berachot*) [i.e., Jews]; only people who do not make blessings [i.e., Gentiles] provide me with my livelihood."

This villager was utterly convinced that his gentile neighbors controlled all channels of abundance providing him with his livelihood. This outlook completely prevented him from having any connection with his fellow Jews.

The same applies to the entire nation (due to our numerous sins). During this lengthy exile, we have become so accustomed to nursing from the breasts of a foreign woman that we think it is impossible otherwise. HaShem complains about this and says to the Jewish nation: "How many years have you been accustomed to this, yet it does not disgust you!" He begs us [to loath the exile]; He even forces us [to do so] by way of current events. For if we do not loath them [the Gentiles], they will loath us. In this way, He will rid us of our Diaspora mentality, in which we have become so accustomed to living together with the Gentiles. Then, He will teach us to live in conjunction and brotherhood with our fellow Jews, without jealousy, hatred, or rivalry; in our Land, the portion of our inheritance. Amen, so may HaShem declare.

We must take matters into our own hands

מא Furthermore, my brother, contemplate and recognize the history of our people throughout the exile. Difficult times were always followed by easier times and freedom. However, the days of freedom only lasted a few decades, and then the hardships began once again. This has been Israel's lot throughout the journey of exile. Therefore, do not put your faith and trust in the cordiality that the Gentiles will show you after the passage of these difficult days, for strength does not last forever.[367] Instead, set your sights and your

366 Based on *Shemot* 16:31.
367 Based on *Mishley* 27:24.

heart upon returning to your mother's house. There, under her wings, you will find eternal and stable rest, with God's help.

Had our predecessors of the past two generations done this (when the *gaonim* of the generation aroused people to this cause, in 5624 [1864])[368] we, their children, would have been spared the severe hardships of this difficult period. However, they completely nullified their personalities and did not try to convince the kings of the nations to allow them to live independently in the Land of their forefathers. Instead, they were satisfied living in exile by the "flesh pots"[369] with the "pottage of lentils"[370] they obtained through a good business or livelihood. They fulfilled all of their desires and wishes with these [material] things while ignoring *Eretz Yisrael* and the holy nation as a whole. This is how our forefathers acted in exile from generation to generation. Therefore, we, their sons, have reached this predicament.

This explains Yirmiyahu's lamentation, *Our fathers have sinned and are no more* (ואינם), *but we bear their iniquities* (*Eichah* 5:7). That is to say, they sinned by nullifying themselves and failing to request to live separately in their Holy Land, like every other nation [does in its respective land]. They acted as if they did not exist (אינם) in this world, as if they were not an individual nation which deserves to live in its land. Instead, they were satisfied being an anomaly among the nations. What resulted from all of this? *We bear their iniquities.* We suffer and have reached our present state because of our fathers' sin.

Therefore, my brothers and friends, let us make sure that we do not commit the same sin as the previous generations. Let us make sure that our children will not cry after us and lament the same lamentation: *Our fathers have sinned and are no more* [i.e., they made themselves nonexistent], *but we bear their iniquities*. Thus, we must strive with all our might to return to our Holy Land, all together. Then we, our children, and our children's children, until the end of time, will gain HaShem's complete blessing. This will lead to the coming of *Mashiach ben David*, speedily in our days. Amen.

מב This explains the following *Mesorah*: The word "continuously" (הלוך) appears four times: הלוך ונסוע – *continuing to journey*

368 See the approbations to this book.

369 *Shemot* 16:3.

370 *BeReishit* 25:34.

(*BeReishit* 12:9), הלוך וחסור – *continuously decreasing* (ibid. 8:5), הלוך ושוב – *continuously returning* (ibid. 8:3), הלוך וגדל – *continuing to grow great* (ibid. 26:13). That is to say, if we are satisfied with *continuing to journey* in the exile as before, then we will *continue to decrease.* For exile constantly diminishes us, as is well known to all. Unfortunately, we saw with our own eyes how much the bitter exile diminishes us, due to our numerous sins. On the other hand, if we *continue to return* to our Holy Land, we will *continue to grow great.* Our Holy Nation will continue to increase in quantity and quality, spiritually and physically. Then, God's name will be sanctified through us, because when the nation grows, so does His holy and exalted name, as is clear from innumerable verses in *Tanach.*[371] With God's help, this is true and clear.

We must not forget what the Gentiles did to us

מג Furthermore, my brother, ponder what is written in the Torah:

> *Remember what Amalek did to you on the way when you were leaving Egypt* (Mitzrayim): *how he met you on the way and smote your hindmost ones, all that were feeble at your rear, when you were faint and weary, and he did not fear God. It shall be that when the Lord your God gives you rest from all your enemies around, in the Land that the Lord your God gives you as an inheritance to possess it, you shall obliterate the remembrance of Amalek from under the heavens; do not forget.* (*Devarim* 25:17-19)

I will now explain these verses based on our situation and the difficult exile that we recently encountered. The *Midrash* states that the word *Mitzrayim* does not only refer to the Egyptian exile. Rather, all of our troubles in exile are termed *Mitzrayim* (מצרים), based on the word *meitzarim* (מיצרים), which means troubles (*VaYikra Rabbah* 13:4). Now, we have seen in our times that when a Jew tries to relieve himself of distress, an "Amalek" comes along, blocks his way, and prevents him from taking action.

King David says, *I am similar to a desert* ke'at (bird)*, I am like a* kos (*owl*) *of the wilderness... All day long my enemies blaspheme me* (*Tehillim* 102:7,9). The Maharsha explains that [in this Psalm] King David describes all of the hardships that will befall Israel in exile. The *ke'at* and *kos* birds live in uninhabitable deserts and wildernesses. They call out for help when they are in distress, but

371 See *BeMidbar* 14:13-19; *Yechezkel* 36; *Tehillim* 2, 79.

no one hears them. The same is true of our exile. When someone oppresses us, we cry out for help, but no one hears us. And, when we go to the ministers of justice to complain about the injustice done to us, they not only refuse to help, but even blaspheme and punish us. Thus, the verse means: I am like a *ke'at* in the desert and a *kos* in the wilderness, where no one hears them. Moreover, *My enemies blaspheme me for this* [for crying out].[372] Indeed, we have recently seen this with our very eyes.

This is the meaning of the verse *Remember what Amalek did to you on the way when you were leaving Egypt* (Mitzrayim). When you are in distress (*tzarah*) and want to escape from it, an "Amalek" meets you on the way and prevents you from taking action. Therefore, you remain in distress. Remember all of the cruelties he did to you: *He smote your hindmost ones, all that were feeble at your rear.* That is, he had no compassion on the weak and sick ones. *You were faint and weary* due to the severe hardships you encountered. *He did not fear God* at all, and he, therefore, committed immeasurable and unfathomable evils against you. However, you must know that I command you to remember this only so that when *the Lord your God gives you rest from all your enemies around*, you will remember to dedicate your energy and strength to *the Land that the Lord your God gives you as an inheritance to possess it.* That is to say, everything has an end, including your afflictions, but do not even consider remaining here in exile [when the troubles end]. Rather, strive to return to your forefathers' inheritance. This way, *you will obliterate the remembrance of Amalek from under the heavens.* However, if you remain here, you will not only fail to obliterate Amalek, but you will strengthen him by dedicating your energy to him... I command you to remember what he did to you only so that you will despise him and his land and go to your own Land, the Land that I give you as an inheritance to possess it.

The verse concludes, *Do not forget.* That is to say, I [God] know your weakness. You quickly forget all the hardships that the "Amaleks" inflicted upon you during difficult times. Their small, cold gestures of affection placate you easily, because you want to retain the meager income you made before the decrees began. And you will certainly forget everything they did to you if they provide you with a profitable livelihood. You will make peace with them

372 Maharsha, *Ta'anit* 15a, s.v. *baruch ata HaShem merachem.*

and disregard your inheritance and possession in order to promote yourself among them. Therefore, the Torah warns, *Do not forget* what they did to you, and never let them appease you. Instead, take hold of your forefathers' inheritance, for that is HaShem's desire. All of these misfortunes befell you in order to arouse you in this matter, as I explained above.[373]

We must choose to dwell in Eretz Yisrael by our own free will

מד Subsequently, I found [this idea] in the *Derashot* of the Chatam Sofer on the verse *He subdues peoples under us and nations beneath our feet. He chooses our inheritance for us, the pride of Ya'akov* (*Tehillim* 47:4-5):

> It is well known that (we fulfill) the entire Torah by choice and not by force... The Ramban explains that the verse, *You shall dispossess* [the inhabitants of] *the Land and dwell in it* (*BeMidbar* 33:53), implies an explicit positive commandment to dwell in the Holy Land. Now, when we are rejected from the entire face of the earth, we fulfill this positive commandment only under duress, and it is not clear that we choose it willfully, for HaShem's sake. However, when we could live in the choicest lands of the nations, but we choose to dwell only in *Eretz Yisrael*, then we fulfill this positive commandment by our own free will.
>
> We already explained that the Holy One Blessed be He guides our destiny and places His hand upon the best portion, saying, "Choose this for yourselves."[374] Thus, the verse says, *He subdues peoples under us and nations beneath our feet*, so that we can dwell in the lands of the nations as we please. But afterwards, *He chooses our inheritance for us* (which means that we must strive to return to our Land). This makes it clear that we [fulfill this *mitzvah*] by choice and not by force.[375]

This is a proof for what we said above.

Therefore, my brothers and friends, now that HaShem has saved Israel, and the nations of the world allow us to dwell wherever we please, we have an even greater obligation to choose our inheritance. This way, everyone will see *the pride of Ya'akov*.

373 See above, note 354.

374 ❖ Rashi states this explicitly on the verse *And you shall choose life* (*Devarim* 30:19)...

375 *Derashot Chatam Sofer*, Sermon given on the 7th of Av (a eulogy for R. Yeshayah Berlin *z"l*), vol. 2, p. 306a. [The parenthetical comments are R. Teichtal's.]

We must learn from our bitter past

מה *Chazal* state in the *Midrash*: "*Israel does not know* (*Yeshayah* 1:3), in the past; *My nation does not contemplate* (ibid.), the future" (*Yalkut Shimoni* 2:387). In my opinion, the explanation is simple. The prophet rebukes Israel for quickly forgetting the hardships they suffered. They should have learned from the difficult times of the past and contemplated the future. Harsh decrees overcame them; their skin was flayed; the verse, *You will sow your seeds in vain* (*VaYikra* 26:16), was fulfilled through them; and their enemies trampled and robbed them mercilessly. They should have remembered this in order to understand the future and no longer trust the Gentiles. But, they forget this quickly and act as if they do not know. Therefore, they do not contemplate the future. Accordingly, the prophet cries out, *Israel does not know*, in the past; *My nation does not contemplate* that in the future these events could repeat themselves, God forbid. Our history proves this to be true. The mournful events are not the main tragedy of the Jewish people. The fact that they do not want to learn a lesson from these events, that is the great tragedy.[376]

How to end our troubles forever

מן The Sefardic version of the *Musaf* prayer on *Rosh Chodesh* (the New Moon) reads, "May this month be the end and the termination (סוף וקץ) of all our troubles, the beginning and the start (תחילה וראש) of the redemption of our souls." There are many repetitions in this prayer: 1. "The end and the termination of all our troubles" is the same as "The beginning and the start of the redemption of our souls." For once the troubles end, the redemption of the soul begins. Alternatively, if there is a redemption of the soul, there is obviously an end to the troubles. Thus, one of these phrases is redundant. 2. "The end" and "the termination" seem synonymous. 3. "The beginning" and "the start" are also synonymous. Undoubtedly, *Chazal* did not institute this wording for naught; there certainly must be some special meaning hidden in these words.

HaShem enlightened me to understand and fathom the depths of this prayer based on recent events. For decades and even centuries we lived and coexisted with our gentile neighbors here in Europe peacefully, tranquilly, serenely, and securely,[377] without anything dividing us. Then, all of a sudden, they became our enemies, persecutors, and oppressors; so much so that HaShem's nation has become despoiled and downtrodden. Yeshayahu's prophecy has

376 [Originally in Yiddish.]

377 Based on the Sabbath *Minchah* prayer.

literally been fulfilled through us, *This is a despoiled and pillaged people; they are all ensnared in holes and hidden away in prison houses; they are despoiled and no one rescues, pillaged and no one says, "Restore"* (*Yeshayah* 42:22, see Rashi). Every word of this verse has come true today. They stole our possessions, afflicted us cruelly, and exiled us to an uninhabited land. There is not enough parchment on which to record all that has befallen us in this bitter exile. They did to us things that are not done, and we have reached the depths of debasement and exile.

This is very perplexing. Why has this happened to us? Why are we any worse than the other nations of the world? Each of the nations has the privilege to live pleasant lives on this earth, but they have robbed us of any such right. They consider us to be even lower than animals, as everyone knows.

There is another perplexing matter. We know that most of our Jewish brethren in Europe have completely assimilated with their gentile neighbors. They have imitated their spirit, language, and conduct, and have abandoned and breached the covenant of the Patriarchs. Logically, then, they should coexist peacefully, amicably, and lovingly with the Gentiles, for similarity breeds love. However, we see the exact opposite. On the bitter day, our enemies persecuted us relentlessly, making no distinction between a devout Jew, who follows the ways of our sacred forefathers, and an irreligious, assimilated Jew. They are all the same in the eyes of our enemies, for they know *Chazal*'s statement "Even if a Jew sins he is still a Jew" (*Sanhedrin* 44a).

The history of our people in this lengthy exile is also perplexing. Every few decades or centuries, the same cycle of events repeats itself. The Jews dwell peacefully and tranquilly among the nations for a few decades. Then pogroms erupt, and the Jews are pillaged, despoiled, and murdered. This is what happened in Spain. The Jews enjoyed many years of tranquillity there, but afterwards they were plundered and expelled. This happened numerous times in Germany and Austria[378] and is happening to us now in practically every country in Europe. Why have we not attained the status of one of the nations which dwell peacefully and tranquilly upon the earth for many long years, without any troublesome years in between?

Perhaps, my brother, you want to answer that we are not at fault;

378 See above, p. 98, n. 17.

it is a Heavenly decree. It is all part of the exile that was decreed upon us until *Mashiach* arrives (speedily in our days, Amen). I disagree, for the Ramban writes the opposite. According to him, the verse, *And yet despite this, when they are in the land of their enemies...* (*VaYikra* 26:44), refers to the "promise of exile." It assures us that as long as we are in exile we will have peace, tranquillity, and prosperity, and we will enjoy the same rights as the rest of the people, and perhaps even more than them.[379] Hence, it is not predetermined in heaven that things must be like this. On the contrary! This Ramban implies that we are to blame for [our present situation]. Therefore, we must understand how and why.

Pay attention and hear my words and you will understand this matter. Each person is made up of two parts, body and soul. Each of these parts needs to be saturated with "food" and sustenance. The body needs physical food, and the soul, spiritual food. Spiritual food includes keeping the proper balance in worldly matters, [which must be utilized] wisely and intelligently, in the [proper] measurements and balance. If a man [eats] more than his body needs, it will deteriorate, and he will die. A man's spirit and intellect arrange his affairs wisely, for the benefit of body and soul. This is how the body and soul should coexist. A person must not emphasize one at the expense of the other; rather, he must use them equally. This is the only way he will succeed in living a long and pleasant life. However, if he loses the equilibrium between the two, emphasizing one over the other, he is destined for perdition and destruction. For example, if he inclines himself entirely to a physical life, and does not use his intellect – i.e., his spiritual side – to regulate and limit his physical existence, he will perish (because an unrestrained physical existence causes bodily harm). [Why will he perish]? Because he listened to the voice of his body which says "Give, Give"[380] and not to the voice of his intellect which says, "No, No."

This is true both of an individual and a nation as a whole. A nation also needs these two parts in order to subsist – a physical and a spiritual existence. The physical existence is the materialism: the economy, trade, industry, and anything which is needed for the nation's subsistence. The spiritual existence is the spirit and soul of the nation. Each country places great value on developing the

379 Ramban, *Devarim* 28:42.
380 Based on *Avodah Zarah* 17a.

nation's spirit in all facets of life, so that it can express its intellectual spirit in every aspect of life. The greater the intellectual spirit of a country, the greater its material strength will be. We see this all the time; the country that excels in the spirit of wisdom called "technique" also excels in material strength. Thus, a country's spirit of wisdom is its vital force, the soul of its body. If a nation completely ignores its spirit, putting all of its energies into physical and material concerns..., it lacks the soul and life-force of the nation. Accordingly, it has absolutely no right to live and exist in this world, and it is destined for perdition and destruction. Sooner or later, it will also lose the materialism to which it devoted all of its strengths, and its name and memory will vanish from the world. Many examples throughout history prove this.

I already explained above[381] that when our condition in exile deteriorates and HaShem removes the "promise of exile" from us, it is a sign that He wants us to leave the Diaspora and strive to return to our Land. We must start the process and HaShem will bring our work to a successful end. Now, just as a distressed man cannot attain spiritual perfection, so too, the nation as a whole cannot perfect its soul when it has nowhere to dwell peacefully. *Chazal* state this explicitly, "There is no greater abrogation of the Torah than when the Jews were exiled from their place" (*Chagigah* 5b).

We will now explain the wording of the above-mentioned prayer.[382] In reality, the expressions that were used have distinct meanings. The word "end" (סוף) indicates the end of something which began at a specific time. For example, today's troubles began in a specific year and ended in a specific year. That year is considered the "end" of the troubles. However, it is quite possible that these troubles will repeat themselves later. The word "termination" (קץ), though, indicates that a particular thing will end and never recur again for all of eternity. Thus, it says at the end of *Daniel*, *at the termination* (קץ) *of days* (12:13). There are many similar verses in Scriptures.[383]

"Beginning" (תחילה) and "start" (ראש) are also two distinct concepts. תחילה connotes beginning, but ראש implies "primary" and "principle." When an action has two purposes, the word ראש indicates which one is the primary and principle purpose, just like the head (ראש) is the primary organ of the body.

381 Pp. 223-24.
382 P. 334.
383 See *Tehillim* 119:96.

One more, brief preface: It is well known that when our enemies prevail over us and take away our very right to live, we cannot do any constructive work, especially if it effects the entire community. But, when the decrees are annulled and we once again enjoy freedom of movement, we begin our projects again, to our hearts content.

This explains the entire text of the prayer. We pray to HaShem that this month should be "the end and the termination of all our troubles." That is to say, we are not satisfied to simply reach the time when our troubles will end, because perhaps they will return later. Therefore, we request that our troubles terminate forever. Then we conclude, "The beginning and the start of the redemption of our souls." This means that whether or not our troubles recur is up to us. It depends on our emphasis when we begin working after the troubles end. If we continue to emphasize the physical and material aspects of life, our troubles may, and probably will, return after a number of years (as history teaches us). This will happen because we are missing the soul of our nation..., and a body without a soul has no right to live and is destined for destruction, God forbid. However, if we emphasize the redemption of our soul, we can be sure that our troubles will terminate forever. I mean that if we toil to improve our soul and the soul of the nation by building and establishing our Holy Land in accordance with the purity and sanctity of *Eretz Yisrael*, in the spirit of the Torah (because the soul of our holy nation will only be redeemed in this way), then our troubles will terminate forever.

Thus, the prayer concludes, "The beginning and the start (תחילה וראש) of the redemption of our souls." That is, after the troubles subside and we achieve peace from our enemies, we must primarily and principally toil for the redemption of our souls. Until now, we did the opposite. We contented ourselves with and devoted all of our strengths to expanding our earthliness and materialism, while we abandoned our Torah, our tradition, the sanctity of our nation, and our Holy Land. We completely neglected our Land for the fragmented and lowly lives we attained in the lands of exile. This doomed us to perdition and destruction. However, if we emphasize the redemption of our soul – first and foremost this means to strive to return to our Holy Land, because *Eretz Yisrael* is the heart of the nation[384] and no

384 ❖ I cited this above (pp. 81, 233) from the godly Kabbalist, Maharam Cordovero, and *Sefer HaMitzvot* of the Rambam.

nation can live without a heart – then we will achieve eternal life and an everlasting end to our troubles. In my opinion, this is a true and clear explanation of this prayer. Amen, so may HaShem declare.

In order to achieve this, the Orthodox, God-fearing Jews must strive to return to our Holy Land, without waiting for a prophet's call.[385] Then, when many Jews who tremble at the word of God gather in *Eretz Yisrael*, we will strengthen and elevate the sanctity of the Land and ensure the fulfillment of the Torah and *mitzvot*, as I cited above from the godly Rebbe of Gur *shlita*.[386] This way, we will achieve the redemption of our souls and put an absolute end to all of our troubles.

Current events indicate God's desire in this world

In addition, everyone will understand the "talk of the times" which tells us that the ôtime of loveö[387] has arrived to return to our dwelling place and inheritance, and that we have nothing more to look for here in the Diaspora. Several times in his writings, our master, the Maharal, asserts that when HaShem wants to reveal His desire in this world, He does so through worldly events. This is His way of telling us what He wants.[388]

The verse says about Eliyahu, *And I* [God] *have commanded the ravens to feed you* (I *Melachim* 17:4). The Chatam Sofer[389] cites the Radak as saying that God did not explicitly command the ravens to do so. Rather, He placed in their hearts the desire to bring Eliyahu bread. That was considered God's commandment.[390]

The *Midrash* states, "The Holy One Blessed be He accomplishes His mission through any means: sometimes through a frog, sometimes through a mosquito" (*BeReishit Rabbah* 10:7). *Yefeh To'ar* comments:

> This does not mean an actual commandment. Rather, HaShem arouses the animal in some way to perform the particular act, even though it seems voluntary and natural. Despite this, the term "mission" is appropriate, because God Himself evokes this novel occurrence. If not for His desire, even nature would not function.

385 ❖ As I cited above (p. 148) from the Ramban *zôl*.

386 P. 312.

387 Based on *Yechezkel* 16:8.

388 See *Kitvei Maharal MiPrague*, by A. Kariv, vol. 2, p. 372.

389 Our author cites the Chatam Sofer's *Derashot* for *Shavuot* as the source for this. We were unable to locate it there.

390 Radak on the verse quoted.

Similarly, one should view recent events as HaShem's messengers to bring us to the mountain of our inheritance.

In exile we toil in vain

מז Yechezkel the prophet tells us, *And I passed by you and saw you wallowing in your blood, and I said to you, "In your blood, live!" and I said to you, "In your blood, live!"* (*Yechezkel* 16:6). It seems to me that the prophet saw, with his *Ruach HaKodesh*, our exile and all that happened to us in the kingdoms of Europe. We toiled by the sweat of our brows and put all of our energy into every facet of life: education, economy, trade. Israel contributed its skill, strength, and ingenuity to help life in Europe flourish. But in the end, the verse, *You will sow your seeds in vain* (*VaYikra* 26:16), was fulfilled through us. Other people eat the fruits of our labor while we wallow in the dirt with no protection from the storm[391] of troubles that rages upon us (due to our numerous sins).

Because of this, the prophet lifts his voice to us and says, *I passed by you and saw you wallowing in your blood* (דמיך). דמים has two connotations – money and actual blood. Thus, he says, you gave your money and strength (blood) to the lands of exile, and still you wallow in the dirt, naked and bare. Therefore, I say to you, from now on make sure that *In your blood live! In your blood, live!* That is, return to your Land and your inheritance and give the two types of דמים to it. Then, ***you*** will live, not someone else. For, if you expend your strength and energy on the Holy Land, [you will benefit from it]. If you build a house in *Eretz Yisrael*, you and your children will dwell in it for many years. If you plant a vineyard in *Eretz Yisrael*, you, not strangers, will inaugurate it and eat from it.[392] Similarly, you and your children will eat the fruits of any work you do in your Land, and you will not toil in vain. Therefore, I exhort you, "In your blood, ***you*** shall live! In your blood, ***you*** shall live!" Contemplate this for it is true.

HaShem enlightened me to find a great and holy "*Tana*" who agrees with this idea; he is none other than our mentor, the Chatam Sofer. The Torah states, *The Lord our God spoke to us in Chorev saying, "You have dwelt long enough at this mountain, turn and take your journey and come to the mountain of the Amorite... Behold, I have set the land before you, come and possess the Land which the*

391 Based on *Yeshayah* 4:6, 25:4.

392 Based on *Devarim* 20:5-6.

Lord swore to your forefathers...to give to them and their seed after them" (*Devarim* 1:6-8). After asking several questions on these verses, the Chatam Sofer explains:

> On the day the Torah was given, Israel gained the right to inherit the entire world and subjugate the nations. For on that day, the foundations of the earth collapsed, and if not for that momentous revelation, the world would have reverted to nothingness. Thus, the entire world exists for Israel's sake. This is true even if we do not fulfill Torah and *mitzvot*, for [*Chazal*] say "Had He brought us near to Mount Sinai, but not given us the Torah, it would have been sufficient for us" (*Pesach Haggadah*). Thus, this momentous revelation, in and of itself, is worthy of sustaining the world.
>
> Accordingly, we have the right to choose a nice portion in which to dwell [from anywhere] in the world, and the nations must accept us based on the preceding logic. But, why should we sustain other nations with our [efforts], while we lack everything and are starving and thirsty?[393] The entire world subsists for the sake of HaShem's nation, but we have no portion nor inheritance in this world, [besides *Eretz Yisrael*]. Furthermore, it is unimaginable that we could reach the level of perfection needed to rectify (*tikkun*) the supernal worlds, outside the Holy Land. Therefore, when we neglect to acquire true perfection, the tables are turned and we bring calamity to the entire world.
>
> Now we will explain the verses mentioned above. The Holy One Blessed be He says to Israel, *You have dwelt long enough at this mountain*. That is to say, you deserve merit and honor just because you dwelt at this mountain, even without accepting and keeping the Torah. Therefore, from now on *Turn and take your journey*, [meaning, journey] for yourselves. When will you provide for your own house?[394] *Come to the mountain of the Amorite* [i.e., *Eretz Yisrael*], for there you will acquire true perfection. He further says, *Behold I have set the land before you*. This means, I have given you the entire world because you dwelt at this mountain. However, I advise you, *Come and possess the Land which I swore to your forefathers*. Why should you toil for others and let the nations of the world eat the

393 Based on *Tehillim* 107:5.
394 Based on *BeReishit* 30:30.

fruits of your labor? Therefore, chose life![395] *Come and possess the Land.*[396]

According to these holy words, the Holy One Blessed be He says to us, "Why do you toil in vain, only to give your strength to others?" And He asks us to strive to possess the Land of our forefathers. This coincides precisely with what we said above. It is all up to us, and HaShem will assist us to complete the process for the good.

The consequences of neglecting Eretz Yisrael

מח We find that Ya'akov Avinu, while gripped with fear, tried to save his money from Eisav's clutches, as it is written, *And he sent over that which he had* (*BeReishit* 32:24). Rashi, quoting the *Midrash*,[397] explains, "[He sent over] the cattle and moveables. He acted like a bridge, taking [them] from one side [of the river] and setting [them] down on the other side." This is puzzling! How could he possibly have sent over this great wealth with his own two hands? The Shelah cites a *Midrash* which states that the gift which Ya'akov sent to Eisav consisted of 600,000 flocks and 600,000 dogs, one dog per flock.[398] Surely Ya'akov had even more than this. How, then, could he send all of this over with two hands, just by putting one leg on one side of the river and the other leg on the other side, like a bridge? Also, why did he need to do this? Surely there were other crossings over which he could have sent his possessions.[399]

It seems to me that *Chazal* allude to an instructive lesson that we, Ya'akov's descendants, can learn. I already cited[400] earlier *gedolim* who say that the events which befell the Patriarchs are signs for their descendants. Now, let us examine Ya'akov's actions in the war against his brother, Eisav. At the outset, it was unknown who would win and who would lose. Therefore, before doing anything else, Ya'akov made sure that his hard-earned money would not fall into Eisav's hands; and he indeed succeeded. The *Midrash* tells us why he succeeded: Ya'akov always made himself like a bridge. A bridge has two "feet," one foot on one side of a river and one on the other

395 *Devarim* 30:19.
396 *Derashot Chatam Sofer*, Sermon given on the 7th of Av (a eulogy for R. Yeshayah Berlin *z"l*), vol. 2, p. 306a.
397 *BeReishit Rabbah* 76:9.
398 *Sh'nei Luchot HaBrit, Torah SheBichtav – VaYeitzei*, 3:23a; citing *BeReishit Rabbah* 73:10.
399 ❖ See the Rashbam there.
400 Pp. 38-39, 222, 224, 314.

side. Ya'akov Avinu, as well, always stood with one foot on the *Eretz-Yisrael* side of the river, and one foot on Eisav's side, in the atmosphere of a defiled land. This is what helped him send all of his possessions to *Eretz Yisrael* and save them from Eisav. Ya'akov Avinu never stood with both of his feet on Eisav's side. Therefore, he was able to transfer his possessions from one side to the other. However, had he stood constantly with both feet on Eisav's land, he would not have been able to save his money and possessions. The *Midrash* and Rashi demonstrate this by saying, "He made himself like a bridge." That is to say, he was like a bridge his entire life. With one foot he stood in *Eretz Yisrael*, and his head and heart constantly thought of ways to send his money there.

The same applies to us, his descendants. Had we not stood with both of our feet, our heads, and our hearts here in the Diaspora, forgetting completely about our Holy Land, our money would not have fallen into Eisav's hands. Woe to all of the Jewish money that fell into Eisav's hands here in the lands of Europe. How much of our Holy Land could we have redeemed and built with that money?! This happened because we stood with both of our feet here in the Diaspora. We put so much faith in our sojourn here in exile that we disregarded our Land and our inheritance. Ya'akov Avinu stood in the Diaspora with only one foot, while his other foot, his eyes, and his heart were in the Holy Land. Therefore, foreigners had no control over his money. We, however, did not follow his example. Therefore, we have reached our current situation. This is the cause of our troubles.

Apparently, this explains the following *Midrash*:

> If we were worthy we would have read, *No man will desire your Land* (*Shemot* 34:24). But now that we were unworthy, we read, *The persecutor spread out his hand on all of her pleasant things* (*Eichah* 1:10). (*Petichta DeEichah Rabbah* 11)

That is, had we been worthy of constantly thinking of *Eretz Yisrael*, and had we not become settled here in the Diaspora, we would have read, *No man will desire your Land.* For then, even our sojourn in exile would have been considered dwelling in *Eretz Yisrael*, as *Sefer Chareidim*[401] and *Sefer HaChayim*[402] (by the Maharal's brother)

401 (Jerusalem: 5718 [1958]), pp. 195-196.

402 Vol. 5, *Sefer Ge'ulah ViYeshuah*, chap. 1.

assert.[403] Then, the Gentiles would have had no control over our money. But now that we were unworthy – because we said, *Here I will dwell, for I have desired it* (*Tehillim* 132:14), and we stood in the lands of exile with both of our feet – we read, *The persecutor spread out his hand on all of her pleasant things.* They took everything from us, as we witnessed in recent times (due to our numerous sins). This is true and clear.

Let this be an instructive lesson for us. From now on we must not stand here in the Diaspora with two feet. Instead, we should always have one foot in *Eretz Yisrael*, and our eyes and hearts should be there at all times. Then, we will receive a blessing from HaShem. Amen, so may it be God's will.

מט The *Midrash* says, "If someone owns land and his ship sinks at sea, he will survive [the loss]. If he has no land, however, there is no greater tragedy [lit., vanity] than this" (*VaYikra Rabbah* 22:1). The author of *Pardes Yosef*, the brilliant and pious magnate of noble lineage, from the family of our mentor, the Rim of Povianitz, comments on this:

> Until Israel returns to its Land and dwells under its vine and fig tree,[404] its wealth and trade are vanity of vanities. The holy rabbi, our master and mentor, R. Yosef, the *Admor* of Kotsk, discusses this at length in *Shalom Yerushalayim* (sec. 200). Also see Responsa *Avnei Neizer* (*Yoreh De'ah* 2:454, 455, 457)...[405]

This concludes the words of the Pardes Yosef. (At this point I do not know what has happened to him. May the merit of his Torah, righteousness, piety, and deeds of kindness stand by his side during these troublesome times.)

We must not alienate any Jew

נ Tangentially, I will quote further from *Pardes Yosef* on *parashat BeShalach*:

> ...This is a clear proclamation against those who pursue the sinful Jews in order to "remove the thorns from the vineyard." They [the pursuers] do not realize that burial is not the only way to deal with corrupt sons. Preferably, they should try to revive their souls and educate them. In most cases, this will

403 ❖ God willing, I will cite them below (pp. 391-92).

404 Based on I *Melachim* 5:5.

405 *Pardes Yosef* (Lodz: 5697 [1937]), vol. 1, p. 77, s.v. *u'beMidrash Rabbah*.

achieve the desired goal. In any event, it is better to revive than to bury. Unfortunately, though, there are many who prefer to defile themselves with their brother's burial than purify themselves with their resurrection.

The Talmud says that Acher, [Elisha ben Avuyah], became a heretic because [a Heavenly voice] proclaimed, "*Return O rebellious sons* (*Yirmiyah* 3:14, 22), except for Acher" (*Chagigah* 15a). However, when we bring them near, many sinners become righteous and pious people. *Avot DeRebbe Natan* states, "Many Jewish sinners drew near to Torah study and bore righteous, pious, and upright offspring" (2:9). The Talmud also states, "One might have thought that we should abandon[406] a person who was sold to idolaters, because he has become a priest to their gods. Therefore, the verse says, *After he is sold, he shall have a redemption* (*VaYikra* 25:48)" (*Kiddushin* 20b, *Arachin* 30b). We must free him, not abandon, pursue, and forcibly push him aside. Also see *Mekor Baruch* (2:152, 3:655).

Furthermore, *Chazal* say, "At all times, the left hand should push away, while the right hand brings near, unlike Elisha who pushed Gaychazi away with both hands" (*Sotah* 47a, *Sanhedrin* 107b). Also see *Eiruvin* (21b): "*Bad figs* (*Yirmiyah* 24:2) refers to wicked people. Perhaps you will say that they have lost all hope..."[407] Also see *Teshuvat HaGaonim* printed in *Sha'arei Tzedek* (sec. 7). The Talmud states, "Even if a Jew sins, he is still a Jew" (*Sanhedrin* 44a). The Radvaz (*Teshuvot HaChadashot* 187) concludes that one must be moderate on this issue.[408]

In *parashat Kedoshim*, the Pardes Yosef states:

> We say in the *Haggadah*, "For not only one (שלא אחד בלבד) has risen up against us to destroy us." That is to say, only the fact that we are "not one" (לא אחד בלבד) – the fact that we are not united – causes us to be destroyed, God forbid.[409]

May HaShem join our hearts one to the other[410] and bring unity to Israel. Amen, so may it be God's will.

406 Lit., "Throw a stone after the fallen man." Rashi explains, "We should push a stone [upon him] so that he not be redeemed."

407 [The Talmud concludes that even the wicked will serve God in the future.]

408 *Pardes Yosef*, vol. 2, p. 102a, s.v. *u'mi'kan*.

409 Ibid., vol. 3, p. 236b, s.v. *be'inyan*.

410 Based on *Yechezkel* 37:17.

VII Refuting the Antagonists

An attempt to censor our author

נא When I reached this point in the printing of my book, I was forced to leave the capital [Budapest] (until HaShem granted me the opportunity to return). I went to a beautiful community whose members are great Torah scholars and God-fearing men. There was also a study house (*beit midrash*) there with *chassidim* and men of deed. For the few weeks I stayed there I decided to pray with the members of this *beit midrash*, because I very much enjoyed their company. The brilliant rabbi and *av beit din shlita* granted me the honor of delivering a sermon in the synagogue. However, there was one *chassid* who heard about my sermons in the capital and knew that I support and defend *aliyah* and the building of our Holy Land. He zealously tried to prevent me from speaking, because he was afraid that I would express this lofty idea and prove that we have a great obligation to build our Land. Satan's scheme succeeded, and I did not speak the first Sabbath I spent there.

Afterwards, however, the city elders asked me once again to deliver a sermon, and I obliged. On the third Sabbath, I addressed a large gathering and spoke about our holy nation's predicament here in Europe. I poured out my soul and spoke so emotionally that the entire audience wept. I concluded that the only way we can recover from this bitter exile is to return to our Holy Land the moment HaShem delivers us from distress, and that each and every Jew has a sacred obligation to strive with all his might to leave the lands of exile and return to his mother's bosom, *Eretz Yisrael*. I explained that HaShem brought this bitter exile in order to awaken us from the slumber of exile and motivate us to yearn and desire to return to our forefathers' inheritance.

I also mentioned what I cited above[411] in the name of the brilliant and pious Nefesh Chayah quoting "the holy angel of the Lord of Hosts," our master, R. Eliyahu of Greiditz *zt"l*. He explains that great *tzaddikim* oppose this matter only because of the strengthening of the *kelipot* (evil forces). The *kelipot* try to prevent the return to the Land because they know that this will cause their downfall. Now, this holy *gaon* said this at his time, when the Jews dwelt peacefully in exile. All the more so today, when the flood of exile has assailed us with numerous waves and violent storm winds, can we possibly

411 P. 15.

be consoled by anything other than our beloved Land? Nonetheless, even today, some people oppose this matter! Can the human intellect comprehend this? The only explanation is that it stems from the strengthening of the *kelipot*, may the Merciful One protect us.❖

❖ Tangentially, I will cite here a short letter I recently received from the brilliant and holy rabbi of a large city here in Hungary. A student of mine fell ill while serving in the army and was taken to the local hospital. I asked this rabbi to keep a watchful eye over him. He responded:

> After conferring greetings and blessings, I will now respond to his honorable letter.
>
> I immediately sent someone over to the hospital, but even after a thorough investigation, your student's whereabouts are regretfully unknown. I sincerely share in his honor's sorrow and in the pain of thousands and tens of thousands of Jews who have been exiled from their homes. The Talmud states: "*And my eye will weep sorely* (ודמוע תדמע) *and run down with tears* (דמעה) (*Yirmiyah* 13:17). Why three tears? One for the First Temple, one for the Second Temple, and one for the Jews ***who were exiled from their place***" (*Chagigah* 5b). Woe to us that this has occurred in our times. May HaShem have mercy on the survivors and gather our dispersed ones, not to their original place in exile, but to our forefathers' Land, which is the desirable Land.

This *gaon*'s words, which came from the depths of his pure heart, effected my emotions so much that I wept sorely, and my eyes shed endless tears.

Observe his closing remark: We do not look forward to returning to our original place in exile, but to our forefathers' Land, which is the desirable Land. Our wounds will not be healed any other way, and our nation, which has been broken into many pieces, will not be cured simply by remaining in its original place, hidden in the shadows of exile. King David referred to this when he said, *The Lord is the Builder of Jerusalem, He will gather the outcasts of Israel. He is the Healer of the brokenhearted and binds up their wounds* (*Tehillim* 147:2-3). That is to say, only building Jerusalem and ingathering the outcasts of Israel will cure the brokenhearted of Israel and bind up their wounds. Subsequently, I found this stated in *Midrash Tehillim* (17:4).

I already proved[412] from many statements of *Chazal* that the Holy

412 Pp. 4-5, 128-29, 161, 164.

These words made that *chassid* very angry, and he prevented me from leading the *Musaf* service the next Sabbath, which was the Sabbath before I had *yahrtzeit*.[414] As *gabbai* of the *beit midrash*, he said that someone else – a certain member of the community who takes precedence – had an obligation to lead the services. In the end, I found out that this was all fabricated. He was simply angry because of my sermon. Indeed, many people rebuked him for this (and behold, the next Sabbath they honored me to lead the blessing of the new month of Av and the *Musaf* service); but the damage was already done.

They refuse to accept the truth

Afterwards, on Monday of *parashat Matot-Mas'ei*, good tidings reached the *beit midrash*. There was a turn for the better in the world.[415] We all rejoiced, because we recognized this as the beginning of redemption. All of the *minyanim* omitted *Tachanun* [the prayer of supplication], because it was like a holiday. At that moment, we rejoiced like the Jews did at the time of Mordechai and Esther.

After all of the *minyanim* finished praying, we remained to discuss the situation. I stood among truly God-fearing men, both young and old, educated in the spirit of true *Chassidut*, offspring blessed by HaShem, with the image of God on their faces. I spoke up and said: Now that the redemption has begun, every Jew must know that he has an obligation to HaShem and His holy nation to leave the defiled

---

One Blessed be He awaits our initiative to return to our desirable Land. Then, He will bring our efforts to a successful end. Thus, after all that has happened to us, how can people still oppose this? It must be that the *kelipot* are gaining strength, as the godly Kabbalist, R. Eliyahu of Greiditz, asserts. We must strengthen ourselves with the help of He Who Possesses Strength, and raise a banner in the name of our God.[413] The *kelipot* will evaporate like smoke, and we will ascend and sanctify HaShem's name. Then, the following verse will be fulfilled through us, *Be strong, all you people of the land, says the Lord, and do, for I am with you, says the Lord of Hosts... And My spirit remains among you; do not fear* (*Chaggai* 2:4-5). Amen, so may it be God's will.

413 Based on *Tehillim* 20:6.

414 [Yiddish for "Year time." It refers to the anniversary of the death of a close relative. Customarily, a living relative leads the prayers on the day of the *yahrtzeit*, as well as on the Sabbath before.

415 [It is unclear to which event he is referring.]

land and yearn to return to our Holy Land. Then, our bitter exile will not have been in vain. However, if we remain here in the atmosphere of the lands of the nations, it will all have been for naught and to no avail.

One of the older listeners responded, "This is not true!" because his rebbe believes differently about *Eretz Yisrael*. He also said that the Hungarian Jews were saved because they did not join the movement to build the Land. It truly pains the heart to hear so many fools say that the Holy One Blessed be He had mercy on the Jews of Hungary because they despised the movement to build the Land and did not take part in it. May the Merciful One protect us from such an opinion. Notice how stubborn they are! One should not argue at all with people like these. Shlomo said about them, *Do not answer a fool according to his folly* (*Mishley* 26:4).

The young men agreed with that elder *chassid*, claiming, among other things, that we must not join the sinners of *Eretz Yisrael*. Every argument I presented failed to convince them. They had one answer: their rebbe is against it. I retorted that although their rebbe is indeed a great man among giants, the Rebbe of Gur is no less than him. He is a profound genius and a holy man of God. Thousands and tens of thousands of Torah scholars and men of deed find shelter under his wings. And he says that if many God-fearing, Orthodox Jews gather in *Eretz Yisrael* they will enhance the sanctity of the Land. Also, I recently heard that the brilliant and holy mentor of *Eretz Yisrael*, R. Yosef Chayim Sonnenfeld *z"l*, said the same thing to our brilliant and righteous master, R. Fischel Sofer Sussman *z"l*, rabbi and *av beit din* of the Orthodox community here. He commented on the verse *You shall see the goodness of Jerusalem* (*Tehillim* 128:5): ôIt is insufficient to criticize the Land and its inhabitants from the outside. Instead, you must enter the Land and enhance its sanctity."[416] Thus, it is obvious that the claim of these *chassidim* is invalid. But they were still not convinced.

Why do people oppose aliyah?

Truthfully, there is reason to lament, for these people are truly upright, righteous, and loyal to HaShem... But, they stubbornly refuse to budge on this lofty issue. All of the *tzaddikim* whom I quoted at the beginning of this book, all of the proofs, and even the Rebbe of Gur are not adequate witnesses for them. The only way

416 See *Eileh Mas'ei*, cited below (p. 506).

to explain this is as R. Eliyahu of Greiditz does: The *kelipot* (evil forces) are gaining strength, and they prevent us from returning to *Eretz Yisrael*, because they know that our return to the Land is their downfall.

Or, we can explain this based on what the brilliant *gadol ha'dor*, the Rebbe of Lublin, said to one of the leaders of Hungarian Jewry: "You are still eating 'fish of light.'"[417] May HaShem help them continue to eat "fish of light" forever, but they should be aware of the suffering of the [rest of the] world. They should also be aware of the fact that the holy man of Israel, the Rebbe of Unsdorf, advocated building the *yishuv* because of Israel's suffering.[418]

Alternatively, people may oppose this matter because of some ulterior motive. They are certainly no better than the spies. The Torah testifies that the spies were upright men, but they were eventually ensnared on the issue of *Eretz Yisrael*, because of selfish concerns.[419]

The *Midrash* says that Moshe Rabbeinu was confident that he was not demanding his own needs, only those of Israel (*Devarim Rabbah* 11:2).[420] The *Midrash* also states:

> The Holy One Blessed be He said: "The righteous Moshe gave of himself for the Children of Israel." He could have lived for as long as he wanted, for the Holy One Blessed be He said to him, *Take vengeance...on the Midyanites; afterwards you will be gathered to your people* (*BeMidbar* 31:2). The Holy One linked his death to the vengeance against Midyan. This demonstrates Moshe's virtuousness, for he did not say, "I will prevent the Children of Israel from taking vengeance, so that I can live..."
>
> Even though he was told that he would die, he did not say, "Why should I take vengeance on Midyan? Tomorrow I shall die!" Instead, he eagerly approached the task. Yehoshua, however, did not do this. When he came to fight the 31 kings, he said, "If I kill them, I will immediately die, just like Moshe did." What did he do? He began with one king and dragged

417 See pp. 318-19.

418 ❖ See above, preface (p. 30).

419 ❖ See above, [second] introduction (p. 49).

420 [*Etz Yosef* explains that when Moshe asked HaShem to forgive the Jewish people after the Sin of the Calf he was confident that he was doing so for Israel's sake and not for personal reasons (i.e., so that he could be the leader of a nation).]

out the wars, as it says, *Yehoshua made war a long time* (*Yehoshua* 11:18). (*BeMidbar Rabbah* 22:2,6)

Thus, even though Yehoshua was perfectly righteous, the verse accuses him of delaying Israel's entry into the Land for selfish reasons. Therefore, it is completely obvious that one should not believe that today's antagonists are free of selfish motives. They fool themselves into thinking that they act for the sake of Heaven, but they are affected by their hidden motives.[421] This is clear and true, in accordance with the truth of the Torah.

There have always been opponents of this sacred cause

The incident in which I was deprived of performing a sacred service is nothing new. Such things already happened to our ancestors who devoted themselves to cherishing the Land. Our mentor, the Kaftor VaFerach, who was one of the Tosafists...from the generation of the Rashba and the Rosh, devoted 27 years to the love of the Land and its settlement, as he writes: "I spent 22 years[422] in the Galilee investigating and searching, and another five years in the lands of the rest of the tribes. I did not stop spying the Land for even a moment. Blessed is He Who gives assistance."[423] In the introduction to his work he writes: "I will ignore the zealous ones who seek excuses [to oppose me]. I would be surprised if this generation is free of such phenomenon, whether publicly and openly, or secretly and privately." Thus, even then, some people stubbornly opposed the sacred and lofty endeavor of settling the Land. They also opposed anyone who wrote about it, even if the author was the greatest *gadol*, like the Kaftor VaFerach. Elsewhere, while discussing Beit She'an, he complains: "There are newcomers here, supposedly knowledgeable people, who are dissuading the women and the simpletons from dwelling here. They say to them that this may not be *Eretz Yisrael*, but *Chutz LaAretz*."[424] Thus, he complained that they disrupted his task. He tried to inspire the masses to love the Land, but these people opposed him and tried to make them despise it.

421 ❖ See what I cited above (p. 50) from R. Yeshayah Muskat of Praga *z"l*. Also see what our mentor, the Divrei Chayim, thinks about those who acted "for the sake of Heaven" in his days; all the more so in our days (*Divrei Chayim*, vol. 1, *Choshen Mishpat* 25).

422 Our version (Jerusalem: A. M. Luntz, 5657 [1897]) reads: "...approximately two years."

423 *Kaftor VaFerach*, chap. 11.

424 Ibid., chap. 7.

I found the same thing in the introduction to *Mitzvat Yeshivat Eretz Yisrael*, by the great *gaon*, our master and teacher, R. Yonah Dov Blumberg of Dvinsk.[425] This booklet was printed in Vilna in 5658 [1898] with the approbations of the *gedolim* of his generation. He was an ordinary man, a lumber merchant, who wrote this wonderful book for the sake of Heaven. He writes there:

> I imagined that everyone agreed on (this sacred issue) and that none of my brethren in the House of Israel would think otherwise... To my astonishment, I saw that my thoughts were incorrect (for many of our brethren are very far from this viewpoint)... Many even have the audacity to widen their mouths and say unrepeatable things. More than once I got into verbal arguments with these "big mouths." Logical reasoning does not effect them, only the "verbal staff" and contentious rebuke.[426]

He also writes that more than once the hand of fate brought him into a discussion with those whom HaShem blessed with wealth and wisdom. When he heard their chatter, which would irritate any good-hearted person, he was unable to tolerate it, and his health suffered greatly from this. He cites *Tana DeVei Eliyahu* which states that this same sin prevailed in the era of the kings: "The inferior [scholar] became jealous of the superior one, and said to him, 'Even though you concur with the *halachah* and I do not, let your words be nullified and mine established, even if it destroys the entire world'" (*Eliyahu Rabbah* 6:9). He writes that incidents like this occurred throughout his journey on the path of the love of holiness. He constantly felt intense sorrow and bitterness, and sometimes even anger, pain, depression, and anguish.[427]

The mentor of the entire Diaspora, the *gaon* of Kutno, writes in his approbation to R. Hirsch Kalischer's *Derishat Tzion*, "Do not become disheartened nor discouraged by the words of the antagonists, for they speak out of ignorance."[428] This shows that many people opposed him on this issue.

Thus, I have demonstrated that there is nothing new under the

425 ❖ See above (pp. 230, 234, 236).
426 *Mitzvat Yeshivat Eretz Yisrael*, introduction, p. 7, s.v. *aval* (end).
427 Ibid., s.v. *hineih ki* (middle).
428 See above, p. 3.

sun,[429] and that my lot is no worse than that of my predecessors, who were much greater than me. Now I will no longer be surprised at those who arrogantly oppose me because of my sacred task. None of this will dissuade me from my work, since I found assistance and support from our earlier and later Rabbis (as I cited above). I will draw strength from the hope that there are also pure-hearted men who will say to me, "Well-done!" and who will encourage my work. I hope that they will recognize its great importance, because the *kelipah* has grown so strong that it sways even the hearts of the *tzaddikim* to nullify this good (as I cited above[430] in the name of the godly Kabbalist from Greiditz *z"l*). *

---

* In the sermon I delivered here in the Linat HaTzedek Synagogue, I explained King David's statement *Do good, in Your favor, to Zion; build the walls of Jerusalem. Then You will desire sacrifices of righteousness, burnt offering and whole burnt offering. Then bullocks will go up upon Your altar* (*Tehillim* 51:20-21). This is difficult! The Talmud asserts that HaShem is not impressed by big sacrifices (*Shavuot* 15a), for "whether one does a lot or a little, the important thing is to direct one's heart to the Heavens" (*Berachot* 5b). If so, what does *Then bullocks will go up upon Your altar* mean? It seems as if David wants to bribe God, as it were, with big sacrifices, like bullocks.

To answer this, I will preface with the words of our holy Rebbe of Lublin *zt"l* on the verse *With this shall Aharon come into the holy place: with a young bullock for a sin offering* (*VaYikra* 16:3). It is well known that the Jewish nation's existence depended on the service of the High Priest in the Holy of Holies on *Yom Kippur*. If he performed the service properly, the Jews ascended and succeeded in every possible way. However, if his service was blemished and unfit, God forbid, they descended. Therefore, Satan and his associates lay in wait to somehow blemish the High Priest's service. The High Priest had to gird his loins and strengthen himself in order to conquer the evil forces and prevent them from causing any damage to his work. He needed great strength for this.

Now, it is well known that the strongest animal is a bullock. Thus, the verse says, *With this shall Aharon come into the holy place: with a young bullock for a sin offering*. This means that Aharon had to come into the holy place with the strength of a young bullock in

429 Based on *Kohelet* 1:9.
430 P. 15.

Do not answer a fool according to his folly

נב In the second edition of *Shimru Mishpat*, the brilliant Kabbalist, R. Akiva Yosef *z"l* (author of *Lev HaIvri*), recounts the following incident:

> While I was involved in the matter of settling *Eretz Yisrael* – to find a place for HaShem in the Land, a habitation for the Mighty One of Ya'akov[434] – I traversed the borders of *Eretz Yisrael*. As I rode my donkey from Tzanan to Jerusalem (may it be rebuilt and established speedily in our days. Amen), I passed through Binyamin's portion. My heart was humming as I meditated,[435] and it appeared that an elderly, respectable

---

order to conquer the sin that ôcrouches at the door"[431] and tries to cause the *tzaddik* to fail at his task.[432]

I already explained that whenever individual Jews devoted themselves to raising Zion from the dust and building the Land, they came up against opposition and many obstacles. Nevertheless, the complete Jew must strengthen his heart, as the *gaon* of Kutno writes, "Do not become disheartened nor discouraged by the words of the antagonists, for they speak out of ignorance."[433] He must realize that this is Satan's doing, as the godly *gaon* of Greiditz writes.

Thus, King David says, *Do good, in Your favor, to Zion; build the walls of Jerusalem*. When HaShem wants to build Zion and Jerusalem, He arouses men to devote themselves to this task. At the same time, however, Satan sets up antagonists and obstacles to prevent it. When this happens, *Then You* [HaShem] *will desire sacrifices of righteousness, burnt offering, and whole burnt offering*. That is to say, just like these offerings are completely burnt up on the altar, so too, the ones who work to build the Land must dedicate all their strengths, all their souls, and their entire lives to this task. *Then bullocks will go up upon Your altar*. This means that they must strengthen themselves like a bullock to overcome all the obstacles and hindrances that stand in the way of this sacred task. For, this task is as important in HaShem's eyes as an altar. Then, their toil will be considered as *a burnt offering and a whole burnt offering*.

431 I.e., the forces of evil; based on *BeReishit* 4:7.
432 *Zichron Zot, Acharei Mot*.
433 See above, p. 3.
434 Based on *Tehillim* 132:5.
435 ❖ Based on *Tehillim* 4:5.

man was approaching me. He said, "You want to settle *Eretz Yisrael* for the sinners and the detestable ones, together with reckless hooligans?" I was completely astounded. I stared at him penetratingly and said, "It seems to me that you are the ministering angel of Edom with the well-known name [Sama'el]. Previously, you were an elderly, foolish king. Now, there is no king in France[436] and you have remained an old fool; and the verse says, *Do not answer a fool according to his folly* (*Mishley* 26:4)." Then, I continued on my way, singing my song.[437]

He explains that he composed a song to arouse his heart for the sacred endeavor of settling *Eretz Yisrael*, so that he would not become disheartened by the pursuers, oppressors, wicked ones, and pseudo-saints.

This coincides with what I wrote above[438] about the claim of the foolish *chassidim* here in Hungary. They say that God's wrath went forth against the Jews of Slovakia and Poland because they engaged in building and settling the Land, while the Jews of Hungary were spared because they refused to participate in this. Woe to the ears that have heard such things, and woe to the generation which has become so foolish and has been raised and educated with such futile teachings. How can they make such a distorted statement about thousands and tens of thousands of Jews who were murdered for the sanctification of God's name? And how can they degrade the *mitzvah* of *Yishuv Eretz Yisrael*, which *Chazal* elevate and equate to the entire Torah?[439] There is no response to this except, *Do not answer a fool according to his folly* (*Mishley* 26:4), as the wisest of all men said. May HaShem forgive them.

The "prohibition" of speaking about Yishuv Eretz Yisrael

נג This past summer, 5703 [1943], while I dwelt here in the capital [Budapest], there was an unusually severe heat wave. In order to breathe some crisp, pure air, I spent a few weeks in the ôVarush Meyerö Orthodox hospital, which stands atop a mountain. On the Sabbath of *parashat Re'eh*, some people implored me to impart some words of reproof relevant to the time of the year (that Sabbath, they were blessing the New Month of Elul) and relevant to the

436 [Apparently, France was the seat of Edom (Rome, Christendom) at the time].
437 *Shimru Mishpat Tanina* (Jerusalem: 5633 [1873]), *Pizmonim*, p. 43b.
438 P. 349.
439 *Sifrei, Re'eh* 28 (on *Devarim* 12:29).

birthpangs of *Mashiach* which we had recently experienced. Two Torah scholars, sons of saints, begged me profusely to accept, because at first I had adamantly refused to accept this honor (for my own hidden reason). But, they beseeched me to no end, and I was no longer able to refuse. Before I rose to speak, these two scholars made a condition: I may not mention *Yishuv Eretz Yisrael*, and if I do they will not come to hear me.* I said to one of the scholars (who is truly great in Torah; he is the rabbi of a large city, a pious man, a complete *tzaddik*, an elder who aged with piety and innocence, and a man who walks with innocence both in and out of his house): I know that you made this condition innocently, but I want to analyze whether or not you are right about refusing to hear a public sermon on the love of the Land and the great obligation we have towards it.

---

* Does the Torah not don sackcloth on account of this? Is *Eretz Yisrael* – our mother – not disgraced and insulted by this? Her sons insult her greatly by interfering with anyone who wants to raise his voice and inspire the masses to strengthen her and raise her from the dust, as the Holy One Blessed be He has commanded us.[440] Today's pseudo-saints defame and degrade her so much that it is forbidden to speak in public for the sake of *Yishuv HaAretz*. And if, by chance, someone courageously and fearlessly states the truth as it is, they say that it is forbidden to listen to his sermon.

With my own ears, I heard not one, but many people say that thousands and tens of thousands of Jews were punished because they engaged in the settlement and rebuilding of the Land. Is this not blasphemy, an insult to our holy Torah? Does this not cause grief and sorrow to the holy *Shechinah*, which is Kingship (*Malchut*), and to *Eretz Yisrael*, the mother of Israel, which is also Kingship?[441] Woe to the ears which have heard this. It is obviously a grave sin to even utter such things.

Every intelligent person with a brain in his head will realize that this is exactly what happened with Yehoshua and Calev. They were not afraid to declare the truth in public, opposing the entire congregation, including the princes who "sanctified" themselves by disrupting and preventing Israel from entering *Eretz Yisrael*.

The brilliant Kabbalist, R. Akiva Yosef *z"l*, cites the *Zohar* (3:158a)

440 ❖ I proved this above at length from the words of *Chazal* and from the profoundly holy *Rishonim* and *Acharonim*.

441 ❖ As I explained above (p. 316).

We must speak about redemption

I told him that I would prove that such talk is Satan's way of blinding us (may the Merciful One protect us). Who is greater than our mentor, the author of *Tzemach HaShem LaTzvi*, one of the foremost disciples of our master, R. Baer [of Mezhibuz] *zt"l*? He was a holy and awe-inspiring man, as is evident from his holy work. He comments on [Moshe's statement to HaShem], *Behold the Children of Israel have not listened to me; how, then, will Pharaoh listen to me?* (*Shemot* 6:12):

> This is difficult! The Children of Israel did not listen to him because of their spiritual anguish and hard work.[443] But Pharaoh, who did not have these problems, might listen to him?
>
> We may answer as follows. Seemingly, there was no reason to send a messenger to the Children of Israel, for they would certainly want HaShem to redeem them. So why did HaShem send Moshe altogether? The explanation is based on the verse *My word that emanates from My mouth will not return to Me empty* (*Yeshayah* 55:11). The Ramban explains that for every good decree that comes from the mouth of the Holy One Blessed be He, a symbolic action must be done here on earth so that the decree can be fulfilled without hindrance.[444] Now, HaShem knew that Pharaoh would not want to listen to the command [to free

---

which states that the spies claimed that they could concentrate better on Torah and divine service in the desert because they received Manna and were not busy making a living. If they would enter the Land, however, they would have to work the ground, and this would disrupt their divine service.[442] Yehoshua and Calev stood up against them and cried out, *If the Lord desires us, He will bring us into this Land... Only, do not rebel against the Lord..., the Lord is with us* (*BeMidbar* 14:8-9). Afterwards it says, *But the entire congregation said to stone them with stones* (ibid. 14:10). Are they not doing the same thing today? But, the verse continues, *And the Glory of the Lord appeared in the Tent*, upon which Rashi comments that the cloud came down to save Yehoshua and Calev. The same will happen whenever a person defends the honor of the Land and refuses to listen to the words of the grumblers, saying, *Do not answer a fool according to his folly* (*Mishley* 26:4). A word to the wise is sufficient.

442 *Tosafot Ben Yechiel* on *Eliyahu Rabbah* 1:2, s.v. *lishmor et derech*.

443 See *Shemot* 6:9.

444 Ramban, *BeReishit* 12:6.

the Jews from Egypt]. If so, HaShem's words would return empty! Therefore, He commanded Moshe to tell these words of redemption to the Children of Israel first, for Israel would certainly listen. By listening, the Jews would perform a symbolic action [which would ensure] that Pharaoh would also listen. Moshe understood that this was HaShem's intention, and he, therefore, wondered, "Since the Children of Israel have not listened to me as a symbolic action, how then will Pharaoh listen to me?"[445]

Behold, when Moshe came to the people of Israel, the time of their redemption had already arrived.[446] Nevertheless, since the Attribute of Justice wanted to hinder the redemption (as is well known), Moshe had to perform a symbolic action first, in order to abolish all the accusers and obstacles. The action was that Moshe would speak about the redemption to the Children of Israel, and they would listen to and accept his words. In the end, the verse testifies that they actually did listen, as it is written, *Moshe and Aharon went and gathered together all the elders of the Children of Israel. And Aharon spoke all the words which the Lord had spoken to Moshe... And the people believed; and when they heard that the Lord had remembered the Children of Israel and that He had seen their affliction, they bowed their heads and prostrated themselves* (*Shemot* 4:29-31). Indeed, the Children of Israel were then redeemed from the bondage of Egypt. This happened because they listened to Moshe when he spoke to them about the redemption. The symbolic action was performed in order to prevent the accusers and adversaries from nullifying the Holy One's decree, so that the word that emanated from His mouth would not return empty.

Now, let us apply this to our issue. We have already reached the era of *in its time* (*Yeshayah* 60:22), and the set time for redemption has already arrived.[447] The only thing that holds us back is the Attribute of Justice.[448] Therefore, we, too, must speak to the Children of Israel

445 The question, but not the answer, appears in *Tzemach HaShem LaTzvi*, p. 138, sec. 81.

446 ❖ See *Midrash Rabbah* on the verse *The sound of my Beloved knocking* (*Shir HaShirim* 5:2)...

447 ❖ I proved this above (pp. 42-43, 155-56) from the words of *Chazal*.

448 ❖ I demonstrated this above (p. 186, also see 380-81) from the Talmud (*Sanhedrin* 97b) and *Midrash* (*Shir HaShirim Rabbah* 2:7) which interpret the verse, *Until it pleases* (*Shir HaShirim* 2:7), to mean, "Until it pleases the Attribute of Justice."

publicly about the redemption, about [the need] to return to our beloved Land, and about other things related to Israel's dwelling in *Eretz Yisrael*. If the Children of Israel listen to and accept these words, they will be performing a symbolic action which will silence and abolish all of the accusers. Then, all wickedness will vanish like smoke,[449] and Israel will leave the exile with a mighty hand. This is what happened during the exodus from Egypt, because the people listened to Moshe when he spoke to them about the redemption. We should do the same today, for every Torah scholar who delivers sermons has a spark of Moshe in him, as is well known...[450]

Therefore, every Torah scholar has an obligation to speak publicly about the love of the Land and about entering it. And every Jew has an obligation to go to the sermon, listen to it, and accept its words. This will draw the redemption closer.

After all of this, my friend (who has been my confidant and colleague from youth; both of us drank from the wellsprings of our master, the author of *Arugat HaBosem*) told me that if I speak about the positive commandment of *Yishuv Eretz Yisrael*, he will not come to hear my sermon. I wonder if this is the truth!

We must inspire the Jews to love Eretz Yisrael

I also told him about the angel's revelation to our master, the Beit Yosef, regarding Moshe's reason for sending the spies. At that time, the people of Israel were not worthy of entering the Land. Therefore, Moshe sent out men expecting that they would return and recount the praises of the Land. This would arouse the people of Israel to desire and love the Holy Land. Then, by virtue of this desire alone, they would deserve to inherit the Land.[451]

Now, why should we not do the same? We, too, must speak publicly about the praises and virtues of the Land, and about the derogation of the lands of exile, in order to inspire our Jewish brethren to desire and love *Eretz Yisrael*. The time for redemption has arrived, but we must become worthy of it. Thus, if we desire and long for the Land we will be worthy to enter it, and we will truly deserve the final redemption. But, we will [only] achieve this goal if the leaders deliver public sermons about loving *Eretz Yisrael*. Hence, I cannot comprehend how his eminence can say that it is forbidden to preach

449 From the *Ata Kadosh* blessing of the High Holiday prayers.

450 See *Zohar* 3:27b; *Tikkunei Zohar, Tikkun* 69, p. 112a; *Sha'arei Zohar, Shabbat* 101b; *BeReishit Rabbah* 56:7.

451 ❖ I cited this above [in its entirety] (p. 258).

in public, or listen to a sermon, about the positive commandment of *Yishuv Eretz Yisrael*.

Ya'arot Devash states:

> What a (great) *mitzvah* it is to desire to go to *Eretz Yisrael*! The Shelah and *Sefer Yere'im* teach that a person should constantly have in his heart a desire and love for *Eretz Yisrael*, as it is written, "And your eyes and your heart shall be there all the days."[452] If a man has all that he desires, he should always remember that he is lacking something, because he is not in *Eretz Yisrael*... He should be sad about that, for the most important thing is missing.[453]

The way to defeat the accusers: Speak to the Children of Israel that they should travel

I also told him something I saw in a particular book (I am now writing without books, so I am unable to specify the source) on the verse *The Lord said to Moshe, "Why do you cry out to Me? Speak to the Children of Israel that they should travel"* (*Shemot* 14:15). Our holy Rebbe, Sar Shalom of Belz *z"l*, asked our mentor, the Noam Elimelech *z"l*, in a dream: What kind of question is this – *Why are you crying out to Me*?! At that moment, the people of Israel were in dire straits. The sea was before them; the Egyptians were behind them; and snakes and scorpions were on the sides. What else was Moshe to do if not cry out to HaShem for help? R. Elimelech answered with a story.[454]

Once, a certain queen went into labor. When the sorcerers, who hated the king, heard about this, they cast a spell on the queen making her unable to give birth. Great howling filled the king's house, for she remained in labor many days. There was a wise man there who advised the king to spread a rumor throughout the kingdom that his wife, the queen, had given birth to a healthy baby boy. "When the sorcerers hear this," he said, "they will assume that their spell did not work, and they will remove it. Once the spell is removed, the queen will be able to give birth." The king did this immediately, and it actually worked.

The same thing happened during the exodus from Egypt. When the Children of Israel reached the Red Sea and needed the great

452 Based on I *Melachim* 9:3.

453 *Ya'arot Devash*, beginning of *Derashah* 14.

454 This is cited in *Tiferet Yonatan*, by R. Yonatan Eybeshitz, (Lemburg: 5633 [1873]), p. 17a.

miracle of the splitting of the sea, the accusers rose up against them (as is well known)[455] and hindered the miracle. Thus, when Moshe cried out to HaShem, the Holy One Blessed be He told him to stop, for, on the contrary, crying will make the accusers assume that HaShem has not yet decided to save Israel, and they will continue to accuse. It is better to simply *speak to the Children of Israel that they should travel.* For, once the accusers see that Moshe Rabbeinu commanded Israel to travel into the sea, they will understand that HaShem already decided to perform the miracle of the splitting of the sea, and they will stop accusing. Then, the sea will actually split. This is the answer that the Noam Elimelech gave our mentor, Sar Shalom of Belz, in a nighttime vision.

The same is true today. We are in labor, but have no strength to give birth, because the accusers are trying to delay the redemption. Therefore, we must follow R. Elimelech's advice and *speak to the Children of Israel that they should travel* to *Eretz Yisrael* and disregard the lands of exile. Then, the accusers will understand and conclude that HaShem has already decided to redeem us, and they will stop accusing. Thus, the true redemption will arrive without any obstacles whatsoever.

Now, how can the pseudo-saints not be ashamed to say that it is forbidden to preach or listen to a sermon about going to *Eretz Yisrael*? I am utterly astounded! The only explanation is that the Adversary blinds them (may the Merciful One save us)! He wants to prevent the redemption with all his might, because he knows that he will fall when the redemption comes.[456]

We must not blindly follow the tzaddikim who oppose aliyah

This is what I said to my friend and colleague (a truly complete *tzaddik* who speaks innocently), and he could not answer me. He remained silent for a while and then said that my proofs are true and correct. He admitted that he never dealt with this question nor examined the issues. Rather, he innocently followed some of the *tzaddikim* of the generation who opposed this matter.

I responded by citing our mentor, the Maharam Schick, on the verse *And I will betroth you to Me in faithfulness, and you will know the Lord* (*Hoshea* 2:22).[457] He explains that if a Torah scholar says something contrary to the words of *Chazal*, we need not believe him

455 See *Zohar* 2:170b; *Yalkut Reuveni, BeShalach*, verse *chel Paroh*.

456 ❖ I mentioned this above (p. 15) in the name of several true *tzaddikim*.

457 ❖ I mentioned this above, at the end of the second introduction (p. 59).

blindly. In fact, it is forbidden to follow his opinion. I subsequently found the same idea in the sacred work, *Sur MeRa VaAsei Tov*,[458] by our holy Rebbe of Zhidachov *z"l* (may his merit protect us).

In addition, I already[459] cited the *Midrash* which states that Moshe Rabbeinu was the only one who cared selflessly for the needs of Israel. Yehoshua, however, was on a lower level and worried about his own needs more than those of Israel. If so, what are we, the people of this generation, to say? Above,[460] I cited the *Yerushalmi* (*Gittin* 6:7) which describes how each successive generation falls from the level of the previous one. Certainly, then, we have fallen greatly from the level of Yehoshua's generation! Furthermore, if the spies, who were *tzaddikim*, slandered *Eretz Yisrael* because of selfish motives, then our generation is certainly [capable of doing so].

Turning a mitzvah into a sin and a sin into a mitzvah

Moshe said [regarding the episode of the spies], *But you* [Israel] *did not want to go up, and you rebelled* (ותמרו) *against the word of the Lord your God* (*Devarim* 1:26). I explain this as follows. *You did not want to go up*, because of your selfish motives. *And you rebelled* (ותמרו) *against the word of the Lord*: ותמרו can also mean transformation, as in the verses *He shall not switch it nor exchange* (ימיר) *it* (*VaYikra* 27:10), and "...in lieu of (מר) a slaughtered animal" (*Chullin* 94a). That is to say, you transform *the word of the Lord* – i.e., HaShem's *mitzvah* – into a sin, and the sin into a *mitzvah*. You take the *mitzvah* of dwelling in the Land, which is a very valuable *mitzvah* according to all the *poskim*,[461] and turn it into a sin. You say that it is forbidden to speak about it in public, and you persecute anyone who devotes himself to it. Furthermore, you take the sin – that is, neglecting and distancing yourself from this *mitzvah* and refusing to support it both physically and monetarily (which is truly a tremendous sin, as *Chazal* state clearly) – and turn it into a *mitzvah*. Thus, the verse says that not only did you refuse to ascend to *Eretz Yisrael*, but you also distorted the words of the living God, turning a *mitzvah* into a sin and a sin into a *mitzvah*.

In their defense, the antagonists say that they oppose this matter because the builders are improper Jews. I already[462] explained at

458 (Lublin: 5672 [1912]), sec. *VaAsei Tov*, p. 45, s.v. *ve'od*.
459 Pp. 350-51.
460 P. 51.
461 ❖ As I proved above at length (pp. 232-39).
462 Pp. 167-75.

length that this is not a good enough excuse. I cited the Talmud's statement: "Why do you involve yourself with the Merciful One's hidden matters? Do as you are commanded..." (*Berachot* 10a). I also quoted the holy men from Gur[463] and Jerusalem[464] who say that if many Orthodox Jews join this undertaking they will enhance the sanctity of the Land. I already discussed this at length, so there is no need to reiterate. The truth is that all of the antagonist's claims are nonsense and have no validity whatsoever. May HaShem help every single Jew recognize the truth and accept it from whence it came. Amen, so may it be God's will.

A great chassidic master agrees that the redemption will occur naturally

נר On Monday of *parashat Eikev*, in the summer of 5703 [1943], I went with my friend and confidant, the famous *gaon*, the outstanding teacher, the great judge of the Orthodox community here, our honorable master and mentor, ***R. Yisrael Veltz*** *shlita*, to greet the great rabbi and foremost *tzaddik* of the generation, ***our revered master and mentor, the holy man of God, R. Ahara'le*** of Belz *shlita*. May the Omnipresent assist him, and may his crown forever blossom by virtue of the fact that he encamped in the capital city[465] after the terrible events and immense dangers that he experienced (due to the sins of the generation). HaShem had compassion on him, and he escaped from the decrees in Poland like a brand plucked from the fire.[466]

Before we entered the inner chamber [to see the Rebbe], we greeted his younger brother, the holy *gaon*, ***R. Mota'le*** *shlita*, *av beit din* of ***Bilgoria***. I knew him when I was young, during those peaceful years before World War I, when, in the months of Elul and Tishrei, I used to sit in the shadow of [his father], "the holy of holies," our master and teacher, ***R. Yisachar Baer*** [of Belz] *zt"l*. I also knew [these two brothers] from when they resided in Rutzfort during the first World War.

This holy *gaon* [R. Mota'le] spoke to us about current events; about the dreadful condition of Polish Jewry, which he had seen with his own eyes; about all that happened to him there, and how HaShem miraculously saved him. In the course of the conversation, the topic turned to *Eretz Yisrael*, and R. Yisrael Veltz told him that I was

463 See p. 312.

464 I.e., Rav Yosef Chayim Sonnenfeld. See p. 349.

465 Based on *BeReishit* 33:18. [I.e., May God reward him for honoring us with his presence despite all that he has been through.]

466 Based on *Zecharyah* 3:2.

writing a book on this issue. R. Mota'le then said that the holy rabbi, the mentor of Israel, the godly *Maggid* and *Admor* of Trisk *zt"l*, writes in his holy work, *Magen Avraham*, that the future redemption will occur naturally. Thus, we must prepare whatever we can through natural means, and HaShem will bring our efforts to a successful end.[467] I am greatly distressed that I do not have this sacred volume in order to see his holy words inside. Nonetheless, I trust the testimony of the holy R. Mota'le.

I especially cherish these words of the holy man of Trisk, because I am a prominent disciple of our holy mentor, the brilliant teacher of Israel, the *Admor* of Zavna, author of Responsa *Yad Shalom*,[468] who himself was a *chassid* of Trisk. For several years he stayed with the Rebbe of Trisk to drink from the waters of his well.[469] Thus, I am a disciple of a disciple of the Rebbe of Trisk. Blessed is HaShem Who provided me with a "redeemer" who concurs with my opinion, a great man like the Maggid of Trisk *z"l*.

A wonderful story about the Rebbe of Trisk

Now, in order to help the masses appreciate the greatness of the Rebbe of Trisk *z"l*, I will recount a story that we heard from R. Mota'le's holy mouth during that very same conversation. He heard it from his father, the mentor of Israel, R. Yisachar Baer *z"l*. The Maggid of Trisk was once in Krakow, and a certain woman came and asked the attendants to let her in to see the Rebbe. After much effort she was permitted to enter. When she came before him she said, "Rebbe, I owe his honor several hundred rubles. Many years ago the Rebbe was here and I asked him to bless me that I may be remembered for the good and have surviving offspring, for I was barren at the time. The Rebbe commanded me to give him a certain sum of money, but since I did not have the entire amount, the balance became a debt. I have not yet paid the debt because it is a long trip from here to the Rebbe's home, and I could not find anyone trustworthy enough with whom to send the money. When I heard that the Rebbe was here, I came to pay the debt myself, because his prayers bore fruits. HaShem has blessed me with proper, healthy sons, offspring blessed by HaShem with Torah and greatness." She

467 *Magen Avraham, VaEira*, s.v. *velakachti etchem*.

468 ❖ [R. Shalom David Unger], who was of very noble descent. He was the grandson and disciple of our mentor, the author of *Imrei Noam* from Dzykov, and the son-in-law of the holy R. Moshe'le of Razwadov.

469 [I.e., to learn Torah from him.]

then gave him several hundred rubles, which he accepted cordially and put into his pocket. With this, the woman went on her way.

The attendants who witnessed this began to talk among themselves, for they knew that their Rebbe, the Maggid, was never in Krakow before. ôThis woman must have made a mistake; she probably mistook him for a different Maggid. Do you think she remembered which Maggid was here the first time, whether it was the Maggid of Trisk or the Maggid of Kaznitz or some other Maggid? They are all the same to her. In any event, it is clear that it was not this Maggid. Therefore, he does not deserve the money. How, then, did he take it from this innocent woman, who was really not his debtor? Even a simple Jew would not do such a thing." (There is a well-known saying about the attendants of *tzaddikim*: Every attendant has a spark of Gaychazi in him).[470]

The righteous Maggid of Trisk realized what they were saying and told them the following incident about the Ba'al Shem Tov *z"l*. During his lifetime there were two, young Torah scholars who had a very hard time making a living. They used to trudge together from place to place and from door to door begging for charity. One day, one of them said to his friend: "Look, we toil all day long and end up with very little. I know how we can attain great relief and make an easy, plentiful, and honorable living." "How? Where? I definitely agree!" said his friend. "Quickly, tell me your idea, I cannot wait to hear it." The first one answered: "You have certainly heard of the famous Ba'al Shem Tov. Everyone longs to meet him. Therefore, I suggest that one of us pose as the Ba'al Shem, and the other as his attendant. Wherever we go we will first write a letter saying that our master, the Ba'al Shem, will be arriving on such-and-such a date, so that the people of the town can prepare a prominent place for his honor. Thus, word of his arrival will spread, people will gather from all over, and the *kvittlach*[471] and redemption money will come in abundantly. Then, we will truly prosper." When his friend heard this appropriate advice, he immediately agreed.

And so they did; and they grew, succeeded, and prospered. For, this Ba'al-Shem-Tov-impostor also performed miracles. Whenever he

470 [Gaychazi was the disgraceful attendant of the prophet Elisha. See II *Melachim* 4 and 5.]

471 Plural of *kvittle*, Yiddish for "a note." Customarily, a person would write his name on a slip of paper and submit it to a *tzaddik* so that he would pray for him.

blessed people – even those with the greatest problems, like a barren woman, a seriously ill person, or an imprisoned Jew – HaShem had compassion and saved them. It was amazing. Once, when the two scholars were alone, they spoke about this incredible phenomenon. They knew the truth, that he was not the real Ba'al Shem, so how could he perform miracles? They feared that perhaps it came from the evil forces (may the Merciful One protect us), and they began to regret the entire scheme (for they were men who feared sin). Afterwards, they began to think, "We have seen that Satan can perform miracles even through someone who is undeserving. Maybe the real Ba'al Shem Tov is no greater than us. Perhaps he also uses the powers of the evil forces, God forbid." Finally, they decided to stop their venture and travel to the real Ba'al Shem Tov, to observe his ways.

When they came before him, even before they uttered a sound, the Ba'al Shem Tov began to speak. "I know all that you have done, and if I did not have pity on your families, I would give you your just deserts. My powers enabled you to perform miracles. You see, I came into this world to strengthen the faith of the lowly masses of Israel. Therefore, the Holy One Blessed be He gave me the power to do miracles, because that is the only way to strengthen their faith.✧ Now, you posed as the Ba'al Shem and conferred blessings and salvations to the masses of Israel. Had these blessings not come true, it would have caused a great desecration of HaShem's name and it would have weakened the faith of the masses, because they did not know that you were an impostor. Therefore, I bestowed some of my powers onto you so that your words would come true and HaShem's name would be sanctified, even though you were not worthy of this."

This is what the Ba'al Shem Tov said to these two scholars, [continued the Rebbe of Trisk], and the same happened to me. Many years ago, an impostor came here, saying that he was the Maggid of Trisk, and gave a blessing to this woman in exchange for a few

---

✧ See *Maggid Meisharim*, where the angel tells our master, the Beit Yosef, that HaShem will grant him the ability to perform miracles so that the masses will believe in him.[472]

472 Introduction to *Maggid Meisharim* called *Azharot VeTikkunim VeSiyagim*, s.v. *shevach ha'rav*.

hundred rubles. In order to avoid desecrating HaShem's name, I bestowed my powers onto him and his blessing came true. Thus, this debt truly belongs to me.

Behold! This great man, our holy and godly mentor, our master and teacher, R. Yisachar Dov of Belz *z"l* – who was crowned by his entire generation as the foremost *tzaddik* of the generation – testifies that the Maggid of Trisk was on the same level as the Ba'al Shem Tov! This is really not surprising, because he was a third generation [disciple] of the Ba'al Shem Tov. He was the son of our mentor, R. Mota'le of Chernobyl, who was the son of our mentor, the author of *Me'or Einayim*, who was a disciple of the Ba'al Shem Tov.

This giant of giants asserts that the future redemption will occur naturally. Who, today, is noble and arrogant enough to contradict his opinion?! Besides which, the greatest *Rishonim*, profoundly holy men from earlier and later generations, agree with him, as I mentioned above.[473] Blessed is HaShem Who lead me onto the true path and aroused me to adhere to this opinion, after I delved deeply into this *halachah*.[474] Undoubtedly, the merit of my holy teacher, the author of *Yad Shalom*, whom I faithfully served,❖ helped me recognize the truth. For, as I mentioned above, my teacher *z"l* was a disciple of the Rebbe and Maggid of Trisk *z"l*. When he was seventeen years old, my rebbe became the *av beit din* of Rakov in Byelorussia. He was a renowned genius, and the people of that ancient city accepted him as their *av beit din*, even though he was so young. While he lived there, he clung to the Rebbe of Trisk, who also lived in Byelorussia. My teacher always mentioned his rebbe and told wondrous things about him. Now I have another iron pillar upon which to rely, my teacher's teacher. This gives me even more courage to study and preach this principle to the masses, for the sake of HaShem's glorious name and for the honor of our holy nation.

❖ When I was seventeen years old, he brought me into his house to teach his young, but clever, son who was engaged to the daughter of our master, the author of *Kedushat Yom Tov z"l*, of Sighet. I stayed in his house for a considerable amount of time and became close with him. He loved me dearly and "gorged me like an ox"[475] with Torah and *Chassidut*.

473 See chap. 2, pp. 134-40.

474 ❖ As I explained in the second introduction (p. 42).

475 Based on *Ketuvot* 50a.

The punishment for slandering the Land and its inhabitants

I am sure that if the Jewish masses, and even the Torah scholars, would be aware of everything I cited in this book, no small-minded individual would say that it is forbidden to preach publicly or hear a sermon on the topic of settling and building the Land. Unknowingly and innocently, they insult and harm our Holy Land and one of the 613 *mitzvot* of the Torah. Unwittingly, they prevent their fellow Jews from doing a *mitzvah*, thus violating one of the 24 things that incur excommunication.[476] This is especially true of such a valuable *mitzvah* like this one, which is equal to the entire Torah, as the *Sifrei* explains (*Re'eh* 28). May the good Lord forgive them. A word to the wise is sufficient.

Furthermore, I already cited[477] Maharam Chagiz's *Sefat Emet* which discusses the great punishment that awaits those who slander the inhabitants of *Eretz Yisrael*. HaShem decreed [after the sin of the spies] that anyone who spreads an evil report about the Land will be included in the punishment of, *And all who provoke Me shall not see it* (*BeMidbar* 14:23). The Maharam explains that this verse refers to the future. Anyone in subsequent generations who opposes *Eretz Yisrael* will be included in the punishment of the spies.[478]

The *Midrash* states:

> That generation (of the spies) could not taste any fruits of the Land. R. Akiva said: "When the merchants would uncover a basket of fruits from the Land, they [the Israelites] would die. Thus, it says, *Surely not one of these men of this evil generation shall see the good Land* (*Devarim* 1:35): [They will not see] any good that comes from the Land." (*Tanchuma, Chukat* 19)

Observe what R. Akiva said. The Holy One Blessed be He withheld all the goodness of the Land from those people who slandered it and its inhabitants; and any pleasure that came from *Eretz Yisrael* was dangerous to them. Now, all those who scorn, blaspheme, and despise the people who settle and build the Land: how can they not fear for their souls?! Perhaps they will fall into the category of the spies and receive their harsh punishment! There is only one thing we can say to vindicate them: they do not realize how far-reaching this matter

476 ❖ See Rambam, *Hilchot Teshuvah* 4:1; *Shulchan Aruch, Yoreh De'ah* 334:43.

477 P. 27.

478 ❖ See what I cited above (pp. 27-28) from *Chesed LeAvraham* and *Nachalah LeYisrael*.

is. It is like a mistake made by a ruler.[479] From now on, however, they will listen and fear, and they will not act presumptuously anymore.[480] And He, the Merciful One, forgives iniquity.[481] A word to the wise is sufficient.

VIII The Exile-Jew

נח Until now, I discussed our issue in a general manner. I proved from *Chazal* that our salvation depends solely on us. We must lift ourselves out of our abysmal and dreadful predicament, ascend higher and higher, and raise our pride with glory. We can attain this only by awakening ourselves to abandon the Diaspora and ascend to our desirable Land. The perfection of the *aliyah* (ascent) is proportionate to the awakening and dedication (שימת הלב) that we have for it. I mentioned this above[482] in the name of our holy Rabbi of Liska *z"l*. He quotes our mentor, the Chida, as saying, "ארץ ישראל has the same numerical value as תת לב (ôput one's heartö or dedicate). If all the Jews put their hearts into ascending to *Eretz Yisrael*, our righteous Savior (*Mashiach*) will arrive."

The exile-Jew refuses to learn from the past

I will now address the "***exile-Jew***" (*golus Yid*), specifically you, "***exile-Jew***." You are so attached to the clods of earth of these lands of exile...that even if oppressors smite you ruthlessly all day long, you become reconciled with your dwelling place the moment they relent. You do not take "tomorrow" into consideration at all. You do not consider that tomorrow the oppressor will, once again, lift his hand against you and smite you. Sometimes "tomorrow" means immediately, and sometimes it means after a while.[483] During almost 2,000 years in exile you received recurring blows, but you have still not learned from the past to contemplate the future.

It seems to me that *Chazal* had this in mind when they said, "*Israel does not know* (*Yeshayah* 1:3), in the past; *My nation does not contemplate* (ibid.), the future" (*Yalkut Shimoni* 2:387). That is to say, the prophet laments that the Jews of exile lack perception. They refuse to learn from the past, and they fool themselves into thinking that

479 Based on *Kohelet* 10:5.
480 Based on *Devarim* 17:13.
481 *Tehillim* 78:38.
482 P. 314.
483 See *Midrash Tanchuma, Bo* 13; Rashi, *Shemot* 13:14.

their situation in exile will improve in the future. Therefore, they do not consider returning to their forefathers' inheritance. And since they do not consider returning, HaShem does not bring them back to the Land, as I demonstrated from Ya'akov Avinu: "If Ya'akov did not consider praying at the place where his forefathers prayed, should God detain him?!"[484] Our mentor, the Mabit *z"l*, explains that this alludes to our exile.[485] The Chida's statement, that our return to *Eretz Yisrael* depends solely on our dedication to it, also demonstrates this, for one can derive the negative from the positive.[486]

In other words, the greatest tragedy of the Jewish people is that they do not want to learn a lesson from the bitter and disastrous misfortunes that befall them. Herein lies the Jewish tragedy...[487] A word to the wise is sufficient.

The exile-Jew lacks a true sense of brotherhood

Furthermore, I am astonished at you, "***exile-Jew***." Your eyes are so blinded that you do not see what is happening around you. You see how the oppressors torture your brethren, beating and afflicting them terribly, and you are not moved at all. You see your brothers' blood flowing on the ground like water and you are not frightened, for you believe that the hour is still propitious. You say in your heart that these things will not affect you at all because you are standing in a safe place, and you bless yourself in your heart saying that you will have peace.[488] If only your words could be true! So may HaShem say.

O "***exile-Jew***" listen and pay heed to my words. Open your eyes and see that your brethren, upon whom this calamity has fallen, also dwelt in a safe place like you do. But in the end, the tables were turned, and they were plundered and murdered (may the Merciful One protect us). How are you so sure and confident that you will be spared this fate? Why are you not afraid? And why is your heart not softened by your friend's misfortune?

In reality, it is impossible to say that you completely ignore the victim's suffering. After all, if someone asks you to donate money to help alleviate his pain, you give as your heart desires. However,

484 See above, p. 162.
485 See ibid.
486 Based on *BeMidbar Rabbah* 9:47. [That is to say, the opposite is also true. If we do not dedicate ourselves to the Land, HaShem will not return us there.]
487 [Originally in Yiddish.]
488 Based on *Devarim* 29:18.

contemplate this: How much do you give? Does it compare to the pain of those who are suffering? Do you give as much as you can, according to the blessing that HaShem has given you? Hence, this donation does not fulfill your obligation.

You act this way because you lack true brotherhood and *ahavat Yisrael* (love for one's fellow Jew). You do not regard an afflicted Jew as your "brother" in the fullest sense of the word, like Moshe Rabbeinu did. *He saw an Egyptian man hitting a Hebrew man of his brothers* (*Shemot* 2:11). [Seemingly], the words, *of his brothers*, are completely superfluous. Furthermore, it already says in the beginning of the verse, *He went out to his brother*! The verse teaches us that the blows which the Egyptian inflicted on the Jew hurt Moshe immensely, as if this Jew was one of his real brothers. Therefore, Moshe endangered himself to save the oppressed from his oppressor. Since he so desperately wanted to save his brother, he did not weigh the extent of his actions so precisely. Rather, he endangered himself in order to save him, without thinking about the [possible] consequences to his own life.

This is a Jew's nature when it comes to saving other Jews. This is also how it should have been today with those who escaped from the land of hell. They came here [to Hungary] to save themselves and their families from the ensnaring trap that was set for them in their homelands. They thought that the local Jews would sympathize with them and band together to extend a helping hand. But instead, they received them coldly and hardheartedly, except for a few people who truly sacrificed themselves to save their fugitive brothers. However, the people in positions of authority and prestige treated them coldly, as if this was not their problem at all.

There is much contempt and wrath[489] at their indifference towards Israel's suffering. All the Jews of Europe are in dire straits. Israel's lives and possessions are completely abandoned (*hefker*). At such a calamitous time the hearts of all Jews should have leaped from their places.[490] But, unfortunately, what do we see? The spirits and souls of the wealthy and prominent men, who dwell comfortably in their palaces,[491] have not moved an iota, and they do not truly share in Israel's pain. Even when they do something to help the refugees,

489 Based on *Esther* 1:18.
490 Based on *Iyov* 37:1.
491 Based on *Tehillim* 122:7.

they do it with a very heavy heart and cold spirit. It is too burdensome for them to bother two or three times for the refugees, so they fulfill their obligation by acting once.

These are the kinds of things we hear from the leaders of this country. However, this is not what *Chazal* say about Moshe Rabbeinu: "That *tzaddik* went out twice, and the Holy One Blessed be He recorded them one next to the other" (*Shemot Rabbah* 1:27). On the first day he went out and killed the Egyptian. On the second day he went out and said to the wicked one, *Why do you smite your fellow?* (*Shemot* 2:13). Our master, the Maharal, explains that the Torah here teaches that even though Moshe should have been afraid to act again immediately on the second day, nevertheless, he acted fearlessly. This is a lesson for all leaders of Israel: When it comes to saving the oppressed from the oppressor, a leader must not worry about himself; rather, he must act over and over again.[492]

Due to our sins, however, today's leaders do not do so. Instead, they exhibit extreme "coldness" [i.e., apathy] when it comes to saving the refugees. Their spirit is cold, their speech is cold, and all their actions are cold. Even that which they do is external; it does not come from the depths of their hearts. This all stems from the fact that they do not see the refugee as the *Hebrew man of his brothers* (*Shemot* 2:11). Their hearts do not feel his pain as they would for a real brother. Moshe Rabbeinu, on the other hand, always saw the Hebrew man as his real brother. Therefore, he assisted his fellow Jew boundlessly and even went beyond the limits of human strength. He devoted his spirit, his soul, his entire body, and obviously his money, to his Jewish brother.

A Jew must feel the pain of his fellow Jew

Rav said, "Whoever is not included in the concealment of God's face is not one of them. Whoever is not included in, *And they will be as prey* (*Devarim* 31:17), is not one of them." (*Chagigah* 5a-b)

Rashi explains: "He is not one of the seed of Israel, for it says, *And I* [God] *will hide My face from them* (*Devarim* 31:17). [When God hides His face it means] that the Jews cry out because of their troubles, but are not answered. *And they will be as prey* means that the Gentiles despoil their money." This is quite puzzling. What did Rav want to teach us? Must a person who escaped misfortune subject himself to other people's afflictions? On the contrary, the *Shulchan*

492 Maharal, *Gevurot HaShem* 18 (end).

Aruch rules that a person must save himself from danger if he can,[493] and the Shelah concurs.[494]

With HaShem's help, it seems clear to me that Rav intended to teach us the following. When a particular person escapes a misfortune that befalls others, and neither his body nor his property are afflicted, he should not say, "Peace unto you, my soul; why should I care about someone else's misfortunes?" In the first chapter of *Ta'anit*, the Talmud states that if a person ignores the suffering of the community, saying, "Peace unto you, my soul," the ministering angels place their hands on his head and curse him that he should not merit to see the community's consolation. See the text inside (at this time I do not have the Talmud in front of me to cite the exact location.)[495] Similarly, Rav states that a person should feel the pain of others to such a degree that he considers himself part of them, even though he is unaffected. He should devote his soul, his body, and his money to them as if he was one of them, as if he himself was actually afflicted. Then, he will do all he can, and perhaps even more, to help save them. He will completely disregard the fact that this might cause him harm, just like he would do for himself if he was in trouble.

This is what Rav teaches us: "Whoever is not included in the concealment of God's face," meaning, whoever does not sympathize with others when God conceals His face from them; and "whoever is not included in, *And they will be as prey*," meaning, a person who sees or hears that the Gentiles are plundering someone else's money and he does not feel as if they are plundering his own money, "is not one of the seed of Israel." Moshe Rabbeinu *a"h* had this quality. He endangered himself not only once, but every time he saw the suffering of *a Hebrew man of his brothers*. He regarded every Jew as his real brother, as his own flesh and blood. Therefore, his self-sacrifice to save the Children of Israel knew no bounds or limits.

The same should be true of every Jew. *Chazal* derive this from the verse *Israel is a scattered sheep* (*Yirmiyah* 50:17): Why is Israel compared to a sheep? When one of the limbs of a sheep (a tender animal by nature) is injured, all of its limbs feel the pain. So too, when one Jew is stricken, all of Israel feels his pain (see *VaYikra Rabbah* 4:6). This is the proper Jewish attitude.

493 *Yoreh De'ah* 116:5 in *Hagah*. Also see *Choshen Mishpat* 427:9-10.

494 *Sh'nei Luchot HaBrit, Sha'ar HaOtiot* 1:44b (marginal note).

495 *Ta'anit* 11a.

One is obligated to endanger himself to save a fellow Jew

Last year, on the Sabbath of *parashat Korach*, the leaders of Bakash-Tshaba honored me to speak in their synagogue. On that occasion, I explained the following *Mesorah*: The word פדה is mentioned twice [in two separate verses]. First, *But, you shall surely redeem* (פדה תפדה) *the firstborn of man* (*BeMidbar* 18:15); and second, *A man can surely not redeem* (לא פדה יפדה) *a brother, nor give to God a ransom for him. For the redemption of their soul is too dear, and he leaves it forever* (*Tehillim* 49:8-9). We must examine the wording of the first verse, for it should have said, "You shall surely redeem your firstborn ***son***," as it says in *parashat Bo*.[496]

It seems to me that [the explanation is as follows]. It is well known that when a fellow Jew is in trouble we are obligated to save him, if we can. The verse states this explicitly, *Do not stand aside when your friend's blood is being shed* (*VaYikra* 19:16). However, today's situation is different than that of years gone by. The oppressors have decreed that it is forbidden to extend a hand to the refugees and save their lives. Severe punishments await anyone who gives them the slightest bit of help. This decree doubles a refugee's hardships. Not only is he forced to abandon everything and run for his life, but no one wants to take him into his house. Where shall he go to escape the troubles of his soul?

However, it is well known that nothing happens in this world by chance. The Holy One Blessed be He did not allow this decree to be enacted for naught. In fact, it came from the heavens. But, let no one imagine that HaShem consented to this decree in order to exempt a Jew from saving his friend. No! This is not true! On the contrary, HaShem consented to it in order to heighten the test. He wants a person to truly sacrifice himself to save his fellow Jew. For, it is well known that when the Attribute of Justice prevails in the world, it is impossible to silence and nullify it except with self-sacrifice. Thus, HaShem made this decree so that we may sacrifice ourselves to fulfill the *mitzvah*, not in order to exempt us from it.

Now, it is well known that double-wording always indicates that there is a great obligation to do something, even a hundred times.[497] It is also known that the people of Israel are called "the firstborn"[498]

496 *Shemot* 13:13.

497 ❖ *Chazal* teach this with regard to, *You shall surely send away* (שלח תשלח) (*Devarim* 22:7), and similar verses (see *Bava Metzia* 31a).

498 *Shemot* 4:22. See Sforno.

(for they are the firstborn of all the nations), while the nations of the world are called "man" (האדם).[499] This explains the *Mesorah* cited above. *But, you shall surely redeem the firstborn of man*: That is to say, you shall redeem Israel who is the firstborn of "man" [i.e., the nations]. Do not think that HaShem made the decree forbidding us to save the refugees in order to exempt us from our obligation. That is not so! On the contrary, *You shall surely redeem* (פדה תפדה). You have a double obligation to redeem them, even if this endangers your own life. Similarly, the S'ma rules (based on the *Yerushalmi*) that a person is obligated to put himself in a potentially dangerous situation to save his friend who is in certain danger.[500]

The second verse refers to someone who does not redeem his fellow because he is afraid of endangering himself.[501] *He does not redeem a brother*: If you do not redeem your brother, claiming that the government forbids you to come to his aid; then, when he becomes ensnared in their trap, *no man will give to God a ransom for him*, and you will be responsible for his blood. However, if you sacrifice yourself to redeem him, then, *the redemption of their soul is* so *dear* to HaShem that He will abolish all of Israel's troubles and harsh decrees and cause them to be forgotten. This is the meaning of, *And he leaves it* (וחדל) *forever*. That is, the decrees will cease (יחדלו) and desist forever.

Esther did the same thing. When she said, *But I have not been called to come to the king* (*Esther* 4:11), Mordechai became angry with her. He understood that she did not want to endanger herself by doing something illegal in order to save Israel. Therefore, he said to her, *If you remain silent at this time, relief and deliverance will arise for the Jews from somewhere else* (ibid. 4:14). Do not think that you are safe and sound, because the opposite may be true. To this she responded, *Go, gather all the Jews together..., and if I perish, I perish* (וכאשר אבדתי אבדתי) (ibid. 4:16). That is, "I already decided to give my life for Israel's salvation (thus, it says אבדתי in the past tense, indicating that I have already perished), but I want Israel to repent." (I elaborated on this in my sermon.)

499 See *Bava Metzia* 114b; *Tosafot, Avodah Zarah* 3a, s.v. *kohanim*.

500 *Sefer Me'irat Einayim* 426:2.

501 [Our author is now interpreting this verse homiletically. Therefore, the translation here differs from above.]

Wealthy Jews must use their money to help save their brethren

Due to our numerous sins, most people do not put this into practice. However, there are always exceptional individuals who dedicate themselves and their money to saving Israel (thank God). But, these individuals do not come from the elite of the nation. Those who sit in the palaces of kings and at the helm of leadership have closed up their wealth and withheld their money. They will always find excuses to exempt themselves from their obligation to help Jews in distress, as we have recently seen during this ôtime of trouble for Ya'akov.ö[502]

Chazal state: "R. Shimon ben Lakish says, 'This nation is compared to a grapevine. The branches are the landowners'" (*Chullin* 92a). Rashi explains: "The branch produces twigs, leaves, and fruits; and it is the main part of the grapevine. Similarly, the landowners perform acts of kindness, support the poor, ***and help their brethren survive by giving money to the government on their behalf.***"

This helps explain David's statement, *You brought a grapevine out of Egypt* (*Tehillim* 80:9). When the landowners act like a grapevine and give their money to help their brethren in distress, they cause Israel to be brought out of Egypt (מצרים). That is to say, they cause Israel to be saved from distress (צרה), for the *Midrash* explains that the word *Mitzrayim* (מצרים) represents any misfortune (צרה) that befalls Israel (*VaYikra Rabbah* 13:4).

The exile-Jew is detached from Klal Yisrael

All of this happened to you only because the exile made you into an "***exile-Jew***." I mean that exile life made you into a man who is detached and separated from the entire Jewish community, for in exile you do not live life as a nation. In other words, in exile you do not lead a nationalistic life to the degree that you feel unified with the holy nation of Israel.[503] You do not feel yourself part of the Jewish nation, which is scattered and dispersed among the nations.[504] Rather, you consider yourself a citizen of the place in which you live. You only [see yourself] and lead your life as a loyal citizen of that place.[505] By this I mean, you do not take your obligation towards the holy Jewish nation into consideration. You are only concerned about your obligation towards the citizens amongst whom you dwell, and you dedicate your entire heart and soul to that. Thus, you have

502 Based on *Yirmiyah* 30:7.
503 [Originally in Yiddish.]
504 Based on *Esther* 3:8.
505 [Originally in Yiddish.]

detached and separated yourself from the holy nation and its collectiveness, and you have become isolated in your place of dwelling in exile. You have exchanged an everlasting world for a transient one. For, the world of the collective, holy nation is everlasting and eternal, but your separate and isolated world is transient. One night it is here and the next night it perishes.[506] Current events prove this, for in one night you lost all of the prosperity that you had in exile. In this way, the "***exile-Jew***" betrayed his true nation and inheritance.

We are not talking about a common Jew who is only concerned with, and completely engrossed in, his business and livelihood. He does not know nor feel that he is part of the eternal and collective Jewish nation, or that he has some obligation towards *Klal Yisrael*. We see examples of this every day. A person knows that he must give to the city, country, and society in which he lives, but if someone asks him to give to *Klal Yisrael*, he becomes very stingy. And even if he gives, he does so against his will, as if he is not obligated. Is there any greater betrayal than this?

But, even Jews who are devoted to Torah and *mitzvot* – learned, God-fearing Jews and pious men of deed – are detached and separated from the collective Jewish nation. They have no connection or bond to the Jewish community at large, for their field of vision does not go beyond the place in which they roam.

Let us take as an example a *chassid* who is devoted to his rebbe and to the other *chassidim* who find shelter with that rebbe. His world revolves only around the small circle in which he travels; his "Sabbath limit" (*techum Shabbat*) only goes until there, and he does not care about anything beyond it. He completely disregards the collective Jewish nation which is scattered and dispersed throughout the world. If someone would ask him to donate to a cause related to *Klal Yisrael*, he would be very reluctant to give; but in his own circles, money is no object.

Let us also consider the upright, Orthodox Jew. He goes to synagogue every morning and evening and participates in all the classes of the Talmud Society (*chevrat shas*). The Talmud Society is his world, but he knows nothing outside of its boundaries. He thinks that he has already fulfilled his obligation and mission towards the Torah and the Jewish nation by attending to the Talmud Society

506 Based on *Yonah* 4:10.

and all of its subdivisions. He does not want to know about anything beyond that.

Is this "***exile-Jew***" not detached and separated from the Jewish nation? However, he is used to this from the time he enters this world and dwells in exile. For he is bound exclusively to the clods of earth upon which he dwells and does not look beyond his own circles. Therefore, it is not surprising that he cannot stir his heart when his fellow Jew, who is far from his own circle and with whom he has never had any association, is in distress. This is a clear and true understanding of this matter.

The cause of this detachment

In the past hundred years, the kingdoms of Europe emancipated the Jew and made him an equal citizen in the land. They allowed him to benefit from the good of the land, to do what his heart desires, to live wherever he pleases, and to study and pursue their wisdom and languages. This freedom gave the final push to detach the exile-Jew from his communal bond and from his connection to the Jewish nation. It caused him to assimilate into the nation with which he dwells. This is the opposite of, *But of Zion it will be said, this and that man was born in her* (*Tehillim* 87:5), [which implies] that the men that are born in her are completely distinguished in their spirit, knowledge, and conduct.

When this freedom was granted, the ôropeö [which connected the Jews] of all different countries to the collective Jewish nation was completely severed, and they were no longer united. Beforehand, when the Jews lived in ghettos, they were less detached from one another. This is evident from the fact that the German, Hungarian, Bohemian, and Moravian Jews hired and respected Polish rabbis. Once freedom and liberty were granted, however, a Polish rabbi would be considered unqualified to serve as a rabbi in Hungary, Germany, or Moravia. All of this occurred because the Jews assimilated into the nations and became as distant from one another as east and west.

This assimilation affected even devout, Torah Jews. We saw and heard that in Germany, and even Hungary, a Jew from Poland was considered inferior, a "Polish Jew." In Germany they called him an "eastern Jew,"[507] which indicated his lowly status. Even rabbis, who bore the banner of Torah, and God-fearing, faithful Jews showed some contempt towards Polish Jews, as if they were from a different

507 Referring to Eastern Europe.

nation. The explanation for this is as I stated above: The exile has made the Jew into an "***exile-Jew***." It separated and detached him from the collective nation and made him live an isolated life in exile. He no longer lives a nationalistic life, nor does he feel for his nation and inheritance. He only knows about his own affairs. This is the true description of an "***exile-Jew***," and this is what has brought us to our present situation.

IX The Unification of Israel Through the Mitzvah of Yishuv Eretz Yisrael

Our redemption depends on unity

נז Ya'akov said to his sons, *Gather yourselves together and I will tell you that which will befall you in the end of days* (*BeReishit* 49:1). Our Rabbis in the *Midrash* comment:

> He said to them, "You shall all be one gathering," as it says, *Now you, son of man, take for yourself one stick and write on it, "For Judah and for the Children of Israel, his companions"* (*Yechezkel* 37:16). [This last word] is written as חברו, *his companion*, (even though we read it as חבריו, *his companions*) to teach that if the Children of Israel become one unit, prepare yourselves for the redemption. What is written afterwards? *I will make them into one nation in the Land* (ibid. 37:22). (*BeReishit Rabbah* 98:2) ❖

Midrash Kohelet says the same thing, commenting on the verse *A time to sew* (*Kohelet* 3:7):

> As it is written, *And join them one to the other...and they shall become united in your hand* (*Yechezkel* 37:17).[508] What is written afterwards? *Thus says the Lord God, "Behold, I will take the Children of Israel from among the nations into which they have gone, and I will gather them from all around, and I will bring them to their Land, and I will make them into one nation in the Land"* (ibid. 37:21-22). This is *a time to sew*. (*Kohelet Rabbah* 3:8)

❖ In addition, a later verse states, *I will purify them and they will be My nation, and I will be their God* (*Yechezkel* 37:23). That is to say, by virtue of the fact that they will all unite, HaShem will send a spirit of purity from above and they will all deserve to be HaShem's nation and to have Him as their God.

508 In our versions, the *Midrash* ends here.

Thus, Israel's redemption depends on sewing all of Israel into one nation. The *Midrash* further states:

> *You are standing today, all of you* (*Devarim* 29:9)... When? When you are all united as one... Similarly, you find that Israel will not be redeemed until they are all united as one, as it says, "In those days and at that time the Children of Israel and the Children of Judah will come together" (see *Yirmiyah* 3:18). (*Midrash Tanchuma, Nitzavim* 1)

The Talmud concurs: "Israel will not be redeemed until they become one group, as it is written, *And He established His group* (אגודתו) *upon the land* (*Amos* 9:6)" (see *Menachot* 27a). In addition, the Jewish nation's existence depends on unity, as the above-mentioned *Midrash* states, "*You are standing today*... When? When you are all united."

This is why the pride of Israel has declined, our nation has sunken to the depths, and we have reached our current situation. It is all because the nation of Israel is torn to pieces and cut into fragments, as I recounted above in my description of the "exile-Jew." The only remedy for our afflictions is to once again become one nation, to bring the people of Israel close to one another and unite them in absolute oneness. Then, we can prepare ourselves for the redemption, as I just cited from the *Midrash*, "If the Children of Israel become one unit, prepare yourselves for the redemption." Our entire existence and future depend on this.

The Kabbalist and divine scholar, our mentor, the Maharal of Prague *z"l*, explains why the Second Temple was destroyed. The *Beit HaMikdash* in Jerusalem is the center which unifies *Klal Yisrael*; it makes us into one nation. Since the Jews were not united, they did not deserve this place.[509] Now, if we unite and rectify this situation, we will deserve the redemption and the place which unifies us as one nation.

Above,[510] I cited the Talmud which asks, "If we are waiting (for redemption) and He (the Holy One Blessed be He) is waiting, then who detains it?" The Talmud answers, "The Attribute of Justice detains it" (*Sanhedrin* 97b). Similarly, the *Midrash* comments on the verse *That you not wake nor rouse the love until it pleases* (*Shir*

509 *Netzach Yisrael* 4.

510 P. 186.

HaShirim 2:7): "Until it pleases the Attribute of Justice." I also quoted[511] our mentor, the Magen Avraham, as saying that the accuser has permission to interfere until the nullifier [i.e., the accuser himself] is abolished. Thus, when Israel unites as one complete unit, we will defeat the Attribute of Justice and silence our adversaries and accusers. Then, our enemies will have no power over us; we will leave this bitter exile with a high hand;[512] and we will merit to see the complete redemption, speedily in our days. Amen.

The Jews are unblemished and invincible when united

Our mentor, the Noam Elimelech, expresses this idea on a verse from the *Brit Bein HaBetarim. He* [Avraham] *took all of these* [animals], *cut them down the middle, and placed each half opposite the other; but the bird, he did not cut up* (*BeReishit* 15:10):

> He placed them all opposite one another. *But the bird*, which represents Israel, *he did not cut up*. That is to say, nothing can measure-up to the merit of the entirety of Israel, for even the wicked ones are filled with *mitzvot* like a pomegranate [is filled with seeds] (*Berachot* 57a).[513]

The Noam Elimelech refers to something he wrote elsewhere:

> The entirety of Israel is righteous (without a single blemish), as it says, *Your people are all righteous* (*Yeshayah* 60:21). Therefore, even though individuals sin, the whole [of Israel] always retains its sanctity, and there is no adversary nor evil affliction in them, God forbid. Their form is forever engraved [before God] above, and the evil forces have no power over them. And, the individual man connects himself to this collectiveness.[514]

Avraham intended this when he placed the bird (which alludes to Israel) opposite the cut pieces (which allude to the nations of the world and the evil forces). When "the bird" is not divided, but united, Israel's merit is immeasurable, and the evil forces have no power over it. *Targum Yerushalmi* and *Targum Yonatan* explain that Avraham's merit annuls all the evil designs that our enemies

511 Pp. 193-94.
512 Based on *Shemot* 14:8.
513 *Noam Elimelech*, p. 7, col. c. (Mossad HaRav Kook edition: vol. 1, p. 37.)
514 Ibid., p. 88a. (Mossad HaRav Kook: vol. 2, p. 472.)

devise against us.* It also protects us and prevents the Gentiles from controlling our money.[515] All of this is true only when the bird, which alludes to Israel, is not divided. That is, when the entirety of Israel is a completely undivided unit, then it is powerful and has no adversary nor evil affliction.

Actually, the Maharal of Prague agrees with the Noam Elimelech that the entirety of Israel always retains its sanctity without a single blemish. He adds that the Omnipresent loves His people and is bound to them with a firm, unbreakable bond.[516] I subsequently found that our mentor, the Rambam, states this explicitly in *Iggeret Teiman*:

> HaShem, may He be blessed, strengthened us with the good tiding that it is impossible for Him to reject us as a collective entity, even if we anger Him and transgress His *mitzvot*. For it is written, *Thus says the Lord: "If the heavens above could be measured and the foundations of the earth searched out beneath, then I too would reject the entire seed of Israel because of all that they have done," says the Lord, God* (*Yirmiyah* 31:36).[517]

---

* This *Targum* helps explain the *Midrash* on the verse *Thus says the Lord of Hosts, "They will build, but I will destroy"* (*Malachi* 1:4):

> A certain philosopher asked R. Elazar: "The prophet said, *They will build, but I will destroy*. But, is it not true that whatever the Romans built is still standing?" R. Elazar responded: "The verse is not referring to buildings, but schemes. The Holy One Blessed be He destroys all of the schemes that you devise and 'build' to annihilate us." He replied: "By your life, this is true! Every year we sit and discuss how to enact decrees to annihilate you, but one elder comes and annuls them." (*Yalkut Shimoni* 2:587)

The commentator there explains that the root-word בנה (build) also pertains to thoughts. It refers to a "spiritual" building. The enemies of Israel continuously devise ways to annihilate us (God forbid), but the Holy One Blessed be He annuls their plans. One elder, which refers to the Elder Israel (*Yisrael Sabba*), arouses one of the advisors of the kingdom to save us, as we find in many Aggadic passages.

Based on the *Targum* mentioned above, it seems obvious that this elder is Avraham, for his merit accomplishes this.

515 *Targum* on *BeReishit* 15:11.
516 *Netzach Yisrael*, chap. 11.
517 *Iggeret Teiman*, p. 128.

Thus, we have three great witnesses – each of whom is worthy on his own, all the more so when they are together – who testify to the immense value of unifying the people of Israel into one unit. For even if they are wicked as individuals, collectively they are unblemished...*

After all that I have presented here, everyone will understand my statement above that our salvation and future depend solely on unity. We must unify all the different types of people that exist among us, from the most extreme right to the most extreme left, until the entire Jewish nation is included in one complete unit. Then, we will defeat the Attribute of Justice, silence our adversaries, and see the fulfillment of the verse *And the Children of Israel were going out with a high hand* (*Shemot* 14:8), speedily in our days. Amen.

---

* This helps us explain the following *Pesikta*:

> Yirmiyah said that [Israel] *will be called "despised silver"* (*Yirmiyah* 6:30), and Yechezkel called them dross, as it says, *The House of Israel has become dross to Me* (*Yechezkel* 22:18). Therefore, Zecharyah said: *And behold, an all gold menorah* (*Zecharyah* 4:2), [meaning], it is [made] entirely of gold. Why? *You are entirely fair, My beloved, and you have no blemish* (*Shir HaShirim* 4:7). (*Piska VaYehi HaMakriv*)

Based on the statements of these three rabbis, the *Pesikta* illuminates like fire. They assert that the entirety of Israel has no blemish, that they retain their sanctity as when they stood at Mount Sinai, that their form is engraved before God's glorious throne, that the Holy One Blessed be He always loves them even if they do not fulfill His will (God forbid), and that sin and iniquity are only found in them when we judge them as individuals, but as a whole there is no adversary, evil affliction, sin, iniquity, or blemish. Now, the Sforno explains that the menorah symbolizes the unification of the entire Jewish nation.[518]... Thus, the *Pesikta* states: Since Yirmiyah said that the Jews are despised silver, God forbid, and Yechezkel called them dross, Zecharyah said: "*And behold, an all gold menorah*; it is [made] entirely of gold. Why? *You are entirely* (כולך)." That is to say, when the Jews exemplify כולך, by uniting together as the menorah symbolizes, then, *You are entirely fair, My beloved, and you have no blemish*. This is a true explanation of the *Pesikta*, with God's help.

518 Sforno, *BeMidbar* 8:2-4.

Unity is part of our nature

נז Truthfully, I know that everyone will look at me in astonishment and ridicule me, saying, "Your words are true, our salvation depends on every Jew gathering together into one unit. But, how can we do this? Who can join them together? How is it possible to include and gather all of Israel from the five parts of the world, with their different ideologies and characteristics, into one assembly?" Indeed, our mentor, the author of *Hafla'ah*, already grappled with the issue of Israel's unification, which [seems to be] impossible [to achieve] nowadays, due to our diverse ideologies.[519]

However, *Chazal* teach us, "Do not underestimate anything" (*Avot* 4:3). Furthermore, the tribulations that we encountered during these abnormal times teach us that things which people consider unrealistic can become very realistic. Things which no one wanted to believe could possibly happen, actually happened in the end. The same applies to Israel's unification. It is certainly realistic and possible, and it is not so far from the nature of the matter, as I will explain with God's help.

Our mentor, the Maharal of Prague *z"l*, writes in his pellucid work, *Netzach Yisrael*,[520] that nature always retains its status. Its existence is so strong and firm that it refuses to deviate from the natural boundaries which the Creator of the Universe established. Even if something occurs which forces nature to stray from its natural boundaries, it will not remain in this unnatural state. Instead, it will return to its natural state, for something which is unnatural cannot endure. Nature, on the other hand, is everlasting.

Accordingly, Israel [will eventually unite], for the Holy One Blessed be He determined that this nation will naturally be more unified and indivisible than any other nation. *Chazal* point out that the Torah says about Ya'akov, *All the soul* (הנפש) *that came with Ya'akov to Egypt* (*BeReishit* 46:26); while it says about Eisav, *And all the soul**s*** (נפשות) *of his house* (ibid. 36:6) (*VaYikra Rabbah* 4:6, *Yalkut Shimoni* 1:137). Unity is part of Ya'akov's nature, not Eisav's. Also, when the Torah was given, *Israel encamped* (ויחן) *there before the mountain* (*Shemot* 19:2), "as one man with one heart."[521] Thus, from Israel's very inception as a nation, the Creator determined that it will be a united nation.

519 *Hafla'ah, Ketuvot* 112b.

520 Chap. 1.

521 Rashi there. [He derives this from the fact that the verse should have said ויחנו, in the plural.]

Therefore, dispersion is unnatural for Israel; it goes beyond the boundaries of nature and cannot endure. Now, just as anything that deviates from the natural order [eventually] returns to its place, so too, the dispersed and scattered fragments of Israel will return to their place, since they are all part of one entity... And, it is impossible to say that [Israel's dispersion will last forever since] it is a result of sin; after all, it is unnatural.

The Maharal uses this principle to explain a *Midrash* on the verse *And He* [God] *said to Avram, "Know for sure"* (ידוע תדע) (*BeReishit* 15:13). *Chazal* comment, "Know (ידוע) that I will disperse them, and know (תדע) that I will gather them" (*BeReishit Rabbah* 44:18). That is to say, the dispersion itself demonstrates that I will gather them. Dispersion runs contrary to the order of existence, [because nature dictates] that everything which is one – like Israel which is one nation – must be together. Therefore, know that I will gather them.

The Maharal demonstrates at length that exile itself is a clear proof that there will be a redemption. For, exile is a diversion and deviation from the natural order. HaShem arranged each nation in its appropriate place and Israel in its appropriate place, which is *Eretz Yisrael*. Thus, exile is a departure from nature. Anything outside of its natural place cannot endure and, therefore, returns to its natural place. So too, Israel will return to its place, which is *Eretz Yisrael*. This matter is clear to any intelligent person. Thus, we can understand the redemption from the exile.

Exile (גלה) and Redemption (גאל)

He also points out that the words גלה (exile) and גאל (redemption) have [virtually] the same letters. The only differences are: 1. גאל has an "א" while גלה has a "ה." 2. In the word גאל the "א" is in the middle, while in גלה the "ה" is at the end. Each word has a specific meaning.

The word גאל alludes to the fact that HaShem redeems us from the four corners of the earth and unites our dispersion, so that we can become the quintessence of oneness. This is why it is written with an "א," which represents unity. Furthermore, all unity in the world is in the center, for the extremes are separate while the center is one. Therefore, the "א," which represents unity and the ingathering of the dispersion, is in the middle of the word, alluding to the fact that HaShem will gather us from the dispersion of our exile only by the merit of unity.

The word גלה (exile) has a "ה" because the letter "ה" (which numerically equals five) represents dispersion to the four corners and to the center – the five directions in which things are scattered. Similarly, the people of Israel are dispersed over the four corners and center of the earth. The "ה" is written at the end of the word to teach that exile is a deviation from the natural order and a departure from [Israel's] appropriate place, which is *Eretz Yisrael*, the center of the world. Therefore, this situation will not last forever, as explained above. Now, even though the center stays in its place and is, therefore, not a dispersion, the fact that the Jews have a center demonstrates that they still have the capacity to unite and gather together, as I will explain. It also teaches that the exile itself is a cause for the redemption, [an impetus] to gather the dispersed and unite Israel.

Israel retains its capacity to unite even in exile

Thus, the letters of גלה are the same as those of גאל, only that the dispersion became unity, as the "א" of גאל implies. The "ה" of the word גלה demonstrates that Israel retains its unity even in exile. The center unites and connects the four dispersions, because the center always unites and connects everything else. This teaches that Israel still has the capacity to unite in exile, and that they have not completely disunited. This remaining capacity to unite will help them unite even more. For, if there was no such capacity left, God forbid, they would not have been able to reunite...*

---

* *And the angel that spoke with me returned and woke me, as a man that is awakened from his sleep. He said to me, "What do you see?" I said, "I looked and behold, an all gold menorah with a bowl* (וְגֻלָּה) *on its top"* (על ראשה) (*Zecharyah* 4:1-2). The *Midrash* comments:

> Two *Amora'im* [dispute this]. One says גולה (exile), and the other says גאולה (redemption). The one who says גולה [claims that this prophecy refers to Israel] who were exiled to Babylonia along with the *Shechinah*... And the one who says גאולה [claims that it refers to] the Redeemer, as it says, *Our Redeemer, the Lord of Hosts* (*Yeshayah* 47:4). It also says, *Their king will pass before them, and the Lord at their head* (בראשם) (*Michah* 2:13). (*VaYikra Rabbah* 32:8)

I believe that this *Midrash* can be explained according to the above-mentioned Maharal. These two *Amora'im* truly allude to his idea. The words גלה and גאל are really equal, for even in exile the Jews retain the capacity to unite, which helps them achieve redemption. Then, *the Lord is at their head*. That is why this vision was of a menorah, for the menorah represents the unity of Israel, as the Sforno explains.[522] When the Jews unite they will deserve to be built up, with HaShem's help.

Now, it is clear from the Maharal that "ה" indicates ingathering and unity, and that גלה and גאולה are the same. The only difference is that the "א" of גאולה is in the middle to hint that the Jews retain the capacity to gather together even in exile. The "ה" [of גלה] hints to the same thing. Then, when all of *Klal Yisrael* becomes one entity, the "א" [אלף], which represents the Master [אלוף] of the Universe, will join with them and bring redemption.

Thus, the meaning of the *Midrash* is obvious. "One says גולהö: Even in exile we must assemble the holy nation into one entity. "And, one says גאולה," meaning, then the redemption will occur. [In reality], they do not argue. One *Amora* says [this idea] in one way and the other says it in a different way. This is clear and true.

This also explains the words of our holy and divine master, R. Menachem Mendel of Premishlan, a disciple of the Ba'al Shem Tov. In the holy work, *Iggra DeParka*, our mentor, R. Tzvi Elimelech *z"l*, relates the following:

> I heard a remarkable story about the holy and divine rabbi, our master, R. Menachem Mendel of Premishlan. [The Rebbe and his followers] were once sitting at a festive meal, and the Rebbe gave the waiter a coin worth four *peshutim* with which to buy beer. However, he told the waiter to bring five *peshutim* worth of beer. The waiter, not looking at the coin, assumed that it was worth five *peshutim*. When he approached the seller, the seller looked at it and said, "This coin is worth only four *peshutim*." So, the messenger returned to the Rebbe and said, "This coin is worth only four *peshutim*." The Rebbe began to argue and said, "It must be five *peshutim*." But, the messenger stood firm, and a squabble ensued. Finally, the disciples of the Rebbe hinted to the waiter that he should concede to the words of the Rebbe (for they understood that he did this for a reason). The messenger agreed and said, "Let it be like the words of my master." Then, the Rebbe stood and prayed, "May it be God's will that all people will know and recognize that four is five."[523]

522 *BeMidbar* 8:2-4.

523 [Originally in Yiddish.] The Rebbe was making a play on words here. The Yiddish word *firer* – a coin consisting of four parts (from the word *fir*, meaning "four") – also means "ruler" from the root *firan*, meaning "to lead." Thus, the Rebbe was probably saying that the Ruler of the Universe, Who conceals

The Maharal also explains why Israel is called by Rachel's name, as it says, *Rachel weeps for her children* (*Yirmiyah* 31:14), and as the *Midrash* states explicitly (see *BeReishit Rabbah* 71:2). He writes:

> The woman is called "the house," as R. Yosi says, "I never called my wife, 'My wife,' but 'My house'" (*Gittin* 52a). Now, Rachel was Ya'akov's primary "house"..., and the one who is called "the house" encompasses and unites everyone else, just like an actual house does. Therefore, Israel is called by Rachel's name (because she gives us the ability to unite, for she is called "the house").
>
> Some unifying force [always] remains within Israel, but [in exile] it is only in potential. Therefore, Rachel – a force that unites Israel, for all of Israel is called by her name... – continues to pray until the people of Israel are completely gathered in their Land... The Holy One Blessed be He answers her, *Refrain*

> This is what I heard, and in my opinion it corresponds to the *Yichud* (Unification) mentioned in the *Zohar*: "[The letter] *heyh* (ה) [represents] four (ד) Tetragrammatons; and when 'The Male' joins with it, it becomes *heyh* (five).ö[524] Contemplate this matter and realize how far-reaching are the deeds and speech of the *tzaddikim*, and you will stand in awe.[525]

In my humble opinion, this hints to the Maharal's principle. "ד" (four) represents the exile, for the people of Israel are dispersed throughout the four corners of the world. "ה" represents the ingathering and redemption, for if we actualize the potential to unite (which remains with us in exile), the redemption will arrive. In addition, it is possible that the *Zohar* also hints to this when it says, "[The letter] *heyh* (ה) [represents] four (ד) Tetragrammatons; and when 'The Male' joins with it, it becomes *heyh* (five).ö This is why the above-mentioned *tzaddik* prayed that four should become five.

Himself in the four corners of the earth, reveals Himself and is, in essence, five with the unifying point.

524 See *Etz Chayim* 39:5. [In effect, the letter ה is made up of the letters ד and ו (ו being the leg of the ה). The *Zohar* teaches that the ד (4) represents four mentions of the Tetragrammaton (י־ה־ו־ה), and the ו represents "The Male." This refers to the male "face" (*partzuf*) of HaShem which is made up of the six (ו) *sefirot*: *Chesed, Gevurah, Tiferet, Netzach, Hod, Yesod*. It goes without saying that it is beyond the scope of this translation to explain these esoteric concepts.]

525 *Iggra DeParka*, sec. 4.

> *your voice from weeping and your eyes from tears* (*Yirmiyah* 31:15), because the merit of Rachel, who is a unifying force, will bring Israel back from their exile. This is the meaning of, *And the children will return to their border* (ibid. 31:16). [Why will they return]? Because there is a force that unifies Israel in their exile, and through this unifying force, Israel will return from their exile.

This concludes the words of the brilliant Kabbalist, the divine scholar, our mentor, the Maharal of Prague, who spoke with *Ruach HaKodesh*. (It is well known that *Ruach HaKodesh* appeared in his study hall.) May his merit protect me and all of Israel. Amen.

We can achieve unity

נח Thus, according to this godly philosopher, unity is natural to Israel, while disunity is unnatural and cannot endure. Unity will not be silent nor rest until it returns to its natural place. I mean that even though the attribute of unity (which is part of Israel's nature) left Israel due to an external circumstance, it will once again establish its abode within Israel, for nature itself helps accomplish this. Therefore, from the standpoint of nature, reuniting Israel is not far-fetched.

Secondly, this godly rabbi reveals to us with his *Ruach HaKodesh* that the capacity to unite remains with Israel even in exile. However, this capacity is only in potential and must be actualized. When the people of Israel collectively take proper action, they will cause this potential to actualize, and unity will return to Israel.

Thirdly, our mentor explains that Rachel, through her merit and prayers, gives us strength to unify and gather all of Israel into one unit, even when we are in exile.

Therefore, from these three perspectives, the concept of unity is neither foreign nor unrealistic to us. We can achieve it, but only if we use true and proper actions and means, and only if we strive to arrive at the truth. We must ask HaShem to show us the path that will lead to this lofty goal, [and to help us] do things that are capable of arousing the unity which is now merely in potential and cause it to actualize in our midst. Then, HaShem Himself will assist us, as *Chazal* say, "He who comes to be purified receives assistance" (*Shabbat* 104a). The *Tikkunei Zohar* explains that the entire Heavenly Host assists him.[526] Our mentor, the Rashba, writes, "All perceptive people

526 *Tikkun* 69. Also see *Sha'arei Zohar, Shabbat* 104a.

realize that HaShem helps those who do sacred tasks, whenever necessary."[527] The same applies to our issue.

We must all unite through the mitzvah of Yishuv Eretz Yisrael

I thank HaShem with all my heart, for after I decided to examine the issue upon which Israel's salvation depends, HaShem enlightened me, and the Great Advisor[528] placed proper counsel in my heart to find the way to actually unify the entire, holy Jewish nation and make it into one assembly. The solution is to choose one *mitzvah* of the Torah in which all of Israel, from small to great, will engage. This *mitzvah* will be the thread that surrounds us, making us into one body and one nation in the land. This way, all of Israel will be one complete unit both physically and spiritually, in holiness and purity.

I already explained[529] that *Klal Yisrael* as a whole always retains its sanctity, and there is no adversary nor evil affliction in it. I also quoted[530] the Rambam, the Ran, and the godly Kabbalist, R. Shalom Sharrabi *z"l* (cited in *Pele Yo'etz*), as saying that if the Jews accept one *mitzvah* they are considered complete penitents and may achieve redemption through it. *Chazal* state this [clearly]: "Anyone who performs one *mitzvah* will receive goodness and long life and will inherit the Land" (*Kiddushin* 39b). This refers to an individual. Certainly, then, if the masses perform a *mitzvah*, its effects are immeasurably great and can give rise to all of the above-mentioned benefits.

I know that many people will ask, which *mitzvah* of all the *mitzvot* of the Torah should *Klal Yisrael* choose to engage in? I will answer with the words of the Ran, cited above.[531] He asserts that in order to be worthy of the World to Come by performing one *mitzvah*, a person must choose a *mitzvah* of great value, one that is equal to many other *mitzvot*. The same applies here. In order to make all of *Klal Yisrael* into one entity, the *mitzvah* that we choose must be greater and more important than the other *mitzvot* of the Torah.

People will still ask, is it possible for us to weigh the relative value of *mitzvot* and decide between them? Does it not say, *The path of life, lest you weigh* (*Mishley* 5:6)?[532] On the other hand, it says, *Weigh*

527 *Torat HaBayit*, introduction.
528 Based on *Yirmiyah* 32:19.
529 Pp. 381-83.
530 Sec. י״, p. 260.
531 Ibid.
532 [See Rashi there.]

the path of your feet, and all your ways will be established (ibid. 4:26)![533] It must be that we are permitted to weigh and choose a *mitzvah* which *Chazal* inform us is greater than the rest. And behold, *Chazal* state explicitly in the *Sifrei* (*Re'eh* 28) and the *Tosefta* (*Avodah Zarah* 5:2) that the *mitzvah* of settling *Eretz Yisrael* is equal to the entire Torah.❖ Therefore, let us choose *Yishuv Eretz Yisrael* as the *mitzvah* which all Jews in the world will engage in together. This *mitzvah* will make us one nation in the Land and cause Israel's unity to return to its proper place. Then, our potential unity will actualize, and we will deserve the final redemption and the great future about which our sacred prophets prophesied.

We can only be one nation in Eretz Yisrael

נט Furthermore, we should choose the positive commandment of *Yishuv Eretz Yisrael* not only because it is equal to all other *mitzvot*, but also because we who dwell in *Chutz LaAretz* cannot become one nation without it. Our holy mentor, the author of *Sefer Chareidim*, cites the great *Tana*, R. Shimon bar Yochai,[537] who says that we are one nation only in *Eretz Yisrael*. Thus, the verse says, *And who is like Your people, Israel, one nation in the land* (II *Shmuel* 7:23). Understand this literally: We become one nation only in the Land.[538] Thus, it is impossible to attain the status of "one nation" in *Chutz LaAretz*.

Those who cherish the Land are considered already there

Besides this, the brilliant Rabbeinu Chayim, brother of the Maharal of Prague, writes that if a person constantly anticipates ascending to *Eretz Yisrael*, setting his eyes and heart there all the time, he is considered as if he resides there. *Chazal* say that people who die outside the Land will be resurrected only after suffering the pain of

---

❖ In addition, the Ramban counts it as one of the 613 *mitzvot*.[534] The majority of the greatest *poskim*, *Rishonim* and *Acharonim*, agree with him.[535] Furthermore, I proved above[536] that the Rambam, as well, holds that it is biblically ordained, even though he does not include it in his count of the *mitzvot*.

533 ❖ *Chazal* discuss this contradiction in *Mo'ed Kattan* 9a.

534 Ramban's Addendum to *Sefer HaMitzvot* of the Rambam, Positive Commandments 4.

535 See *Pitchei Teshuvah, Even HaEzer* 75:6.

536 P. 232ff.

537 *Zohar* 3:93b. Also see there *Nitzotzei Zohar* 3.

538 *Sefer Chareidim, Mitzvat Yishuv Eretz Yisrael*, chap. 2.

rolling through underground tunnels (*Ketuvot* 111a). R. Chayim explains that this refers only to those who do not cherish the Land. However, those who cherish the Land and anticipate redemption during their lifetimes, will not, after their deaths, be separated from that holiness which was etched and engraved on the tablets of their hearts.[539] The brilliant Mabit (colleague of our mentor, the Beit Yosef, and a co-member of his court) concurs:

> We maintain that the resurrection will occur only in *Eretz Yisrael* and that those who die in *Chutz LaAretz* will suffer the pain of rolling through underground tunnels. Nonetheless, those who die (for whatever reason) on their way to *Eretz Yisrael* will be privileged to come back to life outside the Land and complete the *aliyah* that they began during their lifetimes.
>
> Yechezkel's resurrection of the dead, which occurred in *Chutz LaAretz*, in the valley of Beit Dura, proves this.[540] [*Chazal* say]: "The resurrected people proceeded to *Eretz Yisrael* and married women. R. Yehudah ben Beteira stood up on his feet and said, 'I am a descendant of theirs.' Rav said, 'They were the children of Efrayim who reckoned the end [of the Egyptian exile] and erred, as it says, *And the children of Efrayim...: The men of Gat, who were born in the Land, killed them* (I *Divrei HaYamim* 7:20-21)" (*Sanhedrin* 92b).
>
> Thus, they died in *Chutz LaAretz* and afterwards ascended to *Eretz Yisrael*. Why? Since they died while attempting to do the *mitzvah* of *aliyah* (according to Rav who says that they were the children of Efrayim who erred in their calculations and were ascending to *Eretz Yisrael*), the Holy One Blessed be He wanted to give them the privilege of completing the *mitzvah* that they began.[541]

I will add that this is true even of completely wicked people. The *Midrash* states that these children of Efrayim were wicked (*Shemot Rabbah* 20:11). Nonetheless, they deserved to be resurrected because they wanted to ascend to *Eretz Yisrael*. Our mentor, the Chatam Sofer, also states that whoever desires to ascend to *Eretz Yisrael* is

539 *Sefer HaChayim, Sefer Ge'ulah ViYeshuah*, chap. 1 (end).

540 See *Yechezkel* 37:1-14.

541 *Beit Elokim, Sha'ar HaYesodot*, chap. 55. [The comments in parentheses are the Mabit's.]

considered as if he is already there.[542] The Tashbetz also concurs.[543]

In any event, those who cherish the Land and strive to enter it are considered as if they live there. Thus, when we engage in building and settling the Land, we are considered as if we are already there. Therefore, we actually can attain the status of "one nation" even in *Chutz LaAretz*.

From this we may conclude that any *mitzvah* of the Torah other than settling the Land is completely incapable of making us into one nation, as I explained. ❖ Therefore, I was correct when I said that we should choose specifically this *mitzvah* by which to unify, assemble, and weave the entirety of Israel together. Then, with God's help, we will achieve our sacred goal and desire, to elevate our pride, the pride of our holy God, and the pride of the Davidic Dynasty, speedily in our days. Amen.

We will only be redeemed if we unite

מ My brother, do not make light of my assertion that our salvation depends solely on unifying Israel, and that the only way to attain this is by weaving the entire nation together through the settlement and building of the Land. The words of our Rabbis prove this, as I will explain with God's help.

The Holy One Blessed be He says that at the time of redemption, *I will search Jerusalem with candles* (*Tzefanyah* 1:12). The *Pesikta* comments:

> Israel said to Him, "Master of the Universe, is this all of the glory that You promised us – that You will search Jerusalem with candles?! Where is the promise of the prophets, *The sun will no longer be your light by day... The Lord will be a light*

❖ *These are the people of the Country* [*Eretz Yisrael*] *who went up...* (*Ezra* 2:1). All of the commentators[544] are bothered by the fact that it should have said, "These are the people of the Diaspora who went up," because they were not yet in *Eretz Yisrael*. However, based on the above it is clear. The moment they considered ascending, they were called *People of the Country* and were considered as if they were already there. This is a strong proof for my thesis.

542 *Derashot Chatam Sofer*, Sermon for *Shabbat HaGadol*, 5558 [1798]. See below, p. 523.

543 *Teshuvot Tashbetz* 3:288.

544 See Rashi and *Metzudat David*.

> *for you* (*Yeshayah* 60:19). It also says, *Arise, shine, for your light has come, and the glory of the Lord has shone upon you* (ibid. 60:1). And You say, *I will search Jerusalem with candles*?!"
>
> The Holy One Blessed be He replied: "It is not as you think. Rather, it is as I showed Zecharyah in the vision of the menorah, as the verse says, *I looked and behold, an all gold menorah* (זהב כולה) (*Zecharyah* 4:2). This refers to the Assembly of Israel [about whom it says], *You are entirely fair* (כולך יפה), *My beloved, and you have no blemish* (*Shir HaShirim* 4:7)." He [God] also showed this to Moshe, *You shall make a menorah of pure gold* (*Shemot* 25:31). This refers to the Assembly of Israel. (*Pesikta, Piska VeHaya BaEit HaHi; Yalkut Shimoni* 2:567)

This is incomprehensible! How does this answer Israel's complaint?

Above,[545] I explained that the menorah symbolizes Jewish unity. I also explained that the people of Israel cannot be saved unless they are united, because the Attribute of Justice interferes. However, when they are united there is no adversary nor evil affliction, because the entirety of Israel has no blemish. Zecharyah's vision of the menorah demonstrates this very idea, as the verse [and the *Midrash*] say, "*And behold, an all gold menorah*: This refers to the Assembly of Israel." That is, they shine like pure gold only when they are assembled together. Moshe's menorah also alludes to this: *You shall make a menorah of pure gold*. That is to say, Israel will be pure gold only when they are assembled together, as *Chazal* state, "This refers to the Assembly of Israel."

This, then, is HaShem's answer to Israel: "Indeed, I will be a light for you, and you will not need to use any other light. However, I am unable to appear to you with My light until you are completely united as one entity"... Thus, the Holy One Blessed be He replies, "Do not think that I will search for you only with simple candles. Rather, when I say *candles* I mean that you should personify Zecharyah and Moshe's vision of the menorah (candlestick), which represents the Assembly of Israel. You should assemble together into a single unit, and then, *You are entirely fair, My beloved, and you have no blemish*. Then, I will truly be a light for you, and I will say, *Arise, shine, for your light has come, and the glory of the Lord has shone upon you*." In my opinion, this is the explanation of this passage, and it is true and clear, with God's help.

545 P. 383.

An historical proof

סא This actually happened during Ezra's *aliyah*. The people followed Zecharyah's vision of the menorah and joined together like one man for the purpose of building and ascending to the Land. The verse thus says, *The people gathered together as one man to Jerusalem* (*Ezra* 3:1), and, *We together will build for the Lord God of Israel, as King Cyrus has commanded us...* (ibid. 4:3). The Ibn Ezra comments, "*We together*: This alludes to the entire Congregation of Israel." Thus, all the Jews who returned with Ezra joined together, even though some of them were very wicked.[546] But, wickedness is not recognizable in the Jewish collective. This merit [of unity] helped them defeat the adversaries of Yehudah and Binyamin,[547] i.e., the neighboring Gentiles who wanted to stop them.* Had all of *Klal*

---

* The brilliant author of *Siftei Chachamim* comments on the construction of the walls of Jerusalem at the time of Ezra:

> Half of the people held the spears to guard against the enemies who wanted to stop the building, as it says, *So we did the work, and half of them held the spears from the rising of the dawn until the appearance of the stars..., so the night was to us for guarding and the day for work* (*Nechemyah* 4:15-16). This shows how much they sacrificed and bestirred themselves for the building, and it should be a lesson for us.
>
> This explains the [Talmud's] statement: "Perhaps you will say that dawn is not yet considered day and that night begins at sunset, and they [the workers of Ezra's time] arose early and stayed late..."[548] (*Megillah* 20b). That is, [perhaps you will say that] due to their love for *Eretz Yisrael* they were diligent and built even at night, for they sacrificed themselves to build [the Temple], as it says, *and half of them held the spears...*[549]

He wanted to teach us how much we must sacrifice ourselves to build our Land.

546 ∴ As I explained above, pp. 215-16, 291-95.

547 See *Ezra* 4:1.

548 [The Talmud cites these verses from *Nechemyah* to prove that a halachic day begins at dawn and ends at the appearance of the stars. However, it is bothered by the necessity of the second verse, *So the night was...for guarding and the day for work*. The Talmud answers that if only the first verse was stated, "perhaps you will say...they arose early and stayed late." That is, perhaps they were exceptions to the rule. Therefore, the second verse is needed, because it states clearly that they worked only during the day.]

549 *Siftei Chachamim, Megillah* 20b, s.v. *va'anachnu*.

Yisrael joined them, the eternal redemption would have ensued, as I demonstrated above[550] from the words of *Chazal*.

In any event, we see that they successfully reestablished the House of our Lives [the *Beit HaMikdash*] only by joining together as one man with one heart for the purpose of building the Land. Therefore, we must do the same, for this is the only way to successfully fulfill HaShem's desire[551] (may His name be blessed and exalted forever). By virtue of this, HaShem will be a light for us, and His glory will shine upon us, speedily in our days. Amen.

X *Our Age-Old Debt*

The sin of the spies: propaganda against Eretz Yisrael

סב My brothers, in addition to what I have written above..., know that we are obligated to unite all of *Klal Yisrael* by way of this *mitzvah* because of an age-old debt that was loaded upon us at the inception of our nation. We were exiled, we have suffered harsh oppression for thousands of years, and we have wept profusely while dwelling on foreign soil, all in order to pay off this debt. I will preface with the following *Midrash*:

> *The entire congregation lifted up their voice, and the people wept that night* (*BeMidbar* 14:1): This is the meaning of the verse *The words of the talebearer are like blows* (כמתלהמים) (*Mishley* 18:8, 26:22)... R. Eliezer son of R. Yosi HaGalili said, "*The words of the talebearer are* כמתלהמים (כמת להם – as if a relative had died)... So too, when the spies returned from spying out the Land, they spread themselves out among all the tribes of Israel. Each one went to his respective tribe and threw himself down in every corner of his house. His sons and daughters came to him and said, 'What happened my master?' Then, while standing up, he pretended to fall [again], and he said, 'Woe unto me because of you, my sons, daughters, and daughters-in-law. Oh, how the Amorites will mock and rule over you. Who will be able to look at you?... I know what I saw.' All at once, his sons, daughters, and daughters-in-law broke out in tears, until the neighbors heard what had happened, and they, too, began to cry. One family heard from the next until the entire tribe was crying. Each of the spies did the same and caused his tribe

550 Pp. 161, 252-56.

551 Based on *Yeshayah* 53:10.

> to weep. Finally, all 600,000 [Jews] became one group, and they cried bitterly, lifting their voices towards the heavens. From where do we derive this? From the verse *The entire congregation lifted up their voice.*"❖
>
> Another explanation: *Lifted up* (ותשא): The Holy One Blessed be He said to them, "You took a bad loan." ותשא [is understood here like the word תשה in the verse] *When you lend* (תשה) *your friend* (*Devarim* 24:10). "By your lives, you will eventually pay [for this]."
>
> The Holy One Blessed be He said, "You wept in vain; I will establish for you weeping for all generations." At that moment it was decreed that the Temple would be destroyed and that the Jews would be exiled among the nations of the world. Thus, it says, [*They despised the desirable Land...*]; *therefore, He lifted up* (וישא) *His hand against them* (*Tehillim* 106:24-26): a lifting of the hand parallel to a lifting of the voice. (*Yalkut Shimoni* 1:743)

The *Yalkut* explains another verse in a similar way. *You murmured* (ותרגנו) *in your tents and said, "Because the Lord hates us, He brought us out of the Land of Egypt to deliver us into the hand of the Amorite to destroy us. To where shall we ascend? Our brethren have melted our hearts, saying, 'The people are greater and taller than we..., and we have seen the sons of the giants there'"* (*Devarim* 1:27-28). (Rashi comments: "ותרגנו denotes slander, just like, *The words of the tale-bearer* (נרגן), i.e., a person who brings an evil report."):

> This teaches that they sat in their houses and spoke as if a relative had died, as it says, *The words of the talebearer are like blows* (כמתלהמים)... They cried and made others cry as if a relative had died (כמת להם). They took their sons and said, "Woe unto you, O afflicted ones. Tomorrow, they will crucify you." They took their daughters and said, "Woe unto you, O mournful ones, woe unto you, O afflicted ones. Tomorrow, they will murder you, take you captive, and shame you. (*Yalkut Shimoni* 1:805)

Thus, the spies, who were the leaders of Israel, abused and

❖ The *Midrash* is bothered by the words *The entire congregation.* Therefore, it explains that the entire congregation became like one group which wept together because of the dread and fear that each of the spies generated within his tribe...

betrayed the trust that *Klal Yisrael* gave them. The entire nation trusted them and sent them to spy out the Land, in order to discover the most effective way to enter, conquer, and settle their forefathers' Land. This explains Moshe's reproof: *And when the Lord sent you from Kadesh-Barne'a, saying, "Go up and possess the Land that I have given you"* (that is to say, the whole purpose of sending the spies was to go up and possess the Land), *you rebelled against the word of the Lord your God* (*Devarim* 9:23).

Notice, my brothers, that the spies used the same modern technique that people use today when they want to capture the hearts of the masses; it is called propaganda. The spies used this technique so extensively that each prince entered his house and pretended to fall... (as the *Midrash* recounts). Is there any greater propaganda than this? Even nowadays you will have a hard time finding anything like it.

They achieved their goal because they did not spare the trouble of entering (by way of their messengers) the houses of each of the 600,000 Jews and scaring the family members, until the entire congregation, as one group, broke down and cried bitterly. Thus, Israel said, *Our brethren have melted our hearts* (*Devarim* 1:28), by murmuring in each man's tent. This also explains Moshe's statement *You murmured in your tents* (ibid. 1:27). Similarly, David said, *They despised the desirable Land...and murmured in their tents* (*Tehillim* 106:24-25). [Both verses say] *in their tents* to teach that they succeeded in making the desirable Land despicable in the eyes of the entire congregation by murmuring in everyone's tent.

Rectifying this sin: propaganda for Eretz Yisrael

סג Now, my brother, notice that they did not hesitate to use various deceptive and shrewd methods, and that they spared no trouble to mislead the entire nation and arouse them to hate and detest the desirable Land. Their intense propaganda helped them achieve all of this and enabled them to unite the entire nation against our desirable Land. These princes and leaders of the congregation did all of this for their own selfish goals (as I cited above[552] from the holy *Zohar* and the *Shelah HaKadosh*...). They caused the bitter afflictions which we suffered during these past two thousand years and which we continue to suffer to this very day. We see no end to our exile; on the contrary, it intensifies day by day, culminating in our current predicament.

552 P. 49.

This all happened because of the "bad loan" we took back then, as the *Midrash* terms the sin of the spies. The Holy One Blessed be He said, "By your lives, you will eventually pay [for this]," but we have yet to pay up this debt. Therefore, we must endure all [the afflictions] that befall us. Furthermore, *Midrash Eichah* states, "Israel left a 'bad debt' to the future generations with this crying of theirs" (*Eichah Rabbah* 1:23). Thus, as long as this debt has not been paid off, we cannot expect any improvement in our situation, God forbid.

Behold, the Magen Avraham explains that we stay awake on the night of *Shavuot* in order to rectify the sin that our ancestors committed by sleeping through the night prior to the giving of the Torah.[553] Now, if our Rabbis introduced a custom to rectify such a minor infraction, then we must certainly rectify a major infraction like [the sin of the spies]. Our entire existence and honor depends on this; as does the honor of: HaShem, our holy Torah, the Davidic Dynasty, and our Holy Land. Therefore, it is as clear as day, to anyone who wants to admit the truth, that the only way to free ourselves from the horrible predicament in which we have been for close to 2,000 years is to rectify and pay off the "bad debt" that we incurred long ago. Then, when we tear up this bill of debt, we will leave this bitter exile with an uplifted hand, dwell honorably in our Holy Land, and the children will return to their borders,[554] speedily in our days. Amen.

Now, on the night of *Shavuot* we rectify our sin by fulfilling now what we should have done then. We should have stayed awake all night preparing ourselves with bridal ornaments for the designated day when the Holy One Blessed be He would enter into a nuptial covenant with the Assembly of Israel under the canopy of Mt. Sinai.[555] Since we were remiss back then, we make up for it now, each and every year. Similarly, in order to rectify the sin of the spies, which caused us this "bad debt" (for which we pay until this very day) we must fulfill what was lacking then. When we do this, our debt will be paid off, our bill of debt torn up, and we will (God willing) achieve the great and wondrous salvation which all of Israel awaits with great anticipation.

553 *Magen Avraham, Shulchan Aruch, Orach Chayim* 494 (introduction).
554 Based on *Yirmiyah* 31:16.
555 See *Pirkei DeRebbe Eliezer*, chap. 41.

As I already mentioned,[556] the angel of the holy volume, *Maggid Meisharim*, told our master, the Beit Yosef, that Moshe Rabbeinu sent the spies expecting that they would return and extol *Eretz Yisrael* and its special qualities. This would arouse within the hearts of Israel a burning desire and an intense yearning to enter *Eretz Yisrael* as soon as possible. This burning desire would make the Jews worthy of inheriting the Land, even though they were not worthy of it on their own merit. However, because of their selfish motives, the spies did exactly the opposite. Using various methods and expending much effort, they caused the nation to hate and abhor *Eretz Yisrael*, as I explained above.

Thus, if we want to rectify this sin, we must strive to arouse the Children of Israel, wherever they may be, to love and desire the desirable Land of our forefathers. Then, a fire will burn within them to come and inherit the Holy Land, and they will desire it more than anything in the world. This will be the complete rectification of the great sin mentioned above. In this way, we will pay off the ancient debt that we incurred at the inception of our nation, the debt which causes us, to this very day, such diverse and frequent troubles that we have practically perished, God forbid. When we complete this rectification, our bill of debt will be torn up and the day of salvation will arrive with great wonders and grandeur. This is the day for which we have waited, let us exult and rejoice in His salvation,[557] speedily in our days. Amen.

However, my dear brother, you must be aware of what *Chazal* say in the *Midrash*: Righteous people rectify their sins in the same manner that they commit them (*Tanchuma, BeShalach* 24). Therefore, we must inspire the hearts of Israel and kindle within them the fire of desire for *Eretz Yisrael* using the same methods that our ancestors used to undermine Israel's desire for the Land. The generation of the spies united the entire congregation against *Eretz Yisrael* and put a great deal of effort into propaganda. They established an entire propaganda organization - what we would call today a propaganda department - which organized people to convince others to oppose *Eretz Yisrael*. Similarly, we must establish a propaganda apparatus which will permeate every Jewish home and try to convince every Jewish soul to support *Eretz Yisrael*.

With God's help, if we do so we will succeed in uniting all of *Klal*

556 P. 258.
557 Based on *Yeshayah* 25:9.

Yisrael behind *Eretz Yisrael*. Then, the "bad debt" will be paid off; the bill will be torn up; the sin will be rectified; the prosecutor will withdraw; the defender will grow strong; the day of salvation will arrive; and the verse, *Let the heavens be glad and the earth rejoice* (I *Divrei HaYamim* 16:31), will be fulfilled through us. For, the joy will be in both the upper and lower [worlds]. Amen, so may it be God's will.

We must use propaganda just like the Gentiles do

סד *Beit Rebbe*, a book about the Ba'al HaTanya, recounts various lessons that the Rebbe learned from the war between Napoleon and Russia (which he lived through).[558] We, too, must learn from today's war. The warring kingdoms have established propaganda departments whose sole purpose is to promulgate their doctrine and capture the hearts of the masses. Similarly, we must appoint great men, blessed with true wisdom and abounding insight, imbued with fear of God and talent, to convince the masses of the importance of this sacred and lofty ideal. These men must be able to enlighten the holy nation of their obligation towards settling *Eretz Yisrael* and arouse within them the desire to elevate the pride of the Land and raise it from the dust.

Tana DeVei Eliyahu also states that we are permitted to learn this kind of lesson from gentile practices. The *Midrash* explains that Elkanah instructed the Jews to ascend [to Shiloh][559] for the festivals en masse and with great enthusiasm, in order to fulfill the verse *A multitude of people is the King's glory* (*Mishley* 14:28). He said to them:

> Learn the way of worship from the Canaanites and the idolatrous nations. They created an orderly system of worship for their gods, even though these gods are vanity and nothingness. Certainly, then, you must worship HaShem in an orderly fashion and ascend to the ark of the covenant, for HaShem is a living God, blessed be His name for ever and ever. [Then], Elkanah told them to ascend with him. (*Eliyahu Rabbah* 8:8-9)

In order to publicize the matter, they lodged in the main square of each city through which they passed. The *Midrash* describes at length how Elkanah persuaded Israel to ascend with him en masse and joyfully, in order to glorify the King of the Universe. The Holy One Blessed be He was grateful for this and rewarded him with

558 *Beit Rebbe* (Brooklyn: Kahat, 5713 [1953]), vol. 1, p. 110; vol. 2, pp. 152-156.
559 [The site of the *Mishkan* before the Temple was built in Jerusalem.]

Shmuel the prophet [as a son]. *Tana DeVei Eliyahu* concludes: "From here you learn that Shmuel was a reward for Elkanah's deed."

Thus, Elkanah learned from the Gentiles how to utilize organization and propaganda for sacred matters. Therefore, what I said above – that we should learn from them to use propaganda to generate a love for the Land – is not far-fetched. However, for our purposes, we do not need to learn this from the Gentiles, for the spies employed these exact same methods against HaShem and the Land. Therefore, we are obligated to rectify their sin and use these very methods to glorify HaShem and the Land.

I am certain that had we done this from time immemorial – that is, enlighten the nation of the great virtue of cherishing the Land[560] – then, we would not have reached the point in which there are innocent, pure-hearted people, even Torah Jews, who think that it is forbidden to preach or hear public sermons about cherishing the Land.[561] Furthermore, there would not be people who make such ear-splitting statements like, "The reason the Jews of other countries were punished is because they engaged in settling the Land, and the reason the Hungarian Jews were spared is because they stayed far away from this endeavor."[562] I heard this distorted judgment with my own ears. Innocent, simple, God-fearing Jews, and even learned *chassidim*, aroused themselves to speak against those who cherish the Land. They do not realize that they have fallen into the sin of the spies, thereby increasing our age-old debt. Unwittingly, they enkindle HaShem's wrath (God forbid). May the good God forgive them for this, for they speak out of ignorance and do not realize how far-reaching are their words. This all happened because they do not know enough about this important issue. Therefore, we must teach them this great principle, in order to rectify the age-old sin of the spies. We must teach them to desire and yearn for our Land and refrain from arousing hatred against its inhabitants. By doing this, we will appease the Master, HaShem, and merit to see the complete redemption, speedily in our days. Amen.

The leaders must propagandize for Eretz Yisrael

סה Furthermore, my brother, know that in order to rectify our ancestors' sin, everything must be exactly as it was then. At

560 ❖ Which is the only way we can achieve redemption, as the angel told our mentor, the Beit Yosef. See above, p. 258.

561 See above, p. 355ff.

562 See above, pp. 349, 355.

that time, the leaders of the congregation spread evil propaganda against *Eretz Yisrael*. Therefore, today, as well, the leaders of the congregation must propagandize for the sake of *Eretz Yisrael*, in order to pay off their "bad loan." They must be the first ones to open the nation's eyes. They must explain that there is no reason for us to remain in the foreign, impure, and polluted atmosphere of exile, nor to expend our energies in vain while the Gentiles rob the fruits of our labor from before our very eyes. The leaders must speak to the people in this fashion and arouse within them a fire and a spark of love for our desirable Land. This alone will make us worthy of redemption, as I cited above from the Beit Yosef's *Maggid*.[563] The Maharsha also writes that when the people of Israel cherish the stones and dust of *Eretz Yisrael* they bring the appointed time of redemption closer.[564] Thus, the leaders will unite all of *Klal Yisrael* together for the sake of *Eretz Yisrael*, and then our "bad debt" will be paid off.

However, if the leaders neglect this matter, there is a danger that they themselves will have to pay for the bad loan that they took back then. The *halachah* states that if two partners borrow money from someone, the lender can collect the entire debt from whichever partner he wishes, because each partner becomes a guarantor for his friend.[565] The same applies to the "bad debt" that the spies and their entire generation incurred. Since they all joined together [against *Eretz Yisrael*],[566] they became like partners who borrowed from the Holy One Blessed be He. Therefore, if HaShem wants He can collect the debt – which *Klal Yisrael* incurred by causing the exile – entirely from Israel's leaders. Moreover, the leaders have a greater obligation to pay off this debt, because they were the primary cause of this "loan" to begin with.

This explains the words of our mentor, the Or HaChayim. He writes that Israel's leaders throughout the generations will be held responsible for the fact that we are still in exile, because they should have inspired the Children of Israel to love *Eretz Yisrael*.[567] Even though he explains [this to mean] that the leaders must uplift the

563 See p. 258.
564 Maharsha, *Ta'anit* 15a, s.v. *baruch ata HaShem merachem*. ❖ I cited this above (pp. 277-78, 302).
565 See *Shulchan Aruch, Choshen Mishpat* 77:3.
566 ❖ See the *Midrash* I cited above (pp. 396-97).
567 *Or HaChayim, VaYikra* 25:25.

Jews spiritually and make them worthy of redemption, he also asserts that the afflictions of the birthpangs of *Mashiach* will complete the repentance.[568] Now, in our days we have already suffered more than our share of the birthpangs of *Mashiach*. In all of Jewish history there has never been such calamity. Therefore, we do not lack the element of repentance. The only thing we lack is a desire and a love for the Land which will make us worthy of entering it.

Furthermore, the Or HaChayim writes that if Israel does not repent, the redemption will occur naturally.[569] Therefore, now that it is impossible to bring the world to repentance, as we [clearly] see,[❖] we expect only a natural redemption. Thus, the leaders of the generation must inspire the Children of Israel to help bring the redemption closer using the natural means that HaShem has prepared for us. We are not worthy enough for it to occur with manifest miracles, only with miracles disguised in nature, as in the days of Cyrus. Our mentor, the Kedushat Levi expounds on this in his work.[570]

Hence, the generation's leaders must encourage all of Israel to help pay off the loan that they took as partners at the time of the spies. They are considered partners who become guarantors (ערב) for one another... Now too, every Jew is responsible (ערב) for our bitter and lengthy exile. The leaders are even more responsible, because they caused this bad loan, and they have the ability to exhort and arouse the nation to cherish and desire the Land. The brilliant prince of the Torah from Dvinsk concurs in his pamphlet, *Yeshivat Eretz Yisrael*:

> The *gaonim* who sit in the tents of Torah and wisdom and upon the seats of the Rabbinate (may HaShem grant them long life) have a foremost obligation to publicize this beloved, lofty, and profound *mitzvah*, which affects the overall existence and character of our nation.[571] For, the great length of the exile made many people practically forget about this *mitzvah*. There are even those who are stubborn enough to oppose it publicly.

❖ Also, R. Yehudah states that Israel will not repent until Eliyahu comes (*Yalkut Shimoni* 2:595).

568 Ibid., ibid., 25:26.
569 Ibid., *BeMidbar* 24:17.
570 *Kedushat Levi*, First *Kedushah*, p. 337.
571 See above, pp. 233-35.

> This error cannot be uprooted easily, unless our brilliant rabbis, who sit in judgment, arouse themselves to reform these stubborn people.[572]

But, if the leaders fail to do this, they will delay the payment of this age-old debt and, consequently, delay the redemption. Then, the Holy One Blessed be He will collect the entire debt from them (God forbid), in accordance with the law that a lender may collect an entire loan from one of the partners, especially from the partner who causes the delay in payment. This is what the Or HaChayim HaKadosh means when he says that the leaders will be held responsible for this. I demonstrated that this idea is built on a law in *Choshen Mishpat.**

---

* In the introduction to the second volume of my responsa, *Mishneh Sachir,*[573] I explain a verse in *Yechezkel*: *I have made you a watchman for the House of Israel... When I say to a wicked person, "O wicked one, you shall surely die," and you do not speak to warn the wicked one concerning his way, that wicked one will die in his iniquity, but I will demand his blood* (דמו) *from your hand* (33:7-8). I assert that the word דמו can mean either blood or money, as I will explain with God's help.

The *Midrash* says: *"And her tear is upon her cheek* (לחיה) (*Eichah* 1:2), [meaning] upon her *kohanim* (priests), as it says, *They shall give the priest the shoulder, the cheeks* (הלחיים), *and the maw* [of the sacrifices] (*Devarim* 18:3)" (*Eichah Rabbah* 1:25). This is extremely puzzling. Were these trivial priestly gifts the only thing they had to cry about when the Land was destroyed? The brilliant author of *Matta De-Yerushalayim* of Pressburg elucidates this *Midrash* beautifully in the introduction to his work, *To'ar Moshe* (on the laws of *Shechitah*):

The verse says, *This shall be the priest's due* (משפט)[574] *from the*

572 *Yeshivat Eretz Yisrael*, p. 58a.

573 ❖ I printed this book in 5699-5700 [1939-1940], and it is still sitting in the Katzburg Printing House in Tirna. May HaShem grant me the privilege to promptly retrieve it amidst Israel's salvation. I am very distressed about this work, for I took great pains to have it printed, and it is a considerable work both quantitatively (it consists of 150 pages) and qualitatively (it contains 214 responsas on practical halachic issues in all four sections of the *Shulchan Aruch*).

574 [In the following selection, the word "משפט" is used in different ways: due, right, and judgment (or claim). Therefore, we placed the word "משפט" in parentheses next to the translation.]

people... They shall give the priest the shoulder, the cheeks, and the maw (*Devarim* 18:3). We must examine the word *mishpat* (משפט) in the context of the priestly gifts. It seems that the Torah is telling us that both sides – the *kohanim* and the nation – have a *mishpat* towards one another.

The priests of HaShem teach the nation of HaShem the ways of Torah and *mitzvot*, as it is written, *They shall teach your statutes to Ya'akov* (ibid. 33:10). Therefore, the gifts that the people of Israel give them are rightfully (במשפט) theirs, in exchange for the service that they perform for the people.[575] The opposite is also true. Since the priestly gifts are given in exchange for the supervision and instruction that the priests provide for the nation of HaShem, if they fail to fulfill this obligation, HaShem's nation has a claim [lit., judgment (משפט)] against them. The verse thus says, *The Lord will enter into judgment* (משפט) *with the elders and princes of His people,* [saying], *"You have consumed the vineyard; that which you robbed from the poor is in your houses"* (*Yeshayah* 3:14). Since the priests do not watch over the nation of HaShem, their portion and reward is stolen property.

Now, it is well known that *Chazal* explain the verse, *Her princes were like harts* (*Eichah* 1:6), to mean that the princes hid their faces in the ground and did not rebuke the Jewish people (*Eichah Rabbah* 1:33). They failed to watch over them and eventually caused the Land to be destroyed. Now, as long as the Land stood strong and the people continued in the stubbornness of their hearts,[576] without any interference on the part of the *kohanim*..., the people had no ill feelings towards them for their silence. On the contrary, they were grateful for it. However, after the Land was destroyed and they experienced the hardships of the bitter exile, they cried over the fact that the *kohanim* did not watch over them and make sure that they follow the ways of HaShem. They said, "We fulfilled our obligation towards the *kohanim* and gave them their portion, but they did not fulfill their obligation towards us."

This explains *Chazal*'s statement: "*And her tear is upon her cheek*, [meaning] upon her *kohanim*, as it says, *They shall give the priest the shoulder, the cheeks and the maw*." That is to say, we were vindicated in their judgment (משפט) against us, but they were not vindicated in our judgment (משפט) against them. Hence,

575 Based on *BeMidbar* 18:21.
576 Based on *Devarim* 29:18.

סו I explained above[582] that we must unify all of *Klal Yisrael* through the *mitzvah* of settling the Land not only because our redemption depends on it, but also in order to pay off our age-old debt. Now, based on the preceding ideas, we can understand this better. Just as during the time of the spies all of Israel united for evil, to oppose *Eretz Yisrael*; today as well, we must unify all of Israel for good, to support *Eretz Yisrael*. This way, we will pay off our debt, tear up our record of liability, and cause the glory of HaShem to shine upon us with the complete redemption, speedily in our days. Amen.

We will not be redeemed until we pay off our debt

---

all the reward that they received from us is stolen. They are the ones who caused our bitter lot and the destruction of the Land. For they knew how to take the reward and the gifts, but they did not know how to supervise us so that we would not reach our current situation. Therefore, they need to cry and lament, not us.

Subsequently, I found [a similar idea] in the holy work, *Beit Aharon*, by our sacred, awesome, and exceedingly lofty master, R. Aharon of Karlin *z"l*. He wrote a letter rebuking rabbis and teachers who sit upon the thrones of judgment[577] and derive benefit from the consecrated payment that they receive from the community. "If they abuse their divine task, it is as if they commit *me'ilah* (מעילה) and *piggul* (פיגול),[578] God forbid. For they receive money which is holy to HaShem[579] and fill their bellies with divinely consecrated items, without giving pleasure – a pleasing aroma – to HaShem."[580] This is a short excerpt from his lengthy tirade.

Thus, the prophet's statement [above], *I will demand his blood* (דמו) *from your hand*, has a double connotation. 1. Actual blood (דם): I will hold you [the leaders] responsible for the Jewish blood that is spilled, God forbid, as I cited at the beginning of this book from *Tana DeVei Eliyahu*.[581] 2. Money (דמים): I will demand the money and reward that you received from them. For, since you did not watch over them it is [as if] you stole it.

577 Based on *Tehillim* 122:5.

578 [*Me'ilah* – Deriving personal benefit from consecrated items (see *VaYikra* 5:14-16). *Piggul* – Literally, abomination. A sacrifice offered with improper intentions (see *VaYikra* 7:18, 19:7).]

579 Based on *Yirmiyah* 2:3.

580 *Beit Aharon* (Petrokov, 5674 [1914]), p. 296, s.v. *u'mah me'od*.

581 See above, pp. 23-24.

582 See p. 396.

But, as long as we fail to do this, all of our complaints to the Holy One Blessed be He about the lengthiness of our exile are in vain. In vain we pray in our synagogues and study halls, "Our Father, our King, erase through Your abundant mercy all of our bills of debt." For, the debt that we incurred by despising the desirable Land ❖ still hovers over us. How can we pray that God should erase this bill of debt when it is up to us to pay it off and rectify it? This is like a debtor who asks his creditor to rip up the bill of debt before he has paid. The creditor will certainly do no such thing! The same is true of us.

We must ask HaShem to persuade the hearts of all of Israel to recognize the truth and accept my words. For, all that I have written here is built on the foundations of truth – the words of *Chazal*, whose every utterance is true and righteous.

Coope-rating with irreligious Jews

מז I know that the humble ones who separate themselves from the building effort do so for the sake of Heaven. They fear that they and their children may be harmed by joining people whose ways have strayed from the path of the Torah. Behold, we can say about such people that although their intentions are acceptable, their actions are not,[583] for many reasons.

First of all, I already mentioned[584] that the prophet Yeshayahu said to King Chizkiyah, "Do as you are commanded! Why do you involve yourself with the Merciful One's hidden matters?" (*Berachot* 10a). The same applies here. All Jews must be united in order to fulfill the biblically ordained, positive commandment of building and settling the Land. It cannot be accomplished individually. Therefore, do as you are commanded! Why do you involve yourself with the Merciful One's hidden matters?

Furthermore, "One *mitzvah* leads to another" (*Avot* 4:2), and no harm will come to any Jew who participates in this great and exceedingly lofty *mitzvah*. On the contrary, if a large number of Orthodox Jews join in, they will enhance the sanctity of the Land, as I cited above[585]

❖ As it says, *They despised the desirable Land...and murmured in their tents* (*Tehillim* 106:24-25). The *Midrash* comments that Israel took a bad loan at that time (*Eichah Rabbah* 1:23).

583 Based on *Kuzari* 1:1.

584 ❖ Quoting the Talmud and *Tana DeVei Eliyahu*. (See pp. 172-73.)

585 Pp. 312-14.

in the name of the holy Rebbe of Gur (may he live) and the Ramban.

Boaz and Ploni Almoni

In addition, I have a clear proof from the *Tanach* that such a claim is incorrect. At the very inception of the light of our righteous Savior (*Mashiach*), Ruth the Moabite said to Boaz, *Spread your cloak over your handmaid, for you are a redeemer* (*Ruth* 3:9). He responded that there is another redeemer who is a closer relative than he: *Stay this night, and it will be that in the morning if he will redeem you, good! Let him redeem. But, if he does not want to redeem you, then I will redeem you* (ibid. 3:13). *Then, Boaz went up to the gate and sat down there, and behold, the redeemer of whom Boaz spoke passed by. He* [Boaz] *said, "Turn aside, sit down here, Ploni Almoni,"*[586] *and he turned aside and sat down... Then, Boaz said, "The day you buy the field from the hand of Naomi, you must also buy* [it] *from the hand of Ruth the Moabite, the wife of the deceased, to establish the name of the deceased on his inheritance." The redeemer said, "I cannot redeem it for myself, lest I ruin my own inheritance. You redeem it..."* (ibid. 4:1,5-6). This is exactly what Boaz did, he took Ruth and bore her our righteous Savior.

Rashi explains: "*Lest I ruin my own inheritance* (נחלתי), i.e., my offspring, as in the verse *The heritage* (נחלת) *of the Lord is children* (*Tehillim* 127:3). [That is, lest I] cause my offspring to be blemished."

Thus, this redeemer was a "pious Jew" (*frummer*).[587] He was afraid to take Ruth and bring forth the light of *Mashiach*, lest she cause his children to be blemished, [for she was a Moabite]. Scripture denounces him for this, as Rashi writes on the words *Ploni Almoni*: "His name is not written, because he did not want to redeem [her]." Even though he stated his reason, *Lest I ruin my own inheritance*, the verse accuses him of acting improperly. For when it comes to revealing the light of *Mashiach*, one must not be a fool and act overly pious. *

---

* Behold, there is a wise saying told in the name of our holy Rebbe, R. Naftali of Ropschitz *z"l*: A proper Jew must be good, religious, and wise. One without the others is insufficient. Someone who is only good may be an adulterer (may the Merciful One protect us); someone who is only religious may be a fool; and someone who is only wise

586 [Literally, "Anonymous one."]
587 [Yiddish for "Religious Jew."]

may be a heretic. However, someone who is good, religious, and wise is a proper Jew.[588]

Actually, I found this idea stated explicitly in *Tosafot*. They quote a *Midrash* which says that a person must be wise, humble, and God-fearing and that one without the other two is insufficient.[589] *Or Zarua HaGadol* also cites this *Midrash*.[590]

Boaz followed our holy Rebbe's opinion and was not afraid of, *Lest I ruin my own inheritance*. He was God-fearing and wise, and he knew the principle set down in *Chovot HaLevavot*: "One of the components of caution is not to be overly cautious."[591] Therefore, he simply did as he was commanded and let the Holy One Blessed be He do His part. He also knew that when it is necessary to reveal the light of *Mashiach* one must not be overly pious. And since he did his share, he was worthy of revealing the light of *Mashiach*.

The same is true of building the Land. Since we are commanded to build the Land and raise it from the dust, it is forbidden to be overly pious and undermine this endeavor, God forbid. Rather, we must build with whomever it may be and concentrate on enhancing the sanctity of the Land. Then, HaShem will assist us, as I explained above. We must not stop or hinder the building, God forbid, for a wise man would not do that. (A word to the wise is sufficient.)

Above,[592] I cited *Chavot Ya'ir* which states that R. Zeira called the Babylonian Jews "Stupid Babylonians" (*Beitzah* 16a) because of his love for *Eretz Yisrael*.[593] This teaches us how much it pained R. Zeira that so many Jews failed to ascend to *Eretz Yisrael* with Ezra. Because of them, the redemption did not last. Now, R. Zeira was a very earnest man; he never let even the slightest laughter cross his lips. The Talmud describes how R. Yirmiyah went to great lengths to make R. Zeira laugh, but failed (*Niddah* 23a). In addition, R. Zeira used to fast many days for every little thing (see *Bava Metzia* 85a). It goes without saying, then, that he did not speak idly or insult others. [Why, then,] did he call the Babylonians stupid? The answer is as I said above: It pained him greatly that they did not ascend to *Eretz Yisrael* at the time of Ezra, for had they done so the redemption

588 Cited in *Ohel Naftali, Likutim* 312.
589 *Tosafot, Avodah Zarah* 20b, s.v. *anavah*, citing *Derech Eretz Rabbah* 7.
590 *Derush HaAlfa Beta* 44.
591 ❖ I cited this above, p. 25.
592 Sec. י״ד, p. 254.
593 *Chavot Ya'ir* 152.

The same is true of building the Land. I already cited our great and holy Rabbis who say that the light of *Mashiach* will shine when we build and cherish the Land. But, today's "pious ones" claim, like Ploni Almoni, "*Lest I ruin my inheritance.*" Boaz, on the other hand, was wise and ignored this claim; and indeed, the light of *Mashiach* came from him. We must do the same and completely ignore the claim of today's "pious ones." We must cherish our Holy Land and sacrifice ourselves for it. This way, we will cause the light of *Mashiach* to shine forth, with God's help, speedily in our days. Amen.

Why do people oppose this lofty endeavor?

At the beginning of this work,[595] I mentioned that the brilliant teacher of Israel, R. Yusha'le Kutner *z"l*, told the brilliant R. Tzvi Kalischer to ignore the words of the antagonists because they speak out of ignorance. The holy and divine *gaon*, R. Eliyahu of Greiditz,[596] and the brilliant Kabbalist, R. Akiva Yosef (author of *Lev HaIvri*),[597] go even further. They say that these antagonists are blinded by the *kelipot* (evil forces), may the Merciful One protect us. A third possibility is that their opposition stems from the counsel of the spies. I explained above,[598] at length, that the spies' selfish motives prevented them from entering the Land.

In summation, anyone who has a brain in his head and truly believes in HaShem and His Land will let no claim in the world stop him from elevating the pride of our Land. The arguments of those who try to prevent people from building the Land are the arguments of Satan and his associates, may the Merciful One protect us from their viewpoint. In addition, the Ya'avetz refutes the argument that there are sinners in the Land by pointing out that the same is true of *Chutz LaAretz*.[599] This is even more true today after all that we

---

would have been eternal. But, because of some "pious" (*frum*) reasoning they remained behind and caused what they caused. He called them stupid, because when it is necessary to accomplish something as crucial as *aliyah* to *Eretz Yisrael*, one must not engage in nonsense and futility.[594]

594 ❖ See the end of *Ketuvot* (112a) [where the Talmud describes] the extent to which R. Zeira loved the Land.

595 P. 3.

596 See above, p. 15.

597 ❖ See above, sec. נב, pp. 354-55.

598 P. 49.

599 *Siddur Beit Ya'akov, Sullam Beit El*, p. 13b, col. a.

have been through. Where are all the Torah centers of Poland, Lithuania, and Hungary? Do we still have a portion and an inheritance here? Are we not considered strangers by the inhabitants of these lands? They have devoured our money,[600] our bodies, and our spirituality. Thus, any intelligent and truly God-fearing person will realize that there is nothing more to search for here in exile. The time has come for all of us to return to our forefathers' possession. This is true and clear in accordance with the truth of the Torah, and anyone who denies it denies the truth and the Torah.

The power of a talit bag

סח My brother! I will explain this further with a parable, a story that actually happened to me. When I fled the land of hell to save my bare soul, I was unable to take any personal belongings with me. I was even forced to leave my Rabbeinu Tam *tefillin* (phylacteries). The only thing I rescued was my Rashi *tefillin*... I simply could not part with them, because they are worth more to me than anything in the world; they are irreplaceable. I bought them when I was young, before the First World War, and gave them over to the famous, perfectly righteous scribe, R. Chayim Sofer of Munkatch *z"l*, to have them rewritten. This is why they are so precious to me, and I do not make the slightest move without them.

When I arrived here in the capital [Budapest], I was missing Rabbeinu Tam *tefillin* and a *talit* (prayer shawl). I hereby express gratitude to my dear friend, the brilliant rabbi, perfect *tzaddik*, son of saints, our master, ***R. Yisrael David Margolis Schlessinger***, rabbi of the Linat Tzedek study hall, here [in Budapest]. Through his efforts, an honorable, God-fearing man in the community, R. Chayim Mordechai Stern (may his light shine forth), gave me a very beautiful pair of Rabbeinu Tam *tefillin*. This truly gave me new life, for now I had two pairs of *tefillin*, but I was still missing a *talit*. I praise my affluent friend, R. Wolf Reichman (may his light shine forth), for giving me a *talit* with which to pray.

Everything was not yet perfect, however, because I was still missing a prayer belt (*gartle*). HaShem helped me with this as well, for an old student of mine, who learned in our yeshiva, provided me with a *gartle*. But, everything was still not perfect, because although I had all of these sacred articles, I was missing a *siddur* (prayer book). I hereby express my gratitude to my friend and disciple, paragon of Torah and piety, our honorable master and rabbi, R. Zalman Leib

600 Based on *BeReishit* 31:14-15.

Kalman (may his light shine forth), one of the guardians of the Talmud Society here in the capital city, also a disciple of my brilliant and righteous mentor and father-in-law of blessed memory. He gave me a *siddur* with which to pray.

Blessed is HaShem Who provided me with all of the sacred articles I needed for my daily prayers. Nevertheless, every morning when I wanted to pray, I was very distressed, because these items were never available at the same time. Once I was missing Rashi's *tefillin*, once Rabbeinu Tam's, once a *talit*... This happened day after day, and I was barely able to gather them all together at the same time. Why did this happen? Because I did not have a *talit* bag in which to put all of these sacred articles, to hold them together and prevent them from scattering. Finally, my friend and student, R. Zalman Leib, had compassion on me and provided me with a *talit* bag. From then on, I was satisfied and pleased, because whenever I wanted to pray I found everything prepared and ready. I was overjoyed with this *talit* bag because it helped me gather these items together whenever I needed them, and I no longer had to search for each one individually.

I contemplated the great power of this *talit* bag. It has the ability to gather and connect everything together, so that nothing will ever be missing or separated from the rest. It gives these items value and enables them to fulfill their intended purpose whenever necessary. However, after much contemplation, I realized that although it has this great power to gather things together, it is incapable of affecting any change, for better or for worse, in the items that are placed in it. I never found that any of these sacred articles became unholy or transformed into a different object... The *talit* bag only has the power to gather things together, but has no influence whatsoever on the items it contains.

This story of the *talit* bag is a fitting metaphor for the Jews in exile. There are many different levels of Jews. Some are extremely holy, like Rashi's *tefillin*; some are like Rabbeinu Tam's; some are on the level of a *talit*; some are on the level of a *gartle*; and some are on the level of a *siddur* – these are the simple Jews, who are as simple as a *siddur*. And, some are inferior, but they are Jews nonetheless. All of these groups must be united and interconnected, as the *mitzvah* of the Four Species demonstrates.[601]

601 See *VaYikra Rabbah* 30:12; Hymn (*piyut*) for *Sukkot*, *Ekchah BaRishon...*, *Machzor Rabbah*, pp. 132-35.

All Jews are essential to the nation and must unite

Furthermore, we need one another, as the Rebbe of Tzanz explains so well in his commentary on the Torah, *Divrei Chayim*. He compares [Israel] to a body. The human body has various essential, life-supporting organs, like the head and the heart. It also has unessential limbs, like the arms and legs, without which a person can live. Nevertheless, can the head say to the arms and legs, "I do not want to associate with you, because I can live without you," or "I do not want to have anything to do with you, because you are inferior to me"? Of course not! For even though a person can live without arms or legs, what kind of life is that? May the Merciful One spare us from such a life. In reality, the head needs the legs, for they support the entire body; and it needs the arms, for they perform all actions. These limbs perfect man's form and make him complete. The same is true of a nation. Some people are highly perceptive and intelligent, and others are ignorant and inferior. Nonetheless, they are all essential to the nation and compliment one another. They must be united.[602]

However, since we are scattered among the nations, it is impossible to gather us together, and we are always incomplete. This is our weakness and the reason why everyone rules over us. This is also why we are severed and detached from one another, as I explained above in my description of the "exile Jew."[603] It is all because we do not have anything to join us together and ensure that our individual parts do not scatter about.

Thus, if we rectify our age-old sin (with God's help) and reunite all of *Klal Yisrael* through the positive commandment of *Yishuv Eretz Yisrael*,[604] this unification will be the great "*talit* bag" of the holy nation. It will help bring together all the fragments of Israel throughout the world, without necessarily having any detrimental effect on the individual parts. Everyone will be able to continue his former practices. The *chassidim* will build a *kloyz*[605] for themselves

602 ❖ *Divrei Chayim* on the Torah, Addendum to *Parashat Re'eh*. Also see above, sec. לג (pp. 308-9) where I cited the Rambam's introduction to *Zera'im* which says that the Holy One Blessed be He placed the wicked ones [the seven nations] in *Eretz Yisrael* in order to create a society for the righteous ones, so that they will not be lonely.

603 Sec. נה, p. 369ff.

604 ❖ I explained above, at length (pp. 390-93), that only this *mitzvah* can unite all of Israel, making it into one nation.

605 Yiddish for a house of study (*beit midrash*).

in which to learn, pray, and educate their children according to the desire of their pure souls. The holy and pure *perushim* ("puritans"), will also [lead their lives as they see fit]... We will only join together as one man with one heart on the issue of building and settling the Land. All of Israel will be united in this specific area, just as they were in the days of Ezra, as I cited above.[606]

In this way, our debt will be paid, Israel's pride will be raised, and every Jew will find his appropriate place. Then, knowledge [of HaShem] will increase, as I cited above[607] in the name of the Rebbe of Gur *shlita* (*zt"l*) and the Ramban. They assert that large numbers of God-fearing Jews influence their surroundings even without intending to do so, thus causing knowledge [of HaShem] to increase. Then, the words of our mentor, the Rambam, which I cited many times,[608] will be fulfilled. He writes that after many Jews assemble in *Eretz Yisrael*, HaShem will place in their hearts a purifying spirit, and they will join together to serve Him and keep His *mitzvot* wholeheartedly. Amen, so may it be God's will.

Summary

סט In summation, we all need the *mitzvah* of building the Land to make us into one united entity. This is the only way that our efforts will succeed, God willing. That is to say, we must maintain economic solidarity and work together.[609] I proved above that our salvation and redemption depend solely on Israel's unity.

The experience of today's war also proves this. Each of the battling sides [realizes] that its victory depends solely on unifying its [component] nations. These nations must work together as one man with one heart, without any division or dissension, to achieve the goal for which they went to war. Each side [realizes] that if it is plagued with dissension it enables the other side to prevail. Thus, both sides struggle to maintain unity, even against their [members'] will. They force all of the factions that existed among them during peaceful times to unite for the common goal of defeating the enemy which seeks to destroy them. We must do the same, for this is the only way we will reach our desired goal, with the help of God.

The *Brit Bein HaBetarim* which HaShem made with Avraham Avinu also alludes to this. Avraham asked, *By what shall I know*

606 P. 395.
607 Pp. 312-14.
608 See p. 117.
609 [Originally in Yiddish.]

that I will inherit it [the Land] (*BeReishit* 15:8)? The Holy One Blessed be He answered, *Take for Me three heifers... He* [Avraham] *took all of these and cut them down the middle..., but the bird, he did not cut up* (ibid. 15:9-10). HaShem hinted to him that the bird, which represents Israel,[610] should not be cut up into factions. It must be a united assembly, and then the people of Israel will inherit the Land. Thus, the Holy One Blessed be He promised Avraham that the Jews are guaranteed to inherit the Land only when they are completely united.

We must unite and build our Land together

ע Therefore, I implore all Jews throughout the world, small and great, men and women, young and old: Arise! Stand strong! Prepare yourselves to enter into the covenant of building the Land. Not a single soul should be left out (even though, in reality, a majority is sufficient, as is clear from the Talmud [*Horayot* 3a]). Let us all build our Land collectively,[611] for the first and second Temples were eventually destroyed because many Jews failed to participate in its construction. Therefore, if we all join together now, the settlement will last forever, and HaShem will be with us. The verse thus says, *Be strong, all you people of the land, says the Lord, and do, for I am with you, says the Lord of Hosts... And My spirit remains among you; do not fear* (*Chaggai* 2:4-5). Then, we will deserve the final redemption and the renewal of the Davidic Dynasty, because there is no adversary nor evil affliction when the entire congregation is united.[612]

Thus, in my opinion, we must direct our efforts primarily towards uniting the entire holy nation on the issue of building the Land.[613] We must appoint officers to actualize our potential unity.[614] Then, we will merit to see the elevation of the pride of HaShem, His nation, and His anointed one (*Mashiach*). For, I proved above[615] that our salvation and glorification depend solely on this. May HaShem desire this, speedily in our days. Amen. Amen.

610 ❖ See *Noam Elimelech* cited above (p. 381).

611 [Lit., "When you all come," or ôen masse.ö] See Rambam, *Hilchot Terumot* 1:26; Maharsha, *Yoma* 9b, s.v. *ke'chomah*; above, p. 256.

612 ❖ I mentioned this above (pp. 381-83), citing our holy Rabbis who possessed *Ruach HaKodesh*.

613 ❖ As I explained above at length (pp. 390-93).

614 ❖ See what our mentor, the Maharal, says above (pp. 384-89).

615 Pp. 379-81.

XI Words of Admonition to Today's Pioneer Builders

Working the Land is a spiritual endeavor

עא At the beginning of this book,[616] I addressed today's *olim* (immigrants) and builders. I will now elaborate and address them once again.

I proved above[617] that the shining of Israel's salvation depends on all of *Klal Yisrael* joining together in the sacred task of building and settling the Land. That is, we will not achieve our desired goal without the participation of both the God-fearing Jews and the masses, whoever they may be. One must know and understand that the cities of Zion will not be built without the God-fearing Jews, and that the cities of Judah will only be built with the spirit of HaShem.

Even though some of the masses succeeded in beginning to build the Land, they should not think that this is a result of human endeavor alone. Everything was accomplished with God's help. The Cause of All Causes caused the initiation to occur specifically through them, as I explained above at length.[618] However, they still need heavenly assistance to continue to move higher and higher in this undertaking and bring it to perfection. Without heavenly assistance, the entire endeavor can dissolve, God forbid, as happened at the time of Don Yosef HaNasi.[619] If HaShem is displeased with their work, they may lose all the fruits of their labor in one day. Above,[620] I cited the godly Kabbalist, the author of *Hon Ashir*, as saying that if something is contrary to God's will, it is possible that "the end of joy will be sorrow."[621] Therefore, the builders should strive to do everything in the spirit of the Torah and according to the counsel of the wise men of the generation, as I wrote in the foreword. Then, the Master of the World will be pleased and send His assistance from the heavens.

My main purpose here is to awaken the masses who have come to cultivate, build, and settle the Land to realize that settling the Holy Land is not merely a material endeavor as it is in *Chutz LaAretz*. There, it is termed "agriculture" [lit., "land culture"], which implies purely material objectives. When these builders were in

616 P. 82ff.
617 Pp. 390-93.
618 P. 183ff.
619 ❖ See above (p. 180).
620 Sec. לג, p. 310.
621 Based on *Mishley* 14:13.

Chutz LaAretz they became accustomed to and educated in the culture of the nations, as the *Midrash* states: "*They made me the keeper of the vineyards* (*Shir HaShirim* 1:6), for the honor of the nations. *But my own vineyard*, meaning, the Holy One Blessed be He, *I did not guard* (ibid.)" (*Yalkut Shimoni* 2:982). ❖ Thus, when they come to the Land and try to work as they did in *Chutz LaAretz*, we must inform them that their work in *Chutz LaAretz* was considered purely material, while in the Holy Land it is spiritual. Every action that is done to develop and settle the Land – like plowing, sowing, planting trees, building houses, and paving roads – is considered a *mitzvah*. According to our mentor, the Chatam Sofer, it is like someone who prepares *tefillin*, a *lulav*, a *sukkah*, or performs any other preparatory *mitzvah* (הכשר מצווה).[622]

Actually, our brilliant ancestor, the Rashbash, son of the Tashbetz, expressed this idea before the Chatam Sofer did.[623] After explaining this issue at length, he concludes that dwelling in the Land is a positive, biblical commandment. On this point he concurs with his father, the Tashbetz, and his ancestor, the Ramban. [He also asserts] that the main aspect of this *mitzvah* is dwelling in the Land, which depends on two factors: 1. *Aliyah* (ascension): For, if one does not ascend to the Land how will he live there? 2. Settling the Land: For example, planting gardens, orchards, and trees; acquiring land on which to build houses; and [caring for] other human necessities. For, as long as there is food and housing there will be dwelling. [In other words], *aliyah* is the way to attain [the status of] "dwelling," while

---

❖ This is an instructive lesson and a clear admonition to our fellow Jews in the Diaspora who expended all of their spiritual energies on enhancing, elevating, and exalting the European, gentile culture. Most of the countries with highly advanced cultures reached this state only because the Jews expended all of their spiritual energies on these cultures. The Gentiles should have been grateful for this and given the Jews a choice portion of the benefits. Instead, they robbed them of their rights and excluded them from any good portion, while others eat the fruits of their labor. This is the lot of our fellow Jews who neglected to guard the vineyard of the Lord of Hosts and went, instead, to guard the vineyards of the Gentiles or to satiate themselves with gentile culture.

622 Novellae to *Sukkah* 36a, s.v. *domeh le'kushi*. See above, pp. 302-4.

623 *Teshuvot HaRashbash* 1-3.

settlement maintains it. He repeats this idea many times throughout his discussion and concludes as follows:

> Therefore, I say that both settlement and *aliyah* give rise to the *mitzvah* [of dwelling], but one precedes it while the other achieves it. That is to say, settlement helps a person achieve and maintain this *mitzvah*. They are both preparatory *mitzvot*, just like [making] *tefillin*, [building] a *sukkah*, and [purchasing] a *lulav*, which allow a person to fulfill the *mitzvah*.[624]

In any event, we see that the different aspects of settling the Land are preparatory *mitzvot* just like building a *sukkah*, [purchasing] a *lulav*, and making *tefillin* or a *mezuzah*.

Reciting the She-Hechiyanu blessing on Yishuv Eretz Yisrael

Truthfully, if I was not afraid that my colleagues and teachers would ridicule me, I would suggest something novel. *Chazal* state that if a person makes his own *lulav* or *sukkah* he must say the *SheHechiyanu* ("Who kept us alive") blessing (*Sukkah* 46a, *Menachot* 42a). Similarly, I would add, when a person begins tilling his own soil or building his own house in *Eretz Yisrael* he should say a *SheHechiyanu*. Perhaps he should do so even if it is not his own, because one could distinguish between *sukkah* and *lulav*, on the one hand, and settling the Land, on the other. The latter *mitzvah* requires a Jew to make the Land inhabitable; therefore, the soil does not necessarily have to be his own. Even if it belongs to others, there is sufficient reason to require a blessing, because his toil benefits him as well. (I have explained the logic only briefly.)

Furthermore, Tosafot discuss which *mitzvot* require a *SheHechiyanu* and which do not. They conclude that the blessing is recited only over a *mitzvah* which involves joy.[625] Now, the *mitzvah* under discussion certainly involves joy. Therefore, when a person begins to work and build the Land he should certainly recite the *SheHechiyanu* blessing.

This is only a suggestion, not an halachic decision, and it should certainly not be put into practice, unless the generation's *gedolim* acquiesce.

624 ❖ Truthfully, I am astonished that the brilliant author of *S'dei Chemed*, from whom no secret was hidden, did not see this Rashbash, for he does not refer to it at all. (See *Ma'arechet Eretz Yisrael*.) Perhaps he did not have this work in his possession.

625 *Tosafot, Sukkah* 46a, s.v. *ha'oseh sukkah le'atzmo mevarech shehechiyanu*.

HaShem will assist the chalutzim if they work in the spirit of the Torah

עב In any event, all of the workers in *Eretz Yisrael* must realize that their work is not material in nature, but spiritual. Everything they do to settle the Land is imbued with sanctity and godliness. Perhaps this was Yeshayah's intention when he said, *Say to the cities of Judah, "Behold your God"* (*Yeshayah* 40:9). Above,[626] I analyzed the expression *Behold your God* (see there). In addition, one could explain that Yeshayah meant to teach us that every act performed for the sake of the cities of Judah is imbued with sanctity and godliness. For, every such act is a *mitzvah* like all other *mitzvot* of the Torah, and it causes the Land to become sanctified with the sanctity of God's name, as I explained above.

Therefore, every worker must prepare his heart and his mind for this sacred and lofty task. He must discard the foreign concepts which he brought with him from *Chutz LaAretz* and arouse himself to the spiritual side of the work. Then he can be sure that HaShem will send His help from the Sanctuary[627] and bestow blessings upon his handiwork. The settlement will grow and expand until we reach our final objective, the ultimate redemption, speedily in our days. Amen.

For this to happen, it is essential that you [builders] draw close to the God-fearing Jews and take instruction from the wise men of the generation, so that everything is done in the spirit of the Torah. This new Torah-spirit will help you achieve the purpose for which you came to the Land – to build and strengthen it. You will do exactly what you did in *Chutz LaAretz*, with one change for the better. There, you acted in the foreign spirit of the nations, while here you will act in the spirit of the Torah and the Lord of Hosts. You will then see with your own eyes that HaShem's desire will be fulfilled through you and all of the prophetic blessings will come upon you. If the people of the Land act in the spirit of the Torah, all of the world's silver and gold will flow into *Eretz Yisrael*.[628] Our Holy Land will be built and established so quickly that even we will be astonished by the rate at which her borders will expand. HaShem will help us in all of our endeavors, and heavenly angels will assist us, as the *Midrash* recounts:

Once, R. Chanina ben Dosa saw his fellow townsmen bringing

626 Sec. לא of this chapter (pp. 298-302).
627 Based on *Tehillim* 20:3.
628 ❖ See the Rashi that I cited at the end of the foreword (p. 90).

free-will offerings to Jerusalem. He said, "Everyone is bringing free-will offerings to Jerusalem, and I am bringing nothing." What did he do? He went to the outskirts of the city and saw a stone which he cut, chiseled, and smoothed. He said, "I vow to bring this up to Jerusalem."

He then searched for workers to hire. Five men came his way, and he said to them, "Will you bring this stone up to Jerusalem for me?" They replied, "Give us fifty *sela* [coins] and we will take it up." He wanted to give them [their price], but he did not have it. So, they left him and went on their way.

The Holy One Blessed be He sent him five angels in the guise of five men. R. Chanina said to them, "Will you take this stone for me?" They replied, "Give us five *sela* and we will bring your stone up to Jerusalem, but only if you join us with your hand and finger." He put his hand and finger in and they found themselves standing in Jerusalem. He wanted to pay their wages, but he could not find them. He entered the Chamber of the Hewn Stones[629] and asked about them. They [the *Sanhedrin*] told him, "It seems that the ministering angels brought your stone up to Jerusalem." (*Kohelet* and *Shir HaShirim Rabbah* 1:1)

This seems puzzling. Since he had five *sela* with which to pay the workers, why did he not bring a *Shelamim* sacrifice with the money? The answer is: He wanted to demonstrate that when a person helps build or repair the city [of Jerusalem], HaShem accepts his work like a burnt offering. Therefore, he specifically brought a stone up to Jerusalem, because it can be used for the city walls. God assisted him by sending the ministering angels to carry the stone.

Now, if they carried it, why did they ask him to put his finger in? How could his finger help carry it? Did they really need him? It seems to me that the answer is based on something I saw in the name of the brilliant and holy R. Yeshayah Muskat *z"l*, *av beit din* of Praga, near Warsaw. *Chazal* state that the Holy Ark used to carry the ones who carried it (*Sotah* 35a). Nonetheless, HaShem commanded us to carry it. Why? Because HaShem wants an awakening from below, as the *Zohar* writes, ôAn awakening from below elicits an awakening from aboveö (1:77b, 1:88b). Here too, the angels wanted R. Chanina to effect an awakening from below using his finger. Then, assistance would come from the heavens.

629 [Where the *Sanhedrin* (the highest Jewish court) sat.]

My beloved friends! The same is true today. If you work in the spirit of our Torah and tradition, according to the counsel of the Torah scholars and leaders, I am certain that HaShem will send His help from the Sanctuary (מקודש) and support you from Zion (מציון).[630] ❖ You will soar higher and higher in your sacred work and receive blessings from the storehouse of all blessings. All of the blessings of *parashat BeChukotai* and *Ki Tavo* will be fulfilled through you, and HaShem will say: *I am the Lord your God Who brought you out of the land of Egypt* [מצרים] (that is, out of the land in which you were troubled [מיצר] and oppressed),[631] *that you should cease being their slaves; and I broke the bars of your yoke and let you walk upright* (*VaYikra* 26:13). Amen, so may it be God's will.

XII Our Obligation to Support and Build the Land

Harsh decrees are an incentive to return to our Land

עג Behold, thus far in this chapter I have thoroughly explained the *mitzvah* of building and settling the Land. I explored it from beginning to end and in every corner, and I proved unequivocally that all of *Klal Yisrael* is obligated to keep this *mitzvah* at all times. No one can free himself from it.

Today, we have an even greater obligation to arise from our slumber and indolence. Anyone who has eyes and ears and has seen or heard what has happened to us during recent, difficult times will realize that there is enough [incentive] to awaken ourselves for this cause. The historians can entitle the decrees of the past four years "The *Tash, Tasha, Tashab, Tashag* Decrees,"[632] just as they entitled the Crusades "The *Tatnu* Decrees."[633] The mouth will grow too weary to recount them all, and the pen will not suffice to record them all.

However, due to our numerous sins, this has all happened with the consent of the Most High, as the following *Midrash* indicates: "They asked R. Yehoshua ben Levi, 'Where is the Holy One Blessed

❖ The *Midrash* explains that HaShem will send His help because of the sanctity (קדושה) and eminence (ציון) of your deeds (*Midrash Tehillim* 20:5).

630 Based on *Tehillim* 20:3.

631 See above, p. 331.

632 [Hebrew abbreviations (ת״ש, תש״א, תש״ב, תש״ג) representing the years 5700-5703 (1940-1943).]

633 [תתנ״ו – 4856 (1096)]

be He?' He replied, 'In the great city of Rome'" (*Yerushalmi, Ta'anit* 1:1 [3a]). Both the question and the answer are perplexing. What kind of question is "Where is the Blessed One?" Where is He not?! Furthermore, why was this question specifically asked during the time of R. Yehoshua ben Levi? Also, what is the meaning of the answer "In the great city of Rome"? Is it not true that *The entire world is filled with His glory* (*Yeshayah* 6:3)?

The true interpretation is as follows: It is well known that the Gentiles enacted relentless decrees against Israel at the time of R. Yehoshua ben Levi. He lived right after the destruction of the Temple, and Israel suffered greatly from harsh and cruel decrees. Thus, people came to him in dismay and asked: "Where is the Holy One Blessed be He? Why is He silent in the face of all that is happening to Israel?" We hear the same questions today from so many people: "Where is the God of the Jews? Why does He keep silent and restrain Himself in the face of all this?" R. Yehoshua ben Levi responded, "He is in the great city of Rome." All of these decrees emanated from Rome, the seat of the royal advisors. Therefore, R. Yehoshua said to them, "Do you think that these decrees were enacted without the knowledge of the Holy One Blessed be He? No! He too (as it were) participated in the ministerial assembly which enacted these harsh decrees. Everything was done with His consent, because such was His desire."

While I was still in the infamous land of hell [Poland], many people asked me this very question, "Where is the God of the Jews, blessed be He?" I, too, responded that He is in the place where the king and his officers meet, and He has consented to their actions (due to our numerous sins). The reason He has consented is as R. Yonatan writes in *Ahavat Yonatan*: so that the Jews will devote themselves to returning to *Eretz Yisrael*.[634] Our mentor, the Ya'avetz, also writes that when the Jews neglect *Eretz Yisrael* harsh decrees befall them.[635] I already discussed this above, at length,[636] so there is no need to repeat it here.

In any event, there is enough [incentive] to awaken ourselves to return to our desirable Land. Therefore, my friends and brothers, I beseech you: Arise! Wake up! Come forward! Join together! Be

634 *Ahavat Yonatan, Haftarat Eikev*, on *Yeshayah* 49:19.
635 *Siddur Beit Ya'akov, Sullam Beit El*, p. 13a, col. a.
636 See pp. 45, 52-54, 96-101, 121-23, 221-25.

strong and let us be strong for the sake of HaShem, our nation, the cities of our God,[637] and our Torah. Let us unite as one man with one heart for the sake of the cities of our God, because the time has come for all of us to ascend and encourage others to ascend. Our salvation is close at hand, as all the signs indicate. Therefore, everyone must eagerly donate money to help support the *mitzvah* of *aliyah* and building the Land.

Every Jew should forgo the extras and donate to the building effort

עד David said, *Now, behold, in my poverty/affliction* (בעניי) *I have prepared gold...for the House of the Lord* (I *Divrei HaYamim* 22:14). The *Yerushalmi* comments:

> What does *in my poverty* (בעניי) mean? (Did he not have an abundance of gold?) Rebbe answered, "No one is wealthy compared to the One Who Created the World." (That is to say, David called himself poor in comparison to the Holy One Blessed be He.) Another interpretation: *In my affliction* (בעניי, read as בעינויי) – David would fast and consecrate his meal to God (that is, for the building of the *Beit HaMikdash*). (*Yerushalmi, Pe'ah* 4:1 [15b])

Our mentor, the Maharam Schiff, explains this verse based on *Chazal*'s statement "Those who fast are rewarded primarily for the charity they give afterwards" (*Berachot* 6b).[638] [The verse means that] David gave charity every day he fasted.[639] The annotator explains that the brilliant Maharam did not want to interpret the word בעניי as poverty because David prepared a great deal of silver and gold [for the *Beit HaMikdash*]. Instead, he defines בעניי as self-affliction and fasting, as in, "Those who fast are rewarded primarily for the charity they give afterwards."

This is astounding! How did these two fail to realize that the *Yerushalmi* states this explicitly? The *Yerushalmi* asks the annotator's question and answers it the same way the Maharam Schiff does. It is astounding that the Maharam Schiff, from whom no secret was hidden, overlooked this *Yerushalmi*.

In any event, we see that King David *a"h* limited his food intake to help build Jerusalem and the *Beit HaMikdash*. I would, therefore,

637 Based on II *Shmuel* 10:12.

638 [Based on Rashi's interpretation.]

639 *Sefer Maharam Schiff, Chiddushei Halachot* (*Gittin, Ketuvot, Bava Metzia, Chullin*), (5579 [1819]), *Derushim Nechmadim*, p. 8a, s.v. *divrei hayamim*.

like to suggest that all members of our holy nation, wherever on earth they may be, should emulate our holy king and give all of their savings to help build our Holy Land. I do not mean that they should constantly fast and afflict themselves and send the money to *Eretz Yisrael*, as King David did. I simply mean that they should limit their luxuries and consecrate the extra money to help build the Land.

I will explain my intention. All men, women, and children of the House of Israel who regularly attend theaters or various recreational events (called "sport") should resolve not to do so anymore. They should consecrate the amount that they used to spend on these things and donate it to the funds which collect money to help build the Land. If all the Diaspora Jews would do so, we would collect an abundance of silver and gold with which to strengthen ourselves and our Land, not a foreign land. The same applies to all luxuries of life. If only the Jewish people would heed my words and the Master of the Universe would find favor in them!

We must also donate on a communal level

Furthermore, I already cited[640] *Ezrat Kohanim* as saying that all of Israel, together as one, is undoubtedly responsible for building [the Temple]. It is the community's task. The Rambam[641] and the Ra'ah[642] concur: "Everyone is obligated to build and support [it] with their very selves and their money." King David actually did this. He collected money from each tribe of Israel and only then bought the land for the *Beit HaMikdash*.[643] He did this so that the entire nation could have a portion in the edifice.

Behold, we find that (when he was collecting donations for the building of the *Beit HaMikdash*) David said to HaShem, *And now, I have seen Your people, who are present here, offering donations to You with joy* (I *Divrei HaYamim* 29:17). Rashi explains:

> *Who are present here...* But, the wealthy Jews of each city are not present here. Therefore, O Master of the Universe, the donation is humble. For, if the rest of Israel were here, the donation would be greater.[644]

640 Sec. א, p. 217.
641 *Hilchot Beit HaBechirah* 1:12.
642 *Sefer HaChinuch, Mitzvah* 95 (end). [The actual quote is from the Rambam.]
643 ❖ See *Zevachim* 116b; Rashi, I *Divrei HaYamim* 21:25.
644 ❖ See my comments on this Rashi in sec. טו (pp. 256-57).

Thus, David gathered donations for this sacred endeavor from private individuals. Nevertheless, he also made sure to collect fifty shekels uniformly from each tribe. That way, the money would come from the community, and this undertaking would not only be private, but also communal. Study the text thoroughly and you will fully understand my words.

The same is true of building the Land today. It is insufficient for individual Jews to volunteer for this sacred endeavor. It must also be a communal endeavor, for it is a communal *mitzvah*, as the verse says, *Come and possess the Land* (*Devarim* 1:8, see the Ramban). That is to say, in order to fulfill our obligation, each and every Diaspora community must give a specific sum of money each year from the communal fund for the purpose of *aliyah* and building the Land.

Then, the merit of *Eretz Yisrael* will stand by us to deliver us from distress.[645] For behold, David collected money from the twelve tribes immediately after the plague, and Gad the prophet told him that this calamity occurred because the Jews neglected to build the *Beit HaMikdash* (see *Midrash Tehillim* 17:4). The same is true today. All of our troubles are a result of the fact that we neglected *Eretz Yisrael*, as I cited above from many sources in *Chazal*.[646] Therefore, we must engage in this matter on a communal level, as David did, and contribute to it from communal funds. Then, the strength of the many will deliver us from distress.

Furthermore, above[647] I cited a *Yerushalmi* (*Bava Batra* 8:2) which compares the *mitzvah* of inheriting the Land to the *mitzvah* of inheriting the Torah. The word *morashah* (heritage) is used in reference to both: Concerning the Torah it says, *Moshe commanded us the Torah, a heritage of the congregation of Ya'akov* (*Devarim* 33:4), and concerning *Eretz Yisrael* it says, *And I will give it to you as a heritage* (*Shemot* 6:8).[648] Thus, *Chazal* tell us that these two obligations are equal.

Now, the Ramban writes that the Torah is an inheritance of the congregation of Ya'akov, not of individual Jews.[649] In my work,

645 ❖ See the first introduction, pp. 33-35.

646 See above, note 636.

647 Foreword, p. 79.

648 ❖ See the *Yerushalmi* inside, and see the foreword where I elaborated on this concept.

649 Ramban, *Devarim* 33:4.

Mishneh Sachir (vol. 5),[650] I derive a practical *halachah* from this Ramban. That is, we do not discharge our obligation towards the *mitzvah* of maintaining the Torah❖ if individuals hire and pay a teacher. The teacher must be paid from communal funds, for this is a *mitzvah* incumbent upon the congregation of Ya'akov. It is a communal issue, not a private one. As a proof, I cite the fact that David wanted the community at large to contribute to the building of the Temple. He was not satisfied with private donations; instead, he collected [fifty] silver shekels from each tribe and exchanged them for gold.[651] He did all of this so that the building of the Temple would be a communal effort, not a private one. I also prove this...from the *Perishah* (*Hilchot Eiruvin*),[652] but this is not the place to elaborate.

Thus, since the *Yerushalmi* compares the inheritance of the Land to the inheritance of the Torah..., it follows that we do not fulfill the positive commandment of settling the Land if private individuals alone engage in it. Moreover, it is clear from the *Perishah* that even if all of Israel participates, but each individual gives by himself, from his own pocket, the Jews retain the status of individuals. Instead, they must collect the money from individuals, add it to the communal fund, and donate from the community's coffers. This is how Israel achieves the status of a community. Now, although the *Perishah* states this in reference to the laws of *Eiruvin*, we may apply it to all other communal obligations. These words of the *Perishah* are wondrously novel, but I did not come across any *posek* who sensed this.

In any event, since the positive commandment of settling the Land is a communal obligation, as the *Yerushalmi* indicates, every Diaspora community must set aside some communal funds (according to its capabilities) for the sake of this *mitzvah*. This is evident from all of the above, both theoretically and practically. Then, we will fulfill our obligation, and the merit of *Eretz Yisrael* will stand by our side to deliver us from distress. Amen, so may it be God's will.

❖ As it is written, *Cursed is one who does not maintain the words of this Torah* (*Devarim* 27:26), which the Ramban claims refers to the maintenance of the Torah from generation to generation.

650 ❖ It is still in manuscript. May HaShem grant me the merit to publish it at the time of Israel's salvation.

651 ❖ See *Tosafot, Zevachim* 116b, s.v. *gavah*; Rashi, I *Divrei HaYamim* 21:25.

652 He means *Derishah, Shulchan Aruch, Orach Chayim* 380.

Our money is safest in Eretz Yisrael

עה In addition, every Jew should consider what has happened to all of the gold, silver, and property that belonged to the Diaspora Jews of the last few centuries. It has all gone to waste and fallen into the hands of Eisav. These Jews were not wise and intelligent enough to invest their wealth in *Eretz Yisrael*, to buy fields and build houses which remain permanently in Jewish hands. The Rivash writes that *Yishuv Eretz Yisrael* is not a transient *mitzvah*, but a *mitzvah* that endures forever. It benefits the entire Jewish nation that the Holy Land not remain in the hands of the defiled ones.[653]

The Diaspora Jews should have learned from Ya'akov Avinu. While he was battling Eisav, he devised ways to save his money and property from falling into Eisav's hands. He succeeded in doing so by making himself like a bridge. He placed one foot on the *Eretz-Yisrael* side of the river and the other foot on the wicked Eisav's side, outside the Land (*Chutz LaAretz*). I already explained above[654] that this is not to be understood literally, but figuratively. It teaches us that the "bridge" over which he transferred all of his possessions to *Eretz Yisrael* was the fact that he never stood with both feet on Eisav's side. He always stood with one foot in *Eretz Yisrael*, and his eyes and heart were there at all times. Therefore, he was able to transfer his possessions, slowly but surely, to *Eretz Yisrael*. However, had he stood in *Chutz LaAretz* with both feet and forgotten about *Eretz Yisrael*, that would have been the end. All of his efforts would have fallen into Eisav's hands.

This is exactly what has happened today. All of our great and wonderful possessions were consumed, because we stood with both of our feet here in exile, neglecting *Eretz Yisrael*. Therefore, our enemies robbed the fruits of our labor from before our very eyes. Let this be a lesson for us. We should know in the future not to establish ourselves here with both feet. Instead, we should stand with one foot in *Eretz Yisrael* and keep our eyes and hearts there at all times. Then, with God's help, we will successfully transplant our wealth to *Eretz Yisrael* and invest the surplus in building our Land. There, our money will grow for us and our children, for the benefit of our entire holy nation, and for the sanctification of God's blessed and exalted name.

653 *Teshuvot HaRivash* 101, 387.

654 Pp. 342-44.

Whoever acquires the Land has a portion in the World to Come

עו After this bitter exile ends and we find rest from our enemies, we will have an even greater obligation to turn our attention to *Eretz Yisrael* and raise its glory by acquiring fields and building houses. We learn this from Ya'akov Avinu, about whom it says, *Ya'akov arrived complete at the city of Shechem which is in the Land of Cana'an..., and he bought the portion of land* (*BeReishit* 33:18-19). Rashi comments, "Like a person who says to his friend, 'So and so escaped from the lion's teeth and has returned unharmed [lit., complete].'" The Ibn Ezra writes:

> *He bought the portion of land*: a portion in the Land. Scripture mentions this to demonstrate that *Eretz Yisrael* has great virtues, and he who has a portion in it is considered as [if he has] a portion in the World to Come.[655]

Our [holy] books learn from here that [the Jews] became worthy of the World to Come when they inherited the Land. These books explain that the verse, *Your people are all righteous, they will inherit the land forever* (*Yeshayah* 60:21), means: By inheriting the Land, *Your people are all righteous* and worthy of the World to Come.

The *Midrash* states that after Ya'akov was saved from Eisav's clutches he thought to himself, "I will perform a *mitzvah* which the Holy One Blessed be He will deem more important than all other *mitzvot*." He then bought a portion of land in *Eretz Yisrael*.[656] We must do the same, for HaShem had compassion on us and kept us alive. We escaped from the lion's teeth unharmed [lit., complete], at least physically. Therefore, we must emulate Ya'akov Avinu and actively take part in purchasing fields and houses, and settling the Land. The Master of the Universe will surely desire this.

Now that our troubles have waned we must strive to settle the Land

עז The *Midrash* states that Gad the prophet told David that the plague came to punish Israel for failing to demand the building of the *Beit HaMikdash*. Immediately following this revelation, David went to Ornan and purchased a plot upon which to build the *Beit HaMikdash* (*Midrash Tehillim* 17:4). In *Divrei HaYamim* (I, 21:25) the verse says, *So David gave Ornan, for the place, six hundred gold shekels by weight*. But, in the book of *Shmuel* (II, 24:24) it says, *Fifty silver shekels*. Rava points out this contradiction in *Zevachim* (116b). Rashi reconciles it as follows: "...He took fifty shekels from each tribe, which

655 ❖ The Ramban also quotes this (ibid., s.v. *vayichan et p'nei ha'ir*).
656 We were unable to locate this *Midrash*.

equals 600 shekels, so that all of Israel could have a share."[657] Thus, when David bought the site of the *Beit HaMikdash*, he wanted all of *Klal Yisrael* to have a share, so that the Master would forgive them for failing to demand its construction.

The *Midrash* (ibid.) derives a *kal vachomer*: If David's generation, which preceded the *Beit HaMikdash*, was punished for not having demanded its construction; then we, who had a *Beit HaMikdash*, which was destroyed because of our sins, will certainly be punished for neglecting to demand its construction (God forbid). The *Midrash* also cites a parable: A father once beat his son repeatedly. Finally, the son asked, "Why are you doing this?" to which the father answered, "Why do you disregard my commandment?!" This is why *Chazal* instituted three daily prayers for the return to our Land and the building of the *Beit HaMikdash*.[658] Thus, all of our afflictions in exile come because we disregard [our obligation] to return to our Land.

Therefore, now that the terrible blows have ceased, we must do as David did and immediately, without delay, purchase our Land and the site of the ôHouse of our Lives.ö[659] Then, we will no longer be punished, as the parable of the father who beat his son demonstrates.

This is a communal obligation

Furthermore, I explained above,[660] based on David, that it is insufficient for private individuals to buy portions of land in *Eretz Yisrael*. All of *Klal Yisrael*, together, must become involved. This implies that every Jewish community, in conjunction with one another, must help build the Land. Then, the Master, HaShem, will forgive us for neglecting this until now. I also cited[661] the brilliant author of *Ezrat Kohanim* who says that all of Israel, together as one, is undoubtedly responsible to build [the Temple]. If an individual does so, it is invalid, for it is a communal task. He proves this from David (see there).

Moreover, we anticipate that when the war ends, the kingdoms will grant the Jewish nation permission to return to and take hold of its inheritance. Certainly, then, this obligation rests upon the entirety of Israel and is a communal matter, not a private one. The Rashbash, son of the Tashbetz, thoroughly explains the positive

657 Rashi, I *Divrei HaYamim* 21:25.

658 [See the full citation of this *Midrash* above, p. 45.]

659 From the second blessing recited after the *Haftarah*.

660 Pp. 425-26.

661 This chapter, sec. א, p. 217.

commandment of *Yishuv Eretz Yisrael* in his responsa.[662] He writes that the *mitzvah* is for individuals to ascend to the Land, not the entire nation, because we swore not to go up "as a wall" against the will of the kingdoms.[663] Hence, after the nations grant us permission to take hold of and ascend to *Eretz Yisrael*, this *mitzvah* will once again be incumbent upon the entire nation. Then, in addition to the fact that every individual must strive to return, it will also be a communal obligation, as we learn from King David *a"h*.

Chazal explain why the first exile did not begin until the time of Hoshea ben Be'eiri.[664] King Yerovam [ben Nevat] forcibly prevented the Jews from ascending to Jerusalem on the three pilgrimage festivals. Therefore, the blame rested solely on him.❖ In the days of Hoshea, on the other hand, the guards were abolished and the Jews were allowed to ascend; but they did not. Therefore, the entire congregation was to blame, and they were exiled (*Yalkut Shimoni* 2:234, *Tana DeVei Eliyahu Zuta* 9:3). The same applies today. Now that the government has granted permission to ascend to *Eretz Yisrael*, the entire nation is obligated in this *mitzvah*. It is a communal matter, not a private one. Therefore, we must support it with communal funds, as I explained above.

Building the Land with proper intentions

עח I believe it is appropriate to instruct people to say the following when donating money to help build our Holy Land: "I hereby give this donation for the purpose of building our Land, in order to fulfill the positive commandment of settling the Land, which the Creator of the Universe commanded us, in order to rectify its source in the supernal world." This way, the donation will be imbued with exalted sanctity, and the evil forces will be unable to mar the building process or have a portion in it. Then, everything will be done sacredly and according to the will of the Most High.

❖ Even then, those who loved HaShem risked their lives for this *mitzvah* (see *Ta'anit* 28a). This will be remembered in their merit for all of eternity.

662 Sec. 1-3.

663 See *Ketuvot* 111a.

664 [Hoshea ben Be'eiri is the prophet whose book is the first of the "Twelve" (תרי עשר). Apparently, our author means Hoshea ben Eilah, the king who abolished the guards. It is possible, though, that his reference is correct for they both lived around the same time.]

I found a source for this in *Maggid Meisharim*. The angel tells our mentor, the Beit Yosef:

> Behold, in this holy *parashah* it says, *They shall make for Me a sanctuary* (*Shemot* 25:8), and *They shall take for Me a portion* (ibid. 25:2). This alludes to the fact that regarding sacred matters one must say, "This thing is for holiness." Whenever a person does a [holy] act he should say, "This is for the sake of holiness." Similarly, someone who wants to use the chair that is set aside for Eliyahu at a *Brit Milah* (circumcision) must say, "This is the Throne of Eliyahu."[665]

I believe that Rashi also alludes to this when he writes: "*They shall take for Me* (ibid.) – for the sake of My name; *a portion* – they shall set aside from their possessions a voluntary gift for My sake." That is to say, when they set aside the money they should say, "I hereby set this aside for the sake of the holy *Mishkan*." Rashi's words concur with those of the angel.

Subsequently, I saw that *Sh'nei Luchot HaBrit*[666] quotes a *Zohar* as cited in *Reishit Chochmah*:[667]

> Come and see. *And all of the women whose hearts stirred them* (*Shemot* 35:26): While working, the women would say, "This is for the Sanctuary; this is for the *Mishkan*; this is for the partition." All of the craftsmen did likewise, so that holiness would rest upon their hands and sanctify their work. Thus, when [their handiwork] was set in place, it was set in holiness (*Zohar* 3:50a)...
>
> R. Eliezer said, "All of man's deeds must be done for the sake of HaShem's holy name. One must mention the holy name every time he acts, so that everything will be for the service of God, and so that the evil forces will not rest upon his handiwork. For, they are constantly ready and able to rest upon man's deeds" (ibid. 3:51b).

The Shelah comments that before every action one should say, "For the sake of the unification of the Holy One Blessed be He and His *Shechinah*, through the One Who is hidden and concealed, in the name of all of Israel." All of this concurs with the words of the angel.

Therefore, it is proper to make the above-mentioned declaration

665 *Maggid Meisharim, Terumah* (end), s.v. *u'pele*.
666 *Sha'ar HaOtiot - Alef*, 1:44a.
667 *Sha'ar Ahavah*, chap. 9.

when donating to the building effort. Moreover, if all of the workers would say this before plowing, sowing, or doing any work, they would undoubtedly cause a great rectification (*tikkun*). They would also render the external, [evil] forces powerless to attach themselves to any of their actions.

Let it be known, however, that all of this is not essential to the actual *mitzvah* of settling the Land. Even if a person works without making this declaration, or without any intent (*kavanah*) whatsoever, he still fulfills all [aspects] of this positive commandment. This is implicit in the words of the Or HaChayim (cited above)[668] and is consistent with the accepted rule that lack of intent does not inhibit a *mitzvah* which involves an action. Furthermore, the Rashba writes that if the performance of a *mitzvah* is irrevocable, it remains unblemished even when done sinfully.[669] However, in order to perform the *mitzvah* in the best possible way, it is certainly proper to do what I said above. Then, the Most High will be praised above and below. Amen, so may it be God's will.

Yehudah will return first, and the ten lost tribes will follow

עט The prophet Yeshayahu says, *The Lord God Who gathers the dispersed of Israel says, "I will gather others to him, besides those already gathered to him"* (56:8). The Ramban explains that God will first gather many, but not all, of the dispersed of Israel. Then, after the war of Gog, He will gather others to the ones who have already been gathered. This verse refers to those who are lost in the land of Assyria,[670] i.e., the ten [lost] tribes. They will be gathered second.[671]

In his work, *Derishat Tzion*, the brilliant R. Tzvi Kalischer points out a contradiction to this. The Ramban himself writes that the ten tribes will be gathered first![672] R. Kalischer answers that both statements are true. If many Jews who are lost in the land of Assyria assemble in *Eretz Yisrael*, they will surely not come to a desolate and ruined land. Undoubtedly, someone will come before them to bring bread from the Land;[673] and afterwards, the rest of the people

668 Sec. לג, pp. 311-12.
669 Rashba, *Yevamot* 103. See above, p. 85.
670 See *Yeshayah* 27:13.
671 This Ramban is cited by R. Kalischer in *Derishat Tzion*, p. 91. Apparently, he is referring to the Ramban on *Shir HaShirim* 8:13, although it is not clear.
672 Ramban, *Shir HaShirim* 8:13.
673 From the blessing recited before eating bread.

will come to a Land filled with HaShem's blessings. The desert will become a fertile land,[674] full of fields and vineyards in Israel's possession.

This is also evident, [continues R. Kalischer], from a verse in *Hoshea*: *Yehudah, too, has made a harvest for you, when I return the captivity of My people* (6:11). The commentators are very hard pressed to explain this verse. According to my position, however, it makes good sense. Throughout the chapter, HaShem speaks to Efrayim, one of the ten tribes. He says [that Efrayim will say], *Come, let us return to the Lord... He will revive us after two days; on the third day He will raise us up* (ibid. 6:1-2). Rashi explains that this refers to the building of the Third Temple. Afterwards, HaShem admonishes Efrayim saying, *What shall I do to you, Efrayim...* (ibid. 6:4). Then, He returns to His original statement (*On the third day He will raise us up..., and He will come to us like the rain* [ibid. 6:2-3]) and says to Efrayim, *Yehudah, too, has made a harvest for you, when I return the captivity of My people* (Efrayim). [That is to say], Yehudah will harvest for you and prepare an inhabited land before the masses return. Then, the great ingathering will take place, after which *Mashiach ben Yosef* will undoubtedly arrive and reign in Jerusalem. Then, [the war of] Gog will occur; God's great name will be sanctified; HaShem and His name will be one;[675] and everyone will unite to serve Him with one consent.[676] Amen.[677]

Behold, the *Midrash* states explicitly what this *gaon* figured out on his own... Nachum the prophet says, *Behold upon the mountains, the feet of the one who brings good tidings proclaiming peace! Celebrate your festivals, O Yehudah* (2:1). The *Midrash* comments:

> You find that Yehudah is always first. Yehudah is the first to encamp, [as it says], *Those that encamp to the front, eastwards: the banner of the camp of Yehudah* (*BeMidbar* 2:3). Yehudah is the first to travel, [as it says], *The banner of the camp of the children of Yehudah traveled first* (ibid. 10:14). Yehudah is first [to offer] sacrifices, [as it says], *The one who brought his offering on the first day: Nachshon ben Aminadav of the tribe of Yehudah* (ibid. 7:12). Yehudah is first [to go] to war, as it says, *Who shall go up for us first against the*

674 Based on *Yeshayah* 32:15.
675 Based on *Zecharyah* 14:9.
676 Based on *Tzefanyah* 3:9.
677 *Derishat Tzion*, p. 108.

> *Canaanite... The Lord said, "Yehudah shall go up"* (*Shoftim* 1:1-2). And when the one who brings good tidings comes, Yehudah will receive the good news first, as it says, *Celebrate your festivals, O Yehudah.* (*Yalkut Shimoni* 2:561; *Tanchuma, BeMidbar* 14)

This certainly means that he will be the first to return to the Land, the first to celebrate the festival of entering the Land, and then, the first to tell Israel the good tidings of the redemption.

This idea is also stated explicitly in *Zecharyah*: *Woe! Woe! Flee then from the land of the north, says the Lord, for I have spread you out like the four corners of the heaven, says the Lord. Woe! O Zion, escape, O you who dwells with the daughter of Babylonia* (2:10-11). Rashi and Metzudat David explain:

> *Woe! Woe!* This refers to the future redemption. It is as if [HaShem] proclaims: "You children of the ten tribes who were exiled to the land of Assyria in the north, flee from there and return to your Land!" *For...like the four corners of the heaven*: "Just as the four corners of the heaven are distant from each other, so too, *I have spread you out* to a far-off land. Therefore, go quickly, because it is so far." *Woe! O Zion, escape*: It is as if HaShem calls Yehudah and says, "You, congregation of Yehudah who was exiled to Babylonia first..., escape from your current place and come to Zion."[678]

Behold, HaShem called specially to Yehudah who was exiled first. The same thing will happen today. Yehudah will return to the Land first, as the *Midrash* states, "Yehudah is always first."

Thus, R. Tzvi Kalischer's words are correct and true. Had he remembered this *Midrash* he would have rejoiced. I should add that Hoshea intended this as well when he said, *Yehudah will plow, and Ya'akov will break the clods for him* (*Hoshea* 10:11). Consider this matter well and you will understand.

In any event, we see that Yehudah is always first, and that he will also be the first to return to the Land at the time of redemption. Therefore, we, the descendants of Yehudah and Binyamin, must lead the way to rebuilding our Land. Afterwards, the ten tribes will be revealed and the complete ingathering will take place. Amen, so may HaShem say, speedily in our days. Amen.

Eventually, HaShem will widen our borders and grant us rest

678 *Metzudat David* (ibid.).

from all our enemies who surround us like bees and sting us mercilessly (may HaShem take vengeance on them on our behalf). When this happens, all of us will join together and become involved in the building effort (with God's help). For, Nachum's prophecy – *The gates of your Land have been opened wide* (3:13) – has been fulfilled through us (thank God). We will disregard our newfound freedom here in exile and make sure not to use it to remain here as before (God forbid). For if we remain here, the nations will oppress us once again, as the prophet says: *...you who rejoice over nothingness, who say, "Indeed, with our strength we have taken horns for ourselves." For behold, I will raise up a nation against you, O House of Israel, says the Lord..., and they will oppress you* (*Amos* 6:13-14). Thus, the nations oppressed us only because we rejoiced over our lot here in exile. We felt that we were strong, [as if] we had horns with which to gore eastward, northward, southward, and westward. But, HaShem showed us that we rejoiced over nothing and that our greatness here was like a fleeting dream.

Therefore, let us learn from the past and use our newfound freedom to establish great movements to encourage all segments of our nation to ascend to Zion with happy song and eternal joy. Then, HaShem will fulfill His promise to us: *The Lord will be zealous for His Land and have pity on His people* (*Yoel* 2:18). Amen, so may it be God's will.

XIII Essay: The Sanctuary of HaShem[679]

We will build the earthly Temple and God will lower the supernal one upon it

פ The book of *Ezra* states, *They celebrated the dedication of this Temple with joy* (6:16). The Malbim cites earlier sages (*kadmonim*) who explain the expression "*this Temple*":

> Had they been worthy at that time, the ultimate redemption would have arrived and a *Beit HaMikdash*, like the one Yechezkel foresaw,[680] would have descended from the heavens immediately after this edifice [the Second Temple] was

679 [The major thesis of this essay is that man will build the future Temple first, and then God will lower a supernal, spiritual Temple upon it. It is written in extremely complex, halachic language. Only someone who truly studies this essay, including the sources quoted, will fully understand it. Also, most of the ideas mentioned in the essay are not directly related to the rest of the book; it is essentially a separate entity. Therefore, some readers may choose to skip it on the first reading and continue with p. 457.]

680 See *Yechezkel*, chap. 40-43.

> completed. Then, they would have begun the second dedication, mentioned in *Yechezkel* (43:18-27). For the time being, though, they made *the dedication of **this** Temple*. The word *this* indicates that they anticipated the dedication of another Temple.
>
> Behold, Yechezkel's dedication will begin on the 23rd of Adar, as explained there.[681] The dedication [at the time of Ezra] lasted 21 days, until the 23rd of Adar.[682] Had they been worthy, the dedication of the final Temple, which will be built by HaShem, would have ensued immediately.
>
> Now, since the festive and joyous days of Purim fell out during those days, the verse states that their main joy came from the dedication, which was even more joyous than Purim.

It is evident from these *kadmonim* that even though God will build the future Temple, we will build a *Beit HaMikdash* with our own hands first. Afterwards, the hoped-for, heaven-made edifice will descend.

I found the same idea in the holy work, *Aspaklariya HaMe'irah*:

> The Talmud states: "The Holy One Blessed be He said, 'I must pay for the fire I set. I kindled a fire in Zion, as it says, *He kindled a fire in Zion and it has consumed its foundations* (*Eichah* 4:11). In the future, as well, I will build it [Zion] with fire, as it says, *And I will be for it...a wall of fire round about, and I will be in its midst for glory* (*Zecharyah* 2:9)" (*Bava Kama* 60b).
>
> Similarly, the *Zohar* says that the Holy One Blessed be He will build the future Temple Himself..., as it is written, *The Lord is the Builder of Jerusalem* (*Tehillim* 147:2) (*Zohar, Parashat Pinchas* 3:221a).
>
> Galanti cites the *Zohar* (*Parashat Pekudei* 2:240a)[683] which says that not all of the stones and foundations of the [First] Temple were destroyed. Some of them were hidden away. In the future, the Holy One Blessed be He will build the *Beit HaMikdash* from these very stones. ❖

❖ Using this, he explains the verse *The glory of this latter Temple will be greater than the first one* (*Chaggai* 2:9). Why does it not say, "than

681 See Malbim, *Yechezkel* 43:27, 45:18.

682 For they began their dedication on the 3rd of Adar. See *Ezra* 6:15.

683 Also see *Tikkunei Zohar* (R. Reuven Margolis edition) 60b; *Nitzotzei Zohar*, ibid. 13.

Behold, according to the *Zohar* (*Parashat Pekudei*), the Temple will be built with man-made stones, not those made by the Holy One Blessed be He. This contradicts the Talmud (*Bava Kama*) and *Zohar* (*Parashat Pinchas*) cited above (which imply that it will actually be made by God). Perforce, we must introduce a third and deciding opinion – the *Midrash Pesikta*.[685] It says there that the Holy One Blessed be He will lower the supernal Jerusalem upon the earthly one. Thus, both *Midrashim* are true. The supernal Temple will be made entirely of fire, the handiwork of the Holy One Blessed be He. The earthly one will be man-made from the crowning stones which sparkle on the ground since the days of King Shlomo *a"h*.[686]

I am astounded that our mentor, the author of *Aspaklariya HaMe'irah*, made this distinction on his own, based on the *Pesikta*; for behold, it is stated explicitly in *Tikkunei Zohar*:

> At that time, the House of the *Shechinah*, which is the *Beit HaBechirah* [the Chosen House], will be built by the Holy One Blessed be He, about Whom it says, *And I will be for it, says the Lord, a wall of fire round about* (*Zecharyah* 2:9). And its stones (ואבניה): these are the precious stones from which it will be built, as it is written, *That I too may be built up* (ואבנה) *through her* (*BeReishit* 30:3) – sacred plants (נטיעין קדישין)[687]...
>
> The *Beit HaMikdash* will be built of silver, gold, and precious stones. It will be embroidered with every image of creation; and the light of the uppermost Jerusalem [will be] above it, embroidered with every shade of light. The secret of the matter

---

the first onesö [in the plural], since two Temples were destroyed? Based on this *Zohar*, however, the verse is ever so sweet. It tells us that none of the stones of the first edifice were lost. The future Temple will be built with these very stones. Thus, it says, *The glory of this latter Temple will be greater than the first one* (מן הראשון), meaning, it will be built from the same stones as the first one.[684]

684 [מן הראשון can also be translated as, "from the first one."]

685 We were unable to locate this source.

686 *Aspaklariya HaMe'irah* on *Zohar* 2:114a, s.v. *hi*. [The parenthetical comments are R. Teichtal's.]

687 [A reference to some deep, Kabbalistic concept. It is beyond the scope of this translation to explain such references.]

is [in the verse] *The built-up Jerusalem is like a city that is joined together* (*Tehillim* 122:3), for its light is above it.[688]

The author of *Kisei Melech* comments on the statement "The *Beit HaMikdash* will be built with silver...": "This earthly *Beit HaMikdash* will also be a magnificent edifice, decorated with every image of creation. Then, the spiritual light of the supernal Jerusalem [will descend] upon it."

It seems to me that when the *Tikkunei Zohar* states, "And its stones: these are the precious stones from which it will be built," he means that it will be built with the stones of the First Temple, as the *Zohar* (*Parashat Pekudei*) asserts.

Hence, everything that the author of *Aspaklariya HaMe'irah* said above is stated explicitly in *Tikkunei Zohar*. I am very surprised at him, for he was one of the greatest Kabbalists of the earlier generations. How did he neglect to mention this *Tikkunei Zohar*?[689]

In any event, there is no contradiction between the *Zohar* in *Parashat Pinchas* and the Talmud in *Bava Kama*, on the one hand, which imply that the future Temple will be built by the Holy One Blessed be He, and the *Zohar* in *Parashat Pekudei*, which implies that it will be man-made.[690] Both are true. Man will build the earthly Temple first, and afterwards, the supernal Temple will descend upon it.

While I was speaking with my beloved friend, the great *gaon*, prince of the Torah, our revered master, R. Yitzchak Weiss *shlita*, rabbi and *av beit din* of Verba,✣ he added that the verse, *And I will be for it, says the Lord, a wall of fire round about* (*Zecharyah*

✣ As I copy the manuscripts for printing, I do not know what has happened to him. For he, too, was abducted by the cruel ones and taken off to an unknown land (due to our numerous sins). May the merit of his Torah stand by him and help him live to see Israel's salvation, speedily in our days. Amen.[691]

688 *Tikkunei Zohar, Tikkun* 21, p. 60b.

689 ✣ See above (sec. ב, pp. 218-19) where I explained why we must build [the earthly *Beit HaMikdash*] first, and [only] then the supernal *Beit HaMikdash* will descend upon it.

690 ✣ The *Zohar* in *Parashat Toledot* also implies this. (We were unable to locate this source.)

691 Unfortunately, he was killed in the Holocaust. May HaShem avenge his blood.

2:9), alludes to all of this. The words *round about* seem to be unnecessary. Based on the above, however, it is very well understood. Man will build the earthly *Beit HaMikdash*, and then, the fiery, supernal *Beit HaMikdash* will descend upon it and surround it.

When I arrived here in the capital [Budapest], I briefly obtained a copy of *Derishat Tzion*, by the brilliant R. Hirsch Kalischer. In it I found a responsa by the brilliant author of *Aruch LaNer* in which he also determines that Israel will build the earthly *Beit HaMikdash* first, and afterwards, the supernal one will descend upon it.[692] He reiterates this concept in *Aruch LaNer*[693] and uses it to explain the *Midrash* – quoted by Rashi and *Tosafot*[694] – which states that God will build the future Temple (*Tanchuma, Ki Tisa* 13). That is, God will build the supernal *Beit HaMikdash* and place it upon the earthly one. Also, in the above-cited responsa, he explains the words, *round about*, the same way R. Weiss does. However, the brilliant Aruch LaNer does not mention the *Tikkunei Zohar* or *Aspaklariya HaMe'irah*. Had he seen their words, he would have been overjoyed to know that he concurs with them.

The earthly Temple will be built before Mashiach arrives

It seems clear that the earthly, man-made Temple will be built before *Mashiach* comes. First, Jews will gather in *Eretz Yisrael* with the permission of the kings. Then, the earthly *Beit HaMikdash* will be built. (It is possible that the merit of the masses will help reveal the hidden stones.) Afterwards, *Mashiach* will arrive, and then the supernal *Beit HaMikdash* will descend [upon the earthly one].

This is evident from the following *Pesikta*:

> Our Rabbis taught: When the Messianic King reveals himself, he will stand on the roof of the *Beit HaMikdash* and proclaim to Israel: "O humble ones, the time for your redemption has come. If you do not believe me, behold God's light that has shone upon you, as it says, *Arise, shine, for your light has come, and the glory of the Lord has shone upon you* (*Yeshayah* 60:1)." (*Piska Kumi Ori*)

692 See *Derishat Tzion* (Mossad HaRav Kook), pp. 97-98, 157-60.
693 *Sukkah* 41a, on Rashi s.v. *iy nami*.
694 *Shavuot* 15b, *Rosh HaShanah* 30a, *Sukkah* 41a.

Our mentor, R. Efrayim Zalman Margolis, comments in his *Zera Efrayim*:

> "He will stand on the roof of the *Beit HaMikdash*": The *Yerushalmi* (*Ma'aser Sheini* 5:2 [21b]), quoted in *Tosafot Yom Tov* (ibid.), asserts that the *Beit HaMikdash* will be built forty years before *Mashiach* comes. Therefore, "He will stand on the roof of the *Beit HaMikdash*" could very well be taken literally.

Thus, it is explicit that the earthly *Beit HaMikdash* will be built before *Mashiach* comes.❖

To sum up, everyone agrees that we will build the earthly *Beit HaMikdash* first, and afterwards, the supernal one will descend upon it: the Malbim citing *kadmonim* (earlier sages), the *Tikkunei Zohar*, and the *Aspaklariya HaMe'irah*. Perhaps the latter two are the *kadmonim* to whom the Malbim referred. Or, perhaps he saw other *kadmonim*. In any event, the author of *Aruch LaNer* also agrees with them.❖❖

I believe that this matter is alluded to in the verse *Therefore, thus says the Lord, "I have returned to Jerusalem with mercy, My House will be rebuilt in it," says the Lord of Hosts, "and a line will be*

❖ The brilliant rabbi, our master, R. Moshe Shimon Hoffman (may his light shine forth), rabbi of the Orthodox synagogue here in Budapest, showed me the following *Tosefta*: "If Israel is granted [permission] to build the *Beit HaBechirah*..." (*Pesachim* 8:2). [After seeing this], I am surprised that the Minchat Chinuch asserts independently that we have a *mitzvah* to build the *Beit HaMikdash* if the kingdoms allow us to do so.[695] He did not realize that the *Tosefta* states this explicitly. In any event, this source also implies that we will build the Third Temple.

❖❖ Behold, the *kadmonim*, cited by the Malbim, assert that had the Jews of Ezra's time been "worthy," the supernal, future *Beit HaMikdash* would have immediately descended, and the final redemption would have arrived. It seems to me that the "worthiness" mentioned here refers to the Talmud's statement that the miracle of the complete redemption should have occurred at the time of Ezra, but sin prevented it (*Berachot* 4a). The Maharsha explains that the sin was their failure to ascend to *Eretz Yisrael* en masse.[696]

695 *Minchat Chinuch*, *Mitzvah* 95 (p. 93b, col. a, in standard edition).
696 Maharsha, *Yoma* 9b, s.v. *kachomah*.

stretched forth over Jerusalem" (*Zecharyah* 1:16). This means that man will first build a House – i.e., the earthly Temple – in Jerusalem. Afterwards, *a line will be stretched forth over Jerusalem*, meaning, the supernal *Beit HaMikdash* will descend upon it.

Who will build the future Temple – God or tzaddikim?

פא Know that the preceding idea answers an enormous question which I posed in my youth. (It is printed in my responsa, *Mishneh Sachir* [1:34]). Rashi and Tosafot write that God will build the future Temple, as it is written, *The Sanctuary, O Lord, that Your hands have established* (*Shemot* 15:17).[697] This is difficult, for it contradicts their own commentary elsewhere. The Talmud states:

> Bar Kappara expounded: The deeds of the righteous are greater than the creation of heaven and earth. Regarding the creation of heaven and earth it says, *Also, My hand has laid the foundation of the earth* (*Yeshayah* 48:13). Yet, regarding the handiwork of the righteous it says, *Your dwelling place that You have made, O Lord; the Sanctuary, O Lord, that Your hands have established* (*Shemot* 15:17).[698] (*Ketuvot* 5a)

Rashi and Tosafot comment, "The Sanctuary is the handiwork of the righteous." Thus, it is evident that the righteous will build it, not the Holy One Blessed be He!

Now, the Maharsha writes that "the righteous" refers to Betzalel and his colleagues who built the *Mishkan*.[699] According to this, the future Temple could be built by the Holy One Blessed be He, and there is no contradiction at all. However, there is still a question based on Rashi's commentary in *parashat BeShalach*. On the verse, *The Sanctuary, O Lord, that Your hands have established* (*Shemot* 15:17), Rashi writes:

> The *Beit HaMikdash* is beloved, for the world was created with [only] one hand, as it says, *My hand has laid the foundation of the earth*; while the Sanctuary [will be built] with two hands. When will it be built with two hands? When *The Lord will reign for ever and ever* (ibid. 15:18), in the future, when kingship is His.

Thus, Rashi writes explicitly that the future Temple will be built

697 See Rashi and *Tosafot*, *Sukkah* 41a.

698 [Bar Kappara derives this from the fact that the first verse says *hand*, in the singular; while the second verse says, *hands*.]

699 Maharsha, *Ketuvot* 5a, s.v. *gedolim*.

with two hands, and it is clear from *Ketuvot* (5a) that "two hands" refers to the handiwork of the righteous, not that of the Holy One Blessed be He. Therefore, Rashi contradicts himself! This is the question I asked when I was young, and it is a strong question.

In my responsa, *Mishneh Sachir*, I answered based on Rashi's comments on the verse *The Sanctuary, O Lord, that Your hands have established.* He explains that the word *Sanctuary* (מקדש) is marked by a *Zakeif Gadol* cantillation to separate it from the word *Lord* (ה') which follows it.[700] [In effect, then, the verse] says, "The Sanctuary that Your hands have established, O Lord," implying that the Holy One Blessed be He will build it. Nonetheless, it says, *Your hands have established*, that is, two hands [which refers to the handiwork of the righteous, according to *Ketuvot* (5a)]!

Now, Rashi's source is the *Mechilta* (*BeShalach, Parashat HaShirah* 10). Thus, we must say that the *Mechilta* disagrees with Bar Kappara's teaching, which distinguishes between the handiwork of the righteous and that of the Holy One Blessed be He. Instead, the *Mechilta* makes a different distinction, as Rashi cites there:

> The *Beit HaMikdash* is beloved, for the world was created with [only] one hand, as it says, *My hand has laid the foundation of the earth*; while the Sanctuary [will be built] with two hands. When will it be built with two hands? When *The Lord will reign for ever and ever* (ibid. 15:18), in the future, when kingship is His.

That is to say, the *Mechilta* distinguishes between the building of the Sanctuary and the creation of the world. However, when it comes to something as beloved as the future Sanctuary, even the Holy One Blessed be He will use two hands.

Bar Kappara, on the other hand, distinguishes between the handiwork of the righteous and that of the Holy One Blessed be He, not between that which is beloved [the Sanctuary] and that which is not [the world]. He derives this from the fact that it says about the Sanctuary, *Your hands have established.* Therefore, he clearly does not hold that HaShem will build the future Sanctuary. Rather, the righteous will built it with two hands.

This is why Rashi writes [in *Sukkah*] that God will build the future Temple, for he is following his own line of reasoning [which follows the *Mechilta*]. But, according to Bar Kappara, it will be man-made.

700 [The *Zakeif Gadol* cantillation indicates a minor pause in a verse.]

I also used this to explain the Rambam's opinion. He implies that the Temple will be man-made,[701] because he holds like Bar Kappara.

This is what I wrote when I was young, but now I believe that the *Mechilta* and Bar Kappara do not necessarily disagree. Instead, we can answer our question simply. The earthly *Beit HaMikdash* will be built first. Afterwards, the supernal *Beit HaMikdash* will descend upon it, and they will unite. Thus, the work of the righteous will also be involved. This is unlike the creation of heaven and earth, in which only the Holy One Blessed be He was involved. Therefore, only one hand is mentioned. The future edifice, however, will also include the work of the righteous. Therefore, the verse mentions two hands. This answer is very fitting.

Can the Temple be built at night or on a holiday?

פב Furthermore, the principle which I cited above from the *kadmonim* and *Tikkunei Zohar*...helps us understand the words of Rashi and Tosafot in Tractate *Sukkah* (41a). [The Talmud states that the *Beit HaMikdash* may be built either on the night of the 16th of Nissan or at the very end of the 15th, the first day of *Pesach*]. Rashi and Tosafot ask, "Is it not prohibited to build the *Beit HaMikdash* at night, as it is written, *And on the **day** the Mishkan was erected* (*BeMidbar* 9:15)?... And, the building of the *Beit HaMikdash* does not supersede [the prohibition of doing work on] a holiday!" They answer that God will build the future Temple; therefore, it may be built at night or on a holiday.

I find this answer very difficult. Granted, it solves the problem of building on a holiday. [How so]? It coincides with the Talmud's statement that spinning goats' hair while it is still on the goat's back does not violate the Sabbath, because this involves extraordinary wisdom and is an unusual way to work (*Shabbat* 74b). The Chatam Sofer derives from this that miraculous work does not violate the Sabbath.[702] He also uses this to answer the Rosh's question: If Moshe died on the Sabbath, how could he have written thirteen Torah scrolls on that day?[703] The Chatam Sofer explains that since it was done miraculously, in an unusual way, there was no violation of the Sabbath. The same applies to the future Temple, which God will build miraculously. Since this involves unusual work, it does not violate the holiday. It is, therefore, possible that the Temple will be built on a holiday.

701 See *Hilchot Beit HaBechirah* 1:1; *Hilchot Melachim* 11:1.

702 *Teshuvot Chatam Sofer* 6:29.

703 Rosh, *Pesachim* 10:13.

However, Rashi and Tosafot's assertion that since God will build the Temple it may be built at night, is completely incomprehensible. Since night is an invalid time to build the *Beit HaMikdash*, as derived from the verse *And on the* ***day*** *the Mishkan was erected*, it is certainly invalid if built then. This is similar to the rule that night is an invalid time to offer sacrifices, as derived from the verse *On the* ***day*** *He commanded* (*VaYikra* 7:38). How, then, does it help if God builds it? Since nighttime is intrinsically invalid, there is no difference whether it is built by man or God!

At this time I am writing in exile here in the capital, hidden in the recesses of my house, without any books through which to search to see if anyone discusses this matter. Nonetheless, the above-mentioned principle explains it well. Man will build the main part of the Temple during the day, in accordance with the law. Therefore, even if the spiritual Temple descends upon it at night, this will not disqualify it. An example will help explain this. If one slaughters a sacrifice and sprinkles its blood during the day, he may burn its fats and limbs – which completes the offering – at night.[704] The same is true of building the Temple. Since it will be initiated during the day, it may be completed at night. With God's help, this matter is clear.

Minchat Yehudah agrees

פד[705] While writing these words, I came across a small book entitled *Minchat Yehudah* (which I mentioned above).[706] I obtained it here in the capital through Divine Providence, for it is very hard to find. Its author was a great Sefardic scholar and Kabbalist, a disciple of our brilliant and holy masters, the author of *Pele Yo'etz* and the author of *Shoshanim LeDavid*. I noticed that he, too, discusses this issue at length and concludes that the future *Beit HaMikdash* will be built by man first, and only afterwards, the supernal *Beit HaMikdash* will descend upon it.[707]

He cites the following from *Kevod Chachamim*:

> It seems clear that the House of Ya'akov (i.e., the Third Temple) will also be built from the stones of the [previous] Temples of *Eretz Yisrael*, for the original holiness was never annulled. Now, if this is to be understood literally – that the Holy One

704 See Rambam, *Hilchot Ma'aseh HaKorbanot* 4:2.

705 [In the original Hebrew edition, section number פג is missing.]

706 P. 260.

707 *Minchat Yehudah*, sec. 37-38.

> Blessed be He will build the Temple Himself... – the Jews at the time of R. Yehoshua ben Chananyah would not have accepted the opportunity to build it (see *BeReishit Rabbah* 64:10)... Furthermore, R. Yehoshua would not have needed that sermon to placate the people.❖ Rather, he would have thanked HaShem publicly, because the decree was annulled.[708]

Minchat Yehudah also cites the *Zohar* which states that the Holy One Blessed be He will lower the first and second Temples from above (*Zohar, Parashat Pinchas* 3:221a). He explains:

> *Chazal* state that the Holy One Blessed be He will build the Third Temple and lower it from the heavens already built. This refers to the sanctity that will rest on the edifice which the Messianic King will build. (For, *Midrash Shir HaShirim* [4:31] states explicitly that *Mashiach* will build the *Beit HaMikdash*.)... This is (also) the meaning of the verse *The Sanctuary, O Lord, that Your hands have established* (*Shemot* 15:17). Rashi comments, "The future *Beit HaMikdash* will be built with two hands." This means that the Holy One Blessed be He will place the sanctity of the first two Temples upon the future Temple, which the righteous will build.[709]

For, the Gentiles had no control over the first two Temples. The destruction was only a guise, and [the Temples] were hidden away. *Kevod Chachamim* explains that "Their spirituality was hidden away, and that is what HaShem will send from above."

While I was reviewing the words of this brilliant Kabbalist [*Minchat Yehudah*], my heart filled with immense joy. I discovered there that the pious author of *Ma'archei Lev*[710] posed the same enormous question that I posed in my youth. He was hard-pressed to resolve it, but the brilliant author of *Minchat Yehudah* resolved it the same way I did. I was overjoyed that I was privileged, in my

---

❖ The *Midrash* recounts that the enemies of Israel convinced the king to retract his permission to build the *Beit HaMikdash*. The Jews were distressed by this, so the king asked R. Yehoshua ben Chananyah to placate them with a sermon.

708 *Kevod Chachamim*, on the Aggadic passages of the *Yerushalmi* (as cited in *Yefeh Mar'eh*), *Berachot*, chap. 4, *Aggadah* 6.

709 *Minchat Yehudah*, sec. 37-38.

710 R. Refa'el Yosef Chazan.

youth, to concur with these two Sefardic scholars. I will now quote the words of *Minchat Yehudah* verbatim:

> It seems to me that this is the meaning of the verse *The Sanctuary, O Lord, that Your hands have established*. Rashi *z"l* explains, "The future *Beit HaMikdash* will be built with two hands." This means that the Holy One Blessed be He will place the sanctity of the first two Temples upon the future Temple, which the righteous will build.
>
> I believe that this answers an enormous question. The Talmud states in the name of Bar Kappara: ôThe deeds of the righteous are greater than the creation of heaven and earth. Regarding the creation of heaven and earth it says, *Also My hand has laid the foundation of the earth* (*Yeshayah* 48:13). Yet, regarding the handiwork of the righteous it says, *The Sanctuary, O Lord, that Your hands have established* (*Shemot* 15:17) (*Ketuvot* 5a). That is, two hands. Rashi comments, "The Sanctuary is the handiwork of the righteous."
>
> In *Sukkah* (41a), however, Rashi writes the opposite: "The future edifice, for which we hope, will appear and descend from the heavens already built and perfected, as it says, *The Sanctuary, O Lord, that Your hands have established*." His commentary on the *Chumash* agrees: "When will it be built with two hands? When the Lord will reign forever and ever,"[711] i.e., in the future. Tosafot concur: "The future *Beit HaMikdash* [will be] heaven-made, as it is written, *The Sanctuary, O Lord, that Your hands have established*. This is also stated explicitly in *Midrash Tanchuma* (*Ki Tisa* 13)."[712]
>
> I also found that the pious author of *Ma'archei Lev z"l* questions Tosafot's conclusion based on the above-cited statement from *Ketuvot*.❖ He suggests that according to Bar

❖ This is the very same question I posed in my youth. It is printed in my responsa, *Mishneh Sachir* (1:34), which was published 19 years ago, in 5684 [1924]. [On the other hand], I only recently obtained a copy of *Minchat Yehudah*, which was printed in Spain in 5603 [1843] and is very hard to find. Someone brought it from Jerusalem and gave it to me because he knew I was dealing with this issue. There is no end to my joy, because I was privileged to concur with these two Sefardic scholars.

711 Rashi, *Shemot* 15:17.

712 *Tosafot*, *Shavuot* 15b, s.v. *ein*.

Kappara the verse, *The Sanctuary, O Lord...*, refers to King Shlomo's Temple as well, [not only the future one]. And, when the *Tanchuma* explains that the verse refers to the future Temple, it agrees that the prophecy also applies to Shlomo's Temple.[713] ❖

This is difficult. According to him, everyone agrees that the verse refers to the future Temple which will be built by God, as Rashi and Tosafot explain. If so, how does he know that the deeds of the righteous are great? Also, if everyone admits that the verse also refers to Shlomo's Temple, how does he know that the Holy One Blessed be He will build the future Temple?

Based on the above, everything is clear. The Third Temple will be built (speedily in our days) by the righteous men of deed..., the shepherds of Israel, as Bar Kappara taught and Rashi explained. Then, God will permanently establish this edifice with two hands. That is, He will place the sanctity of the first two Temples upon it, as the *Zohar* and *Tanchuma* state. This is a proper explanation. ❖❖

The "Chief Shepherd," our mentor, the "High Priest," [R. Eliyahu HaItamri] (author of *Sheivet Mussar*), writes something similar in *Midrash HaItamri*: "It is well known that there are contradictory statements [about *Mashiach*]... Some imply that the Messianic King sits in the Garden of Eden. This can be found in *Eichah Rabbah* (1:57), concerning the baby who was born on *Tish'a B'Av*; Tractate *Ta'anit*;[715] and other sources. But, there are innumerable statements which imply that he is alive... The explanation is as follows: When the Holy One

---

❖ Apparently, the brilliant author of *Ma'archei Lev* did not see the Maharsha on *Ketuvot* which states that ["the righteous" in Bar Kappara's statement] refers to Betzalel and his colleagues. For, this answers his question, as I explained above. However, this answer does not suffice for Rashi, as I explained above. Therefore, he was compelled to answer that the verse refers to both.

❖❖ This is exactly what I answered above. Rejoice, my innards,[714] for you have been privileged to concur with a great Kabbalist.

713 *Ma'archei Lev, Derush* 95.

714 Based on *Bava Metzia* 83b.

715 We were unable to locate this reference. See, however, *Yerushalmi Berachot* 2:4 (15b).

Blessed be He wants to redeem Israel, He will implant *Mashiach*'s soul in the appropriate man. Hence, his body sits in this world, and his soul sits in the Garden of Eden."[716]

[717]The language of the verse, *The Sanctuary, O Lord, that Your hands have established* (כוננו), also implies this. The [main] edifice is not the one that our eyes behold, as the verse says, *It* [David's throne] *shall be established* (יכון) *forever like the moon* (*Tehillim* 89:38). It also says, *The work of our hands, establish it* (כוננהו) (ibid. 90:17).[718]

The verse, [*The Sanctuary*...], refers to both Shlomo's Temple and the future one, as the pious rabbi writes [in *Ma'archei Lev*]. Thus, the future edifice proves that the deeds of the righteous are greater than the creation of heaven and earth. Regarding the creation of heaven and earth it says, *Also, My hand has laid the foundation of the earth, and My right hand has spanned the heavens* (*Yeshayah* 48:13), with one hand. This means that heaven and earth have no existence beyond this world, for in the future *The heavens will vanish like smoke and the earth will wear out like a garment* (ibid. 51:6, see Rashi). On the other hand, regarding the deeds of the righteous it says, *The Sanctuary, O Lord, that Your hands have established*, two hands. That is to say, they exist in this world and in the next, for the Holy One Blessed be He will place them [the first two Temples] upon the future edifice. This will demonstrate...how great and desirable are the deeds of the righteous. Then, the *Shechinah* and holiness will rest upon their handiwork.

Regarding the *Tanchuma*'s statement that the Third Temple will be surrounded by a wall of fire (*Ki Tisa* 13): perhaps this means that the sanctity which God will lower from above, which the entire world will see, will have the appearance of a burning fire reaching the pinnacle of the glorious heavens. Alternatively, it is a metaphor signifying that this Temple will be eternal.[719]

A strong question against this principle

פה However, we are still faced with a strong question against the principle which we proposed in the name of our Rabbis – the

716 *Midrash HaItamri, Derush* 18.

717 [Minchat Yehudah now returns to his assertion that "God will permanently establish this edifice with two hands." See the paragraph before the last.]

718 [These verses indicate that after man "builds" something, HaShem establishes it.]

719 *Minchat Yehudah*, sec. 38.

authors of the *Midrash* and the *Zohar*, as well as earlier and later scholars. They assert that the future Temple will be built by man first, and afterwards, the supernal one will come down upon it from the heavens.

[The *Mishnah* states that] R. Yochanan ben Zakkai instituted a prohibition [against eating new grain] the entire day of the waving [of the *Omer*].[720] The Talmud asks, why should the entire day be forbidden? Until midday should suffice, because *Beit Din* (the High Court) is not indolent![721] The Talmud replies: [Perhaps] the Temple will be built immediately before sunset [on the 15th] (*Rosh HaShanah* 30a, *Sukkah* 41a). Rashi and Tosafot explain that the Temple will suddenly come down from the heavens, and *Beit Din* will have no time to prepare the *Omer* beforehand. Therefore, it will take the entire day [to prepare and offer it].

Now, if the earthly *Beit HaMikdash* will be built by man first, it will not happen suddenly. We will surely know that it is under construction. Therefore, *Beit Din* will have time to prepare the *Omer* beforehand, and the Talmud's question remains: ôWhy should the entire day be forbidden? Until midday should suffice!ö This is a formidable question against those who hold [that man will build it first].

Ezrat Kohanim's answer

I was very bothered by this question, until HaShem enlightened me and showed me a passage in *Ezrat Kohanim*, a commentary on Tractate *Middot*[722] by one of the *gedolim* of the generation in Byelorussia.[723]

Perchance, I came across the newly reprinted edition of

720 [According to Torah law one is permitted to eat new grain (*Chadash*) immediately after the *Omer* offering is brought on the 16th of Nissan. When there is no Temple, it is permitted from the very beginning of the day. However, R. Yochanan ben Zakkai prohibited it the entire day. The Talmud explains the reason for this: We are worried that the *Beit HaMikdash* may be rebuilt speedily, and people will say, "Last year we ate the new grain at daybreak. We will do the same this year." But, they will not realize that since the *Beit HaMikdash* was rebuilt, they must wait until the *Omer* is offered. The Talmud attempts to determine which specific case causes concern. One possibility is that the *Beit HaMikdash* will be built on the 15th of Nissan.]

721 [I.e., even if the Temple is rebuilt on the 15th, *Chadash* will be permitted by midday, because *Beit Din* will surely offer the *Omer* by then.]

722 *Ezrat Kohanim* (Warsaw, 5633 [1873]), part 3 – *Pinot HaAzarah*, vol. 2, p. 260, s.v. *achar kotvi*. [The parenthetical comments are R. Teichtal's.]

723 R. Yehoshua Yosef HaKohen, *Av Beit Din* of Mard.

Minchat Chinuch on the Ra'ah's work.[724] There, I found the following: "It is possible that today, as well, ...there is a *mitzvah* to build the Temple. Accordingly, the *Midrash* recounts that at the time of R. Yehoshua ben Chananyah, [the king] permitted the Jews to build the *Beit HaMikdash*, and they began construction (*BeReishit Rabbah* 64:10). Also, *Kapot Temarim* states that Rabbeinu Netanel, one of the Tosafists, wanted to offer sacrifices in Jerusalem.[725] The same applies to building the *Beit HaMikdash* [today]..."[726] This concurs with what I wrote above, and it is clear from the *Midrash* that we will build the *Beit HaMikdash* ourselves.[727]

Now, R. Yehoshua certainly consented to this great undertaking, and the *halachah* always follows his opinion. It is unlikely that the people acted without his consent, for he was the greatest sage of that generation, as the *Midrash* there states. [Had he opposed this], they certainly would have listened to him, just like they did afterwards (when he told them to stop building), as I stated above.

I discussed this matter with the revered, brilliant, and sacred rabbi, the holy luminary, the pious and virtuous *Admor*, our master and teacher, R. Ya'akov of Radzin *shlita*. He told me with his holy tongue that we will build the *Beit HaMikdash* ourselves. (See the *Haggadah* of R. Tzvi Kalischer *zt"l*.[728] The *Midrash* mentioned above also proves this.)

I then said to this revered and holy man that although, thank God, I have some knowledge of the structure of the *Beit HaMikdash*, I am still unsure how to build [the Third Temple], whether according to the form and dimensions of the Second Temple or according to those of Yechezkel's edifice. The only one [who addresses this issue is the] Tosafot Yom Tov, who writes that we will build Yechezkel's edifice. For, although the *Mishnah* describes the structure of the Second Temple, indicating that we will follow its dimensions, nevertheless, one could argue that Rebbe Yehudah HaNasi describes the Second Temple only because of the few things that it has in common

724 I.e., *Sefer HaChinuch*, attributed to the Ra'ah.

725 *Kapot Temarim, Sukkah* 34b, s.v. *shel ma'aser sheini beYerushalayim*.

726 *Minchat Chinuch, Mitzvah* 95.

727 ❖ This is also clear from the *Tosefta* I cited above (p. 441).

728 Called *Yetzirat Mitzrayim*. [This parenthetical statement is from *Ezrat Kohanim*.]

with Yechezkel's edifice. Alternatively, as the Tosafot Yom Tov writes, "The description of the Second Temple helps us analyze and understand Yechezkel's edifice."[729] Indeed, we find that Scriptures describe Yechezkel's edifice, implying that we will follow its [dimensions]. Therefore, it seems more likely that we will build Yechezkel's edifice.[730]

The brilliant and holy *Admor shlita*...answered me as follows. Undoubtedly, we will build the future Temple according to the form and dimensions of the Second Temple. However, afterwards, at the time of the complete rectification, when *Mashiach* arrives, Yechezkel's edifice will be built by itself [and descend] from the heavens.[731]

When I heard this from his holy mouth, I was overjoyed, because it opened up gates of wisdom for me. It enabled me to mediate between...the *Targum Yonatan*[732] and the *Midrash Tanchuma*[733] on the one hand (which state that God will build the *Beit HaMikdash*), and the *Yerushalmi* and the holy *Zohar* on the other hand (which state that it will be man-made). [The same argument exists] between the Rambam (man-made) and Rashi (heaven-made).

We can explain that Rashi and Tosafot's statement, that the future Temple will be built by God, is based entirely on the Talmud's assumption that the day of the waving [of the *Omer*] is forbidden merely by Rabbinic law (*Rosh HaShanah* 30a). Because of this and because of the Talmud's question,[734] we are forced to say that God will build the future Temple from the very outset. Thus, we must also say that the *Tanchuma* argues with the *Yerushalmi* and the holy *Zohar*, holding that we will not build it by ourselves at all. Rather, God will build it instantly, and it could be built at night or on a holiday. Therefore, R. Yochanan ben Zakkai instituted a prohibition [against eating new grain] the entire day of the waving, as the Talmud explains. For if you do not say this, the Talmud's

729 *Tosafot Yom Tov*, Introduction to Tractate *Middot*.

730 ❖ See what the Chatam Sofer writes about this in his *Teshuvot, Yoreh De'ah* 236.

731 ❖ See *Kol HaRemez* on the Tosafot Yom Tov's introduction to *Middot*.

732 Perhaps he is referring to *Targum Yonatan* on *Shemot* 15:17.

733 According to *Tosafot, Shavuot* 15b, s.v. *ein binyan*. (Ezrat Kohanim's note)

734 ["Why should the entire day be forbidden? Until midday should suffice, because *Beit Din* is not indolent!" See above, p. 450.]

question remains unanswered. Hence, we are forced to say that the Talmud holds that God will build the future Temple instantly...

However, according to Rav Nachman Bar Yitzchak's determination (ibid.) that [the new grain is prohibited] the entire day of the waving by Torah law, we need not say that the Temple will be built at night or by God. Therefore, we can explain that the *Tanchuma* agrees with this assumption, and when it asserts that the Temple will be built by God it refers to the edifice which will be built afterwards. Nevertheless, the *Tanchuma* agrees with the *Yerushalmi* and the holy *Zohar* that we will first build a structure in the form of the Second Temple, by ourselves. Thus, our Sages do not argue with one another. Perhaps, in this same manner we can reconcile the words of the Rambam in his commentary [to the *Mishnah*] with those in his treatise, [*Mishneh Torah*].[735]

Hence, the brilliant author of *Ezrat Kohanim* answered the question which we posed earlier against the opinion which says that we will build the earthly *Beit HaMikdash* first, and afterwards, the supernal one will descend from the heavens. I already mentioned[736] that the *Tikkunei Zohar* and *Aspaklariya HaMe'irah* (citing the *Midrash*) also agree with this. I subsequently discovered the same thing in *Emunot VeDe'ot*, by R. Sa'adya Gaon. He writes that we will first build the *Beit HaMikdash* with the permission of the kingdom, and this will be the foundation for the edifice that will descend from the heavens.[737]

Thus, this opinion is established like a fixed peg. May it be God's will that we merit to see this, speedily in our days. Amen.

Minchat Yehudah's answer

פו Once again, I looked into the holy work, *Minchat Yehudah*, and found that he was also aware of this formidable question from the Talmud in Tractate *Rosh HaShanah*..., and he answered it properly:

735 Apparently, he is referring to his own comment in *Sha'ar Kri'at HaBinyan*, the introduction to *Ezrat Kohanim*: "The Rambam *z"l* writes in *Hilchot Melachim* (chap. 11) that the Messianic King will build the *Beit HaMikdash*. Nonetheless, he writes [in his Introduction to the *Mishnah* (chap. 5)] that the purpose of Tractate *Middot* is to teach us how to build [the Temple] at the end of days. *Tosafot Yom Tov* also cites this. "

736 Pp. 437-39.

737 *Emunot VeDe'ot* 8:5.

Chazal state, "R. Yochanan ben Zakkai instituted a prohibition [against eating new grain] the entire day of the waving [of the *Omer*]," and they delve into [the issue of] when the Temple will be rebuilt. Only God knows the hidden things. It is possible that after the Temple is built it will remain closed until the sanctity descends from the heavens. We similarly find that Shlomo's edifice was closed for twelve months, and the *Mishkan* was folded up from the 25th of Kislev until *Rosh Chodesh* Nissan.[738] Therefore, R. Yochanan ben Zakkai was worried that this sanctity would be revealed on the 16th of Nissan.

Alternatively, it is possible that this entire Talmudic discourse is not definitive, rather, one possible scenario. For, if Israel is worthy, the Holy One Blessed be He may build and perfect the Temple instantaneously, as *Chazal* state, "A miracle should have occurred in the days of Ezra, but sin prevented it" (*Berachot* 4a). Similarly, statements like, "This *halachah* applies when *Mashiach* arrives" (*Sanhedrin* 51b), are only possibilities. ❖

My master and teacher states explicitly in *Shoshanim LeDavid*[739] that all of these statements (asserting that the future [redemption] will occur miraculously) are according to R. Yochanan. Shmuel, however, disagrees (holding that everything will occur naturally). This is why we do not find that our Rabbis *z"l* prohibit Israel from building the Temple based on these statements. ❖❖

❖ They do not determine that this is definitely the way it will be. So too, [the conclusion of] the discussion in *Rosh HaShanah* is not a definite statement of the way things will be, but a possible scenario. If Israel is worthy it will happen instantaneously. Thus, R. Yochanan ben Zakkai instituted his prohibition in case it happens this way.

❖❖ The *Midrash* which states that R. Yehoshua ben Chananyah began to build the *Beit HaMikdash* with his own hands, unconcerned with the statement that it will be built by God, proves this point. I would add that the *Tosefta*[740] also states this explicitly: "If Israel is granted [permission] to build the *Beit HaBechirah*..." (*Pesachim* 8:2). Clearly, the *Tosefta* is not concerned with the notion that God has to build it. It must be that such statements are only according to R. Yochanan.

738 See *Yalkut Shimoni* 2:184.

739 *Shoshanim LeDavid*, introduction to *Middot*.

740 ❖ See above, p. 441.

> This matter needs to be examined and analyzed further. [Nonetheless], I presented my opinion with awe and reverence.
>
> Anyhow, the way to cause the initial rectification (*tikkun*) is to appoint elders. Then, when we are fortunate to bring together the chosen assembly of seventy one, all hidden matters will be revealed to them.[741]

In any event, he was also aware of our question, and he answered it conclusively with his great wisdom. Thus, the principle that we will build the earthly Temple first..., to which the overwhelming majority of our Sages adhere, remains clear and valid. May we be fortunate to see its fulfillment speedily in our days. Amen.

An unanswered question

פז Since we are discussing the Talmudic dialogue from Tractates *Rosh HaShanah* and *Sukkah*, I will present here a question that I posed when I was seventeen years old. At that time, I was studying under my master and teacher, the holy and profoundly brilliant *Admor* of Zavna, author of Responsa *Yad Shalom*.❖ He greatly admired my question. I asked as follows. *Chazal* state:

> R. Yochanan ben Zakkai instituted a prohibition [against eating new grain] the entire day of the waving [of the *Omer*]. Why? [Perhaps] the *Beit HaMikdash* will be rebuilt speedily and people will say, "Last year, we ate [the new grain] at daybreak. We will do the same this year." But, they do not realize that last year, when there was no *Omer*, daybreak permitted [the eating of the new grain]. Now that there is an *Omer*, the *Omer* permits it. (*Rosh HaShanah* 30a, *Sukkah* 41a, *Menachot* 68a-b)

The Talmud concludes that we are concerned that the Temple may be built suddenly, and there will be no time to prepare the *Omer*. Therefore, the Sages prohibited the new grain the entire day.

Behold, the author of *Kereiti U'Peleiti* determines that when our righteous Savior (*Mashiach*) arrives, speedily in our days, all grain will be prohibited as *Chadash*, even the grain in the storehouses.[742]

❖ He took me into his home to teach his fourteen-year-old son, Elazar, who had become engaged to the daughter of our master, the author of *Kedushat Yom Tov*.

741 ❖ *Minchat Yehudah* holds that all of *Klal Yisrael* will assemble and choose seventy one elders. (See there, sec. 38.)

742 [This grain would normally be permitted, because it is presumed to be at

This coincides with Tosafot's statement that when the Jews entered *Eretz Yisrael* all of their grain became prohibited, even the grain in the storehouses.[743] Based on this, the Peleiti explains R. Yom Tov's opinion, cited in the Mordechai,[744] that *Chadash* is not considered "a prohibition which will eventually be permitted" (דבר שיש לו מתירין),[745] because it will once again become prohibited [when *Mashiach* comes].[746] I subsequently discovered that our master, the Chatam Sofer, also agrees with this.[747]

However, I have a problem with the opinion of these two great scholars... We maintain that the first time a *kohen* performs the Temple service, he must first offer an inaugural *Minchah* sacrifice.[748] *Torat Kohanim* is of the opinion that this offering is inhibitive; meaning, if a *kohen* serves without it, his service is invalid.[749] R. Yochanan agrees in *VaYikra Rabbah* (8:4).

Now, we also maintain that one may not bring any *Minchah* offering before the *Omer*. If one does, the offering is disqualified (*Menachot* 68b), because it is not "*From the feasts of Israel* (*Yechezkel* 45:15), i.e., from the permitted foods of Israel" (*Menachot* 6a).[750] Thus, when the *Beit HaMikdash* is rebuilt and the *kohanim* want to offer the *Omer*, which is a *Minchah*, they will have to offer an inaugural *Minchah* first, in order to be inaugurated into the service. But, according to the Peleiti and the Chatam Sofer, who say that all grains will be prohibited because of *Chadash*, the *kohanim* will not be able to offer this inaugural *Minchah* because it is not *from the feasts of Israel*. It follows, then, that they will not be able to offer the *Omer* or perform any of the other services. What will they do?

We must say that at that time, as well, daybreak will permit the new grain. This will enable the *kohanim* to offer the inaugural *Minchah* and perform all of the other services. However, if this is

least a year old. Therefore, the 16th of Nissan has already passed, making it permissible.]

743 *Tosafot, Rosh HaShanah* 13a, s.v. *de'ikrivu*.

744 *Beitzah*, chap. 1.

745 [Even though it becomes permissible on the 16th of Nissan.]

746 *Kereiti U'Peleiti* 102:1.

747 *Torat Moshe* (5641 [1881]), *Parashat VaYeishev*, p. 35a, s.v. *haMordechai*.

748 ❖ See *Menachot* 51b; *Shekalim* (*Yerushalmi*) 7:3 (28a).

749 ❖ This *Torat Kohanim* is cited in *Mishneh LaMelech, Hilchot K'lei HaMikdash* 5:16.

750 [*Chazal* derive from this verse that all sacrifices must be brought from kosher food.]

true, why does the Talmud say, "Now that there is an *Omer*, the *Omer* permits it"? [According to what we just said], daybreak will permit it...!

Do not answer: the Rambam rules that the inaugural *Minchah* is not inhibitive,[751] and it is, therefore, possible that the *kohanim* will not offer it first. I could still raise an objection. Yechezkel says, *And on the day that he* [a kohen] *enters...into the inner court..., he shall offer his sin-offering* (44:27). The Talmud comments, "This is the [inaugural *Minchah* which measures] one-tenth of an *eifah*" (*Mo'ed Kattan* 15b). That is to say, the inaugural *Minchah* will be the first offering that a *kohen* will bring on the day he begins to perform the sacred service. Now, it is well known that Yechezkel's prophecy refers to the future. Thus, it is clear that HaShem wants the *kohanim* to offer the inaugural *Minchah* first. But, how is this possible [according to the Peleiti and the Chatam Sofer], seeing that everything will be prohibited because of *Chadash*? This matter needs to be examined.

I presented this question to the most brilliant scholars of the generation, and they were unable to answer it, despite their efforts. See my responsa, *Mishneh Sachir* (1:92).

This concludes the essay: The Sanctuary of HaShem

XIV Conclusion

Thoughts on Rosh HaShanah

פח Today is the 23rd of Elul, 5703 [1943], close to the forthcoming "appointed day."[752] Thus, I will conclude this chapter with an idea that I originated last *Rosh HaShanah* in Nitra. I recorded it in my journal the next day, *Tzom Gedalyah*.[753]

In the middle of Elul, in the year, *You turn* (תשב) *man back to dust* (*Tehillim* 90:3),[754] my family and I were exiled from Pishtian. The savages

751 [I.e., if a *kohen* serves without it, his service is still valid.] *Hilchot K'lei HaMikdash* 5:16.

752 I.e., *Rosh HaShanah*. See *Tehillim* 81:4 and *Rosh HaShanah* 8a-b.

753 [The author kept a journal during the stormy Holocaust years. It contains descriptions of events, *divrei Torah* pertinent to the times, words of encouragement to his beloved people, and a rough draft of this book. Miraculously, it survived the Holocaust and was discovered 49 years later. R. Teichtal's son, R. Chayim Menachem, is presently working on its publication. One volume has already been published under the title, *Emunah Tzerufah B'Kur HaSho'ah*.]

754 [The numerical value of תשב is 702, corresponding to the year 5702 (1942).]

tormented us to the brink of despair, so we fled to Nitra in the middle of the night, with absolutely nothing. We stayed there until after the holidays, at which time HaShem helped us escape to our present location [Budapest]. May He cover us with His wings[755] until salvation comes to all of *Klal Yisrael*, speedily in our days. Amen.

He who seeks Eretz Yisrael seeks God

In our High Holiday prayers we beseech HaShem, "And so, grant honor, O Lord, to Your people..., happiness to Your Land, joy to Your City, and a flourishing of pride to David Your servant." A commentary which I found in an old *machzor* explains this prayer based on a Tana'itic statement:

> The people of Israel were exiled because they despised three things: the kingdom of Heaven, the kingdom of the House of David, and the *Beit HaMikdash*. R. Shimon ben Menassiya said, "Israel will not be shown a good sign until they return and seek out these three things." (*Yalkut Shimoni* 2:106)

That is to say, "Grant honor to Your people" corresponds to the kingdom of Heaven; "Happiness to Your Land, joy to Your City" refers to the *Beit HaMikdash*; and "A flourishing of pride to David" refers to the kingdom of the House of David.

Behold, after living among the Gentiles for close to 2,000 years, we have mingled with the nations and learned their ways.[756] Most of today's Jews have absolutely no concept of Judaism. We cannot expect them to return and seek out the kingdom of Heaven and the kingdom of the House of David, because they have no idea what these things are. Rather, what do they seek? *Eretz Yisrael*, which includes all of these things, as I explained above at length.[757] *Chazal* allude to this when they say, "He who dwells in *Eretz Yisrael* is like one who has a God" (*Ketuvot* 110b). For, the kingdom of the House of David and the kingdom of Heaven are one in the same, as is well known to the Kabbalists.[758] And since we see that [today's pioneers] sacrifice themselves for *Eretz Yisrael*,[759] they seek out these three things without even knowing it.❖

❖ I wrote this a while ago, independently. But now I discovered that

755 Based on *Tehillim* 91:4.
756 Based on *Tehillim* 106:35.
757 P. 45.
758 See *Zohar* 1:33b; *Sha'arei Orah* 1.
759 ❖ See above (pp. 169, 257).

Furthermore, the *Pesikta* states:

Ya'akov is completely holy

> *Sing joyously to God, our strength, cry aloud to the God of Ya'akov* (*Tehillim* 81:2). R. Tanchuma son of R. Abba began: *He beheld no iniquity in Ya'akov* (*BeMidbar* 23:21). Why did Bil'am mention Ya'akov and not Avraham or Yitzchak? Because, he saw that Avraham begot unworthy offspring – Yishmael and the children of Keturah. Yitzchak begot unworthy offspring – Eisav and his chiefs. Ya'akov, on the other hand, is completely holy, as it is written, *All these are the twelve tribes of Israel* (*BeReishit* 49:28).[762] Therefore, Bil'am did not mention any of the Patriarchs except Ya'akov. *Cry aloud to the God of Ya'akov.* (*Pesikta Harninu, Parashah* 40)

This seems difficult. Today, Ya'akov also has many unworthy offspring, due to our numerous sins. Why, then, is he greater than the other Patriarchs?

Apparently, the answer is that everything follows the root. If the root is good, all of the branches are considered good, even those with deficiencies. Since they absorb moisture from the root, they will flourish once again. However, if the root is bad, it blemishes everything.[763] Thus, Ya'akov, who is completely holy, is a perfect root. He will give new life to all of his descendants until the end of time, and they will flourish once again. Most importantly, his descendants must stay connected to the root, so that they can absorb new vitality from it.

This explains Bil'am's statement *From its beginnings I see it like a rock, and from the hills I behold it* (*BeMidbar* 23:9). That is to say, their root is completely good. Therefore, *He beheld no iniquity in*

---

the author of *Minchat Yehudah* concurs.[760] He cites the *Zohar* which says that the Holy One Blessed be He is called "King" only in *Eretz Yisrael* (*Zohar* 3:276a).[761] Therefore, *Chazal*'s statement that Israel will seek out the kingdom of Heaven means that they will return to *Eretz Yisrael* so that the Holy One Blessed be He can be called "King." Our entire repentance depends first and foremost on this.

760 *Minchat Yehudah*, sec. 17 (vol. 1, p. 237).
761 Ibid., sec. 18.
762 See Rashi there.
763 See *Chullin* 64b.

Ya'akov and saw no perverseness in Israel (ibid. 23:21). Their perverseness and iniquity are merely "wayfarers," and the moment the sinners connect to their roots they will once again flourish like a rose.[764]

Thus, our main task on *Rosh HaShanah* is to connect ourselves to Ya'akov Avinu *a"h* so that his sanctity will permeate us and rectify all of the defects that we caused in the previous year, and ever since we entered this world. Accordingly, the verse says, *Blow the shofar at the new moon... Because it is a statute for Israel, an ordinance for the God of Ya'akov* (*Tehillim* 81:4-5). It specifies *Ya'akov* for he is completely holy and we are rooted in him. We, the branches, will draw life and sanctity from the root so that we can once again flourish. The *paytan* (poet) thus says, "When there is no advocate..., speak for the sake of Ya'akov regarding the statutes and ordinances."[765] It specifies "Ya'akov" because the root is good, and through it everything will be rectified for the good. With God's help, this seems to be the explanation of the *Pesikta*. May HaShem help us connect ourselves to Ya'akov Avinu at all times. Amen.

The virtue of judging matters based on the future

פט The *Pesikta* continues:

Another interpretation: Why Ya'akov of all the Patriarchs? Our Rabbis taught, "A person is treated like he treats others." This can be compared to a king who had three friends. He wanted to build a palace, so he summoned the first friend and said, "Look at the place in which I want to build my palace!" The friend replied, "I remember it as a mountain at first." He summoned the second one who said, "I remember it as a field at first." The king dismissed him and summoned his third friend who said, "I remember it as a palace at first." The king replied, "By your life! I will build it into a palace and name it after you."

So too, Avraham, Yitzchak, and Ya'akov were friends of the Holy One Blessed be He. Avraham called the *Beit HaMikdash* a mountain, as it says, *On the mountain the Lord will appear* (*BeReishit* 22:14). Yitzchak called it a field, as it says, *See, the smell of my son is like the smell of a field* (ibid. 27:27). Ya'akov called it a palace, as it says, *How awesome is this place! This is none other than the House of God* (ibid. 28:17). The Holy One

764 Based on *Hoshea* 14:6.

765 Hymn recited after *Kedushah* on the High Holidays.

Blessed be He said to him, "You called it a house before it was even built; by your life, I will build it and name it after you." [Thus, it says], *O House of Ya'akov, come and let us walk in the light of the Lord* (*Yeshayah* 2:5); and, *Many nations will go...to the House of the God of Ya'akov* (ibid. 2:3). Yirmiyah also states this, *Behold, I will return the captivity of the tents of Ya'akov* (30:18). Asaf also confirms this matter, [for] he mentions only Ya'akov in connection with the *teruah*, as it says, *Sound the* teruah *to the God of Ya'akov* (*Tehillim* 81:2). (*Pesikta Harninu, Parashah* 40)

With God's help, I believe the explanation is as follows. The first two friends, who called the site of the palace a mountain and a field, meant that the site on which a king's palace is to be built must be inherently prepared and fitting to receive such an honorable edifice. Thus, the first one said, "I remember it as a mountain at first," and the second one said, "I remember it as a field at first." That is to say, they saw it as a simple mountain and a simple field which are not inherently suitable to house the palace of the king. On the other hand, the third friend said, "I see the palace with my spiritual eye. I am not looking at the present, when this site is merely a mountain or a field. I am looking into the future, when the palace will sanctify this place and elevate it to the highest heights, making it fitting for the king's honor." The Omnipresent was so pleased with this outlook that He called the *Beit HaMikdash* exclusively by Ya'akov's name.

Thus, Ya'akov distinctively appraised matters based on the future. Anything which had the potential to be holy, he considered holy now, even if it was not yet inherently worthy. Therefore, Ya'akov called the *Beit HaMikdash* "The House of God" even before it was built. The Holy One Blessed be He was so pleased with this quality that he called the Temple by Ya'akov's name, showing that He approved of this characteristic.

This is true of all matters, including ours. On *Rosh HaShanah* we must accept the yoke of the kingdom of Heaven. But, how can we proclaim HaShem as our King when we failed to do His will throughout the year? The answer is, we can proclaim Him as our King by virtue of the future. That is, if we resolve to do His will and serve Him wholeheartedly from now on, we can call Him our King, even though we [presently] have no merits. That was Ya'akov Avinu's quality: he identified things based on the future.

This explains the *Pesikta*'s statement "Asaf also confirms this matter, [for] he mentions only Ya'akov in connection with the *teruah*, as it says, *Sound a* teruah *to the God of Ya'akov*." That is to say, by virtue of our acceptance to heed His voice and fulfill His will in the future, the Holy One Blessed be He is our King even now, and we accept upon ourselves the yoke of His Kingdom.[766] May it be God's will that the upcoming year be one of redemption and salvation. (This concludes the idea that I originated last *Rosh HaShanah*.)

Summary: Two ways to come closer to God

Thus, we have before us two good ways to elevate the simple man from his lowly, spiritual state. 1. He could connect himself to his root, i.e., Ya'akov Avinu, who is completely holy. That way, life-giving waters will flow upon him and implant within him new life and abundant sanctity. 2. He could be accepted from the very outset based on his future [deeds].

Today's *olim* (immigrants) possess these two characteristics, no matter how simple or bad they may be (God forbid). We find that Ya'akov Avinu valued living in the Land more than all the money in the world. He gave all of his exceedingly great wealth to Eisav and said, "*Chutz-LaAretz* possessions are worthless to me."[767] Therefore, since today's *olim* sacrifice themselves for the love of the Land, as is well known, they connect themselves to their root, which is Ya'akov Avinu. This connection will also elevate them spiritually. Furthermore, Ya'akov judged maters based on the future; and *Chazal*[768] promise us that after the Jews assemble in *Eretz Yisrael*, HaShem will bestow upon them a purifying spirit and inspire them to do His will wholeheartedly.[769]

We must all unite to build the Land

Therefore, it is obvious that every Jew must join the *olim* and [help] sanctify HaShem's name through all of *Klal Yisrael*. We say this in our holy prayers on the Days of Awe: "And may they all become a single society to do Your will wholeheartedly. For we know, O Lord our God, that dominion is Yours, strength is in Your hand, and might is in Your right hand."[770] That is to say, if all the Jews

766 [One of the reasons we blow the *shofar* (*teruah*) on *Rosh HaShanah* is to proclaim HaShem as our King (see *Rosh HaShanah* 16a). Therefore, Asaf specifically mentioned Ya'akov in connection with the *teruah* to teach us that we can only proclaim HaShem as our King if we emulate Ya'akov's trait of judging matters based on the future.]

767 Rashi, *BeReishit* 46:6.

768 See *BeReishit Rabbah* 76:2.

769 ❖ I cited this above (p. 117) from the Rambam and other *gedolim*.

770 From the *Ata Kadosh* blessing.

form a single society, they will add strength and might to God's dominion (as it were), and He will elevate their pride to the utmost heights. Amen, so may it be God's will.

This coincides with the *Midrash* cited by the Ramban on the verse *He was King in Yeshurun when the heads of the people gathered, the tribes of Israel together* (*Devarim* 33:5): "When is the Holy One Blessed be He established above? When Israel forms a single society below" (*BeMidbar Rabbah* 15:18).

This concludes the third chapter, on the 23rd of Elul, 5703 [1943], here in the capital, Budapest. May HaShem fulfill the verse, *On the third day He will raise us up* (*Hoshea* 6:2), and may we live before Him, speedily in our days. Amen.

Addendum to Chapter Three

An apparent refutation of our author's entire thesis

A man came up to me with an open book in his hand and asked if he could show me something. I took it from him and saw that it was *Divrei Yechezkel* by our holy Rebbe of Shinev *z"l*. He then showed me that this man of God disapproved of working the fields of *Eretz Yisrael*. Rather, we must strengthen the settlement of the Land only by sending an abundance of "holy coins"[771] to those who are engrossed in Torah and divine service, until HaShem elevates our pride and returns our captivity, speedily in our days. Amen.[772]

I responded with the comments of our mentor, the Chatam Sofer:

> Students study under their teachers primarily to [learn how to] compare one case to another. The Rosh writes, "One can say that nowadays, as well,[773] not every case is found in the Talmud, and [the arbiter] simply compares cases. Therefore, there is concern that his comparison is incorrect."[774] For this reason, there is a custom that when a person originates his own idea we say in German, "*gleich*" or "*um gleich*," similar or dissimilar. That is, [we ask] whether the comparison is a good one or not.
>
> Profound and extremely fine logic is needed to distinguish between two cases, but by doing so several questions are

771 [I.e., charity.]

772 *Divrei Yechezkel, Likutim* (end).

773 [In addition to earlier generations.]

774 Cited in *Beit Yosef, Bedek HaBayit, Yoreh De'ah* 242.

> resolved... Therefore, the teacher analyzes the cases and shows his students the fine line between the two... This way, they learn the true method of deciding *halachah*.[775]

Thus, the determination of practical *halachah* depends primarily on the comparison between cases. If the case at hand is similar to the one from which we would like to learn, with all of its conditions and details, [then we may derive the law from that case]. However, if there is the slightest distinction between the two, the law changes and we cannot derive one from the other. Therefore, if inadequately trained students want to apply the laws of one case to another, because they think that the two cases are similar, a sage may analyze the issue and show explicitly that the comparison is incorrect. Thus, the law that they originally derived, whether it be a stringency or a leniency, is annulled.

This principle will help me refute your findings in the holy work, *Divrei Yechezkel*, which you thought would contradict my entire thesis. Realize, my son, that these words of the Rebbe of Shinev are not new to me. I already alluded to them above[776] and made a distinction between his era and ours... I wrote as follows: "Similarly, the statement of the holy Rebbe of Shinev, at the end of *Divrei Yechezkel*, refers to his era when Israel enjoyed tranquillity in exile. Today, however, when our very lives have been taken from us, even the Chatam Sofer, the Ahavat Yonatan, and the Rebbe of Shinev would admit that HaShem is ordering us to leave the lands of exile and go to the Land that the Lord our God seeks out." I explained there, at length, that all of our troubles are a divine command to return to our beloved Land.[777]

Thus, I was also bothered by your finding and by the comparison you wanted to make between the two cases. However, I made a distinction and showed that they are not comparable. Therefore, you cannot apply his words to our situation, and my words remain valid both theoretically and practically.

All agree that one may go to Eretz Yisrael in times of danger

With God's help, I will now further prove the veracity of my words. *The Lord said to Avram, "Go forth from your land"* (*BeReishit* 12:1). Rashi comments: "Did he not already leave that place and go to Charan with his father? Rather, HaShem said to him, 'Go even

775 *Chiddushei Chatam Sofer, Chullin* 7a, s.v. *u'po matzati*.

776 Chap. 3, sec. ו (p. 227).

777 See ibid., sec. ד, ה, ו.

further away from there and leave your father's house.'" The Shelah elaborates:

> The Holy One Blessed be He knew that Avraham kept the entire Torah, even Rabbinic injunctions. Presumably, Avraham also took upon himself every stringency. Therefore, it is possible that he did not want to ascend to *Eretz Yisrael* and live there on a permanent basis because he wanted to fulfill R. Yehudah's dictum: "He who ascends from Babylonia to *Eretz Yisrael* transgresses a positive commandment, as it says, *They will be brought to Babylonia and there they will stay* (*Yirmiyah* 27:22)" (*Ketuvot* 110b). Even though this was not yet applicable, all of Avraham Avinu's experiences alluded to future events.
>
> Therefore, the Holy One Blessed be He first commanded him to uproot himself from his original place, which was in Babylonia. Avraham then went to Charan..., where the Holy One Blessed be He commanded him, "Go even further, for you are now permitted to ascend to *Eretz Yisrael*. R. Yehudah only prohibited ascending from Babylonia to *Eretz Yisrael*, not from other lands to *Eretz Yisrael*.ö
>
> Do not ask, how was he allowed to go from Babylonia to Charan when it says, *They will be brought to Babylonia and there they will stay*? If it is prohibited to emigrate to *Eretz Yisrael*, it is certainly prohibited to emigrate to other lands! The answer is that Avraham left in order to save his life, for one may not rely on miracles. When he was cast into the fiery furnace[778] it was a hint that he should go far away from there. [HaShem wanted him] to first settle in Charan and then ascend to *Eretz Yisrael*.[779]

Thus, even though Avraham Avinu accepted R. Yehudah's prohibition..., HaShem forced him to leave Babylonia, because his life was in danger. And even though HaShem saved him from the fiery furnace, He prohibited him from staying in Babylonia, because his salvation occurred miraculously. Instead, HaShem forced him to go to *Eretz Yisrael*. Even though there is a prohibition to leave Babylonia..., Avraham was permitted to leave, because...saving lives overrides all of the Torah's prohibitions, as the Talmud teaches:

778 [In Ur Kasdim, which is in Babylonia. See Rashi, *BeReishit* 11:28.]

779 *Sh'nei Luchot HaBrit*, vol. 3, *Torah SheBichtav, Lech Lecha*, p. 11b, col. b, in a note.

"*And live by them* [the *mitzvot*] (*VaYikra* 18:5), but do not die by them" (*Yoma* 85b).

Avraham was prohibited from staying in Babylonia because he had been saved miraculously, and one may not rely on future miracles.[780] Now, after the miracle at Ur Kasdim everyone feared him and recognized that he was a man of God over whom Divine Providence vigilantly watched. Everyone exalted him greatly, as the *Midrash* describes.[781] Therefore, he no longer had any reason to fear that his life would be in danger. Nevertheless, since he was exposed to danger there once, and we maintain that one may not rely on miracles, HaShem prohibited him from remaining there.

Now, our mentor, the Shelah, asserts that all of Avraham Avinu's experiences allude to future events. Thus, Avraham taught his descendants that if they are ever saved from mortal danger in a particular place, they may not remain there. Instead, they must move far away and go to *Eretz Yisrael*. This is what the Shelah implies.

Let us apply this to our situation. Behold, the Jews who lived in the parts of Europe which fell under the influence of the infamous oppressor, [Hitler], experienced greater danger than Jews have ever experienced in exile. Some were killed, some were burnt, some were stripped naked, and all of them suffered innumerable torments. The oppressor schemed to destroy the entire nation, God forbid; and due to our numerous sins, he succeeded in executing his plot against a significant majority of our people, as is well known. Only a minority survived, which in itself is a great miracle that the Holy One Blessed be He performed for His nation. For, that wicked man also gnashed his teeth at the few who remained, and they were in constant danger of falling into his trap, God forbid.

We were in mortal danger more than once. I remember the fear and confusion that prevailed throughout Hungarian Jewry in the beginning of this summer, when the evil oppressor [Hitler] urged the Prime Minister to solve the ôJewish question" here. His solution to this question is well known – to send the Jews to an uninhabited land, or as the oppressors call it, "deportation" (and the outcome of this deportation is known to all). This is what [Hitler] wanted to do to the Jews of this country, as well, and he urged and pressed the Prime Minister to acquiesce. Rumors spread that the Speaker of

780 See *Pesachim* 64b.
781 See *Zohar* 1:77b.

Parliament was going to deliver a speech and express his opinion on this matter. Dread and great darkness fell upon all the Jews.[782] We were in grave danger. All that was missing was the stroke of a pen [lit., quill] and Israel's verdict would be sealed, whether for the staff (God forbid) or for benevolence.✣ Had HaShem not performed a great miracle on our behalf, we all would have perished. He made the Prime Minister decide to solve the ôJewish question" as the evil oppressor requested, but only after the war.

Ever since then, dread and fear hover over us. At the very moment I write these lines, all of the Chassidic Rebbes of this country are making efforts to flee to *Eretz Yisrael* out of fear of the oppressor. They ignore the fact that this causes Israel to despair. One can hear the masses complain, "The Rebbes are fleeing! What will be with us?!" The *Midrash* states that Elimelech was punished for this very reason; he fled at a time of trouble, causing Israel to despair (*Ruth Rabbah* 1:4).

We have great faith that HaShem will save us from the oppressor. However, everyone knows that when we were in mortal danger before, HaShem saved us [only] with true miracles. Therefore, we must do as our venerable patriarch [Avraham] taught. We must move far away from here and go to *Eretz Yisrael*, because our lives are in danger, and one may not rely on miracles.

Now, after all I have shown you, tell me my friend, are the words of the Rebbe of Shinev – that we must not go to *Eretz Yisrael* until HaShem elevates our pride and returns our captivity – applicable today?... On the contrary, we are not allowed to remain here any longer. Instead, we must take the initiative ourselves, and then HaShem will assist us, as He did with Avraham Avinu.[784]

✣ The *Midrash* suggests a similar idea on the verse *Rebuke the beast of the reed* (*Tehillim* 68:31). When *Mashiach* comes, the fourth kingdom (Edom) will want to bring him a gift. The Holy One Blessed be He will say to Gavriel, *Rebuke the beast of the reed*. What does this mean?... R. Chiya bar Abba said in the name of R. Yonatan: ôHe (God) will say to him (Gavriel), 'Rebuke the beast whose every action is written down with one quill'"[783] (*Yalkut Shimoni* 2:800). That is to say, he [Edom] solves "the Jewish question" with the stroke of a pen.

782 Based on *BeReishit* 15:12.

783 [Quills can be made from reeds, hence the connection to the verse.]

784 ✣ See *Zohar* (1:77b) cited in *Sh'nei Luchot HaBrit*, ibid., p. 11a, col. b, s.v. *rabim*.

The Rebbe of Shinev only referred to a time when Israel dwelt peacefully in exile, not to difficult times such as these. Just think about it. You surely heard what happened to the sacred rabbi, the holy luminary, the pious and virtuous R. Yeshaya'le Krakauer, the youngest son of the Rebbe of Tzanz and brother of the Rebbe of Shinev *z"l*. He was hiding in Bachniya, near Krakow, with hundreds, or thousands, of other Jews. Meanwhile, people here in the capital tried to save him and bring him here. They spent great sums of money to accomplish this, but time ran out; all of them were killed in sanctification of God's name. O land, do not cover up their blood, nor the blood of the thousands and tens of thousands of Jews that has been spilt! May their merit stand by us and help put an end to our troubles. ❖

Now, tell me, my friend, if the holy R. Yeshaya'le...had an opportunity to escape from Bachniya to *Eretz Yisrael*, what would the holy Rebbe of Shinev have said to him? Would he have insisted that he remain here until HaShem raises our pride and returns our captivity? Undoubtedly, the Rebbe of Shinev would have answered, "Of course! Do not stay here for an instant. Run for your life to *Eretz Yisrael*." For, his statement [in *Divrei Yechezkel*] does not refer to times like these, when lives are at stake.

The same applies to us. Since we escaped danger miraculously, our situation is considered one of life and death, as the story of Avraham Avinu demonstrates... Thus, HaShem commands us to move far away from this dangerous place and...go to *Eretz Yisrael*.

❖ The verse says, *For the Lord will judge His people, and He will repent regarding His servants* (*Devarim* 32:36). The Or HaChayim HaKadosh comments:

> *For the Lord will judge His people*: This means that He will bring to judgment the "cups of bitterness" that they suffered, and He will see the troubles that befell the righteous. Some were killed, some were burnt, and some were stripped bare. *And He will repent* for the sake of the righteous who suffered. This is the meaning of, *And He will repent regarding His servants*. That is, He will repent for their sake and say to the hardships of exile, "Enough!"

Amen! So may HaShem say today, when all of these [troubles] have actually befallen us.

The author's admission

I have heard that many people try to defame me because of a letter I wrote in *Tikkun Olam*,[785] published by the holy Rebbe of Munkatch *z"l*. For in that letter I spoke out against *aliyah*, while now I advocate it. However, the preceding idea resolves this contradiction quite well. When I wrote that letter, it was a time of peace and tranquillity. We had not yet reached this state of mortal danger, and no lives were at stake. Now, however, times have changed. Therefore, the ruling has also changed, as the above-cited *Shelah* demonstrates.

Besides this, I already explained in the introduction[786] that I had never delved deeply into this issue. Now, however, after examining this *halachah* in depth, I realize that I was mistaken. Therefore, I am emulating many of our Talmudic Sages who admitted their mistakes and said, "What I originally told you was mistaken."[787] We also find that the *poskim* sometimes retract rulings that they made previously.

May HaShem bring us to His holy mountain speedily in our days. Amen. I wrote and completed these words on Tuesday evening, the fourth day of the Ten Days of Repentance, 5704 [1943], here in the capital, Budapest.

Belief in Mashiach must be accompanied by action

Behold, we say every day, "I believe with complete faith in the coming of *Mashiach*. And even though he may tarry, nevertheless, I yearn every day for his coming." Likewise, *Chazal* state:

> We find that our forefathers were redeemed from Egypt only by virtue of their faith, as it says, *And the people believed* (*Shemot* 4:31)... So too, the exiles will be gathered only on account of their faith, as it says, *Come with Me from Lebanon, O bride... Look from the top of Amanah* [lit., faith] (*Shir HaShirim* 4:8); and, *I will betroth you to Me forever... I will betroth you to Me with faith* (*Hoshea* 2:21-22). (*Yalkut Shimoni* 1:240)

However, you must know that faith without action is insufficient and ineffective. The *Midrash* states:

> *Let this be written for the final generation* (*Tehillim* 102:19): This refers to the generations which are on the verge of death. *So that the newly created people will praise the Lord* (ibid.): In the

785 Pp. 104-107.
786 Pp. 41-42.
787 See *Mesoret HaShas* on *Shabbat* 63b.

future, the Holy One Blessed be He will make them into a new creation. And, what must we take? A *lulav* and *etrog*, and praise the Holy One Blessed be He. Therefore, Moshe commands Israel, *You shall take for yourselves on the first day, [the fruit of a citron tree, branches of palm trees...]* (*VaYikra* 23:40).[788]

The godly scholar, R. Yosef Tzarfati,[789] asks the following in his wondrous work, *Yad Yosef*. What is the connection between the fact that the Holy One Blessed be He will make us into a new creation and the question "And what must we take"? Why must we take something just because He will make us into a new creation? The end of the *Midrash* is also difficult. Who says that this is why Moshe commanded us to take these things?

He explains that the Four Species demonstrate the belief that it is up to us to rectify all of our sins with complete repentance. Complete repentance refers to thought, speech, and action, as the verse says, *The matter* (i.e., repentance) *is very near to you, in your mouth and in your heart, to do it* (*Devarim* 30:14). He explains that the Four Species allude to thought, speech, and deed. (I will not elaborate here.)

In effect, then, the *Midrash* tells us that repentance is so powerful that it tears up the evil decree:[790] *Let this be written for the final generation* refers to the generations which are on the verge of death because of their sins. However, when they repent, the Holy One Blessed be He will make them into a new creation. Now, ***faith without deed is transient and ineffective***. The Rambam thus writes in *Moreh Nevuchim* that [we observe] the Sabbath in order to substantiate our belief in the creation [of the world].[791] Therefore, the *Midrash* asks, what must we take to demonstrate the belief that it is up to us to repent? We must take a *lulav* and an *etrog* to demonstrate that all of the tools of repentance are in our hands: thought, speech, and action. Therefore, Moshe commands Israel, *You shall take for yourselves on the first day*.[792]

In any event, this godly scholar teaches us that faith without an action to strengthen it is ineffective. He cites this principle in the

788 See *Midrash Tehillim* 102:3, *Yalkut Shimoni* 2:855, *VaYikra Rabbah* 30:12.

789 ❖ He was the rabbi of Andrinapol in 5377 [1617].

790 *Rosh HaShanah* 17b.

791 *Moreh Nevuchim* 2:31.

792 *Yad Yosef*, Second Sermon for Sukkot.

name of our mentor, the Rambam, and also fits it into the words of the *Midrash*. According to him, when our Rabbis ask, "What must we take?" they mean that we must put our beliefs into practice, for faith alone is insufficient.

Prayer without action is insufficient

This also helps explain the verse *The Lord said to Moshe, "Why do you cry out to Me? Speak to the Children of Israel that they should travel"* (*Shemot* 14:15). All of the commentators ask: What else should a Jew do at a time of trouble, if not cry out to the Holy One Blessed be He? Rashi explains: "All they have to do is travel, for the sea will not stand in their way. Their forefathers' merit, and their own, combined with the faith that they put in Me by leaving [Egypt], are sufficient to split the sea for them." *Siftei Chachamim* elaborates:

> If they travel, the sea will split when you [Moshe] raise your staff. On the other hand, if they do not travel, the sea will not split, even if you raise your staff over it. For, "their forefathers' merit..., combined with the faith...are sufficient to split the sea for them." According to this, the words, *Why do you cry out to Me*, mean: You think that your prayers will help?! Not so! Rather, *They should travel.*

This seems difficult. Since they had faith in God, why should Moshe's prayers be ineffective? Furthermore, the very fact that Israel was frightened by the Egyptians is puzzling. The verse says, *The Children of Israel lifted up their eyes, and behold, Egypt was coming after them, and they were very frightened* (ibid. 14:10). Immediately before this it says, *And the Children of Israel were going out with a high hand* (ibid. 14:8). Rashi explains, "With high and outstanding strength." Thus, they already saw their strength over Egypt, so why should they be frightened by them now?[793]

Based on the rule which the greatest of our earlier Sages established, that faith without action is ineffective, everything is clear. From the exodus until this point, the Children of Israel had only faith. They did not reveal the strength of this inner faith with actual deeds. During that period, they encountered no danger whatsoever, for their exodus and journey occurred miraculously. HaShem carried them on the wings of eagles.[794] Obviously, then,

793 ❖ I subsequently discovered that the Ran deals with this question. See *Derashot HaRan, Derush* 10.

794 Based on *Shemot* 19:4.

leaving Egypt and traveling in the desert were not considered acts which strengthen faith. Therefore, the Holy One Blessed be He put them in a dangerous situation. The Egyptians were behind them, the desert and ferocious beasts were on the sides, and the sea was in front of them. Then, He commanded them to travel into the sea while it was still full of water, as it is written, *The Children of Israel went into the midst of the sea* (ibid. 14:22). It became dry land only afterwards, as is well known.

Thus, by entering the sea they demonstrated their faith with concrete action and became worthy of the splitting of the sea. This is what Rashi means by saying, "All they have to do is travel, for the sea will not stand in their way..." That is, just like the *Midrash* says about the *lulav*, "What must they take?" – teaching that we must substantiate our faith with action – so too here, faith alone is insufficient. They must travel into the sea, and then the sea will not stand in their way. However, without concrete action, even Moshe's prayers will be ineffective, as *Siftei Chachamim* explains.

The same applies to our belief in *Mashiach*. All of us, young and old alike, believe in him so much that all of the storms and upheavals in the world cannot uproot this belief from our hearts. However, belief alone is insufficient; we need some action to substantiate it, as our Rabbis taught. Therefore, we must do as they did during the exodus...and speak to the Children of Israel that they should travel to *Eretz Yisrael*... Then, the Holy One Blessed be He will deliver us. When we take concrete steps to ascend to *Eretz Yisrael*, HaShem will grant us success, and we will achieve the final redemption, speedily in our days. Amen. But, if we do not take any action, our prayers will be ineffective...

Thus, the Rambam lays down the rule that every belief needs an action to strengthen it. Otherwise, it is very weak and short-lived. Let us apply this to the belief in the coming of *Mashiach*. A person who refuses to take action, simply waiting for *Mashiach* to come and carry him off to *Eretz Yisrael*, shows that he does not believe in *Mashiach* at all. His faith is only external, and it causes him to fool himself. However, a person who takes action shows that he believes in *Mashiach*, and this belief will encourage him to take further action on his own. Thus, his belief will be strengthened, and HaShem will grant assistance from the heavens.

This is what happened in Egypt during the first redemption, which is the prototype for all future redemptions. HaShem became impatient and said, "*Why do you cry out to Me* in prayer? Prayer will not help you at all in this situation. Instead, *Speak to the Children of Israel that they should travel*." Even though this journey was dangerous, for their only choice was to go in the middle of the raging sea, [HaShem commanded them to go]. Indeed, this act perfected their belief in redemption, and the Holy One Blessed be He granted them the true redemption.

We must act the same way they did in Egypt. The prophet thus states, *As in the days of your leaving the Land of Egypt, I will show him wonders* (*Michah* 7:15). Then, HaShem will show us wonders, [as well]. Amen. *Selah*!

CHAPTER FOUR

UNITY AND PEACE ISRAEL'S RESTORATION

In the sacred work, *Ohev Yisrael*, our holy master from Apt points out that the numerical value of אוהב ישראל (lover of Israel) equals that of תקנה (restoration). This demonstrates that loving one another is Israel's only means of restoration.[1]

Disunity causes destruction

א The *Midrash* comments on the verse *He has worn away my flesh and my skin; He has broken my bones* (*Eichah* 3:4):

> *He has worn away my flesh* refers to the community. *And my skin* refers to the *Sanhedrin*. Just as the skin protects the flesh, so too, the *Sanhedrin* protects Israel. *He has broken my bones* (עצמותי) [refers to] the strengths (עיצומי) of people who were like the sons of the mighty (עיצומים). (*Eichah Rabbah* 3:2)

This is puzzling! How did *Chazal* apply this verse to the community, the *Sanhedrin*, and the great and mighty people among Israel? What did they mean?

HaShem enlightened me to understand their profound words. They intended to teach a practical lesson on how to deal with the community in a way that will bring it success and blessings. They also wanted to define the obligations of the leaders with relation to the people and explain how they should lead and direct the people onto the path which will bring them true perfection in all of their affairs.

I will preface with an observation made by "two prophets who prophesied in the same manner."[2] The wonderful sage, R. Shlomo

1 *Ohev Yisrael* (introduction).
2 Based on *Sanhedrin* 89a.

Verga,[3] in his *Sheivet Yehudah*,[4] and our scholarly mentor, the Maharam Schiff,[5] both point out that this verse is inverted. In reality, first comes the skin, then the flesh, and then the bones. Therefore, the verse should have begun with the skin and proceeded inward: "He has worn away my skin and my flesh; He has broken my bones." Alternatively, it should have begun with the bones and proceeded outward... Now, however, there is no order! They suggest a tenuous answer: God's plague is situated in the middle, in the flesh. Sometimes it moves outward, as it says, *and my skin*; sometimes it enters inward, as it says, *He has broken my bones*; and sometimes it moves inward and outward.

However, this does not explain why Yirmiyahu[6] specifically described the plague as beginning in the middle and spreading inwards and outwards? Why did he not describe it as beginning in the skin, entering the flesh, and proceeding to the bones, as we find in the Torah, *When a man will have in the skin of his flesh...* (*VaYikra* 13:2)? Alternatively, why did he not describe it as beginning in the bones and spreading outward to the skin, which is, at least, in order? What was Yirmiyahu's intention in presenting it specifically this way?

It seems to me that he had a special reason for this. He wanted to hint to the reason why we lost our Land, the *Beit HaMikdash* was destroyed, and we were exiled from our soil. All of this happened even though we were a strong nation and all the inhabitants of the land feared us, as it says, *The kings of the earth and all the inhabitants of the world did not believe that the adversary and the enemy would enter the gates of Jerusalem* (*Eichah* 4:12). Lack of unity among the Jewish nation was the sole cause of the destruction. Had we been unified and undivided, no nation in the world could have conquered our Land. But, the plague of disunity broke out in our midst. We became segmented, and each faction fought the other. What this one built the other destroyed. There was chaos, as the history books describe and as our Sages allude to in the Talmud[7] and

3 ❖ The author of *Korei HaDorot*. He lived in Italy, three hundred years ago.

4 (Jerusalem: Mossad Bialik, 5707 [1947]), *HaShemad* 41, p. 114, lines 29-33.

5 *Sefer Maharam Schiff, Chiddushei Halachot* (*Gittin, Ketuvot, Bava Metzia, Chullin*), *Derush* for *Parashat Devarim*, p. 2a.

6 [Literally "The Lamentor," meaning, the author of *Eichah* (Lamentations), i.e., Yirmiyahu HaNavi.]

7 See *Yoma* 9b, *Gittin* 55b-57a.

Midrash.[8] Thus, at that time, the plague came out of the very midst of Israel and spread inwards and outwards. Once the foundation of Israel was destroyed from within, the enemies from without were able to descend upon the Jews and conquer them. They were attacked from both within and without.

Thus, the prophet laments, *He has worn away my flesh*. That is to say, the plague came from the very midst of Israel, as the verse says, *Your ruiners and your destroyers will come forth from you* (*Yeshayah* 49:17). The chaos that arose in the camp of Israel caused the plague to eventually spread both outwards (*and my skin*) and inwards (*He broke my bones*). This is the meaning of the *Midrash*'s statement "*He has worn away my flesh* refers to the community." That is to say, the plague afflicted the community of Israel itself. The Jews were torn apart into separate groups and factions, each one with its own methodology and ideology, and each group fought the other for the sake of its own ideology. Thus, all law and order ceased from the Land, and chaos reigned. This caused only misfortune and darkness in all of Israel's camps, and it allowed the enemy to enter from without to destroy everything.

The leaders must unify the people

This also explains the *Midrash*'s statement "*And my skin* refers to the *Sanhedrin*; just as the skin protects the flesh, so too, the *Sanhedrin* protects Israel." The members of the *Sanhedrin*, in their capacity as leaders of the nation, must unify the Jewish people. Just as the skin unifies and covers all parts of the flesh, so too, the leaders must try with all their might to unify all parts of the nation and make them into a single society. Then, the Jewish nation will survive, flourish, and blossom[9] to the highest heights, and there will be no adversary (*satan*) nor misfortune. If, however, the leaders do not strive to unify the nation, they will cause the plague to spread to the community and to themselves, as well. They will lose their influence over the people, the foundations will be destroyed, and everything will wear away. "*He has worn away my flesh* refers to the community." Afterwards, *and my skin*, meaning, the *Sanhedrin* will also lose its place. And finally, "*He has broken my bones* [refers to] the strengths of people..." That is to say, even the great and mighty people who were destined to help the nation, will be broken and lost, without bringing any benefit to the generation.

8 See *Eichah Rabbah* 1:31.
9 Based on *Yeshayah* 27:6.

This actually occurred at that time. Disunity caused destruction and exile, and it continues to cause the exile to persist (due to our numerous sins). For, Satan still dances among us. The leaders will eventually suffer the consequences for this,[10] because they do not attempt to unify the Jewish nation into a single society. This is the only cure for our ailments, as *Chazal* state.[11] *

---

* Our holy mentor, R. Shaptil the son of the Shelah, writes in *Vavei HaAmudim*:

> Know that our Sages state in the name of R. Yehoshua ben Levi: "The Holy One Blessed be He said to Israel, 'You caused the destruction of My Temple and the exile of My children; pray for the sake [lit., peace] of the Temple and I will forgive you.' How so? *Pray for the peace of Jerusalem* (*Tehillim* 122:6). It also says, *Seek the peace of the city* (*Yirmiyah* 29:7). It also says, *May there be peace within your walls* (*Tehillim* 122:7). It also says, *For the sake of my brethren and my companions I will now speak of peace in your midst* (ibid. 122:8)" (*Derech Eretz Zuta, Perek HaShalom*).
>
> Thus, peace is great, for if we are at peace the Holy One Blessed be He forgives us, even though we caused the destruction of the *Beit HaMikdash*. Therefore, he who supports dissension overturns peace.
>
> In addition to the sins which caused the destruction of the Temple and the exile from our Land, the destruction of the Temple itself is considered a sin on our part. This is the meaning of Yirmiyahu's outcry, *The crown of our head has fallen; woe to us, for we have sinned* (*Eichah* 5:16). This is difficult. What is he adding here? He has already stated many times, *Jerusalem has grievously sinned* (ibid. 1:8)! The answer lies in what I just said. *The crown of our head has fallen* refers to the *Beit HaMikdash*. *Woe to us, for we have sinned* implies that the destruction itself is considered a sin on our part, since we caused it.
>
> I discovered that the *Midrash* states, "Any generation which does not witness the rebuilding of the *Beit HaMikdash* is considered as if it destroyed it" (*Yerushalmi, Yoma* 1:1 [4b]; *Midrash Tehillim* 137:10). This is puzzling. Why should it be so? Our fathers sinned and are no more.[12] They caused the destruction of the Temple,

10 See *Or HaChayim HaKadosh, VaYikra* 25:25.

11 See *Midrash Tanchuma, Nitzavim* 1; *Yalkut Shimoni* 2:549; *BeReishit Rabbah* 98:2. Also see above, chap. 3, sec. נו, pp. 379-83.

12 Based on *Eichah* 5:7.

so why should every generation be considered the destroyers? In addition, I have come to eliminate the complaints that the Children of Israel level against HaShem.[13] They doubt His ways and say, "We have yet to be redeemed even though we worship the Lord our God, cling to His Torah, put our faith in Him, and fulfill His commandments. Why has HaShem done this to us?[14] Why has He banished us from His house? And why has the son of Yishai [*Mashiach*] not arrived?"

Truthfully, there is no question... We are still plagued with groundless hatred, selfishness, and gossip..., and these were the sins of the Second Temple era. *Chazal* declare, "Why was the Second Temple destroyed, seeing that the Jews were involved in Torah, *mitzvot*, and acts of kindness? Because of groundless hatred" (*Yoma* 9b).

This explains *Chazal*'s assumption that we mourn more intensely for the Second Temple than the First (*Rosh HaShanah* 18b). This is difficult. On the contrary, we ought to mourn more intensely for the First Temple, because the Second Temple did not have the Ark, its cover, the Cherubim, or the Tablets![15] The answer lies in what I just said. Since we are plagued with groundless hatred, our mourning for the Second Temple is more intense, for if this sin caused the destruction, it certainly prevents *Mashiach* from coming.

This can also help explain the Talmudic debate in the story of Kamtza and Bar Kamtza: "Bar Kamtza went and told the Caesar that the Jews were rebelling against him... The Caesar sent the Jews a sacrifice... On the way, Bar Kamtza placed a blemish in the animal's upper lip. Some say it was in the upper membrane of the eye" (*Gittin* 56a). It seems to me that both of these opinions are the words of the living God. Since the Jews of that time gossiped, one opinion holds that Bar Kamtza placed a blemish in the upper lip. And since they were also selfish [lit., "evil eyed"], the other opinion holds that he placed a blemish in the upper membrane of the eye.

We now understand the *Midrash* cited above. "Any generation which does not witness the rebuilding of the *Beit HaMikdash*" – that is to say, since they continue the practices of the Second

13 Based on *Shemot* 16:8.
14 Based on *Devarim* 29:23.
15 See *Yoma* 21b; *Yerushalmi, Horayot* 3:2 (12b); *Tanchuma, BeHa'alotcha* 6.

Unity vs. Disunity

ב Before his death, our mentor, R. Baer [of Mezeritch] *zt"l*, told his students: "My children, stay together! Then, you will survive and move only forwards, not backwards (God forbid). A hint to this is, *He is one, and who can turn Him back?* (*Iyov* 23:13)."

The same lesson applies to our nation as a whole. A certain poet expressed this beautifully when he said about Israel:

My fortunate and wretched nation!
You are fortunate when you are unified,
You are wretched when you are divided.
You are weak when you are divided, and you are strong when your desires are one.
My fortunate and wretched nation!
You are wretched because of your abundant factions, for abundant factions are a curse in your tents.
You are fortunate when you are unified, for unity is a deathblow to your enemies.
Upon your factions lie the slain![18]
Destroy your factions, raise up your walls, and gird your loins with iron to become united.
Then, you will arise, become established, and stand forever.

Disunity makes Israel vulnerable

ג I later discovered that everything I said above is stated clearly in Yirmiyahu's lamentation: *The kings of the earth and all the inhabitants of the world did not believe that the adversary and the enemy would enter the gates of Jerusalem. It was for the sins of her prophets, the iniquities of her priests* (Rashi explains, "This calamity occurred because of the sins of her false prophets.")... *For they quarreled* (כי נצו) *and also wandered* (גם נעו). *The nations said they will no longer fear. The anger of the Lord has divided them* (*Eichah* 4:12-16).

The commentators interpret the words כי נצו parallel to, *when men*

Temple era, "it is considered as if they destroyed it." This is why our miserable and bitter exile has lasted so long. We have practically perished; we are all lost[16] because of our sins. May HaShem have mercy on us.[17]

16 Based on *BeMidbar* 17:27.
17 *Vavei HaAmudim, Amud HaDin*, chap. 27 (end).
18 Based on II *Shmuel* 1:19.

shall fight (כי ינצו) (*Shemot* 21:22). They fought one another, therefore, גם נעו, meaning, their position became shaky (התנענע), and their existence crumbled beneath them. *The nations said...*: When the nations heard that the Jews were fighting and even killing each other, they said *they will no longer fear*. That is to say, at first, they did not believe that they could conquer Israel, for it was a strong nation. But now they said that *they will no longer fear* (לגור) the Jews,[19] because *the anger of the Lord has divided them*. HaShem's anger separated and divided them into many parts, thereby weakening them. This all happened because of *the sins of her prophets and the iniquities of her priests*, meaning, the sins of the leaders who did not attempt to unify them and make them into a single society. This explanation coincides with what I wrote above.

A certain wise politician put it this way, "Disunity of a nation is its downfall."[20]

Groundless hatred is worse than the three cardinal sins

The *Yerushalmi* states:

> R. Yochanan bar Torta said: "We find that the First Temple was destroyed because the Jews committed idolatry, adultery, and murder. But at the time of the Second Temple, we know that they studied Torah diligently, observed *mitzvot* meticulously, and possessed all of the good character traits. [Nonetheless, they were exiled] because they loved money and hated one another for no reason; and groundless hatred is worse than these three cardinal sins." (*Yoma* 1:1)❖

The *Yerushalmi* also points out that the sin of jealousy, which existed at the time of the Second Temple, caused greater destruction than the sins of the First Temple era. The enemies only destroyed the ceiling of the First Temple, while the walls remained. When it came to the Second Temple, however, they destroyed and demolished even the walls and the foundations, as it is written, *Raze it, raze it to its foundations* (*Tehillim* 137:7).

The *Yerushalmi* concludes, "Any generation which does not witness

---

❖ In *Asarah Ma'amarot*, the brilliant and godly Kabbalist from Panow explains that their groundless hatred stemmed from their love of money. They were jealous of each other's wealth and power.

19 ❖ The word לגור means to fear, as in *Moav was afraid* (ויגר) (*BeMidbar* 22:3).
20 [Originally in Yiddish.]

the rebuilding of the *Beit HaMikdash* is considered as if it destroyed it." That is to say, since Satan still dances among us in the form of groundless hatred and jealousy, we cause the exile to continue and the *Beit HaMikdash* to remain in ruins. Therefore, it is considered to have been destroyed in our days.

Consider what *Chazal* say! Although the Jews of the Second Temple era studied Torah diligently and observed *mitzvot* meticulously, their jealousy caused a greater destruction than that of the First Temple. Even the foundations were destroyed! We can derive from this that those who find excuses to rouse jealousy, hatred, and disunity destroy the entire edifice of Israel, even if they study Torah and observe *mitzvot*. They destroy the foundations of Israel's existence and cause the exile to persevere. David said about them, *When the foundations are destroyed, what has the righteous man accomplished* (*Tehillim* 11:3)? What good is his righteousness and divine service if his deeds cause Israel's foundation and existence to be destroyed. May HaShem help us coexist with love and brotherhood, so that no nation will rule over us. Amen, so may it be God's will.

A united Jewish nation is invulnerable

ד *Chazal* state that when the Jewish people are united no nation can rule over them.[21] HaShem helped me discover a true and novel explanation for this based on Rabbeinu Bachya's interpretation of the verse *Like a muddied fountain and a polluted spring, so is a righteous man who bows before the wicked* (*Mishley* 25:26). He explains that a fountain clouded with mud and other substances will eventually clear up. The impurities will settle to the bottom, leaving the upper waters clear. Similarly, a righteous man who bows before the wicked will eventually become pure and rise to the top, while the wicked one will fall to the bottom. The stories of Pharaoh and Israel and Mordechai and Haman prove this.[22]

Adding to Rabbeinu Bachya, I claim that this is only true if the waters of the fountain or spring are calm and quiet and "dwell peacefully with one another," without moving from their place. Then, the pure and clear waters will rise to the top, while the intermingled impurities will settle to the bottom. However, if the waters move from place to place and "fight each other," they will

21 See *VaYikra Rabbah* 30:12; *BeMidbar Rabbah* 15:18; *Ketuvot* 66b; *Menachot* 27a; Rashi, ibid. s.v. *behartza'ah*; *Tanchuma, BeHa'alotcha* 11; *Yalkut Shimoni* 1:953, 2:213.

22 Rabbeinu Bachya, *VaYishlach* (beginning).

make themselves cloudy. For when the different particles of water move and "fight," they stir up the mud that has already fallen to the bottom.

The same is true of the Jewish people. If they dwell together peacefully and tranquilly, the wicked people will fall to the bottom. But if they fight and disunite, the intermingled substances – i.e., the sinners of Israel – will be stirred up, the fountain will become cloudy, and the wicked ones will rise to the top (God forbid).

Apparently, Esther had this in mind when she warned Mordechai, *Go, gather all the Jews together* (*Esther* 4:16). Make sure that they gather together with love, affection, and mutual respect. Then, they will be purified and rise to the top, and the wicked Haman will bow before the righteous Mordechai. They did this and immediately felt its effects. Haman began to fall, as Zeresh said, *You have begun to fall..., you will surely fall* (ibid. 6:13) further and further down. This happened because when the water is calm it clears up and rises to the top.

This is what *Chazal* mean when they say that no nation can rule over the Jews as long as they are united. For then, the following verse will be fulfilled, *The righteous one falls seven times yet rises* (*Mishley* 24:16), while the wicked one falls but once.[23]

The leaders must unify the people

ה Thus, the leaders of Israel have a foremost obligation to strive with all their might to make peace within Israel and help the Jews live together with love and unity. Observe how the Chatam Sofer explains the verse *The people that survived the sword found grace in the desert; when Israel goes to its place of rest* (*Yirmiyah* 31:1):

> I explained elsewhere that strife disbands a settlement and makes it into a desert. Furthermore, it has been said that strangers (in a foreign land) live together very peacefully. Therefore, the prophet says with bewilderment, *The people who survived the sword* should love one another. But behold, they *found grace* being a *desert*, disunited because of strife. Then, *Israel goes to its place of rest.* It says, *goes* (הלוך), in the present tense, as if to say: "Israel, which refers to the Torah scholar appointed over the Jews, should continuously seek out a place of rest [for the Jewish people] and engender peace and tranquillity among them."[24]

23 Based on *Mishley* 28:18.

24 *Derashot Chatam Sofer*, vol. 1, p. 1b, s.v. *haftarah*.

His words are especially relevant today, for we indeed are the people who survived the sword. We escaped the sword of the oppressor[25] which has consumed thousands, tens of thousands, and hundreds of thousands of Jews. But, HaShem has protected us. We give thanks for the past and pray for the future: "HaShem, hear our voices! Support and aid the impetuous ones! Please, assist the remnants! Bring near the reckoned time of consolation! Have pity on the unpitied nation!" Therefore, we, the last remnants, should love one another and remove anything that causes disunity. We should not provoke one another, but act as one man with one heart.[26] The Torah scholars who are appointed over the various communities must strive to achieve this goal, as the Chatam Sofer explains.

A wonderful parable

ו Our holy Rebbe of Tzanz *zt"l* was fond of telling over a wonderful parable. Once, there was a man who lost his way in a vast desert. For many days he was unable to find the path which would lead him to an inhabited city. As he wandered to and fro, he saw an elderly man coming his way. He was overjoyed, for he thought that this man would certainly lead him to the straight path out of this terrible desert. He asked the elderly man, "From where do you come, and where are you going?" and told him that he has been wandering in this awful desert for many days, unable to find his way to a city. He begged him to have compassion and lead him onto "the path of righteousness"[27] and save him from this labyrinth. The old man responded, "The same thing happened to me. I, too, have been lost in this desert, not only for many days but for many years, during which time I became old. I have yet to find a path leading out of this vast desert. My lot is no better than yours, but allow me to make a suggestion. Let us not take the paths we have already taken. They certainly do not lead to the "path of life," for we have yet to reach our destination. Rather, we must seek a new path and walk on it together, for two are better than one.[28] Then, we can hope to attain our goal, with God's help."

We must abandon our old ways and find a new path

The same applies to our generation. Our enemies gathered us into a fiery furnace and annihilated the majority of our Jewish brethren in Europe (due to our numerous sins). The few remnants

25 Based on *Yirmiyah* 46:16.
26 See Rashi, *Shemot* 19:2.
27 Based on *Tehillim* 23:3.
28 *Kohelet* 4:9.

are like a brand saved from a fire[29] and people who survived the sword.[30] Behold, we now realize that the path we took thus far in this lengthy exile did not lead us to our desired destination, for it was full of strife, disunity, factionalism, and groundless hatred. It only led us to destruction. Our mentor, the Rama, writes that he saw several communities destroyed by dissension.[31] Many countries which once housed thousands of holy communities, large and small, are now desolate and destroyed. The paths of Zion are mourning.[32] All of this can only be ascribed to the abundance of strife in Israel.

R. Chisdai, cited in *Or Zarua HaGadol*, explains that strife is loathsome because it brings Israel to financial ruin and causes the *Shechinah* to depart. And when there is no *Shechinah* in Israel, there is no protection for Israel. (See the responsa inside. I do not have it in front of me at this time.)[33]

Our master, the Noda BeYehudah, wrote to the brilliant R. Isaac'l Hamburger *z"l* that there is no such thing as a dispute for the sake of Heaven today.[34] Now, if he wrote this in his generation, which was still learned, what are we, orphans of orphans, to say?

Therefore, we, the few remaining survivors of the sword, must follow the Chatam Sofer's advice.[35] We must mediate peace between ourselves, bring people close to one another,[36] and strengthen our unity. We must begin a completely new life and break away from our old shackles of disunity. We must lead unified lives with common goals.[37] We must gather all the remaining strength of our nation's last remnants and live as one man with one heart. Then, HaShem will help us rebuild the ruins[38] and establish ourselves firmly in the world. We will no longer be a disgrace among the nations, for HaShem will place His *Shechinah* in our midst and protect us. I derived this from R. Chisdai's responsa, for one can infer the positive from the negative.

29 Based on *Zecharyah* 3:2.
30 Based on *Yirmiyah* 31:1.
31 Apparently, he refers to responsa 11, which discusses the pursuit of peace.
32 Based on *Eichah* 1:4.
33 *Or Zarua HaGadol, Hilchot Tefillah* 1:115.
34 Apparently, the reference is to *Noda BeYehudah* (First Edition), *Yoreh De'ah* 1, although this letter was not sent to R. Isaac'l Hamburger.
35 See above, p. 482.
36 Based on *Yechezkel* 37:17.
37 [Originally in Yiddish.]
38 Based on *Yechezkel* 36:36.

Unity is the only remedy for widespread adversity

ז Do not wonder how all of the different segments of Israel can possibly be included in one unit. I will answer that Mordechai and Esther also gathered all the Jews together as one. Now, do you think that all the Jews of Mordechai *HaTzaddik*'s generation had the same convictions?! They, too, had differences of opinion, and many of them even assimilated. Open your eyes and see that the *Midrash* describes how Mordechai begged them not to defile themselves with the king's food,[39] since the feast was not compulsory. Nevertheless, 18,000 Jews ignored the *tzaddik* and defiled themselves with prohibited foods and abominable acts (*Esther Rabbah* 7:18). This demonstrates that they, too, had diverse opinions.

Nonetheless, when a general decree was issued against the entire Jewish nation – irrespective of whether they were devout Torah observers or sinners – they understood that gathering all of *Klal Yisrael* into one, unified entity was the only remedy for this affliction. All Jews had to unite, from the most extreme left to the most extreme right, without differentiating between various types. Thus, Esther said, *Go, gather all the Jews together* (*Esther* 4:16). For, just as the affliction came upon all of Israel, the remedy had to come by uniting all of Israel. Therefore, she specifically said, *all the Jews*, without distinguishing between the various types. In *Eshkol HaKofer*, the great Kabbalist, R. Avraham Sabba (the grandfather of the Beit Yosef's wife), also explains that the various salvations [mentioned in the *Megillah*] paralleled the troubles.[40]

This helps me explain the verse *It is a time of trouble for Ya'akov, but he shall be saved from it* (*Yirmiyah* 30:7), and the prayer "From the midst of trouble, provide them relief."[41] That is to say, since the salvation arises in the same way as the trouble, we can learn the remedy from the trouble itself. Just as the trouble affects all of *Klal Yisrael*, so too, HaShem will provide relief, healing, and salvation when we unite for His sake.

This is exactly what Mordechai did. He succeeded in uniting the Jews because he cared about the troubles of the generation and grieved over Israel's [fallen] glory. He paid attention to the *Zohar*,

39 Based on *Daniel* 1:5.

40 *Eshkol HaKofer, Esther* 8:16.

41 *Selichot* for Thursday, *Yisrael Nosha BaHaShem*. Based on *Yalkut Shimoni* 2:311.

Talmud, and *Midrashim*[42] which state that we must love and befriend every single Jew, even the greatest sinners, for they, too, are the offspring of Avraham, Yitzchak, and Ya'akov. He befriended them and showed them love until he was able to influence them, slowly but surely, to repent and accept the Torah anew.[43] The Eshkol HaKofer concurs with this in his interpretation of the verse *For Mordechai the Jew was...accepted by the multitude of his brethren; he sought the good of his people* (*Esther* 10:3). He explains that Mordechai became involved in their concerns and tried to make peace between them. He assisted them and spoke to them kindly. He also taught them true beliefs. (See the commentary inside.) But, he did all of this with a gentle reply,[44] without shouting and screaming.

We learn from the above that when adversity strikes all of Israel, we must, likewise, bring all of Israel together in peace... Only then, HaShem will send us relief and salvation. In chapter three,[45] I discussed this at length and proved that our redemption depends on uniting all of the extremes within the Jewish nation. I also proved that we are capable of doing so, and that our joint effort in rebuilding the Land is the force that will surround and unify us. See there; it is unnecessary to repeat it here.

Disunity is worse than idolatry

Here, in the chapter dealing with unity, I simply want to reinforce what I wrote above and demonstrate that our Father in Heaven wants us to unite. The Shelah writes that we are called 'The Assembly of Israel' (*Kenesset Yisrael*), "because we are all assembled and united in the secret of HaShem's unity."[46] Therefore, we must put an end to quarreling and controversy within Israel. The Shelah continues:

> The worst thing in this world is dissension. It is even worse than idolatry. *Chazal* state that Achav's generation won its wars, even though the people were idolaters, because there was peace and harmony among them. Sha'ul's generation, on the other hand, lost its wars even though the people were guiltless, because there were slanderers among them who instigated arguments (*Yalkut Shimoni* 2:213; *BeMidbar Rabbah* 19:2).

42 See above, pp. 104-14.

43 See *Shabbat* 88a.

44 *Mishley* 15:1.

45 Sec. נו־סו, pp. 379-408.

46 *Sh'nei Luchot HaBrit, Sha'ar HaOtiot* 1:42a, note s.v. *od*.

The secret of this matter is as I explained above. We, the Assembly of Israel, are united in the secret of the genuine "One." Thus, when there is strife [below], there is division and disunity above, and the "cutting of the shoots,"[47] God forbid... Therefore, he who yearns for the *Shechinah* should flee from the filth of the serpent and stay far away from even the slightest hint of discord. But, why must I describe how disgraceful strife is when all of the holy books are filled with such descriptions? Just remember this rule: The sin of (disunity and) dissension is worse than the sin of idolatry, as we find by Achav and Sha'ul. *Chazal* also state, "The Holy One Blessed be He pardoned the sin of idolatry three times, but He did not forgive the sin of discord"[48] (*Midrash Lamed Bet Middot, Mishnat R. Eliezer* 4).[49]

Hence, my friends and brothers, do not believe those who attempt to break Israel's cohesiveness by saying that it is impossible and dangerous to unify all segments of Israel. For even if they are right and there is some danger involved (God forbid), the Holy One Blessed be He prefers that the Jewish people be united, not separate. Our mentor, the Shelah, proves this from *Chazal* and reiterates the proof from Achav and Sha'ul.

Uniting all the Jews is not dangerous

In reality, there is no danger at all. On the contrary! If the Orthodox Jews would draw close to the irreligious, the irreligious would come close to us and incline their hearts to the good. *Pardes Yosef* cites from *Avot DeRebbe Natan* that many Jewish sinners produced righteous, pious, and upright offspring because they drew close to Torah scholars.[50]

We trust *Chazal* and the Shelah more than those who separate the unified people, no matter who they are, even if they are important individuals. Furthermore, I already cited[51] the godly scholar, our master, the Maharal (who spoke with *Ruach HaKodesh*), as saying that unity is part of Israel's nature. He also says that Rachel Immeinu's merit helps ensure that our unity will not be a stumbling block, God forbid. In addition, the people of our generation can be

47 [I.e., heresy. See *Chagigah* 14b.]

48 ❖ See the text inside where the Shelah enumerates these cases.

49 *Sh'nei Luchot HaBrit, Sha'ar HaOtiot* 1:45a.

50 ❖ I cited this above in chapter 3, sec. נ (p. 345).

51 Pp. 384-89.

influenced to the good, for they went through an iron furnace; and those who survived, with God's help, emerged purified and softened. Also, the Shelah asserts that Israel's unity is God's unity.[52]

The brilliant author of *Teshuvah MeAhavah* writes, "If the only way to build the *Beit HaMikdash* is through strife, it is preferable not to build it."[53] Thus, when it is possible to rebuild our Holy Land, which is the first step of redemption, and in this way expedite the rebuilding of the *Beit HaMikdash,*[54] which depends on Israel's unity, it is certainly imperative to unify all of Israel, prevent strife, and build our Land as one.

Mahari Anzil *z"l* cites the following in the name of our mentor, the Maharal. It is well known that HaShem's name is Shalom (Peace),[55] and His seal is Truth.[56] Now, which is closer to a man, his name or his seal? Everyone certainly agrees that a person's name is closer to his essence than is his seal. The same is true of the Holy One Blessed be He. His name, Shalom, is more important to Him than His seal, which is Truth. Therefore, we must often forgo the truth, which is merely God's seal, and pursue peace, which is His name.[57] This concludes the Maharal's divinely inspired words.*

---

* *Chazal* state, "Just as a *mikvah* purifies the unclean, so too, the Holy One Blessed be He purifies Israel" (*Yoma* 85b). The brilliant "light of the Diaspora," R. Amram Bloom *z"l*, explains the comparison between Israel's purification by God and a *mikvah*. A *mikvah* purifies only *be'ashboren*,[58] that is, when the waters are gathered together, calm, and "pleasant with one another." The same is true of the Holy One Blessed be He. He purifies Israel only when their hearts are close to one another, when they are gathered together in one group, and when they live together peacefully.

52 See note 46 above.

53 *Teshuvah MeAhavah* 1:205.

54 ❖ As I cited above (pp. 55, 180) from *Mishnat Chassidim*.

55 *VaYikra Rabbah* 9:9; *BeMidbar Rabbah* 11:18.

56 *Shabbat* 55a.

57 *Teshuvot Mahari Anzil* (Jerusalem, 5730 [1970]), *Chiddushei Halachah VeAggadah, Derush BeMa'alat HaShalom VeHaAchdut*, p. 94b, s.v. *vegodel*; citing Maharal, *Netivot Olam, Netiv HaShalom* 1.

58 [Meaning, when the waters are contained in an enclosed area, as opposed to flowing water. See Rambam, *Hilchot Mikva'ot* 9:8.]

Those who unify belong to Ya'akov's camp, and those who divide belong to Lavan's

ח I found a manuscript, written by a great man,[59] which explains the verse *Thus, the feeble* [sheep] (העטופים) *went to Lavan and the strong ones* (הקשורים) *to Ya'akov* (*BeReishit* 30:42). It is well known that Ya'akov's defining quality was truth (אמת), as it is written, *Grant truth to Ya'akov* (*Michah* 7:20). Now, the word אמת consists of letters which are very distant from one another, as the Talmud points out (*Shabbat* 55a). The "א" and the "ת" are on the two extremes of the alphabet and the "מ" is in the middle. But, truth (אמת) joins them all together. This demonstrates that the attribute of truth has the power to join even the most opposite extremes. Even though the "א" is on the rightmost extreme and the "ת" is on the leftmost extreme, the "מ," which is the middle letter, joins them together. It is well known that the letter "מ" is made up of the letters "כ" and "ו", as the Beit Yosef explains.[60] These two letters numerically equal the Tetragrammaton (י־ה־ו־ה, 26). This hints to the fact that when we strive to bring the two extremes together, HaShem assists us. He wants to unify the extremes, therefore, His seal is truth (אמת).

The Shelah writes that "truth" alludes to unity, as the poet (*paytan*) says, "His seal is truth, to demonstrate that He is one."[61] This was also Ya'akov Avinu's quality, to join and bind everyone together, even those who were distant from one another. This is the meaning of the verse *And the strong ones* (הקשורים) *to Ya'akov*. Ya'akov would bind (לקשר) and join everyone together, for holiness is in the domain of unity. Those who follow this path are part of Ya'akov's camp. Thus, the קשורים [those who bind people together] belong to Ya'akov.

But, the עטופים[62] – those who attempt to disunite the united ones and who enwrap (עוטפים) their words in pious wrappings – belong to Lavan's camp. For Lavan attempted to act pious, even more pious than Ya'akov. We see this from his statement to Ya'akov, *Such is not done in our place* (*BeReishit* 29:26). Lavan brought destruction to the world through this "piety." The Kabbalists explain that had Rachel been given to Ya'akov first, he would have borne the twelve godly tribes from her. Then, the world would have

59 ❖ The opening page of the manuscript does not indicate the author's name. But, it is clear from the work that he was a great man.

60 *Beit Yosef, Orach Chayim* 36. That is to say, in the script used in Torah scrolls, the מ is formed by writing a כ and a ו adjacent to one another.

61 *Sh'nei Luchot HaBrit, Sha'ar HaOtiot* 1:42b.

62 [Translated in the verse as "*feeble ones*," it can also mean "the enwrapped ones."]

immediately reached perfection and we would not have been subjected to the Egyptian, or any other, exile.

This explains the verse *An Aramean destroyed my father, and he descended to Egypt* (*Devarim* 26:5). Rashi is hard-pressed to explain how Lavan destroyed Ya'akov. The preceding idea, however, explains it well. He actually destroyed him with his "piety" and caused the Egyptian exile. Thus, the verse says, *An Aramean destroyed my father*. How? *He descended to Egypt*. Lavan caused Ya'akov to descend to Egypt, thereby destroying him until this very day. Lavan caused our current exile by tricking Ya'akov and attempting to be more pious than him. Similarly, those who attempt to be "pious," causing dissension while enwrapping their ways in pious wrappings, belong to Lavan. They cause destruction and damage to Israel, just like Lavan did.

I will supplement the words of this great man with a *Midrash* on the verse *You rescue me from the strife of the people* (*Tehillim* 18:44): "Ben Azzai says: 'David said, "I prefer to reign over the entire world, but not over two [people] wrapped in sheets"'" (*Midrash Tehillim* 18:34). The commentator[63] explains that this refers to those "who are wrapped in *talitot* and *tzitzit*," i.e., "good Jews." This is shocking! King David prayed for the Holy One Blessed be He to rescue him from the strife of the "good Jews"! He even declared that he preferred to reign over the entire world, but not over those who enwrap everything in *talitot* and *tzitzit*, meaning, pious wrappings. In reality, David saw them as mere people of strife. This is a great and strong proof for this *gadol*'s idea.

In any event, we see that King David, as well, trembled before such people and prayed to be saved from them and their cohorts. He did not include all of the "good Jews" in his prayer, God forbid, only those who cause strife among Israel, justifying their actions with excuses. These people bring destruction to the Jewish world;[64] they must be cast aside and kept far away from the Congregation of Israel. A truly "good Jew" strives to bring other Jews closer, not further, as our mentor, the Chatam Sofer, writes regarding Shammai and Hillel.[65] Shammai characteristically distanced others, while Hillel brought them near. The Chatam Sofer explains that Shammai acted according to the law, for he only distanced those who deserved

63 ❖ Mahari Kohen, the son-in-law of the Maharal.

64 ❖ As the *Yerushalmi*, cited above (p. 480), indicates.

65 ❖ I cited this above, in chapter 1 (p. 105).

such treatment. Hillel, on the other hand, acted contrary to the law, for he befriended those who rightfully should have been distanced. The Chatam Sofer concludes that, despite this, the *halachah* follows Hillel.

Our mentor, R. Pinchas'l of Kuritz, was known to possess *Ruach HaKodesh* and receive revelations from Eliyahu. In *Midrash Pinchas*, his disciple writes, "The last summer before he died he said that Israel must abandon all dissension, so that no Jew will be disunited."[66] This implies that we must not dissociate from even the most corrupt and lowly Jews. They are also Jews, as the Talmud states, "Even if a Jew sins, he is still a Jew" (*Sanhedrin* 44a).

Keep in mind that these things were said by great *tzaddikim* like the Chatam Sofer and R. Pinchas of Kuritz, from whose mouths the *Shechinah* spoke. This is the true characteristic of a "good Jew" who is really a "good Jew." A word to the wise is sufficient.

When the Jews unite HaShem listens to their prayers and blesses them

מ *Chazal* expound the verse הן אל כביר ולא ימאס, כביר כח לב – *Behold, God is mighty and He does not despise; He is mighty in strength of heart* (*Iyov* 36:5):

> From where do we learn that the Holy One Blessed be He does not despise the prayers of the community? It says, הן אל כביר לא ימאס – *Behold, God is mighty, He does not despise.* (*Berachot* 8a)

Seemingly, the Talmud cites the verse incorrectly, for it really says, ***and*** *He does not despise*, with the letter "ו"! In *Shivrei Luchot*, the divine Kabbalist, our mentor, the Rama of Panow, explains that this is Talmudic style:

> The first *mighty* of the verse praises the Omnipresent... The second *mighty* praises the community when they are united [with a] *mighty heart*, which refers to prayer. The Talmud only mentions one *mighty* in order to be brief, and it omits the "ו" in order not to interrupt the idea. It is as if the Talmud says, "הן אל, את כביר לא ימאס – Behold, God does not despise the mighty" [i.e., the prayers of the community]. This is simple.
>
> Now, the repetition of *mighty* (כביר) in this verse is similar to the repetition of *He will bless* (יברך) in the verse *The Lord Who remembered us will bless, He will bless* (*Tehillim* 115:12). Both of these words (כביר, יברך) have the same numerical value,

66 *Midrash Pinchas*, p. 62b.

72+63+45+52 (which equals 232, and these are the four expansions of the Tetragrammaton).[67] When the people of Israel are united they are the name of the Holy One Blessed be He.[68]

I, humble of men, will embellish his sacred words. כביר (*mighty*) has the same letters as יברך (*He will bless*), which alludes to a very lofty concept regarding unity. When the Jews are *mighty in strength* – i.e., unified – HaShem will immediately remember them for the good and bless them. Thus, the Rama's assertion that the repetition of *mighty* is similar to that of *He will bless* demonstrates that these two verses parallel each other. When the Jews are *mighty in strength* – i.e., unified – then *The Lord Who remembered us will bless* [us]. Thank God, this is very true.

When we are united we are God's great name

My brothers and friends, observe how great the power of unity is. Our mentor, the Rama (whose every utterance was Kabbalah), says that when the people of Israel are united they are actually the name of the Holy One Blessed be He. And, they are not simply an ordinary name of God, but the great name, with all of its four expansions (72, 63, 45, 52).

This helps us explain the verse *For the Lord will not forsake His people for the sake of His great name* (I *Shmuel* 12:22). That is to say, when they are united, at which time they are actually His great name, He will not forsake or despise them. This is true even if they are on an extremely low level (God forbid), as the verse says, *Behold, God is mighty and He does not despise; He is mighty in strength of heart*. Since it says, *He does not despise* we can infer that they deserve to be despised (God forbid). Nonetheless, when they are *mighty in strength of heart*, meaning, unified as one man with one heart, He does not despise them. He will even bless them, as it says, *The Lord Who remembered us, will bless...*

67 The Tetragrammaton is made up of the four letters י־ה־ו־ה. Each letter can be spelled in different ways: "י" is always spelled יוד. "ה" is spelled הא, הי, or הה. "ו" is spelled וו, ויו, or ואו. Using the numerical values of these spellings, we arrive at four different sums. יוד (20) + הי (15) + ויו (22) + הי (15) = 72. This is the Tetragrammaton expanded with "י". יוד (20) + הי (15) + ואו (13) + הי (15) = 63. This is the Tetragrammaton expanded to form סג (63). יוד (20) + הא (6) + ואו (13) + הא (6) = 45. This is the Tetragrammaton expanded with "א". יוד (20) + הה (10) + וו (12) + הה (10) = 52. This is the Tetragrammaton expanded with "ה". Adding all four together comes to 232.

68 *Shivrei Luchot*, p. 101, s.v. *vechein*.

I would like to add another idea based on a statement of the Ari *z"l*, as cited by the Shelah.[69] He writes that יהי אור – *Let there be light* (*BeReishit* 1:3) – numerically equals the four expansions of the Tetragrammaton (232). Thus, if we are *mighty* – i.e., unified – we will deserve *Let there be light*, as in the days of Mordechai: *The Jews had light, and gladness, and joy, and honor* (*Esther* 8:16). Amen, so may it be God's will.

The preservation of the Jewish people depends on unity

יא In *parashat BeHa'alotcha*, Rashi writes that when Aharon saw the tribal leaders dedicating the *Mishkan* he became disheartened by the fact that he did not participate. "The Holy One Blessed be He said to him, 'By your life! Your portion is greater than theirs, for you will kindle and set the lamps in order.'"[70] This requires explanation. In what way was his portion greater than theirs? Furthermore, the *Midrash* adds that the Holy One Blessed be He said to him, "Do not fear; you are destined for something greater than this. Sacrifices are only brought when the *Beit HaMikdash* is standing, but the lamps are forever, as it says, *towards the face of the menorah* (*BeMidbar* 8:2)" (*BeMidbar Rabbah* 15:6). This is also difficult. How do the words, *towards the face of the menorah*, indicate that it is everlasting? Moreover, in reality, the lamps were only lit when the *Beit HaMikdash* stood!

With God's help, I believe the answer is as follows. I will preface with a *Midrash* on the verse *On the day that Moshe finished erecting the Mishkan* (*BeMidbar* 7:1):

> R. Yehudah bar Simon said: "The day that the *Mishkan* was erected, Moshe entered it and heard glorious sounds, pleasant sounds, and praiseworthy sounds. Moshe said, *I will hear what God, the Lord, will speak* (*Tehillim* 85:9). The Holy One Blessed be He said to Moshe, 'I speak peace to them' as it is written, *For He will speak peace to His people and to His pious ones, but let them not revert to folly* (ibid.). Afterwards it says, *Surely His salvation is near to those who fear Him, that they may dwell honorably in our Land* (ibid. 85:10). When? On the day that the *Mishkan* was erected." (*Tanchuma, Naso* 25)

This entire *Midrash* is puzzling and needs explanation.

As a rule, it is more difficult for man to preserve what is already

69 *Sh'nei Luchot HaBrit* 1:19b, s.v. *beit HaShem*.

70 Rashi, *BeMidbar* 8:2.

made than to make it in the first place (as is well known). True, in the beginning a person has to exert himself and gather all of his strength to overcome the obstacles and deterrents that stand in his way. And if he is stubborn, he completes his task despite great difficulties. Nonetheless, it is more difficult to preserve his handiwork and ensure that it does not dissolve over time. He needs much greater effort to protect it from damage and destruction, as a certain wise man said, "Time is harsh, for it diminishes and destroys everything."

We see this all the time. A person creates something with great devotion, and eventually it disintegrates and fades away. This is certainly true of efforts upon which a man's life depends, and even more true of efforts upon which the lives of the masses depend. It is certainly difficult to finish such a task, and it requires great effort. But, even more effort is needed to preserve and keep it for the future so that it will be able to accomplish its purpose and bestow its goodness upon mankind. This is a well-known law of nature.

Now, let us apply this to our issue – the building of the *Mishkan*. The Holy One Blessed be He commanded, *Let them make a Sanctuary for Me, that I may dwell among them* (*Shemot* 25:8). Its purpose was to be a center for the Jewish people. The Holy One Blessed be He would let His *Shechinah* rest there in order to be close to His people and bestow upon them all sorts of beneficial influences. This center would allow the Children of Israel to continuously connect and cling to their Father in Heaven.

Certainly, such a great and precious venture, which was destined to generate a strong bond between the Holy One Blessed be He and Israel, would require great efforts to prepare, explore, and complete it, so that it could achieve its lofty purpose. Indeed, every Jew did his share. Only one man remained distant, not taking part in this exalted undertaking. This man was none other than the sacred and awe-inspiring man of God, Aharon the High Priest of Israel. Understandably, he was greatly disheartened and upset that he did not participate in this lofty endeavor, as if, for some reason, HaShem was pushing him aside. Finally, the Holy One Blessed be He Himself calmed and pacified him, saying, "Aharon, My son, you are destined for something greater than this."

The explanation for this is based on what I said above. Preservation is the most important part of any endeavor, that is, ensuring that it lasts forever so that it can accomplish its predestined purpose uninterrupted. Now, the purpose of the *Mishkan* was to consolidate all the people of Israel in one place and connect them to their Father in Heaven. The Jews needed to select one man who would ensure the continuous preservation of this center, so that it would not be abolished, God forbid.

It is well known that the *Beit HaMikdash* was destroyed due to lack of peace within Israel. Groundless hatred, strife, and disunity intensified until the Temple was destroyed. Therefore, after the building, completion, and dedication of the *Mishkan*, it was essential to maintain peace among Israel, so that the *Mishkan* could accomplish its predestined purpose. It was necessary to uphold unity, love, and brotherhood so that the *Mishkan* could endure and achieve its goal. However, if division among Israel would disturb the peace, the *Mishkan* would be destroyed, God forbid, and this entire, precious endeavor would dissolve and go to waste.

Thus, although the building of the *Mishkan* was truly a lofty endeavor, its preservation was even more lofty; and peace was the only way to ensure it. Now, for the most part, disunity and strife are caused by people who consider themselves pious, Torah scholars. They refuse to associate with the masses, because they consider them inferior. In the meantime, the peace is disturbed and the *Shechinah* leaves Israel.[71]

This explains the *Midrash* mentioned above.[72] On the day the *Mishkan* was erected, the Holy One Blessed be He was truly gratified by His children, for they had constructed an exalted and sublime structure and had dedicated it with great joy and enthusiasm. Moshe Rabbeinu thought in his heart that strength and joy are certainly in God's place,[73] and that HaShem has not been so happy since the day of creation. (The *Midrash* says that the day the *Mishkan* was erected was as great as the day the heavens and earth were created [see *Shabbat* 87b].) Moshe said to himself, *I will hear what the Lord will speak*, as if to say, "The Holy One Blessed be He will certainly speak contentedly about His children, Israel, and He will praise them before me." He thought that hearing the praises of Israel from the mouth of the Holy One Blessed be He would be his greatest joy.

But, the Holy One Blessed be He said to him, "My beloved Moshe, I am truly pleased with My children, but there is one fear which

71 ❖ As the *Or Zarua* (1:115) states in the name of R. Chisdai.

72 P. 493. [It will help to review the *Midrash* before continuing.]

73 Based on I *Divrei HaYamim* 16:27.

hovers over Me: the preservation of this lofty endeavor. I want it to last forever and not dissolve, for the preservation of something is greater than its creation. There is only one solution: 'I speak peace to them' – there must be peace between them. All I demand of My children is that they *speak peace to His people and to His pious ones*." That is to say, there must be peace between the pious ones and the simple folk, referred to as *His people*. *But let them not revert to folly* – the *Yeitzer HaRa*'s folly – which says that it is impossible for devout people to join together with lowly people. This is the *Yeitzer HaRa*'s scheme to cause division and discord among Israel. *Surely His salvation is near to those who fear Him*, for in reality they all fear God. Even the "empty ones" among them are as full of *mitzvot* as a pomegranate [is full of seeds].[74] Then, when they dwell together peacefully as one man, they will achieve *His salvation..., that they may dwell honorably in our Land*. This refers also to the future, indicating that it will always be this way. When the people of Israel unite, they will deserve to dwell honorably in our Land.

When did the Holy One Blessed be He reveal the secret that the *Mishkan*'s preservation and our honorable dwelling in the Land depend solely on peace and unity? On the day the *Mishkan* was erected. On that day, HaShem revealed to Moshe that the secret of Israel's existence and the key to our freedom from exile and our honorable and glorious settlement in the Land is simply, *when he will speak peace to His people and to His pious ones*, i.e., when there is peace among all types of Jews, for HaShem loves them all.

The Or HaChayim HaKadosh comments on the verse *He will say, "Where is their God, the Rock in Whom they trusted?"* (*Devarim* 32:37):

> Israel will say, *Where is their God?* Even though the Jews act improperly, they will plead to God, to Whom the word *Rock* alludes. And He is the One *in Whom they trusted*. For even though the people of Israel sin and violate some of HaShem's commandments, they put their trust in HaShem. They suffer poverty and degradation for His sake and die for the sanctification of His name. But, they arise and anticipate the Rock of their salvation. This is the meaning of *The Rock in Whom they trusted*.

During these difficult times, we see how true are our holy

74 *Berachot* 57a.

mentor's words. May his merit protect us and all of Israel.

Now, let us explain Rashi's comments.[75] After the Holy One Blessed be He revealed to Moshe that preserving the *Mishkan* is greater than constructing it, and that preserving it depends on peaceful coexistence between all segments of the Jewish people, He needed to select one man who would be able to maintain peace among the people. Who was more fitting for this than Aharon, whose attribute was to love and pursue peace (*Avot* 1:12)?

The Sforno explains that the purpose of making and kindling the menorah was to unify the different segments of the people, those on the right and those on the left; meaning, those who occupy themselves with the Torah, which is called "right," and those who occupy themselves with the mundane. [The goal was] to fulfill God's will in a way that everyone participates in achieving His purpose. Then, they will exalt His name together, as they accepted upon themselves [at Mt. Sinai]: *All the people answered together and said, "Everything that the Lord has spoken we will do"* (*Shemot* 19:8). That is to say, we will all accomplish His purpose. The menorah's function was to demonstrate unity which is directed towards one purpose.[76]

Thus, the kindling of the menorah was intended to generate unity and strengthen peace within Israel, which would ensure the preservation of the *Mishkan*. Hence, the Holy One Blessed be He said to Aharon, "Your portion is greater than theirs [the tribal leaders], for you will help preserve the *Mishkan* and see to it that it performs its task continuously. Your strength is greater than theirs, for preserving something is more honorable than building it." This also explains the *Midrash* which adds that the Holy One Blessed be He said to Aharon, "But, the lamps are forever." This means that the purpose of the lamps, which is to bring about the unity of Israel, is forever. Israel's preservation always depends on unity. Contemplate this explanation for it is very accurate, thank God.

Our situation will improve only when we unite

יב This concept also applies to us today. All of our troubles and hardships have made us physically and spiritually weary. We have reached a state of despair, and many people are saying, ôWe shall totally perish,ö[77] God forbid. There is no vision or hope of

75 Above, p. 493.

76 Sforno, *BeMidbar* 8:2. [He derives this from the fact that the six outer flames all faced the middle one.]

77 Based on *BeMidbar* 17:28.

any change for the better.

It seems to me that King David had our generation in mind when he composed chapter 85 of *Tehillim*. *Tosafot Yeshanim* explains that King David composed the book of *Tehillim* for a time when the Jews are in exile.[78] (I have mentioned many times that as I write this book I have no access to *sefarim* in order to quote exact sources.) David prayed on Israel's behalf:

> *Return us, O God of our Salvation, and annul Your anger with us. Will You be angry with us forever? Will You let Your wrath endure from generation to generation? Will You not revive us again, that Your people may rejoice in You? Show us Your kindness, O Lord, and grant us Your salvation.*[✧] *I will hear what God, the Lord, will speak, for He will speak peace to His people and to His pious ones, but let them not revert to folly. Surely His salvation is near to those who fear Him, that they may dwell honorably in our Land.* (*Tehillim* 85:5-10)

That is to say, bend an ear and listen to what HaShem will say about David's request that He should annul His anger and show us His kindness and salvation from now on. HaShem responds, *For He will speak peace to His people and to His pious ones, but let them not revert to folly*. We cannot expect any improvement until peace is restored, until all segments of Israel are united, from the "good Jews," referred to as *pious ones*, to the simple and wicked Jews, referred to as *people*. For, even the most sinful Jew is part of the Jewish nation. Thus, the verse says, *For He will speak peace to* ***His people*** *and to* ***His pious ones***. Peace must be restored to all parts of the nation, from those called *people* to those called *pious ones*. *But, let them not revert to folly*: They must not revert to their old, foolish ways of causing division and strife. They must not divide themselves into factions, as I mentioned above,[79] for division is the cause

✧ David, in effect, was saying, "Master of the Universe, have we not suffered sufficient hardships? It seems as if Your anger and wrath will endure forever, from generation to generation, God forbid. The time has already come for You to revive us again. Show us Your kindness, and grant us Your salvation." David answers his own question, [as the verse continues]:

78 See *Tosafot Yeshanim, Yoma* 71a, s.v. *zeh makom*.

79 This chapter, sec. א, pp. 475-76.

of all our troubles and brings only curses and destruction upon Israel. However, when we unite and become one nation, no adversary nor evil affliction will harm us.[80]

When Israel is united HaShem protects even the sinners

The *Midrash* also states:

> R. Elazar the son of R. Elazar HaKappar said: "If there is peace [among the people of Israel], then even if they worship idols, the Holy One Blessed be He says (as it were), 'No adversary will harm them.' As it says, *Efrayim is attached to idols, let him be* (*Hoshea* 4:17). But, when they are divided it says, *Their heart is divided, now they shall be found guilty* (ibid. 10:2)." (*BeMidbar Rabbah* 11:7; *Sifrei, Naso* 42)

When we are united, HaShem considers us all God-fearing, observant Jews. Our mentor, R. Elimelech *z"l*, asserts that it is only possible to find blemishes and sins in individual Jews. But, when they are all part of one whole, they retain their sanctity, and their appearance is engraved before HaShem.[81] Then, the verse – *Surely His salvation is near to those who fear Him, that they may dwell honorably in our Land* – will be fulfilled through us. That is to say, HaShem will be near us and grant us the complete redemption; and we will return to our glory and our Land. This is the only way we can achieve the salvation for which we so desperately yearn. This is a true Torah interpretation.

Above,[82] I cited R. Avraham Sabba's notion that one can discover the remedy from the affliction. If the affliction affects the entire Jewish people, the only remedy is for all of Israel to join together and become one entity. Then, no adversary nor misfortune will harm them. This is what the Jews did at the time of Haman's decree, and we must do the same, for our affliction has befallen all those who bear the name of Israel.

Rebuilding the Land is the only mitzvah capable of uniting us

יג Therefore, I lift my voice to the people of our generation who have been through a dreadful and brutal, fiery furnace; people who have suffered all of Iyov's afflictions, if not more; people for whom there is no vision or hope for a cure. ***Please, let us try, just this once, to fulfill the words of Chazal according to their***

80 ❖ As I cited above (pp. 133, 381) from our mentor, R. Elimelech.

81 ❖ See above (ibid.).

82 P. 485.

simple meaning. They informed us numerous times that our only hope is to unite completely and avoid division, as I demonstrated above from the Midrash and Talmud. If we do this we will see the truth of their words, for we will reach our desired goal, the true redemption, with God's help. Therefore, we must unify* (להבריח) *the entire nation, from one end to the other. Only the task of building and settling our Holy Land can be that "middle bar"* (הבריח התיכון)[83] *which will bring us all together. This is the only mitzvah capable of doing so, as I explained in the previous chapter.*[84] *We must also do this because of the age-old debt that hovers over us from time immemorial, as I discussed above.*[85] *Then, when we unite, HaShem will be pleased with us, and He will remember us according to the promise of redemption and compassion,*[86] *speedily in our days. Amen.

This gathering and unification will not harm the Orthodox Jews in any way, God forbid. Let me illustrate this with an example. A factory building is surrounded on the outside by a great wall. Even though the inside of the building contains many types of rooms, cubicles, and sections – each one serving its own specific purpose, the large surrounding wall makes them all into one unit called a factory. The same applies to uniting all of Israel through the holy task of rebuilding the Land. This task is only the surrounding wall; but inside, each Orthodox Jew can do as he pleases. For example, he can educate his children in accordance with the written Torah and the oral traditions of our sacred forefathers. We will only unite to build and settle the Land, as it is written, *The people assembled as one man to Jerusalem* (*Ezra* 3:1); and, *Rather, we, together, will build for the Lord, God of Israel* (ibid. 4:3). The Ibn Ezra explains that the words, *Rather we together*, "allude to the entire Congregation of Israel."

Above,[87] I cited the Rambam's introduction to *Zera'im* which states that wise men need the masses in order to keep the land from becoming desolate:

> The masses were created in order to form a society for the

83 Based on *Shemot* 26:28.
84 Pp. 390-91.
85 Pp. 396-416.
86 From the *Ya'aleh VeYavo* prayer.
87 Pp. 308-9.

> wise men, so that they will not be alone... The Holy One Blessed be He placed the wicked ones [the seven gentile nations] in *Eretz Yisrael* to...eliminate loneliness... Our Sages explained this and said, "What is the meaning of, *This is man's entire duty* (*Kohelet* 12:13)? The entire world was created only to accompany the [righteous one]" (*Berachot* 6b).

Thus, even the masses are beneficial. Therefore, it is clear that everyone must join together to build the Land. The masses will also bring honor to HaShem, as I cited above in the name of the brilliant R. Shlomo Kluger *z"l*.[88] We must hope and pray that after many of our Jewish brethren gather in *Eretz Yisrael*, HaShem will direct their hearts to love Him and His Torah. The Rambam, Chatam Sofer (who quotes the Rambam), Or HaChayim HaKadosh, and Ahavat Yonatan write that all this will occur before *Mashiach* arrives.[89] Therefore, we must not be overly wise. Instead, we must do our share and HaShem will do His, as Rashi writes in *parashat BeMidbar*.[90]

Every person has a specific task to fulfill

יד The *Midrash* states, "The entire world borrows from one another" (*Shemot Rabbah* 31:16). In *Divrei Chayim*, the Rebbe of Tzanz explains that this connects the people of the world together like one man with one heart. Now, man's limbs are interconnected; if they were not, he would perish. Man is built in such a way that some of his limbs need the others and some serve the others. Every intelligent person knows that the hands do not boast that they do everything for the other limbs, because the entire body is one. Also, the other limbs have no reason to feel sad and discontented by the fact that they cannot do what the hands can do, for the hands also have a deficiency, they lack intelligence. Only the mind has intelligence. Therefore, none of the limbs feel inferior or superior to the others, for the body as a whole is one entity which consists of some limbs which act and some which think. In this way, man is perfected.

However, if one of these types of limbs were missing, or if the head would act and the hands would think, the human race would surely cease to exist. Why was man created in this fashion? There is no explanation other than, such was HaShem's will (just like there

88 The author cites as the reference, "chapter 3, sec. ג, in a footnote." However, he means sec. ל (pp. 296-97).

89 ❖ I discussed this at length above (pp. 117-20, 170-71, 174-75).

90 *BeMidbar* 3:16.

is no explanation why the entire creation was created as it was). The *Yerushalmi*[91] and *Midrashim*[92] state that HaShem consulted the heavenly court (as it were) about how to create each and every limb. Furthermore, *Chazal* say that all the different creatures "were created with their own consent and in the form that they chose for themselves" (*Rosh HaShanah* 11a, *Chullin* 60a). Therefore, this must certainly be true of man. He was created with imperfect limbs which need to be complemented by others. The entire world was also created in this manner. (This concludes the Rebbe of Tzanz's words of wisdom and truth.)[93]

The same applies to our national existence. We need one another. We need people to serve as "hands," that is, the laborers; and we need people to serve as "the mind," the eyes of the congregation. All together they form one complete nation. But, when there is division, the state ceases to function and the people will never reach the paths of life.

Therefore, we need every Jew to help build our Holy Land, and all of us must unite as one man with one heart. God wants all individual Jews to join together as one, as the *mitzvah* of the Four Species demonstrates. *Chazal* tell us that the Four Species represent the four types of Jews who need to be bound together into one group, as is well known (*VaYikra Rabbah* 30:12). Unity connects us to the Creator of the Universe and sweetens our judgments. With His great mercy, HaShem will bestow upon us an unlimited abundance of life and blessings, and He will fulfill the verse *The Lord your God will place you high above all the nations of the land* (*Devarim* 28:1).

HaShem uses the wicked as ôseedsö for future generations

Therefore, ***my brothers and friends***, our only option is to unify all of *Klal Yisrael* and make them into a single entity through the positive commandment of *Yishuv Eretz Yisrael*. The prophet also states, *For there will be the seed of peace; the vine will give its fruit, and the Land will give its produce, and the heavens will give their dew. I will bestow all these things upon the remnant of this people* (*Zecharyah* 8:12). The *Midrash* derives from here that the Land's prosperity depends on peace.[94] Now, why did the prophet say, *seed of peace*, and not, "sons of peace"? It seems to me that he was

91 See *Sanhedrin* 1:1 (1b).

92 See *BeReishit Rabbah* 8:3.

93 *Divrei Chayim* (Jerusalem, 5706 [1946]), *Re'eh* (addendum), vol. 2, p. 230.

94 We were unable to locate a source for this.

alluding to the comments of the brilliant Kabbalist, Rabbeinu Chayim,[95] in *Sefer HaChayim*:

> We find that the Holy One Blessed be He promised the people of Israel that He would never destroy them. Therefore, He always refers to them as "seeds," as in the verse *And all this Land...I will give to your seed, and they will inherit it forever* (*Shemot* 32:13), and many other verses in *Tanach*.[96] The reason for this is as follows. Many onions and other vegetables harden in the ground and become inedible. Nonetheless, [the farmer] does not uproot them. Instead, he leaves them [in the ground] to serve as seeds, for he hopes that these seeds will sprout edible fruits the next season.
>
> Similarly, the Holy One Blessed be He does not destroy an evil generation. For even though they are guilty, HaShem needs them to bear the seed of the sacred Patriarchs. He hopes that completely righteous people, who will live at the time of redemption, will sprout from the roots of this lowly generation. Then, *The Lord will rejoice in His works* (*Tehillim* 104:31), and *On that day the Lord will be One* (*Zecharyah* 14:9). The eternal redemption (גאולת עולם) will emerge from the exile (גלות) with the addition of the letter "א" which represents the oneness of HaShem's name. May He be blessed and may His remembrance be exalted for all of eternity.[97]

Thus, the Holy One Blessed be He uses even an unbefitting generation as seeds for future meritorious generations. This concurs with the Rashbam's statement that it is possible that a thousand sinful generations will pass, after which a virtuous generation will sprout from them.[98]

This is also true of the generation which will assemble in *Eretz Yisrael*. They, themselves, will be completely unworthy of the name "Israel," for it will be impossible to tell that they are Jews. Despite this, they will be important to the Holy One Blessed be He, and He will bring them to the Land. He will use them as seeds for future generations to produce blessed offspring worthy of having God's *Shechinah* rest upon them. Therefore, the verse uses the word *seed*

95 ❖ The brother of the Maharal of Prague and colleague of the Rama *zt"l*.

96 See *Devarim* 10:15, *Yeshayah* 61:9, *Esther* 9:28.

97 *Sefer HaChayim, Sefer Ge'ulah ViYeshuah* (end).

98 Rashbam, *Devarim* 7:9.

to demonstrate that we must make peace even with those who serve merely the function of a "seed." Then, HaShem will bestow all of these things upon the remnant of His people, [as the verse concludes].

Invoking merit upon the chalutzim

מט Recently, HaShem brought to my attention a pamphlet entitled *Eileh Mas'ei* which recounts the journeys of our brilliant and righteous master, R. Fischel Sofer Sussman *zt"l*, mentor and *av beit din* of the capital city, Budapest. In this pamphlet I saw a statement of the brilliant and righteous R. Yosef Chayim Sonnenfeld *zt"l* in which he invoked merit (לימד זכות) upon today's corrupt pioneers (*chalutzim*):

> These corrupt *chalutzim* display a great amount of self-sacrifice and patience for the sake of working the Land! This demonstrates such a love for the Land that we can anticipate that this love will bring them back to the proper path.[99]

In passing, I would like to quote a responsa of the brilliant and righteous mentor of *Eretz Yisrael*, R. Yosef Chayim Sonnenfeld *zt"l*. R. Fischel Sofer asked him to express his opinion on buying fields in *Eretz Yisrael*. The following is his answer:

> With God's help, from the holy city of Jerusalem, may it be rebuilt and established speedily in our days. Friday, the day before the holy Sabbath of *parashat Emor*, the 31st day of the *Omer*, 5681 [1921].
>
> Life, blessings, peace, and all that is good from Zion to my beloved friend and in-law the ... rabbi, the "*Tana* of the House of the Nasi," our famed, praiseworthy, and honorable master, R. Fischel Sofer Sussman. May his light shine forth and may he be privileged to see the goodness of Jerusalem, speedily in our days. Amen.
>
> After inquiring about his honor's well-being, I say: Be strong and courageous in your sacred task. When the righteous assemble it is good for them and good for the world.[100] May HaShem, in His mercy, have compassion upon His nation and His pious ones, and may He grant a complete awakening for His salvation and a swift redemption to the entire nation and to each individual.

99 ❖ *Eileh Mas'ei*, p. 32. See above (chap. 2, sec. ט-ח, pp. 165-75), what I wrote concerning these *chalutzim*.

100 *Sanhedrin* 71b.

Concerning your question: I say that the time has certainly come for the men of means to awaken themselves and pay attention to the holy settlement. Ever since the hearts of the holy Jewish nation began to yearn for a closeness to sanctity [i.e., *Eretz Yisrael*], they only supported those few remnants who strove to ascend to the Holy [Land]. Apparently, however, they did not arouse themselves to try to expand the holy settlement. The brilliant and righteous Ya'avetz *zt"l* already discussed this holy matter adequately in the introduction to his *siddur*,[101] and he stirred and chastised the readers.

In any event, even though the *Agudat Yisrael* took action, and the *gedolim* of Poland became involved and made a great impact, they only did so after they decided to send messengers to the Holy Land and contemplate the matter. All those who volunteer for this endeavor must do the same. They must choose from their midst erudite men who know about worldly matters, and contemplate this sacred matter. Afterwards, they can take council with the *gedolim* of the land.

Apparently, the verse, *That you not wake or rouse the love until it desires* (*Shir HaShirim* 2:7), has been fulfilled through us. And apparently, this "desire" means a divine awakening. May HaShem, in His mercy, bring salvation to His nation, speedily in our days. Amen.

I would be glad to greet his honor when he visits the Holy Land. I will end this letter as I began it, with a blessing. May you succeed greatly in Torah, *mitzvot*, and good deeds, and may you soon see salvation in accordance with the wholehearted prayers of he who awaits it. I seek the welfare of his honorable self and of his son-in-law, the brilliant and holy elder, *shlita*.

Yosef Chayim Sonnenfeld.[102]

Afterwards, when R. Fischel Sofer traveled to the Holy Land and met the brilliant and righteous R. Sonnenfeld, he said to him, "So, the Rebbe agrees?" "What do you mean, 'agree'?" he answered excitedly. "I look forward to this (that is, to labor for the settlement of the Land), and I beg you to come and buy fields in our Holy Land and keep the *Shemittah*, of course, like others do." He was referring to the Rebbe of Gur's B'nei Brak and Petach Tikvah.

101 *Siddur Ya'avetz, Sullam Beit El*, p. 13a and on.
102 This letter is found in *Eileh Mas'ei*, pp. 28-29.

We must avoid the sin of the spies

מז I also saw in *Eileh Mas'ei*[103] an idea which the righteous mentor of *Eretz Yisrael*, R. Sonnenfeld, used to say [on the verse] *And you shall see the goodness of Jerusalem* (*Tehillim* 128:5): One must always see only the good of *Eretz Yisrael*, that is, the positive sides of Jerusalem. One must be careful not to be a "spy," God forbid. The spies were punished because they slandered *Eretz Yisrael* at a time when there were no Jews there; how much more so now, when there are many Jews in the Land.[104]

Praise to my beloved friend, the young and exceptionally sharp scholar, the magnate, our master, R. Eliezer Sussman *shlita*, the son of our brilliant and righteous master, R. Efrayim Fischel Sofer *z"l*, rabbi and *av beit din* of [Budapest]. He copied for me parts of a manuscript of his father's eulogy for our brilliant mentor, R. Yosef Chayim Sonnenfeld:

> Who will have pity on you, O Jerusalem, and who will bemoan you, O beloved Land! He never cursed anyone, under any circumstances. He was distressed more than anyone else about those who came and defiled the Land by desecrating the holy Sabbath, eating forbidden foods, and eating leavened bread on *Pesach*. He invoked merit upon these lost souls, saying, "The Land which they work with such great devotion will bring them back to the proper path and purify their hearts."
>
> He would rebuke anyone who even slightly slandered the residents of the Holy City. He once told me that the *Shulchan Aruch* states that righteous people fast on the seventeenth of Elul because the spies, who spread the evil report about the Land, died on that day.[105] The Magen Avraham asks, does it not say, *When the wicked perish, there is jubilation* (*Mishley* 11:10)?[106] The Shelah answers that the spies were righteous men (*tzaddikim*). Thus, ***even tzaddikim can be spies!***

The Torah says that HaShem constantly seeks out *Eretz Yisrael* (*Devarim* 11:12). Also, the sanctity of the Land is connected with the sanctity of our Creator, may His name be blessed.[107] Hence, just as

103 P. 14.

104 ❖ See what I wrote on pp. 27-28, quoting *Chesed LeAvraham*, *Sefat Emet*, and *Nachalah LeYisrael*.

105 *Orach Chayim* 580:2.

106 *Magen Avraham*, ibid.

107 ❖ I cited this in previous chapters from *Tzror HaMor* (see pp. 16, 234).

the Holy One Blessed be He is the essence of unity, so too, our Holy Land is bound up with the essence of unity.[108] Therefore, the Land does not tolerate the people of Israel unless they, too, are bound up in the essence of unity. The verse alludes to this when it says, *And who is like Your nation Israel, one nation in the Land* (II *Shmuel* 7:23). That is to say, the Land carries and tolerates the Jews only when they are united and undivided. Thus, we must do as I said and join all of Israel together in rebuilding the Holy Land. Then, we will become unified.

An important lesson to be learnt from today's war

יז I stated above[109] that the Ba'al HaTanya learned a lesson relevant to the Jewish nation from the war that broke out in his days. I also quoted the *Tana DeVei Eliyahu* which indicates that we should learn how to serve God from the nations. Therefore, we should also learn a lesson from today's war.

We see today that countries which were on the two opposite extremes of the political spectrum joined together to reach the lofty goal which they set for themselves. They united and put aside all of the divisive issues, in order to combine and increase their strengths. They realized that this is the only way to achieve their goal. We must do the same and combine all of our strengths for our sacred goal.

Similarly, I saw in the daily newspaper that a distinguished priest from this country said at a gathering in his honor: "May god help us stop looking for those things which cause division and disunity, and look only for those things which engender solidarity and harmony. Even though during peaceful times we allow ourselves to divide into factions, during difficult times like these it is forbidden to separate from one another. We must ensure that we remain as one man with one heart." [Now, if he said this about the Gentiles], what are we to say in our terrible and frightful situation! How can it be morally correct for us to remain separate?

I also saw in the newspapers that the Prime Minister of [Hungary], Count Teleki, said at a certain gathering: "I am only the captain of the ship. My objective is to steer the ship successfully to its destination. But, I can only accomplish this if the ship is intact. If it breaks into pieces, however, I will be unable to steer it

108 ❖ The Maharal of Prague discusses this at length in *Netzach Yisrael* 1.
109 P. 401.

successfully, for it will sink to the depths before it can reach its destination."

I also saw that Sweden's Prime Minister said that man must take current situations into account and plan accordingly. During troublesome times like these, someone who behaves the same way he does during normal times, when everything runs naturally and smoothly, is insane.

Chazal tell us that if a gentile sage says something wise, he is called a wise man (*Megillah* 16a). They also state, "If someone tells you that there is wisdom among the Gentiles, believe him" (*Eichah Rabbah* 2:13). Furthermore, I already explained[110] that we are permitted to learn good things from the Gentiles. Therefore, I cited these statements to teach us how to act during these difficult times.

In reality, though, we do not need to learn this from them, for our holy mentor, the Noam Elimelech, already said this: "We should see the good qualities in our friends, not their shortcomings, and we should speak justly to one another..."[111]

Unity is the cure for adversity

Whenever Israel was in distress, the leaders of the generation tried more than anything else to make peace among the people and unite them into one perfect unit. We find that when the Philistines attacked Israel, Shmuel said, *"Gather all of Israel to Mitzpah, and I will pray to the Lord for you." And, they gathered at Mitzpah and drew water...* (I *Shmuel* 7:5-6). The *Yerushalmi* comments, "R. Shmuel bar R. Yitzchak said, 'Shmuel wore the cloak of all of Israel'" (*Ta'anit* 2:7). This is puzzling! What is "the cloak of all of Israel"? It means that he enwrapped all of Israel in one cloak and unified them. Through this initial act, Shmuel caused Israel to be saved from the Philistines.

This also explains Shmuel's statement *Gather all of Israel...and they gathered*. That is, they gathered and joined together. Later on it says, *Then, Shmuel took one rock...and called it Even-HaEzer* (*the Rock of Help*) (ibid. 7:12). This demonstrates that becoming like "one rock" was the only thing that helped them defeat the Philistines.

The verse about Ya'akov Avinu, *And he took from the stones of that place* (*BeReishit* 28:11), also alludes to this. *Chazal* comment that he took twelve stones and they became one (*BeReishit Rabbah* 68:11). At that moment, Ya'akov foresaw the destruction and taught us to

110 P. 401-2.

111 From the Noam Elimelech's prayer recited before the morning prayers.

become like one rock. Immediately, when they became one, *Behold, the Lord stood over him* (ibid. 28:13) and promised Ya'akov that He would protect him. Understand this for it is correct and true.*

This book concludes with life

חי Says the author: God willing, I intend to complete this work – and in particular this fourth chapter dealing with unity and peace – with this section (18), which equals life (חי). Our Sages have already taught us that omens have significance (*Horayot* 12a). The Ya'avetz writes as follows:

> A wondrous thing happened in the numbering of the sections of *Tur Orach Chayim*. By chance, the laws of the *shofar* fell out in the section whose numerical value equals that of the word *shofar* (שופר – 586). Even though the author did not intend for this to happen, the truth fell in its place. This demonstrates that HaShem approved of the work, because the author wrote it for the sake of Heaven; and anyone who works for the sake of Heaven is shown an unexpected, good sign.[113]

---

* After I wrote this, one of my colleagues showed me that our mentor, the Malbim, already explained Ya'akov's stones in this way. I borrowed a *Chumash* with the Malbim's commentary and found it there. I was overjoyed to have concurred with him. Allow me to quote his words succinctly:

> The *Midrash* says, "R. Yehoshua ben Levi explained that the verse, *And Ya'akov went out* (ibid. 28:10), refers to exile, as it says, *And all the splendor went out from the daughter of Zion* (*Eichah* 1:6)" (*Yalkut Shimoni* 1:119). Now, the exile was caused by the sin of groundless hatred, and it is impossible for us to be redeemed until we unite and become one nation, as it says, *Take for yourself one stick...and one stick...and join them one to the other* (*Yechezkel* 37:16- 17). Therefore, HaShem made a sign for Ya'akov: If the stones of the Tribes of God unite and become one, [Israel will be redeemed]... Then Ya'akov saw that all the stones will unite and become one stone. Hence, it says, *And he took the stone* (*BeReishit* 28:18).[112]

Ya'akov foresaw that the Jews will eventually unite, at which time they will be redeemed from their troubles. Therefore, *he took the stone*.

112 Malbim, *BeReishit* 28:17.

113 *Siddur Ya'avetz, Dinei Tekiyat Shofar* 6:7 (p.324a). Also see ibid., *Hanhagat Leil Shabbat* 3:17.

Similarly, the Rashba writes, "All perceptive people realize that HaShem helps those who do sacred tasks, whenever necessary."[114] The same is true of this book. God is my witness that I did not intend to conclude my work with the letters חי (life). But, when I numbered the sections, I found that the last one spelled the word חי. I was overjoyed, for I saw this as ***heavenly approval*** for everything written in this book.

Allow me to explain further. We find that the Men of the Great Assembly – some of whom were prophets and men of *Ruach HaKodesh*[115] – concluded the *Shemoneh Esrei* (The Eighteen Blessings) with the blessing, "Grant peace, goodness, etc. Blessed are You, O Lord, Who blesses His people Israel with peace." This hints to the fact that peace is the foundation of everything. If there is no peace, there is nothing.[116] The previous blessing reads, "And all the living shall thank you forever." Why did the authors specifically use the words "And all the living"? To indicate that if we want life we must have peace, as the next blessing states, "Grant peace..." This is similar to the verse *My covenant was with him,* ***life and peace*** (*Malachi* 2:5). That is to say, these two concepts are bound together.

Love of Israel is the defining line between good and evil

We find many times in the Torah, *And the Lord said to Moshe,* ***"Speak to the Children of Israel"*** (*BeMidbar* 15:37-38). Now, it is well known that our holy Torah is eternal and relevant to each and every generation. Thus, an aspect of Moshe exists in every generation[117] in the form of Torah scholars; and at all times, the Holy One Blessed be He tells him ["Moshe"] to speak to the Children of Israel.

I thought about this and discovered that the numerical value of the first letters of the words דבר אל בני ישראל (*Speak to the Children of Israel*) equals the numerical value of the word טוב (good) (17). Further, the numerical value of the last letters (ר,ל,י,ל) equals that of the word רע (evil) (270). This alludes to the verse *See, I have placed before you today life and good, and death and evil* (*Devarim* 30:15). (Rashi explains, "One depends on the other. If you do good, you will have life; but if you do evil, you will have death.") *Choose life so that you and your offspring will live* (ibid. 30:19). (Rashi explains,

114 *Torat HaBayit* (introduction). ❖ I already cited this above (pp. 389-90).

115 *Megillah* 17b.

116 ❖ As Rashi writes on *VaYikra* 26:6.

117 ❖ This is well known from the *Tikkunei Zohar* (*Tikkun* 69) which states that there is a manifestation of Moshe in every generation.

"I instruct you to choose the portion of life.ö) The numerical value of the middle letters of the words דבר אל בני ישראל equals 553. If we add [two to this sum, which represents] the two letters of the word אל, which does not have a middle letter, we end up with 555, the numerical value of the words אוהב ישראל (lover of Israel). This alludes to Israel's restoration, as the Rebbe of Apt states (see the beginning of this chapter).

This teaches that love of Israel is the defining line between good and evil and between life and death. If the Jews unite and love one another, "good" will tip the scales and they will be rectified. But if, God forbid, they do the opposite, "evil" will tip the scales. Therefore, love of Israel is placed between good and evil in this verse. The Torah scholars of every generation must tell these things to the Children of Israel. They must inform them that their only hope for restitution is to love every single Jew, even the greatest sinners.❖

The greatest peace is when opposite extremes unite

The prophet says, *I create expression of the lips: Peace, peace for the far and near, says the Lord, and I will heal him* (*Yeshayah* 57:19). This verse is difficult to understand for two reasons. First, it should have said, "for the near and far," because a person first needs to be at peace with those who are near to him and only afterwards with those who are far. Second, what is the connection between the phrase, *says the Lord, and I will heal him*, and the previous statement, *Peace, peace...*?

In order to answer these questions, allow me to preface with something I heard from my brilliant and righteous brother-in-law, our master, R. Shlomo, *shlita*.[120] He related that his grandfather, our

❖ In *Tomar Devorah*, the godly man from Cordovero discusses the great obligation we have to love our fellow Jews even if they are inferior and lowly, God forbid. He also elaborates on the great rectification achieved when Jews love one another.[118]

The author of *Mikdash Me'at* on *Tehillim* quotes the holy Rebbe of Lublin as saying that he loves the wicked man who knows that he is wicked more than the righteous man who knows that he is righteous.[119] The holy man of Peshischa *zt"l* explains the reason for this (see there).

118 *Tomar Devorah*, chap. 1: sec. 4, 9, 12; chap. 2 (end).

119 *Mikdash Me'at* (Warsaw, 5650 [1890]), vol. 1, p. 290, s.v. *ve'harav miPeshischa*.

120 ❖ He is the son of my brilliant and righteous mentor and father-in-law, our master, R. David Friedman *zt"l*, *av beit din* of Tzahlim. R. Shlomo served

brilliant and godly master, R. Menachem Katz,[121] summoned the burial society (*Chevra Kadisha*) prior to his death (for he had told them that he would call them when it was time and that they need not stand next to him waiting). The entire community gathered around him, and he blessed them. He also cautioned them about the importance of peace, explaining *Chazal*'s statement "Great is peace, for the name of the Holy One Blessed be He is erased for it"[122] (*Chullin* 141a, *VaYikra Rabbah* 9:9). There are two types of peace: 1. A "negative" peace, in which people do not join together. Everyone turns to his own affairs and has nothing to do with other people. Obviously, there is no strife between them, but this is not true peace. 2. True peace, in which people join together and live as one, with love and affection.

Now, in the case of a *sotah*, the husband and wife become separated and distanced from each other because he suspects her [of being unfaithful]. But, when the Holy One's name is erased, they reunite and make peace with one another. Thus, *Chazal* state, "Great is peace." Which peace is so invaluable and primary? The one in which "the name of the Holy One Blessed be He is erased," that is to say, a peace which unites those who are far apart and enables them to live a life of peace and brotherly love. This kind of peace is great and exceedingly lofty.

These were his last words, and with them he passed on to the next world. May his merit protect his descendants and all of Israel.

Behold, *Chovot HaLevavot* states that speech was created in man to unite those who are divided, for speech unites people.[123]

as the rabbi of Baden near Vienna. At this time, however, he is exiled in Switzerland. May HaShem help him see Israel's salvation.

121 ❖ R. Menachem Katz, better known as R. Menachem Praznitz, was the *av beit din* of Tzahlim. He was one of the foremost disciples of our mentor, the Chatam Sofer, under whom he studied for fifteen years during his youth and five years after his marriage. He was a man of lofty stature. When he was together with the Rebbe of Tzanz, they ate from the same plate. When I visited my brother-in-law, the brilliant R. Mordechai Rottenberg, *av beit din* of Antwerp, I found one of R. Menachem's manuscripts. It was a large notebook filled with practical Kabbalah, which he had received from his mentor, the Chatam Sofer... I asked my brother-in-law to let me have the notebook, but he did not want to give it to me. And now, we do not know what has happened to my brother-in-law and his family. May HaShem have compassion on him and all of Israel. Amen.

122 [In the case of a *Sotah*. See *BeMidbar* 5:11-31.]

123 *Chovot HaLevavot, Sha'ar HaBechinah* 5.

Furthermore, I already explained above (based on many sources)[124] that the Holy One Blessed be He loves Israel primarily when all segments of the nation are at peace, even if they worship idols, God forbid. When they unite, HaShem will grant them a purifying spirit and direct their hearts to return to the proper path.

This explains the verse mentioned above. *I create expression of the lips*: The main purpose of creating speech was to engender peace. Therefore it says, *Peace, peace for the far* (the repetition of the word *peace* demonstrates its primacy). The verse specifically mentions *the far* first to demonstrate that we must make peace between people who have been far from each other until now. This is the greatest peace, as I mentioned above. Afterwards, the verse says, *and to the near*, meaning, we must also strengthen the peace between those who have been close from the beginning, but not close enough.

Alternatively, the verse means that we must establish and strengthen the peace between those who are at the extremes, far from one another, as well as between those who are not so far from one another. Do not fear that making peace between the extremes will harm you, for *Says the Lord, and I will heal him.* You must do your duty, and HaShem will do His. He will cure everyone, both spiritually and physically. With God's help, this is a true Torah interpretation.

Do not denounce the chalutzim

Thus, my brother, every Jew must speak peace to his nation[125] and avoid dividing the united ones. Our entire salvation depends on this. Therefore, I am extremely saddened that there are still people among us who publicly condemn and antagonize the builders and settlers of the Land. They read, *Let Jerusalem know of her abominations* (*Yechezkel* 16:2),[126] and they examine the abominations of our holy mother, [*Eretz Yisrael*]. They provoke hatred and enmity against her builders by calling them heretics, sinners, and infidels, and by saying that it is forbidden to associate with them. In this way, they bring disunity to the united and prevent the entire nation from unifying through this exceedingly lofty *mitzvah* [*Yishuv Eretz Yisrael*].

I call out to you incessantly, O people of Israel, young and old alike: Do not pay attention to such comments, even if they come

124 See pp. 486, 497-99.
125 Based on *Esther* 10:3.
126 See *Megillah* 25b.

from a distinguished and important person. He is wrong, and the Master of the World is displeased by such statements. For, as I mentioned above,[127] the actions of these builders, whom the complainers call sinners and rebels, will give rise to exceedingly lofty events, including the elevation of Israel's pride, the elevation of the pride of *Mashiach*, and the building of the House of David. I also cited our mentors, the Maharal of Prague, the Midrash Shmuel, the Shach, and the Noam Elimelech (who all possessed *Ruach HaKodesh*) as saying that great and holy things must develop from mundane matters and through sinners. These sacred rabbis are more reliable than all of today's distinguished men. How can these men compare to those "lions"?!

On the contrary, every God-fearing Jew must join the builders in their sacred task. In this way, the religious Jews will enhance the sanctity of the Land after the secular Jews succeeded in initiating the building.[128] Furthermore, the merit of Israel's complete unity will cause HaShem to rest His *Shechinah* among us. He will then bestow a purifying spirit upon the secular Jews and cause them to return and serve Him wholeheartedly. Thus, the prophet says, *And I will remove the iniquity of that Land in one day* (*Zecharyah* 3:9), and HaShem says, *Peace, peace for the far and near, says the Lord, and I will heal him* (*Yeshayah* 57:19). That is to say, you will see that you will live peacefully even with those who you call sinners. Building the Land will unite you, for this *mitzvah* alone is capable of bringing unity, as I explained above, at length.[129] Do not worry [about the secular Jews], for I [God] will heal them with a heavenly spirit of purity. Those who "sanctify themselves" and publicly advocate division, speak out of ignorance, as the brilliant and holy R. Yusha'le of Kutno writes.[130]

Today's spies

Do not be surprised that righteous and distinguished men speak ignorantly, for I will show you an even greater [example] of this. I already stated[131] that the angel of *Maggid Meisharim* told our mentor, the Beit Yosef, that Moshe chose the wisest and most righteous men to be the spies. Nonetheless, the *Midrash* refers to them as "foolish

127 Chap. 2, sec. י״ג, pp. 186-94.

128 ❖ Above, I cited profoundly brilliant and sacred men who support this. (See pp. 312-14.)

129 Pp. 390-91.

130 See above, p. 3.

131 Pp. 258-59.

messengers," since they spread an evil report about the Land (*BeMidbar Rabbah* 16:3; *Tanchuma, Shelach* 2). The same is true today. Our *tzaddikim* are certainly no more righteous or learned than the spies were. Even R. Zeira, who was very careful about his speech,[132] called the Babylonians "foolish" (*Beitzah* 16a). He did so even though they were *gedolei Torah*, because they did not ascend to *Eretz Yisrael* at the time of Ezra.[133] Furthermore, now that we have remained few in number, due to our numerous sins, and we are the survivors of the sword,[134] logic dictates that we embrace each other and extend a hand to one another.[135]

Therefore, my friends and brothers, do not pay any attention to those who slander the Land, even if they are truly righteous. For, I mentioned above[136] that the brilliant mentor of *Eretz Yisrael*, R. Yosef Chayim Sonnenfeld *z"l*, derived from the words of the Shelah that even *tzaddikim* can be spies. Realize that all those who oppose *aliyah* and the building and resettlement of the Land belong to the camp of the spies. But, all those who choose *aliyah* belong to Yehoshua and Calev's camp.

Our mentor, the Ari *z"l*, revealed to his disciple, R. Chayim Vital *z"l*, that when one chooses a *mitzvah* for which a certain *tzaddik* sacrificed himself, the soul of that *tzaddik* comes to his aid. The author of *Midrash Shmuel* once entered the study hall and [the soul of] the Ari HaKadosh stood before him, as is well known. The same is true today. Yehoshua and Calev sacrificed themselves for *aliyah*. The entire Jewish nation wanted to stone them, but they said, *Let us go up* (*BeMidbar* 13:30). Similarly, if we sacrifice ourselves for *aliyah*, the souls of Yehoshua and Calev will come to our aid. This is as clear and true as the Torah of Moshe from the Almighty.

Thus, we must decide (as Ya'akov Avinu did during his time of trouble)[137] that when HaShem rescues us from our enemies we will sacrifice ourselves to elevate the pride of our Land. Then, the merit of *Eretz Yisrael* will save us from misfortune and deliver us from distress. But, we will only achieve this when all Jews unite, because

132 See *Megillah* 28b, *Ta'anit* 20a.

133 ❖ I discussed this above, at length, in chap. 3, sec. טו (pp. 408-11).

134 Based on *Yirmiyah* 31:1.

135 ❖ As I cited above (p. 482) from our mentor, the Chatam Sofer.

136 P. 506.

137 ❖ See the first introduction, pp. 36-38.

they are all descendants of Avraham, Yitzchak, and Ya'akov, and they all need it.

Conquering Eretz Yisrael precedes the destruction of idolatry

My beloved colleague, the elderly rabbi, the perfectly righteous son of saints, our brilliant master, R. Yisrael David Margolis *shlita*, rabbi of the Linat HaTzedek synagogue here [in Budapest], showed me the following Talmudic statement: "R. Yehoshua ben Levi said, 'Conquering *Eretz Yisrael* precedes the destruction of idolatry'" (*Avodah Zarah* 45b). Rashi explains, "After conquering [the Land], they will search [for idols] in order to uproot and destroy them." In my opinion, this is why Ezra did not separate the people of his generation from their abominations [– idols] immediately upon entering the Land.[138] He did so only twenty years after he built the *Beit Ha-Mikdash* and Jerusalem, because he did not want to cause strife and condemnation while he conquered and built the Land. He fulfilled R. Yehoshua ben Levi's rule that conquering *Eretz Yisrael* precedes the destruction of idolatry. The same applies to us. We need all the strengths of our holy nation for the sacred task of building the Land. We must proceed arm in arm, and then the Holy One Blessed be He will accept the work of our hands and bring it to a successful end. The complete redemption will develop from this, speedily in our days. Amen.*

Who am I to reprove the Children of Israel?

We must convey these and similar ideas to the Children of Israel, to fulfill our obligation deriving from the verse *The Lord said to*

---

* I just discovered that the author of Responsa *Imrei Aish* concurs:

> The great virtue of dwelling in *Eretz Yisrael* is well known, as elucidated in *Ketuvot* (110b ff.), so there is no need to elaborate. The Ramban counts it as one of the 613 *mitzvot*. Thus, we must make sure that our Land does not remain desolate, God forbid. This is a *mitzvah* incumbent upon all of Israel, and [every Jew] must arouse his brethren to ascend to HaShem's chosen place.[139]

Thus, he agrees that this is a *mitzvah* incumbent upon all of Israel, a public concern, and that we are commanded to inspire others to ascend to HaShem's chosen place. The Ramban also writes, "Settling *Eretz Yisrael* is a *mitzvah*, and it is beneficial to all of Israel that the Holy Land not [remain] destroyed.[140]

138 ❖ This is stated explicitly in *Ezra* and *Nechemyah*. See above (pp. 295-96).
139 *Imrei Aish, Yoreh De'ah* 101.
140 Novellae, *Shabbat* 130b.

Moshe, "Speak to the Children of Israel" (*BeMidbar* 15:37-38). I explained above that this refers to the Torah scholars of each generation who must generate *ahavat Yisrael*, unity, and peace, in order to tip the scales in Israel's favor and bring them merit, life, and peace.

If someone should ask, "Who appointed you the man[141] to lift his voice and speak to the Children of Israel?" I will give two answers. First, every Torah scholar has the right to lift his voice and speak to the generation. The great halachic authority, our mentor, the Mabit, writes this explicitly in the introduction to *Beit Elokim*:

> The *Midrash* comments on the verse *This is the book of the descendants of Adam* (man) (*BeReishit* 5:1): "This teaches that the Holy One Blessed be He showed Adam the preachers of each generation (דור דור), the wise men of each generation, and the leaders of each generation" (*BeReishit Rabbah* 24:2)... The fact that the *Midrash* says, "each generation" (דור דור), and not "...a generation" (דור), alludes to the fact that HaShem will not forsake His nation.[142] In every generation, without exception, there will be preachers, wise men, and leaders, or at least one or two of them. Not a single generation will be left without "shepherds." Therefore, a man who is completely engrossed in Torah must act as if he is from "the book of the descendants of Adam," one of the preachers, wise men, or leaders of his generation. This is not arrogant, because by doing so he adorns himself...to become worthy and bring merit to others.[143]

Second, the Rambam writes that the fixing of a leap year is treated like a case of capital punishment (דיני נפשות) – therefore requiring a majority of two – because it alters the year's regular course.[144] We see from this that altering something's regular course makes it similar to a case of life and death (דיני נפשות). Now, let us apply this to our discussion. Since we want to detach the Jewish people from the customs they learned in exile, our situation is like a case of life and death. Moreover, since exile actually involves life and death issues, as we see today, our situation is certainly similar to a case of capital punishment (דיני נפשות).

Now, the *halachah* states that the least significant judge speaks

141 Based on *Shemot* 2:14.
142 I *Shmuel* 12:22.
143 *Beit Elokim*, Introduction, s.v. *u'mipney she'yeish*.
144 See Rambam, *Hilchot Kiddush HaChodesh* 4:10.

first in cases of capital punishment.[145] Thus, since I am the least significant of this generation, it is certainly fitting for me to speak first and express my humble opinion on the rectification and restoration of our people, with God's help. The great ones (*gedolim*) of the generation will hear me and accept the truth from whence it came. They will fulfill *Chazal*'s statement "Fortunate is the generation in which the great ones listen to the small ones" (*Rosh HaShanah* 25b). In truth, I did not invent even one idea in this book. I drew everything from the wellspring of living waters, the well dug by the princes of the Torah,[146] our Rabbis of the Talmud, *Midrash*, *Zohar*, and other holy books. I built this book, which I present before you, upon the foundations of their words.

The truth is the truth no matter what

Our mentor, the Gra, teaches us a most important principle of life in his work, *Sh'not Eliyahu*:

> *Torat Kohanim* explains the verse, *You shall leave* [the gifts to the poor] (*VaYikra* 19:10), as follows: "Place the gift before the poor and let them grab it, even if one strong man says, 'Put it up for grabs.'"[147] We listen to the strong one (even if ninety-nine weak men say, "Divide it"), because his claim coincides with the *halachah*. This is so even though he is biased (for he can grab more than the weak ones). The rule is, we listen to someone whose opinion coincides with the *halachah* even if he is biased about that particular thing. This is evident from the *Torat Kohanim*.[148]

Therefore, realize that everything I wrote and cited in this book is in accordance with the *halachah*. This is the Torah's outlook and the will of the Creator. Therefore, you must listen to me. [Everything I wrote] is true and clear *halachah*, like Moshe's Torah from the Almighty. May HaShem sway the hearts of all the Children of Israel to accept the truth from whence it came. And, may His blessed name be praised [in the heavens] above and [on the earth] below. Amen, so may it be God's will.

I know that not everyone will be pleased by my words and that some will shout thunderously at me. But, before anyone lifts his voice, let me remind him of a story in the *Yerushalmi*. Reish Lakish

145 *Sanhedrin* 32a, Rashi s.v. *min hatzad*.
146 Based on *BeMidbar* 21:18.
147 *Torat Kohanim* on *VaYikra* 19:10.
148 *Sh'not Eliyahu, Pe'ah* 4:1. [The parenthetical comments are R. Teichtal's.]

said, "A prince who sins receives lashes." R. Yehuda the Prince heard this and became angry, so Reish Lakish fled. Afterwards, R. Yehuda himself looked for him and said, "Why did you disgrace me with that statement?" Reish Lakish retorted, "Do you think that I will refrain from relating the teachings of the Merciful One because I fear you?!" (*Yerushalmi*: *Sanhedrin* 2:1 [7b], *Horayot* 3:1 [9a-b]).

I say the same thing. Do you think that I will refrain from relating the teachings of the Merciful One because of the animosity of those people whose honor will be damaged by the ideas written in this book (which are all based on *Chazal*)?! Whatever I wrote or cited in this work is the truth of the Torah, and anyone who subscribes to truth will admit to the truth. I am prepared to debate anyone who wishes to do so, but only a halachic debate, as Tosafot write,[149] and as I cited in the second introduction in the name of the Maharival and the Mabit.[150]

Conclusion

My heart is filled with more thoughts on this issue, but since this work has already grown quite large, I will stop here. God willing, I will return to you, people of this generation, in writing and speech, and through the healing tongue of the sages.[151] May HaShem bind the breach of His people and heal the wound of their blow,[152] speedily in our days. Amen. Amen. So may it be God's will. Blessed is the Merciful One Who assists us.

I completed my book on Thursday night, the eve of the holy Sabbath [on which we read], *And your seed will inherit the gate of its enemies* (*BeReishit* 22:17, *parashat VaYeira*), in the year: *Israel, in whom I will be glorified* (בך אתפאר)[153] (*Yeshayah* 49:3),❖ here in the capital,

❖ *Yalkut Shimoni* states: "The Holy One Blessed be He said to Moshe: 'Moshe, praise Israel before Me any way you can. Glorify them any way you can, for I will be glorified through them in the future,' as it says, *Israel, in whom I will be glorified*" (*Yalkut Shimoni* 1:376, 2:315). The statement, "For I will be glorified through them in the future," clearly demonstrates that even if they are currently unworthy for Me [God] to be glorified through them, I request that you, Moshe,

149 ❖ *Horayot* 2a, s.v. *hacha*, explaining *Chazal*'s statement "We do not derive *halachah* from stories" (*Bava Batra* 130b).
150 P. 49.
151 Based on *Mishley* 12:18.
152 Based on *Yeshayah* 30:26.
153 [בך אתפאר numerically equals (5)704, i.e., 1943.]

Budapest. I am in the midst of the exile.[154] May the Holy One Blessed be He transform exile (גלות) into Israel's redemption (גאולת ישראל) by adding an "א" which represents HaShem's unity.[155] Let us be glad and rejoice in the salvation of the Lord to Whom we hope.[156] May HaShem's glorious name be blessed for ever and ever. Amen, so may it be God's will. Amen. Amen.

Finished and completed. Praise God, Creator of the World!

Addendum

When you cry out, let your collection [of idols] *save you; but the wind will carry them all away... But, the one who trusts in Me will possess the Land and inherit My holy mountain* (*Yeshayah* 57:13). The *Midrash* comments: "It has been taught: Ya'akov's gathering [i.e., uniting] and the gathering of his sons saved him from Eisav. *The wind will carry them all away* refers to Eisav. *But, the one who trusts in Me will possess the Land and inherit My holy mountain* refers to Ya'akov" (*BeReishit Rabbah* 84:1, *Yalkut Shimoni* 2:488). This teaches that the only thing that saved Ya'akov from Eisav was the fact that he gathered together. So it was, and so it will always be. When Ya'akov and his sons are assembled and gathered together, the wind will carry Eisav away, and Ya'akov will inherit and possess the Land and His holy mountain. So may it be God's will, speedily in our days. Amen. Amen.

---

praise and glorify them any way you can. This is a definitive proof for everything I wrote in this book.

154 Based on *Yechezkel* 1:1.

155 ❖ As I cited above (pp. 385-89) in the name of our mentor, the Maharal of Prague. I recently discovered that Rabbeinu Chayim, the Maharal's brother, concurs (end of *Sefer Ge'ulah ViYeshuah*, see above, p. 503). Thus, the word of HaShem shall stand forever according to two witnesses (based on *Devarim* 19:15 and *Yeshayah* 40:8).

156 Based on *Yeshayah* 25:9.

ADDENDUM[1]

HaShem awakens us to return to the Land

א Since I found some empty space, I will present a few more brief ideas related to this book. It says in Zecharyah's prophecy, *I will whistle to them and gather them, for I have redeemed them; and they will increase as they had increased before* (10:8). Rashi explains, "*I will whistle to them*, like one who whistles to those who have lost their way as a signal for them to come towards him. *And I will gather them*, in the future, at the time of the end (קץ)." *Metzudat David* explains:

> *I will whistle* to the Jews of exile as a sign that they should come, and in this way *I will gather them*. That is to say, I will awaken their hearts to return to their Land, *for* then *I will redeem them* from exile. *And they will increase*, with sons and daughters, *as they increased* in Egypt.

The prophet further states, *I will sow them among the nations; and they will remember Me in faraway places; and they, with their children, will live, and they will return* (ibid. 10:9). *Metzudat David* explains:

> *I will sow them among the nations*: Even though I scattered them like a person scatters seeds for sowing, they will remember Me in the faraway places to which they were scattered. Therefore, they, with their children, will live and return to their Land.

Thus, the prophet foretold that the redemption will occur by way of a hint. HaShem will call His children who are lost in the lands of exile, the same way a man shows a sign to someone who is lost in a desert, to help him find a way out. This will happen when the Holy One Blessed be He awakens the Jews to return to their Land. However, if the redemption were to occur with manifest, publicized miracles, it would not happen with a hint and a sign. When *Klal Yisrael* is unworthy, though, the redemption must occur in this fashion, as I explained above.[2]

1 [In the Hebrew edition, this addendum appears at the beginning of the book. However, as the first sentence indicates, this choice of location was completely arbitrary. Therefore, I decided to place it at the end, where it is more appropriate.]

2 See pp. 134-36.

Now tell me, O people of Israel, is this prophecy not fitting for our times?! This awakening to return to the Land has already entered the heart of every Jew. We fulfill the verse *And they will remember Me in faraway places; and they and their children will live, and they will return.* That is to say, even Jews in the furthest places will remember to return to their Land. For they and their children will only find a safe haven when they return to their Land. Every detail of this prophecy coincides with current events.

Above,[3] I mentioned that the Sages of the Talmud, whose every utterance was said with *Ruach HaKodesh*, revealed that unclean birds will bring us a hint and a sign of our return to the Land. We will be lost in the desert of the nations, greatly bewildered, and we will cry out, "To where shall we flee? To where shall we flee?"[4] Then, the Holy One Blessed be He will whistle to us and give us a sign to come towards Him. He will do this by way of unclean birds, meaning, men who have strayed from the path of Torah and fear of God due to the foreign influences they absorbed in exile. I already explained above[5] that no one can fathom the searchings of God.[6] The thoughts and deeds of He Who is Perfect in Knowledge[7] are beyond our thoughts.

In any event, we see clearly that this prophecy refers to our era. Therefore, no one should oppose the return to the Land, for even if his intentions are desirable, his actions are certainly not.[8]

The settlement of Eretz Yisrael is a divine visitation of redemption

In *Megillah* (12a), Rava states [that the visitation (פקידה) mentioned in the verse, *After seventy years are completed for Babylonia, I* (God) *will visit* (אפקד) *you* (*Yirmiyah* 29:10), is] "only a visitation," [not the complete redemption]. The Maharsha explains that the visitation was "that a few Jews settled in *Eretz Yisrael*."

Thus, any settlement of Jews in *Eretz Yisrael* is a visitation of redemption. At that time, only a few thousand Jews settled there (I do not have a book of *Ezra* right now in order to indicate the precise number.)[9] Today, close to a million have settled there! So

3 See pp. 184-85.

4 ❖ The *Pesikta* explains that we will be greatly confused prior to the redemption (*Pesikta Rabbati, Piska Aseret HaDibrot* 1).

5 See pp. 184-85.

6 Based on *Iyov* 11:7.

7 Based on *Iyov* 37:16.

8 Based on *Kuzari* 1:1.

9 See *Ezra* 2:64-65, *Nechemyah* 7:66-67. The precise number is 42,360.

may this number increase and so may it multiply, with God's help. There has not been an ingathering like this ever since we were exiled from our Land. This is certainly a visitation of redemption.

Therefore, every Jew must certainly join the settlement effort with all of his physical and monetary strength. Not a single Jewish soul should be left out, and no claim in the world should prevent the entire Congregation of Israel from joining together. Then, with God's help, we will achieve complete redemption, and God's great name will be exalted and sanctified, speedily in our days, forever and ever. Amen, so may it be God's will.

Salvation comes through those who desire to ascend to Eretz Yisrael

ב The verse says about Gideon, *Go with this strength of yours and you shall save Israel from the hand of Midyan* (*Shoftim* 6:14). Our mentor, the Chatam Sofer, explains:

> In order to save Israel from its enemy's clutches, a generation needs four *tzaddikim* who join together in the mission of salvation. Scripture calls them, *four craftsmen* (*Zecharyah* 2:3),[10] and we say in our prayers, "Four craftsmen as in the vision." The verse says about this, *How good and how pleasant it is when brothers* (אחים) *dwell in unity* (*Tehillim* 133:1). The word אחים is an acronym for אהרן חור יהושע משה.[11] The same is true of every generation.
>
> Now, Rashi explains the verse, *A roasted* (צליל) *barley bread* (*Shoftim* 7:13),[12] as follows: "[The word צליל] is written as צלול (clear), for Gideon's generation was clear of *tzaddikim*." [That is to say], Gideon did not have three helpers in that generation. However, *Chazal* state, "One Torah scholar from *Eretz Yisrael* is like two from Babylonia. And, one of us [from Babylonia] who ascends to *Eretz Yisrael* is like two of them" (*Ketuvot* 75a). Thus, any *tzaddik* from the Diaspora who ascends to *Eretz Yisrael* is equal to four *tzaddikim*. Now, it seems to me that he does not have to actually ascend. Even if he just desires to ascend, but fails, he is considered like four *tzaddikim* and is worthy to have a miracle occur on his account. For, anyone who contemplates doing a *mitzvah*, but is unable to do so, Scripture considers it as if he did it (*Berachot* 6a).
>
> Now, in those days it was unanimously accepted as *halachah*

10 See *Sukkah* 52b.

11 [The four people who were responsible for the redemption from Egypt.]

12 [From the story of Gideon.]

> that *Eretz Yisrael* had the status of *Chutz LaAretz*, and Gideon was distressed by this. Thus, he was exactly like a *tzaddik* in the Diaspora who sorely wants to ascend to *Eretz Yisrael*. Therefore, he was equal to four *tzaddikim* and was able to save Israel. This is the meaning of *Go with this strength of yours and you shall save Israel.*[13]

Behold, it is well known that Gideon was one of the "empty ones."[14] He had no merits, other than the fact that he invoked merit (לימד זכות) upon Israel[15] and sorely wanted to ascend to *Eretz Yisrael* (as the Chatam Sofer writes). This alone made him a *tzaddik* equal to the "four craftsmen" and enabled him to save Israel. Therefore, it is forbidden to degrade anyone who sacrifices himself for the public welfare and sorely desires to ascend to *Eretz Yisrael*. For it is possible that today, as well, salvation will come to all of Israel through a person like this, as it came to our forefathers through Gideon. A word to the wise is sufficient.[16] May HaShem speedily gladden us with salvation and compassion. Amen, so may it be God's will.

Conclusion

The printing of this book began on *parashat VaEira*, 5703 [1943], and was completed successfully on Thursday, *parashat Miketz*, the second day of *Chanukah*, 5704 [1943]. May HaShem recall the miracles that He performed for our forefathers in those days and renew them for us today.[17] May the following verses be fulfilled through us, *He puts an end to the darkness* (*Iyov* 28:3) and *The Jews had light and gladness and joy* (*Esther* 8:16). So may it be for us,[18] speedily in our days. Amen.

This week's Torah portion states, *He* [Yosef's servant] *said* [to the brothers], *"Peace be to you, do not fear"* (*BeReishit* 43:23). The godly author of *Megaleh Amukot* writes:

> He was hinting to them, "When you live together peacefully, you need not worry.ö If he [Israel] is attached to idols, let

13 *Derashot Chatam Sofer*, *Derush* for *Shabbat HaGadol* 5558 [1798], vol. 2, p. 233a, s.v. *u'bazeh yuvan teshuvat HaShem yitbarach*.

14 See *Rosh HaShanah* 25a.

15 *Tanchuma, Shoftim* 4; *Yalkut Shimoni* 2:62. See above, pp. 113-14.

16 ❖ See above, beginning of chapter 2 (p. 131).

17 ❖ As the Taz writes in the name of the Levush (*Orach Chayim* 682:5).

18 From the *Havdalah* service.

him be,[19] because peace is Eisav's adversary, as he is called *The hater of peace* (*Tehillim* 120:6). This is the meaning of the verse (above): *Peace be to you*, therefore, *do not fear*, because Eisav's adversary [i.e., peace] is present.

It is well known that all of his words were said with *Ruach HaKodesh*.

I thank HaShem with all my heart that he granted me the privilege to complete this work successfully. So may He grant me the privilege to publish all of my works, to glorify His blessed name. May our eyes behold Jerusalem rebuilt like the high heavens.[20] May His eternal kingdom be exalted. Amen. Amen.

At this time, at the completion of the printing, I will make it known that the incident mentioned at the end of the second introduction happened to me! Blessed is HaShem Who performed this wonderful kindness for me. May He never abandon or forsake me. And, may I behold Israel's solace and salvation, speedily in our days. Amen.

19 Based on *Hoshea* 4:17. [*Megaleh Amukot* interprets the verse homiletically: If the Jews are attached - i.e., united - then, even if they worship idols, HaShem says, "Let him be." See above, p. 499, where R. Teichtal cites a similar interpretation from the *Midrash*.]

20 Based on *Tehillim* 78:69.

*GLOSSARY**

Acharonim – "Later ones." The collective title for the Torah authorities of the past five hundred years (approximately).
Admor – Acronym for אדוננו מורינו ורבנו – our master, our mentor, our rabbi. It is used as a title for chassidic rabbis.
Aggadah (pl. *Aggadot*) – The homiletic sections of the Talmud.
a"h – Acronym for עליו השלום, may he rest in peace.
Aliyah – "Ascension" or emigration to the Land of Israel.
Amora'im – The Sages of the Talmud.
Asei – A biblically ordained positive commandment.
Aseret Yemei Teshuvah – The Ten Days of Repentance, between *Rosh HaShanah* and *Yom Kippur*.
Av Beit Din – The chief judge of a rabbinic court.
Avinu – "Our Father." An appellation used for the three Patriarchs: Avraham, Yitzchak, and Ya'akov.
Baruch HaShem – Thank God.
Beit HaBechirah – "The Chosen House," i.e., the Holy Temple in Jerusalem.
Beit HaMikdash – The Holy Temple in Jerusalem.
Beit Midrash – A study hall.
Beraita – A Tana'itic teaching found outside the *Mishnah*.
Brit Bein HaBetarim – "The Covenant Between the Pieces," made between God and Avraham (see *BeReishit* 15).
Brit Milah – Circumcision.
Chacham – "Scholar." Usually used as a title for a Sefardic Torah scholar.
Chalutzim – The pioneer builders of the Land of Israel at the turn of the century.
Chassid (pl. *Chassidim*) – Lit., "pious ones." It is now widely used in reference to the members of the Chassidic movement.
Chassidut – The Chassidic movement.
Chazal – Acronym for חכמינו זכרונם לברכה, Our Sages of blessed memory.
Chiddushei – Novel Torah insights on...
Rosh Chodesh – The beginning of a new Jewish month.
Chumash – The Five Books of Moses.
Chutz LaAretz – Anywhere outside the Land of Israel.
Derashah – Sermon.
Derech Eretz – "The way of the land." Proper ethical behavior.
Eirev Rav – "Mixed multitude." Originally: the non-Jews who joined the Jewish people during the exodus from Egypt.
Eretz Yisrael – The Land of Israel.
Etrog – The fruit of a citron tree, taken on the holiday of *Sukkot* (see *VaYikra* 23:40).
Gadol (pl. *Gedolim*) – A great Torah scholar.

---

* This glossary does not include words which were explained in context.

Gadol Ha'dor – The greatest Torah scholar and leader of the generation.
Gaon (pl. *Gaonim*) – A brilliant Torah scholar.
Gabbai – Sexton, or synagogue caretaker.
Gezeirah Shavah – One of the methods through which the Torah is elucidated. Using it, a new interpretation or law is derived based on the similarity of words found in different biblical verses.
Haftarah – A section from the Prophets read after the Torah on the Sabbath and Holidays.
Halachah – Jewish law.
HaNavi – The prophet.
HaShem – Lit., "The Name": God.
Hashkafah – Outlook or world view.
Havdalah – Ceremony marking the end of the Sabbath.
Hefker – Ownerless, abandoned.
Immeinu – "Our Mother." An appellation used for the four Matriarchs: Sarah, Rivkah, Rachel, and Leah.
Isru Chag – The day after a holiday, considered somewhat joyous.
Kal Vachomer – One of the methods through which the Torah is elucidated. Using it, an inference can be made from a lenient law to a strict one (or vice versa).
Kashrut – Jewish dietary laws.
Kavanah – Concentration or devotion during prayers or the performance of *mitzvot*.
Kedushah – Prayer in which we sanctify God's name as the angels do.
Keitz – A reckoned time for the coming of *Mashiach*.
Kelipah (pl. *Kelipot*) – Lit., "husks," referring to the evil spiritual forces.
Kenesset Yisrael – The Assembly of Israel.
Kerem Rivai – The fruits of the fourth year of a tree's life, which must be eaten in Jerusalem.
Kiddush – The sanctification of the Sabbath, said over a cup of wine.
Klal Yisrael – The entirety of Israel, the Jewish collective.
Kohen (pl. *Kohanim*) – "Priest(s)." The descendants of Aharon who perform the sacred service in the Temple.
Levi'im – Levites, members of the tribe of Levi who work in the Temple.
Lo Ta'asei – A biblically ordained negative commandment.
Lulav – A palm branch taken on the holiday of *Sukkot* (see *VaYikra* 23:40).
Ma'asrot – Tithes (one tenth of a Jew's crop) given to the Levites and the poor.
Machzor – A holiday prayer book.
Maggid – 1. A preacher. 2. An angel who reveals the secrets of the Torah to deserving individuals (like the Beit Yosef).
Mashiach – Lit., "The anointed one," i.e., the Messiah.
Matzah – Unleavened bread eaten on Passover.
Mesorah – Glosses on the Scriptures, written in the early medieval period, designed to establish precise texts of the Bible.
Mikvah – A bath used for ritual purification.
Minchah – An offering made of flour.

Minyan (pl. *Minyanim*) – A quorum of ten men praying together.
Mishkan – The Tabernacle.
Mishnah – Tana'itic teachings compiled by Rebbe Yehudah HaNasi.
Mitzvah (pl. *Mitzvot*) – Divine commandment(s).
Musaf – An additional prayer recited on the Sabbath and holidays.
Olam HaBa – The World to Come.
Olim – Immigrants, specifically those who ascend from the Diaspora to the Land of Israel.
Omer – Grain offering brought on the sixteenth of Nissan (see *VaYikra* 23:9-15).
Orlah – The prohibition to eat a tree's produce for the first three years of its life.
Parashat – The weekly Torah portion of...
Pasul – Halachically invalid or disqualified.
Paytan – A liturgical poet.
Pesach – The Passover holiday, commemorating the exodus from Egypt.
Piyut – Liturgical hymn or prayer.
Posek (pl. *Poskim*) – Decisor, or authority on Jewish law.
Rabbeinu – Our teacher, or mentor. Also used as an appellation for Moshe (Moses).
Rasha (pl. *Resha'im*) – Wicked person(s).
Rishonim – "Earlier ones." The collective title for the Torah authorities of the 11th to 15th centuries (approximately).
Rosh HaShanah – The Jewish new year.
Ruach HaKodesh – Divine Inspiration.
Sanhedrin – The highest rabbinic court, based in the Holy Temple in Jerusalem.
Sefer (pl. *Sefarim*) – Book(s).
Sefirah (pl. *Sefirot*) – Kabbalistic, heavenly spheres.
Selichot – Prayers of supplication recited before *Rosh HaShanah*, during the Ten Days of Repentance, and on fast days.
Shavuot – The Festival of Weeks, commemorating, among other things, the giving of the Torah.
SheHechiyanu – "Who has kept us alive." A blessing recited on happy occasions.
Shechinah – The Divine Presence.
Shelamim – An animal sacrifice partially eaten by the owner.
Shemittah – The Sabbatical year.
Shemoneh Esrei – A prayer recited three times a day, originally consisting of eighteen blessings (it now has nineteen).
Shevi'it – The Sabbatical year.
Shlita – Acronym for שיחיה לאורך ימים טובים אמן, may he live a good, long life. Amen.
Shofar – A ram's horn blown on *Rosh HaShanah*.
Siddur – Prayer book.
Simchat Beit HaSho'eivah – A joyous celebration which used to take place in the Temple on the holiday of *Sukkot*, celebrating the water libation.
Sotah – An unfaithful wife (see *BeMidbar* 5:11-31).

Sukkah – A temporary booth used on the holiday of *Sukkot*.

Sukkot – The Festival of Booths, commemorating the Jews' journey through the desert.

Tachanun – Daily prayer of supplication, omitted on happy occasions.

Talit (pl. *Talitot*) – Prayer shawl with the traditional fringes (*tzitzit*).

Tana (pl. *Tana'im*) – The Sages of the *Mishnah*.

Tanach – Acronym for תורה נביאים וכתובים, i.e., the Holy Scriptures: Torah, Prophets, and Writings.

Techum Shabbat – "Sabbath Limits." The boundaries past which a Jew may not walk on the Sabbath.

Tefillin – Phylacteries.

Teruah – A *shofar* blast.

Terumah – A gift set aside from a Jew's produce and given to a *kohen*.

Teshuvot – Responsa. Answers to halachic questions collected and published by an authority on Jewish law.

Tetragrammaton – God's great, four-letter name: י-ה-ו-ה.

Tikkun – Spiritual rectification.

Tish'a B'Av – The ninth day of Av. The saddest day of the Jewish calendar, commemorating, among other things, the destruction of the two Temples.

Tzaddik (pl. *Tzaddikim*) – Righteous individual(s).

Tzara'at – Commonly translated as leprosy, it is some type of disease caused by the transgression of various sins.

Tzitzit – Fringes worn on the four corners of a male Jew's garments.

Yeitzer HaRa – The Evil Inclination.

Yichud – Spiritual unification.

Yishuv Eretz Yisrael – Settling the Land of Israel.

z"l – Acronym for זכרונו לברכה, of blessed memory.

zt"l – Acronym for זכר צדיק לברכה, may the memory of the righteous be blessed.

ztvk"l – Acronym for זכר צדיק וקדוש לברכה, may the memory of the righteous and holy be blessed.

INDEX

F

G

T